WORD CRIMES

WORD CRIMES

Blasphemy,
Culture,
and
Literature
in
Nineteenth-Century
England

JOSS MARSH

THE UNIVERSITY OF CHICAGO PRESS
CHICAGO AND LONDON

The University of Chicago Press, Chicago 60637
The University of Chicago Press, Ltd., London
© 1998 by The University of Chicago
All rights reserved. Published 1998
Printed in the United States of America
07 06 05 04 03 02 01 00 99 98   1 2 3 4 5
ISBN: 0-226-50690-8 (cloth)
ISBN: 0-226-50691-6 (paper)

Library of Congress Cataloging-in-Publication Data

Marsh, Joss.
    Word crimes : blasphemy, culture, and literature in nineteenth-
century England / Joss Marsh.
        p.   cm.
    Includes bibliographical references and index.
    ISBN 0-226-50690-8 (cloth : alk. paper). — ISBN 0-226-50691-6
(pbk. : alk. paper)
    1. English literature—19th century—History and criticism.
2. Blasphemy in literature. 3. Foote, G. W. (George William),
1850–1915—Trials, litigation, etc. 4. Christianity and literature—
England—History—19th century. 5. Trials (Blasphemy)—Great
Britain—History—19th century. 6. Language and culture—
England—History—19th century. 7. Hone, William, 1780–1842—
Trials, litigation, etc. 8. Freethinkers—Great Britain—History—19th
century. 9. Atheism—Great Britain—History—19th century.
10. English language—19th century—Euphemism. I. Title.
PR468.B55M37   1998
820.9′353—dc21   97-49344
                                                                CIP

♾ The paper used in this publication meets the minimum requirements
of the American National Standard for Information Sciences—
Permanence of Paper for Printed Library Materials, ANSI Z39.48-1992.

In memory of Nora Wrapson

Contents

List of Illustrations ix
Acknowledgments xi
Introduction 3

CHAPTER ONE

Blasphemy, 1817–30
— 18 —

1. "You know me now, the Arch Blasphemer":
The Three Trials of William Hone 24
2. Three Epilogues 39
3. Carlile, the Volunteers, and the *Age of Reason* Struggle 60

CHAPTER TWO

Trials of the 1840s
— 78 —

1. "Knowledge is Power," or, the Cheap Press as Blasphemy 78
2. The Moxon Case and the Growth of the Poet's Income 90
3. Jacob Holyoake and other "Priests" of the *Oracle* 109

CHAPTER THREE

England, 1883
— 127 —

1. The "Celebrated Case" of G.W. Foote and the *Freethinker* 128
2. Two Codas 163

CHAPTER FOUR

Literature and Dogma
— 169 —

1. "Bibliolatry" and "Bible-Smashing" 170
2. The Heretic Trope of the Book 181
3. Literary Law and the Authority of Literature 191
4. When "Literary Difference" Became a "Criminal Offence" 197

CHAPTER FIVE

Words, Words, Words
— 204 —

1. Mr. Foote's Trial for Obscenity 207
2. Victorian Euphemism and the Fear of Language 215
3. The Systematization of Silence 230
4. Jacob Holyoake, "Master of Sentences" 240
5. The Victorian Crisis of Language 249

CHAPTER SIX

Hardy's Crime
— 269 —

1. Committing Literary Blasphemy 271
2. "Get It Done and Let Them Howl" 279
3. Hardy the Degenerate, Pooley the Obscure 295
4. Modern Words, Modern Crimes 319

Notes 329
Abbreviations and Archival Collections 379
Bibliography 379
Index 409

Illustrations

1 Foote the "Martyr" pictured on the *Freethinker*'s cover 4

2 Liberty defends the printing press from the "Guilty Trio" 23

3 Hone and Cruikshank collaborate 58

4 The Clerical Magistrate, pictured by Cruikshank 64

5 Carlile's bishop arm-in-arm with a devil 73

6 Blasphemy memorabilia 116

7 Commemorative notice of Holyoake's daughter's death 119

8 George Jacob Holyoake as a near-Eminent Victorian 125

9 Nightmare educational image by Harry Furniss 130

10 Fake culture's potential for mob violence 131

11 "Divine Illumination," *Freethinker* 1882 141

12 Offensive literalism: notorious Bible cartoon 142

13–14 Comic strip in the *Freethinker*'s Christmas number 145

15 The *Freethinker* for 16 July 1882 146

16 *Punch*'s view of the "Bradlaugh Bill's" defeat 195

17 Holyoake records his progress in language 247

18 Staging blasphemy: One of Hatherell's *Jude* illustrations 276

19 The "Master" (Thomas Hardy) in his study   281

20 Holyoake's sketch of the Reverend Bush's notorious gate   299

21 Collage of materials in the Pooley case, 1857   303

22 Hatherell's final image for *Jude,* November 1895   312

Acknowledgments

This study is indebted to the librarians at Santa Barbara and throughout the University of California system who made possible early research; the curators of the John Johnson Collection, Oxford (especially Julie) and the Bodleian Library generally; the National Secular Society (with thanks to Terry Mullins); reference librarian David Webb of the historic Bishopsgate Working-Men's Institute, housing the Holyoake Collection and the library of the National Secular Society; Gillian Lonegan at the Co-operative Union, Holyoake House, Manchester; the Huntington Library, California, home to the Carlile Collection; the Public Records Office at Kew; the British Library in Bloomsbury and at Colindale (newspapers); the staff and volunteers of the Dorchester Country Museum who maintain the Dorsetshire and Thomas Hardy Collections; the Dorchester Reference Library; the Cornwall County Records Office at Truro; and the caretakers of Bodmin Goal and Bodmin Asylum. I am grateful to Rodney Phillips and the curatorial staff of the Berg Collection, New York Public Library, for access to materials on William Hone and George Cruikshank, and to manuscripts librarian Robert Matuozzi and secetary Frank Sciamanda of Washington State University at Pullman, who graciously facilitated distance access to holdings. Special thanks are due to Maggie Kimball and the Department of Special Collections of Stanford University, who generously assisted the photographing of rare materials, and to Sonia Moss and the staff of Stanford's Inter-Library Loan Office for their incomparable helpfulness and good cheer.

I am deeply grateful to the University of California, Santa Barbara, for the Summer Research, Dissertation Year, and General Affiliates' Fellowships that enabled me to carry out preliminary research, and to write a doctoral thesis that laid out some of the groundwork for this completed study. I was enabled to undertake archival research between 1989 and 1991 by a postdoctoral fellowship from the Mellon Foundation: I thank not only the foundation but my colleagues and the superb support staff at the California Institute of Technology, to which I was attached for the duration of the fellowship (and, in a different sense, still am attached), especially John Sutherland. I owe my deepest debts to him; to the best of all possible doctoral supervisors, Garret Stewart, now at the University of Iowa; and to my colleagues at Stanford University, especially David Riggs (who *dared* me to get a draft done), Rob Polhemus (most indefatigable of readers), John Bender, Terry Castle, Herbert Lindenberger, Jason Camlot, Marjorie Perloff, and Elizabeth Traugott. This study also benefited from opportunities to present and discuss my research provided by Patrick Parrinder of Reading University and Michael Slater of Birkbeck College, London. In 1994–95, writing was made possible by an American Council of Learned Societies fellowship, and residence at the Stanford Humanities Center. In 1996–97, the last stages of editing were greatly assisted by my friends Reinhart Lutz and Caron Cadle, and by the good efforts of Erika Mikkelsen, Phin Younge, Bruce Suttmeier, Lisa Jenkins, Ryan Johnson, and (especially) Renee Fox. My thanks to Ann Donahue for an excellent job of copyediting.

WORD CRIMES

I think that there is an interesting subject of investigation, for the student of traditions, in the history of Blasphemy, and the anomalous position of that term in the modern world. It is a curious survival in a society which has for the most part ceased to be capable of exercising that activity or of recognizing it.

T. S. Eliot, *After Strange Gods*

BEAUFORT. Pope, Swift, Shakespeare himself, and every other name you can mention . . . is hateful to my ear, and detestable to my remembrance.
LADY SMATTER. I am thunderstruck!—this is downright blasphemy.

Fanny Burney, *The Witlings*

INTRODUCTION

In the summer of 1988 I was in the Ephemera Room of the Bodleian Library, Oxford, doing one of those "quick" favors for a friend that takes all day. Half an hour before closing, the librarian, taking pity, asked me what I was working on myself. I wasn't sure, I said: atheism, perhaps; heresy, possibly; what the Victorians summed up as "Freethought." Would I like to take a look at a cardboard box in the back room that was stumping her to catalogue, she asked? I wiped off the dust, and found inside a tattered and yellowed memoir: *Prisoner for Blasphemy* by G. W. Foote, editor of the *Freethinker,* 1884 (fig. 1). I had never heard of the man, his atheistical penny paper with its front-page "Comic Bible Cartoons," or the "celebrated" case of 1883 (E. Coleridge 1: 251). Yet it had produced three separate trials, the last in the Court of Queen's Bench before the lord chief justice of all England; a year in Holloway Gaol with hard labor for Foote (six and three months for his associates); and a historic ruling that, under the cloak of religious liberality, mandated the policing of language and ensured blasphemy's survival into the twentieth century: "I now lay it down as law, that, if the decencies of controversy are observed, even the fundamentals of religion may be attacked without a person being guilty of blasphemous libel" (J. Coleridge 28). If the decencies were not observed, the culprit was guilty.

Foote's prison memoir was an unlikely find for more reasons than first appear. It is a fragile paperback; I have traced five surviving copies in Britain and the United States. The British Library at Colindale holds an imperfect set of the *Freethinker;* the only full run used to be kept in a North London basement, periodically flooded, by a beleaguered atheistical organization, founded in 1866, called the National Secular Society (N.S.S.).[1] Foote sur-

PROSECUTED FOR BLASPHEMY.

THE FREETHINKER.

EDITED BY G. W. FOOTE.
Sentenced to Twelve Months' Imprisonment for Blasphemy.
Interim Editor, EDWARD B. AVELING, D.Sc., Fellow of University College, London.

William James Ramsey, as Proprietor, sentenced to Nine Months' Imprisonment; and Henry Arthur Kemp, as Printer and Publisher, sentenced to Three Months' Imprisonment.

Vol. III.—No. 26.]   JULY 1, 1883.   [PRICE ONE PENNY.

GEORGE WILLIAM FOOTE.

MR. FOOTE, whose counterfeit and certainly unflattering presentment is given to our readers this week, is still a young man, but it is many years since he first threw his well-filled and well-trained mind into the Freethought service. An early love of literature had brought him into contact with the writings of such men as Mill, Carlyle, Ruskin and Darwin, and while still in his teens, a thoroughgoing spirit of inquiry resulted in his complete emancipation from the superstitions in which he had been nurtured. Restless in propaganda, in 1869 he was concerned in starting the Secular Sunday School of which he became superintendent. In the same year he formed a Young Men's Secular Association, with the object of organising the young men of the Secular party in London and training them for debate. He afterwards conducted classes in logic with the same purpose. He contributed to the *National Reformer* from as early as 1870, and many of his early papers such as the one entitled "Joys and Sorrows" and those upon "The Poetry of William Blake," bear witness to his poetic insight, as well as to his critical ability and purity of style.

Orthodox Christians who take it for granted that opposition to their creed must proceed from some bad qualities of head or of heart, probably look upon Mr. Foote as a very vulgar person, justly incarcerated for coarse and offensive attacks on the religion of the land. Nothing could be further from the mark. Justice North, who made it evident how inferior in all the qualities of a gentleman a judge could be to the person he convicted, was constrained to speak respectfully of his intellectual abilities, and Lord Coleridge spoke in the most admiring manner of his striking and able defence in the Court of Queen's Bench. Mr. Foote has the culture which is incompatible with vulgarity; but he has also the earnestness which is above hypocrisy. In the volume entitled "Arrows of Freethought," some of Mr. Foote's most trenchant onslaughts upon Christianity have been reprinted.

[No. 99.]

The reader will find smart wit, satire, vigorous home-thrusts, ridicule, and relentless logic, but he will fail to find coarseness or scurrility there, or indeed in any line of our paper, for editing which he is now herded with criminals. Strange as it may seem to the Christian, Mr. Foote has something of the fastidiousness which goes with the poetic and artistic temperament. His love of art is intense but particular. In painting he prefers Titian, Agelico, Turner. In music, Beethoven, Wagner, Chopin. In poetry, Shakspeare, Byron, Shelley; and among moderns, Browning. George Meredith is his favorite novelist. In the course of his itinerant apostleship of Freethought he has very frequently lectured on the poets of progress and the prose teachers of our time. The very first public discussion on the merits of Darwin *versus* Moses was, I believe, that held for two nights in Glasgow between Messrs. G. W. Foote and H. A. Long. Mr. Foote has also defended Freethought in set debates with Dr. Sexton, the Revs. Harrison, Woffendale, and others. On the platform his bearing is easy and impressive. His speech is deliberate but unhesitating—well-chosen words and sound arguments, seasoned with mother wit, wide reading, and upon occasion, impassioned eloquence.

In 1876 Mr. Foote started the *Secularist*, a publication in which many thoughtful and high-toned articles appeared. In 1879 he became editor of the *Liberal*, a Radical and Freethought magazine. The principal contributions, both political and anti-theological, were from his pen. Some papers on Gambetta, a favorite of whom he always speaks with enthusiasm, are certainly among the best that have ever appeared on that statesman. Looking on the clerical party as the obstructives and *obscuranti* of Europe and believing that our hopes centre round the French Republic, Mr. Foote has for many years taken the keenest interest in watching every turn of the ever-shifting game of French politics.

Thinking the time had come for a thorough clearing of the ground from the wreck and 'lumber of the past; and deeming that its best work was to be done by attacking superstition, he started the *Freethinker* with the avowed

Figure 1. Foote the "Martyr" pictured on the *Freethinker*'s cover three months into his imprisonment. Notice the banner headline and legal details. Reprinted by permission of the British Library.

vives today only as a caricature in Arthur Calder-Marshall's genealogy of 1960s "alternative" societies, and as a bit player in a few works about the N.S.S. and its charismatic Cockney leader Charles Bradlaugh, Britain's first openly atheistical, working-class member of Parliament. Leonard Levy dismisses Foote as a bigoted specialist in "sleaze, ridicule, and hate" (*Blasphemy* 479). In effect, the *Freethinker* and its editor have vanished into an Orwellian memory hole. The story they cap and conclude, the history of blasphemy in nineteenth-century Britain, seems an atrophied branch on culture's evolutionary tree, a history deliberately forgotten.

Piecing it together looked like digging a grave for my own scholarly burial in 1988. Chadwick, Cockshut, and Willey had settled the matter of the Victorian loss of faith, advisers said; the novel of doubt, the genre graced by Newman, Froude, Pater, and Mrs. Ward, seemed set forever to eke out existence as a dreary compendium of sociological data. Tidy professional distinctions among theology, political studies, and history masked the identity of religious and political protest into the last decades of the nineteenth century, and their eventual divergence minimized in hindsight the importance of what had gone before.

Besides, Mr. Foote, the son of a low-ranking Plymouth customs officer, and (it turned out) his two hundred blaspheming predecessors of the nineteenth century were not born to rub shoulders with the Tennyson of *In Memoriam* or the Arnold of "Dover Beach." All except a handful belonged to what the *Freethinker* called "the *elite* of the working class" (5 February 1888: 42); of the rest only two ranked higher than a bookseller or a penny journalist, and they were anomalies. (For convenience, this study calls this combination of upper working and lower middle classes "lower class.") We do not have time for the subliterary in our literature seminars; and neither the study of "culture" as Arnold remade it nor the cultural study of material reality as Marx construed it accommodates popular Freethought. It is easy to forget that Bernard Shaw admired Foote, or that Bertrand Russell lectured on N.S.S. platforms. And while a tenderness of elegy lingers on Victorian agnosticism, vulgar unbelief gets a snobbish or fearful dismissal: the one was "honest doubt," the other (in period phrase) a plot to "rob" people of their compensations in heaven.[2] The growing pile of papers on my desk—transcripts, cuttings, letters, pamphlets, diaries—told an impossible story. Blasphemy in the nineteenth century, in the age of achieved democracy and religious toleration, was a crime that could not have existed; blasphemy in the twentieth, a decade and more since the last (scandalous) prosecution in Great Britain in 1977, was obsolete and uninteresting. Our cultural memories are short. But the two hundred cases remained. And then Salman Rushdie published the *Satanic Verses.*

Almost none of the two hundred cases were isolated events. The people who fought them made up a distinct tradition of conscious protest and willful "martyrdom" that stretches back to 1817 and beyond into the 1790s, tying the Romanticism and rough radicalism of the 1810s to the respectability of the 1880s, shoving the French Revolution and Tom Paine's plain-spoken Bible criticism full in the face of Victorian society. G. W. Foote entered Holloway Gaol in 1883 not only as that tradition's inheritor but as a confirmed leader of the movement that grew out of it, the most important "advanced" lower-class political grouping to emerge in Britain between the decline of Chartism and Owenism in the 1840s and the rise of socialism in the late 1880s: the indigenous atheistical movement christened "Secularism," circa 1851, by its founder, George Jacob Holyoake. Terra incognita to literary or cultural studies, though it has had some able historians, Secularism had an importance out of all proportion to its size in its "heroic" and "militant" decade of the 1880s, reorganized by Bradlaugh as the N.S.S. Its writers and orators focused the most contentious and dramatic issues of the day: the religious oath that secured legal and civil proceedings; blasphemy; birth control; freedom of speech, of meeting, and of publication; access to political power. All three of the Secularist movement's national leaders were prosecuted for blasphemy: Jacob Holyoake, imprisoned 1842; "Iconoclast" Bradlaugh, whose legal skills helped him slip the net in 1883; and G. W. Foote, who became N.S.S. president in 1890. Though they may look today like history's "losers," men who followed "blind alleys [and] lost causes," they loomed large in history "as it in fact occurred" and as E. P. Thompson urges us to remember it (12).

"When . . . 'God is dead,' Atheism dies also," Bernard Shaw wrote in the *Freethinker* in 1908 (1 November: 689). But the same cannot be said of blasphemy: Shaw's own *Blanco Posnet* invoked that very charge in 1909. An American judge once rightly described it as a "chameleon" crime (Levy, *Treason* 336). The verses that establish blasphemy as the crime of crimes in the Judeo-Christian tradition (Leviticus 24.11–16) omit to tell us what it consists in. How did the "stranger" stoned to death by the community "blaspheme the name of the LORD"? How was this different from "curs[ing]"? English law followed suit, from the crucial first statutes "On the burning of heretics" in 1400, until the Reformation forced a distinction of heresy and blasphemy.[3] But the failure to define blasphemy qua blasphemy persisted through passage of a severe statute "for the more effectual suppressing of blasphemy and profaneness" in 1698, into the nineteenth century.[4] When Joseph Hume demanded a definition in Parliament in 1823, Wilberforce answered, "If you desire to go as near as you safely can to blasphemy, I only hope that you will find that you have overstepped the mark, and incurred the punishment which you tempted" (qtd. in Thomas, *Long Time* 206). The prevailing vagueness, said the century's wittiest miscreant, William Hone, reminded him of the tyrant of Syracuse, who wrote his laws high up on the walls "in very small letters," and brutally punished the malefactors (i.e., *all* malefactors) who were unable to read them (W. Hone, *Three Trials* 154). No authoritative interpretation of the law of blasphemy has ever been given. It was even doubtful, declared Lord Sumner in 1917, if its foundations had ever been fully investigated. "Blasphemy," Bradlaugh concluded, pleading for abolition in the House of Commons in 1889, was simply "an ever-changing word" (*Speeches* 157).

On the one hand, confusion had practical uses; and definitions are only needed when consensus breaks down, as the leading Victorian theorist of the criminal law, Sir James Fitzjames Stephen, remarked in 1882 (*History* 2: 396). On the other hand, there is a real sense in which blasphemy was— and is—genuinely indefinable. On one side it slides into "obscenity," on another into "treason" and "sedition." Blasphemy finds cognate offenses in slander and libel; "hate speech" and "fighting words" are its descendants. "In a world of superstition," said American infidel Colonel Robert Ingersoll in 1885, "reason is blasphemy. In . . . a world of lies, truth is blasphemy" (*Real Blasphemy* 5). To play on the legal adage, the greater the "truth," the greater the "blasphemous libel," as the crime can be technically known. Like Foucault's deceptively simple concept of transgression, blasphemy marks the moving boundary line between the permissible and the prohibited: it is always what you may not say; always whatever affronts what the people, or the people in power, put their faith in—God, religion, nature, art, even democracy, freedom, or childhood innocence.

It is partly for these reasons that *Word Crimes* does not unfold a single theory of blasphemy. There is little to learn from a naked and reductive formula, shorn of historical context: *Blasphemy is the speaking of the unspeakable.* Rather, this study seeks to uncover the uses and meanings of blasphemy for English culture by pushing steadily to its limits the question of how and why the *Freethinker* case came to trial in 1883, forty years after Jews were admitted to Parliament and the last penalty on dissent was erased, and a generation after the crime was declared dead in 1857.[5] Drawing on a bulk of archival and manuscript material, as well as extant published historical sources, *Word Crimes* reconstructs a unified and particular account of nineteenth-century blasphemy from the close of the Napoleonic Wars to the *Freethinker* case and its aftermath.

The blasphemy of G. W. Foote emerges as a necessary and inevitable historical event. The third trial of the *Freethinker*, 24 April 1883, when editor Foote and Lord Chief Justice Coleridge faced each other across the highest

court in the land, figures here as a transforming spectacle, a kind of blasphemous primal scene. But it was not a trial for "blasphemy" as we have traditionally understood it: as the contradiction of dogmas, especially the Trinity
(the "blasphemy" of the Unitarians, relieved in 1813); as the denial of the
Holy Bible's divine inspiration, a profound threat to Protestantism; as the
reviling of religion; or more generally and anciently, as "treason against
God." Blasphemy's nineteenth-century renaissance not only signaled an obsolete law's acquisition of a Foucauldian "disciplinary" and "normalizing"
function but the positive transference of faith to new objects of worship:
class-coded Respectability, "serious" Literature, and "nice, clean English"
(Du Maurier 120). The case of G. W. Foote and the *Freethinker* proves a
cultural watershed. For forty years, Leonard Levy writes, his research as a
legal historian centered on freedom of speech, and blasphemy "lurked . . .
in the background" (*Blasphemy* x). My own feeling is stronger. Blasphemy
holds up a looking glass in which we seem at first to see nineteenth-century
history upside down but end by wondering if the inversions of ideology
have not disturbed our vision for two hundred years.

Reverence for the new idol of Respectability determined blasphemy's
ultimate transformation into a class crime of language. Lord Coleridge's
momentous ruling, binding to this day, consolidated several hundred years
of secular evolution from "sin" to "crime," officially recreating blasphemy
as what the nineteenth century had covertly made of it: a mechanism of
sociopolitical control. On the eve of the Third Reform Act that gave a
"voice" in government to every working man in the country, the ruling
clawed back what might best be called "language power" by establishing a
single standard for public discourse that it was impossible for the less educated to observe. It criminalized vulgarity, especially Cockney vulgarity.

But as Foote himself perceived, blasphemy's class transformation also
told the tale of how a "literary difference" became a "criminal offence"
(*Prisoner* 42). Trial by trial, 1817 to 1883, we can trace the process whereby
the Bible—once protected by blasphemy law, and the century's primary
"fetish" (Foote, in Herrick, *Vision* 39), the Book that entered the nineteenth
century as the sacred repository of Truth—was demoted to literary "masterpiece," while Literature was installed as England's cultural policeman and
primary standard of value.[6] (As Richard Webster tartly remarks, Ayatollah
Khomeini "blasphemed" that very same "sacred cow" in issuing his *fatwah*
against the *Satanic Verses*.) Ironically, Foote's own legal *succès d'estime* completed the process. At his third trial for blasphemy, he was allowed to do
what no defendant had been allowed to do since 1817, by the lord chief
justice of all England: he read aloud, in court, for comparison, side by
side, indicted items from the *Freethinker* and extracts from the works of

Swinburne, Arnold, Huxley, and "other heretics whose works are circulated by Mudie['s Circulating Library]" (*Prisoner* 14). Prisoner and judge alike called on Literature as Evidence, Literature as Authority. The third trial of the *Freethinker* thus marked an extraordinary moment. For in making that defense, Foote won a liberating admission of the real source of Victorian values, to which Freethinkers too could subscribe. But by consecrating the authority of high Literature, he also confirmed his own and his ilk's construction as its subliterary and criminal "other."

Blasphemy's literary history pointed in turn to another story. What made it England's original sin of language was the nation's investment of faith *in* the language, a faith that both dramatically surged and yet was also at risk in the 1880s. The prosecution of Foote's penny paper gave legal and public outlet to the fear of words endemic in a culture addicted to euphemism—blasphemy's exact etymological, linguistic opposite—at exactly the moment when the "holdfast" offered English (S. Coleridge, qtd. in Dowling 29) by the revered idiom of the King James Bible was taken away by publication of the Revised Version, issued 1881–86. At the same time—developments germane to but outside the main scope of this study—English was called on to bear the burden of "universal" tongue and instrument of rational imperial rule, and it began its sacral monumentalization at the hands of James Murray and the *Oxford English Dictionary.* These contradictory events demanded and even produced the outburst of blasphemy, the historical manifestation of the imagined "word crime" of *1984:* the apparent oddity of blasphemy in fact proves vital to our understanding of central strands in nineteenth-century culture. Certainly, only its history welds those strands into the interlinked chain of cultural phenomena that they were. Nor could anything else so weld them in light of the persistent will to faith that could canonize Literature when it lost faith in the Bible, or transfer to "mere" words the sacred awe it once owed to the Word.

Foote's three trials were the notorious cap to seventy years of blasphemy martyrdom. "The laws are not enforced consistently," a 1914 committee for repeal complained to the prime minister, "and they are enforced at irregular intervals" (*Prime Minister and the Blasphemy Laws* 4). Exactly so. The laws against blasphemy were invoked at times of special political stress and cultural pressure throughout the century: the 1810s; the "Hungry Forties"; and the troubled and atheistical 1880s, that transitional decade between the heyday of "high Victorianism" and the excesses of the "naughty nineties" perennially neglected by literary and cultural scholars. These are coincidences of date in the richest and most literal sense of the term: blasphemy marks the lines of convergence between public political trauma and aesthetic, personal, and class transformation.

Chapter 1 explores the trials of the 1810s. Tried three times on three consecutive days in December 1817 for three parodies on the catechism, the creed, and the Litany, a dusty middle-aged bookseller called William Hone caused a national sensation when he defended himself—and *won*. His case and his strange subsequent career open a dramatic prospect on the politicization of blasphemy; the threat and "treason" of laughter; the theory and offense of parody as a type of literary "decomposition"; parody's relations with forgery, apocrypha, impostordom, and popular literature; and the blasphemous risks and class dangers faced by the celebrated novelist who cracked jokes over Hone's grave in 1842, Charles Dickens.

Hone was a solitary and a near genius. His fellow blasphemer of the 1810s was a different animal. Plainspoken Richard Carlile won the right of free publication for revolutionary Tom Paine's critique of the Bible, *The Age of Reason*, through six years of incarceration; he figures by sheer force of will in the evolution of an "intellectual vernacular," as Olivia Smith has finely called it (x), and its fight for a public hearing against the voices of class and established power. As importantly, his individual struggle inspired perhaps 150 working-class volunteers to take up the cause. Most earned their places in history, although some at all times and all at some times were "impudent, vulgar, over-earnest, or 'fanatical' " (E. Thompson 732). They account among them for perhaps three quarters of the blasphemy cases of the nineteenth century, and served two centuries in jail. Blasphemy made their claim to "independence" and intellectual being; the printing press was their engine of "Knowledge" as "Power."

That Baconian slogan was the motto of Henry Hetherington, champion of the "unstamped" cheap newspaper press and the first subject of chapter 2. His name is familiar to history, though his blasphemous role in the people's "leap into literacy" is not: it should stand, where it does not, in the history of the mass-market paperback and the genealogy of the book club. In fact, put names to the individuals who made up the whole century's "United Order of Blasphemers" (Holyoake, qtd. in *Trial of Thomas Paterson* 80), and you experience an uncanny sense of déjà-vu. They are exactly the same names that figure in the struggle for freedom of the press and of publication in the nineteenth century: that story is their same story too.

Indicted in 1840, Hetherington also put in train the very public prosecution for blasphemy of Edward Moxon, high-class publisher of the *Complete Works* of Shelley. These included, of course, the atheistical *Queen Mab*, the favored underground text of radical activists and piratical publishers, which (with Byron's *Cain*) had offered government its best target for prosecution of a major and reputed author through the 1810s and early 1820s. Moxon was found guilty, though never called up for sentence. His case was important, nevertheless. In his defense, counsel Thomas Noon Talfourd advanced literature's claim to cultural status and authority in terms that startlingly prefigured the trial of Penguin Books for *Lady Chatterley's Lover* 120 years later, and in rhetoric that revealed the powerful influence of his friend William Wordsworth. Literature's claim was recognized a few months later in passage of the landmark Copyright Act of 1842. The bill had failed repeatedly from 1837, when Talfourd first introduced it. The specter of a cheap press directed from below and configured as blasphemous per se, glimpsed through Moxon's subjection to Henry Hetherington, may well have hurried it into law.

Hetherington's friend Jacob Holyoake, the other subject of chapter 2, was almost an eminent Victorian. Prosecuted for an aside during a lecture on home colonization in 1842, he really went to jail for "devilism," that is, Owenite socialism (McCabe 1: 65, 66), and for his connection to the first openly atheistical journal published in England, the outrageous *Oracle of Reason*. His trials, and those of his flamboyant *Oracle* colleagues, focus issues of "blasphemous" lower-class literary ambition and claims to "[their] own words" (Holyoake, *History of the Last Trial* 65);[7] they uncover the underground identification of language with property and a "voice" in politics; and they reveal respectable bourgeois fear of "publicity" and the unwashed "public."

Chapters 3, 4, and 5 explore the cultural-political, literary, and linguistic meanings of the climactic *Freethinker* case as they are described above, adding in chapter 5 the after-tale of Jacob Holyoake's exemplary chastening by the "law" in language. Finally, chapter 6 brings the century's blasphemous inheritance to bear on a single literary text. The prosecution of G. W. Foote and his comic atheist penny paper laid the mines Thomas Hardy exploded in *Jude the Obscure*. Understand the pressures producing as well as punishing blasphemy in 1883, and you re-create the offensive context and the censoring mechanisms that pronounced Hardy's last novel "dirt, drivel, and damnation" in 1895 (*Pall Mall Gazette*, in Lerner and Holmstrom 111).[8] But Foote is not *Jude's* only blasphemous ghost. This final chapter also recovers the most forgotten of the martyrs to blasphemy law, a Cornish laborer sentenced to twenty-one months' imprisonment in 1857. The indebtedness of Hardy's novel to the story of Pooley "the obscure" restores scandal, pathos, and political edge to the swan song that closed the book on Victorian fiction.

The novel here invoked has several roles to play in this study. Its first burden is one of proof and demonstration. As the era's most characteristic literary form, and a prime producer of sociability and community, the novel is our most sensitive surviving measure of Victorian culture's *epistēmē*. Moreover, as Noel Annan remarks, the "most severe" of those restraints on freedom, which a society will always impose upon its "most influential" medium, fell in Victorian times on the novel (67). Anglo-Irish George Moore, who walked into the well-policed world of English fiction in the 1880s from the free air of France and a private income, left posterity the most disgusted record of the infantilization and commodification fostered by the circulating library system and the costly thirty-one shilling and six-pence, three-decker format it favored, *Literature at Nurse, Or, Circulating Morals*.[9] Quiet commercial censorship by Mudie's, Smith's, and the other book-lending outfits, combined (later in the century) with the profitable practice of serial publication in general interest periodicals, together created a bourgeois novel that lived more and more by encoding, indirection, and strategic compensatory maneuvers. If "advanced" ideas were "inserted edge-wise so to say," as Hardy wrote his publisher, they might become "the most attractive remarks of all," not foci for outraged offense (Seymour-Smith 85). A novel, like a successful crook, had to have a good alibi; the "supply of family fiction" was a job (Seymour-Smith 411)—Trollope compared it unfavorably to stone breaking (98). While Hardy chafed against the form's constraints, Moore helped to smash the system that fed on it, not only by launching his polemic against "Tradesman" Mudie and his "intolerable jurisdiction" (28, 32) but by publishing his own novels in one-volume, six-shilling editions.[10] That assault begs comparison with the rupture in public discourse that was the *Freethinker*'s contemporary crime of blasphemy.[11]

What is at stake in the whole history here retold, then, is what is always at issue in literary studies: the inscription of social relations; the status and dynamics of literature; the interplay of accepted "licence" and fictional of-fense; and the power and possibilities of words. It is indeed "[b]ecause blasphemy is a linguistic act," as David Lawton writes, "and a place where one sees whole societies theorizing language" that it demands fine-grained literary analysis (17). The subliterary texts that bore the blasphemous brand deserve to be treated—as Christopher Herbert says of nineteenth-century scientific and philosophical works—"as if they were poems" (25). What follows seeks not to use the history of blasphemy as a quarry for a disquisi-tion on "representing" protest or "fictionalizing" the lower classes. Rather, it also finds in the history of blasphemy a unique key to what made Victo-rian fiction tick. The will to transgression and the urge to avoid it may be integral elements in all literary production, and our relative critical judg-ments of both may profoundly affect our sense of what has artistic merit at any moment. Thus, blasphemy and its opposite, euphemism or "reti-cence," may prove as germane to understanding Victorian fiction as the disciplinary mechanisms at work in David Miller's *Novel and the Police.* They are certainly more culturally specific phenomena. In hearkening to the "howling" voice of the "hooligan" working classes, *Word Crimes* hopes to give back to the era's fiction a context and a method of understanding it has lacked.[12]

For like language, literature regenerates itself from below as much as from above; "trickle-down theories" do not always or even most often apply.[13] It is true that both Foote and Hardy read Mill, but that does not mean that Foote can be derived from Mill, or that the primary influences on Hardy were as respectable as *On Liberty. Word Crimes* attempts to read Victorian culture not as we have habitually read it, and as our resources and methods make it easier to read it, from the top of the social ladder down, but from the bottom up. As it does so, it tries also to beware of inverted snobbery and the assumption of "authenticity." Thomas Hardy was also a tuft hunter, and blaspheming Mr. Foote bashed the Salvation Army for using boot camp English.

The *Freethinker* case of 1883 had abiding real consequences for that "freedom and sincerity in literature" that J. M. Robertson, as editor of Secularism's earnest other face, the *National Reformer,* like Foote himself, put at the top of the movement's agenda (qtd. in Royle, *Radicals* 331). We owe those benefits today not to literary "heroes," "advanced" writers, and daring novelists, or even to legal pioneers and resolute jurists, but to the obscure blasphemy martyrs of the nineteenth century who fought the cause of free publication with their incarcerated bodies, and exploited their legal "privilege" to conduct their own defenses publicly to stage their right to a "voice." Foote is perhaps their best single representative, as he is the perfect example of the extinct "militant" Secularist, an outlawed Victorian archetype. "[M]en are now benefited by his exertions," as Jacob Holyoake wrote of Richard Carlile, "who remember him not, who knew him not, and who would disown or revile him if they did" (*Life and Character of Richard Carlile* 38).

This study has three obvious limitations. A very few of the men and women convicted in the nineteenth century were not members of the tradition of blasphemous martyrdom but religious extremists and idiosyncratic "prophets." One was a crippled shoemaker, "Zion" Ward, who inherited the mantle of visionary zealot Joanna Southcott, and drew enormous crowds for his messianic lectures in the summer of 1831. Early the next year he was locked away for declaring, "The Bishops and Clergy are Religious Impostors, and as such by the laws of England are liable to Corporal Punishment" (qtd. in E. Thompson 800). The anticlerical anger matched that of the Secularists and their predecessors, who took advantage of his fervor. But Ward's blasphemy seems to have been the result of religious mania. It is for this reason that he has no place in this story.

A second limitation concerns gender. A courageous few of the two hundred martyrs were women. Carlile's wife and sister were the first to carry on the fight when he was jailed in 1819. "Had [they] flinched," he said, all would have "gone to wreck" (*Republican,* 12 October 1819: 97–98). One of the volunteers in his shop, Susannah Wright, was "committed for a contempt of Court" at her blasphemy trial in 1822 for deciding that "I shall plead for myself" (*Speech of Mrs. Susannah Wright* 3). "[H]andsome" and "invincible" Harriet Adams hawked the notorious twenty-fifth number of the *Oracle* about the streets when her husband was arrested in 1842. Matilda Roalfe, prosecuted in Edinburgh in 1844, refused to plead feminine ignorance or subordination (Holyoake, *Sixty Years* 1: 110), though her story literally makes an appendix to a male drama of blasphemy (*Trial of Thomas Paterson* 75–80).

I use the term "male drama" deliberately. For blasphemy, like common cursing and "strong language," progressively gendered itself male as Victoria's reign lengthened. The book that might do these women justice would set them in different company, with the female "heretics" who denied nineteenth-century England's association of femininity and faith: with Carlile's masterful lover, Eliza Sharples, England's first atheistical woman lecturer and equal-rights magazine editor (*Isis,* 1832); escaped wife and Owenite Emma Martin, whose unbelieving deathbed became the locus of unseemly controversy; political economist Harriet Martineau; unorthodox publisher's reader Geraldine Jewsbury; Eliza Lynn Linton, witch-hunter, antifeminist polemicist, and author of the *True History of Joshua Davidson, Christian and Communist;* colonial heretic Olive Schreiner; Hardy's fictional Sue, in *Jude the Obscure;* and Mrs. Humphry Ward, author of *Robert Elsmere.*

The National Secular Society was the first political organization to make women's suffrage an open objective of policy: enough, said Foote, of doing as St. Paul bid them, "play[ing] second fiddle in a minor key" (Herrick, *Vision* 30). Free the nation's domestic "angels" of the religion that salved and suppressed them, he argued, and you would break religion's hold on the nation. The Secularist movement brought women to the fore: Mrs. Harriet Law, editor of the Birmingham *Secular Chronicle,* a florid middle-aged farmer's daughter who "had what some devotees of 'culchaw' do not possess—a great deal of natural ability" (Foote, *Freethinker,* 15 February 1891: 73); Bradlaugh's daughters, early students at London University; and, most famously, Annie Besant, birth control advocate and leader of the

Matchgirls' Strike of 1888, a luminary successively of Secularism, socialism, and Theosophy, who began her rebellion against God and her clergyman husband by mounting the pulpit in his empty church to send "my voice roll[ing] down the aisles," possessed by a "feeling of power" (*Autobiographical Sketches* 72). The women heretics await their due.

A third limit to this study is geographical, and brings with it important legal distinctions. The history here told is not Anglo-American nor European nor even truly "British," but specifically English. The Irish case of Catholic Redemptorist Father Vladimir Petcherine, spuriously charged with burning a Bible in Dublin in 1855, is not part of this mainland history, though it works well towards establishing the central point of David Lawton's *Blasphemy*, that "[t]he issue . . . normally arises in a community that is divided, and it normally arises because the community is divided" (118). The 1844 Edinburgh trials of Thomas Paterson, Thomas Finlay, and Matilda Roalfe do not qualify as "Scotch Trials," though this is how Holyoake catalogues them. Finlay was a native, but Paterson and Roalfe, the main antagonists, were sent up from England by committee to take propaganda advantage of the 1843 disruption of the Church of Scotland (Matilda Roalfe, letter, 7 November 1844, in HL).[14] Blasphemy was a capital offense in England until 1677, but in Scotland until 1813; the country's harsh background of dogmatic Calvinism sharply inflects the fictions of Scottish writers from James Hogg to Robert Louis Stevenson.

England is a very different country from France, a secular state inhabited by a nominally Catholic people, or from other European neighbors like Sweden, where a major writer like August Strindberg could not only be brought to trial for blasphemy in 1884 but could also be acquitted. England is very different, too, from the United States, which has no established religion, although until recently it did have prosecutions for blasphemy.[15] Persistent British class divisions, today haphazardly mapped on to race, and that habit of reticence that found its most invidious institutionalized form in the Official Secrets Act of 1889, create a culture in which the crime of blasphemy must be differently constructed than in a nation that enjoys the right to free speech under the First Amendment.

English law has its differences too. In England, "common" or "case" law has existed side by side with statute law for centuries, and it is "a well established and general principle," as a chief justice declared in 1819, that a statute which "is made agreeable to the common law . . . does not take away the original right to proceed on the common law" (*British Press*, 17 November: 3). The statute of 1698 was not once invoked in any of the two hundred trials for blasphemy in the nineteenth century; it performed its function merely in "supplementing" and therefore stiffening the law (Bradlaugh, *Speeches* 152). All two hundred proceeded under common law, in which decisions and interpretation depend on developments in earlier and comparable cases, with special status accorded to the rulings of chief justices, like Lord Coleridge's in the *Freethinker* case. Jeremy Bentham compared such "judge-made" law to the kind of ad hoc rules we make for our dogs (Pannick 144): like the Victorian novel, common law reflects and records the pressures of the times. But it also lets the past live in the present: "Crown law[y]ers," as Hone wrote Carlile in 1819, "stand still like the mile stones of an old road, over which nobody passes" (undated note in CC). The cultural resistance that scotched parliamentary attempts at abolition of the 1698 statute on blasphemy in 1883, 1886, 1889, 1913, 1914, the 1920s (three times), 1930, and 1936 persists to this day.[16] The statute was wiped from the books in 1969, but blasphemy remains a criminal offense in common law. The *Freethinker,* sole contemporary survivor of the thirty-odd periodicals into which Victorian Freethinkers poured their energies, devotes much space to attempts by pressure groups and politicians not to stamp it out but to extend its scope.

Here Salman Rushdie and blasphemous Mr. Foote shake hands. The case of the *Satanic Verses* recalls the "militant" atheists of the 1880s whose memory has faded over the horizon of history. A slender chain of names, obscure and notorious, besides a variety of minor actions and (Home Office papers reveal) unrealized repeat prosecutions of Foote between 1887 and 1908, form links between the trials of the *Freethinker* and the Satanic eruption of 1988:[17] Harry Boulter, prosecuted in 1908 and 1909; J. W. Gott, an ailing diabetic of fifty-five who did a record third "stretch" for a joking pamphlet called *God v. Gott* in the year Joyce published *Ulysses,* 1922, and died a few weeks after he got out of jail; and Dennis Lemon, respected editor of *Gay News,* who was handed the same stiff sentence of nine months in 1977, eight years after abolition of the 1698 statute (see below, 5.2).[18]

The *Freethinker* case disrupted and confirmed the closed circuit of a still largely homogeneous society. The affair of the *Satanic Verses* plays itself out across international borders and on the postcolonial streets of cities like Bradford, where Rushdie in 1988 (like Tom Paine in 1792) was burned in effigy: blasphemy came home, and "home" came apart. For while blasphemy law has survived, despite the fact that Christianity has lost hold over the vast majority of the population, it is an exclusive law that gives Islam no protection.[19] It shelters only the Church of England, the historical established religion of the state and the ruling classes. In Britain, where (in the language of blasphemy indictments) the Roman Mass could and still can be "depraved and reviled" with impunity (an open invitation to Ulster Protestant extremists), modern Hindus, Sikhs, and Muslims find themselves no less "strangers" in law than the worshippers of Baal (Judges 6.25–32) or the unbelieving vulgarian who put out the *Freethinker*, amongst other reasons, to protest a shameful political plot to deprive "Iconoclast" Charles Bradlaugh of his hard-won seat in Parliament.[20]

The trials of a penny paper and its blasphemous editor, however sharp-tongued and talented, may not dramatize the 1880s in the way that the global affair of the *Satanic Verses* did the 1980s, or in the manner that Oscar Wilde's crucifixion epitomizes the 1890s. But the *Freethinker* case was nevertheless the defining trial, and a defining event, of its decade. We live with its consequences.

CHAPTER ONE

BLASPHEMY, 1817–30

"You shall not revile the gods, nor curse the ruler of thy people" (Exodus 22.28). In the nineteenth century, an offense against the one came to be read as a crime against the other: blasphemy remembered its ancient interest in state control. And as the crime began its passage to political offense and treasonable practice, so it revealed its potential for class rebellion and popular protest.

The first important judicial distinction, 1656, between blasphemy and heresy—*"Crimen Judicii,"* "a purely ecclesiastical offense" (Odgers, *Libel and Slander* 455)—laid grounds for the crucial dictum that made blasphemy the province of civil control. Denounced by Jefferson and English radicals as a canny "judiciary forgery" (Jefferson 16: 50), it crystallized common law for the next two centuries. "Christianity being parcel of the laws of England," pronounced Chief Justice Hale at the 1676 blasphemy trial of a man called Taylor, "to reproach the Christian religion is to speak in subversion of the law" (Bonner 31). "Hale's law" was confirmed by the Blasphemy Act of 1698, and practically tested in the prosecution of Thomas Woolston in 1728. When it was moved, in arrest of judgment, that the secular wing had no authority in his case, "[t]he court declared," recorded Thomas Starkie's authoritative *Treatise on the Law of Slander and Libel* (1812), "they would not suffer it to be debated, whether to write against Christianity in general was not an offense of temporal cognizance" (2: 137).

The Woolston case was an important prelude to the trials with which this chapter deals for other reasons too. A well-educated Deist, Woolston had nevertheless used "forcible" and occasionally funny "homely" language, in a cheap pamphlet entitled *Six Discourses on the Miracles,* to argue for the nonliteral, allegorical interpretation of the Scriptures. He was rewarded with sales of thirty thousand copies, sixty rebarbative pamphlets in reply, and effective life imprisonment (Bonner 35). The case gave a pronounced class twist to official suspicion of all who threatened to spread the power of language, as if literacy were a political virus. Suspicion deepened with the 1763 case of Peter Annett, who compounded his crime by publishing in his own cheap magazine, the *Free Enquirer,* and became ingrained at the 1797 case of a bookseller named Williams, who was prosecuted for peddling Deism, republicanism, and egalitarianism in the plain English of revolutionary Tom Paine's *Age of Reason.* This was the book Carlile would make the national symbol of the struggle for "blasphemous" free publication in 1819.

By 1812, Starkie confirmed, it seemed "absurd" to "attempt to redress or avenge insults to a supreme and omnipotent Creator." Blasphemy was a crime "properly cognizable by municipal laws" only in so far as it "tend[ed] to weaken and undermine the very foundation on which all human laws must rest," thus immediately encouraging "acts of outrage and violence" (2: 127–30).[1] Its prosecution protected "the peace and good order of civil society" (2: 127), a formulation that quietly acknowledged the influence of Jeremy Bentham, through whose 1789 *Introduction to the Principles of Morals and Legislation* the concepts of public interest and public order entered mainstream legal thinking. (Ironically, Bentham actively supported Hone and was sympathetic to Carlile.) Starkie's further citation of blasphemy's "gross insult" to believers (2: 130), and of blasphemy as "licentious and contumelious abuse" (2: 146) by which "the general right of inquiry and discussion" was suspended (2: 144), would prove useful to government throughout the century in its attempts to put down blasphemy as a political crime whilst masking the motive of prosecution.

The state church whose ecclesiastical courts had long lost jurisdiction over blasphemy retained enormous power in the 1810s. Until reform (from 1835) and the revival of Evangelical fervor, the Church of England was politically corrupt, bloated with wealth, scandalously disorganized, and apparently indifferent to the spiritual fate of the new urban masses.[2] The total income of the twenty-one bishops in the House of Lords was 528,698 pounds a year, giving an average of over 25,000 pounds at a time when 300 pounds was considered a minimum income for gentlemanly living.[3] All but one were Tory appointees; all but two opposed parliamentary reform; and a few controlled their own pocket boroughs. To them, sneered the pioneer popular journalist, ex-Tory William Cobbett, "Reform . . . mean[t] *Revolution;* and that Revolution mean[t] a revolution like that in France, which . . . stripped the Church of all its property" (*Political Register,*

27 January 1820: 760–61). When the First Reform Bill was voted down in 1831, mobs stormed episcopal palaces and the bishops were burnt in effigy (Chadwick, *Church* 1: 28).

Parsons too were openly political, and nearly all Tories (Chadwick 1: 46). Nationally, only 4,413 of 10,533 actually lived in their parishes; the bulk of the work was done by underpaid curates, though the incumbents pocketed pew fees and collection offerings. Half the nation did not worship as Anglicans, and bitterly resented the church's tithe. It was claimed even in impoverished Ireland.[4] "What is the Church but one unvaried system of fraud and robbery?" asked the radicals (Chadwick 1: 35). "[T]he state of the poor and that of the Church," concurred Thomas Arnold, "are melancholy proofs of the folly of . . . 'letting well alone.'" Anglicanism was sick of an "incurable pestilence. . . . and no human power can preserve it" (Stanley 1: 281).[5]

The church survived, however, and retained its class power and social prestige throughout the century. Parsons were local potentates with broad control over housing, schooling, Poor Law administration, public health, even the granting of alcohol licenses. Crucially, they were magistrates, a typical doubling of roles in the period, giving point to one blasphemer's request to know whether his offense meant anything more in law than what a witness in a fellow "martyr's" case had called *"bringing a scandal upon the religion of the magistrates"* (Holyoake, *History of the Last Trial* 45; *Trial of Charles Southwell* 21). England's parsons hunted and laid down their wine cellars like any squires: one central objective of the Church of England, publicly professed and repeatedly reaffirmed, was to put a gentleman in every parish. Gladstone's description of state religion in the Roman Empire sums up Anglicanism's real position in the nineteenth century: "weak and effete as a religious discipline," but "of extraordinary power as a social institution" (*Nineteenth Century*, May 1888: 775).

Not that there was no religious faith among the upper classes. The French Revolution had shocked them into piety. "It was a wonder to the lower orders," reported the *Annual Register* in 1798, "to see the avenues to the churches filling with carriages" (G. Trevelyan 506). All revolution's "horrors," they believed—"absurd[ly]" but "devoutly"—were "brought about by religious freethought";[6] the work of Hume and Gibbon was utterly undone. For nearly a century after the Terror, the upper ranks of society lived in fear of popular "Reason" and irreligion. "[T]hough Christianity could not be overturned, yet it might for a time be suppressed," Carlile's judge told his jury in 1819; "and in their own times in an adjoining country that was actually the case. The worship of Christ was neglected. . . . They knew what took place; the bands of society were torn asunder, and a dreadful scene of anarchy, of blood, and confusion followed" (*British Press*, 15 October 1819: 3). "The gospel is preached particularly for the poor," the attorney-general concurred; "It is calculated to show them the vanity of earthy things" (*Report of the Mock Trials of Carlile* 13).

But the revolution that appalled the haves had given hope to the have-nots. Revolution in France cemented an enduring English bond between radical politics and unbelief. The bogey the nineteenth century opposed to the gentleman clergyman was the urban "artisan atheis[t]" (Rossiter, title). The threat he posed increased in proportion to his independence, and the opportunity his trade afforded for reading or quiet reflection: printing, shoemaking, tailoring. It is no accident that silly Mrs Nickleby, reading of a murder in Dickens's serial entertainment of 1838–39, should remark, "somehow or other . . . they always are journeymen shoemakers who do these things" (*Nickleby* 569).[7] The figure of the "artisan atheist" condensed and embodied fearful national memory; he was the quintessential "underground actor" and "proscribed man" (Holyoake, *Sixty Years* 1: 1); he made a class specter of Locke's threat in a *Letter Concerning Toleration*: "Lastly, those are not at all to be tolerated who deny the being of a God"* (93).

For only fear of justice in the next world could ensure its operation in this: Blackstone underscored the belief in his foundational *Commentaries on the Laws of England* (4: 43). Few "underpinning assumption[s]" of modern society, as David Wootton remarks, have been so taken for granted (79). Those who most threatened it were those who already lived on the fringes of law as a property-owning society construed it, the impoverished working classes. "Everything . . . in the nineteenth century," as E. P. Thompson writes, "was turned into a battle-ground of class" (832); "the Atheist" was a man who "ignores God, just as a rude man might ignore the presence of his superior in rank" (*Spectator*, 28 April 1883: 542). Despite abundant evidence that social danger lay in the beer-sodden indifference and bestial ignorance of the urban poor, what colored the genteel imagination black was the considered unbelief that drove working men to sign the pledge and invest in Freethinking libraries.[8] Not all the blasphemers of the nineteenth century were outright atheists: the large majority before 1840 were Deists. But they were labeled atheists anyway. The word was a powerful weapon.

1817, the year William Hone came to trial, was a terrible year for the English common people. Depression and economic dislocation had followed two decades at war. Wages dipped, while bad harvests and new Corn Laws designed to save land values from collapse made starvation imminent. The Tories had a stranglehold on power, which they would keep until 1830, and used it to ward off—in the words of a House of Lords committee—

all prospect of insurrectionary "general plunder and division of property" (E. Thompson 639). Three quarters of the 658 members of Parliament were appointed more or less directly by peers or wealthy magnates. The only panaceas on offer were platitudinous dribblings like Hannah More's ballad on the workingman's duties, hawked about the streets to the tune of "A cobbler there was":

> So I'll work the whole day, and on Sundays I'll seek
> At church how to bear all the wants of the week.
>
> (qtd. in Hackwood 132)

Some took it for satire (Routledge 329); it enraged William Hone.

Englishmen were threatened where once they had justly been proud. The *post facto* system created between 1695 and Fox's Libel Act of 1792 had fostered a press that was the envy of Europe: "licensing" was swept away; an Englishman might "publish anything which twelve of his countrymen think is not blamable" (Lord Kenyon, qtd. in Odgers, *Libel and Slander* 10), unlike his compeer in France or Russia, where prima facie censorship lasted through the nineteenth century and politics were an open motive for preemptive prosecution.[9] These unique freedoms now stood at risk. Government was determined not to extend them to the cheap press born with Cobbett's "twopenny trash" in 1816. Cobbett himself had already been jailed for an attack on flogging abuses in the army; his satirical rival, T. J. Wooler, stood trial twice for the red-hot *Black Dwarf* in 1817. That year saw over twenty prosecutions of radical pressmen for "seditious libel." Many more were imprisoned without trial.

Indeed, constitutional liberty lay dying under a weight of new "gags" that reenacted the panic stricken repressions of the years following the Revolutionary Terror: the Treasonable Practices Bill; the Army and Navy Seduction Bill; the Seditious Meetings Bill, suppressing clubs and debating societies. "Our present rulers," Shelley wrote Leigh Hunt, "[are] creating a military and judicial despotism" (*Letters* 2: 148). In February 1817, the Liverpool Ministry suspended habeas corpus: moving the motion, Home Secretary Sidmouth singled out William Hone from all the suspect ranks of publishers, printers, and booksellers (fig. 2) for special denunciation. Shortly afterwards, in a notorious circular, Sidmouth abrogated to magistrates, including clerical magistrates, the power to issue warrants for the arrest of any person suspected of seditious or blasphemous libel, a startling, not to say unconstitutional extension of power to an untrained body of state officials, most of them Tories.

The stage was set. In December 1817, Hone was tried at the London Guildhall for publishing three outrageously popular political parodies: the

'The body of the people, I do think,
are loyal still,'
But pray, My L—ds and G—tl—n,
don't shrink
From exercising all your care
and skill,
Here, and at home,
TO CHECK THE CIRCULATION

OF LITTLE BOOKS,
Whose very looks—
Vile ' *two-p'nny trash*,'
bespeak abomination.
Oh! they are full of blasphemies
and libels,
And people read them
oftener than their bibles.

Figure 2. Liberty defends the printing press from the "Guilty Trio" of Tory ministers, caricatured as machine breakers: Castlereagh, Canning, and Home Secretary Sidmouth. From Hone's *Man in the Moon* (January 1820).

Late John Wilkes's Catechism of a Ministerial Member, the *Sinecurist's Creed
or Belief,* and the *Political Litany.* They were probably all his own productions.[10] His liability lay in the fact that they were modeled on the church
catechism, the creed, and the order for Anglican services, which included
the Lord's Prayer and the Ten Commandments. The three parodies were
tried separately before England's greatest judges by three separate juries.
All three declared Hone guiltless of blasphemy. He emerged from trial "a
kind of political martyr" (Tegg iii).[11] But the political motives that took
him to court taught the nation some literary lessons.

1. "YOU KNOW ME NOW, THE ARCH BLASPHEMER": THE THREE TRIALS OF WILLIAM HONE

Born in 1780, William Hone was a small-time publisher-bookseller and
amateur antiquarian who displayed his wares at "67, Old Bailey, three doors
from Ludgate Hill" (Hone, 1817 title pages, passim). He was a "seedy" and
retiring man in a rusty coat, said a witness of his trials, "with a half-sad,
half-merry twinkle in his eye," a clutch of old books always under his arm,
and another clutch of seven (later twelve) hungry offspring at home (Hackwood 155). Individualist and autodidact, possessed of a passion for justice,
Hone was the founding type of the nineteenth-century blasphemer: he was
the little man in excelsis, and he shuffled for his living between the worlds
of "high" and "low" literature.

That balancing act was easier to accomplish in unrespectable pre-
Victorian England. But it was precarious, nevertheless. This is part of the
Hone problem, and it is at once a political and literary problem. In his
own day, the distinction between high and low literature was not yet set
in stone; satire and parody were still equally tools of both. Immediately
after his trials, six hundred "fine" subscribers, John Keats wrote his brothers
(1: 199), made "William the Conqueror, the Game Cock of Guildhall," not
only the most popular man in Britain but also by far its wealthiest bookseller (title to 1818 lithograph, Patten 1: 139).[12] "Hone the publisher's . . .
Not Guilty," Keats thought, had done all writers "an essential service" (1:
191). He made Hone the personal poetical offering of his cryptic and colloquial sonnet "Nebuchadnezzar's Dream": understandable only in light of
events of 1817 and the tradition of biblical parody, it was considered spurious by De Selincourt forty-two years after discovery of Keats's manuscript
(A. Ward 177n), a meaningful denial. A "Lady unknown" sent "25 one,
and 5 five pound notes" (*Trial by Jury* 21); "Percy B. Shelley, Marlow,"
remitted five pounds (23); one of Hone's jurymen subscribed a pound (22);
the Earl of Sefton sat up on his deathbed to protest, to the tune of a hundred

guineas, the "spiteful imbecility" that had motivated the trials (copy of letter, facing p. 20 of *Trial by Jury,* in Hone Berg). Ominously, however, many donators signed themselves "No Parodist, but an Enemy to Persecution," or "My name wou'd ruin me" (*Trial by Jury* 21, 23).

Hone had "genius," "heroism," and "extraordinary talent," decided such well-known antiparody well-wishers as the Reverend Samuel Parr (Hone BL 40,108: 9–10). Successive years established him as a major player in English print culture, involved in every activity and innovation from the time of his trials to his death in 1842: radical journalism; political squibbery; serial publishing; popular history; cheap magazines; the miscellany and the almanac; the affordable illustrated book. But the mere accusation of blasphemy branded him: " 'Parodist!' rang in his ears to the last" (Routledge 281). The "glooms" that "outmastered me" shadowed even Hone's triumphant dedication of his 1825 *Every-Day Book* (see below, 1.2) to "CHARLES LAMB, Esq.," as a man who could "dare" to publish himself Hone's friend (1: v). The "blasphemy" of which Hone was accused in 1817 crystallized in history as a violation of the border between the subliterary and "proper" literature, scripture and fiction, the "literary" and the "political." And at his trials there took root dangerous taboos against profane and popular laughter, ridicule and parody.

Thus, in the decorous 1870s, publisher William Tegg, inheriting Hone's properties from his father, needed the excuse of public interest to condone republication of the trial transcripts, conveniently revived by James Routledge's 1876 *Chapters in the History of Popular Progress, 1660–1820.* Tegg's introduction is a squirming testament to bourgeois Victorian piety: "The publishers," he pleads, "must not . . . be in any way held responsible for the doctrine or teaching elicited," since the *Trials* contained the full texts of the parodies (v). Routledge more simply omitted painful "vulgarisms" (365) and other material, which to defend "now . . . would surely be pronounced an absurdity" (281). Hone's Edwardian biographer, F. W. Hackwood, suppressed the political import of his trials for blasphemy, refiguring his subject as a "gentle and innocuous" bibliophile, while he trumpeted his own revulsion for "burlesques" that "grate" upon the feelings (Hackwood 165, 112–13). His friend G. T. Lawley, the Wolverhampton antiquarian who gave Hackwood access to the family papers (passed to him from Hone's granddaughter in about 1900), left in manuscript a study of Hone's *Purely Literary Productions,* which consigns the "amateur" political half of his "dual" life to the dustbin of history (Lawley, preface in Hone WA). But Hone was political *and* literary, a man of the 1810s. To this day, he is misunderstood. Even so good a critic as Peter Manning allows him to play second fiddle to Byron only if he does it off-key, though Edgell

Rickword, J. Ann Hone, and Olivia Smith do justice to different phases of his career, and Robert Patten intuits some of Hone's long-standing right to our attention.

The Ministry had had its eye on William Hone since he published his first "squib" in 1815. *Buonaparte-phobia, or Cursing made Easy to the Meanest Capacity* announced a dangerous talent for political satire. Then, in February 1817, Francis Place (later replaced by Jeremy Bentham) backed the launch of Hone's *Reformist's Register*. Radical, though not insurgent, the journal had much in common with Cobbett's bluff *Political Register,* though it took its own line on "Political Priestcraft."[13] When habeas corpus was suspended, Hone's *Register* kept Cobbett's name alive while he fled to America, and Hone himself was left to face the music weeks after suffering a stroke.

Hone's *John Wilkes's Catechism, Sinecurist's Creed,* and *Political Litany* were extraordinarily inventive parodies by literary as well as political standards. Critics have dismissed them as "crude" (Manning 219) and "brutal" (Altick 4), picking up precisely the class-coded terms of judgment of the nineteenth century. But, like Blake's *Songs,* the parodies work backwards through sophisticated invention to a wholly willful simplicity, both bridging and widening the gap between holy language and political jargon, implicitly exposing the corrupt relationship of church and state. Hone's coolly moving *Political Litany,* for example:

> spare us good rulers, spare the people who have supported ye with their labor, and spilt their most precious blood in your quarrels; O consume us not utterly.
> *Spare us, good Prince!* (*Political Litany* 4; *Three Trials* 78)

Or his reworking of the Lord's Prayer as the "Minister's Memorial":

> OUR Lord who art in the Treasury, whatsoever be thy name, thy power be prolonged, thy will be done throughout the empire, as it is in each session. Give us our usual sops. . . . [And t]urn us not out of our places, but keep us in the House of Commons, the land of Pensions and Plenty; and deliver us from the People. Amen. (*John Wilkes's Catechism* 6; *Three Trials* 11)

Well might the "Member" imagined reciting it first have to "put on the helmet of impudence," as required by his interrogator (*John Wilkes's Catechism* 4; *Three Trials* 8). The three ministers petitioned in the *Sinecurist's Creed,* Lord Chancellor Eldon, Castlereagh, and Home Secretary Sidmouth himself, the "coeternal" "Co-Charlatans," had personal reasons not to forgive the comic logic of Hone's Trinitarian satire: they never shook off the nicknames Hone gave them in this and previous squibs—"Old Bags," "Derry Down Triangle," and "the Doctor."[14]

And yet they are not three Humbugs: but one Humbug.

As also they are not three incomprehensibles, nor three Mountebanks: but one Mountebank, and one incomprehensible. (*Sinecurist's Creed* 4; *Three Trials* 144)

The Ministry's literary beneficiaries likewise remembered Hone's name. In the "Place everlasting" of the *Sinecurist's Creed,* "COLERIDGE shall have a Jew's Harp, and a Rabbinical talmud, and a Roman Missal: and WORDSWORTH shall have a Psalter, and a Primer, and a reading Essay: and unto SOUTHEY'S Sack-but shall be duly added," and they shall "HUM [their] most gracious master," the Prince Regent, "whose kingdom shall have no end" (*Sinecurist's Creed* 7; Three *Trials* 145).[15]

The Ministry wisely refrained from prosecuting Hone's most wickedly apposite effort. Its immediate excuse for the suspension of habeas corpus was a so-called assassination attempt on the regent in January 1817; a semiofficial "Form of Thanksgiving" for his "Escape" was printed in newspapers and read in churches after the incident. In reality, his carriage had been struck by a stone; the flurry of prayer, said the radical Sir Francis Burdett, was "solemn mockery and impiety" (*Examiner*, 16 February 1817: 97).[16] *The Bullet Te Deum* was Hone's straight-faced riposte. "There shall be read distinctly, with an audible voice," runs the preamble, "the Leading Article of the *Courier*. . . . And after that, shall be said or sung, in English, daily throughout the week, as followeth" (*Bullet* 3):[17]

> We praise thee O Stone: we acknowledge thee to be a Bullet.
> All the Corruptionists doth worship thee: the Place-giver everlasting.
> To thee all Placemen cry aloud: the Treasury, and all the Clerks therein.
> To thee Pensioners and Sinecurists: continually do cry,
> Bullet, Bullet, Bullet: from thee our power floweth. . . .
> O ALL ye workers of Corruption, bless ye the Stone: praise it, and *magnify* it as a Bullet for ever. (3–4, 6)

Such a "brilliant" talent had to be silenced, by fair means or foul.[18] Hone had withdrawn the parodies, so his shopmen were plied with bribes for stray copies (Patten 1: 129). Seditious manuscripts were planted on his printing premises. (Hone handed them in at the Treasury, much to the government's surprise.) Finally, on 3 May 1817, he was apprehended on an ex officio "information" filed by the attorney-general and signed by Chief Justice Ellenborough, "the most terrible judge of the age" (Routledge 277), a bishop's son, and—like Home Secretary Sidmouth—a personal butt of Hone's satire, vilified at close of the *Canticle* Hone appended to his *Bullet Te Deum* (8). This anachronistic proceeding by information, nearly abolished in 1808 (when instead it was invoked forty times) allowed government to side step normal process in the case of "offences so high and dangerous" that "a moment's delay would be fatal" (Blackstone, 4: 309).[19] It hardly applied to a man who had voluntarily suppressed the publications three months before (*Yellow Dwarf,* 3 January 1818: 1).[20] Hone was held for forty-eight hours in a smelly sponging house before being brought before Ellenborough to make his plea. He had not been given a copy of the "information" against him, he said. Ellenborough replied that he had no right to one until he had pleaded. Moreover, the court had "no funds out of which to pay for it," and "[i]f a copy of the information were given to you, by the same rule every person charged with a crime might claim a copy of the indictment." Hone "bowed assent" to that startling proposition (*Reformist's Register,* 10 May 1817: 491–92). Bail was set at the vindictive figure of two thousand pounds. Hone was dispatched to King's Bench Prison to await trial.

That browbeating hardened all his resolve. "I have no wish to goad government to extremity," Hone wrote John Hunt on 8 May 1817, "but were all their force in array against me and if I stood single handed, *in a just quarrel,* I should defy their efforts" (Hone BL 38,108: 189–90). He refused on principle to ask friends to stand surety for him; two months later, he was released on his own recognizances. Government's final, deliberate cruelty was to "cut . . . one crime into piecemeal," not only by demanding a separate trial for each of the twopenny productions ("three hooks" to catch a very small fish [W. Hone, *Three Trials* 167]), but by staging the three trials on consecutive days: 18, 19, and 20 December. The problem this offered Hone was compounded by a crucial decision. For in face of the forces that worked to silence him, he had a card up his sleeve: the right, in legal parlance, to "speak for himself."[21] In deciding to exploit this right by conducting his own defenses, he set a powerful precedent for nineteenth-century "martyrdom."

In one sense, the decision was a return to an earlier tradition of testimony. Representation by a legal professional, particularly for the defense, did not become standard practice until well into the eighteenth century, while the sheer cost of access to "equal" justice meant that "the poor might as well have no law at all" (Foote, *Prisoner* 37). The copy of his indictment Hone asked for cost eight shillings and sixpence, a good working week's wages. However, poverty was not the real reason he found himself "reduced to the necessity of standing . . . before the Court" (W. Hone, *Three Trials* 41). A London banker had offered to pay all his costs. But Hone had "objections" against every lawyer his friends suggested: "Some from motives of etiquette, could not attend upon him in prison. Others . . . had not *courage* to undertake his defense" (*Three Trials* 154–55). Not one would "defend a heretic without apologizing for his opinions" as Holyoake put it years later

(*Sixty Years* 1: 158). And no lawyer could speak Hone's cause so passionately as he could himself: a man on trial for his voice wants no interposition between himself and his jury. Following Hone's lead, the blasphemy martyrs of the nineteenth century sometimes retained legal counsel, but "for watching and advising not pleading" (Ryall to Holyoake, letter, 4 January 1842, in HL). Hone now put his desultory teenaged years as a solicitor's clerk to good use. The economic and class partiality of the legal system backfired dramatically on this score of self-representation. The card up his sleeve proved a trump.

To "speak for himself" was to entitle himself to "all the privileges of counsel" (Foote, *Three Trials for Blasphemy* 74): the right to call witnesses; the right of cross-examination; the right to review the case for the jury in a final speech. It was to claim "a rare audience and still rarer liberty" (Mac-Cabe 78). Before the First Reform Act of 1832, while severe constraints were placed on public meetings, trials held a special place in political consciousness. "A Jury is the only system of representation that exists in this country" Carlile told his twelve jurymen (*Times,* 17 October 1819, cutting in CC). Open to spectators, packed with reporters, the courtroom inherited all the potential for subversive publicity that James I had sought to strip from public execution by his decree of 1611: "Hereticks hereafter, though condemned, should silently and privately waste themselves away in prison" (Fuller 10: 64). In its privileged space the accused might *"say everything"* that elsewhere could not be said (Foucault, *Discipline* 60).

Hone's trials took him to the edge of prostration. That, after all, was the point, as he said on the third day:

> It was hoped, he had no doubt, by certain *very grave* members of the Cabinet . . . that William Hone . . . would sink under his fatigues and want of physical power. "He can't stand the third trial," said these humane and Christian Ministers; "we shall have him now; he must be crushed." (Great shouts of applause.) Oh, no! no! he must not be crushed; you cannot crush him. (*Three Trials* 163)

When some respite was at last offered, he turned it down. The role of underdog made for better histrionic effect: "Had he not been able to walk, he should have ordered himself to be brought in his bed, and laid upon the table" (149). Even the rusty suit was a dramatic prop: "I did resolve to get a suit of clothes for these trials," Hone told his last jury, "but the money I had provided for that purpose I was obliged to give for copies of the informations against me" (160). Eventually, he spoke for a total of twenty-two hours over the three separate days. He had read for the martyr's role, suggests Olivia Smith, ever since, at the age of eleven, he had saved up to buy the *Trial* of John Lilbourne, acquitted of treason under Cromwell's nose: Hone had a ripe sense of his trial as a "literary event" (Smith 178).[22]

His manuscript memoirs, still extant at the British Library, suggest also the models of Bunyan's *Pilgrim's Progress* and Fox's *Book of Martyrs,* books Hone "reveled in" as a boy (Hone BL 40,121: 11, 14).

Hone was brought up in strict nonconformity, inheriting his father's violent dislike of the established church and its clergy. "At a very early age I observed intensely, felt intensely, & inquired intensely" (Hone BL 40,121: 6); and what he inquired, observed, and felt most "intensely" about was the Bible. It was not just his childhood spelling book and solitary primer but the instrument of family punishment. By the age of twelve he "began to hate the sight of [it]" (22). "One morning," after some childish infraction, his father

> enjoined upon me to learn by heart an entire chapter before he returned to dinner. . . . While he said this and put the Bible into my hands, I felt petrified. I knew it was utterly beyond my power. . . . [I] closed the book in reckless despair; nor reopened it until my father came home. . . . he inflicted upon me the severest chastisement I had ever received; I believe the severest of which his arm was capable. (22–23)

"I secretly resolved never to read [the Bible] again unless compelled" (23)— a resolve dramatized in an unreliable memoir as the child throwing the Bible down the stairs, saying, "When I am my own master I will never open you" (Rolleston 8). When he was about thirteen, Bishop Watson's "Apology for the Bible in answer to Paine's *Age of Reason* was given to my father," and Hone realized "that the Bible had been or could be doubted or disbelieved" (Hone BL 40,121: 29–30). By his seventeenth year, he was a Deist, involved in the pro-revolutionary London Corresponding Society. While we shall never know the exact motives that pushed him to publish his biblical parodies in 1817 or, three years afterwards, his *Apocryphal New Testament,* revenge on the all-mastering Book to which he owed both literacy and misery was surely part of the mix. In this too, as we shall see, he set a pattern for the century.

Hone never "laughed away" Christian feeling, however (Hone BL 40,121: 6). The parodies were withdrawn immediately when they offended his pious father (*Three Trials* 41). Alone amongst all his works, they were never republished. The loss of a child, penury, and the severe illness of a favorite daughter in 1832 turned him back to Christianity (Hone BL 40,121: 60). In 1833, another stroke precipitated a near-death experience that convinced him he had seen God and must pay "public homage to his sovereignty"— or so declared the replica of a letter to Thomas Chapman, 18 July 1834, pasted into the Reverend Samuel Prince's copy of the *Every-Day Book,* an addition that gave it cash value, to judge by its conspicuous reference in the cutting from a bookseller's catalogue later pasted into the inside back cover (Hone Berg; the copy was later bought by Jerome Kern). In later life, his past embarrassed him. Thus when a neighbor was alerted to his identity as "The Hone" and withdrew from their usual chat over the garden wall, he exclaimed, "with an expression of the greatest self-abasement":

> "Then you know me now, the arch blasphemer! . . . and will you now converse with me?" (Hone BL 40,121: 82–84; Rolleston 7, 79)

Hone died the subeditor of a dissenting journal, the *Patriot,* and a member of the Weigh-House Chapel, Eastcheap, in 1842. His neighbor, Miss Rolleston, published her *Account* of his "remarkable conver[sion]" (5) in 1853: it was heartfelt, but it was also excellent propaganda. Misrepresenting Hone as an "Atheist"—an overstatement that the self-dramatizing humility of the new convert also demanded (Rolleston 10; W. Hone, *Early Life* 48)— her sole intent was to prove his resubmission to "the one" Book, "the Bible!" (6). "Oh!" she remembers him saying on the day he reopened his New Testament, in the best style of the religious tract, "what a flood of light burst in upon me!" (11, 48). Until that "conversion," Hone kept a determined public silence about his beliefs; they were not and are not the issue. He almost certainly never strayed beyond Deism, and probably leaned towards Unitarianism (*Early Life* 47).[23] In 1817, he volunteered to "go to the stake and burn," if he were truly "guilty of blasphemy" (*Three Trials* 18). The purpose of the parodies was not to revile religion but to rebuke a repressive government.

Their political pedigrees shrieked from their titles. "The Late John Wilkes," for example, was an evil name to Torydom: radical jester, free press campaigner, editor of the *North Briton,* and M.P. for the "open" seat of Middlesex, he had paid dearly for his own parodic squibs of the 1760s.[24] The Ministry knew Hone's intent: it even indicted the *Political Litany* both as an "impious and profane" libel and as "a wicked and seditious libel of and concerning the Prince Regent" (*Three Trials* 73). But the charge of blasphemy was a better stick to beat opposition down in 1817. The "Friends of Liberty of the Press and Trial by Jury," meeting to raise Hone's subscription at the City of London Tavern shortly after his trials, had good reason to pass a resolution, widely reported:

> That a hypocritical prostitution of Religion, and a pretended zeal for its defense, when used by corrupt Statesmen as a mask for political persecution, must ever be held by all sincere Christians as the worst profanation of its sacred name. (*Trial by Jury* 9)

Standing on a table to make himself heard, Sir Francis Burdett hammered home the political point: "They had no security for the Liberty of Press" without "a free, fair and honest representation of the people.—(*Great Applause*)" (5).

The government was serious. Eight other booksellers who had sold pirate copies of the parodies were also charged.[25] The law officers of the Crown described them as *"infamous and atrocious blasphemies"* in the House of Commons (*Trial by Jury* 19), while "the official preacher of an official sermon" at St. Paul's denounced Hone from the pulpit in the "official" presence of his future judges (W. Hone, *Aspersions* 60). For nine months he was "held up to general execration" (60). "See the odds against me," Hone exclaimed at the third trial, "it is one farthing against a million of gold" (*Three Trials* 159).

But Hone was main attraction as well as prime target. Twenty thousand people attended his three battles of 1817, crowding the courtroom, spilling into the halls and streets. The big guns were rolled out for the first encounter. Attorney-General Sir Samuel Shepherd prosecuted; Mr. Justice Abbott took the judge's seat. But Hone did not face a "packed" special jury drawn from narrow lists of property freeholders, with each man paid a guinea per case as an inducement to do his duty, as was the corrupt norm at political trials—the equivalent, said the radical Horne Tooke, of "offering a man a basket of rotten oranges, from which he was at liberty to take his choice" (*Trial by Jury* 8). Thanks to the intervention of a sympathetic city solicitor, his jury was picked at hazard from a list of eligible men (19). They trusted their common sense, and took at face value the injunction of Fox's Libel Act of 1792 that it is juries who decide criminality, not the judges before whom they sit. It took them only fifteen minutes to read through the Ministry's motives and reach the verdict of "NOT GUILTY." The courtroom and corridors erupted in applause: *"Long live the honest jury, and an honest jury for ever"* (W. Hone, *Three Trials* 69). Chief Justice Ellenborough dragged himself furiously from his sickbed to preside in person over the second and third trials. But those juries acquitted Hone too: their names were immortalized on congratulatory posters.[26] The final verdict was "followed by a tremendous burst of applause, which [Ellenborough] could not even attempt to quell" (Campbell 4: 233). Rarely, except in Victorian fiction, has one small man faced so powerful a battery—and won.

Nothing more earned Hone's acquittals than laughter. If a comedian had scripted the trials, he could not have dreamed up procedures more skewed to his ends. To prove the criminality of the parodies, Attorney-General Shepherd first had to prove how close they were to their originals, which meant reading them aloud, in full. *The Late John Wilkes's Catechism,* for example:

I believe in GEORGE, the Regent Almighty, . . . And in the present Ministry, his only choice, who were conceived of Toryism, brought forth of WILLIAM PITT, suffered loss of place under CHARLES JAMES FOX, were execrated, dead, and buried. In a few months they rose again from their minority; they re-ascended to the Treasury benches, and sit at the right hand of a little man in a large wig; from whence they *laugh* at the Petitions of the People. . . . (*Catechism* 3–4; *Three Trials* 4).

"[E]very separate clause produced an irresistible burst of laughter" (Rolleston 42). It was in vain that Judge Abbott rebuked the audience or that Ellenborough directed, "The first man I see laugh shall be brought up" (*Three Trials* 90).

For Hone had hit upon a beautifully simple strategy for courtroom success. Almost his entire defense consisted in quoting aloud—voluminously and hilariously, thanks to a stock of curious books and a team of sympathizers—from the works of "venerable and respectable" fellow parodists: Martin Luther, who had parodied the first Psalm; martyred Bishop Latimer, who compared Christianity to a card game; the Dean of Canterbury, who intoned from the pulpit, circa 1613, "Our Pope, which art in Rome, hellish be thy name" (*Three Trials* 26); men like Mr. Reeves, publisher of both the prayer book and a penny parody of the catechism. The roll call was swelled by such lawyers and politicians as that "unblushing hypocri[te]," "the *Right Honorable* President of the Board of Control" (*Three Trials* vii), and George Canning, who had once even lampooned his superiors, Sidmouth and Castlereagh. Canning's 1798 parody of the *Benedicite,* "The New Morality," was a hit at supporters of the French atheist Lepaux, paid for by Pitt and the Whigs. Earl Grey pointedly read it aloud in Parliament on 12 May 1817, a week after Hone was arrested:

> Whether ye make the Rights of Man your
> theme,
> Your country libel, and your God blaspheme,
> Or dirt on private worth and virtue throw,
> Still blasphemous or blackguard, praise Lepaux!
>
> (*Anti-Jacobin,* 1798, qtd. in *Three Trials* 48)

The occasion was an inspiration. Here was Hone's keystone to a tracery of risible references:

> He was dragged before the Court, from behind his counter—and for what? For doing that which a Cabinet Minister had been suffered to do with impunity. . . . He had been advised to subpoena Mr. Canning as a witness, but he had really abstained from a regard to Mr. Canning's feelings. (*Three Trials* 45–46, 50)

Now consideration began to crumble under the stress of feeling:

> George Canning come into Court! make way for him if you please. (163)

Till finally truth demanded outlet:

> He should at least go down to posterity with George Canning. If this right honor-
> able parodist ascended after Mr. Pitt, he would lay hold of his left leg, and ascend
> along with him. (183)

The point was decisive: Judge Abbott might claim that "The New Morality" was a parody of Milton, but Hone demonstrated beyond doubt that
it derived from Genesis, Job, and the Forty-eighth Psalm (49). Common
sense won, for the day: Hone literally "laughed [the Ministry] out of court"
(*Three Trials* [1818] ii); his "merits as a parodist" were publicly "acknowledged by the highest authorities in the State," as the *Monthly Magazine*
later ironically put it (December 1819: 453). He walked away a comic hero,
celebrating an enforced spell of government leniency with an edition of his
transcripted *Trials* that sold like hot cakes (some enterprising authors based
stage entertainments upon them), and an exuberant legal satire called *Great
Gobble, Gobble, Gobble, and Twit, Twittle, Twit.* "What!" blusters Turkeycock Ellenborough, "must I stay here for ever, the object of profane diversion?!" while the Geese cackle at Tom Tit's performance: "O law! O law!
. . . This twitting is most blasphemous" (Hackwood 172–73). Hone's "extraordinary powers of language and argument" had defeated the attorney-
general (*Gentleman's Magazine,* January 1843: 98); he had even tripped Ellenborough up on a point of law, quoting his own episcopal father's verdict
on the Athanasian Creed against him (Routledge 430). He was, quite simply, better read than his privileged opponents, and used his learning with
greater wit. The presumption of it disturbed serious literary people: "The
acquittal of Hone," wrote Wordsworth's sister Dorothy, "is enough to make
one out of love with English Juries" (Selincourt 410).

But no courtroom hilarity or popular triumph, no catcalls and punctur-
ing of dignities, were sufficient to dislodge what was seeded at the three
trials of William Hone: a legal veto on profane laughter; a taboo on vulgar
ridicule. "Wherein lay the triumph," asked a ministerial paper, "in a
crowded court laughing at and sneering against the guardians of the law?
Was that victory? . . . The writer thought not" (qtd. in Routledge 438).
What the Geese witnessed in the Guildhall court was as much a literary
debate as a legal-political battle, and it had no less distinct class consequences. At issue was the status of parody. Tom Tit and the Turkeycock
had clashed on a matter of genre and interpretation.

Was parody a suspect "imitation" of original work as Johnson and the eighteenth century had declared it? Was it irremediably "common" and "low," as Schiller decided in 1802, part of the negative hierarchy that count-erweighs the sublime and pathetic? All laughter, so Hobbes had written, sprang from a sudden conviction of superiority: was not parody from pens like Hone's, then a form of sedition?[27] Parody was incapable of "serious" intent, the lowest form of mimesis, undeserving of literary status. The "cer-tificate of popularity" it gave a writer was no mitigation for the "maim[ing]" and "mutilat[ion]" of his work (Paull 139): parody willed nothing less than the destruction of its paternal "target." Or was parody not a mere "piece of buffoonery, so much as a critical exposition" which "will only strike at what is chimerical and false?" (D'Israeli 2: 460). Could parody sympathize with its parent text, laughing with it at human folly?

The latter view had few supporters in 1817. One was Hackney clergyman Robert Aspland, editor of the Unitarian *Monthly Depository,* who put out a thoughtful *Inquiry into the Nature of the Sin of Blasphemy* and stood by in court to help Hone with his books. The Bible depicts Elijah scoffing at the priests of Baal, Aspland reminded his countrymen; ridicule "is not the peculiar property of infidelity and profaneness" (vi). Hone reinforced the point with a literary distinction between form and content: the creed, the catechism, and Lord's Prayer were merely the vehicles, not the targets, of his satire. To parody the Ten Commandments was not to undermine them but rather to demonstrate that the "principles" of the substitute Decalogue were "as detestable and noxious as those of the first were respectable and beneficial" (W. Hone, *Three Trials* 53). His *Catechism* was a sweeping indict-ment of institutionalized euphemism, such as parody longed to unmask:

> VI. Thou shalt not call starving to death murder.
> VII. Thou shalt not call Royal gallivanting adultery.
> VIII. Thou shalt not say, that to rob the Public is to steal. (*John Wilkes's Catechism* 5; *Three Trials* 9)

Hone and Aspland were in a small minority. "Did not this [blasphe-mous] libel take the name of the Almighty in vain?" asked Judge Abbott, "Did it not . . . apply the sacred appellation of the Creator to light and trivial matters?" (*Three Trials* 68). For Hone to parody the catechism was necessarily to bring it into contempt, argued Attorney-General Shepherd; the very manner of Scripture deserved law's protection. The claim implied a right to regulate the varieties of literary expression to the point of declaring some outlaw. For if parodies like *John Wilkes's Catechism* were to be permit-ted, what would become of "sacred fear" and "reverential awe" (Three *Trials* 65)? A *"tincture of the ludicrous"* would linger (66). It was the "conjunction," said Lord Ellenborough, of "both the subject and the object of the parody" that created ridicule and therefore guilt (*Three Trials* 194). In short, parody produced blasphemy.

The lawyers' contentions spoke to a coming piety of taste. As the Hone subscription list suggested, even those who backed him in 1817 also backed away from his productions. The *Philanthropic Gazette* wondered in the same breath why he did not quote the Masons' parodies and wished that the Masons "would avoid the ridicule of sacred things" (28 January 1818: 26). "[T]hat [Hone's] parodies are very censurable admits of no doubt," concurred the *Aberdeen Chronicle,* while it offered up Swift's famous "COURTIERS' CREED" for comparative delectation. The "spurious wit" that dictated all such productions might "shock the mind of any well-meaning Christian" (cutting, 12 July 1817, in Hone BL 40,108: 143). In less-civilized times, Ben Jonson might parody the Litany with impunity and the queen for audience, as he does in *Cynthia's Revels.* For Ellenborough, however, taking down two lines in court—"That all the books of Moses / Were nothing but supposes" (a couplet straight out of Gene Kelly's mock paean to elocution in *Singin' in the Rain:* "Moses supposes his toeses are roses")—and prohibiting further "recital of such profanations," the songs of older days "would deserve severe punishment if [they] were . . . modern publication[s]" (W. Hone, Three *Trials* 104).

Parodies "were as old at least as the invention of printing" (*Three Trials* 23), Hone countered, "In no age of the world was there before a prosecution for parody" (175). But Judge Abbott spelled out the classist subtext and the fear of the uncensored printing press that loomed behind the historical smokescreen: "I don't care what the common people have had for centuries. If the publication be profane, it ought not to be tolerated" (44). Hone's trials for parody thus marked a moment of separation between literature and the subliterary. Proscribing popular parody, like putting down Bartholomew Fair, was a way to stifle the people's voice, or at least to force it underground. "Was a laugh treason?" Hone asked his juries, and they answered "no" (126). But as Blackstone had declared, "Contumely and contempt" are "what no establishment can tolerate" (4: 59): "exposing" Scripture to "ridicule" brings up the rear in his catch-all list of everything that might constitute blasphemy.

Thus, a few months after Hone's trials, a small-time Birmingham printer named Russell was arrested for selling the *Political Litany:* three times called into court with his witnesses, at ruinous cost, he was dispatched to jail at the Warwick Summer Assizes (W. Hone, *Don John* 36–37n). Two years later, Judge Abbott, now chief justice, went a great deal further than Blackstone's *Commentaries:* "Reason and discussion, properly conducted, are always lawful; calumny, scoffing, and ridicule are always contrary to law" (Bonner 48). The new taboo was the price of toleration. Twenty years later, the humorlessness so often associated with the Victorian period was carved into precedent. Henry Hetherington's 1840 trial for Haslam's *Letters to the Clergy* provoked a judgment from Chief Justice Denman that singled out as especially blameworthy those cases of blasphemy "where ridicule or invective were had recourse to [sic]" (*Trial of Henry Hetherington* 22). Jacob Holyoake, on trial in 1842, was too earnest to realize that he got six months in jail for what sounded like a joke about putting God on "half pay" (*History of the Last Trial* 5).

Here were powerful judicial reasons for the decline of satire in the nineteenth century. Within two decades of Hone's trials, ridicule could be found criminal, and parody was subject to careful limitations. The *Essays of Elia* by Hone's friend Charles Lamb were blackballed for "levity" by Woodbridge Quakers in 1823 (*Prose and Poetry* xi–xii); "levity" helped his reputation dwindle quickly after his death in 1847. Victorian literature disengaged from overt relationship with "personalities" and public affairs; parody became "general" and private, self-consciously middle-class. It also became strenuously "purely literary": only when the parodist was "legitimate" could parody achieve legitimacy in the later nineteenth century (Paull 133). And it eschewed altogether religious subjects. Hone came to epitomize the Victorian conception of "the objectionable form of parody" (Paull 134). Not one of the works collected in Walter Jerrold and R. M. Leonard's 1913 Oxford volume *A Century of Parody and Imitation* had any political bearing, or was written by anyone other than an established high-literary author, with the vivid exception of the antirevolutionary parodies of Hone's ministerial foe, the honorable George Canning.[28] Hone's parodies were erased from literary history until Jerome McGann included his extraordinary 1819 *Political House That Jack Built* in the *New Oxford Book of Romantic Period Verse*, 1993.

It was not that the Victorians did not love to laugh. They delighted in Dickens and his Pickwickian jollities—except when, as in *Little Dorrit*, he sailed too close to political winds; they embraced *Punch*, for which parody was meat and drink—once it shed its burden of social criticism; they made national figures of "nonsense" writers like Lewis Carroll and Edward Lear. But as those two practitioners in the delicate art of controlled transgression very well knew, the descent from the sublime to the ridiculous remained fraught with danger throughout the nineteenth century. The parodic impulse survived and prospered within a defined circuit; theatrical burlesque's targets through the 1850s and 1860s were Shakespeare, star melodramas, the classics, and English history; literary reference modulated even political caricature. Polite media respected the nation's sacred cows: the Anglican Church and the royal family. They gave credence to the psalmist's line: "The fool hath said in his heart, There is no God" (Psalms 14.1, 53.1). Under Victoria, "true lovers of Fun" needed and received surety that their "mirth" was "innocent."[29] Attorney-General Shepherd lost the case in 1817, but he won the battle. With that "solemn bigotry" (*Three Trials* [1818] iii) which is the "outward visible sign," in the words of Hone's *Catechism*, "of an inward intellectual meanness" (*John Wilkes's Catechism* 7; *Three Trials* 10), he succeeded in having it laid down in law that the familiarity induced by parodies bred contempt, and the precedent bore fruit.

Greek *para,* from which the word "parody" derives, is an ambiguous prefix: it means at once both "beside" and "opposite." The Greeks attributed Homeric parodies to Homer; the Middle Ages accepted for its mnemonic value the parodic *Cena Cypriani,* in which biblical figures indulge at a Saturnalian feast;[30] the great novels of the Renaissance, *Gargantua* and the *Quixote,* were parodic works. But the later nineteenth century preferred an "either/or" to a "both/and" model of relationship; the Arnolds, father and son, were typical in rejecting parody as "debasing," "spurious," and "vile" (Paull 133, 137). The age of "Literary Conscience" classified it as a literary "misdemeanor" (10).

Yet there had been far more at work in the *Late John Wilkes's Catechism* and the *Political Litany* than jeering vulgarization. Parody may perhaps best be described as a type of literary "decomposition." This is indeed the view of modern theorists: parody is "metafiction" and "self-reflexive" "demythification." Its imbrication in Russian formalism, through key texts by Rabelais, Cervantes, Sterne, and Dickens, was germ for the concept of "intertextuality" that Kristeva made current in an essay of 1966.

Its subject was Mikhail Bakhtin. He came to believe in "authentic and productive" parody by way of folklore and the figures of rogue, clown, and fool (*Dialogical Imagination* 364, 413). The laughter of the carnival "brings together, unifies, weds, and combines the sacred with the profane, the lofty with the low, the great with the insignificant, the wise with the stupid" (*Problems of Dostoevsky's Poetics* 123); it "bears the stamp of the public square where the folk gather" (*Dialogical Imagination* 159–60). Laughter never "took on an official character" (236); it was the free expression of "the people's unofficial truth" (*Rabelais* 90). These were beliefs Bakhtin shared with William Hone: his trials were a kind of carnival; and the subtitle of his *Bullet Te Deum* was a front-page joke—*Imprimatur F. RABELAIS,* repeated in all advertisements.

The nineteenth century, however, preferred the other and darker vision Bakhtin developed in *Problems of Dostoevsky's Poetics,* of parody as the quintessential "double-voiced" and "dialogical" discourse (185). William Hone's "referential object" was corrupt and repressive government, but the Liverpool Ministry chose to see only his work's "second context," the scriptural (185). It suited repression to believe that "once having made its home in the other's discourse," the "second voice" of parody would inevitably "clash hostilely with its primordial host," until discourse became "an arena of battle between two voices" (193). We are not far here from the nineteenth-century language of treason, rebellion, and (as we shall see [2.3]) linguistic property rights. The Ministry's view has been reinforced by subsequent theorists. For Linda Hutcheon, parody is a "stylistic confrontation" producing "repetition with critical distance" (8, 6). For John Felstiner, parody may erupt in a form of "patricid[e]"; "eras[ing] its original," it "spoil[s] the innocence" of our reading (156, 144, 161). And when the "straightforward, serious word" that parody ridiculed (Bakhtin, *Dialogical Imagination* 52) was still believed to be the Word of God, and the world in which that word was "parcel" of law was rigidly divided along class lines, parody could not be found other than blasphemous. Parody in the nineteenth century thus became an irreligious danger to rival those of science, historical biblical scholarship, and radical politics: G. W. Foote would found his criminal career of the 1880s on that very premise. For parodic "decomposition" reveals the problematic inventedness—the *literariness*—of what is parodied. Sacred texts treated as mere literary constructs are demoted to such. Parody cancels Scripture; only Literature remains.

2. THREE EPILOGUES

The meanings of Hone's three trials were reinforced by three important epilogues. The first continued the parodic and populist trajectory, the second reiterated the threat to religion in literary activity, and the third offers new insight into the career of the most famous novelist of the century. In the five years after his trials, Hone turned out an enormously successful series of squibs: *The Man in the Moon* (1820), *The Political Showman—at Home!* (1821), and many others. But he balanced his life as political parodist with labor that satisfied the antiquarian instincts that helped him triumph in 1817.

In February 1819 Hone announced a "Superb Edition" of his *Three Trials,* "To be published by Subscription, in Royal Octavo," "price £2 2s in extra boards." The work would "contain verbatim Copies of all the Parodies, and every other production, either quoted or referred to in each defence" (Hone BL 40,108: 17). As such, it was a risky undertaking: "Are you quite sure that [it] may not subject you to a second prosecution?" wrote his friend the Reverend Samuel Parr on 13 April (Hone BL 40,108: 8). But gradually Hone's sense of the project developed, until he sketched out a title page that relegated his personal victories to a final chapter, and made plain the project's claim to serious scholarly consideration:

> A History
> of
> English Parody
> being
> an arrangement of the
> most Remarkable Parodies
> by royal noble ecclesiastical
> legal and other writers
> from the reformation
> ending with
> The Author's
> Three State Trials
> in MDCCCXVII
> and including
> Singular Specimens of the
> Literature of the Multitude
> Popular Facetiae, Foreign Parody
> Allegory and Antithesis
> By William Hone.
>
> (Hone BL 40,108: 31)

The final clauses were crucial. "Connected with *Parody*," he alerted potential subscribers, "an Abundance of Articles will be presented, which . . . have scarcely ever been noticed by the bibliographical inquirer, and are wholly unknown to the general reader," despite the fact of parody's "contributing largely to the amusements of the illiterate, and hourly influencing their motives and character" (27). Hone's projected "History of Parody" was to be a manifesto and a model for the study of popular literature. Issued in eight monthly parts, with five engravings per part (5, 17), it would grant its subject immediate status.

Alas, the "History" was never finished.[31] Time and energy drained away on other projects. Then, in 1827, his business affairs hopelessly entangled, William Hone was imprisoned for debt. More than 600 of the 850-odd pamphlets, books, and manuscripts he had collected towards the project were sold by auction; he was given one day, sitting on a packing case, to write a catalogue by which to remember them. Hopeful to the last, and "conscious of having excited . . . strong curiosity," he put out a final advertisement for the "History of Parody" on the flyer announcing the auction (Hone BL 40,108: 17), and kept careful note, in his own copy of Southgate the auctioneer's catalogue, of who bought each item: friends like Aspland, collectors like Cotton, and the many who offered a disappointing one shilling and sixpence for "A Whip for the Devil, *rare*" (*Catalogue* 8, Hone Bath) or a mere six shillings for an "EARLY AND VERY RARE" copy of a Catholic satire on the text of "I am the door," lot 471, showing Luther et al. dragging "the sheep" through the sides of "the fold," and "Calvin & c. breaking in through the roof" (22). He was gazetted a bankrupt in September 1828, and languished in the Rules of King's Bench for two and a half years. When G. T. Lawley deposited the "mass" of Hone's papers towards the project at the British Museum some time after 1924, he included a snobbish prefatory note regretting that political "rancor" should have dictated the terms by which "the bookseller and blasphemer" selected his examples (Hone BL 40,108: 4). The very inclusion of Hone's own *Three Trials* perhaps canceled out his emphases on "Different Forms of Parody," "Allegory Antithesis & c." (W. Hone's headings 40,108: 46). A hundred years after the trials, Hone still posed a threat to the "purity" of literature: the literary and the political, the literary and the subliterary, the popular and the high-brow, still could not be seen to coexist.

The second and parallel project in which Hone immersed himself after 1817 was unequivocally "purely literary." In fact, it was dangerously literary. The germ was a "memorable moment in my humble existence," 19 December 1817, when "the late Lord Chief Justice Ellenborough observed that 'the first scenic performances were Mysteries or representations of incidents in Sacred Writ'" (*Ancient Mysteries* ii). The remark spoke to Hone's delight in "old literature," which took the place of the classics denied him by his family's poverty in the imaginative education of his childhood; it stirred his instinct for literary reconstruction. If the germ were to be cultivated, he would need access to the British Museum.

This was easier said than done. Hone had a citizen's right of entry, but it took a year's petitioning, with repeated assurances of his "purely literary" intentions, and the personal intervention of William Godwin and museum trustee Dr. Birkbeck to secure him "ye ticket which openeth . . . ye wyckett-gate too ye temple of knowledge," as Hone put it in a celebratory mock medieval letter to the keeper of manuscripts once it was in his hands (Lawley 12–13, in Hone WA). He began reading on 29 May 1820 (Hone BL 40,113: 43), at first simply copying extracts from old and arcane parodies. But opening the ancient manuscript of the anciently popular "Coventry Mysteries" of Cotton Virpassian D. VIII, he was at once deflected from his "History" and sharply reminded of Ellenborough's remark. Speeches like Mary's reply to the "holy gost" begged deeper investiga-

tion from a man who had been accused of too freely mingling the sacred
and the profane:

> A! now I fele, in my body be,
> Parfyte god, & parfyte man;
> Havyng al schapp of chyldly carnalyte:—
> Evyn, all at onys, thus God be gan!
>
> (*Ancient Mysteries* 44; Hone BL 40,116: 49)

The result of Hone's investigation was *Ancient Mysteries Described,* an ana-
lytical condensation of eight medieval miracle plays, with extensive textual
quotation and a glossary to enable reading of the extracts. The manuscripts
had never previously been searched; the plays had never been published:
the book was an event—"remarkable" and "extraordinary" (*Times, British
Press,* qtd. in Lawley 17a, in Hone WA). It encapsulated his determination
to "violat[e], step after step, the circumscription by which the aristocratic
compasses . . . defin[e] the scope of the knowledge proper for a man of
my condition" (Foster, qtd. in W. Hone, *Ancient Mysteries* i–ii). Hone had
rediscovered materials "from which a new history of medieval life could be
written," inaugurating a "new era" of research (Lawley 16, in Hone WA).
    Most importantly for this study, Hone's reading had also taken him to
various tracts on the text of the "three heavenly witnesses" (1 John 5.7).
Thence he had come, accidentally, to "certain of the Apocryphal Gospels."
The study of parody—what the *Aberdeen Chronicle* dismissed as "spurious
wit"—had led to the discovery of spurious *writ.* And "violation" of the set
limits "of the knowledge proper for a man of my condition" now blurred
the boundary between Christian learning and literary knowledge. In only
six weeks from the discovery, Hone sped into publication "a work of mere
curiosity" for fellow bibliomaniacs (*Ancient Mysteries* ii), "theological student[s] and ecclesiastical antiquar[ies]" (*Apocryphal* xi): *The Apocryphal New
Testament* (1820). Here, he intuited, "the lover of old literature" would
find "the obscure but unquestionable origin" of the "monkish mysteries
performed as dramas at Chester, Coventry, Newcastle and in other parts
of England" (xi–xii). Victorian and modern scholarship has borne out his
perception.[32]
    Several of the twenty-four contested texts Hone collected had once al-
most been accepted as part of the canon, such as the Similitudes of Hermas
and Paul's Letter to the Laodiceans, the latter of which was included in all
eighteen printed German Bibles before Luther's translation. But the bulk
had never enjoyed the status of the Old Testament Apocrypha, which made
part of an extended canon in the Latin Vulgate and was printed in English
Bibles until the eighteenth century with explanatory prefaces.[33] Hone's vol-

ume included such dubious texts as the Protevangelium, or "An Historical Account of the BIRTH of CHRIST, and the perpetual VIRGIN MARY" by "James the lesser, cousin and brother of the Lord Jesus" (*Apocryphal* 8), and the Infancy Gospel of Thomas, in which magical play is made with foreskin and swaddling clothes (the cause of four separate miracles), and the boy Christ is imagined bringing clay animals to life and striking dead his schoolmaster. Most contested in 1820 was the Gospel of the Birth of Mary, in which the annunciatory angel sent to her barren mother promises that the unborn Virgin shall "be filled with the Holy Ghost from her mother's womb" (2.10, *Apocryphal* 3). This was the "horrible blasphemy" that the editor of the *Monthly Magazine,* an opponent of Catholic Emancipation, declared "he sh[ould] not wonder to see . . . become the subject of many commentaries, expositions, and pious discourses" (qtd. in *Quarterly Review,* July 1821: 364).

Hone's *Apocryphal New Testament* included a short editorial preface and introductory headnotes briefly giving details of each text's reception and use among ancient Christian sects. Occasional footnotes provided cross-reference to canonical books. The late miraculous birth of Mary, for example, was thus connected to the births of Samson and Samuel (Judges 13.2; 1 Samuel 1.6). The volume was rounded out with a table listing "Apocryphal pieces not now extant," like the Gospels of Eve and Judas Iscariot; the "False Gospel" of Hesychius; the provegetarian Ebionite Gospel; and the Book of the Helkesaites, which fell down from Heaven (*Apocryphal* 266–68); a second table listed "Christian Authors of the first four Centuries, whose Writings contain Catalogues of the Books of the New Testament" (269–71).

Almost nothing had been written on the apocryphal texts in English or any other language until the eighteenth century, when "blind acceptance" of received and unreceived texts gave way to "critical examination" (Paull 29). The commentaries remained few.[34] Hone's main source was Jeremiah Jones's 1726 *New and Full Method of Settling the Canonical Authority of the New Testament* (reissued 1798), three volumes of scholarly commentary squarely aimed at consolidating the status of the twenty-seven canonical books, in which each "trifling and idle" apocryphal text (2: 246) was not only preceded by a note on provenance and reputation but followed by as many as four separate chapters proving its spuriousness: Jones presents the antidote with the poison.

What drew Hone to the *New and Full Method,* however, was a unique feature of the work: Jones was the first scholar to print the apocryphal fragments and texts both in their original languages and in English translation, in double columns. Some of his translations were heavy handed in the extreme. "Think not, Mary, that you shall conceive in the ordinary way," announces the angel, for example (Gospel of Mary 7.17, *Apocryphal* 7), while Joseph is exhorted not "to entertain any suspicion of the Virgin's being guilty of fornication" (8.9, 7). Nevertheless, Hone was so excited that he literally "*tore* out the Gospels for the printer," and "rushed through" the rest of the *New and Full Method* "for the purpose of extracting matter for the introductions" (*Aspersions* 58). Haste bred errors, though surprisingly few, most notably Hone's conjectural dating of the closing of the New Testament canon to the Council of Nice in AD 325 (*Apocryphal* iv). (The date was both too early and too late.[35])

Hone's *Apocryphal New Testament* remains a landmark: the first publication, in English, at a price and in a form "peculiarly adapted for common reading and extensive circulation" of the Apocryphal gospels and epistles (Rennell I). It was in print until the 1880s, and was republished as recently as 1979.[36] It caused an immediate outcry. Few critics saw Hone's "Curious volume" as an opportunity for healthy Protestant meditation upon the clergy's "secret" and "esoteric" access to holy texts, as "Sirachius" wrote to the *Monthly Magazine* (1 December 1820: 422–23). Rather the book was "the most dangerous" of "various recent attacks" upon Scripture and Christianity (Rennell i). Hone's three most vocal critics, all clergymen, were an anonymous reviewer in the *Quarterly;* the rector of Kensington, Thomas Rennell, writing as Christian advocate for 1821; and Dr. Butler, headmaster of Shrewsbury School and archdeacon of Derby, whose charge to diocesal clergy on the subject was "published at their request" (Dr. Butler 3). All were shocked to find the texts available in a six-shilling volume, rather than "in a form infinitely more useful and satisfactory" (*Quarterly,* July 1821: 365), that is, in expensive and popularly impenetrable Hebrew, Latin, and Greek. All forgot that six shillings was still a large sum to "the common people," by which Hone understood Butler to mean "the ignorant and uninquiring among hard-working men" (*Aspersions* 47). All had different people than Hone in mind when they spoke of "theological students."

The key point at issue for all three critics was Hone's introductory question: "After the writings contained in the New Testament were selected from the numerous Gospels and Epistles then in existence, what became of the books that were rejected by the compilers?" (*Apocryphal* iii). Hone had based it upon Mosheim's comment in his *Ecclesiastical History: "these sacred writings were CAREFULLY SEPARATED from several human compositions upon the same subject"* (Mosheim 1: 108, qtd. in *Aspersions* 35, W. Hone's emphasis). "All I did," he later claimed, "was to frame a question, almost in the very language of Mosheim." Indeed, the "question" itself was suggested by Mosheim's use of the word: the "important question" of how the New Testament canon was formed, Mosheim had written, "is attended with almost insuperable difficulties" (qtd. 35). "[S]o far was I from uttering . . . a syllable," Hone contended, citing the *Quarterly*'s charges, "to 'inspire suspicion of the canonical writings,' that . . . I wholly abstained from mentioning or hinting at difficulties" (36).

To his critics, Hone's "question" only "appear[ed]" to be "natural" and "simple" (Dr. Butler 13). The words "selected" and "compiled" were the flash points: like parodic decomposition, they implied literary judgment and critical method; they turned a process of secure "collection" into a sorting through of "promiscuous and unauthenticated writings," in which "choice may have been influenced by caprice, dictated by fraud, or misled by error" (Dr. Butler 16).[37] In presenting the *Apocryphal New Testament,* Hone had represented the process of Christian canon formation as a historical literary event, and thus had laid it open to common question. *"[H]e who possesses this* AND *the New Testament has,* IN THE TWO VOLUMES, *a collection of all the historical records relative to Christ and his Apostles now in existence and considered sacred* BY CHRISTIANS *during the first four centuries after Christ":* Butler pulled out the other most offensive line, with an ambiguous suggestion that the capitals and italics emphases were Hone's own (Dr. Butler 17n; *Apocryphal* vi); they were not. Hone's misdating helped, since it put already-accepted canonical texts "in competition" with "spurious" works of later date (Dr. Butler 19), a blanket statement no biblical scholar would make today. His book undermined the very concept of "canon" in the sense in which we inherit it from Athanasius, as not a mere "Catalogue" but the *"rule or standard, by which other things were to be examined and judged"* (J. Jones 1: 19–20).

The very method of Hone's preface to the *Apocryphal New Testament* in fact plunges us into a world of dialogical relativity. Its body introduces the texts in straightforward fashion. But subversive speculation rises up from the footnotes. Four of ten prefatory pages are actually taken up with small-type commentary on the verse that had first drawn him to the apocryphal texts, long disputed by Unitarians: "For there are three that bear record in heaven, the Father, the Word, and the Holy Ghost: and these three are one" (1 John 5.7). "[I]f, in spite of all objections," Hone concluded, in a tone in which sarcasm competes with simplicity for the greatest unsettling effect:

> [the verse] be still genuine, no part of Scripture whatsoever can be proved either spurious or genuine; and Satan has been permitted, for many centuries, miraculously to banish the finest passage in the N.T. from the eyes and memories of almost all the Christian authors, translators, and transcribers. (*Apocryphal* xn)

Alternately, Hone suggests, the verse might owe its existence to editorial practice and scribal error: the verse was set up "in small types, or included in brackets" in Bibles printed under Henry VIII, Edward VI, and Elizabeth (vii*n*); it might have slipped into John's epistle "from a gloss or paraphrase that was at first put in the margin or between the lines" (vii*n*–viii*n*).[38] When the Revised Version of the Bible began publication in 1881, that very matter of *margins* would return to unsettle biblical scholarship and bibliolatrous belief.

Worst, to compound his literary crime, Hone had granted his uncanonical texts a strictly scriptural *style*. "[I]magining that such a compilation would bear the same relation to the New Testament that the Church Apocrypha does to the Old Testament," he said, "I divided the books into chapters, and the chapters into verses; putting contents to each chapter, and running head-lines on each page" (*Aspersions* 56). The arrangement "render[ed]" the volume "more gratifying to the reader, and more convenient for reference" (*Apocryphal* x). Its actual "mischievous and malevolent" effect, charged Archdeacon Butler, was compounded by Hone's headnotes and a contents list "made to resemble, as closely as possible, the table of the works of canonical scripture" (Dr. Butler 21): thus, "Mary hath Chapters 8," and so forth. The "great danger" of the *Apocryphal New Testament* was that it *looked* like "a continuation or supplement to the sacred volume" (Rennell ii). Antiquarian Hone had a black letter precedent, of course: "a translation of the Shepherd of Hermas, made a hundred and sixty years ago, by John Pringle, is divided into verses; the book is in my hand" (*Aspersions* 43). But at some level of consciousness, he had more motives for what he was doing.

For, if parody is a form of (sub)literary forgery, a " 'fraudulent imitation' or diabolical double of the meaningful artifact" (Haywood 10), invested with *"spurious wit,"* what were the apocryphal gospels as Hone presented them but fakes and impositions, "mockeries" of the real Testament in all senses of that word? To his critics, there was a compelling identity between Hone as the "arch blasphemer," and Hone as the charlatan who designed to "palm" "counterfeit" Gospels for works truly "stamped with the divine superscription and authority" (Rennell ii–iii). To "plac[e] . . . spurious gospels, as like in form and phraseology as they can be made to the originals" before "the common people," Archdeacon Butler concurred, was to invite them to take false for true, apocrypha for Scripture (Dr. Butler 13).

Butler's refutation relied heavily on the methods of biblical criticism that Protestantism had developed in default of such authenticating claims as that still made by the *Catholic Dictionary:* "it is only from this very Church, and on her authority, that Scripture is received" (Addis 108). They too were in essence literary. To distinguish false from true, Butler turns to "direct" (that is, external), "traditional," "inferential," and "internal" evidence (Dr. Butler 10). The very closeness of the apocryphal "imitations" to their "model[s]," he argued, bore "testimony" to the "priority" of the models' existence (31, 30, 35). Hone's "sole aim" and "great object," seconded the *Quarterly*, was "to raise the positive evidence for the Apocryphal writings as high as possible, because then another process hardly less direct, for deducing the spuriousness of the New Testament, is opened" (July 1821: 348, 354): apocryphal "authority" would destroy canonical "credit" (355, 348). In effect, the scandal occasioned by Hone's *Apocryphal New Testament* anticipated by a generation the storm that would surround reception of the German "Higher Criticism" in England from the 1840s through the 1880s. Here was a first homegrown threat to the exclusive status and authority of the Holy Scriptures—what G. W. Foote of the *Freethinker* would later call the preeminent Victorian "fetish." It was not to be "finally" turned off by any "small supplement" to Paley's *Evidences* or "popular compendium" of reasons for textual belief and unbelief (Rennell v). "AN ENEMY HATH DONE THIS" (Dr. Butler 30). Hone's second act of blasphemous decomposition was thus the second originating point of nineteenth-century Christianity's "literary problem" (Mrs. Ward, introduction to *Elsmere* [1911] xxv). Clearly, the "wicked" and "contemptible" parodist of 1817 had only "escape[d]" conviction by his juries' collusion or his talent for fooling them (*Quarterly*, July 1821: 348). This time, his critics tried, condemned, and attempted to execute him by review.

Hone responded to the attacks only when stories about his own brother repudiating him as an "advocate of 'blasphemy'" found their way into the Tory scandal sheet *John Bull*, and from there spread to the *Sun* evening newspaper and the local papers (*Aspersions* 8).[39] In the sixty-eight pages of his retaliatory pamphlet *Aspersions Answered*, Hone finished the research he had curtailed in rushing his apocryphal volume to press. But he also exposed in learned detail the scholarly incompetence and stunning duplicity of his respected opponents—transpositions, misreadings, omissions, "perversions" of meaning (15), and even insertions, all of which (cross-checking proves) Hone was right in imputing to them. His refutation is witheringly funny. When the *Quarterly* reviewer declines to "penetrate deeper into the dark recesses" of the volume's "falsehoods" than Mary and Protevangelium (*Quarterly*, July 1821: 362), Hone erupts:

> What an amiable deficiency of moral courage! . . . just at the moment when he
> ought to have acquainted his readers that these "dark recesses" are the parts of the
> Apocryphal New Testament . . . translated and published by Wake, archbishop of
> Canterbury, under the title of "The Genuine Epistles of the Apostolical Fathers."
> (*Aspersions* 32–33)

Then there was the recurrent question of forgery. The *Quarterly* reviewer cinched his case by citing Hone's "insinuation" that "[t]he whole story" of the fixing of the New Testament canon

> may be an imposture; at all events, we may not have received the true and genuine history of it—we can have no certain accounts of the doctrines promulgated by the first teachers; and indeed the simple fact that no formal recognition of the official documents took place, is of itself a very suspicious circumstance and quite enough to cast an air of doubt over the whole transaction. (*Quarterly,* July 1821: 350)

The citation seemed a "master stroke." But it was indeed what Hone pronounced it, "an impudent forgery" (*Aspersions* 37): his "reverend slanderer" had simply made the sentence up (33). "[B]y such a man am I accused of . . . 'a systematic disregard of truth,' 'a deep and desperate malignity,' and 'notorious infidelity,' " Hone concluded (37; see *Quarterly* 355, 364). As Ian Haywood remarks, "The point to note is that forgeries often expose . . . vested interests" (13–14).

Refutation brought Hone little joy. There was no stopping the "critical fraud" from trickling down (W. Hone, *Another Article* 3). The *Quarterly's* reviewer publicly declared in August 1824 that Hone's well-thought and bookish reply was "written in a spirit of the most vulgar and contemptible ferocity," descending to actual "menace" (qtd. in *Another* 3). *"INFIDELITY is not so good a TRADE as it was,* . . . and therefore, Mr. Hone has . . . announc[ed] that his character has been quite mistaken" (qtd. 25, Hone's emphasis). Hone stuttered out *Another Article for the Quarterly Reviewer* in protest. But the world would read the *Quarterly,* and would read Hone through its pages. His reviewer was presented to a living "upon consummation of his crime" (*Aspersions* 38).[40] Hone was "to be written down at any rate" (*Another Article* 32). And the writing down continued into the twentieth century, when the provost of Eton, Montague Rhodes James, prefaced his new translation of the *Apocryphal Gospels, Acts, Epistles, and Apocalypses* in 1924 with a diatribe against Hone's "misleading," "unoriginal," and "very bad" book (xv). ("Only," he added, "I cannot forget that it was the very first book on the New Testament Apocrypha which fell into my hands, and . . . it exercised a fascination which has never lost its hold upon me" [xv].)

There was some comfort for Hone in Archdeacon Butler's recantation (Hone BL 34,586: 4), secured by some masterly self-ingratiation.[41] It extended to a generous review of *Ancient Mysteries* and a private admission of slipshod scholarship and quite crass error in his *Charge* to diocesan clergy, with its weighty claim to Christian learning and its class advantage of training in Latin and Greek.[42] But Butler never saw "ground to alter my opinions as to the mischievous tendency" of the *Apocryphal New Testament,* he wrote Hone in October 1824. It would be "a convenient text-book" for unbelief (34,585: 379). In 1827 the British and Foreign Bible Society finally banned the Old Testament Apocrypha from British Bibles: the decision put the *Apocryphal New Testament* absolutely beyond the pale of allowable print.

A capping insult still begs consideration for its bearing on the nineteenth-century history of blasphemy as a history of class insurgency and class repression. The *Quarterly* reviewer, Reverend Rennell, and Archdeacon Butler all reached the same conclusion in their reviews of the *Apocryphal New Testament:* the man responsible for broadcasting it must himself be an impostor. "Th[e] *ostensible* editor," Butler had asserted, "is a man whose name is but too well known to the ranks of disaffection and infidelity" (Dr. Butler 12, qtd. in *Aspersions* 48, W. Hone's emphasis). But "the book under our consideration *undoubtedly* is not . . . his own production. I grieve to say that the *real* editor is a man of talents and attainments" (12, qtd. in *Aspersions* 50, first emphasis Hone's). "It is indeed a source of real gratification," agreed the *Quarterly* reviewer,

> that . . . we may at once dismiss Mr. Hone from our consideration. He is described to us as a poor illiterate creature, far too ignorant to have any share in the composition either of this, or of his seditious pamphlets. He only supplies the evil will and the audacity: the venom is supplied by the dastard behind. Our future observations will, therefore, be confined to the real editor of this nefarious publication. (*Quarterly,* July 1821: 348)

Here was no "respectable" scholar or "writer of credit" (*Quarterly,* July 1821: 350, 356). Such "low abuse," as one friend wrote Hone, deserved only "silent contempt" (Hone BL 40,856: 8); but the sense of metaphysical annihilation it induced was hard to bear.[43]

For class insult and political catcalling were not the only values attached to the charge of impostordom. It had a disturbing logic. "Considered as a whole, criminals are nothing less than madmen," Foucault quotes the reformer Ferrus (*Discipline* 254), but it did not need the "normalizing" and "disciplinary" "transformation" of the eighteenth and nineteenth centuries to put the English blasphemer "outside the pact" of society (101). His "impostordom" was a legacy of early Protestantism, a product of the theory evolved sometime between 1540 and 1570 that no individual who denied the "reality" of religion could be trusted (Wootton 64). Hence the title of a report on the trial of "The Impostor, Susannah Fowles, . . . for Blaspheming Jesus Christ" (Nokes 163n). The statute of 1698, uninvoked but powerfully suggestive, provided for the blasphemer's complete civil disabling: deprived of office; stripped of the right to sue, plead, prosecute, or testify; debarred from executing a will, coming into a legacy, or standing guardian to a child. The "Rights of Man" from which our modern concept of "human rights" descend was a catchphrase of the French Revolution, not a foundation stone of English law. An "impostor" could not claim legal rights, indeed could hardly be said to exist. The blasphemer was bereft of human status, a false person, a no-body, cut off from the Word of God and the community of human language. "Gentlemen," prosecuting counsel invited a blasphemy jury of the 1840s, "if this man's opinions are true, what becomes of the sanction under which law and justice are administered— including the oath they had just taken?" (*Trial of Charles Southwell* 14). Unbelievers were always already "outlaws" in law; "without [its] pale," as one blasphemer put it, the defendant was subject to startling illegalities and lapses of process.[44]

Moreover, no unbeliever, convicted or not, had any "word" to give. Not until 1888, after thirty years of legal struggle, did the Oaths Act finally secure the right of witnesses to "affirm" rather than swear upon the Bible, enabling an atheist to give evidence in a court of law.[45] (It also legally qualified him to become a judge, technically able to try a case of blasphemy, a paradox worth pondering.) And not to be competent to give evidence in a legal system that had come to rely upon evidence, as Alexander Welsh demonstrates in *Strong Representations,* was tantamount to nonexistence. An "inviolable Oath" testified to belief in a future state, in which perjury would be punished (Burke 85). It was the paradigmatic transaction of a society structured by confession, a state countersigned by its citizens. Without an oath, Starkie summarized, "no question of property could be decided, and no criminal brought to justice" (2: 131). John Stuart Mill viewed its requirement as a national prescription for hypocrisy, reaching for the example of Jacob Holyoake, prosecuted for blasphemy in 1842: proposed as a juryman at the Old Bailey in 1857, he was turned down in "grossly" insulting terms (*On Liberty* 34); later, when his nine-year-old son was knocked down before his eyes by a reckless cabman, he was told he "could not give evidence" at the inquest as he was "unable to take the oath" (Holyoake, *Sixty Years* 1: 79). Before 1888, no defendant in a case of blasphemy could even qualify as a competent witness in his own defense; and in prosecutions for "blasphemous conspiracy" did not become so until ten years later. "How many . . . men," Holyoake asked,

> have been paralyzed in all that made life valuable to them, have been ruined in their profession, their prospects, and their fame—have been excluded from public service, insulted, bullied in public courts, imprisoned, fined in purse and fatally in health [sic], and no paper vindicated their claim, no public opinion would tolerate their defense, nor did any means exist whereby it could be circulated if they made it? (*Case* 30)

In a lighter moment, he preserved amongst his papers a slip recording the presentation of a pianoforte by Rochdale Freethinkers to a Mrs. Maden, "Who was non-suited in an action" because of her inability "to affirm her belief in certain speculative propositions." The piano was intended not for mere consolation but as "a Protest Against a State of the Law, which converts the Witness-box into an instrument of Ecclesiastical Inquisition" (in HC). One hopes she made a lot of noise with it.

Finally, the career of William Hone suggests a last literary inheritance which may at first surprise. The beneficiary was Charles Dickens. Hone's transformative delight in urban bustle; his gifts for metaphor and nickname; his odd fusion of reportage and improvisational comedy; and his ability to slip under his reader's guard by invoking familiar passages of Bible, folktale, and nursery rhyme, make him Dickens's forgotten subliterary father. The boy who "made stories for myself, out of the streets, and out of men and women," like his most famous child hero (*David Copperfield* 224), the journalist who imagined "Boz" and his urban *Sketches* when he realized the narrative potential of a display of old boots and clothes in Monmouth Street (*Sketches* 98), is the rich relation of the "seedy" bookseller whose inspiration for a political squib might be a playbill on a brick wall or a child's toy "absently" glimpsed in a shop window, the germs for Hone's parodies the *Maid and the Magpie* and the *Queen's Matrimonial Ladder*, respectively. Fielding, Sterne, and Smollet were not "Boz"'s only ancestors. We have colluded in Dickens's bourgeois imagination of himself. Dickens did not "write what the people wanted," as G. K. Chesterton once put it. Not only did he "*want* what the people wanted" (*Dickens* 106) but his imagination moved to the same profane and playful urban tunes as popular progenitors' like William Hone's: "[P]recisely here," as Bakhtin writes, in such "popular laughter" as Hone evoked, "the authentic folkloric roots" of the nineteenth-century novel as Dickens created it are indeed "to be sought" (*Dialogical Imagination* 21).

In 1825 Hone found the format that made him most famous, and almost respectable. The *Every-Day Book* he launched in that year was a hybrid of almanac and encyclopedia, popular antiquarian miscellany and literary treasury. Stuffed with facts and legends, "[it] had a charm for every book lover" (1883 notice, qtd. in Hackwood 355). But unlike earlier ventures, like *Time's Telescope* and *Arlis's Magazine*, it was no "mere compilation" but "entirely original" (Lawley, facing 3, in Hone WA). Although it introduced an entire generation to the literary inheritance that was previously locked up in costly and out-of-print volumes, its greatest success "lay in [its] homely or vernacular character" (John Timbs, *Leisure Hour*, 29 July 1871: 470).[46] New editions were followed by similar ventures, the *Table Book* (1827) and *Year Book* (1832). In short, these "most valuable books of modern times" (Hall 320) anticipated by a full generation the familial atmosphere and the popular-educational objectives of Dickens's magazine ventures: *Master Humphrey's Clock*, 1840 to 1841; *Household Words*, twopence a week from 1850 to 1859; and its 1860s successor, *All the Year Round*. Hone's "Books" were "as attractive to the man of 'lettered leisure,' as to the worker in field, forge and factory" (Lawley 22, in Hone WA); a decade before *Pickwick*, they intended and achieved the fusion of high and low audiences on which Dickens's impact and celebrity would depend (1825 advertisement, in Hone WA).

Hone's Londoner's delight in urban rambles and *rus in urbe* anticipated the feel of *Nickleby* and *Chuzzlewit*, and readers responded to his sketches with the same delight in realism and idiosyncrasy that drew them to *Sketches by "Boz"*: "some of the characters are exquisitely drawn," one fan wrote Hone, "the 'drat that Butcher,' of the housemaid followed by the qualifying 'God forgive me,' page 483," for example (letter from C. Ewing, 3 April 1826, in Hone WA). And if Dickens "invented" Christmas as a secular family celebration in the Christmas stories he published from 1843, Hone supplied him with a blueprint. The *Every-Day Book*'s intent is summed up in an epigraph from Herrick: "I tell of festivals, and fairs, and plays, / Of merriment, and mirth, and bonfire blaze; / I tell of Christmas mummings, new year's day, / Of twelfth-night king and queen, and children's play. . . ." Hone's original advertisement of 1824 set out a list of contents all Dickensians will recognize, from "Misers—Quacks—Incantations—Crickets" to "Dwarfs—Giants . . . Betrothings—Phenomena" (in *Every-Day Book* 1: x). "Here were riches," as Squeers might have said.

But there was more behind. The *Every-Day Book* and its successors were serially published in cheap weekly numbers cumulated monthly and annually, a strategy of radical publishing in the 1810s (inherited from the eighteenth century) that Hone perfected for general use.[47] "A number, or sheet of thirty-two columns, price three pence," he explained to the as-yet-uninitiated public, "will be published *every Saturday* till the undertaking is completed"; "NOTE.—*This Leaf and the Title are to be cut off, and thrown aside, when the Volume is bound*" (1: x). This was exactly the method by which Dickens and his publishers would reach a broad readership, both for his magazines and for his novels. Publication of the *Table Book* in particular "commenced on New Year's Day, 1825, and ended in the last week of 1826" (preface v), so that Hone's writing kept exact pace with his audience's reading, fostering the illusion of ongoing conversation that Dickens in his turn also cherished. The public felt a proprietorial interest in his success. "Having accidentally heard that you had been ill," Charles Dilke forwarded a few items to fill the gap in July 1825 (Hone BL 40,856: 17). "I beg of you to accept the enclosed," wrote a local historian, "it is almost an act of duty for every antiquary to supply you with accounts" (40,120: 258). Publishers ingratiated themselves with "the Esteemed Ed[ito]r" on the off chance he might print an extract from their latest volumes (40,120: 256). Hone had invented both a communal treasury and a powerful literary organ.

To respectable William Tegg, whose opportunist father took over and cashed in on Hone's stock and properties, these "wholesome," "popular," and "really valuable" works were "THE ANTIDOTE" to the *Parodies'* "BANE" (Tegg iii–v). To Dickens they may have been a gold mine. Copies of the *Every-Day Book, Table Book,* and *Year Book,* four volumes half bound in calf, dated 1838, were listed in the catalogue of books sold after his death, price two pounds and ten shillings (Stonehouse 60); they appear in Dickens's household inventory of May 1844 (appendix, *Letters* 4: 716). Also catalogued in 1870 was a large bound volume of *Hone's and Cobbett's Political Tracts,* a rarer proposition. Dickens was not a great reader; the fact he acquired and kept these books is meaningful.

Five years after his bankruptcy, Hone's star was declining fast. He lost that cherished control over his own production that had let him (as he wrote Francis Place in 1824) *"do things in my own* way" (Hone BL 37,949: 144). It was Thomas Tegg who published the *Year Book* in 1832, while Hone wrote items on demand for Tegg's *London Encyclopedia* (Hone BL 40,120: 376). But he was an awkward proposition as a house author. The new publishing conditions and "complex machinery" of the 1830s left no scope for his habitual last minute "expedients" (Hone BL 40,120: 373); he proved unable to write "under restraint of any kind" (374); he protested at having Tegg's house drawn as a frontispiece to the *Year Book* (Lawley 118, in Hone WA); and his handwriting had deteriorated after another stroke. In 1836, Tegg turned his eyes to a rising star. In August, he offered Dickens one hundred pounds to write the text of a children's book to be called *Solomon Bell the Raree Showman.* Dickens was halfway through the *Pickwick Papers* but agreed to deliver by Christmas (*Letters* 1: 162). He had stepped directly into Hone's shoes. Stepping out of them only two weeks later, when Bentley made him a better offer, he may have preferred to forget the episode and the affinity it spoke with déclassé literary bankrupts and blasphemers like William Hone.[48] "Mr. Tegg" of his courteous replies quickly turned into "Timothy Twigg," the parvenu butt of jokes in Dickens's circle of friends.[49]

"With a lively conception of wit, and an irresistible propensity to humor," wrote William Hone in 1817, "I have likewise so profound a regard for the well-being of society . . . that I know of no temptation capable of inducing me to pen a line injurious to social happiness, or offensive to private morals" (*Reformist's Register,* 25 October: 430). They are words Dickens might have spoken and probably did on some unrecorded occasion: he was feted for his perfect realization of what Hone's Books aspired to provide, wholly *"innocent"* pleasure (Dickens to Talfourd, August 1837, *Letters* 1: 685). Crucially, if the "Inimitable" novelist saw much worth imitating in William Hone, he also saw what was to be avoided. Hone's fame was never unmixed with notoriety; he remained always a kind of unholy holy fool. "[G]ood-natured readers," he knew, would "find something to be amused with" in exactly the same work that would "offend those I despair of pleasing" (*Ancient Mysteries* vi). It may have been doggedness or simple out-of-datedness that led him to advertise the projected "History of Parody" on the same flyer that carried his "Explanatory Address to the Readers of the Every-Day Book" (*Every-Day Book* 1: ix). The days were numbered in which a correspondent might thank him for *Aspersions Answered* and order a copy of that *Book* in the same letter (Hone BL 40,856: 14).

Charles Dickens never "despaired" of "pleasing," and was determined that no "prejudice" should stand in the way of thoroughly respectable and remunerative success. Not for him Hone's irrepressible "trespasse[s]" into religious doctrine (W. Hone, *Ancient Mysteries* vii). He must not "pander . . . to vulgar prejudices about serious things" (*Quarterly* 1839, Hollington 1: 273) nor stoop too much to "cockney vulgarity" (review of *Sketches by "Boz," Mirror,* Hollington 1: 262).[50] The lower-class dissent that he freely lambasted was a much safer target than the Anglicanism that Hone assaulted; and Dickensian anticlericalism never implied unchristian feeling. While Secularists and agnostics claimed him for their own throughout the nineteenth century, Dickens the Unitarian kept in the shadows. Christianity is assiduously incorporated into sentimental vision; "keynote" texts at the core of the novels are a standing assurance to readers of biblical truth within fictional structure.[51]

Dickens understood how to write "satire by *implication,* not personality," shorn of the specificity that made Hone's parodies bite (G. H. Lewes, *National Magazine,* in Hollington 1: 248). His "skill as a parodist," instantly recognized, rarely tempted him to the mis-"application of ridicule" (*Edinburgh Review,* 1838, 1: 251–52). *Little Dorrit* would become a favored example of Bakhtinian "double-accented, double-styled *hybrid construction*" (*Dialogical Imagination* 304); Shaw pronounced it "a more seditious book than *Das Kapital*" (in Wall, *A Critical Anthology* 290). But it was an index of Dickens's superb "fineness of tact" that even this novel, which was harshly reviewed, should not too deeply have disturbed its readership (Lewes, Hollington 1: 246).

Indeed, it would not be fanciful to trace Dickens's anxiety over the strong language and slang that were a marked feature of his first "real" novel, *Oliver Twist* (1837–38), in part to a need to distinguish himself from the Hone model. As later novelists like Thomas Hardy were to discover, the project of realism *Twist* inaugurated could be construed as a kind of blasphemy, the speaking out of the unspeakable; between its publication in 1837 and *Jude the Obscure*'s in 1895, "coarse" and "shocking" language was progressively criminalized. The very efforts of some early reviewers to clear Dickens of "vulgarity" pointed towards his problem and its class basis (see Lewes, 1837, in Hollington 1: 248). Moreover, cheap publication on the Hone model added to Dickens's risk: the form was hardly "indicative of high literary pretensions" (*Edinburgh Review*, 1838, in Hollington 1: 250); it located him on the dangerous borderline between literature and the subliterary. "[C]ritical contempt" would be a life-long condition of his "immense popularity," not the paradox Lewes remarked on in 1872 (*Fortnightly Review*, in Wall, *A Critical Anthology* 192).

The inheritance of blasphemy loomed large in the year *Twist* began publication. In the twenty years since 1817, as we shall see, perhaps 150 trials for blasphemy took place in England, the bulk between 1819 and 1827. Between the first and third editions of *Oliver Twist* in 1837 and 1841 several more high-profile cases were initiated, one involving the close friend who was the dedicatee of Dickens's *Pickwick Papers* (see below, 2.2). Several more trials were pending. Dickens's *Twist* fears blasphemy.

The famous preface of 1841 is a defense against the charge. In *Oliver Twist* he had "attempt[ed]," Dickens testifies, "to dim the false glitter surrounding" the criminal underworld "by shewing it in its unattractive and repulsive truth." Nevertheless, "I endeavored . . . to banish from the lips of the lowest character I introduced, any expression that could by any possibility offend" (xxvii). The preposterous central premise of the child's inherent goodness expresses itself linguistically: fallen among thieves, Oliver is not to be defiled even by speaking the word "th——" (111). That suppression fits into a network of avoidance and invocation. Sometimes blasphemy is comically implicated, as when "the clerk and the jailer coughed very loud just at the right moment" to smother Fang the magistrate's swear words (65), or circumlocution (what the *Quarterly* called "brimstone in silver paper") sidesteps offense (Tillotson xii). Or indirect discourse describes the words Nancy "pour[s] out . . . in one continuous and vehement scream" (101). But while Dickens vilifies euphemistic avoidance in the figure of

Fagin—"Civil words, . . . we must have civil words" (100)—he also demonizes its blasphemous opposite in Bill Sikes. In 1841 Dickens claimed not to have "abated" the "stern and plain truth" he had told in 1837. But in the third and subsequent editions of the novel he actually eradicated every "damn" that Sikes had originally uttered. Still, blasphemy escaped into peculiar euphemistic substitutions—*"Burn my body!"* (100, 116, etc.), the traditional punishment for Sikes's "blaspheming" (90)—just as it had already surfaced in the curious maneuver whereby Sikes's own name was rendered unutterable: "None of your mistering," he challenges Fagin; "You know my name: out with it!" (76).[52] Blasphemy left its mark at the birth of Victorian fiction.

So too did England's "arch blasphemer." Hone hovers behind Brownlow's pseudocriminal jest that "We won't make an author of you, while there's an honest trade to be learnt" (83), and dictates the finale to innocent Oliver's trial for pickpocketing. At the moment when Magistrate Fang passes summary justice, suddenly "an elderly man of decent but poor appearance, clad in an old suit of black, rushed hastily into the office: and advanced towards the bench."

> "Stop, stop! Don't take him away! For Heaven's sake stop a moment!" cried the new-comer: breathless with haste. . . . "What is this? Who is this? Turn this man out. Clear the office!" cried Mr. Fang. (66)

The man is William Hone, still in his famously rusty old suit, still possessed of his passion for justice. Allan Stewart Laing, the notorious magistrate of Hatton Garden, is not the only historical personage to make his appearance in *Oliver Twist:*

> "I will speak," cried the man; "I will not be turned out. I saw it all. I keep the book-stall. I demand to be sworn. I will not be put down." (66)

Here is the spirit that bowed Chief Justice Ellenborough in 1817: "The man was right" (66). In the figure of the "worthy book-stall keeper" Dickens tips his hat to a forgotten rival. Why else should so inconsequential a character be ushered into Brownlow's coach while the action pauses to admire his bravery and good humor?[53]

The question remains of where Dickens could have learned details and atmosphere from the trials of twenty years ago. Perhaps from Leigh Hunt; perhaps from Tegg, or the poet-publisher Edward Moxon, himself accused of blasphemy in 1841 (see below, 2.2); perhaps from the wide circle of literary acquaintances he shared with Hone, including Charles Dilke, Hone's admirer and later editor of the *Athenaeum* (1830–46), who once gave Dickens half a crown while he was drudging at Warren's blacking factory.

But Dickens most likely got his details where he got the famed illustrations to *Sketches by "Boz"* and *Oliver Twist*. It was his cordial partnership with William Hone that launched George Cruikshank's career as an artist (fig. 3), though it is Dickens's renown that has kept his alive while Hone's has evaporated. From 1816 most of Hone's political "squibs" were illuminated by the young "Cruiky's droll designs" (*Slops's Shave at a Broken Hone* 12); their friendship may date back as far as 1809–10, when Cruikshank was seventeen (Lawley n. pag., in Hone WA). In the two years from 1819, they collaborated on sixteen pieces that together sold more than a hundred thousand copies. Cruikshank's "genius," Hone claimed, "had been wasted on mere caricature till it embodied my ideas and feelings" (*Aspersions* 49n); "By exciting a taste for art in the more humble ranks of life," his squibs as enlivened by Cruikshank first "created a new era in the history of publication" (49n).[54] Cruikshank sat sketching in court while Hone faced Justice Ellenborough, and even rehearsed Hone's defense with him beforehand (Patten 1: 131). It was Cruikshank who turned out the copies of old and new prints "successively commented upon and exhibited to the inspection of the Juries" (Hone BL 40,108: 17), for example, a copy of Gillray's 1798 "Doublûres of Characters;—or—Striking Resemblances in Physiognomy," like that between "A Friend to his Country" and "Judas selling his Master" (Cruikshank, *Album* 2: 89–94, in Hone Berg).

Besides affection and security, Cruikshank took political coloring from Hone, though he was not above taking Tory money in 1820 to caricature him as "the *Blasphemer,* of infamous fame," with his printer's devil at his side (Patten 1: 188). He provided illustrations for *Ancient Mysteries* and the superbly produced *Every-Day Book,* on which Hone laid out six hundred pounds in wood engravings (Hackwood 248; John Timbs, *Leisure Hour,* 29 July 1871: 470). Far from exploiting his talent (an oft-repeated charge), Hone paid some of the best rates going and was a soft touch for loans (even occasional *"wackers,"* as Cruikshank called them [note, 14 September 1824, *Album* 1: 19, in Hone Berg]), while Mrs. Hone kept a bed made up in the "Hall of Parody" for the protégé her husband wished would "forswear late hours, blue ruin," and gin-and-water (Rickword 29).[55] From Cruikshank, Dickens could have learned the same details of his arraignment that Hone wrote John Hunt on 8 May 1817 (Hone BL 38,108: 189) and that Hunt's *Yellow Dwarf* partially reported on 3 January 1818: they strikingly recall Oliver's fainting fit in the magistrate's court. From Cruikshank too Dickens may have inherited details that find their way into the heart of *David Copperfield*. The mixture of heroic dignity and astonished incompetence with which Hone met bankruptcy in 1828 is pure Micawber (he was, moreover, a dab hand at the ceremonial begging letter, as well as a master of comic-pompous circumlocution);[56] its root cause in the "evil machinations" of a

" We twa hae paidl't"—   BURNS.

Figure 3. Hone and Cruikshank collaborate. Title page to Hone's *Facetiae and Miscellanies* (1827).

"confidential business adviser" who "wormed" his way into the family (in the words of a Hone family letter) exactly prefigures the entrapment of Mr. Wickfield by Uriah Heep (Hackwood 195). In a very real sense, Dickens was Hone's inheritor.[57]

Those "worming" "machinations" drove a wedge between Hone and Cruikshank. The estrangement was not healed until Hone was on his deathbed fifteen years later, feebly reading the *Old Curiosity Shop*. Dickens was the mediating figure in their reconciliation. "I am going out to Tottenham this morning," he wrote Forster on 5 October 1842:

> on a cheerless mission I would willingly have avoided. Hone, of the *Every-Day Book,* is dying; and sent Cruikshank yesterday to beg me to go and see him. . . . There is no help for it, of course, so to Tottenham I repair. (*Letters* 3: 337)

The old man's desire to pass the baton, his recognition of similarity, may have dictated the tone of gracelessness under compulsion. Hone, however, was "greatly delighted" with the half-hour's visit, and held Cruikshank's hand for its whole duration (Hackwood 345).

After the funeral Dickens exacted a storyteller's revenge. "You know Hone of the Every Day Book, I dare say," he wrote an American friend on 2 March 1843:

> Ah! I saw a scene of mingled comicality and seriousness at his funeral some weeks ago, which has choked me at dinner-time ever since. (*Letters* 3: 453)

Cruikshank, with his straggling enormous whiskers "like a partially unraveled bird's nest"; Hone's miserable family "crying bitterly in one corner"; and "the other mourners—mere people of ceremony" made an "irresistible" compound of contrasts (453). And then stood forth the Reverend Binney, Hone's friend and pastor from the Weigh-House Chapel, to lecture George on "a paragraph respecting our departed friend" in the morning papers, which "stated, that when Mr. Hone failed in business as a bookseller, he was persuaded by *me* to try the Pulpit." That statement, Binney thundered, was "false, incorrect, unchristian, in a manner blasphemous. . . . Let us pray." With which, "in the same breath," Dickens reported, he and the company dropped to their knees, and "George (upon his knees, and sobbing . . .)" whispered him "that if he wasn't a clergyman, and it wasn't a funeral, he'd have punched his head." Whereupon: "I felt as if nothing but convulsions could possibly relieve me" (454).

Dickens's rewriting of the dead rival's departure reduced it to what Hackwood calls it—a "Dickensian Episode" (title, ch. 28). It was a "grossly" distorted account (Hackwood 347). Forster first footnoted the letter, then suppressed it entirely in revised editions of his *Life of Dickens* in 1874 and 1876. Cruikshank called it a "fiction" (qtd. in Hackwood 353). At least Dickens had had the decency to push through a gift of fifty pounds from the Literary Fund for "the Destitute widow and children of the late Mr. Hone" (*Letters* 3: 366). "They are very poor," he had added in a private letter to the editor of the *Chronicle,* "and he was not a common man" (3: 373). But "a story of th[e] kind" Dickens had fabricated of Hone's interment "cannot be easily forgotten"; "nor," believed the *British Weekly,* "is the tomb of oblivion altogether desirable for a story which . . . throws [light] upon Charles Dickens's methods." Here was its "value" (Hackwood 347–48). The "arch blasphemer" was thus incorporated into literary posterity, reduced to Dickensian caricature. Of all Dickens's biographers, only Ackroyd mentions Hone, and only because of this death scene (379, 386). Dickens had avoided the blasphemous brand.

But Cruikshank felt marked forever. He began the summary work of his career, the *Omnibus* of 1842, with an answer to libels in James Grant's *Portraits of Public Characters* (1841). Worse than imputations of low-life drunkenness was the insinuation that *"With Mr. Hone"* ("afterwards designated 'the most noted infidel of his day,'" Cruikshank remarked) *"he had long been on terms not only of intimacy but of warm friendship"* (*Omnibus* 3). Cruikshank's reply, no less than the friend whose memory he muddled in making it, was "regulated by the strictest morality." He *"had nothing whatever to do"* with the detestable parodies, "and the instant I heard of their appearance, I entreated him to withdraw them" (3). Dickens encouraged the counterattack (letter to Cruikshank, 2 May 1841, *Letters* 2: 276–7; Patten 2: 177).

The story of blasphemy in the nineteenth century begins here, in the life—and the death—of William Hone, because in this one career there came together all the strands in the history of blasphemy in the nineteenth century: parody and ridicule, apocryphal investigation, a threat—and a claim—to literary authority, popular literature and cheap publication, "coarse" and "vulgar" language. The last of these three fused together at heat in the crucible of the Carlile trials of 1819–27.

3. CARLILE, THE VOLUNTEERS, AND THE *AGE OF REASON* STRUGGLE

Richard Carlile was a contrary and hotheaded printer-publisher with a taste for confrontation and the grit to carry it through. What he had done to call "blood" and "anarchy" into court in 1819 (*British Press,* 15 October: 3), was to republish the *Age of Reason* (1793–96), the last work of Thomas Paine, the "rebellious needleman" (Holyoake, *Life and Character of Richard Carlile* 36) who became the darling of American rebels and French sansculottes. Carlile proclaimed him "our great and only prototype" (*Republican,* 27 August 1819: 1): he was the original bogeyman artisan infidel. His *Rights of Man* sold between 50,000 and 100,000 three-shilling copies in a few weeks in 1791 (legend says 1.5 million), partly thanks to his relinquishing of copyright. He fled to France at the urging of William Blake but was condemned for sedition *in absentia;* he died in exile in America in 1809. The anticlerical sequel to his Jacobin handbook, the *Age of Reason* was both a Deist's guide to biblical deconstruction and a startling claim to power for the plain speech of the common man. The case of Richard Carlile dramatically investigates how contempt for the "blasphemous" plain speech of the common man could spin into fear of linguistic "violence."

The Age of Reason took an ax to the Christian "engine of power" (Paine,

Letter to Erskine, qtd. in introduction 35) conceiving the Bible as a political instrument for crushing the people. Its pious explication of natural religion understandably went unheard in the crash of falling idols. The ahistorical simplicities and repetitiveness that flawed Paine's book were of a piece with its quality of personal testament. Half of it was written from memory in France, during the Terror, under a threat of execution that lent urgency to its iconoclasm. All of it was colored by a devout Deist's horror of the "insult" Scripture offered the "Almighty Lecturer" (Paine 76). Following the trials of Richard Carlile and his army of volunteers, the book became the anti-Bible of all lower-class nineteenth-century infidel agitators. For this, Paine was vilified across two continents as a "demi-human archbeast" (Foner 40) and, in Theodore Roosevelt's words, "a filthy little atheist" (48).

The *Age of Reason* was the very book proscribed in the 1797 trial of the bookseller Williams (see above, 1.1), and apparently put down by the 1812 prosecution, pillorying, and imprisonment of the man who had first published it in 1795–96, Daniel Isaac Eaton.[58] He was finally cornered by the Society for the Suppression of Vice, privately founded in 1802 to combat the "poisonous effects of infidelity" and "undue freedom of thinking," and deeply suspicious of anyone who handled books (1802 address, qtd. in Wiener 34).[59] Liberals like Shelley were stung into protest. His *Letter to Lord Ellenborough* is a powerful protest against the first "reviv[al]" of "antiquated precedents" in "a nation that presumptuously calls itself the sanctuary of freedom," but where "we need not despair of beholding the flames of persecution rekindled in Smithfield" (*Shelley's Prose* 73–76). It was too hot to publish in 1819, but such reactions indicate the intense interest writers took in the trials of common booksellers and pressmen, even when the defendant, like Richard Carlile, had little taste or gift for literature.

The historic resurgence of the *Age of Reason,* Carlile's Christmas present for 1818, must have seemed to government like the return of the blasphemous repressed. It was perhaps because repression had seemed so total, because of the book's inheritance of "vituperation" (Carlile, *Life of Paine* iv), that Carlile turned to it as his weapon of choice against the established powers. "Let me have the *Age of Reason* to preach from," he later told his jury, "[and] let the Attorney-General take the Bible, and you will soon see who makes the greater number of converts" (*Report of the Mock Trials of Carlile* 186–87). History has proved him dramatically wrong, though he was believed right through the 1880s and in some quarters is so believed to this day.[60] But the importance of his fight remains. It has entered history as a struggle for free speech and freedom of publication: it was couched throughout in the less-mentionable terms of blasphemy.

The *Age of Reason*'s exposé of Bible "Immoralities," "Absurdities,"

"Atrocities," and "Contradictions" granted common people access to eighteenth-century rationalism's critique of the Bible in terms they could fully
understand. It yoked together what had been thought impossible fellows:
sacred and lofty subjects and the idiom of the secular and lowly. Paine's
English was resolutely logical, shorn of allusion and ornament; and the
plainness dictated by principle extended also to occasional jokes and images
drawn from everyday life. Thus, the world turns around the sun, for example, just as meat turns on a spit (Paine 87n). Like Benjamin Franklin, Paine
excelled in folksy idiom: the legend of Jonah was a "whale of a miracle"
(95); the Jewish kings were "a parcel of rascals" (124). Thomas Jefferson
thought no writer excelled Paine "in ease and familiarity of style, in perspicuity of expression, happiness of elucidation, and in simple and unassuming
language" (qtd. in Foner 42).

The eleven passages picked out in the eleven "counts," that is, the charges
or sections of Carlile's indictment for blasphemy for republishing Paine's
Age of Reason in 1819, are eleven of the frankest passages in the work.

> *1st Count.*
> Whenever we read the obscene stories, the voluptuous debaucheries, the cruel
> and torturous executions, the unrelenting vindictiveness[,] with which more than
> half the [Old Testament] is filled[,] it would be more consistent that we called
> it the word of a Demon than the Word of God. It is a History of wickedness
> that has served to corrupt and brutalize mankind. (indictment, in CC; Paine 60)

"What would your feelings be," Attorney-General Gifford asked in court,
"if you found such a paper had been put into the hands of your offspring
and domestics?" (*Report of the Mock Trials of Carlile* 8). "The story" of the
Annunciation, "taking it as it is told," read the fifth count:

> is blasphemously obscene[; i]t gives an account of a young woman, engaged to
> be married, and while under this engagement she is[,] to speak plain language,
> debauched by a ghost. (indictment, in CC; Paine 156–57)

"I do not think there is a man existing," remarked Gifford, as the words
passed his lips, "who will not say that this is a direct attack, *couched in the
coarsest terms*" (*Report of the Mock Trials of Carlile* 11, my emphasis). "Carlile's publications," the *Age* and other works of the same deistical variety,
the *Morning Herald* reported, "were not only blasphemous, but *studiously
brutal*" (17 November 1819: 2, my emphasis).

Government knew that the people would not so easily be reduced to
cloddish and animal muteness as the phrases I have italicized would desire.
Paine had given them a language of criticism, "a language that was alleged
not to exist," Olivia Smith's "intellectual vernacular" (36). That fact had
political meaning in it. Edmund Burke had used vulgar terms, but Paine's

usage, partly learned in the United States, disrupted "traditional class align-ments" (O. Smith 39), and his ability to communicate threateningly repre-sented what any member of his audience might achieve. Carlile's 1819 re-publication of the *Age of Reason* allowed the fear of plainspokenness that had colored the Woolston case of 1728 and lurked in the wings at Hone's trials to erupt in a specifically political context. It ensured the identification of plain English and insurgency, word crime and class crime, for the rest of the nineteenth century.

1819 was also the year of the "Peterloo Massacre," when magistrates sent in the troops, sabers drawn, to cut down 60,000 men, women, and children gathered for a peaceful mass meeting on St. Peter's Fields, Manchester. Their "panic of class hatred" resulted in the deaths of 11 people and the injuring of 421 (E. Thompson 686). One of the magistrates, a clergyman, was rewarded with the two thousand-pound living of Rochdale for his ser-vices in putting away the "offenders"—not the military he had sent in but the victims they had cut down. Peterloo inspired Hone and Cruikshank's most famous collaboration, the flagrantly disrespectful *Political House That Jack Built* (1819), a satire with the mnemonic force of nursery rhyme (fig. 4).[61]

In a sense, it was on St. Peter's Fields, like much else in the history of England, that the history of blasphemy as an organized method of political protest began. Richard Carlile stood shoulder to shoulder with Henry Hunt, the main speaker at the mass meeting, and paid for it with immediate confinement in jail, while "Orator" Hunt's attendance at Carlile's blas-phemy trial was later conspicuously noticed.[62] More, Carlile came to stand for freedom of the press and publication at a time when those freedoms mattered most, since government's outlawing of political meetings made the cheap press—like *Sherwin's Weekly Political Register,* which printed Car-lile's eye-witness account of the "Horrid Massacre at Manchester"—essen-tial in focusing radical feeling and creating working-class consciousness. Trying Carlile for blasphemy had "the double purpose of getting rid of me as evidence and of drawing the public attention from the Manchester affair" (*Republican,* 14 January 1820: 2). Shelley took the point, and this time his protest was printed in the *Examiner:* Peterloo's "troop" of "enraged master manufacturers," he wrote, "let loose with sharpened swords," were co-conspirators with those who could try Carlile for "some inexplicable crime, . . . one of the features of which, they inform us, is the denying that the massacring of children & the ravishing of women was done by the immedi-ate command of the Author & preserver of all things" (Shelley to Leigh Hunt, 3 November 1819, *Letters* 2: 136).

A journeyman tin-man (like Bunyan, his first biographer, Jacob Holy-

THE CLERICAL MAGISTRATE.

Figure 4. The Clerical Magistrate, pictured by Cruikshank after "Peterloo." From Hone's *Political House That Jack Built* (December 1819): "THIS IS A PRIEST, / made 'according to Law,' / Who . . . 'Gainst his spiritual Oath, / puts his Oath of the Bench. . . ." Carlile's first *Republican* editorial, dated from Dorchester Gaol, 30 December 1819, vows to record "in the PEOPLE'S BOOK" the misdeeds of "the Rev. Parson Hay" who chaired the Manchester Quarter Sessions (for a fee of four hundred pounds) and all his colleagues (xi–xii). Reprinted by permission of the New York Public Library from the Berg Collection, Astor, Lenox and Tilden foundation.

oake, liked to say [*Life and Character of Richard Carlile* 8]) and the son of a shoemaker, Carlile began his print career in vociferous and sometimes unwanted defense of the radical press. His immediate spur was Sidmouth's 1817 circular to magistrates and the suspension of habeas corpus; as he dryly recalled, they put "a damp among the newsvendors" (10). Carlile borrowed a pound from his employers, and set out to hawk the hundred *Black Dwarfs* it bought, in a handkerchief, for a profit of eighteen pence. Then he became legal publisher of Sherwin's *Register*.[63] His willingness to risk prison, Carlile knew, would grant Sherwin unusual indemnity in a system that prosecuted not the author of a work but the agent of its "publication," that is, its "communication" to other persons (Odgers, *Libel and Slander* 150). In law, a "publisher" could thus be a bookseller, shopman, street vendor, or "publisher" in the sense we understand today. This was and to some degree still is a division of responsibility that creates covert censorship: a publisher must be willing to risk prosecution for what another man or woman has written. Thus, complete freedom for writers from William Blake to D. H. Lawrence, who had *Lady Chatterley's Lover* printed in Italy, has meant becoming their own publishers. Hence the happy reverie of Virginia Woolf, coproprietor of the Hogarth Press, in 1925: "I am the only woman in England free to write what I like" (*Writer's Diary* 112).

It is thus misleading to say in one breath, as Leonard Levy does, both that Carlile "achieved more for the freedom of the press than any other person in the country's history" and that his capacity as a "theorist" was strictly limited (*Blasphemy* 352–55), particularly when that judgment is based on Carlile's clear-cut statement that "every free-minded literary man ought to have given me his support, for my long imprisonment was in fact a sort of penal representation for the whole" (qtd. 355). Carlile was not an eloquent man, though he "burned to see himself in print" through the 1810s (Holyoake, *Life and Character of Richard Carlile* 10) and went on to edit from prison, amongst other publications, "one of the premier working-class journals of the early nineteenth century" (Wiener 43), the twopenny *Republican* (1819–26).[64] But he understood exactly the theory of the system he opposed. His true métier was to offer his incarcerated body as a "vicarious sacrifice" in the cause of a free press and "forbidden books" (Holyoake, *Life and Character of Richard Carlile* 18–19).

Trouble first loomed in 1817 when Carlile republished Hone's parodies—much to Hone's chagrin, who had hoped suppression might avert his own prosecution. (By some reports, Hone threatened to sue for breach of copyright, an irony that will need elucidation.)[65] Carlile increased Hone's risk by strategic deletions, advertising the parodies as "Sold by those who are not afraid of Incurring the Displeasure of His Majesty's Ministers, their

Spies or Informers, or Public Plunderers of any denomination" (*Bullet Te Deum* [Carlile pub.], title page), an unpleasant insinuation of cowardice. He also put out a slew of derivative squibs, including his own *Order for the Administration of the Loaves and Fishes* and *A New Catechism for the Use of the Swinish Multitude. Necessary to be had in all Sties.*[66] He was quickly arrested—only to be released, without drama, after Hone's acquittals four months later. But that first anticlimactic spell in jail was decisive in pushing him towards blasphemy as his chosen method of political protest. His resolution was made "never to cease any publication so long as any prosecution or intimidation menaced it" (Holyoake, *Life and Character of Richard Carlile* 18). "[I]t is the slave who makes the tyrant," Carlile summed up (Foote, *Heroes and Martyrs* 154). "[W]hilst the present deficient representation exists," declared his opening address "TO THE PUBLIC" in the *Republican*, 27 December 1819, "the Editor humbly stands forward to fill the post of danger, ambitious of incurring, (if martyrs must be found) even *martyrdom*, in the cause of liberty" (1).[67] The aristocratic elite of the literati, like Byron, might sneer at "that fool Carlile and his trash" (*Letters* 4: 256). But even Byron recognized that the government of the time "would re-crucify Christ himself if he reappeared in his old humble accoutrements" (4: 256). And Carlile, not the aristocratic author of *Cain* (see below, 2.2), now made good his claim as pioneer of the freedoms by which the literature and press of England still live.

The struggle he undertook for publication of the *Age of Reason* needed all the "sturdy independence" by which "[e]very British bookseller has profited" (Foote, *Heroes and Martyrs* 148; Holyoake, *Sixty Years* 1: 190). If Carlile was a loud-mouthed "Anti-Christ" come to "change the condition of the whole of mankind," then "the Printing Press" was indeed his "forerunner" (*Republican*, 3 January 1823: 1–2). He *believed* in books with a devoutness that makes him an unlikely Victorian before there were Victorians, in spite of his disturbing connections to the criminal core of the London "ultra-radicals," some of whom exploited lax regulations on the licensing of "ministers" to found carnivalesque "counter-Christian" "blasphemy chapels" that were hotbeds for violent conspiracy (McCalmain 146).[68] In prison, he set an example of autodidacticism, and nourished a national network of "Zetetic" or "truth seeking" self-improvement societies.[69] His several trials for blasphemy are a crucial link in the chain that connects the revolutionary 1790s to the radical 1810s and thence—directly, through Holyoake—to the Victorian era.

Carlile took his step into history in 1819 "fully anticipat[ing]," reads his preface to the *Age of Reason*, the senseless and unmeaning charges of "impiety" and "blasphemy," that will be exhibited against him by the ignorant and the interested; by the bigot and the hypocrite. (qtd. in Wiener 37)

This first Carlile edition was priced at half a guinea. Even so, sales were brisk; once prosecution loomed, despite constant harassment, four thousand copies were sold within months. "[T]hey are afraid to prosecute," Keats wrote his family, "[T]he Trials would light a flame they could not extinguish. Do you not think this of great import?" (2: 194). By October the Vice Society had made Carlile Public Enemy Number One. He faced between eight and a dozen private indictments and ex officio informations. Two of these were tried, both for blasphemous libel and both before well-packed special juries. One trial concerned the *Age of Reason,* the other a blunt tract by Connecticut Deist Elihu Palmer, *The Principles of Nature,* which referred to Christ as "a murderer in principle" and to the Scriptures as "a vast variety of fact, fable, principle, wickedness, and error" (96).[70] "The eyes of the country," said Attorney-General Gifford, were "upon [the] proceedings" (*Report of the Mock Trials of Carlile* 13); "Never did any judicial proceeding of late years, excite more public interest" (*Observer,* 17 October 1819: 1). "To cry out against CARLILE, PAINE and 'blasphemy,' was the order of the day amongst all the enemies of freedom" (*Political Register,* 27 January 1820: 776). Newspapers testified to the fact in voluminous and biased reports, though many loyalist papers followed the line of the *New Times* (Hone's "Slop-Pail," beneficiary of regular government handouts) in printing all of the indictment against Carlile, two and a half full columns, but none of his defense.[71]

Disappointment was in store for all Carlile's supporters. His day in court was no saturnalia of confrontation. Carlile had the brash naiveté to think he might win, but he was no speaker. Hone buried their disagreements to write out some well-turned paragraphs for his use: they provided not only the most eloquent but also the most humble moments of the proceedings.[72] Carlile's own manuscript notes towards his speech in his own defense are a hopeless litter of worshipful anecdotes about Martin Luther, Galileo, and other fellow "martyrs" who "despised all danger" for their opinions, in the dissenting tradition of protest in which, to dissenters' horror, he claimed a place (RC 544, in CC). ("The blood of the martyrs," as a blasphemous associate put it, "is the seed of every church" [*Republican,* 18 June 1824: 785].)[73] From such sources he cobbled together a rambling thirty-hour harangue, "an extraordinary example of the observation of a Lord Chief Justice," sneered the *Sunday Monitor,* " 'That he who pleads his own cause, has a fool for his client' "(undated cutting, in CC).[74] On the second day the "immense multitude" that the *Morning Chronicle* reported had "cheered him as he passed along" the streets, under the eyes of three hundred constables, happily vacated the courtroom seats they had fought over twenty-four hours before (13 October 1819: 2–3).

Attorney-General Sir Robert Gifford, for the government, and John Gurney, prosecuting Palmer's *Principles* for the Vice Society, made mincemeat of these understandably "very hoarse" productions (*Morning Herald*, 16 October 1819: 3). Gifford "proceeds with a smile apparently contemptuous," Carlile scribbled furiously on the reverse of a sheaf of notes, as he listened to the ripostes (RC 554, in CC). The court refused Carlile's contention that the Trinity Act of 1813, which confirmed Unitarians in their newly won respectability, opened the door to Deism and undermined the law against blasphemy. Not for the defendant, on the day, the freedom enjoyed by Wooler in an exuberant parodic *Dialogue on the Approaching Trial of Mr. Carlile* to bring into court Mr. Unitarian, Mr. Freethinking Christian, and "Mordecai, an honest Jew," to testify to faithful differences of "honest doubt" (the term is claimed and repeated with pride [6, 15]). "His ludship" (the misspelling puns on the name of the imaginary folk "king" of machine breakers) shrugged aside Carlile's attempts to call the archbishop of Canterbury, the chief rabbi, and the astronomer royal, all of whom he had subpoenaed to testify to allowed differences of religious belief, or to implicate the attorney-general and Chief Justice Abbott in unorthodoxy.[75] He was reduced to providing witnesses to his moral character, who proved he had always paid his rent on time, in an attempt to demonstrate that an unbeliever could be a responsible citizen. The "truth" of religion was not at issue, and strictly enforcing the law on the subject promised to stop the mouth of the popular press.

On 16 October 1819 Carlile was sentenced to three years in prison— two for Paine, one for Palmer—and fines totaling fifteen hundred pounds. Moreover, he was condemned to find sureties of twelve hundred pounds for his future good behavior, something no prisoner for blasphemy had ever been asked to do, save in an isolated case of 1703. This gave a total of twenty-seven hundred pounds. All idea of payment was doubly scotched when the authorities twice illegally raided his shop, ostensibly to secure payment of the fines. Thousands of pounds' worth of goods simply disappeared, including Carlile's prized "Figure of Paine with Pedestal cost £20 worth £50," and the sofa-bedstead on which he napped, value 3 pounds (*Account of Goods Seized,* in CC). The idea, of course, was to put him away indefinitely. "It is a mockery to say that I may, if I please, purchase my liberty," as Carlile said on another occasion (qtd. in Holyoake, *Life and Character of Richard Carlile* 15). "Honest doubt" had been robbed.

But if Carlile's courtroom performance backfired, it was enormously effective towards one simple end: to make so great a noise about the *Age of Reason* that no one in the kingdom could ignore it. At his first trial Carlile took advantage of legal process to read the entire book aloud to the jury, as the main part of his speech in his own defense, thus ensuring its re-publication under protection of legal "privilege" in the "verbatim report" of the trial his wife could then legally publish. More copies of this new "reprint" were snapped up in a month—at twopence each—than he had sold in a year, and more prosecutions guaranteed; for, as lawyer Gurney remarked, "if this were to be endured, prosecution would sanction the publication instead of suppressing it" (cutting, 6 November 1819, in CC). This was exactly Carlile's aim: money was a secondary motive, and the prosecution's assertion that he "traffick[ed] in blasphemy for base lucre," inspired by "Hone's success," was largely an empty class sneer (*Morning Herald*, 17 November 1819: 2). Keats's enthusiasm was warranted after all: "I am convinced that apparently small causes make great alterations. . . . This makes the business about Carlisle [sic] the Bookseller of great moment in my mind" (*Letters* 1: 194).

It was not in the courtroom but in and through the prison cell that Carlile assumed a kind of greatness. He eventually served nine and a half years: six years for blasphemy (three of them in lieu of fines) and three years for related offenses. But his capacity to endure imprisonment was not the whole story. What also mattered was his ability to inspire an army of working-class volunteers to do the same. From his cell in Dorchester Gaol he orchestrated a print war of attrition, vowing to provide, as Gurney feared, "a weekly case for prosecution until all harassment ceased" (qtd. in Wiener 87).[76]

The women stepped forward first. Carlile's wife Jane and sister Mary Anne followed him into the shop, the dock, and the prison in 1821, even into the same cell, where Jane gave birth to a baby.[77] Spurred by their self-sacrifice, 150 obscure young men and women joined battle under Carlile's banner, hawking the *Age* in the streets of London, Oxford, Manchester, Edinburgh, and Nottingham and manning Carlile's Fleet Street shop.[78] There was much to brave. Volunteering in the shop technically made them criminal "publishers" of what they sold. Soon government was supported in its promise to prosecute every one of them by the newly formed Constitutional Association, which rapidly collected six thousand pounds towards defraying the cost.[79] Members of this group were known for the place the association met as the "Bridge-Street Gang." In Hone and Cruikshank's famous squib, *A Slap at Slop* (1821), they appear as well-heeled thugs smashing a printing press over the legend "An Interior View of the Den . . . with the Gang at Work." Carlile's volunteers faced long sentences, in which (as one was told), "if hard labor was not expressed[,] . . . it was implied" (qtd. in Linton, *Watson* 13). There was a grave principle at stake: "If a precedent be now set for prosecuting every intermediate agent between the original publisher and the public," the *Morning Chronicle* worried, "it will be in the power of the crown, whenever it pleases, to destroy the sale of any journal whatever" (undated cutting, in CC).

The volunteers rose to the challenge. Carlile was invested as the "GEN-ERAL who will stand by us," said one, "and let us enlist under his banners; and batter down tyranny" (John Jones, *Republican*, 1 February 1822: 140). He worked closely with them from prison, providing legal advice, writing notes towards their defenses, and providing each a weekly "gaol allowance" of up to five shillings—the fruit of a subscription machine to counter the Gang's that raised up to five hundred pounds a year in sixpences and half crowns at the height of the battle.[80] It was palliative subsistence, not an inducement. By their willingness to face incarceration for no personal gain, the "Little Honorable House of Blasphemers" risked and won far more than any twentieth-century publisher—Penguin testing the law with *Lady Chatterley*, for example, in 1960, or Viking gingerly weighing the risks of releasing the paperback of the *Satanic Verses*. Neither "ignorance" nor "frantic poverty," declared one in court, "drove" them to volunteer, "yet no title in the gift of the proud sovereign of these realms is more eagerly sought, than a situation of so honorable a nature" (William Haley, *Republican* 23 July 1824: 70). "I commence my defense," another began his defense, "with a declaration, that . . . I am morally and solemnly impressed with the importance of what I have done and am doing in this case" (William Carpenter, 18 July 1824: 772).[81]

In all, Carlile's volunteers served between them two centuries in jail, irrevocably turning one man's personal struggle into a public political battle and confirming the protest method of martyrdom that was Carlile's other great legacy to the nineteenth and twentieth centuries. Holyoake's "moral" or "passive resistance" ("Richard Carlile," 1012; *History of the Last Trial* 69),[82] Foote's refusal to do his hard labor, the Chartists' jailhouse refusals, the suffragettes' hunger strikes, the self-starvations and blanket rebellions of I.R.A. terrorists and internees: all alike look back to Richard Carlile. Through a humiliation that was also a sanctification, remaking the prison cell as "an admirable school for study and reflection" (qtd. in Wiener 65), tapping into government's own "technology of power" (Foucault, *Discipline* 23), he actually accomplished the subversive transformation of punishment. Law in 1819, the common law of "custom" and "precedent," was seen through Carlile's efforts, for all those who would see, openly to serve the interests of the ruling class: the blasphemous popular lawlessness that he personified and inspired was its inevitable, no less political, and frighteningly disciplined inverse.[83] There was "a rebellious principle in the human heart," he and the "army" declared, that multiplied "like Cadmus' teeth" in direct proportion as it seemed buried down (J. Jones 9). Against government's bid to "establish a general system of despotism over the human mind" (12), they asserted the right of every person freely to use "that divine ray of light transmitted from his Creator," Reason, the guide of revolution (7).

Not all the volunteers' names survive. The first was William Campion. Two dozen are memorialized by surviving trial transcripts, like that of Carlile's associate Thomas Davison, a struggling writer and Smithfield bookseller, editor of the ephemeral hard-line *Medusa: Or Penny Politician*. The trials of John Clark, William Carpenter, and others were recorded in the *Republican,* Clark's and Carpenter's in the summer of 1824. Volunteers' names are reverently listed by Jacob Holyoake in his *Life and Character of Richard Carlile* (13) and by the young G. W. Foote in *Heroes and Martyrs of Freethought* (150). One volunteer figured in court records as "A Man with Name Unknown." (His name was Humphrey Boyle, and "he conducted his defense with astonishing skill and articulateness" [Levy, *Blasphemy* 388].) Many were printers, many shoemakers. One, Benbow, was a shoemaker turned bookseller. Others were carters, flax dressers, and warehousemen. A solitary "itinerant comedian" brought his love of Shakespeare to the cause.

All were swiftly dispatched by justice. Some lasted only a day before arrest; everyone who served in Carlile's shop in May 1824 was seized. Yet "[l]et them apprehend twenty men weekly," one of them, William Haley, declared in court, "and they will be as far from their object as ever" (*Republican,* 23 July 1824: 69). "I am a hundred times more formidable than in 1819," Carlile had reason to boast in 1824 (qtd. in Levy, *Blasphemy* 393). "From December, 1818, to December, 1822, I . . . sent into circulation near 20,000 copies" of the *Age of Reason.* "Let corruption rub that out if she can, as Mr. Cobbett said [of] his 40,000 *[Political] Registers*" (qtd. in Holyoake, *Life and Character of Richard Carlile* 19). "Whatever may be the success of *wholesale* persecutions," volunteer Campion rubbed in the point with a vulgar commercial metaphor, "they have never as yet succeeded in *retail*" (*Republican,* 18 June 1824: 785). Jamming the courts, packing the prisons, inflaming public opinion, Carlile and the volunteers literally wore out the government. Between them they secured the *Age of Reason* immunity from further prosecution. In 1825 the attorney-general struck his standard and discontinued prosecution. There were no further arrests, though existing sentences were served to the day (Holyoake, "Richard Carlile,"

1011).[84] By resorting to the law of blasphemy for the purposes of political and class oppression, the government had won a Pyrrhic victory.

Ingenuity was one prerequisite of the battle. Spies posing as customers were baffled in their survey of the Fleet Street shop by a clockwork apparatus that might have gladdened the heart of Charlie Chaplin in *Modern Times*.[85] Customers turned a dial to the name of the "forbidden book" desired, and "Carlile's invisible shopman" (Holyoake, *Life and Character of Richard Carlile* 19), the blasphemy vending machine, dispensed the goods without incriminating touch of human hands through a series of chutes, flaps, and pulleys. Speaking tubes were also tried. Publicity, naturally, was the other prerequisite, and defiance and the image of the persecuted individual the fuels for generating it. "THE SHOP IN FLEET STREET WILL NOT BE CLOSED AS A MATTER OF COURSE," Carlile announced (qtd. in E. Thompson 725). Carlile publications included facsimiles of his indictment at four pence each, as well as medallions and engraved portraits of Paine to suit all purses: everything was grist to the mill.

As the tidal wave of prosecutions gathered speed, trial transcripts poured from Carlile's press: they had something of the appeal and some of the phenomenal selling power of broadside records of condemned criminals' last dying words. Parliament was forced into debates when David Ricardo, the liberal economist; Joseph Hume (leader of the radical faction); patrician radical Sir Francis Burdett; and even Henry Brougham all presented petitions for the release of the volunteers.[86] Francis Place, later architect of middle-class rapprochement with working men, who was losing faith in open agitation, worked grudgingly behind the scenes. Seventeen-year-old John Stuart Mill protested the volunteers' imprisonment in three letters to the *Morning Chronicle* (January–February 1823), following them in July 1824 with an excoriating anatomy of "Religious Persecution" in the *Westminster Review* that ironically estimated "that at least one hundred thousand persons have . . . been led to the perusal of [the *Age of Reason*] under circumstances highly favorable to its making an impression on their minds" as a result of the prosecutions (*Mill on Blasphemy* 16).[87]

Carlile was not an intellectual originator. But he resembled his hero in a number of important ways. First, like Paine, Carlile viewed religious protest as political protest and "crime" as legitimate political action. That identification matters more, as Iain McCalmain writes, because Carlile's was "the only overt political radical movement to function through the first half of the decade" 1820–30 (185), so that blasphemy casts a deep shadow over what are widely accepted to have been the "formative years" of working-class British history (E. Thompson 9). It is impossible to say which came first, chickens or eggs. Government's commandeering of the laws

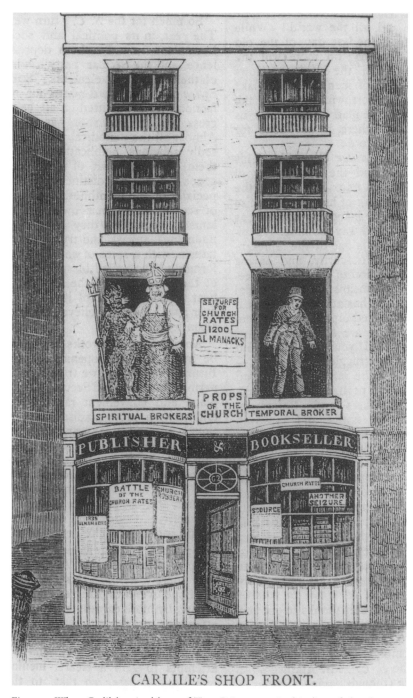

Figure 5. When Carlile's prized bust of Tom Paine was seized in lieu of church rates in 1831, he responded by placing effigies of "temporal" and "spiritual" brokers in his upper shop windows. The bishop was later placed arm-in-arm with a devil, as here. From the *Secular Chronicle*. Courtesy of the Bishopsgate Institute Library, National Secular Society Collection.

against blasphemy was prompted by the failure of prosecutions for sedition,[88] but it was also a response in kind to gestures like that of Carlile's
associate Henry "Orator" Hunt who, in the interval between Peterloo and
his arrest for his role in it, staged a "triumphal" entry into London with
two hundred thousand to witness, not in any spirit of offensive parody but
in invocation of the leveling Christ, still a powerful folk figure.[89]

Secondly, Carlile could speak for Paine because he shared his commitment to the plainest of plain speech, surpassing even Cobbett's. *The Age
of Reason* was its apogee. Those it outraged labeled the author a brute who
was "ignorant even of grammar" (Foner 16): Paine's enemies attacked him
first and foremost through his language. This was Carlile's fate too, and it
had consequences for nineteenth-century law and culture.

For Nicolas Walter of the present-day Rationalist Press Association, the
survival of the *Age of Reason* through thirty years of persecution from 1797
meant that "from the 1820s onwards the crime of blasphemy no longer
covered the mere denial of Christian doctrine but had to contain some
element of genuinely abusive or outrageous language" (*Blasphemy: Ancient
and Modern* 38). Not exactly so. As the subsequent history of blasphemy
was abundantly to demonstrate, the endurance of Carlile and the volunteers
had won the common man some limited right to privileged and volatile
information, but the plain language that was his natural idiom had become
the site of contestation and criminality. Walter slurs over the crucial fact
that at these trials plain English was reconfigured as itself "abusive" and
"outrageous." The *Age of Reason* struggle almost tolled the hour when the
words "plain," "coarse," "common," and "vulgar" took on pejorative
meaning.

Shelley, insisting in another letter to Leigh Hunt on the true and "most
extensive sense of the word 'vulgar' "(15 August 1819, *Letters* 2: 108) was
swimming against the class current of linguistic evolution. Cobbett understood what really was afoot. The publicity of Carlile's trial, coming hard
on the heels of Peterloo, triggered passage in December 1819 of one of the
notorious Six Acts of Tory repression. A warning extension of measures
passed in 1795 and 1817, the 1819 act "for the more effectual Prevention and
Punishment of blasphemous and seditious libels" was introduced, debated,
and signed into law in under a month.[90] What struck Cobbett most about
it was not even its extraordinary instating of "banishment" to New South
Wales as punishment for a second offense but the terms in which the act
was debated. His eloquent "Letter to the Bishop of Landaff" recurs again
and again to that prelate's declaration, in the House of Lords, that when
plainspoken writings like the *Age of Reason* "were placed in the hands of
the vulgar, there was little chance of persuading them of its fallacy *by argu-*

ments they were not equal to comprehend" (*Political Register,* 27 January 1820: 722). "The vulgar," Cobbett bristled, chewing over the loaded new term, "meaning by the word . . . *ignorant*" (734; see also 737–38, 761). Plain language, the sort he also wrote, Cobbett recognized, had become bad language.[91]

This was not a matter of mere snobbery. Paine's *Age of Reason* was legible proof that the plain voice of the vulgar classes could express complex and powerful ideas, which those classes might therefore appropriate and possess themselves of; Carlile was Paine's ideal insurgent reader, the government's nightmare. The book was democracy in your mouth, and its power to offend restores to history and criticism not only a sense of the revolutionary potential of such contemporary texts as *Lyrical Ballads* and their preface of 1800 but an awareness, no less acute, of the class-conscious sensitivity with which gentlemen writers like Wordsworth contained and defused the offense. "The *real* language of men," he writes in the preface, to become a "plainer and more emphatic" poetical idiom, is first "purified" by a mind that has "thought long and deeply," and then safely directed to other men of "an *accurate* taste," which, "as Sir Joshua Reynolds has observed," is "an acquired talent" (Wordsworth and Coleridge 241, 245, 246, 271).

We should pause over the words "insurgent" and "revolutionary." Another of Paine's opponents charged him with "bring[ing] about a revolution in language" (qtd. in O. Smith 45). It was pointless to contend, as the defense had done at the 1797 prosecution of Williams the bookseller for the *Age of Reason,* "that the book is a genuine argument against the Christian religion, . . . however violent . . . in some of its language" (J. Stephen, *History* 2: 471–72). The same charges were made against Carlile. "A half-employ'd Mechanic is too violent" was even Cobbett's judgment (qtd. in Holyoake, *Life and Character of Richard Carlile* 10). Carlile's first efforts as a writer were crude pastiches stuffed with slogans. Even after he developed a workmanlike style, evident in his calmly plain, utilitarian *Life of Paine,* the verdict stuck. His courtroom performance drew down editorial encomiums on that "gentleness" (in itself a loaded term) that must answer linguistic "violence" (*Sunday Monitor,* 16 October 1819: 2). As in the 1790s, so in 1819, fear of insurrection inflated the charges of coarse "grossness" and vulgar "brutality" to produce a belief in the potential and even actual revolutionary "violence" of plain speech. The charge is of the essence to the Paine-Carlile tradition.

It had more than a flavor of vindictive nastiness. Hyperbole and bluntness are the natural outlets of powerless men, "pitted against an armed establishment, with little to do but talk," as E. P. Thompson remarks (677). The spy Castle, champion whistle-blower on conspiracy, parodied the radical style to perfection in his revolutionary toast to the Cato Street conspirators: "May the last of the Kings be strangled with the guts of the last Priest" (qtd. 634).

Carlile himself never overtly renounced the use of force, "although he never did see reason to sanction any particular act," and he abhorred plotting and secrecy (Foote, *Heroes and Martyrs* 153–54). But the whole thrust of the *Age of Reason* campaign was towards what the Chartists later called "moral force." The volunteers chose and took "words and arguments" as alternatives to "fire & sword." It was by words alone, volunteer John Jones declared, that they hoped to "batter down" tyranny: "The pen should be [our] only weapon" (*Republican,* 1 February 1822: 140). The government of 1819, however, took their plain words as a substitute and a promise of physical action. Metaphor and rhetoric ("batter down," "fire and sword") were read as factual statement and legal contract. England had no test or requirement of "overt acts" in establishing criminality (as the state of Virginia enjoyed, for example, by an early statute). Government had neither the legal grounds nor the political will to believe a free press the "safety valve" that Secularists liked to declare it sixty years later, which might "settle . . . every public question without appeal to senseless violence" (Foote, *Heroes and Martyrs* 145). Anxiety and policy pushed out of mind the technical legal meaning of linguistic "violence"—merely "strong words"—to produce a disturbing sense of threat to the established hierarchy. A horror cliché was born.

It was fostered by Carlile's next campaign, an attempt to secure blasphemous free speech or "public oral discussion." On 7 February 1828, a defrocked priest called Robert Taylor was imprisoned for blasphemous "sermons" at a "chapel" in Cannon Street (Cutner, *Robert Taylor* 18). (He had been "perverted" from Christianity by reading the *Age of Reason* [8].) Carlile's response was "immediately" to "convert a large room in his house," 62 Fleet Street, "into a Sunday School of Free Discussion" on "all useful political subjects on the Sabbath Day." "This had not been done before by any one anywhere," Holyoake emphasized (qtd. in Foote, *Heroes and Martyrs* 152). After Taylor's release, in 1830, he persuaded Carlile to take over the ramshackle Rotunda Theater on the south bank of the Thames, which had a capacity of several thousand. Meetings here "became so frequent and so large that the Government took alarm, and the prophecy of the day was, that the Rotunda would cause a Revolution in England" (Holyoake, qtd 152). Not surprisingly, Taylor—who had a taste for girls, finger rings, and inflated rhetoric, and delivered his lectures in full canonicals—was rearrested in 1831, while Carlile was put away for seditious libel in 1830 for publishing his support of farm workers caught up in the "Captain Swing" Riots of that year.[92] The Rotunda survived as an institution of London radical life into the 1840s: its strange history exceeds and overlaps the limits of this study.

However, on 9 July 1831, the first issue of an extraordinary new journal, *The Poor Man's Guardian,* carried a report of Taylor's case that disapproved equally of his flamboyance and of his "SLOW MURDER" by harsh conditions and two years' worth of solitary confinement "for the crime of speaking [his] mind" (9 July 1831: 5). For a penny a week, the *Guardian* promised to spread the "violent" potential of Paine and Carlile's plain speech anew through the "violent" segments of society. Government had seen the *Age of Reason* sold for twopence; it wanted no more truck with cheap publication. England's authorities now turned their attention to a frontal assault on the printing press that Carlile had declared his blasphemous "fore-runner," and that Hone had claimed as the people's champion.

CHAPTER TWO

TRIALS OF THE 1840s

"The history of the mass reading audience," Richard Altick discovered, "is the history of English democracy seen from a new angle" (3). The history of blasphemy sharpens that angle. The men who supplied the new audience and set up the "pauper press" against which government railed were, to a striking degree, determined participants in the tradition of blasphemy "martyrdom": what Altick calls the "worst sort" of illegal "printed demagoguery" (132) proves also to have been a valuable inheritance of his English Common Reader. Tracing the curve of unrest, the "Hungry Forties," decade of Chartism, Corn Law Riots, mass unemployment, revolution in Europe, and famine in Ireland, witnessed a second eruption in blasphemy prosecutions. The numbers do not compare to the Carlile years. But again the seven or eight major cases were forced on by committed teams of activists and volunteers.

1. "KNOWLEDGE IS POWER," OR, THE CHEAP PRESS AS BLASPHEMY

The new storm broke first over the head of the wily printer-publisher of the newly proscribed newspaper the *Poor Man's Guardian,* Henry Hetherington. He conducted it from 1830 to 1835, "d[oing] for the . . . [periodical] press," wrote Jacob Holyoake, "what Carlile did for Freethought works" (*Sixty Years* 1: 102). In 1840, he stood trial for blasphemy, and what was latent in the *Guardian* leapt into forward view. Atheist and blasphemer, a "Christ of Labor" (Holyoake, *Life and Character of Henry Hetherington* 7), Hetherington was the nineteenth century's greatest champion of *cheap* as

well as *free* publication, and the two facts together created blasphemy as
the rest of the century viewed it.

Hetherington's struggle had roots in the decade of Hone and Carlile.
The Tory administrations of 1815–19 had loaded the dice against all forms
of popular print. Newspapers were the first primary target, and therefore
later became Henry Hetherington's. The only press recognized as legitimate
was that which supplied "intelligence" to the commercial middle classes
who had created it. To ensure that exclusivity, in 1815 the tax or "stamp"
on newspapers had been raised to the prohibitive sum of four pence: the
"Tax on Knowledge," a society for repeal dubbed it. To evade it, in 1816
William Cobbett put out his *Political Register* as a single unfolded sheet.
His reward was sales of forty thousand in a country where circulation of
established newspapers, even the *Times* or the *Morning Chronicle,* had rarely
moved above three thousand copies.

The Ministry's response to this unsettling new phenomenon was embedded in two of the six acts of 1819. Besides deprecating the "vulgar" intellect
during passage of the Blasphemous and Seditious Libels Act, the bishop of
Landaff had also asked whether there were not "strong reasons" for making
"blasphemous libel" (as distinct from "blasphemy") "something like a new
offence" (*Political Register,* 27 January 1820: 722). The act targeted the press
per se as much as "blasphemy" and "sedition"—the free and cheap press,
that is, *viewed as* blasphemy and sedition. It sped through the unreformed
House of Commons with the unanimous vote of all members, amongst
them fifteen or sixteen "active and talkative" non-Christian "[h]ypocrites"
(Francis Place, qtd. in Wickwar 153). Never separately invoked in a trial
for blasphemy, there was "no more important dead-letter upon the Statute-
book in modern times" (Wickwar 154). Besides its other effects, it gave
birth to the invidious "Securities" system, requiring deposits against the
appearance of criminal matter in any issue of any suspect publication: three
hundred pounds in London and two hundred pounds in the provinces.

Worse, a second act in 1819 concerning Newspaper Stamp Duties
stopped the loophole Cobbett had slipped through. Henceforth a publication had either to conform to the "requirements" of a "pamphlet" or the
"requirements" of a "newspaper." If a newspaper, it must carry a fourpenny
stamp and retail at seven pence, like the *Times.* If a pamphlet, priced less
than sixpence, it should appear at monthly and not daily or weekly intervals.
Hybridity was outlawed. The measure "deliberately strangled the working
class press" and its twopenny trash; those few papers that survived, like
Cobbett's *Register* and Carlile's *Republican,* "turned pamphlet and doubled
their price" (Hollis, introduction to *Poor Man's Guardian* 1: xiii). "Small
reading societies, consisting of three or four families," Carlile urged, were

"now more essential than ever," since "our enemies" were "straining every-where to stop the reading going on now. . . . for they well know that 'Knowledge is Power' " (*Republican*, 30 December 1819: xvi).

For the thirst for print could not be so easily turned off. Already, estab-lished newspapers passed through the hands of as many as thirty poorer readers before the sturdy rag paper gave out; coffee shops and public houses regularly took in journals and papers for less wealthy patrons; workmen in quieter trades (tailors especially, according to Place) often paid a work-mate to read aloud by doing his quota as compensation (Webb 34); and the extension of reading hours brought about by the introduction of gas lighting soon intensified the demand. Even by such expedients, however, less than one percent of the adult population was supplied with "intelli-gence."

It was this situation, and Carlile's Baconian slogan, that Henry Hether-ington inherited in October 1830.[1] His response was simple: the law was unjust; he would defy it. The penny weekly *Poor Man's Guardian* was the most famous of several hundred "unstamped" papers that sprang into being shortly after the Second French Revolution of July, as agitation for the new Whig government's promised parliamentary reforms hotted up;[2] they quickly became "part of the very structure of London working-class radical-ism" (Hollis, introduction to *Poor Man's Guardian* 1: xiv). The *Guardian* flaunted its illegal status. A cheeky motif on the front page imitated the missing government stamp: a printing press, clearly inscribed with the legend "Liberty of the Press," is theatrically discovered between parted curtains, while at top and bottom, creating a medallion effect, run the words "KNOWLEDGE is POWER." Hetherington had style: his paper was carried in broad daylight under constables' noses, snugly packed in coffins, while the "Guardian" himself slipped past dressed as a Quaker; on one occasion he absconded through a window and over the rooftops, like a robber-hero of melodrama.[3] Two prison terms (six months in 1831, another half-year in 1832) disrupted business but hardly touched his deter-mination.

The fourth number of the *Guardian* ran the back page advertisement that truly launched the "War of the Unstamped":

WANTED

Some hundreds of POOR MEN out of employ *who have* NOTHING TO RISK, some of those *unfortunate wretches* to whom DISTRESS has made PRISON a desirable HOME.

An HONEST and moral way of finding *head* and *gaol shelter . . .* now presents itself to such *patriotic* ENGLISHMEN as will . . . sell to the poor and ignorant

THE POOR MAN'S GUARDIAN
A Weekly "Newspaper" for the People
Published contrary to "Law" to try the Power of "Might" against "Right."
N.B. A *Subscription* is opened for the *relief, support,* and *reward* of all such persons as may become VICTIMS of the *Whig Tyrants.* (30 July 1831: 32)

Carlile had created the method of protest by which to grind down a government: Hetherington added to it the capitalistic common sense that said if his vendors gained a littleby the enterprise, he might bank on finding more than 150 volunteers. (The *Big Issue,* a weekly paper put out by Britain's homeless of the 1990s, inherits the tactic.) Well upwards of five hundred men, women, and children stood up to sell the *Guardian,* at an average cost of three months in prison apiece for hawking an illegal paper (Barker 16, E. Thompson 729). Among them, they got to know "the inside of every gaol in the kingdom" (Holyoake, *Sixty Years* I: 102). The "War of the Unstamped" forced the stripping back of the hated duty to a penny in 1836.[4]

However, Hetherington did not exactly win the war when he obtained from a jury (in 1834) the verdict that the eight-page, sub-tabloid-sized *Guardian* was not strictly a newspaper, and was therefore exempt from the stamp. Late-century Secularists and free pressmen, like his biographer, Ambrose Barker, liked to see Hetherington as a straightforward hero by whose power "Right" triumphed over "Might." Patrica Hollis more accurately sees his "victory" as part of a government plot to erode "the moral basis of Hetherington's crusade . . . and with it the sales appeal of the *Guardian*" (introduction to *Poor Man's Guardian* I: xxiii): it ceased publication within a year of the verdict. But Hetherington's crusade "to give the people cheap knowledge" (xxiii) was not over. It shortly and overtly took on the blasphemous character that always glimmered under the surface, whispering through the "martyr" tone of the *Guardian's* addresses.[5]

All along, the *Guardian* had set out not only "to excite hatred and contempt of the Government and Constitution of the tyranny of this country," as Hetherington put it in his opening address, but "to vilify the ABUSES of Religion" (9 July 1831: 1). The words were a direct quotation from the preamble to the Newspaper Stamp Act, which the address liberally and sarcastically quoted.[6] The *Guardian* indeed did (as Hollis puts it) "graft new socialist and co-operative theory on to the traditional political radicalism" of Paine, Cobbett, Hunt, and Carlile, with its loathing of "Old Corruption" (introduction xxix). It was a resolutely "political" paper. But it also, and no less politically, concerned itself with the church, the clergy, anti-Semitism, and—especially—"true religion" and religious "toleration"; only the vote and constitutional reform merited more attention in its pages.

The first number's hard-hitting report of Taylor's prosecution was not an aberration. The potential commission of blasphemy was not only a motive force in the launching of the outspoken, unstamped *Poor Man's Guardian.* Hetherington and his comrades made in a positive fashion exactly the same connection that government made negatively: the cheap press and "free speech" *were* "blasphemy."

What is more, a large number of the campaigners in the War of the Unstamped, including many of the major figures, were veterans of the *Age of Reason* campaign, convicted blasphemers who retained and in some cases later resumed their blasphemous identities. The fact is easily submerged in histories of the press that lay emphasis elsewhere, divorcing "civil" from "religious" liberty in a way the nineteenth century did not, even when (like Hollis's admirable study, *The Pauper Press*) they try to prevent the wholesale "incorporat[ion]" of the unstamped "into the intellectual lineage of Chartism" (Hollis, introduction to *Poor Man's Guardian* 1: viii). In fact, Chartism itself partly grew out of the Society for the Promoting of a Cheap and Honest Press, founded in 1836 to pay off Hetherington's fines for the *Guardian;* and after the collapse of 1848, remnants of the people's Charter Union turned into the Association for the Repeal of the Taxes on Knowledge: the greatest struggle for a political "voice" in the nineteenth century folded back naturally into the struggle spearheaded by the forgotten martyrs to blasphemy.[7] We tend to remember that Kingsley modeled the eponymous radical hero of *Alton Locke* (1850) on shoemaker Thomas Cooper, the "Chartist poet" and jailhouse autodidact extraordinaire, while suppressing the fact that Cooper was an outspoken atheist and (like Chartist leader William Lovett) a close friend of blasphemers Henry Hetherington and Jacob Holyoake.[8]

"Anti-Christ" Carlile himself has a claim to have cofounded the unstamped press with his *Prompter,* begun in November 1830, for which he was imprisoned the following year. So too does William Carpenter, who had paid dearly with an extraordinary three years in prison for his eloquent defense of free publication and Paine in 1824. He served six months for his unstamped *Slap at the Church* in 1831: a significant number of unstamped papers were directed at the unreformed Church of England.[9] James Watson, a former warehouseman who went on to become the leading Freethought publisher of midcentury, served time both for the *Age of Reason* and for the *Poor Man's Guardian.*

Others reversed the order of experience, moving from the War of the Unstamped to later blasphemous martyrdom. No more than in the case of the *Age of Reason* veterans can their identities as blasphemers be disentangled from their identities as political free press campaigners. Hetherington ranks first among them. But there was also John Cleave, an ingenious strategist who made a third in the "trio of newsvendors" (remembered Holyoake) "whose names were known in every town and village in the three kingdoms—'Hetherington, Watson, and Cleave' " (*Sixty Years* 1: 102).[10] Their task, and the task of all the five hundred–plus vendors of the *Poor Man's Guardian* was completed by "Iconoclast" Bradlaugh in the 1860s. His refusal to provide securities totaling over three million pounds against the appearance of blasphemy or sedition in every copy of every issue of the *National Reformer* made him liable for fines in excess of half a million. Fighting the case technicality by technicality through the courts, he won repeal of the Newspaper Stamp Act in 1869. Holyoake had the honor of being the last person indicted under it: "The story of his requesting the Chancellor . . . to accept payment in weekly installments," the *Biograph and Review* recalled in October 1880, "as he had not the amount by him, is well known (304).[11] Thus blasphemers finished the struggle for press freedom that blasphemers began in 1819.

Back in 1840, its reforming impulse in church and state long exhausted, government had not finished with Henry Hetherington. After Carlile's insurrections and the reform crisis of 1831–32, the Home Office had left the task of quashing the pauper press to the Treasury's stamp collectors; now it returned to the fray. Revenge is a powerful motive, and what Hetherington represented looked powerfully frightening as pressure for the popular vote denied by the Great Reform Act of 1832 began dangerously to mount up again.[12] "Men who did not know him have called him *violent*," Holyoake recalled after Hetherington's death in 1849 (A. Barker 15, my emphasis). It was the old charge of linguistic insurrection class-coded by government during the Carlile years. In February 1840 Henry Hetherington was indicted for blasphemy.

His ostensible crime was the serial "publication" of C. J. Haslam's one-penny *Letters to the Clergy of All Denominations,* typical Deist fare in the plainspoken Paine tradition. Hetherington had no desire to serve a third stretch in jail: he was aging; his bones were tired. Besides, he had merely sold the *Letters,* and Cleave, who had been convicted for doing the same, had had his sentence remitted; while Abel Heywood, the actual publisher, had escaped scot-free.[13] But, from government's point of view, conceding defeat after defeat did not yet mean surrendering entirely to the enemy of cheap publication. Thus, similarly, in 1842 Strauss's landmark *Life of Jesus* was threatened with prosecution when it was issued in England in cheap numbers; but it was published without major incident (though it was refused advertising space in the *Times* [*God v. Paterson* 92]) in Chapman's expensive edition of 1846, in George Eliot's translation (Chadwick, *Church* 1: 487n).

At the time Henry Hetherington openly assumed his identity as blasphemer, books were prohibitively expensive, even more so than in the late eighteenth century, when government had granted monopolistic privileges to publishers "with the intent of *diminishing* the circulation of books" (Charles Knight, preface to *Penny Magazine,* 18 December 1832: iv). "[R]emarkably few . . . were even published": an average of only 580 titles a year between 1802 and 1827, and "[o]ld second-hand copies were the only cheap copies available" (O. Smith 155). There were almost no secondhand copies of recent works. Many working-class readers would never see any other book than the Bible or perhaps the *Pilgrim's Progress,* let alone read one. Hence the attraction of Hone's serial innovations and the two-penny pamphlet. But merely to publish at low cost, as Chief Justice Ellenborough had authoritatively declared in 1817, was automatically to be guilty of "gross" purposes (W. Hone, *Three Trials* 76); his Lordship had steamrollered over Hone's reply that a price of two pence was "commensurate with [the] size" of his parodic publications (85).

"The true crime," Henry Hetherington challenged Attorney-General Campbell, prosecuting, when he was brought to court on 8 December 1840, was "that Haslam's *Letters* are sold at a penny" (*Trial of Henry Hetherington* 16). As in the *Poor Man's Guardian,* so too through penny pamphlets like Haslam's *Letters* did Hetherington consciously put knowledge-power, Foucault's *pouvoir-savoir* by its English name, into the hands of the "great unwashed." And when knowledge becomes "common knowledge" it becomes dangerous knowledge. "The Defendant accused him," the attorney-general replied, "of not objecting so much to the matter of the publication, as to the price at which it was sold." However, "Notwithstanding what the Defendant had said on this point, he . . . contended that the low price at which it was sold made the publication doubly mischievous, as it caused it to circulate among the working classes of society" (*Trial* 20–21). The issue was not price but insidious motive: a nice legal distinction.

Lawyer Thomas Starkie had laid the foundations for the point, as for many others, in his *Law of Slander and Libel:* insinuations "calculated to mislead the ignorant and unwary" were hallmarks of the crime of blasphemy (2: 146). Cheap price was now construed as one such. "The Court has a duty to society," Mr. Justice Bayley refined the self-serving point passing sentence on Mary Anne Carlile in 1821, but especially "to the poor who have not the means of examination," and whose minds might all too easily be filled "with light and trivial matters" (Bonner 53, 44). Chief Justice

Denman, presiding over Hetherington's trial, was still more keen to protect the morals of *"the unthinking working-classes"* (my emphasis). "From their habits," Denman replied to a speech in his own defense that gave vivid proof to the contrary, they were "incapable of thought or discrimination." "Their time was so entirely occupied, that it was impossible they could devote sufficient time to reading to guard themselves against the evil tendency of such works" as Haslam's *Letters* (*Trial of Henry Hetherington* 21).

This was a cruel statement. It was true that men, women, and children who worked a sixteen-hour day, six days a week, before minimal factory legislation was fought through Parliament, were by and large too drained for serious reading, if not as utterly brutalized as it was feared in the 1840s. The decision to deny them knowledge for that reason retains its power to trouble. In court in 1840, the stolid assertion of the prosecution's "plainly-educated" witness, policeman Alexander Kerr, cross-examined by Hetherington, that Haslam's *Letters* had produced no effect on him whatsoever, was quietly ignored (5). If paternalism stood doomed to die from the moment the working classes learned to read, as Mill shortly declared in his 1848 *Principles of Political Economy,* all the more reason, Hetherington's judges implied, preemptively to protect them from their own fatal taste for alphabetical "poison" (*Trial of Henry Hetherington* 21). Never mind that those who read "poison" could also take in the "antidote," as one concerned clergyman put it.[14] George III's pious hope that every child in his kingdom might learn to read the Bible, which had prompted Wesleyans, Methodists, and Sunday school philanthropists to action on literacy, positively alarmed reactionaries. A people nursed on Holy Writ, feared libel expert W. Blake Odgers as late as 1881 (words he repeated in 1905), would "implicitly believe every word they see in print" (*Libel and Slander* 4). The multiple ironies in his statement hardly need teasing out.

The fear of popular knowledge-power contributed largely to the failure of nineteenth-century educational policy, as well as putting "disheartening obstacles" in the way of mechanics' institutes and free libraries (Altick 3). Overfaced by the quadrupling of population between 1751 and 1871, and encumbered by sometimes vicious religious factionalism, England, the richest state in the world, was the last country in Western Europe, trailing despotic Austria by a full century, to set up the basics of an organized national system of public education.[15] "Upon the speedy provision of elementary education," W. E. Forster declared in 1870, seeking passage of his historic education act, "depends our industrial prosperity" (qtd. in R. Williams, *Revolution* 162); "We must educate our masters," government said when the Second Reform Act of 1867 granted a prosperous minority of workingmen the vote.[16] But if the literacy that minimal education might guarantee was truly the "enabling cultural condition" of industrial expansion as modern commentators have claimed, fostering "greater uniformity and control over output" (Godzich 10), and if its extension went "hand in hand" with a general "increase in governmental authority over the Citizens" (Lévi-Strauss 300), then the governors of England were remarkably slow to capitalize on the advantages.[17] Even their preference for prosecuting blasphemy under the common law, one of Carlile's shopmen implied, was a reflection of unease at the "important extent" to which "letters have reached"; "it is abominable that any unwritten law should be in existence, or any but shall be written in language plain and intelligible to every man who shall read it" (trial transcript fragment, RC 563, in CC). In the end, when an educational system did slowly develop, it proved rigidly class determined.[18]

The "leap into literacy" in fact was taken by the working classes largely under their own steam, with many families putting aside hard-won pennies to pay for voluntary schools, often in preference to anything "the Master" might provide in the factory or the town. "[A]ny appearance of a percolation" of knowledge and literacy "downwards from the top of society to the bottom," F. M. L. Thompson records, "was a mirage of chronology rather than a fact of emulation" (82); the spread of education depended on "the rise of an organized working class," which demanded it (R. Williams, *Revolution* 161). And the leap was taken well before 1870 or 1867. The decade and a half from 1832 to 1848, a period that corresponded almost exactly with blasphemer Henry Hetherington's criminal activities in cheap publication, were the crucial years (Webb 21), when literacy rose to roughly two-thirds of population.[19] A working-class reading public not only existed but "was very much larger than has been generally thought" (23).

Crucially, that public was not only startlingly secular in its tastes, "brought into being" by the plain and proscribed works of Paine (O. Smith 57), but deeply indebted to infidels and blasphemers for their satisfaction for most of the nineteenth century, both directly and indirectly.[20] As in the sixteenth century, atheism was inextricably linked with the spread of literacy:[21] it may not exclusively have been by religion's "accursed influence," as one blasphemer testified, that "the multitude are kept in gross ignorance, fit victims for the vampires of society" (*Trial of Charles Southwell* 3), but it was partly by irreligious effort that their right to "intelligence" was won, and their "mind-forged manacles" were broken (Blake, "London" line 8). Blasphemy is as much a chapter in the English story of the newspaper press as it is integral to the history of the book.

The printing press pictured on the front of the *Poor Man's Guardian* was the people's own dynamo, and was more conducive to independent thinking than the monitorial school system that middle-class educators called the "STEAM ENGINE of the MORAL WORLD" (Andrew Bell, National Society, qtd. in R. Williams, *Revolution* 157).[22] Thousands, like Carlile, believed quite literally that "The art of Printing is a multiplication of mind" (qtd. in Wickwar 214). It was with relish, then, that Henry Hetherington reminded his jury in 1840 how recent semiofficial manias for "useful" knowledge had helped the monster of cheap publication to thrive and grow.

The Society for the Diffusion of Useful Knowledge (S.D.U.K.) to which Hetherington referred, founded by Brougham in 1826, entered a period of energetic action in 1832. Its aim was to circulate the kind of information that might make working men more profitable "hands." It took smart commercial advantage of the reductions in printing costs brought about since the teens by steam printing.[23] One of its first productions was an almanac. Next, the organization issued condensed treatments of important subjects as thirty-two page sixpenny pamphlets. The idea was to promote reading efficiency, as well as to keep down costs. These were not Christian productions. As its name proclaimed, the S.D.U.K. was a utilitarian organization, and utilitarianism in its pure aspect was unequivocally atheistical: Bentham had bankrolled Hone's *Reformist Register,* and corresponded with Carlile in prison; the S.D.U.K.'s rules forbade works on religion and morality, a fact that guaranteed the Victorian counter-resurgence of the dormant eighteenth-century Society for the Promotion of Christian Knowledge (S.P.C.K.).

The S.D.U.K.'s most famous publications, the *Penny Magazine* (1832–45) and the *Penny Cyclopaedia,* were the brainchildren of a less-unorthodox man called Charles Knight. They became standard purchases for new schools and aspiring families. "[T]his little work," announced Knight's preface to the first volume of the *Penny Magazine,* "has been justly regarded as one of the most remarkable indications of the extent to which the desire for knowledge has reached in the United Kingdom" (18 December 1832: iii). It offered no gossip, no party politics, not even many pieces on the blessings of machinery. The *Magazine's* staple fare was rather short and digestible articles on natural history and art; "Biographies of men who have had a permanent influence on the condition of the world" (iii); expositions of basic mathematics and political economy; and so forth. Articles in the first volume introduced readers to the British Museum and the excavations at Pompeii, and gave practical advice "On the Choice of a Labouring Man's Dwelling" and "How to Endure Poverty" (28 April 1832). Early series included "An Emigrant's Struggles." Knight was not above insinuating a low-key message of quasi-Christian cultural reverence through a heavily illus-

trated series on the great churches of England and Europe, and entries on
the saints in a regular column entitled "The Week." The *Magazine* provided
a "species of reading" that could "never inflame a vicious appetite," a "consideration" that Knight prematurely hoped would "furnish . . . the most
convincing answer to the few (if any there now remain) who assert that
General Education is an evil" (18 December 1832: iii). The more a man
knows, asserted the first article published, in the loaded terms of blasphemy prosecution, "the less hasty and less violent will be his opinions"
("READING FOR ALL," 31 March 1832: 1).

It was indeed one thing, Hetherington declared in court, for "Penny
Magazines and Penny Cyclopaedias" (*Trial of Henry Hetherington* 5) to
bring knowledge to the working classes. It was quite another for the laboring masses to help themselves to information and distribute it by their
own efforts. "Hands" might grow independent heads. Unlike the *Guardian,*
but like religious tracts and other subsidized productions, S.D.U.K. publications were never prosecuted for their equal violation of the Newspaper
Stamp Act. The *Penny Magazine,* wrote Hetherington's associate James
Bronterre O'Brien, gave the people real "trash," since "the only knowledge
which is of service to the working people is that which makes them . . .
worse slaves" (*People's Conservative [Destructive],* 7 June 1834: 137). Another
described it as fit for the water closet. Parody societies for the diffusion of
"Really Useful Knowledge" were formed to assist the unstamped press (E.
Thompson 729). Knight's promotion of "Knowledge for the million" had
"taught us the way," one blasphemer declared in 1844; "Blasphemy for the
many! then—'Atheism for the Million!' " (*God v. Paterson* 60).[24]

In fact, the fellow martyr of 1844 was wrong. There is a mythical element
in the belief, propounded by some of our best scholars, that the evangelicals
and the utilitarians "together worked to widen the reading audience" (Altick 132). The S.D.U.K. had learned as well as taught, and it had learned
the most from two famous blasphemers: William Hone and Henry Hetherington.

It was Hone, the "Arch-blasphemer" himself, who wrote the article,
"READING FOR ALL," that launched the *Penny Magazine,* though his
authorship was not common knowledge. His *Every-Day* and other "Books"
inspired Knight's innovations, especially the liberal use of woodcuts about
which Knight bragged in his preface (*Penny Magazine,* 18 December 1832:
iii), though Hone's ill health and Knight's aggressive editorial practices excluded him from regular participation, and, therefore, from regular remuneration (Knight to Hone, 18 March 1832, Hone BL 40,120: 373–74). Hone
was even widely believed to have suggested the very idea of the *Magazine*
in the first place (Lawley 123, in Hone WA). Moreover, it took the same

eight-page, double-columned format as the *Guardian* and innumerable other unstamped and radical publications. Knight's catchy and apparently prototypical title, which gave rise to innumerable imitations, was actually taken from Hetherington.[25] The *Poor Man's Guardian* began life in 1830, two years before the *Penny Magazine* first appeared, as Hetherington's *Penny Papers for the People*, only changing its name in July 1831. Knight acknowledged the inspiration: the *Magazine* was a serious and gratifying response to a powerful phenomenon, a co-option of popular knowledge-power.

Burke had reckoned that there were eighty thousand "readers" in the whole country in the 1790s, while "it has been shown by sales of the *Penny Magazine*," claimed Knight's preface of 1832, "that there are two hundred thousand *purchasers* of [this] one periodical work" (18 December: iii). The figure was both optimistic and misleading: optimistic, because *Magazine* readership in fact bottomed out at around sixty thousand, and misleading in its suggestion of mass penetration, since Knight calculated on five readers per purchaser whereas Hetherington could count on twenty. The *Penny Magazine* was a great endeavor but did not succeed in eliminating its dangerous competition in reaching out to the working classes. It was bought primarily by middle-class or aspiring middle-class families. A determined and freethinking element among the lower orders preferred to keep offering their pennies for the kind of "Really Useful Knowledge" that Hetherington and his unstamped and blasphemous colleagues provided. By 1834, thanks to a legacy, Hetherington too was operating a steam press, and might have become a rich man if he had not been committed to radical causes.[26] In the 1840s, eschewing the attractions of ever cheaper Bibles and better-produced S.D.U.K. productions, thousands still scraped to buy the one-shilling "Cabinet of Reason" series published by veteran volunteer and blasphemer James Watson, or individual home study volumes with titles like the *Logic of Facts*.[27] Educational and propagandist drives converged to make bookselling and publishing the life of Freethought, its inheritance from the 1810s. "Every new copy bought increases our power," as the first in a series of little pamphlets called *Wayside Points for New Roads* put it in 1852; "The number we sell is a fact having a moral influence with it" (2).

That belief sustained organized Secularism to the end of the century. The Secular Book Depot of the early 1880s never turned enough profit, raised enough subscriptions, or begged enough cash to support an overambitious "Book Fund, enabling us to give cheap editions of Freethinking classics" (1884 circular, in HC). But C. A. Watts (Foote's associate) did much better. From 1884, his sixty-four page, sixpenny *Agnostic Annual* secured contributions by leading figures like T. H. Huxley; from June 1893, monthly supplements to his *Literary Annual* similarly offered a better-

educated younger generation four-page summaries of works by Leslie Stephen, Lecky, Frazer, Buckle, Herbert Spencer, Winwood Reade, and other
"advanced" writers, as well as reviews of new books. The logical next step
was to publish a series of similar works and to form the "Thinker's Library"
of the Rationalist Press Association. Watts's own translation of Haeckel's
Riddle of the Universe sold two thousand copies in under a year; between
1890 and 1914 Rationalist Press Association membership grew to three thousand. Its famous sixpenny reprint series commenced with Huxley's *Lectures
and Essays;* by 1905 twenty volumes had been published, and no less than
three-quarters of a million books sold. The last great fruits of nineteenth-
century unbelief, blasphemy's legacy to modernity, were two of the most
important concepts in modern publishing: the subscription book club and
the mass-market and paperback reprint at "the people's price."[28]

2. THE MOXON CASE AND THE GROWTH OF THE POET'S INCOME

There was one trial for blasphemy in the nineteenth century during which
it was not a cheap printer or a penny journalist who occupied the dock,
or even a lapsed priest and class traitor like Taylor, but a respected middle-
class publisher. Hetherington's role in history is not exhausted with the
record of his career as blasphemous martyr in the cause of a cheap press.
He had time on his hands between indictment in February and trial in
December, and—partly on the advice of Francis Place—he used it to advertise the partiality of the law by exercising his right as a private citizen
and taking Edward Moxon, publisher, to court for the crime of blasphemy.

Moxon was a sonneteer and litterateur, the high-class publisher of high-
class literature, whose editions of Tennyson and others secured their Victorian reputations. He was also a pioneer of the scholarly edition. It was this
last enterprise that got him into trouble. In 1840 Moxon published a one-
volume edition of the *Complete Works of Shelley* that he had put out with
profitable success the previous year "in a form similar to that in which he
had published the collected works of the greatest English poets" (*Modern
State Trials* 2: 364). The 1840 edition included, amongst other "hot" items,
the atheistical *Queen Mab,* "the verse equivalent of the *Age of Reason,*" as
Nicolas Walter dubs it (*Blasphemy: Ancient and Modern* 38), privately
printed in 1813, quickly withdrawn from circulation, and a motive factor
in Shelley's being denied guardianship of his children in 1816. The indictment had an embarrassment of passages to pick from. Only one was quoted
in full in an edited transcript of the trial:

*They have three words: well tyrants know their use, well pay them for the loan, with
usury torn from a bleeding world! God, Hell, and Heaven . . .* (Talfourd, *Speech for
the Defendant* 9)

The innuendo, lest we should miss it, was carefully spelled out: *"meaning
thereby that God, Hell, and Heaven, were merely words"* (9). Moxon must
have felt sick to read it: this was one of the too atheistical passages he had
persuaded Mary Shelley as widow-editor to omit from the 1839 edition
(Merriam 116); it had been restored after protests from the dead poet's
friends.[29] Such passages invited the ire of all establishment advocates of
blasphemy prosecution, including Bishop Philpotts of Exeter, who had
pushed hard for Hetherington's own.

The fascination of the case is not its verdict. In the event, although it
took a common jury only fifteen minutes to find Moxon guilty, a sympathetic judge (who summed up in his favor) never called him up for sentencing; nor did Hetherington push the point. "Everybody knew the defendant
must be convicted, and would not be punished" (1854 memoir, qtd. in
Merriam 103). Deeply distressed, Mary Shelley volunteered to make declaration that Moxon had published the "objectionable passages . . . at my
request" (M. Shelley, *Letters* 3: 9). Hetherington offered to pay all his
fines—and was reportedly sternly refused (Merriam 102). Rather, as we
shall see, the Moxon prosecution, 23 June, 1841 in the Court of Queen's
Bench, had a powerful and unforeseen impact on passage of the landmark
Copyright Act of 1842; and it set an unexpected seal on what must best be
called the literary redefinition of the crime of blasphemy from the 1810s
through the 1840s.

That latter process concerns us first. On 3 May 1841, the Royal Commission on the Criminal Law appointed in 1834 published its sixth report.
The section on offenses against religion has rightly been described as an
"intellectually reprehensible performance," "muddled," and "chaotic"
(Levy, *Blasphemy* 441). But the distinguished lawyers who labored to produce it had a fine sense of cultural context. For new standards in law,
especially common law, need authorization other than that of courtroom
precedent. The report's crucial paragraph was a coproduction of naked social anxiety and pragmatic legal revisionism of a peculiarly literary kind.
Respecting blasphemy, the report said as follows:

> The course hitherto adopted in England . . . has been to withhold the application
> of the penal law, unless in cases where insulting or contumelious language is used,
> and where it may fairly be presumed that the intention of the offender is not
> grave discussion, but a mischievous design to wound the feelings of others. . . .
> [I]t is only where irreligion has assumed the form of blasphemy, in its true and

primitive meaning, and has constituted an insult both to God and man, that the
interference of the criminal law has taken place. (*British Parliamentary Papers* 3:
85)

The report gave official sanction to the subterranean shifting of law's attention from the religious "matter" to the stylistic "manner" of the crime's
commission that had taken place since Hone's three trials of 1817. Moreover, it begged an important question: If ridicule and parody were to be
judged "improper means" of "discussion," what must one do positively to
avoid blasphemy? Words like "grave" pointed the way forward.

"[A]ny man," confirmed Judge Erskine in the case of Jacob Holyoake,
1842, "may, without subjecting himself to any penal consequences, *soberly
and reverently* examine and question the truth of [religious] doctrines"
(Odgers, *Libel and Slander* 447–48, my emphasis). "The only safe and, as
it seems to me, practical rule," seconded his colleague on the bench, "depends on *the sobriety, and reverence, and seriousness* with which the teaching
or believing, however erroneous, are maintained" (448, my emphasis). The
limits of toleration were extended by such rulings. But it needs to be added
that the "sobriety," "reverence," and "seriousness" that are here recommended constitute an approved style, a legitimate "manner." Rulings like
these wrote into law, in effect, what had become upper-class literary and
cultural practice in the late 1830s and early 1840s. The English strain of
Bible criticism, for example, took its distinctive flavor from Charles Hennell's *Inquiry Concerning the Origin of Christianity* (1838), a book couched
throughout in terms of hushed "reverence." "Sincerity" and "earnestness,"
other new indices of legal innocence, have the stamp of the reformed
public-school culture built by Arnold at Rugby.

Catching the wind of change, from prison, Holyoake forlornly hoped
to find grounds for reducing his sentence in convincing the secretary of
state that he had "unwarily uttered language" which "disingenuousness
would have concealed or art have polished" (*History of the Last Trial* 73).
The "sincerity" of Haslam's *Letters to the Clergy*, Henry Hetherington likewise argued in court, was evidence in his favor (*Trial of Henry Hetherington*
9). Lord Denman listened to such arguments, he declared, "with feelings
of great interest, aye, with sentiments of respect too" (22): they may have
been one motive for his light sentence of four months in prison, which
Hetherington spent in the Marshalsea Debtor's Gaol, under humane conditions.[30] Nor was Denman the only occupant of the bench endowed with
"feelings." Erskine's were "most deeply affected" by visiting the bookseller
he had prosecuted in 1797 for first publishing the *Age of Reason:* shut up
in a room ten feet square with his emaciated wife and children, he was

"sewing up little religious tracts" to make a few pennies (qtd. in *Westminster Review,* July 1883: 5).

However, "feeling" found its way into law not as a spur to tolerance but as a prosecutorial criterion and an alibi against guilt. The act of "insulting" and "wounding" believers, especially younger believers, was criminalized by the 1841 commissioners' report and Erskine's 1842 ruling.[31] One might expect to encounter such emotive constructions of crime in the proper realm of "sensibility": Victorian literature. Certainly when a crime begins to look as if it might "bring a blush," as arch-prude Mr. Podsnap puts it in Dickens's *Our Mutual Friend,* "into the cheek of the young person" (175)—the shibboleth of Victorian fiction reviewers—it has started to look very much like a literary crime. Law's new sensitivity to "feeling" produced a new quasi-literary criterion of "intent" to "shock." Thus, "[i]t gave him pain," declared the attorney-general in Hetherington's case, "that it should be necessary for the Jury to hear" such "shocking" language as was contained in Haslam's *Letters* (*Trial of Henry Hetherington* 5). Step by step, new standards and criteria of guilt and innocence were taking shape.

Almost all the key terms of approval reappeared in Lord Coleridge's landmark ruling of 1883 in the case of the *Freethinker:* "reverent," "sober," "serious," "sincere," "earnest," "decent." "Tasteful" was another, more problematic criterion: "I readily admit," as Hetherington pleaded, "that [a] passage in the eighth number of Mr. Haslam's *Letters* is highly objectionable in phraseology. . . . but is that a reason for sending a bookseller to prison, because he has sold a book written in bad taste?" (*Trial of Henry Hetherington* 13). The terms of condemnation are no less clear: "mocking," "insulting," "coarse," "vulgar," "shocking," "outrageous." Thomas Paterson spat the whole list back at his prosecutors in 1844; Edinburgh's lord justice clerk nevertheless used them all again in passing sentence upon him (*Trial of Thomas Paterson* 56). They are touchstones of Victorian criticism—hardy perennials that sprang up anew with each year's crop of novels. Established within ten years of Victoria's accession, they were the standards, for example, by which Lady Eastlake tried and condemned Charlotte Brontë for a "coarse and brutal" work penned in a spirit of insurgent and godless "vulgarity" (in Olmstead, *Essays in British Periodicals* 1: 612, 609), and an outspoken heroine—Jane Eyre—whose "language and manners . . . offend . . . in every particular" (1: 613); "The humor is frequently produced by a use of Scripture," added the *Christian Remembrancer,* "at which one is rather sorry to have smiled" (*Jane Eyre* 439). The terms remained the standards by which Mrs. Oliphant excoriated Thomas Hardy in 1895 (see below, 6.1). The Moxon case of 1841, the only trial involving a major work of literature in the nineteenth century and the only such trial for 120 years, was not only soaked in these literary terms of legal reference but was an extraordinary demonstration of how, in the case of blasphemy, the parallel tracks along which law and literature move can actually converge.

Language itself alerts us to the relationship: to "indict" means to write as well as to condemn; "dead letter" was a term in law before it became a catchphrase of literary theory. "Forensic oratory" was as much a branch of rhetoric as of law (*Modern State Trials* 2: 358, 360); revenge was both legal prototype and literary genre. Trial and novel, as Alexander Welsh persuasively demonstrates, are both arts of "representation," readings from the evidence; and trial was a central trope of Victorian fiction, from Dickens's *Pickwick* to Trollope's *Phineas Redux*.[32] Moreover, of the alternative professions to which failed novelists resorted, or from which practitioners emerged, the law is by far the most important in the nineteenth century. Dickens, the critic of Chancery, the creator of vampiric lawyer Vholes in *Bleak House,* seems an unlikely descendant of judge-novelist Henry Fielding, or lawyer-romancer Walter Scott, but even he enrolled as a student at the Inns of Court in 1839 and stayed enrolled for many years (Dickens to Madame De La Rue, 17 April 1846, *Letters* 4: 534). Trial by review had a great deal in common with trial by jury, except that anonymous Victorian reviewers enjoyed more "licence" than the most "privileged" of lawyers.[33] It is not enough for literary studies to register Victorian fiction's legal turn of mind, or for legal theorists to apply literary methods of textual analysis to statutory texts. The peculiar literariness of Victorian law demands special attention, and expresses itself most peculiarly in relation to blasphemy.

The crime reenters literary history as Edward Moxon stands trial for *Mab.* The ghost of Percy Shelley stood in the dock at his side. But our interest centers first on the counsel for the defense, Thomas Noon Talfourd. "Serjeant" at law (later judge), member of Parliament for Reading, critic, essayist, and playwright, Talfourd personified the literariness of Victorian law. Born in 1795, he was an early champion of the older Romantics; by the late 1830s, he was a minor literary lion in his own right. In *Glencoe, The Athenian Captive,* and his most famous play, *Ion*—a sententious flirtation with radical rebellion that turns into a bowdlerized Oedipal parable of right reform by the fifth act—Talfourd revived the "classical" verse tragedy, that overbred racehorse of early Victorian literature flogged with desperate energy until the century's end.[34] (The real presiding genii of literature as early Victorians conceived it were bewigged lawyers and other gentlemen penning tragedies of stunning derivative mediocrity, like Bulwer's fabulously successful verse drama the *Lady of Lyons,* and long-forgotten Henry

Taylor's "noble dramatic poem" *Philip van Artevelde* [preface to *Ion, Tragedies* ix].)

Moxon could not have chosen a more suitable counsel. Talfourd answered to his own inflated sense of his literary standing, and probably prevailed upon him to "bear the first attack" for the edition, rather than two "mere vendors," booksellers called Fraser and Otley who were also indicted (*Modern State Trials* 2: 364). The "celebrated case" of Moxon, Shelley, and *Mab* elicited Talfourd's most "celebrated speech," "the only one of his forensic efforts" he himself decided to publish (*DNB* 55: 344), and officially embalmed nine years later in the 1850 edition of *Modern State Trials* as "the best defense that could be urged" in a case of blasphemy (2: 362). On the inside back cover of Talfourd's own edited transcript of the trial, as if to emphasize the seamless continuity of his literary and legal interests, were printed advertisements for his *Tragedies*, "by T. N. Talfourd, Sergeant-At-Law." The *Speech* was reviewed (as the *Metropolitan Conservative Journal* said of another Talfourd production) as much for its "sweet harmony of composition" as for its "fine logical and judicious distinctions."[35] An over-ambitious blasphemer of 1843 thus had models in view when he had "Favourable Notices" printed on the inside front cover of his trial transcript: " 'greatest blasphemy ever uttered.'—*Times*. 'An abomination.'—*Chronicle*," etcetera (*God v. Paterson*, inside front cover). Another naively hoped that Richard Carlile would pay him five pounds the year before for the copyright of his speech in his own defence (Carlile to Holyoake, 25 October 1842, in HL). Publication hoped to turn blasphemy, like "forensic oratory," into a literary act.

Talfourd's speech in Moxon's defense sought to establish his client's immunity, and Literature's (the capital is Talfourd's), as embodied by P. B. Shelley, without admitting any affinity of either with "mute inglorious Hetherington" (Talfourd, *Speech for the Defendant* 41), who is not dignified by name for six dense pages of transcript. "The success of such a prosecution," Talfourd prefaced the record, "proceeding from such a quarter, gives rise to very serious considerations":

> for although, in determining sentences, Judges will be able to diminish the evil, by a just discrimination between the publication of the complete works of an author of established fame, for the use of the studious, and for deposit in libraries, and the dissemination of cheap irreligion, directed to no object but to unsettle the belief of the reader—the power of prosecuting to conviction every one who may sell, or give, or lend any work containing passages to which the indictable character may be applied, is a fearful engine of oppression. (11–12)

A "principle of distinction" is needed (12). It is laid out in Talfourd's high-literary defense.

Girding himself in his own credentials, Talfourd eulogizes Moxon as the friend "of the good and the great in our Literature" (*Speech for the Defendant* 16). Literariness breathes through every line of the speech: "teeming with poetical illustrations, running over with images of grace, rich to gorgeousness in diction," it is indeed the "finished production" of an "accomplished professional" (*Modern State Trials* 2: 362). But even extended meditations on Milton's imaginative Satanism in *Paradise Lost,* and Romantic rhapsodies on the "divine" origin of poetry, "the beatings of the soul against the bars of its clay tenement," are minor parts of Talfourd's literary strategy (*Speech for the Defendant* 42).

His speech has two main lines of argument. One echoes the central proposition of the greatest "contemplative poem" of the age, Wordsworth's unpublished *Prelude,* with uncanny exactness (Talfourd's term, in *Speech for the Defendant* 24). *Queen Mab* must be published, Talfourd maintained, because if we cannot read the early works of the poet, we cannot trace "the growth of [his] mind" (24). In the case of Shelley, we would lose the development from infidel towards his posthumous Victorian incarnation as soulful "angel"; he was temporarily pent up in the "gross" materialistic philosophy of his youth like "Ariel in the rift of the cloven pine" (46). Shelley "fancies himself irreligious, and everywhere falters or trembles into piety" (35); moreover, *Mab* as printed in Moxon's edition "is accompanied by his own letter in which he expresses his wish for its suppression" (32). "Shall this life, fevered with beauty, restless with inspiration, be hidden; or, wanting its first blind but gigantic efforts, be falsely, because partially revealed?" (24). Was it "blasphemy" to present the first "awful mistakes" and "imperfect victories of such a spirit, because the picture has some passages of frightful gloom" (21)? The myth of the solitary "genius" who does not live by ordinary rules—or criminal laws—was ingrained in Romantic ideology and now asked legal recognition. More, Talfourd subscribed entirely to the belief that "the value of literature reside[s] in the author" (Vanden Bossche 57), each work an "embodiment" of that proprietary individual (M. Rose, *Authors* 114): his own *Sketch* of Lamb's life—published by Moxon in 1837—became "a sort of classic" of Victorian literary biography (Fitzgerald xii). In effect, Talfourd justified the crime of blasphemy by resort to a biographical alibi. Literary criticism and cultural history require and sanction complete access to the poet's works.

Talfourd's second line of argument was no less literary, and no less important to the history of criticism and censorship. In his record of the case, Talfourd recalls how the indictment of Moxon proceeded after the first charge (above):

to recite a few more lines, *applying very coarse and irreverent* but not very intelligible comments to each of those words. It then charged, that the libel contained, in other parts, two other passages, also in verse, and to which the same character may be justly applied. (*Speech for the Defendant* 9, my emphasis)

Here was a cunning co-option of the very terms of blasphemy prosecution. The service of Literature, Talfourd suggests, makes a greater claim to taste and sensibility than the law that can be so "coarse and irreverent." In a footnote he adds, "It has not been thought necessary to the argument to set out these passages" (9n). There was an extra motive for the suppression, however. It turned on Talfourd's "admission, that, separately considered," the indicted passages from *Mab* are indeed "very offensive both to piety and good taste" (9n).

"Separately considered." Herein was the rub. It is the very layout of an indictment, Talfourd contends, its procedure of excerpting—in short, its ignorance of literary context, especially in a dramatic poem like *Queen Mab,* or *Paradise Lost*—that makes writers like Shelley and publishers like Moxon liable to criminal charges. "[S]election might be made even from the greatest of all prose romances, *Clarissa Harlowe,* which the Society for the Suppression of Vice would scarcely endure" (*Speech for the Defendant* 23). Individual passages, "like details and pictures in works of anatomy and surgery" (which had been liable to obscenity prosecutions in recent years) "are either innocent or criminal, according to the accompaniments which surround them" (18–19). Thus, Talfourd next led the jury through a step-by-step contextualization of the "self-refuted" query put to Ahasuerus, the wandering Jew, in *Mab: "Is there a God?"* (31). What seems offensive taken in isolation is in fact sanctified by the "spirit, and *intent,* and *tendency"* of the work as a whole (23): with those words Talfourd's literary co-option of legal terms was complete.

Summing up, Talfourd warned that "if the government were consistent in carrying out prosecutions for blasphemy," Milton, Byron, Southey "might be prohibited"; Gibbon would be especially vulnerable, if his notorious chapters of religion were "published at a penny each" (*Speech for the Defendant* 51);[36] even Shakespeare might "be placed at the mercy of an insect abuser of the press" like Henry Hetherington (54). From the bench in his charge to the jury, Chief Justice Denman (to whom Talfourd had dedicated his *Athenian Captive*) posed a series of questions that implicitly endorsed Talfourd's arguments, and reemphasized how important the literary issues of shock and sensibility had become in judging criminality:

Were the lines indicated [from *Mab*] calculated to shock the feelings of any Christian reader? Were their points of offence explained, or was their virus neutralized by any remarks in the margin, by any note of explanation or apology? (*Modern State Trials* 1: 388–89)

There was, of course, such a "note."[37]

Though the verdict went against him, and Moxon grieved, "the sympathies of even the opposing counsel"—not surprisingly—"were with Talfourd" (*DNB* 55: 344). His "failure to convince the jury entails no discredit" (*Modern State Trials* 2: 362); "it would argue the extreme of credulity to imagine" homely jurymen so quickly "made . . . poetical" as to judge *Mab* not guilty (2: 361). Talfourd had won a victory: the safe publication of "serious" heretical works was henceforth assured; there were no further prosecutions of major authors, dead or alive, until the *Gay News* case of 1977.

I move us forward in time deliberately. There are reasons why Talfourd's claims and Denman's instructions sound hauntingly familiar. The lines spoken in the Court of Queen's Bench in 1841 were repeated 120 years later, during a trial for a different crime—the 1960 trial of Penguin Books, indicted for obscenity for the publication of *Lady Chatterley's Lover*. The case is a well-known turning point. The 1959 Obscene Publications Act, replacing the 1857 law, made it possible to argue that literary merit and the mitigation of context absolved offending texts of criminality: that is, Penguin and D. H. Lawrence were cleared of blame on exactly the grounds that Talfourd created in 1841. The histories of the two crimes, blasphemy and obscenity, are tightly intertwined, as we shall further see. What the Moxon case already demonstrates, beyond reasonable doubt, is that a shift towards Literature as a preeminent standard of cultural value occurred very much sooner than has been recorded. It was simply registered in a different court, by means of blasphemy prosecution.

"Would you want your servant to read this book?" prosecuting counsel famously asked in 1960, with a paperback copy of *Lady Chatterley* in his hand, repeating the clichés of this entire history. And how could you stop him if Allen Lane published it at the price of a packet of ten cigarettes (Rolph 24–25)? In 1841, Talfourd envisaged other checks on the circulation of literature than trial for blasphemy: the higher prices and control of literary property that the new copyright law he first proposed in 1837 would secure.

For Talfourd survives in today's literary histories not as the author of *Ion* or as Moxon and Shelley's defender but as the original dedicatee of the *Pickwick Papers*. Smarting under the depredations of Pickwickian plagiarists, Dickens warmly appreciated the "inestimable service" Talfourd hoped to "render . . . to . . . the authors of this and succeeding generations" in introducing his Private Member's Bill on Copyright into Parliament in 1837 (*Pickwick* 39). Opposed by a vocal minority of utilitarians, radicals, and free traders, it failed, and failed again by increasingly depressing margins in 1838, 1839, 1840, and 1841, when Talfourd lost his seat in a general election. But in 1842, pragmatically modified and sponsored by Lord Mahon, the historic act was passed. Widely imitated, the basis of British law until 1911, it secured to authors a lifetime interest in their work plus seven years, or a flat period of forty-two years, whichever was longer.

It is to Talfourd, then—like his friend Dickens, and like Moxon, a type of the successfully self-made gentleman[38]—that we owe the modern conceptualization of literature as a form of property in which the author and his family have posthumous patrimonial rights, displacing eighteenth-century ideas, promulgated by publishing interests, of books as works made for hire, and despite lingering counterbelief in perpetual copyright. What is not known, however, is that Talfourd's work for copyright intersected intimately with his work as defense counsel in the Moxon case, and that Moxon's most distinguished living author, William Wordsworth, turns out to have been behind both. To disentangle the threads that tied copyright to blasphemy law, we must first return to the years in which this history began.

The crucial word in the 1842 legislation was *lifetime*. The decision to link a literary work to the life of its author was a last-minute innovation of an unsatisfactory copyright measure of 1814, with no precedent in the first ancestral Copyright Act of 1710; its resuscitation in every bill introduced from 1837 to 1842 was an index of a deep water shift in understanding of the value of literature and the status of the author.[39] So muddled was that measure of 1814, however, that the entire question of copyright law was reopened in 1817, when confusion was piled on confusion by the intrusion of allegations of blasphemy and sedition.[40]

Somehow, the radical publishers Sherwood, Neely, and Jones had come by the unpublished manuscript of Poet Laureate Southey's drama *Wat Tyler*, a youthful indiscretion of the Jacobinical 1790s. In 1817 the trio put out a pirate edition. Desperate to suppress it, Southey applied to the Court of Chancery for protection of his copyright, but Lord Chancellor Eldon was obliged to refuse an injunction when the defense quoted back to him his own decision in a similar case of a few years before: "[T]here can be no property in what is injurious" (qtd. in *Quarterly Review*, April 1822: 133). Though he could not exactly say so, since that would prejudge a criminal case, Eldon could not but view *Wat Tyler* as seditious and therefore shorn of protection.

Southey's end might have been served, since Sherwood et al. withdrew their edition, had not William Hone now stepped forward. His three shillings and sixpence edition, with a preface by Hazlitt "suitable to recent circumstances" (qtd. in Rickword 13), sold perhaps sixty thousand copies (Manning 218).[41] Between them, Hone and the lord chancellor had made piracy, like blasphemy, another strategy of the aspirant disenfranchised, linking the two crimes together.

It was hawking twenty-five thousand pirate copies of the hapless laureate's red-hot poem that had first "decided the success" of Carlile's "attempts to become a bookseller" (*Republican*, 3 November 1826: 524): "The world does not know," he crowed, "what it may yet owe to Southey" (30 May 1823: 675). Like parody—and like forgery—piracy challenged the notion of art as intellectual property with a single originator; and Eldon's stickling insistence on the letter of law had made suspect texts *"a sort of common property"* (8 February 1822: 343, my emphasis). The *Wat Tyler* case set a precedent that radicals, freethinkers, and simply disreputable types wholeheartedly exploited. Law now allowed any man to issue anything he thought Chancery might think was criminal without the issue going before a jury. And the crime of choice was blasphemy. If in law the blasphemer was a nonperson, an "outlaw," it naturally followed that a blasphemous publication became, as lawyer Henry Folkard put it in 1876, a *"non-book"* (612).

From the other side of the high-low literary divide, as the *Quarterly* realized in a worried review of four recent cases of unhampered piracy, Eldon's decision laid high literature open to "an indirect censorship of the press" (April 1822: 137). By this logic, dangerous works "circulated without restriction *because* it was supposed their tendency might be injurious to the best interests of society" (123). One pirate even told the lord chancellor directly that "the evil tendency of the work he was publishing was as clear as the sun at noon" (130). Better try offending authors separately for their crime, the *Quarterly* thought, and let them claim damages for infringement until the work was proved guilty, than "leave these unhallowed profits . . . in the hands of the libelous pirate" (138). The entangling of blasphemy and copyright could blight the national literature, since "[m]en who have much at stake"—that is, gentlemen authors—will "prefer . . . obscurity" to the "stigma" of "having published what the Court of Chancery would not protect" (137). The cases considered included Southey's (discreetly handled by his *Quarterly* friends); Sir William Lawrence's action against Smith for pirating his materialist *Lectures on Physiology, Zoology, and the Natural History of Man;* and publisher John Murray's Chancery action against William Benbow, who had put out a bootleg edition of Lord Byron's *Cain, A Mystery* in 1821. This last was the crucial case.

Byron's fame in his lifetime owed much to the pirates: William Hone, for example, whose one-shilling volume of *Lord Byron's Poems* (1816), "the Genuine Edition" (W. Hone, advertisement, in *Official Account* 15), and *Hone's Lord Byron's Corsair,* "Adapted as a Romance" for popular taste, were more government black marks against him.[42] Piracy confirmed Byron in his anomalous role as popular revolutionary (Manning 216), and was a thorn in the side of his publisher, John Murray. Worried by their tendencies, Murray had removed his name from the first cantos of *Don Juan* in 1819, only to find the feint of anonymity exploded four days after publication by Hone's "*Don John,*" [Murray] or *Don Juan Unmasked,* which (besides quoting liberally from the work for one-fifteenth of its original one-and-a-half-guinea cost) noted that Murray, a "Government publisher" (38), proprietor of the *Quarterly Review,* and a "strenuous supporter" of the Bible Society (30), had published a "PARODY ON THE TEN COMMAND-MENTS" in stanzas 205 and 206 of canto 1 (35). Robert Aspland in the Unitarian *Monthly Repository* called it the "grossest . . . of modern times" (November 1819: 716).[43] Hone's spurious canto the third, meanwhile, published just after the Peterloo Massacre, transformed Juan into a radical pressman (Manning 232; Wickwar 266). *Don Juan* was pirated outright by William Benbow and William Dugdale, future famous pornographers. The depredations ironically ensured that the bulk of Byron's masterpiece would be published by Hone's close friend, John Hunt of the *Examiner.* A work denounced as "scornful," "filthy," and "impious" (*Blackwood's Magazine,* August 1819: 515, 514) had no protection at law, and the lord chancellor duly dissolved Murray's injunction against *Juan's* pirates in August 1823. The issue of blasphemy was the issue of copyright, as poet and publisher were well aware.

Before they parted company, however, Murray put out Byron's "Mystery," *Cain.* It caused a far louder outcry. As if alerting readers to the parallel between *Cain* and Hone's scandalous *Apocryphal New Testament* of 1820, with its prefatory discussion of "monkish mysteries" (x), Byron's preface declared, "The following scenes are entitled 'a Mystery,' in conformity with the ancient title annexed to dramas upon similar subjects," which were—incidentally—"very profane productions" (*Cain* 155). In Milton's *Paradise Lost* literature had resanctified the sacred, "justify[ing] the ways of God to Man," amplifying on biblical text. In *Cain,* Byron challenged not only Milton but Scripture itself, asserting his literary right to radical reinterpretation, and hoisting scriptural literalism on its own petard:

> The reader will recollect, that the book of Genesis does not state that Eve was tempted by a demon, but by 'the Serpent.' . . . Whatever interpretation the Rabbins and the Fathers may have put upon this, I must take the words as I find

them, and reply with Bishop Watson upon similar occasions . . . 'Behold the Book!'" (155)

Cain went further, rewriting the first murderer in Byron's own image as a "deliberate criminal seeking the conditions for his art by violating the moral sanctions of his society" (Bloom 253). When the Lord rejects his offering, Scripture tells us that "Cain was very wroth, and his countenance fell" (Genesis 4.5). But Byron's Cain knows beforehand that God will accept only animal sacrifice; he makes his gift of "the fruit of the ground" (4.3) in willed subversion of the "Omnipotent tyrant" (*Cain* 1.1.138). Above all, the killing of Abel (Genesis 4.8) is represented as accidental—"I smote / Too fiercely, but not fatally . . . / . . . 'twas a blow / And but a blow" (*Cain* 3.1.326–31)—and is made motive for Byronic remorse and egotistical introspection: "Oh! for a word more of that gentle voice, / That I may bear to hear my own again!" (3.1.356–57). Byron knew what he had wrought: "I dare say your opinion about *Cain* is the right one," he wrote a disapproving friend, John Cam Hobhouse, "but I can't burn it" (23 November 1821, *Letters* 9: 67–68). On publication, Murray suppressed lines in which Lucifer spelled out the costs to sons of not rebelling against their fathers, though his plea to cut a sneer at Christ's Atonement (*Cain* 1.1.161–66) was ignored.

That "scoff" was duly reprimanded by *Blackwood's* (February 1822: 216). The poem "may very properly be called a literary *devil,*" the review concluded, the quintessential production of the "satanic school" of poetry (February 1822: 215).[44] Carlile gleefully noticed the king's disapprobation: "Why the Vice Society does not attack Murray, the publisher of *Cain,* it is difficult for an honest, impartial man to divine, for Jehovah, the God of the Jews, is exhibited in it as a capricious, murderous, and implacable tyrant" (*Republican,* 8 February 1822: 192). A month later, when prosecution was "threatened," he grandly took *Cain* "under my protection," and announced a pirate edition as a "stimulant" to initiate proceedings (15 March 1822: 343), at sixpence—an almost "nominal" price (*Quarterly,* April 1822: 123).

Other voices bestowed on Byron the "hackneyed and lavished title of Blasphemer," as he put it in the preface to cantos 6 and 7 of *Don Juan* (3: 5), and called for Murray's indictment. "[N]othing but an over cautious deference to the peculiar temper of the times," declared "Oxoniensis" (the Reverend Henry John Todd) in a threatening *Remonstrance,* "would allow the prosecutor of Hone"—the attorney-general—"to permit the publisher of 'CAIN' to escape with impunity" ("Oxoniensis" 8). It was true that Hone had "escaped," but "Carlile and his miserable associates are in gaol" (20): action was possible and deserved. For although Murray again had removed his name from the title page, he had "loaded" the literary gun (8), and it would be he, not "the Nobleman, by whom you are employed" (5), who would face trial for its "blasphemous impieties" (13). "In conclusion," asked his inquisitor, "are you prepared to go all lengths with him? . . . will he find in you a willing instrument?" (19). Meanwhile, club-footed Byron was frankly pictured with the "reprobate pack"—Hone, Carlile, et al.—"Who Blasphemy, Treason, Rebellion, exhibit," in a Tory imitation of Hone and Cruikshank's *House That Jack Built,* as "THE DEVIL, / . . . By mischief disguised in the dress of a Peer.— / Pursue the old method, you'll find out the cheat, / And the Imp stand confessed, if you look at his feet" (*Dorchester Guide* 7, 31).

For the first time, a high-literary author and his high-Tory publisher were thus yoked together in serious condemnation with the "insect abusers" of the press. Publicly, Byron was baffled. "How—or in what manner *you* can be considered responsible for what *I* publish—I am at a loss to conceive," he wrote Murray on 8 February 1822, a letter the publisher forwarded to the papers for circulation:

> I desire you will say, that both *you* and Mr. *Gifford* remonstrated against the publication . . . that *I* alone occasioned it—& I alone am the person who legally or otherwise should bear the burthen. (*Letters* 9: 103)[45]

Gifford, the *Quarterly*'s editor, was an old friend. "[He] is too wise a man to think that such things can have any *serious* effect—*who* was ever altered by a poem?" (Byron to Murray, 3 November 1821, *Letters* 9: 53). But the *Quarterly* came out for prosecution, and despite the "intimidating intellectual task for counsel and judges alike" (Thomas, *Long Time* 125), Byron might have faced it as well as Murray. Indeed, he promised him to return from Europe to do so.

The point, explained the *Quarterly,* was not Byron's authorial intentions but the "tendency" of his play's "effects" upon those new thousands of readers to whom cheap piracies introduced it, "on whom its poison would operate without mitigation" (April 1822: 127–28). The *London Magazine* was "far from imputing intentional impiety," though "[the work's] language sometimes shocks us" (January 1822: 71), but agreed that it was "calculated to extinguish in young minds all generous enthusiasm" (*Edinburgh Review,* February 1822: 451). "Mock[ing]" and "argumentative blasphemy" were the "great staple[s] of the piece" (449, 438); its very mention of the old mysteries was "offensive" (437). In short, Jeffrey concluded, poets made "unexceptionable *witnesses*" but "suspected *judges*" and "not often very safe advocates, where great questions are concerned": those who could not "confine" themselves to the "established creed and morality of their country" ought to be "banished" (438). Again, Eldon refused to grant copyright, and *Cain* sold like hot cakes in pirate editions. "If Cain be 'blasphemous,' " Byron protested, "Paradise Lost is blasphemous"; the "personages" speak only "according to their characters; and the strongest passions have ever been permitted to the drama" (Byron to Murray, 8 February 1822, *Letters* 9: 103). He was ignored. The *Quarterly* was right: a work was "susceptible of . . . literary outlawry" in precise "proportion to its originality" (April 1822: 136). But one of Byron's critics at least took the lesson of *Cain* to heart. It was Talfourd who wrote that careful review in the *London Magazine*. Twenty years later, he reproduced Byron's argument in defending Shelley's *Mab*: it took one generation for a statement of literary defiance to become a means to establish the authority of Literature, with a capital L.

What we might call the "Byron effect" on copyright law and literary property reached a last peak in January 1824, when John Hunt was found guilty of libeling the late George III for publishing the poet's *Vision of Judgment*, a savage parody of Southey's verse obituary. This was the first criminal trial for publishing a poem.[46] (Carlile promptly reprinted it.) The end result might have been the unthinkable: a high-literary prosecution for blasphemy initiated by government itself. But three months later Byron was dead, two years after the "striking" "visitation" that conveniently drowned "Mr. BYSHE SHELLY [sic], the author of that abominable and blasphemous book called QUEEN MAB" (*John Bull,* 11 August 1822: 693; see also *Real John Bull,* 18 August 1822: 663). The pirates ran out of fresh texts, and government—worn out by Carlile's volunteers—finally stopped the policy of nonstop prosecution in which Hunt had been embroiled. Death quieted what had not been resolved. The issue of blasphemy's bearing on copyright was held over until the 1840s when a different cultural climate and a strengthened sense of Literature's value made for a different outcome.[47]

By the 1840s, *Queen Mab* was long established as *the* inspirational underground text: "Compared with this," said the *Investigator,* "*Don Juan* is a moral poem and *Cain* a homily" ("Licentious Productions in High Life," October 1822: 361). Pirates, blasphemers, and the foot soldiers of the unstamped had remained loyal to *Mab* through twenty years. Shelley secretly fostered their interest in his own lifetime; when he died, Carlile interrupted coverage of his sister's blasphemy trial to announce, "This beautiful poem is again in full sale at a reduced price," in response to renewed Vice Society activity (*Republican,* 1 February 1822: 145).[48] *Queen Mab* had an enormous popular circulation, doing sterling duty as radical "cannon shot" (Wickwar 259). Thus, it turns out, Henry Hetherington had a subsidiary motive for indicting Moxon: he himself had just put out another pirate edition of this favorite work, and attaching Moxon for blasphemy might baffle the matter of copyright, and keep *Mab* cheaply in public domain.

The resurgent connection of blasphemy and copyright was further demonstrated in the exact identity of the arguments Talfourd employed in his copyright speeches and his 1841 defense of Moxon. In his 1837 copyright speech, as in his argument for Shelley and *Mab,* he told and retold the lives of the English poets; he insisted on the special individuality of the author, as opposed to a mere "mechanical" inventor (deserving only a patent of seven years); he linked copyright to "the familiar Romantic values of permanence, totality, and expressive wholeness" (Vanden Bossche 45). In making this argument, the living example of William Wordsworth was crucial. An important twenty-page essay of 1815 had first set the Lakeland Seer at top of the nation's poetic hierarchy; in 1837 Talfourd confirmed the assessment. It was entirely natural that he should have done so: he was himself the precocious author of the earlier, influential "Estimate [of] the Poetical Talent of the Present Age" for the *Pamphleteer;*[49] and Wordsworth reached the peak of his influence during his lifetime following Moxon's triumphant six-volume collected edition of his *Works* in 1836–37, reprinted at least six times by 1850.

Moreover, Talfourd was not indebted to Wordsworth for his example alone. His rhetoric in the copyright debates draws particularly on Wordsworth's prefaces; as Martha Woodmansee puts it, Wordsworth "virtually orchestrat[ed]" the legislation.[50] And Wordsworth's influence deeply penetrates Talfourd's 1841 speech in Moxon and Shelley's defense: the uncanny echoes noticed above were not uncanny at all. Talfourd was part of the circle within which the *Prelude* circulated in manuscript, and direct echoes of that great poem create his most effective courtroom moments, especially the central plea for publication of the *complete* works of any poet, since without access to early mistakes we cannot trace "the growth of his mind" (*Speech for the Defendant* 24).

Copyright legislation passed out of Talfourd's hands in 1842, but he was not un-instrumental in securing its passage. Feather ascribes Mahon's success and Talfourd's failures from 1837 to 1841 to the one's politic decision to compromise in the face of radical opposition to any more "taxes on knowledge," and the other's inexperience (besides his subsequent loss of his seat in 1841).[51] But Mahon's bill also passed in 1842, as Feather records, because Thomas Macaulay threw his support behind it and helped reshape it, although fourteen months earlier he had dramatically denounced the entire principle of monopolistic postmortem copyright, which would impose a "tax on readers for the purpose of giving a bounty to writers" and excessive profits to publishers (Macaulay, *Speeches* 164), and might result in the suppression of "questionable" works.[52]

What had caused Macaulay's "conversion" (Feather 146)? It needed more urging, I think, than Mahon's carrot of compromise, the reduction of the

postmortem period from sixty to twenty-five years that Macaulay argued
away in favor of a flat forty-two year term. It needed the public spectacle
of Moxon's arraignment for "blasphemy" by that "insect abuser of the
press," Henry Hetherington; it needed the lining-up of that "Champion
of the Unstamped" against Her Majesty's distributor of stamps for Westmoreland, William Wordsworth, luminary of the *Quarterly* coterie that had
skewered Hone in 1822 and thundered against Byron's *Cain,* and the author
of a Jeremiad *Warning* to national leaders against capitulating to radical
demands (1833 [published 1835]);[53] it needed the blasphemous counterclaim
of the unwashed to a cheap share in high-literary Shelley's dangerous commodity. The "celebrated" trial of Edward Moxon, Wordsworth's publisher
and friend of poets, and the terms of Talfourd's defense, not only permanently impacted the evolution of blasphemy but raised all the stakes of the
copyright debate. Between them, unwilling Moxon and martyr Hetherington may have ensured the passage of the act of 1842.

It was not that Moxon blasphemes against God, Talfourd suggested in
1841, but that "mute inglorious" Hetherington who indicted him (and
whose figure conveniently occluded the legal establishment's that oversaw
the prosecution), "blaspheme[s] the Muse!" (Tennyson, "Princess" 5.119).
Twenty years before, literature *was* blasphemy—atheistical *Mab,* heretical
Cain. In 1841 Hetherington and his ilk were seen to blaspheme *against*
Literature. England had come to recognize, as one reviewer of Tennyson
put it in 1831, how far poets "can command the sympathies of unnumbered
hearts; they can disseminiate principles" (*Westminster Review,* January 1831:
224). The transformation had roots in the late eighteenth century, and
would take forty years to consolidate; it is one of the contexts and motive
forces in the *Freethinker* trials of 1883.[54] But passage of the Copyright Act
of 1842 was a long first step in that consolidation. Litterateur Monckton
Milnes even retorted to radical criticism during the debates of 1841—picking up the thread of Talfourd's argument for *Mab*'s noncriminality—that
the Bible itself could seem immoral when quoted out of context. He went
on to reinforce the idea that the individual poem gained its value in relation
to the complete oeuvre, ultimately looking for its value to the sacred person
of the author. Talfourd's own Wordsworthian emphasis on death as the
moment that consecrates literary fame similarly put down a legal foundation for belief in the nation's writers not only as Carlylean "heroes" but as
secular saints, "divine" types (*Speech for the Defendant* 24), fit prophets of
the "genuine Church-*Homiletic*" that Carlyle himself declared extant in
English Literature in *Sartor Resartus,* 1833–34 (191). The conveniently pre-
mature deaths of the younger Romantics not only curtailed the danger they

represented to the literary property system and the operation of criminal law but also allowed their recuperation for that replacement religion.

Above all others, Talfourd said, Wordsworth had dedicated his life to a "high and holy course, gradually impressing thoughtful minds with the sense of truth made visible in the severest forms of beauty" (*Speech of Serjeant Talfourd* 13). He was the prime and perfect type of the spiritual literary guide to whom the nation owed a gentlemanly living, a fact Wordsworth himself felt so urgently that, as support for Talfourd's copyright bills dwindled between 1837 and 1841, he stepped out of Talfourd's shadow to campaign in person, persuading Carlyle and thirty-odd others to join him in petitioning Parliament.[55] He had hoped for complete restoration of "the ancient rights of authorship" (*Speech of Serjeant Talfourd* 6), "perpetual copyright," which was "never disputed until literature . . . received a fatal present in the first act of Parliament for its encouragement" in 1710 (3–4). Talfourd's bills in all their successive versions were thus already a disappointment; Mahon's act of 1842 as Macaulay reshaped it fell well short of expectations. The will to faith, towards a Literature that could stabilize and uplift a nation, and the urge to capitalistic accumulation have rarely shown their potential for close relationship so very clearly.

The Moxon case of 1841 had thus lifted high-literary works beyond reach of criminal action; blasphemy had solved the legal equation—arrived at with copyright passage—that separated authors from "insect abusers" of the press, genuine books from pirate thefts, and works of the "Imagination" from "illegitimate" parodies and plain works for the people: Haslam's *Letters,* say, from George Eliot's translation of *Das Leben Jesu,* or Hone's *Political Litany* from Byron's parody of the Ten Commandments. The Romantic claim to "inspiration" became not only a subversive counterclaim against the exclusive status of Scripture in the very terms by which its apologists distinguished "the word of God" from "the word of man" (Rennell viii) but also an excluding claim to differentiation from popular print. High Literature was truth, the rest was an imposture; and blasphemy was the figure through which both extremes expressed the equation. Talfourd had his own editorial role in enforcing the separation. He minimized mention of his mentor Lamb's friendship with "Arch blasphemer" William Hone in his influential *Sketch of his Life,* and expunged all of Lamb's many irreligious jokes. Lamb became a literary saint, never to be imagined breaking his nose when "inspired with new rum" (*Letters* 1: xiv), never to be heard uttering flippant "impieties" about Wordsworth and other "idols" (De Quincey 1848, in Lamb, *Charles Lamb* 25–26). "In [Talfourd's] hands," as a later editor remarked, "all vulgar associations disappear" (Fitzgerald xi).[56]

Moxon, publishing the volume, likewise forgot Lamb's devotion to the "Esteemed Editor" whom he himself had once courted.[57]

By all these developments, mere popular "literacy" such as Hetherington had promoted was sundered from "Literature," a division pending for twenty years and evident in the differing uses to which the latter word was put by 1819: when Cobbett called the Blasphemous and Seditious Libels Act of that year an assault on "those engaged in literary pursuits" in his famous letter to the bishop of Landaff, he did not have in mind the same "gentlemen of literary attainments" whom Canning thought should not be "exposed" to so "odious a punishment" for the crime as the public pillory (*Political Register,* 27 January 1820: 720, 772). In extolling the virtues of copyright in 1837, Talfourd wiped from consideration "the words of ill omen" and radical promise attached to the Copyright Act of 1710, "the further encouragement of learning," substituting instead the phrase "justice to learning" (*Speech of Serjeant Talfourd* 8). The people who bought two-penny trash and pirate works were not the "nation" whose right to great Literature was established in 1842 but an undeserving "mass"; national "gratitude" to the literary great would no longer be thwarted by "leaving . . . the[ir] fame to be frittered away by abridgments—polluted by base intermixtures" of the kind the cheap pressmen produced (11).

The nation needed Moxons, not Teggs. In the 1840s Wordsworth's publisher also became the source of a new model series of cheap reprints of English authors, all duly paid for and modestly priced at two shillings and sixpence per volume, without "conform[ing]," as the *Quarterly* put it, "to the tactics of the enemy" (April 1822: 133).[58] The idea of *stealing words* made Moxon weak at the knees: as an "unlettered, self-taught" young man, he had once proudly defended an unwitting plagiarism from Goldsmith and Pope in his first slender volume of poems, *The Prospect,* 1826 (viii); he worked closely with Talfourd and Wordsworth on changing the copyright law.[59] Thomas Tegg, Hone's actual and Dickens's would-be employer, put out perhaps four thousand cheap reprints in his career (Feather 127); he was Cleave's partner in the piratical *Parley's Penny Library;* and he was a vociferous opponent of copyright, who fought his self-interested cause with some eloquence. It was in the "interest of this nation to keep this protection down to the minimum point at which the object can be accomplished— in other words, to secure to the public the freest possible access to the best possible work upon the cheapest possible terms" (1842, qtd. in Vanden Bossche 53). He was dismissed with contempt, nonetheless: "Mr. Tegg seems to think literary labor as easy to be valued as any other labor," sniffed the *Eclectic Review* (qtd. 56); while Wordsworth and Carlyle declined to "fall prey" to an "extraneous person,"[60] and the Dickens circle made jokes about the *"Tegg*-rity of literary property" (*Letters of Charles Dickens* 4: 581n).

Piracy as practiced by blasphemers and radicals from the 1810s "permanently enlarged the book-reading public" (R. Williams, *Revolution* 185): "There is more than one kind of hunger that will break through barriers," one blasphemer wrote in the "Hungry Forties," "and I have taken with an unlicensed hand . . . what I know to be wanted by those who stand at the anvil and the loom" (Holyoake, *Logic of Facts* iv). In publishing *Queen Mab* as part of his edition of Shelley's *Works,* Moxon reclaimed as a literary property—reclaimed for Literature—a text that had been in common, not to say vulgar and blasphemous, domain for nearly thirty years; *Mab* was included in a new edition of 1847 without any incident. And in bringing an action against him, Henry Hetherington not only exposed the classist partiality of the law against blasphemy but also ironically started a historical chain reaction that may yet end in the utter contraction of common domain. After 1842, the law's defense against piracy was greatly strengthened. As Martha Woodmansee suggests, spinning out the "Author Effect" to the Disney copyright hearings of 1995, copyright may yet prove the most effective "tax on knowledge" capitalism could have devised.

3. JACOB HOLYOAKE AND OTHER "PRIESTS" OF THE *ORACLE*

It was in recognition of his services to cheap publication and mass education that Jacob Holyoake, prosecuted for blasphemy in 1842, founder of organized Secularism, was made the first chairman of the Rationalist Press Association. He was the workingman hungry for knowledge who "t[ook] with an unlicensed hand . . . what I know to be wanted by those who stand at the anvil and the loom" (*Logic of Facts* iv). Education was "Self-Help" by the people, Holyoake believed; and "Self-thought, which is the original name for Freethought, . . . is the first means of self-help," since "[p]eople who think for us, sometimes do for us" (*Logic of Life* 4,7). This was not exactly what Samuel Smiles meant by the term he made famous in his bestseller of 1859, *Self-Help,* so that it comes as no surprise to find an 1841 rejection letter from him amongst the papers in the Holyoake Collection, London, turning down Holyoake's manuscript and incidentally regretting that he has lost it.[61] The "Cabinet of Reason" was Holyoake's child as well as Watson's, and the *Logic of Facts* one of the shelf full of home study books he wrote from the mid-1840s. He forwarded Freethought's mission when he opened the London Bookstore, 147 Fleet Street, with its "Eclectic Catalogue" of literature and "Works of Inquiry" on "proscribed subjects" (catalogue, in HC); scanty financing kept him writing begging letters through the 1850s for his overambitious Central Secular Book Depot.[62] Holyoake's *Movement: anti-persecution gazette, and register of progress* (1843–46) kept the atheistical and educative impetus of Owenite socialism alive in difficult years; his *Reasoner* (1846–61) was the solitary journal to keep the Freethought flag flying through the 1850s.[63] Jacob Holyoake was almost a Victorian sage, almost one of the radical colossi of the nineteenth century. His recovery from blasphemy and his other life as what one critic called "this new Master of Sentences" (Martin 6) will concern us later (see below, 5.4). Our first concern is with the circumstances and the political aftermath of his trial for blasphemy in 1842.

Holyoake was the son of a Birmingham whitesmith and followed his father's trade from the age of nine until he was twenty-three. But he was a product of the city's Mechanics' Institute and lively radical culture as much as of its industry. He joined the Birmingham Reform League in 1831 at age fourteen, the Chartists in 1832, and the Owenites in 1838. Shortly afterwards he was appointed a "Social Missionary." "[A]ll the religions of the world were wrong," Robert Owen had declared at the London Tavern in 1817, the year Holyoake was born (Holyoake, *Sixty Years* 1: 4): Holyoake came quickly to share his unbelief, though Owenism accommodated a wide range, from atheists to "Rational Religionists" to nonconformist Christians.
Between 1840 and 1842 the tension of that accommodation suddenly increased. Bishop Phillpotts of Exeter denounced Owenite circulation of "blasphemous and immoral" publications in the House of Lords. Several openly heterodox "Social Missionaries" lost their jobs, while others "sought safety" by taking an oath of belief in the Bible (*Sixty Years* 1: 141–42). Owenism's organ, the *New Moral World*, justified the policy of compromise: "the wet blanket of orthodoxy," Holyoake wrote, "[was] drawn around the shoulders of Socialism" (*Spirit of Bonner* 4). His response was to join the "Defiant Syndicate of Four" that began issuing the *Oracle of Reason*, the first outspokenly atheistical periodical published in English, perhaps in any language, in Bristol in 1841 (*Sixty Years* 1: 142). Its aim was to "deal out Atheism"—not the Deism of Paine's *Age of Reason* or Haslam's *Letters*, but straightforward unbelief—"as freely as ever Christianity was dealt out to the people" (opening editorial, *Oracle of Reason*, 6 November 1841: 1). The plain "voice" of "undisguised Atheism" demanded to be heard (Holyoake, qtd. in Grugel 37). Horror was the inevitable reaction. Holyoake would be the *Oracle*'s second editor: the first did not last long.[64] His name was Charles Southwell. He merits attention as Holyoake's first mentor in blasphemy.

Southwell aspired to be the "Oracle" in a more literary fashion than Hetherington made himself the "Poor Man's Guardian." He had read widely, the benefit of youthful friendship with a middle-class mentor.[65] Nearly every piece in the first numbers came from his pen, and those that did not carried their authors' names, an innovation in journalism later revived by G. W. Foote: denying the divine author developed a fascination with authorship, and anonymity would not serve the purpose of confrontation that was the *Oracle*'s whole raison d'être. "Whether this paper . . . will be permitted by the authorities of this country time alone can determine," Southwell began by declaring (6 November 1841: 1). Blunt investigations of the "evidence" for God's existence, with articles on science, mathematics, and natural history (the pre-Darwinian "Theory of Regular Gradation"), were not enough to provoke prosecution, however, and three issues without battle joined were enough to try his patience to the limits. Competitiveness was in the blood: Southwell was the youngest of thirty-three children, and "the liveliest of them all" (Holyoake, *Sixty Years* 1: 109).

What is more, one brother was an actor who "appeared some 15 or 16 years since at Drury Lane as Romeo," and Southwell himself had "smelt the lamps" (letter to Holyoake, 3 April 1842, in HL). For the aspirant first "Priest" of the *Oracle,* trial was drama and living literature. That belief links him to Carlile's associate the "Reverend" Robert Taylor, would-be author of Byronic tragedy and the actual author of *Swing: Or, Who Are the Incendiaries?* His severe two years' sentence for blasphemy immediately demonstrated the political risks of dramatic effect: Southwell fancied himself the hero much as Taylor featured himself on stage as "Robert the Devil, Or the Genius of Reason," plotting dramatically to "catch the conscience of the King!" (*Swing* 18; 1.1).[66]

As manuscript letters reveal, the *Oracle* gang communicated among themselves in a private language of subversive Shakespeareanisms: "rank disease befouls" Owenism's looks (Chilton to Holyoake, 24 December 1841, in HL); Southwell will persist in blasphemy "though hell should gape" (Southwell to Holyoake, 1 March 1842, HL); he "dare not write all I feel, yet I dare do all that may become a man" (19 February 1842, HL); Holyoake's note "screw[s] my courage to the sticking point" (26 October 1842, HL). Shakespeare gave gloss and heritage to atheistical materialism: "Gentlemen," Southwell told his jury, when he finally faced trial, "the learned counsel told you that I wished to reduce man to a level with the brutes. No: I wish to elevate [him] . . . for as it is said—'What a piece of work is man! How noble in reason! how infinite in faculty! in form and moving, how express and admirable!'" (*Trial of Charles Southwell* 30). Not to see his meaning, the prosecution's mind must be "cabin'd, cribb'd, confin'd"

(31). The *Oracle* whose outlandish style of plain speaking owed much to its authors' access to Shakespeare finished life heavily subsidized by a free-thinking Shakespearean scholar from Oxford, W. J. Birch (later Holyoake's benefactor), while the editor who thought to play Hamlet to Holyoake's Horatio (Southwell to Holyoake, 19 February 1842, in HL) ended up shuf-fled off as Polonius (Southwell to Holyoake, 3 APRIL 1842, HL).

The *Oracle*'s Shakespeare was the same radical prophet who penned epi-graphs to the *Three Trials of William Hone* and Holyoake's *History of Co-operation:* "Thrice the brindled cat hath mewed.—*Macbeth*"; "Distribution shall undo excess, / And each man have enough.—*King Lear.*" For the blasphemers as for the Chartists of the 1840s—like Thomas Cooper—liter-ature retained the revolutionary power Shelley claimed for it, and Shake-speare offered an alternative authority to Holy Writ's. If *Mab* was the "Chartist's Bible," Shakespeare's *Works* were the "Bible of Humanity" and the "Bible of Genius": "Its light is the light of daily life. Its wisdom is human and can be judged by [the] common sense of common people" (Holyoake, *Secular Review*, 6 August 1876: 3). Nor did graduating from the one to the other (like Kingsley's hero of 1850) necessarily turn a firebrand into a citizen, or divorce political from religious discontent. The *Oracle*'s Shakespeare was a different author than the Bard exalted in the expensive volumes put out by the Shakespeare Society from 1841, though a similar desire for a text with "relic-status" led the society's director, John Payne Collier, to forge (and profitably to publish) "contemporary" marginal emendations to a 1632 folio.[67] (Dickens subscribed from the society's found-ing [diary, 31 December 1840, in *Letters* 2: 462], and Talfourd was on its council; Mr. Wopsle's appearance as Hamlet in *Great Expectations* remains the perfect comic mediation between common literate and literary apprecia-tion of Shakespeare.) Shakespeare was not easily molded to the disciplinary ends of high Victorian culture: "[I]f some of the finest writers," as Southwell said in court, "give vent to . . . blasphemy, it becomes necessary that you should consider more deeply . . . what blasphemy is; and whether it may not be a good thing" (*Trial of Charles Southwell* 74).

Where Shakespearean self-assertion led in 1841 was to number 4 of the *Oracle of Reason.* Its main feature was Southwell's confessedly "rash" and perhaps "absurd" savaging of the Old Testament (*Trial* 71). He took up the cudgels where Haslam laid off. "[T]hat revoltingly odious . . . [p]roduc-tion called 'Bible' " was "a history of lust, sodomies, wholesale slaughtering, and horrible depravity" (*Oracle of Reason* 27 November 1841: 25). Its proph-ets were "impudent mouthers" who "vomit[ed] . . . sublime balderdash:" Isaiah, for example, "who talks of eating his own dung." If its heroes were to "play their villainous pranks in these times," they would be "strung up to the first lamp post." "Of course," Southwell mocked, "the *better-to-be-safe* 'TRUE believers,' will call this blasphemy, in which they have our full permission; while *infidels* who . . . have acquired a sort of shabby-genteel character with the orthodox, will . . . talk about 'respecting prejudices,' 'public mind not prepared,' & c." (25). Other passages featured in court, but it was this diatribe that sparked an indictment.[68] As Levy remarks, it "beggars paraphrase" (*Blasphemy* 450). Distastefully titled "The Jew Book," the piece retains its power to offend.

What offended in 1841 was not what offends today, however. Victorian atheists were as likely to stoop to racial sneering as the rest of Victorian society. Speculations like Emile Burnouf's in *La Science des Religions* that we owe the seeds of Christianity not to the "Semite" with his "frizzled hair, thick lips, small calves, flat feet," and stunted brain, but to the manly "theological" Aryan, whose "brain . . . may go on growing all his life," were given a wide hearing, though, as Matthew Arnold remarked in 1873, they "almost take away the breath of a mere man of letters" (*Literature and Dogma* 135–37). Or think of the ludicrous late-century fantasy of Christianity's lost "Egyptian" heritage fed by popular writers like Marie Corelli. The anti-Semitism of the Freethought movement was more limited and more functional; even Southwell later played Shylock sympathetically—too sympathetically for the taste of the Melbourne *Age,* to whom his flights of "rhetorical declamation" indicated a fundamental forgetting "that the character represented was a crafty, sordid, revengeful Jew; and not a bold open declarer of a conscious wrong" (Pearce 10).[69] By identifying the Old Testament exclusively with an unpopular minority and a more "primitive" people, Freethought's assaults on the Bible incidentally gained ground: anti-Semitism was an alienation tactic. The *Freethinker* turned several of the same tasteless tricks, even under Foote's Jewish successor, Chapman Cohen; the magazine's notorious "comic Bible" cartoons feature caricature Jews with exaggerated features.

What the Victorian establishment saw in the *Oracle of Reason,* however, was the offense of cheap publication, an insult to the Bible, and an attempt to undermine the intellectual class system (*Trial of Charles Southwell* 7–9). Above all, there was the threat offered by "language as abominable and execrable as is the [atheistical] principle inculcated," of which the "Jew Book" article was the "concentrated" example (101). Southwell had announced his offensive policy in the first number: "[A]ll articles admitted into these columns will be studiedly plain and simple." He would suffer no "cant," "ornament," "glare of language," or "wordy uncertainty" (*Oracle of Reason,* 6 November 1841: 2). "[T]hose who may be shocked at the coarseness of our language," he followed up in the "Jew Book" article, "should study the holy fathers and early saints, who if they had . . . finished their *divine* studies in Billingsgate, could not have been more coarse or indecent" (27 November: 26–27).[70] Class identity and overidentification with the "old and rude language" that Hone also had loved about earlier literature copro- duced Charles Southwell as a Victorian word criminal.

Legal vengeance was swift. "[I]t is for you, by your verdict," Tory Judge Wetherall ominously instructed the jury, "to state whether you are prepared to go along with the writer of these publications in the establishment of Atheism" and the setting-up of "an atheistical press" (*Trial of Charles South-well* 102). They took only ten minutes to find Southwell guilty. He was sentenced to twelve months in Bristol Gaol and a fine of a hundred pounds. He cooled his heels but not his rhetoric in Bristol Gaol, surviving to inflame Australia and New Zealand a few years later, before an ostentatious submis- sion to Christianity. Each of his successors as editor of the *Oracle* met a similarly harsh fate, Holyoake first.

Holyoake was not directly prosecuted for the journal. The route to trial at Gloucester Assizes, 15 August 1842, took several detours. On 24 May, Holyoake tramped to Cheltenham, Gloucestershire, en route to Bristol to visit Southwell in jail and to look for work. It was not an inviting venue for the Owenite lecture he was to give: "genteel and thin," a Chartist friend called it (qtd. in A. Taylor 30). His topic was a pressing working-class issue of the day, "Home Colonization as a Means of Superseding Poor Laws and Emigration."[71] The subject should hardly have laid Holyoake open to a charge of blasphemy. But the *Oracle* made him a target. It marked him out even within Owenism. "Commenced editing *Oracle of Reason or Philosophy Vindicated* for Charles Southwell," reads his diary entry for 24 and 25 Janu- ary 1842. And immediately, "Menaced by Board with loss of lectureship" ("Log Book," no. 1, in HC). He resigned.[72] If Sheffield Owenites wanted no "Priest of the *Oracle*" as their teacher and "Social Missionary," then the burghers of Cheltenham had understandably stronger prejudices, against Owenites as well as atheists, and saw its chance to smear the one by associa- tion with the other.

Holyoake had given ample cause for alarm. The self-righteous plain speaker of twenty-five was both too eager for martyrdom and too hopeful of leniency.[73] In the first number of the *Oracle* that he edited, he gave out the "Jew-Book" article as the "lesson" of the day, and "engage[d] to defend" "every word" of its "boldness" (*Spirit of Bonner* 3). Holyoake wrote the description of Christianity's "hellish mission" that the court singled out as blasphemous during the trial of his friend George Adams, sentenced to a month's imprisonment for merely selling the number that contained it (no. 25), half an hour before he stepped into the same dock.[74] "How sickly is that morality," Holyoake pronounced in his most red-hot production, an account of Southwell's arrest, "which will look upon crime and shudder if [it is] called by its right name" (*Spirit of Bonner* 10). Without morality for "salt," the "stench and putrefaction" of Christianity were overpowering (5). To his own judge, he declared himself "incapable of employing language you are fortunate in being able to adapt to your conscience" (*History of the Last Trial* 43–44). "The principle on which we proceeded with our *Oracle*," Holyoake explained in his 1850 memoir, *The History of the Last Trial by Jury for Atheism in England,* "was that every man should express himself in his own words and in his own way" (65). He clarified the point in 1843 as secretary of the Anti-Persecution Union: "We demand . . . unlimited freedom of expression . . . in writing, reading, or speaking, in all the varieties of language, the strongest or the mildest, which make man intelligible and different from the brute" (preface, *God v. Paterson* iii).[75] The free use of "his own words" was one of the "rights" of man (88). But the next forty years of Holyoake's life would see the secure establishment of "Received" or "Standard" English, born around 1750 and "embalmed" by the new public schools, "with their cult of uniformity" (R. Williams, *Revolution* 247). His demand was a recipe for criminal class confrontation.

It produced immediate effects in 1842. At the end of his Cheltenham lecture, a local teetotaler and preacher named Maitland asked whether Holyoake envisaged chapels in the utopian community that he had sketched. He wanted a statement of unbelief and he got it, in words that were not only "frank" but "indecorous," as the *History of the Last Trial* characteristically understates it (5), and criminally "distinct."[76]

> Our national debt already hangs like a millstone round the poor man's neck, and our national church and general religious institutions cost us, upon accredited computation, about twenty millions annually. Worship being thus expensive, I appeal to your heads and your pockets whether we are not too poor to have a God? If poor men cost the state as much, they would be put like officers upon half-pay, and while our distress lasts I think it would be wise to do the same thing with deity. (5)

"Terms of audacity" indeed (*Sixty Years* 1: 143). Holyoake added,

> I, not being religious, cannot propose [chapels]. Morality I regard, but I do not believe there is such a thing as a God. The pulpit says "Search the Scriptures," and they who are thus trepanned get imprisoned in Bristol jail, like my friend Mr. Southwell. For myself, I flee the Bible as a viper, and revolt at the touch of a Christian. (*History of the Last Trial* 5)

An outraged report in the conservative *Cheltenham Chronicle,* a local clergyman's organ, produced an indictment. Quixotic Holyoake, who had already left for Bristol, walked all the way back to "defend myself from attacks"

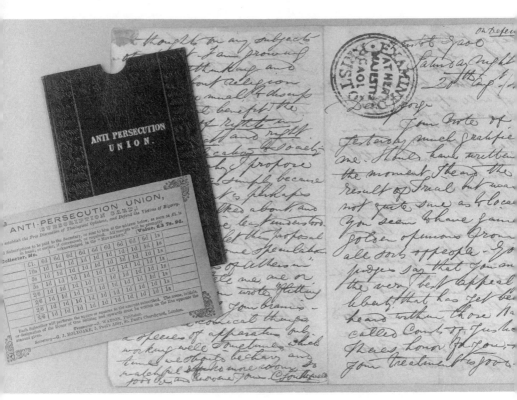

Figure 6. Blasphemy memorabilia: a letter from Southwell to Holyoake, stamped as "Examined at Her Majesty's Gaol, Bristol"; and Holyoake's Anti-Persecution Union membership card, with its case. Courtesy of the Co-operative Union, Manchester, Holyoake Collection.

("Log Book," no. 1, in HC). Policemen joined a new audience, on 2 June, to hear him descant on free speech. They never showed him a warrant when he finished, but he was arrested anyway ("Apprehended for blasphemy," he wrote in his diary ["Log Book"]). The whole audience joined in the procession to the station. Next morning, he was brought before the magistrates, two of them clergymen; summarily committed for trial; and held in a cell for two weeks prior to trial because he refused on principle to swear an oath to his own recognizances to the amount of a hundred pounds (*Sixty Years* 1: 153). In revenge, the warders withheld the books he needed to prepare his defense, and the magistrates gloated in telling him the court would not listen to it (1: 157).

The case quickly became a cause célèbre, national and local. Questions about the "brutal" irregularity of Holyoake's arrest were asked in parliament (Grugel 26); Home Secretary Sir James Graham's swift passing of a bill assigning all trials for "opinion" to assize courts obviated the possibility of more magistrate-administered "Cheltenham law." In Cheltenham, the *Free Press* devoted almost half its closely printed columns to a report of the trial on 20 August 1842; ordinary offenders like William Buy, arrested for stealing a jacket, were dismissed to ten years' transportation in two lines.

What most offended "thin and genteel" Cheltenham, it turned out, were two particular phrases in Holyoake's response to Maitland's question. His parting shot—"I flee the Bible as a viper, and revolt at the touch of a Christian"—was not quoted in the indictment; Judge Erskine was astounded to hear Holyoake himself repeat to the jury what had so "strong" a "sting" (*Free Press*, 20 August 1842: 270). The first of the phrases at issue was "I do not believe there is such a thing as a God." The word "thing" was the problem: mechanical, mundane, derogatory. Holyoake could not remember using it, nor does it appear in the *Oracle*'s 4 June report of the event. But he accepted the burden of dealing with it, as in his cross-examination of the prosecution's witness, a *Chronicle* compositor called James Bartram:

> *Prisoner*—Did you think I uttered those words maliciously and wickedly[?]
> *Witness*—According to my opinion you uttered them wickedly. I felt horror run through me when I heard them. . . .
> *Prisoner*—Did I use the word "thing" in a contemptuous manner? Did I lay particular emphasis on the word "thing"?
> *Witness*—You did not lay any particular emphasis on the word "thing" but you used the word. (*Free Press*, 20 August 1842: 267)

Above all, Cheltenham was outraged by the proposal to put the deity, like common soldiers in peacetime, on "half pay." The term made God a wage slave. It had earned "a general expression of applause" from Holyoake's audience, Bartram had told the magistrates who first examined him (deposition, in HL); it was what the jury "could not get over," the foreman later confided (Carlile to Holyoake, 1 September 1842, in HL). In court, Judge Erskine offered a way of escape: if Holyoake meant only to imply that clergymen's salaries should be reduced, an accommodation might be reached. But Holyoake was "plead[ing] for free speech," recorded his biographer Joseph MacCabe, and left "no alternative" but to convict (1: 77).

"Every man" had the "right to be heard in his own way, and in his own words," Holyoake claimed (*God v. Paterson* 88). But "his own words" were precisely the problem. The charge that he had used outrageous language was absolutely founded in class prejudice. "I do not like always to speak in grave and measured phraseology," Holyoake said (*Free Press*, 20 August

1842: 270). Terms like "half pay" were not chosen to be deliberately "offensive" or "shocking," but because they were suited to his lower-class audience. "I made use of that figure of speech because I thought they would
understand it better, and they did understand it" (*History of the Last Trial*
44).

This was not acceptable argumentation in a community (as expressed
by its *Chronicle*) that had slapped on Holyoake the classist label "poor mis-
guided wretch" before the indictment was even served (*History of the Last
Trial* 32). When it arrived, it turned out to have demoted him from the
"Mathematical Teacher" (22) he was into a common "laborer"; he shortly
after declined into "miscreant" and out-and-out "monster" (*Free Press*, 20
August 1842: 267), while the socialism he expounded was "devilism" (Mac-
Cabe 1: 65). Holyoake wondered if the jury "had expected to see some
griffin appear before you" (*Free Press* 267). Trial for blasphemy became a
ritual of social degradation. After arrest, he was forced to walk nine miles
to Gloucester in handcuffs and conspicuously attended by two policemen
(Holyoake, *History of the Last Trial* 12). Passing judgment, Mr. Justice
Erskine put the crowning touch to the proceedings: "George Jacob Holyoake," he intoned, *"You have been convicted of uttering language"* (*History
of the Last Trial* 64, my emphasis).[77] Two minutes of "his own words" cost
Holyoake six months in Gloucester Gaol. In his absence, his family struggled to eat and his little daughter died (fig. 7). The human consequences
of the defiance that had elated him during trial, and sustained him in imprisonment, as his letters reveal, suddenly came home.[78]

Judge Erskine's extraordinary terms—dry, judicial, terminologically correct—are worth meditating on. They exposed in its unpleasant nakedness
the class assumption that the poor man had no right to use "his own language" to express his own opinions. In fact, he had no right to language
at all. Locke's pronouncement—words can be "no man's private possession" (qtd. in Willinsky 40)—holds less practical force for the nineteenth
century than Humpty Dumpty's linguistic challenge: "which is to be master?—that's all" (qtd. 136). In exactly the same terms Holyoake might have
been found guilty of "uttering" forged banknotes, "the most dangerous
crime" one could commit "in a commercial country" (James Boswell, qtd.
in Haywood 61). The death penalty for passing fake one-pound notes was
a recent memory, abolished shortly after Hone and Cruikshank whipped
up a scandal in 1819 with a caricature "Bank Restriction Note" signed by
hangman "Jack Ketch."[79] There is more at work in Judge Erskine's phrase
than the oddity of legal terminology,[80] or a recognition that words are the
"counters, or paper money" of another signifying system, as in a passage
from W. J. Fox that Holyoake quotes in his workingmen's primer of 1853,

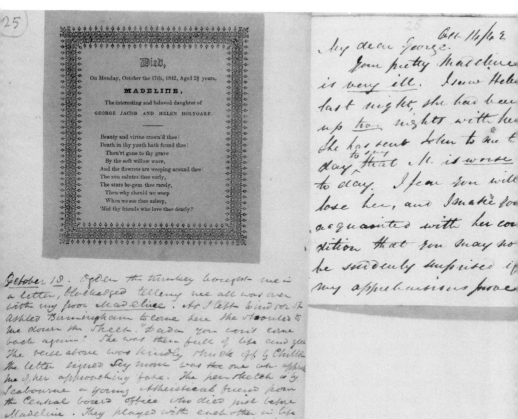

Figure 7. The human cost of blasphemy martyrdom. Commemorative notice of his daughter's death, pasted into Holyoake's prison diary. Courtesy of the Bishopsgate Institute Library, Holyoake Collection.

A Logic of Facts (49). The words, *"You have been convicted of uttering language,"* are early anticipations of the recognitions and disturbances anatomized by Mark Shell in *Money, Language, and Thought.*[81]

The imagery of money informed every aspect of the nation's life, just as the property standard underwrote its book of laws, from copyright to matrimony. Thus, when Hone claimed to hold "independent" views, he was playing on an economic pun, for "[n]o-one is supposed to be independent without property" (*Three Trials* 159); workingmen preferred the term "self-dependent." Campbell's influential *Philosophy of Rhetoric* (1776) called vulgar idiom "counterfeit money, though common not valued" (qtd. in O. Smith 26); Walpole feared the poet Chatterton might pass from "counterfeiting styles" to faking "promissory notes" (Haywood 61); a hundred years later, John Duke, later Lord Coleridge, disproved an impostor's claim to a fortune by his "Wapping preterite[s]" (breaked, teached, thinked) and slaughterman's "howsomdever" (in E. Coleridge, *Life and Correspondence* 2: 186).

To government it seemed that the blasphemer's aim, like the forger's, was to put into circulation words with no stamp of authority, regal or divine; he was a "coiner" of phrases.[82] Language itself anticipated the view of words as a form of property—Bourdieu's linguistic capital, an intellectual medium of marketplace exchange—that Judge Erskine's sentence endorsed: ideology works most powerfully through assumption and metaphor. With no birthright in all one could "utter," money or words, Jacob Holyoake was a pretender to any role that involved them, from bank teller to storyteller.[83] Like Christopher Marlowe, England's most famous literary atheist, he was suspected in the same breath of forging and blasphemy.[84] But unlike modern iconoclast André Gide, he did not revel in the role of "Counterfeiter." "My lord," Holyoake anxiously asked immediately after sentence, "am I to be classed with thieves and felons?" "No," replied Erskine, "thieves and felons are sentenced to the penitentiary, you to the Common Gaol" (*History of the Last Trial* 64).[85] Holyoake, the man of no *property*, violated linguistic *propriety*: the two words are etymologically joined at the hip. As much as it was an apologia for unbelief, Holyoake's defense (like Hone's, and other martyrs') was an attempt to conjure himself from voiceless impostordom, to revel for a few privileged hours in the contested claim to "his own words."

The period political discourse that defined power in terms of property tied both to the concept of "voice." When the Great Reform Act of 1832 established a flat ten-pound householder franchise, and the thousands of workingmen who had held votes under haphazard local conditions were disenfranchised, they understood their loss in terms of language. "Hold your tongue," the magistrate ordered a man called up for selling the *Poor Man's Guardian*, a veteran of the *Age of Reason* battle named Joseph Swann. Defying him, Swann protested that he sold the *Guardian* precisely "[b]ecause I have no voice in [tax]ing . . . publications" (Barker 12).[86] No taxation without representation: "voice" was another term for "vote." Language was a political property; the blasphemer's struggle for its possession was a political struggle; the politics of nineteenth-century England were driven by class; and "classification is at the basis of language" (Hodge and

Kress 62). Hegemonic ideas about language "justified class division," as Olivia Smith writes, "and even contributed to its formation" (3). Beginning in 1793 and especially in 1817–19 Parliament rejected working-class petitions explicitly on the grounds of "disrespectful" language (30).[87] In the 1840s, the law of blasphemy was invoked to imprison its "utterer." Holyoake and his *Oracle* comrades' campaign for "their own words," no less than Hetherington's championship of cheap publication, was as integral a part (though a much smaller one) of the long battle for universal suffrage as the "monster" petitions that Chartists presented to Parliament: only the vote could justify, though it would hardly ask, the "tax on knowledge" that Swann and the rest defied.

In the 1840s, then, the crime of blasphemy took on a different coloring from the insurgent protest of Carlile's campaign or the revolutionary fervor of his more "ultra-radical" criminal colleagues of the 1810s. The ultras aimed to turn the world upside down; they might take their place with modern speakers of "anti-languages": gangs, cults, prisoners, the military (see Halliday, "Anti-languages," passim). The blasphemers and free pressmen of the 1840s wanted recognition that "their own words" qualified as words; they wanted a voice and a voting role in the public sphere. Access to language was power in a world that modern publishing technologies were "convert[ing] into one large conversational party" (Holyoake, *Sixty Years* 1: 155).

Class thinking dictated not only law's views of the workingman's "own words" but its view of where he had said them. For Holyoake to "utter language" before an audience attending a lecture in a hall that had been hired for the purpose was to violate the ear of the Cheltenham public. The prosecution even suggested that Maitland was a "plant" whose question allowed Holyoake to spring unbelief on his audience, and that posters deliberately misrepresented his lecture. Both insinuations turned an unpremeditated declaration into a "diabolical" attempt to unsettle unsuspecting minds in a public place (*History of the Last Trial* 3).

This same issue of public space and public sphere much occupied the court during the 1843 prosecution of Holyoake's successor in blasphemous martyrdom, Thomas Paterson, bookseller, of Number 8 Holywell Street, London. It was highly contentious. Paterson began his career as "Holyoake's curate" in Sheffield (*Sixty Years* 1: 111), and inherited from him the *Oracle* editorship, though he too was not directly indicted for it. In Edinburgh, where he ran a "Blasphemy Depot" supplied by agitators from London, Paterson was prosecuted for blasphemy in 1844; he turned out then and later to be an unstable ranter (Holyoake was as duped by Paterson's gift of the gab, Southwell warned him, as he once had been by Southwell's own [letter, 23 May 1844, in HL]). In 1843, however, he was three times

convicted under a new police act of "exhibiting" three "profane" papers to
general view in a "public thoroughfare." The prosecutions were a new ploy
by authorities to avoid the publicity of a jury trial;[88] and the word "thoroughfare," admitted the presiding magistrate, Mr. Jardine, was somewhat
problematical. Paterson's offending placards were in fact displayed inside
his shop, a foot or so back from the window, through which they could
be read only with difficulty. A policeman caused a public nuisance by
blocking the "thoroughfare" while he labored to take them down as evidence (*God v. Paterson* 63). But for the purposes of prosecution the term
"thoroughfare" was stretched to include the inside of Paterson's shop: private premises were thus magically transformed into public space.

For the lower classes enjoyed no such extended rights of privacy as
upper-crust "pagans" like Algernon Swinburne. He might "belch out
blasphemy and bawdry" at the Arts Club in Hanover Square without running more risk than that of being expelled by fellow members (Thomas,
Swinburne 138). Privacy was a middle-class cult, as the idiom of the period
more than hints: to the "private" gentleman the "private" home, made possible by a "private" income; to the worker the public house, where law
could seize him if he talked politics or (until 1825) even spoke about working
conditions with more than four fellow laborers.[89] Law clung to the eighteenth-century paradigm of the trustworthy reader as the "gentleman in
his closet." Only he enjoyed the right of "private judgment." For Holyoake,
Paterson, and—later—G. W. Foote, the case was altered. Their very placards and publications were taken as unwarrantable intrusions into public
space. Their works were plots, even though—as Foote pointed out at his
trial—they announced their infidel identities on their masthead. The *Freethinker*, for example, was hardly a "surreptitious" publication with an "insidious" title (*Defence* 47), a well-worn ruse of pornographic publishing
(the *Englishwoman's Domestic Magazine*, for example).[90] Customers had deliberately to enter a shop to purchase a copy; and "no Freethinker shoved
it into [people's] hands, saying, 'I want to scarify your sense of decency' "
(Foote, *Daily Telegraph*, 6 March 1883: 3). Nevertheless, in 1883, prosecution, press, and government considered and presented it as an offensive
annoyance.

"We put the thing in progress by asking for it," Carlile wrote, "whilst
we practice Free Discussion in spite of persecution" (*Republican*, 5 November 1819: 749). Holyoake's blasphemous colleague Charles Southwell applied the same principle to learning, flaunting his "Knowledge" as "Power."
His speech in his own defense, 76 of 102 printed pages of the trial transcript,
marshals surprisingly scholarly arguments for the ahistoricity of Christ and
the Protestant right of biblical interpretation. Works cited range from the

quality quarterlies and the *Penny Cyclopaedia* (whose utilitarian sense of the "crime" of blasphemy Southwell cites with satisfaction [95–96]), to Locke, Gibbon, Mosheim's *Ecclesiastical History,* and the contemporary *Tracts for the Times;*[91] classical authors include Socrates, Aristotle, and Epicurus.

Southwell's bravura performance also bears remarking, however, because he did not prepare it on his own. In the 1840s, as in the 1810s, the martyrs closed ranks. Southwell's defense committee was a cooperative research team, a "combination" of talents. Hetherington stood by in court "to assist him in turning to his books" (*Trial of Charles Southwell* i), and published a transcript commissioned from Carlile volunteer William Carpenter, with a view to "the utmost publicity" (*Trial* iii). Months later, Carlile himself sat by Holyoake's side for fourteen hours at the Gloucester Assizes, and "handed me notes for guidance" (Holyoake, *Life and Character of Richard Carlile* vi).[92] Paterson's Edinburgh trial was a committee-planned effort; when he was imprisoned, Thomas Finlay and Matilda Roalfe stepped forward to run his "Blasphemy Depot." Defendants and defense committees made the most of the new penny post.[93] Trials were eagerly reported in the radical press.

The blasphemous method of working-class protest as Hetherington, Southwell, and Holyoake reinvented it—strategic, learned, and intellectually intense—eventually required too much of too small a base. Courage dwindled as prison treatment worsened; fifteen months' solitary confinement in harsh Perth Penitentiary turned loud-mouthed Paterson into a hysterical Christian convert.[94] Around 1844 government stopped prosecuting, declining to make further martyrs; the gathering prestige of the "Higher Criticism" and geological investigation made cases awkward to contemplate. But this matter of *cooperation* merits further attention.

A social critic like Jürgen Habermas might see in Holyoake as he emerged around 1850, eight years after trial and imprisonment, a convert from the aggression that is means-end oriented to the "communicative action" which seeks to enter conversation and reach collective agreement. To the theorist, the crime of blasphemy for which he served his time may seem to "sever and withdraw" the social bond (Lawton 4). But the efforts of defense committees and antipersecution leagues demonstrate that in nineteenth-century fact blasphemy was not a denial but an *assertion* of community. The cooperative martyrs and their supporters of the 1840s did not merely constitute a small countercommunity, but through trial for blasphemy publicly staged the broad questions: What kind of community are we to have? What are its principles of inclusion?

It is no surprise, then, that a large number were also prominent in the organized cooperative movement, an interest that a superficial view of the

blasphemer as individualist and courtroom performer would seem to ne-
gate. "Without knowledge there can be no union," the *Poor Man's Guardian* declared, "without union, no strength" (22 December 1832: 654). Hetherington joined other printers in the pioneer London Co-operative and
Economical Society (founded 1820). Watson joined the Co-operative Trad-
ing Association in 1824, and became its store manager in 1828. Carpenter
edited the *Magazine of Useful Knowledge and Co-operative Miscellany*.
Cleave was an early unionist and cooperator. Jacob Holyoake, preeminently, presided at the opening of the Rochdale Co-operative Store two
years after his release from prison in 1845. He is venerated today as the
father of the mass movement it inaugurated. His 1875 *Self-Help by the People*
brought cooperation widespread recognition and a literary existence; its
preface even stakes a wry claim to cooperativism in the writing (vii). Cooperative work continued the educative trajectory of the blasphemous struggle
for cheap publication. To charge blasphemy against people like these was
not a simple move to restore community but also and simultaneously an
attempt to smash all idea of a different community, conceived along different political lines, in which language, like property, might be held in common, and each man's "own words" be as good as the next's.

Holyoake built another movement, Secularism, within little more than
a decade of leaving his cell.[95] The "Practical Philosophy of the People" (as
his first pamphlet on it is titled), Secularism as Holyoake constructed it
preached the restriction of human effort to the knowable world, and sought
to provide a material foundation for morality and social relations. Its in-
forming ideas were not original. Holyoake took them from Hume, Locke,
Volney (*Ruins of Empire*), and the French philosophes (especially D'Holbach); Paine's common sense, Bentham's utilitarianism, Mill's humane rationalism, and Comtean positivism all added to the mix. Organized Secularism inherited a North of England power base, an urban radical flavor,
several leaders, and a good many of its members from Chartism and Owenism.[96] In the 1850s, Holyoake even made the movement marginally respectable. That fact is deeply important.

As historian F. M. L. Thompson amply demonstrates in the *Rise of Respectable Society*, the mid-Victorians raised an altar to an idol whose dictates
came to replace God's commands, Respectability; by century's end only
the upper crust were immune ("We are above respectability," Lady Wilde
instructed her son [Ellman 9]). Jacob Holyoake had been ripe for "conversion" to the new creed even before his Gloucester ordeal. His *Oracle* colleagues privately called him "the *pet*" of "all *respectables* of society" (Chilton
to Holyoake, 24 December 1841, in HL). It gave him comfort that "[m]any

Figure 8. George Jacob Holyoake in later life as a near-Eminent Victorian. Cabinet portrait by Elliot & Fry of Baker Street. Courtesy of the Bishopsgate Institute Library, Holyoake Collection.

ladies were present" at his trial, including "the wives of clergymen, and some of the nobility" (*History of the Last Trial* 21). A few even offered him lunch. From here it was a small step to a principled craving for Respect-ability: what does respect-able originally mean, after all, but able-to-be-respected? Henry Hetherington's 1849 funeral gave Holyoake a solemn public occasion to proclaim (over the grave) Freethought's conversion to "good taste," "reverence," and "sensibility" (Holyoake, *Life and Character of Henry Hetherington* 16). By 1852 Holyoake was backpedaling on universal suffrage, "sacrific[ing] truth to respectability" in the view of former comrades on the Chartist Executive Committee (C. Murray 2); in 1859 he proposed instead an "intelligence franchise" that set "brains before bricks" by directly linking the vote to education (*The Workman and the Suffrage* 8). His Secularist "Principles" of 1854 were ironically similar to those set out in a parody of Lord Chesterfield's "New Creed" that Hone had quoted in court: "I believe, that this world is the object of my hopes and morals; and that . . . there is no sin, but against good manners" (*Three Trials* 164).

When Bradlaugh appropriated the leadership in the 1860s, Secularism became a nationally important movement. But the price of political power under the Cockney "Chief" and his lieutenant G. W. Foote was to lose the respectability that the former inmate of Gloucester Gaol had fought so hard to secure. Blasphemy as it re-erupted in the *Freethinker* case of 1883 was a class crime of language against a new idol: Respectability.

CHAPTER THREE

ENGLAND, 1883

Every strand in the history of blasphemy in the nineteenth century was woven into the three trials of G. W. Foote and the *Freethinker* in 1883. The case recapitulates and compresses into a three-act drama the episodic narrative of class control and cultural anxiety in which Hone, Carlile, Hetherington, Holyoake, and the rest played their parts. Like them, Foote defended himself, and much of the impact of the case depends on his "powerful" and "very able" speech at his third trial (in J. Coleridge, *Life and Correspondence* 24, 13), a "masterpiece of its kind" (*Times,* qtd. in *Pall Mall Gazette,* 26 April 1883: 12). That political narrative is the concern of this chapter. Blasphemy as the 1880s understood it was no longer primarily regarded as an insult to God and his Church. "Blasphemy," as Foote declared, "is simply skepticism expressed in plain language and sold at the people's price" (*Blasphemy No Crime* 22). As the next chapter demonstrates, the *Freethinker* case also caps and expounds the process by which Literature replaced the Bible as primary standard of cultural value. There were not really "two G. W. Footes," as Edward Royle suggests. But the momentary separation in this chapter of the deliberate political vulgarian from the talented literary critic and "armchair thinker" (*Radicals* 100) of chapter 4 will help to clarify the complex meanings of the *Freethinker* trials. Chapter 5 attempts their final recontextualization, locating the blasphemy of the *Freethinker* as a crucial episode in the history of the English language. Here we are rather concerned with a dense story of cultural control and classist assumption.

1. THE "CELEBRATED CASE" OF G. W. FOOTE
AND THE *FREETHINKER*

The *Freethinker's* decade began uncertainly. Empire entered its jingoistic phase, while British industrial and commercial supremacy began slipping. Fear of anarchist uprising sped passage of Home Secretary Harcourt's Explosives Act in the same month that G. W. Foote went to trial, March 1883. Municipal reform, Irish Home Rule, and affairs in India, Transvaal, and Egypt dominated public attention in that year, together with the "Bradlaugh Bill" to allow secular affirmation, which failed (again), immediately after the trials.[1] Class tensions were screwed to a new high. A *Punch* cartoon of a young rough in a battered top hat, cudgel in hand and toes sticking out of his shoes, on 24 May 1883, gave pictorial shape to "what we've heard a good deal about recently, *i.e.*—MANIFESTOES!" (142). Secularists joined agitation for the Third Reform Bill, which would dramatically extend the vote to every man in the country (against one in three in 1867), adding to the rolls two million of the unemployed, the rough, the vagrant, the unrespectable. After its contested passage, *Punch,* that epitome of the middle-class mind, could produce a comic "Alarmist's Year-Book" for 1885:

> *February 14th.* Sir William Harcourt receives a Valentine which on being opened carefully at the Home Office blows his hat and the roof off. . . . The Governor of the Bank of England while on his way to luncheon tarred and feathered amidst tumultuous rejoicings. (*Punch Almanack,* 1885: 4)

But the years and months before passage of the act were a different matter.

The extension of the franchise was seen as a mob threat to culture, as *Punch's* yearly almanacs testified. After the act, Mr. Punch figures in cartoon as "*The Benefactor* of the Centuries," leading a jolly procession of board schoolchildren and handing out votes to rustics, while cheerful banners in the background flaunt the once-dreadful messages "Museums—Galleries—Open Sunday 2 to 4," "Music for the People," and so on. But the *Almanack* for 1881, the year the *Freethinker* was launched, featured several derogatory cartoons under the very title of "CULTURE." In one, a mistress declines the services of an overdressed "Young Person" because she has no "character," that is, a written reference from a previous employer: the term is expressive. "I have three school-board certificates, Ma'am," the girl replies. "Oh well—I suppose for Honesty, Cleanliness—" "No, Ma'am," the girl interrupts proudly, "for 'Literatoor,' Joggr'phy, an' Free 'And Drawrin!" (4). Such were the fruits of putting pens into pauper's hands. Only a fool would do so, like the silly bespectacled spinster seen handing over a book labeled "CULTURE" to three turnip-headed yokels in the year's two-page engraving, "A Vision of Utopia." Nothing, however, sums up the prevailing atmosphere of class hostility and anxiety better than *Punch*'s 1884 *Almanack*'s large engraving, "Education's Frankenstein—A Dream of the Future" (fig. 9).[2]

Gladstone's liberal government, which swept into office in 1880 with the biggest majority since 1867 and hung on for six troubled years, satisfied no one. It had promised change but in the first year delivered only a coercion act in Ireland. "The working classes were grievously disappointed," wrote Ambrose Barker, Secularist secretary of an East End radical club (qtd. in A. Taylor 161). There was deep industrial and agricultural depression. Tension exploded one fateful day in 1886 when unemployed workers streamed westwards to throw bricks and stones through the windows of gentlemen's clubs. On "Bloody Sunday," 13 November 1887, 300 people were arrested and 150 injured (one fatally) in confrontations with police in Trafalgar Square. The disorders, strikes, and bread riots of the decade, however, seem in retrospect less distressing than the everyday spectacle of dockhands tearing each other's clothes, even each other's ears, in the desperate competition for work.[3] In the 1880s, the nation's capital became the class-divided city it remains to this day. The "Bitter Cry of Outcast London," in the title words of the 1884 pamphlet that shocked government to attention, demanded to be heard; yet measures like the Housing of the Working Classes Act, made more crucial by the yearly influx of eastern European immigrants into the slums and sweatshops of the East End, were not passed until 1890. The general frustration fueled the rise of Continental Socialism in England.

But that was in the late 1880s. For the ten years before it was Secularism that had the public ear, and stood for a solitary moment at the center of unfolding history. Bradlaugh, the Cockney coal heaver, late private in the army, and a lawyer's clerk by day, had thrown Secularist respectability to the winds, and the numbers showed the difference; he was a staunch Republican also, and the aftermath of the Paris Commune of 1870 seemed to prove the futility of not embracing a "militant" approach. A marked upsurge in prosecution, harassment, and general aggression towards unbelievers "ushered in," writes Edward Royle, "a golden age of Secularism in reply" (*Radicals* 265): the 1880s were its "heroic" decade.

"Active" membership in Bradlaugh's London-based National Secular Society (N.S.S., founded in 1866), a risky proposition, jumped from three hundred in 1875 to six thousand in 1880 (*N.S.S. Almanack* for 1870: 19), and by over two thousand more between 1880 and 1882. "Passive" members "whose position does not permit the publication of their names" (17) swelled the number; and ten or even twenty times as many nonmembers were likely to attend lectures.[4] The movement's national audience at this

Figure 9. The vulgarization of learning: nightmare image by Harry Furniss from *Punch's Almanack for 1884.*

Mrs. M. "OH, YOU MUST SEE MY CABINET OF CUR'OSITIES. I'M AWFUL PARTIAL TO BRIC-BATS!!"

Figure 10. Fake culture's potential for mob violence: bric-a-brac as "bric-bats." *Punch* ran this cartoon opposite its first notice of the *Freethinker* case on 17 March 1883.

point approached sixty thousand. Between 1882 and 1884, the trials of G. W. Foote and the *Freethinker* brought another 3,630 new members into the Freethought fold (Royle, *Radicals* 29). Secularism had become the "creed of London working-class club life" (48), almost what Holyoake had hopefully named it, the "Practical Philosophy of the People." The N.S.S.'s ten "approved" and crowd-pulling lecturers traveled thousands of miles a year to service local branches, 120 of them at the movement's height in 1883, and independent regional secular societies.[5] They thrived on debate with the Christian Evidence Society, the Anti-Infidel League, and other religious groups.[6]

For the most part, the Secularists of the "heroic" decade were "converts."[7] "The Freethinker," read a *Freethinker* editorial in 1905, "or at least the open Freethinker, is an exceptional person. He must have some originality of mind, some independence of spirit, and some positive courage" (10 September: 578–79). He made saints and heroes of men like Darwin and Huxley; Mill's *On Liberty* was a holy book. He might also be solitary and contrary, and an individualist to the point of eccentricity, one reason why many Secularists were hostile to socialism in the late 1880s: it was a *mass* movement in a way that Secularism could never be. Ironically, its eventual triumph was assisted by the network that Bradlaugh made available in the interests of open debate: Secularist lecture platforms and the columns of his *National Reformer* and other secular journals.

By the time the *Freethinker* case came to trial in 1883, better-off agnostics and "honest doubters" had made great gains. Jews might now become members of Parliament and judges, and thus technically competent to try cases of blasphemy. But little had changed in the day-to-day experience of lower-class unbelievers since midcentury. The Secularists, Freethinkers, and "infidels" of the 1880s still lived an extreme version of the marginalized impotence that strikes doubting Mr. Hale in Elizabeth Gaskell's *North and South* (1854–55). They "smart[ed]" under "the cruel pressure continually put on [them] by Christian employers," and spoke only under "constant threats of prosecution" (Besant, *Autobiography* 173). Outright atheists remained the one group in Victorian Britain subject to the full range of legal penalties upon opinion. The majority of citizens still believed with the *Tablet*, in 1883, that "when religion goes the protection of all civilized society is a hempen rope" (qtd. in Wootton 57), and with *John Bull* that "adultery, perjury, communism are the natural offspring of atheism" (3 March 1883: 137). The title of George Gissing's 1892 novel encapsulates their fate: *Born in Exile*. They were still society's "lepers and outcasts" (Holdreth, *Secular Miscellany* no. 3 [1854]: 14), the public butts of "bitter prejudice" (*Prime Minister and the Blasphemy Laws* 6).

Popular evangelism still found the figure of the dying unbeliever a temptation impossible to resist. H. L. Hastings, an American missionary who worked London with Moody and Sankey, made rhetorical mileage as late as 1881 of "a letter written to me by Mrs. Mary Benjamin, who at the age of eleven years was an *eye-witness* to the death-bed agonies" of Tom Paine: one moment he "call[ed] on Jesus Christ for mercy" and the next he "blasphem[ed]," with eyes "glaring, rolling," while "his screams could be heard at a great distance" (*Prime Minister and the Blasphemy Laws* 6n).[8] Atheists could not bury their dead in their own way until 1880, and even then the Burial Laws Amendment Act effectually forbade unchristian speeches over the grave (Odgers, *Libel and Slander* 454). A handful of avowed atheists were elected to the new school boards created in the late 1880s, but few unbelievers could educate their children as they wished. Twenty years later, a secular amendment to the 1906 Education Bill was lost by 477 to 63 votes. Trusts and contracts into which they entered in the normal course of business might be declared null and void.[9] Known atheists could still— like Shelley—lose custody of their children. (One father was deprived of guardianship for denying the efficacy of prayer [Hunter, *Blasphemy Laws* 18–19].)

The "heroic" 1880s, then, were years of dogged struggle for changes in persistently discriminating law; for a voice in government; for consolidation of the freedom of the press; above all, for the Affirmation Bill, which finally passed in 1888. At bottom this was a struggle for the simple right to exist, not only for individual unbelievers but for the Secularist movement itself. The N.S.S.'s financial basis was not, and could not be made, sound. Aside from the perennial problem that many members were too poor to pay subscription dues, until 1917 the illegality of willing money for Secularist purposes repeatedly invalidated bequests and denied the N.S.S. the right to large donations.[10] Most of Secularism's leaders died in debt on its account.

The "heroic" decade was a time, too, of large-scale propagandizing. The traces are evident in the pages of Secularist publications: the *Secular Chronicle* (Birmingham); Watt's *Agnostic Annual* (founded 1884) and *Secular Review* (1876); the *Secularist*, which Foote briefly coedited with Holyoake in 1876 before merging it with Watt's *Review;* Holyoake's rather feeble *Present Day;* G. W. Foote's *Liberal*, a promising literary monthly that died in the year it was born, 1879, *Progress* (1883–87), and *Freethinker* (founded 1881); Bradlaugh's *National Reformer*, the preeminent political organ, with an excellent team of writers; and Annie Besant's *Our Corner*, founded in 1883 partly in response to the *Freethinker* scandal, and as resolutely respectable as a female infidel could make it, with its fireside chat about science, politics, and gardening, its children's games, and its lively theater reviews by George Bernard Shaw, whose unpublished youthful novels were serialized in its pages.[11]

As important as journals in their day were Secularist speeches, lectures, and debates, especially at London's notorious "Blasphemy Shop," the Old Street Hall of Science, a "tabernacle of infidelity" erected by subscription in 1868 with a corrugated iron roof, usually filled to its eleven hundred–

person capacity, and expressing "all that is horrid and hideous in politics as politics and religion are understood . . . in Mayfair" (*Weekly Dispatch,* 8 June 1879: 12).

For this was an age of oratory. The platforms, waste grounds, parks, soapboxes, and street corners of Freethought speaking offered a mirror to the testing grounds of the Victorian establishment: the Oxford Union, the courts, the House of Commons, the pulpits. The issues of the day, large matters of law and of public opinion, were Secularist issues, giving drama and news value to every Secularist speech on affirmation and the oath, blasphemy, free speech, and freedom of publication. The movement epitomized the common man's right to a voice, craving and breeding speakers. Hence its susceptibility to con men like Dr. Edward Aveling, who edited the *Freethinker* while Foote was in prison. He had "every aesthetic disadvantage," said Shaw, "except a voice like a euphonium of astonishing resonance and beauty" (qtd. in Pearson 128).[12] Hence the meteoric ascent of gifted Annie Besant.

Hence above all the ascendancy of Charles Bradlaugh, "the lad" who became "the Chief," ousting respectable Holyoake, and the founder in 1866 (at age thirty-three) of the N.S.S.[13] "A true description of him . . . recalls the leaders of the French Revolution," wrote Irish journalist T. P. O'Connor in his *Weekly:*

> Imagine . . . a huge creature, some six feet one or two high; conjure up a vision of a man who looked at once like a coal heaver or a pugilist and a great thinker, and a protagonist in the fight of ideas, and you have some idea of what the figure of Bradlaugh suggested. (21 August 1903, rpt. in Gilmour 43–44)

"Iconoclast" Bradlaugh was the most extraordinary figure to rise up from the working classes in the nineteenth century. A legal genius, "brawling, swaggering Bradlaugh," as the catchphrase ran (qtd. in A. Taylor 150), was the "artisan atheist" reincarnate, the ogre of middle-class nightmare. Even to clerical heretics like notorious Charles Voysey he was "the Devil himself" (qtd. 47). But he was one of the great voices of the century. Every aspiring speaker, her friend the eclectic doyen of South Place "chapel," liberal Unitarian Moncure D. Conway told Annie Besant when she came to London, must hear Bradlaugh speak at the Hall of Science (A. Taylor 71). The prime aim of vicious name-calling by his numerous enemies seemed not merely to strip "the Bradlaugh" of his humanity but to deny him his miraculous faculty of speech: he was the archetypal "blatant, brazen, howling Atheist" (*Freeman's Journal,* 22 May 1880: 5). Not so. Next to radical member of Parliament John Bright, Bradlaugh was acknowledged the finest orator of his time. Fifteen thousand people at one time could hang on his words.

In him, Annie Besant wrote, "Tory squires and lordlings" heard "the masses speak" (*Law and Law Breakers*, qtd. in A. Taylor: 151).

The 1880s were Bradlaugh's decade. He had made two parliamentary bids before, standing for the Northampton seat on a Republican ticket and as an avowed atheist. He made a poor showing in 1868, and lost again in 1874, but by a smaller margin. In 1880 the free electors of Northampton returned him to Westminster as their member of Parliament. (They included, inevitably, a large number of shoemakers, urged to vote Bradlaugh by their comrades in the London Trade Boot and Shoe Makers Society.) "An absolute separation," Gladstone declared when Bradlaugh made secular affirmation under the problematic acts of 1855, 1869, and 1870, and took his seat on 23 June 1880, "has been drawn in the spirit of the law of the land, and, as I believe, in the letter of it, between secular duty and religious belief" (qtd. in *Westminster Review*, July 1883: 6): the Victorians devoutly believed the myth of their own tolerance. But it was a myth nonetheless. On 2 August 1880, Britain's first openly atheist member of Parliament was seized at the door of the chamber, and dragged by policemen "down the steps of the House of Commons," O'Connor reported, "with torn coat and shirt, . . . resisting, shouting, defiant," instantly transformed into a "hunted and outraged outcast" (*Weekly*, rpt. in Gilmour 45). A large number of men were needed to hold him down.

It took six years of struggle and spectacle to take his seat, to which he was repeatedly reelected, from 1880 to 1886: Bradlaugh administering the oath to himself with a Bible; seizing the mace; imprisoned in the Clock Tower while a crowd milled outside, waiting for the signal he never gave to turn angry words into violent action; agitating for the Affirmation Bill that would give him his rights as Northampton's representative. A total of 1,153 petitions containing 263,259 signatures protesting his exclusion was presented to the House of Commons; eighty thousand people gathered in Hyde Park at just one meeting in his support in May 1882. "He was closer to the people than anyone," said Thomas Burt, the miners' leader (qtd. in A. Taylor 162). He was, said Bernard Shaw in 1890, when the dust had settled and Bradlaugh was dead, prematurely, "quite simply a hero" (rpt. in Gilmour 49). No other Secularist leader had been able or would be able to hold together the movement's conflicting impulses towards political engagement and intellectual withdrawal.

Few could stand at Bradlaugh's side and not look dwarfed. In the short term, Annie Besant did best; in the long term, George William Foote. The drama of his *Freethinker* magazine played out in the middle years of the "Bradlaugh struggle" (Foote, in Herrick, *Vision* 7). G. W. Foote (he never used the full name) was a man in a different mold from his "Chief," whom he succeeded as N.S.S. president from 1890 to 1915. He was "very proud of the 'apostolic succession,'" but wise enough not to compete (*Freethinker*, 31 October 1915: 699). Unlike Bradlaugh, he refused to write his memoirs for the Freethought faithful, disliked personal reference, and kept a happy private life separate from his career as atheist agitator. A few details survive from entries in biographical dictionaries of Freethought (a growth subgenre in the last quarter of the century) and the tributes in the *Freethinker* that followed his death in 1915. It would have pleased the pacifist in him that several were from soldiers at the front. A paean written from one mourner's own sickbed with a pencil held between the teeth might have made him cringe: "He is not dead; he lives and reigns in the hearts of all who loved him. . . . As I write his portrait looks down on me saying 'courage'" (*Freethinker*, 31 October 1915: 701). "[T]o us who lived in those days," another admirer recalled, "Bradlaugh and Foote were the giants—the 'great twin brethren' who fought together" (698).

The son of a lowly Plymouth customs officer who died when he was four years old, in 1854, Foote grew up in poor circumstances. Intellectually acute and better educated than his background promised, he had gravitated as a teenager through Anglicanism (his own choice; his mother was a Wesleyan) to Unitarianism by the time he came to London and a job in a large West End library in 1868. In the city he quickly became involved with Freethought. Foote was a founder of the Young Men's Secular Association in 1869, superintendent of the Hall of Science Sunday School, a contributor to Bradlaugh's *National Reformer* from 1870, and secretary of the London Republican Club by 1871 and of the new National Republican League by 1873. A soft, strong voice, of which he was naively vain (he was to fret about his throat in Holloway Gaol), led him to the platform.

It was as a lecturer that he first caught the attention of the N.S.S. leadership, giving his maiden lecture on "Miracles and Special Providence" in 1873. The following year he engaged in his first public debate on the respective merits of Christianity and Secularism: such platform stagings of the issues were to become increasingly popular, and Foote a star on the bills. At his crowded funeral service on 21 October 1915 at dingy Ilford Crematorium, his successor as N.S.S. President, Chapman Cohen, recalled that "nearly everyone had sat tense with emotion or laughing with pleasure under the magic of his oratory," swayed by a "living voice" and a "master of speech" (*Freethinker*, 31 October 1915: 689). He had a gift for the logic of argument and "a reputation for saying hard and bitter things" (Cohen 690); the image obituarists reached for most was that of a sharp, drawn sword. But the congenital good humor that expressed itself as a "Micawber-like faith" that "something will turn up" (Cohen 690) also flowered into a "wondrous gift of improvisation," the "bubbling over of a copious mind" (William Heaford 696). That "playful imagination" (698) shall prove important.

Foote rose to N.S.S. vice-president, first lieutenant to the "Chief," in recognition of services during the 1874 Northampton election. He seemed an unlikely candidate for the post at the time. He was as devoted to his books (which he guarded jealously and never marked) as to the platform, and an habitué of the British Museum reading room: one imagines him mingling there with the seedy cast of Gissing's *New Grub Street.* There he polished up the "scholarly and studiously polite" style in which he produced pamphlets and *National Reformer* pieces on knotty problems of biblical interpretation and Freethought policy. "They were the articles," wrote Chapman Cohen, "of one who felt that the difference between himself and the Christian religion was a purely intellectual one" (rpt. in Herrick, *Vision* 7). He soon made a name for himself as a capable journalist, and as a useful advocate for Sunday opening of museums.[14] There was a rupture in 1877 when Foote left the N.S.S. with several colleagues to set up the rival British Secular Union. It had several causes: Bradlaugh's tendency to dictate; Bradlaugh's overrapid promotion of Annie Besant; distress over her embroiling Bradlaugh in a risky obscenity trial over a birth control pamphlet in 1876 (see below, 5.1); qualms of conscience about their relationship (irregular only in appearance, Besant's latest biographer thinks [A. Taylor 88–95]); and Foote's own prickliness, which sometimes made him a difficult colleague.

But the "Bradlaugh struggle" changed forever the course and tenor of Foote's career. "Mr. Bradlaugh's infamous treatment by the bigots revolutionised my ideas of Freethought policy" (Foote, *Prisoner* 18). His first actions were to bury their differences, officially rejoin the N.S.S., and launch the *Freethinker* in May 1881.[15]

The new venture embodied the change that swept over him. Outrage stung him into populism. The "absurdities of faith" were to be "slain with laughter" (*Freethinker,* 2 March 1884: 65). Foote's plainspoken penny weekly purposefully broke with the publishing traditions of forty years, during which, since the *Oracle* case, no Freethought publication had attracted prosecution; it eschewed the soft spokenness of Holyoake's *Reasoner* and the level-headed and scrupulous seriousness that made Bradlaugh's news-oriented *National Reformer* maddeningly difficult to indict.[16] The *Freethinker* had more than a mocking resemblance to *Punch.* Interspersed amongst its eight pages, doubling to sixteen as the paper caught on, of sharp-tongued articles on Bible, church, sects, Freethought history, public issues like the oath, the milestones of "advanced" publishing, and the excesses of religious fervor and daily persecution, there are pages of mock correspondence and a riot of Punchian puns. As we shall see (below, 6.2), Foote's literal-minded humor made him a particularly dab hand at fake "advertisements" in the *Punch* style ("*The Wooden Leg. A new novel by the Author of The Golden Calf,*" and so forth [*Punch,* 17 March 1883: 130]). And he sought out like-minded contributors.

The *Freethinker* gave the world the shop-counter, below-stairs version of religion. "The friends and favourites of Jehovah were a 'fishy' set," reads an item for 26 March 1882, representative of the *Freethinker* at its worst: "You might boil the lot down without extracting an ounce of virtue from the whole crew" (99). Here was Christianity as it might have played in a music hall. The evangelist Talmadge celebrates "five great victories of Joshua," Foote wrote in a piece of 9 April 1882, for example, but

> He omits two mighty achievements. General Joshua circumcised a million and a half Jews in a single day. . . . [And this] surprising old Jew was as great in oratory as in surgery. On one occasion he addressed an audience of three millions, and everyone heard him. . . . No wonder the walls of Jericho fell down when Joshua joined in the shout. (113)

Here was plainspokenness battering at the laws it knew must be invoked against it:

> Adam, not being up to the tricks of the law, pleaded guilty; and was summarily dealt with. In a rage, God cursed the ground, the serpent, the woman, and the man. A judge should have been more temperate; but then God had no examples to follow, no precedents to guide him. (J. Symes, "God?" 7 May 1882: 150)

> The last way of damnation . . . is very efficacious. It is warranted on the highest authority as a short and easy method of being damned. We allude to that awful and mysterious act, the sin against the Holy Ghost, to which Christ (Matt. xii., 31, 32) so darkly alludes. (W. Heaford, "What Shall I do to be Damned?" 21 May 1882: 174)

One of Foote's aims was to give those beyond the pale the strength that comes from belonging to a community, and one that declined any longer to creep through life in earnest shame, the prevailing tone of contemporary novels and memoirs of lost faith like the *Autobiography of Mark Rutherford* (1881), the perpetual butt of other people's jokes. This was the function of a weekly roundup of news, good and bad, including clerical mishaps and misdemeanors, under the titles "Sugar Plums" and "Acid Drops"; of columns of correspondence, real as well as fictive; and of extensive information about lectures and publications. It was one aim of the "Profane Jokes" that filled the back page: many were sent in by readers.

The laughter was also designed to offend, a large subject to which the next chapter returns. From the first, Foote's *Freethinker* indulged in forbidden lashings of ridicule. And lest danger should not know she was being courted, articles were signed, a decisive break with contemporary journalistic practice and a revival of Southwell's *Oracle* initiative. But Edward Royle overstates his case when he speaks of Foote's "prostitution" to "vulgarity" and "scurrility" in his penny paper (*Radicals* 100). The *Freethinker* was a Freethought forum with a flair for the offensive, born of extraordinary frustration at a critical moment in history. It cannot be understood, let alone condoned or condemned, outside its context. "Those Christian people—yes, and those Freethinkers," wrote F. J. Gould, one of the most accomplished of the cultivated Leicester Secularist circle,

> entirely misunderstand the man if they suppose he "blasphemed" out of sheer anarchism or just for jeering. He felt that the hour was come, in our British evolution, when certain ancient modes of thought must be broken, . . . and concentrating with extraordinary tenacity on this destructive task, he went in and out amongst the democracy, and eloquently uttered his purging and uncompromising satire. (*Freethinker*, 31 October 1915: 695)

Not surprisingly, such boldness made for constant financial difficulties, largely due to a paucity of advertisers.[17]

Some of the *Freethinker*'s offensiveness was a pure function of format and prevailing upper-class hostility to mass culture. Foote's paper was the forerunner of contested changes in journalistic and commercial practice; it was the new tabloid press in its openly blasphemous manifestation. The public sphere was expanding and "dumbing down" in the 1880s. Newnes's weekly *Tit-Bits* and the halfpenny *Evening News* were both founded within months of the *Freethinker* in 1881.[18] The *News*'s first issue set the standard for later cheap papers: twenty-four one-line items made up a front-page "Epitome"; items were reported by telegram from Reuter's or condensed from the *Times* and the *Telegraph;* subjects like the oath got one paragraph while "The Theatres" earned half a column. The eight-page radical *Star,* however, launched a few years later, was the best example of the new mass-market newspaper's generally offensive tendencies. A front-page editorial "Confession of Faith" on the first day of publication promised it would eschew "the hackneyed style of obsolete journalism," presenting "the men and women that figure in the forum or the law court . . . as they are," in language "terse, pointed and plain-spoken" (17 January 1888: 1). That policy, as Raymond Williams remarks, was a "landmark," not a "revolution" (*Revolution* 221): the *Star* brought to a mass readership the same style and language as Foote's blasphemous penny paper; and on three of the four "fundamental freedoms" for which it stood—"free speech, free writing, free meeting, and free combination"—the *Star* was anticipated by Foote's journalistic campaign and regular Secularist agitation.[19] Not surprisingly, it was disdained by the guardians of culture.

For the *Freethinker,* outspoken comic offensiveness brought immediate and lasting success: Foote's paper is the only Secularist publication still alive today. Sales peaked at ten thousand during 1882, and never fell below four thousand, giving actual readership figures of approximately thirty thousand and twelve thousand, extraordinarily high for a paper liable to seizure by the post office, and which libraries and news agents repeatedly refused to stock.[20] A milestone in tactics and impact was reached in November, after Foote's eye was struck by an advertisement in the *Times* seeking assistance in suppressing a "scurrilous" French book.

La bible amusante was one of several paperbound, part-issued publications of the *"Librairie anti-cléricale."* Written by Leo Taxil, it had 401 unnumbered full-page "dessins par Frid'rick." Other titles included *La Vie de Jésus,* a cartoon-book with text by Taxil *("en quelque sorte L'Évangile pour rire"),* which may have inspired the strip cartoon "New Life of Christ" that later spiced up the *Freethinker*'s Christmas number for 1882.[21] Like Foote, Taxil and Frid'rick had a taste for incongruous modernization: *"l'ange exterminateur"* totes a machine gun; Abraham bids farewell to Lot at a railway station, where a sign in the background reads *"Sodome et Gomorrhe—Train de plaisir."* As that example obliquely indicates, they delighted in salacious and earthy moments: Lot eyeing up his daughters; David spying on Bathsheba in a bathing-cabin; Jeroboam apparently administering an enema; Jacob revealingly tearing his garments; Israelites queuing outside a public convenience, a consequence of "la peste"; the cause of an earthquake visually traced to the movements of the Almighty's bowels. Much of this—the smut, the toilet jokes—was too much for Foote. But he decided at once to add to the *Freethinker*'s weapons of ridicule a front-page "Comic Bible" cartoon.

There were crucial differences, however, between the *Freethinker*'s and Taxil and Frid'rick's efforts. First, Foote picked and chose his cartoons: none of those listed above appeared, though the cartoons were "chosen deliberately with the purpose of exciting" that "confidence" which comes from going on the offensive (*Freethinker,* 1 July 1883: 202). Secondly, the captions to *Freethinker* images were not translations from Taxil's sly narration of biblical tales, on which *La bible amusante* relied for comic effect, but actual lines of biblical text to which the "Comic Bible" cartoons now became literal illustrations: "And God said, Let there be light: and there was light" (Genesis 1.3), in which a merry old gentleman lights ("illuminates") his pipe by means of "Divine Illumination" (i.e., a "lucifer" match; 28 May 1882: 169) (fig. 11), a different image from Frid'rick's thin old man

DIVINE ILLUMINATION.

" And God said, Let there be light: and there was light."—
Genesis i., 3.

Figure 11. "Divine Illumination," *Freethinker* 28 May 1882. This "Comic Bible"
cartoon alone earned three counts in the first indictment.

MOSES GETTING A BACK VIEW.

And it shall come to pass that I will put thee in a clift of the rock, and I shall take away my hand, and thou shalt see my back parts.—EXODUS xxxiii., 23.

JOCULAR JEHOVAH.

THE parson is blaring his balderdash perched in his pulpit to
    people below,
Persuading his hearers to praise the good God who ordains all

Take Abe for an instance—the party I mean who enjoyed
    distinction of friend,
Whom the parsons trot out as a model for those on the ladder
    Faith who descend.
"I Am," it appears, had some troublesome doubts if his pa
    as green as the rest,
So paid him a visit and wished him to sacrifice Ikey by way

Figure 12. Offensive literalism: notorious Bible cartoon from the *Freethinker*'s 1882 Christmas number.

striking a light on his buttocks, but nonetheless resoundingly offensive;[22] or (most notoriously, an image not found in *La Bible amusante*) God's promise to Abraham, "I shall take away my hand, and thou shalt see my back parts" (Exodus 33.23), imagined as the prophet's glimpse from a mountaintop, through the clouds, of the Lord's posteriors clad in checked trousers, with a scrap of shirt projecting through an ill-patched hole (Christmas no. 1882: 7) (fig. 12).

This last was that very same passage about which the Wolfman inquired at age four and a half, "whether Christ had a behind too," which Freud read as a latent query whether his father, as God, could use him "from behind" as he had used his mother (Lawton 164). Readers were not invited to take the *Freethinker*'s cartoons so luridly, and a certain intelligence was needed to appreciate all the jokes, but the combination of image and text was a volatile one, a return to the days of Hone and Cruikshank's collaborations, to the early radical days of *Punch* in the 1840s, or to the short-lived *Tomahawk*'s visual assaults on retrograde policies in the early 1870s.[23] English newspapers were chary of visualization through the 1880s. Picture advertisements were restricted to the back page of the *Daily News*, for example; not till the founding of the *Daily Mail* in 1896 did newspapers begin using illustrations or even large type; the *Daily Mirror*, the first picture newspaper, was not founded until 1903. Twenty-two years before, therefore, Foote's Secularist colleagues were worried.[24] Reprinting and refining Taxil and Frid'rick's cartoons was not what the framers of the *Times* advertisement had anticipated. The "loathsome" "Comic Bible" series was a clear assault on the verbal inspiration of the Bible (see below, 4.1, 5.5.i), and a potential assault on the public peace, since (as the attorney-general eventually told Foote's first jury) if the offenders "once had a blasphemous shop established and the windows of it placarded with such pictures, [we] might be sure that, in a population of millions, some injury would be done" (*Daily Telegraph*, 6 March 1883: 3), especially to children, for whom visual material had instinctive attraction.[25] (Foote already had a shop. "I went to [it]," testified Robert Sagar, city constable, however. "It is an ordinary bookseller's shop, and outside it is written 'The Freethinker' " [*Daily News*, 2 March 1883: 6].) The *Freethinker* was indicted for blasphemy on 11 July 1882.

The facts in the case are complicated but very largely recoverable, thanks to the combatants' obsessive memorialization of the truth as they saw it in fliers, pamphlets, rival newspapers, and magazines, and to the Home Office's careful monitoring of proceedings. There were three immediate reasons why the *Freethinker* case came to trial, and some gray areas of morality and motivation that warrant immediate elucidation.

First, one major factor, as might be expected, was what Foote called a naked desire to "cripple Mr. Bradlaugh" (*Defence* 19). He was implicated because his Freethought Publishing Company had put out the first issues. The prosecution was pushed forward from behind the scenes by Bradlaugh's archenemy, Tory member of Parliament Sir Henry Tyler, "full of the piety of the Stock Exchange" (Foote, *Blasphemy No Crime* 6), who wrung from his championship of the anti-Bradlaugh party a little of the fame he had failed to earn elsewhere. The *Freethinker* case was firmly planted in the nineteenth-century tradition of political prosecutions. Tyler rightly calculated that a conviction would prevent Bradlaugh from bothering the House of Commons or the voters again, since a convicted blasphemer would be legally disabled from pursuing his litigation over the parliamentary oath, and barred from standing (again) for reelection: a neat solution, digging a quiet grave for the awkward issues his presence raised in Westminster.

Second, Foote evidently sought the stature he would gain within the Secularist movement if he too could print after his name—like Carlile and Holyoake—the words "Prisoner for Blasphemy." They became in due time the title of his memoir. "In for a penny, in for a pound," he decided (*Prisoner* 49): as the *Freethinker* moved inch by inch up the scale of offensiveness, from its launching and first issues, to the decision to run the "Comic Bible" cartoons, to the printing of the justly notorious Christmas number of 1882 (figs. 13 and 14), Foote was always both orchestrating a campaign and theatrically creating his own image—the hero as blasphemer, the blasphemer as martyr. When the paper was finally indicted, subsequent issues proudly displayed the banner headline "Prosecuted for Blasphemy" above the title (fig. 15).

But Arthur Calder-Marshall overemphasizes Foote's ambition in his *Lewd, Blasphemous, and Obscene.* Foote understood the importance of the courtroom as stage and public forum. The most "celebrated" blasphemy trial for over forty years—in terms of law and abiding consequences, of the whole century, indeed of modern times—could be guaranteed wide publicity and press coverage. Ambition was a necessary element in the martyr spirit, and not merely or only personal. Foote paid for his actions in personal terms: the distress of his young wife and the mental breakdown of his closest friend, the *Freethinker*'s subeditor Joseph Mazzini Wheeler. The fact of the trial, regardless of verdict, would brand him forever a "monster" of vulgarity: like Bradlaugh, Foote figured in the press as "artisan atheist" bogeyman, ignorant of all literature except the works of Tom Paine. He would remain all his life "an Ishmael among [his] fellows, misunderstood, reviled," for disturbing "the supposed peace and good order" of English society (*Freethinker*, 31 October 1915: 693).

In court in 1883, every small detail of the proceedings seemed calculated to sting. His first judge, Mr. North, for example, bluntly addressed him as "Foote," omitting the "Mr." that Lord Chief Justice Coleridge's politeness required in presiding over the third trial. Unnecessary details were offered of Foote's life in humble lodgings, with no "settled servant of his own" (*Three Trials for Blasphemy* 58). Imprisonment would set a limit upon his future, debarring him from polite intellectual society, a significant consideration for a talented and sociable man with literary aspirations. It would also deprive him of income, and throw his wife upon the charity of Secularist friends and supporters, none of them well off.

Moreover, Foote knowingly ran the risk of imprisonment as a common

13. He ordereth the infirm to take up their beds and walk.　　14. He rideth into Jerusalem'

15. He is run in for Blasphemy.　　16. He visiteth Hell and preacheth to the Devils.

A　NEW　LIFE　OF　CHRIST.—Concluded.

17. He surpriseth his disciples.　　18. He vanisheth.

Figures 13 and 14. Last six frames in the *Freethinker*'s Christmas number's comic strip "New Life of Christ." Obvious anti-Semitism was no part of the offense as seen in 1883.

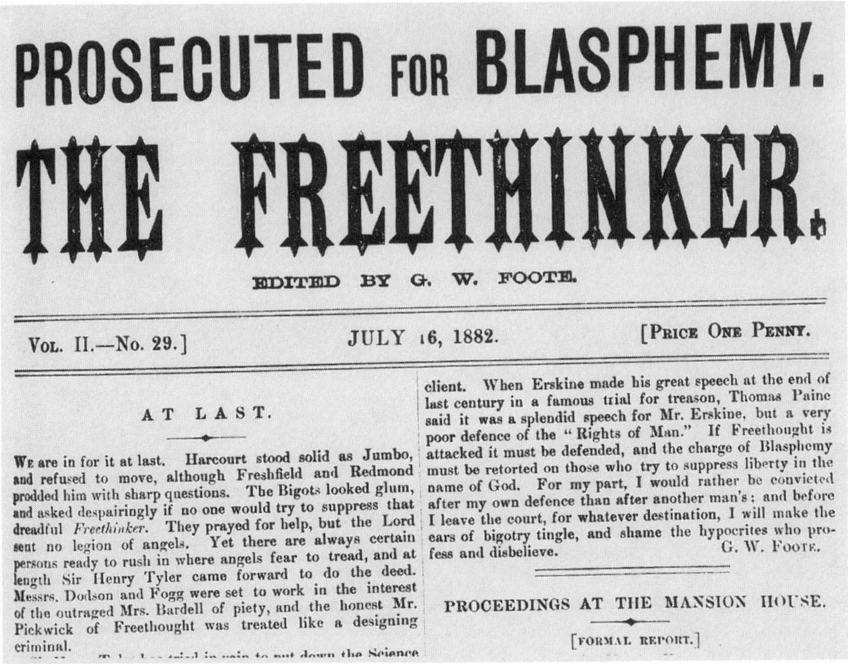

PROSECUTED for BLASPHEMY.
THE FREETHINKER.

EDITED BY G. W. FOOTE.

| VOL. II.—No. 29.] | JULY 16, 1882. | [PRICE ONE PENNY. |

AT LAST.

WE are in for it at last. Harcourt stood solid as Jumbo, and refused to move, although Freshfield and Redmond prodded him with sharp questions. The Bigots looked glum, and asked despairingly if no one would try to suppress that dreadful *Freethinker*. They prayed for help, but the Lord sent no legion of angels. Yet there are always certain persons ready to rush in where angels fear to tread, and at length Sir Henry Tyler came forward to do the deed. Messrs. Dodson and Fogg were set to work in the interest of the outraged Mrs. Bardell of piety, and the honest Mr. Pickwick of Freethought was treated like a designing criminal.

client. When Erskine made his great speech at the end of last century in a famous trial for treason, Thomas Paine said it was a splendid speech for Mr. Erskine, but a very poor defence of the "Rights of Man." If Freethought is attacked it must be defended, and the charge of Blasphemy must be retorted on those who try to suppress liberty in the name of God. For my part, I would rather be convicted after my own defence than after another man's: and before I leave the court, for whatever destination, I will make the ears of bigotry tingle, and shame the hypocrites who profess and disbelieve.   G. W. FOOTE.

PROCEEDINGS AT THE MANSION HOUSE.

[FORMAL REPORT.]

Figure 15. Front-page consummation: the *Freethinker* for 16 July 1882.

felon, with hard labor, picking cocoa-nut fiber and sewing sacks. (His publisher—really his business manager—who shared some of the confinement with him, W. J. Ramsey, had been a shoemaker in his youth and begged to be allowed to repair prison boots, but the governor refused, apparently on instruction from the home secretary [Ramsey 13].) Southwell's judge, amongst others, had directed he serve his time in the civil wing of the jail, an implicit recognition that blasphemy was a press offense rather than a crime. In the "militant" 1880s, Foote rightly anticipated no such latitude. And prison regulations had changed dramatically since Carlile conducted business from his Dorchester cell. The improvements in hygiene since Holyoake's day were more than compensated for by draconian new regulations: plank beds, flogging, and the forbidding of outside gifts of food, warmth, and money. Starfish-shaped Holloway was a model prison built to Bentham's panoptic plan, and allowed for constant oversight of its inmates. Two years of such incarceration helped Oscar Wilde to an early grave; nine months were the death of J. W. Gott in 1922–23.

Foote suffered enough his year inside. The meager diet (he jokes in *Prisoner for Blasphemy* about hunting for the sole piece of bacon in his dish of beans), gave him chronic diarrhea; every month saw him thinner. Thus was the prophecy of the deputy-governor fulfilled when, on the day Foote's prison clothes were issued him, he replied smilingly to a protest that they were too small: "Come, Mr. Foote, don't be so particular; the clothes don't quite fit you now, but they *will*" (*Prisoner* 118). He lost about twenty-eight pounds.[26] "Close" confinement to his cell in block A, second floor, number 2, a provision enforced "only in the case of habitual criminals of the worst class" (Ramsey 13), with the lack of light and air, further undermined his health. When he refused to perform prison labor, he was left locked up all day, every day, in a "loathsome brick vault about the size of a grave" (*Free-thinker*, 29 April 1906: 67), except for one hour in the open yard "walking round and round . . . like a squirrel in a cage" (*Daily Telegraph*, 6 March 1883: 3). The twelve- by six-foot cell contained his bed; a stool; a wash bowl; a slop pail; and a shelf holding a Bible, a brush, and a comb. Cards on the wall spelled out prison regulations and the form of prayer for morning and evening. A late Victorian prison term was a stiffer penalty than we now imagine. "I did not know, and I believe it is hardly known or understood," Lord Coleridge told Foote, "what the punishment of imprisonment as has been inflicted upon you really means" (*Times*, 27 April 1883: 3). The sentence "burdened his constitution with the seeds of the malady," probably tuberculosis, which made the last fourteen years of his life painful (W. Heaford, *Freethinker*, 31 October 1915: 696). It was in these prison conditions that Foote prepared his defense for his climactic third trial in the Court of Queen's Bench before the Lord Chief Justice.

The third immediate reason why the *Freethinker* case came to trial, and the most important, was that Foote had enraged the vocal core of middle-class society. Vicars, colonels, businessmen, and justices of the peace wrote complaints to the Home Office, as its archives reveal, about the "infamous" and "horrible" "blasphemous periodical," sending "specimens" to prove their point.[27] ("A disgraceful publication!" one official paused to scrawl on the back of a letter he was docketing for the home secretary's attention [HO 45, pieces 9,536/49,022/71 and /79e].) If Tyler had not engineered a prosecution, someone else would have commenced proceedings. In Secularism's "heroic decade" of the 1880s, Foote had offended against the same deity Holyoake had come to worship and Wilde would repudiate a decade later: Respectability.[28] Several Christian magazines called for his prosecution (to their credit, more later denounced it). But it was the worshippers of Respectability, he knew, who clamored loudest to have him crushed: "the stupid multitude whose goddess is Mrs. Grundy," imaginary dictatress of the bourgeois novel reviewer, "and great Bumble its god" (Foote, *Blasphemy No Crime* 4).

They were not to be ignored. Victorian government took the horrified correspondence about the *Freethinker* far more seriously than the gigantic petitions presented to Parliament during the six years of the Bradlaugh struggle. People who mattered were outraged "[t]hat such an infamous periodical," as Mr. Walter Grover of Hemel Hempstead wrote on 13 August 1882 (perhaps appropriately, on black-bordered notepaper), "can be disseminated in our public thoroughfares without restraint—while in other respects . . . our national morality is ostensibly the subject of such vigorous supervision" (HO 45, piece 49,902/77).

Home Secretary Sir William Harcourt shared his correspondents' feelings. He wanted to prosecute, and was pressed to do so in the House of Commons.[29] He deferred unwillingly to the attorney-general's advice that seizures or legislation against cheap publications would lead to complications in Ireland, where tricky questions would be raised about the *United Irishman*.[30] His considered refusal to initiate public proceedings against the *Freethinker* rather stemmed from his disinclination to grant the "blasphemous periodical" the publicity he knew it sought and would exploit; the same concern later ensured that a repeat prosecution contemplated in 1887, for the fourth time since 1883, did not go ahead. In the throes of the Bradlaugh struggle, a blasphemy trial was the last thing the Home Office wanted (HO 45 piece 10,406/A46,794/1). When Harcourt refused to act, correspondents appealed to Gladstone and even the queen. Like Under Secretary of State E. R. Henry, meditating legal action against a *Freethinker*-style paper in 1902, Harcourt must have felt he might eventually have to prosecute simply "in self defence," or be "inundated with complaints" (HO 45, piece 10,406/A46,794/1). The *Freethinker* case was a necessary action, reflecting deep social investment in respectability and class hierarchy, let alone religion.

Eventually, a private prosecution for criminal blasphemy was brought against a variety of pieces from issues of the *Freethinker* published between 29 January and 28 May 1882. It was initiated by an angry Notting Hill butcher and revivalist named Henry Varley, member of Parliament Henry Tyler's tool and confederate. Foote had delighted in goading him, and now got the confrontation he wanted. An "Acid Drop" for 29 January 1882 read, "We understand that Butcher Varley has a large stock of the blood of the Lamb, which he is willing to sell at cost price" (36). This, of course, made an item in the indictment. Foote greeted it and its real mover in a front-page editorial for 16 July 1882: "We are in for it at last. Harcourt stood solid as Jumbo, and refused to move. . . . [But] there are always certain persons ready to rush in where angels fear to tread, and at length Sir Henry Tyler came forward to do the deed" (226).

The Varley-Tyler prosecution almost immediately failed in its object of "crippling" Bradlaugh. The "Chief" successfully maneuvered for counts against the early issues to be dropped, thus providing himself with an impeccable defense; for a separate trial, at which he adroitly sloughed off any involvement with the offending numbers; and for the postponement until March 1883 of legal proceedings against Foote, Ramsey, and the paper's printer, Henry Kemp (replacing a man named Whittle, who suffered from cold feet, in time to print the offensive Christmas number of 1882). Five people were eventually tried: Foote and his two confederates plus (separately) two booksellers accused of vending the *Freethinker* in the wake of its successful prosecution.[31] Bradlaugh ensured perhaps most importantly that his own trial, and those of Foote and his colleagues, should be transferred to the superior Court of Queen's Bench, where they were more likely to get a fair hearing, before a reformed special jury.[32]

There were sixteen counts in the indictment. The "Comic Bible" cartoons figured prominently: "Divine Illumination" alone accounted for three. Other offensive items were a satirical piece by William Heaford with a slangy title sure to grate, "What Must I Do To Be Damned?"; Heaford's article on "Christian Humbug"; most of Josiah Symes's "Sermon" on "God?"; and Foote's own sketch of "General Joshua" as a "Bible Hero," all quoted above. Foote's article "Was Jesus Insane?" was also indicted, along with several entries from the *Freethinker*'s regular "Acid Drops" column, one of which was a verbatim report of a Salvation Army meeting in Halifax—not so odd a fact as it sounds, events were to prove.

Another, completely separate, prosecution officially initiated by the city solicitor, Sir Thomas Nelson, was brought against the entire 1882 Christmas number of the *Freethinker,* defiantly pasted up under threat of the imminent Varley-Tyler proceedings. Foote's description of it was precisely accurate: an outspoken comic "budget of blasphemy" (*Prisoner* 50), heavily and offensively illustrated, it quickly became "well known" to London (*Tablet,* 10 March 1883: 366). Home Secretary Harcourt trumpeted his pleasure: "I am glad that Sir T. Nelson is about to take the course which if I was not withheld by the Law Officer's Opinion I should wish to take myself" (HO 45, piece 9,536/49,902/79a).

Once started down the slippery slope of prosecution, the *Freethinker* case gathered emotions and momentum like a giant and rather dirty snowball. The two separate indictments led to three separate trials. In the dock with Foote at the first and second were Ramsey and Kemp; at the third,

Ramsey alone.[33] The first trial (like the second) concerned the second indictment, for the Christmas number. It took place on 1 March 1883 at the Central Criminal Court, Old Bailey, before Mr. Justice North, a devout Roman Catholic. The chief prosecutor, who would appear at all three of the trials, was Sir Hardinge Giffard, former solicitor-general and a determined foe of vulgar Secularism; a few days later he was to appear against Bradlaugh (as he had several times before), representing an informer hot for the five hundred pounds he would earn under an obscure parliamentary regulation if the anathematized member of Parliament could be convicted of having voted in the House of Commons without having sworn the oath, as Bradlaugh had done for a brief time when it seemed he would be allowed to affirm.[34] Foote conducted his own defense, subject to continual interruption and hostile overrulings by Judge North. After the first jury failed to reach a verdict, a second was found to convict four days later, at the second trial; in the interim, against precedent, North peremptorily refused to let the defendants out on bail. He sentenced Foote to twelve months in prison, Ramsey to nine, and Kemp to three, "vindictive and excessive sentence[s]" that were (later) "universally condemned" (*Pall Mall Gazette,* 26 April 1883: 1); on the same day, he sent down for three months a man who killed the proprietor of an early morning stall when he was refused a second cup of coffee (*Daily News,* 3 March 1883: 6). "I do not think the documents we have seen emanated from you," North told Ramsey, "for they show marks of intelligence and ability, however perverted" (*Daily Telegraph,* 6 March 1883: 6). The *Freethinker* editor's "withering" response to pronouncement of sentence against himself instantly entered Freethought folklore: "Thank you, my Lord; the sentence is worthy of your creed" (*Freethinker,* 31 October 1915: 698). As they were taken away in the prison van, Ramsey noticed how some of the "previous occupants had written their names and sentences on the panels; one had put in large capitals: 'Ratty from Plaistow, 12 Moon, out July 1883' " (2). On the second day of their confinement, the chaplain (a humane but fervent fundamentalist) visited Ramsey in his cell, and "after a little talk . . . told me that he had not seen the prosecuted number himself, but his son had, and his son's opinion was that we ought to be transported for life" (7). When he did see the Christmas number, the chaplain decided they ought to be in an insane asylum instead.

The blanket press coverage of the two trials was almost universally hostile. Cheers at the end of Foote's speech at the first trial "were with some difficulty suppressed" (*Daily Telegraph,* 6 March 1883: 3). When sentence was announced, reported the *Daily News,* for which the case merited equal attention with the trials of the Dublin Phoenix Park Murderers, "the prisoners' friends made so much disturbance that the gallery had to be cleared," and "even then the roar of the crowd in the street could be plainly heard inside" (*Daily News,* 6 March: 6). A "storm of hissing, mingled with . . . loud ironical cries of 'Christian! Christian!' rent the air," said the Tory *John Bull,* "and were re-echoed by the large crowd." "A woman"—probably Foote's wife—"was carried out of the gallery in a swoon, while others also uttered cries of lamentation": it was "a scene such as was seldom witnessed" (10 March: 158). "[D]oubtless the scum of East London was gathered to watch the trial of their champions, and hence the indecent exhibition" said the pious *Tablet;* "It is with a strong sense of satisfaction that we announce that the prosecution . . . has been crowned with the completest success" (10 March: 358). The *Spectator* was unusual in giving the case extended front-page attention (10 March: 309): though blasphemy should be "punishable and punished," the editors believed, "it should be very lightly punished when committed by men . . . [whose] only scholarship consists in the study of Tom Paine and Mr. Bradlaugh" (309, 313): "It is very painful to our feelings to have a man come to dinner with dirty face and hands and using coarse forms of speech, but however much annoyance that might cause us, no one would think of making conduct of that kind criminally punishable" (314). "We do not know," sneered *John Bull* in reply, "whether our contemporary contemplates the subjection of the offender to an examination in general culture" (24 March: 185). Even the Unitarian *Inquirer* convicted the prisoners of "irredeemable vulgarity of soul" (10 March: 151): a mere handful of papers called the proceedings anachronistic.

"No law can touch a *Freethinker,* which is a most inappropriate name for any publication," *Punch* concluded, with unusual directness:

> but it can and ought to restrain the free speaker and the too free-and-easy writer who offends against good taste. . . . Pity there are not a few more Mr. Justices NORTH further South, where even the Freethinker's Christmas Number is outdone by the style of paper recently hawked about the streets of some Continental cities. The worship of Respectability in England is something better than merely the homage paid by Vice to Virtue. (17 March 1883: 130)

On 28 April the inevitable pun was finally given utterance: "Mr. BRADLAUGH has been successful in keeping himself out of prison; but hasn't he somehow managed to put his FOOTE in it?" (197). On 24 March a *Punch* piece on "How to Make a Modern Magazine," the imaginary *Contemporary Century,* included "the ex-Editor of *The Freethinker*" among the "High-Class Contributors," writing on "The Limits of Belief: with an Excursus on the Diet in our Convict Prisons" (141). This was an animadversion on the fact that the vulgar blasphemer had had the temerity to launch a new monthly, *Progress,* immediately before he was put away in January 1883. A serious intellectual endeavor, it was doomed to death (in 1887) by inadequate financing and competition from Besant and Holyoake, who launched his *Present Day,* "A Journal Discussing Agitated Questions without Agitation," in direct protest at the *Freethinker* case. On the inside, fellow inmates in Holloway Gaol assisted in putting the *Freethinker*'s crime into perspective. "[Ramsey] was confident[ial]ly asked by an old hand what he was in for," Foote recalled in his memoir, *Prisoner for Blasphemy.* " 'Blasphemy,' said Mr. Ramsey. 'What the hell's that?' said the fellow" (138).

It was no joking matter at the time. So powerful had the pressure of public opinion now become that Foote and Ramsey, from prison, feared they would face another conviction and longer sentences if the third trial came on, particularly if it were delayed until the next law term, when a less sympathetic judge than Lord Chief Justice Coleridge would likely try it. Reluctantly, they empowered their advisers to try any technicality that might abort it. Meanwhile the prosecution applied to the attorney-general for a plea of nolle prosequi, enabling them to abandon the case without admitting effective acquittal. Lord Coleridge, as we shall see in this study's last chapter, had motives of his own for deciding it should take its course (*Times,* 25 April 1883: 3).

A law reformer and a staunch Gladstonian Liberal, Coleridge had served as solicitor-general from December 1868 to November 1871, and as attorney-general from November 1871 to October 1873; during a brief spell as member of Parliament for Exeter, he had guided through Parliament the University Tests Bill that gave dissenters entrance to Oxford and Cambridge, and he had voted decisively for disestablishment of the Church of Ireland. He was the first lord chief justice of the whole realm, an office created by the Judicature Act of 1880. Immediately before the third *Freethinker* trial, he ruled for Bradlaugh and against prosecutor Giffard's informer-client on the matter of the oath, a coincidence that increased the reflective care with which he handled the "celebrated case of *Regina v. Foote*" (E. Coleridge, *Life and Correspondence* 1: 251), one of the four or five most important cases he judged in his fourteen years in office.

On 24 April 1883 Coleridge presided over Foote and Ramsey's third trial, at which "through the kindness of the governor of [Holloway] gaol," noticed the *Daily News,* "they appeared . . . in their ordinary dress instead of prison garb" (27 April: 3). It produced another hung verdict, despite four and a half hours of jury deliberation: a dramatic result. Needless to say, the newspapers that had scrambled to cover the first and second trials passed over this less-acceptable development in silence, though several (like the staunchly Anglican *Rock*) hoped beforehand to stir Coleridge's resolve to protect "civilization" from "slime" with impassioned editorials on the "Blasphemy-mongers" (20 April 1883: 255), and several more objected afterwards to "the effusive and offensive sympathy" he "conceive[d] to be due to an Atheist from a Liberal Judge" (*John Bull*, 5 May 1883: 281). When the prosecution pushed for a fourth trial, going so far as to impanel another special jury, the lord chief justice made no secret of his displeasure at a proceeding "so entirely unusual" (*Times*, 27 April 1883, 3). Only repeated and public upbraidings on his part stopped further action; but his attempts after the trial to reduce the prisoners' sentences had no effect. Also ineffectual were "an extraordinary number of letters" and a wave of petitions to the home secretary requesting their release, both from Freethinkers and libertarians and from Christian sympathizers (Home Office memorandum of 5 October 1894, in HO 45 10,406/A46,794/8); three of the jurymen at the second trial signed (*Freethinker*, 23 March 1884: 90).[35] Foote and his colleagues served out their time as common felons. Respectability's revenge on blasphemous vulgarity was complete when some of Foote's Secularist colleagues added their voices to the chorus of condemnation.

Foote's bitterest critic was Jacob Holyoake. Ill-assorted yoke-mates, the two men had lasted only a few weeks as co-editors of the *Secularist* in 1876: Foote was "a costermonger in rhetoric," Holyoake charged (*Alien Features* 5).[36] The *Freethinker* outraged his sense of self, mission, martyrdom, and respectability. Holyoake refused the telegram summons from Reverend Sharman, secretary of the National Association for the Repeal of the Blasphemy Laws: "Cannot you get *Daily News* to demand instant release of prisoners for blasphemy—you ought not to be silent" (HL). And he chose not to attend the "Mass meeting in Favour of the Release of Messrs. Foote and Ramsey," Wednesday, 11 July 1883. Social duty demanded his presence instead "At Mrs. Knowles party," opposite which laconic diary entry he silently pasted the handbill that announced the meeting (HC). The entry belongs alongside those for Friday, 23 February—"Rector called in to chat"—and Wednesday, 14 March—"Breakfasted with the Marquess of Queensberry," whose support was giving Freethought some aristocratic cachet, though it did not do much for its respectability. (Queensberry wrote Holyoake, who was angling for an invitation, however, "I cannot say I feel satisfied with the associations I find Secularism has drawn me into" [1883, n.d., in HL].) Only grudgingly did Holyoake write to Home Secretary Harcourt, to plead for remission of the blasphemers' sentences (diary, 3 August 1883, in HC), and then only on the grounds that "it was no business of the State to protect Freethinkers from the excess of their own enthusiasm, and that, since Christians were allowed unbridled license to ridicule their adversaries, and did it, both parties should be imprisoned, or neither" (*Sixty Years* 1: 112).[37] In Secularism's "perilous hour," as American "Infidel" Colonel Ingersoll called it (*Ingersoll on Holyoake*, n. pag., in HL), with Foote in prison and Bradlaugh struggling for his voice in the House of Commons, such ungenerous squeamishness amounted to hypocrisy and betrayal.

Had the third trial not come on, the case of G. W. Foote and the *Freethinker* would be nothing more than a footnote in legal history. Foote's assumption of the role of counsel at the first and second trials gained him no quarter before a judge who repeatedly interrupted and upbraided him for introducing "irrelevant" material. But at the third trial, Lord Coleridge handed down a ruling consecrated by his position as lord chief justice that fundamentally changed the definition of the crime of blasphemy. And the condition of his doing so was that at the third trial he allowed G. W. Foote to make the kind of defense that Judge North had repeatedly ruled out of court. Now, too, Foote put aside all the peripheral issues he had taken up before, such as the history of Christian "vituperation." Given his last opportunity to speak, without interruption, Foote collected and crystallized the ideas we have seen develop across the nineteenth century: that class discrimination, property thinking, and political motives were inherent in his culture's use of blasphemy law, even in the teeth of the tacit admission of the 1880s that doubt and unbelief were widespread.

In effect, on 24 April 1883, Foote was officially granted and triumphantly vindicated that right to a public voice for which Secularism and the long tradition of martyrs had struggled. Coleridge was himself, "first and foremost, an orator" (in E. Coleridge, *Life and Correspondence* 2: 386). In summing-up, he described Foote's speech as "powerful" (J. Coleridge 24), and "well worthy" of attention (26); and he gave the jury a day's delay before he did so as "a full opportunity of reflecting calmly *on the very striking and able speech you have just heard*" (qtd. in *Freethinker*, 2 May 1915: 278). To Foote's successors in the Secularist movement, it was "easily the greatest ever delivered by a prisoner on trial for blasphemy" (Cutner, introduction 7). One of the jurors who stood out against a verdict of guilty, Foote proudly recalled, declared, quite simply, "he was not going to assist in imprisoning like a thief 'a man who could make a speech like that' " (*Prisoner* 162).

His masterstroke in court was strikingly simple, and sprang naturally from the tradition of which he was part. He read aloud in court, as he was explicitly forbidden to do by Judge North, side by side with indicted passages from the *Freethinker*, strongly worded extracts from Matthew Arnold, T. H. Huxley, Mill, Herbert Spencer, John Morley, Froude's *Nemesis of Faith*, Professor Clifford, Swinburne's poetry, James Thomson ("B.V." of the *City of Dreadful Night*), Leslie Stephen, and "other heretics whose works are circulated by Mudie" (*Prisoner* 14) or displayed for sale on Mr. Smith's railway station bookstalls (J. Coleridge 27). The technique was reinforced by his codefendant, publisher Ramsey, who instead of naming names among established and unprosecuted blasphemous writers, named their ultrarespectable high-class publishers: Longman, Macmillan, Chapman and Hall. The technique had the incidental benefit of dramatically undermining the public image of Foote's own and his movement's and his class's unlettered ignorance.

Ridicule, the *Freethinker*'s chosen weapon, and very plain speaking indeed, mark the whole impressive range of Foote's quotations from the best literature of the day. Arnold lays aside his earnestness to joke over the seventeenth-century theological poser of whether Jesus had his clothes on at the Ascension, and to imagine God as "a sort of infinitely magnified and improved Lord Shaftesbury" (qtd. in *Defence* 34–35), a passage which he discreetly cut from the next edition of *Literature and Dogma*. Morley snaps in his *Voltaire:* "a religion which has shed more blood than any other has no right to quarrel over a few epigrams" (qtd. 35). Swinburne, in his "Hymn To Man" (the lines apostrophizing Christ on the cross, a favorite selection of Secularist songbooks) shrieks anti-Christian defiance:

> Lo, thy blood-blackened altars, lo
> The lips of priests that pray and feed
> While their own hell's worm curls and licks
> The poison of the crucifix. (qtd. 40)

Huxley declares that orthodoxy is "as willing as ever . . . to visit, with such petty thunder-bolts as its half-paralysed hands can hurl, those who refuse to degrade nature to the level of primitive Judaism" (qtd. 31–32). Herbert Spencer's ironical explanation of the Trinity, meanwhile, would not have been out of place in the indicted Christmas number of the *Freethinker* (qtd. 32).

The utilitarian philosopher James Mill, as his son vividly remembered, once described God as "the most perfect conception of wickedness which the human mind can devise" (*Defence* 33). "In one of [our] libels," Foote paused to remark, "it is said that the deity of the Old Testament is as ferocious as a tiger." "What is the difference," he asked, "between a phrase like that and the extract I have read?" (33). No one could rationally cling to the idea that there is a difference in culpability between a "cold statement" and a "burning metaphor" (*Prisoner* 42). Rather, "[t]he difference," Foote charged, "is that one is the language of a nine-shilling book, and the other the language of a penny paper" (*Defence* 33).

Echoes of Henry Hetherington resonate in that climactic question. "Why," he had asked, "should two-guinea blasphemers be tolerated and penny ones prosecuted?" (*Trial of Henry Hetherington* 16). The law allowed,

Holyoake had added, "Blasphemy in guinea volumes," but "exhibits the holiest horror at it when in penny pamphlets" (*History of the Last Trial* 55). Why should blasphemy and profanity "only be cooked up in an expensive way" (*God v. Paterson* 59)? Shakespeare, Foote's idol, had spoken true: "Great men may jest with saints: 'tis wit in them, / But in the less, foul profanation" (*Measure for Measure* 2.2.128–29, qtd. as epigraph, *God v. Paterson*).

What Foote added to the tradition he inherited was a profound understanding that not only the price of the paper but its class-marked language was at issue. His question, which packed in a nutshell the essence of Freethought's case after three generations of struggle and martyrdom, and his inescapable conclusion, were repeated again and again during the full hour of his three-hour speech, fourteen of forty-five transcript pages, that Foote devoted to his quotations. The upper-class "propagators of heresy," he hammered the point home, were not prosecuted because "it would be perilous to touch them" (*Prisoner* 35). Secularists were being made "the scapegoats[s] of the cultured agnostics of the day" (34). Late Victorian society, he emphasized, and the *Freethinker* case demonstrably proved, no longer primarily regarded blasphemy as an insult to God and his church. Blasphemy had become a class crime of language: it was simply "skepticism expressed in plain language and sold at the people's price" (*Blasphemy No Crime* 22).

Foote had his facts right. It was indeed on record, for example, that the archbishop of Canterbury had recently "pathetically complained" that "it is dangerous to introduce high-class magazines to the family circle, because they are nearly sure to contain a large quantity of skepticism" (*Prisoner* 35). But action was not forthcoming against such publications. Occasionally, a society for the prosecution of blasphemy and blasphemous literature would spring up, but nothing happened. One was formed during the *Freethinker* trials; it planned to "get up cases, as . . . funds will allow, against Professor Huxley, Dr. Tyndall, Herbert Spencer, Swinburne, the author of Strauss's works, Leslie Stephen, John Morley," all of whom Foote had quoted, plus "the editor of the *Jewish World*." "If the promoters of the anti-blasphemy crusade were determined on getting the law altered in favor of the blasphemers," the *Tablet* commented, "they could not have decided on a better course than this" (10 March 1883: 366). These were writers "we should no more expect to see in the dock than the Archbishop of CANTERBURY" (*Pall Mall Gazette,* 2 March 1883: 1). Back in 1861–62, even the celebrated trial for heresy of the authors of the Broad Church collection, *Essays and Reviews,* in the ecclesiastical Court of Arches, had resulted in impasse. A verdict of guilty (which carried the threat of excommunication) was overturned on appeal by the Lords in 1864, "dismissing eternal punishment," in the epigram of the day, "with costs" (qtd. in Bonner, *Penalties* 89). Six years after the *Freethinker* trials, the 1889 publication of a second collection of progressive theological essays, *Lux Mundi,* caused no legal ripples.

In effect, since the beginnings of mass literacy, even as far back as the Woolston case of 1728, the drive to suppress vulgarity and plain speaking had proven more and more powerful a motive in blasphemy prosecution than the apprehension that what might most damage Christianity was serious scholarship and sophisticated irony, what Byron in *Childe Harold* called "sapping a solemn creed with solemn sneer" (3.107.5). "It was most unjust," Brougham told the House of Commons in 1825, on the occasion of a petition by Carlile and four of his shopmen, that "whilst [the] subtile poison" of Hume and Gibbon and Bolingbroke "was left unpunished, . . . the poor man should be sent to prison" (appendix, *Trial of Thomas Paterson* 71). But to attack those influential, high-literary authors in the courts would have been a daunting intellectual task. Lesser fry are easier targets.

If an upper-class author was circumspect in the latter decades of Victoria's reign, and particularly if he veiled his criticisms in the revered and cloudy language of Christian tradition (see below, 5.5.i), he could publish with impunity. Even when John Morley, editor of the *Pall Mall Gazette* and noticeably hostile to Foote's case before the commencement of his trials, openly took to spelling "God" with a lower-case *g,* the only retaliation was the *Spectator's* decision to spell Morley with a small *m* (*Three Trials for Blasphemy* 77): one punishes a gentleman's joke with another joke. "Mr. JOHN MORLEY and Mr. CHARLES BRADLAUGH are believed to think alike," commented *John Bull,* "but they speak very differently" (5 May 1883: 280).

Writing in the *Westminster Review* during the Carlile prosecutions, John Stuart Mill had first perceived the class danger of not abolishing the law on blasphemy: "It would be most unfair to judge the poor, unrefined, uneducated man by the same standard we apply to the man of 'culture' " (*Mill on Blasphemy* 10). A great deal lies behind that statement. Theoretically, gentleman and working man were equally capable of belief in or denial of the "Being or Providence" of God and his Revelation. The unfairness Mill perceived lay in the kind of "standard" used. Herein lies the danger of celebrating too quickly the requirement, post-Carlile, that "the crime of blasphemy" should no longer "cover . . . the mere denial of Christianity," but "had to contain some element of genuinely abusive or outrageous language" (Walter, *Blasphemy: Ancient and Modern* 38). The workingman's language *was* "abusive"; it *was* "outrageous." By the 1880s, even Locke's "simplicity" looked "uncouth" (*Saturday Review,* 20 January 1883: 88). The climactic case of the *Freethinker* allows us finally to understand the relationship between the linguistic class prejudice that doomed Jacob Holyoake to jail for "uttering" "his own words" and the literary redefinition of blasphemy undertaken between Hone's trials of 1817 and Hetherington's case of 1841. It vividly demonstrated how the shift in emphasis from what law called the religious "matter" to the stylistic "manner" of the crime, which had covered and helped enable the secularization of blasphemy while it helped to mask its politicization, bore hard on the "unrefined" man of no "culture." Tolerance was paid for by class repression.

The traditional interpretation of blasphemy stood until the 1810s. Whatever else they did, the few rulings between the Woolston case of 1728 and Eaton's 1812 trial for the "Third Part" of the *Age of Reason* also explicitly confirmed it: up to the time of Hone's trials, the religious "matter" was considered primary, while the "manner" of the crime's commission was a secondary factor, whether (in Blackstone's phrase) by measured argument, "contumelious reproaches," or "ridicule" and "profane scoffing" (4: 59, 60). In the year of the *Freethinker* trials, judge and legal authority Sir James Fitzjames Stephen handed it down as law that "[e]ven in our own days, it is an offence for anyone brought up as a Christian to deny the truth of Christianity, however respectfully" (*History* 2: 437–38), though the law that made it so was "obsolete" and barely "theoretically" workable (2: 396). This was the case, he emphasized, in an article in the *Fortnightly Review,* months after that "obsolete" law was invoked to imprison G. W. Foote, during the case of Henry Hetherington: "Though the language used . . . was violent and indecorous, the court do not in their judgement refer to that fact."[38] "What, I ask, has happened since 1841"—the date of the muddled Royal Commission Report on the Criminal Law—"to change the law?" ("Blasphemy," March 1884: 304).[39]

Stephen was being disingenuous. His chapter "Offences against Religion" was not a description of existing law but a blueprint for its rationalized abolition (*History* 2: 476), as an insult to his generation—"the first in which an avowed open denial of the fundamental doctrines of the Christian religion has been made by any number of serious and respectable people" (2: 437–38). In his 1878 *Digest of the Criminal Law* Stephen himself had printed side by side, in facing columns, the competing definitions centered on "matter" and "manner." Hot for conviction, Judge North perhaps followed his lead in 1883. At the first trial, he defined the crime, for the jury's benefit, as denial of the truth of the Bible per se; at the second, it meant the use of "offensive," or "profane" language that might disturb the feelings of a Christian community.

As we have seen, a great deal had happened after—and before—1841, as Stephen well knew. Starkie's authoritative 1812 *Treatise on the Law of Slander and Libel* gave considerable leeway to judges who wished to shift emphasis from the "matter" to the "manner" of the crime. The "criterion and test of guilt," he had concluded his long description of blasphemy, in words that Lord Coleridge pondered carefully in summing up at the third *Freethinker* trial, was a "wilful intention to pervert, insult, and mislead others, by means of licentious and contumelious abuse applied to sacred subjects" (2: 146). We recognize "honest" criticism by its "spirit of temperance, moderation, and fairness" (2: 144), a spirit to which the common Everyman whom Starkie hesitatingly admitted had "a right, . . . legally speaking, to publish his opinions" (2: 144) could rarely aspire. It is easy to see why Fitzjames Stephen dismissed this formulation as "flabby verbiage" ("Blasphemy" 312).[40] But it stuck. More, as we know, the Hetherington case was not the straightforward support for definition centered on "matter" that Stephen presents. Chief Justice Denman had paraphrased these very sections from Starkie in his judgment (*Trial of Henry Hetherington* 22). Other trials of the 1840s had given the definition centered on "manner" clear precedent (Paterson's 1844 Edinburgh trial, for example).[41] Moreover, Starkie was the senior member of the 1841 royal commission whose muddled report had balanced respect for evangelical public opinion with concern for bad publicity. Thus, "[t]he law distinctly forbids *all* denial of the being and providence of God or the truth of the Christian religion." Yet, since the Woolston case of 1728, only legal action against those who stoop to an abusive "manner" has "met with the cordial acquiescence of public opinion" (*British Parliamentary Papers* 3: 85). When "manner" was finally criminalized, Mill's "poor, unrefined uneducated" culprit had a very big problem indeed. A man who can produce only "gross" "errors" and "blunders" in his presumption "to teach and enlighten the rest of mankind," as Starkie put it, would be bound to be wanting in "manner" (2: 44): the word has a social as well as a literary bearing.

And the theoretical equality of all men before the law breaks down when the crime in question is a crime of words, language, style. A single standard for adjudging guilt created "one law for the refined, another for the vulgar disputant" (Mill, *Mill on Blasphemy* 10). As Fitzjames Stephen contended:

> If you allow coarse and vulgar people to discuss [sacred] subjects freely, they must and will discuss them coarsely. . . . You cannot . . . send a man to gaol for not writing like a scholar and a gentleman when he is neither one nor the other, and when he is writing on a subject which excites him strongly. ("Blasphemy," 315)

In court in 1883, G. W. Foote took up the point with plainspoken aplomb. "To imprison every person guilty of 'vulgar' language," he later remembered

warning the court, "would be to make one half the population maintain
the other" (*Freethinker,* 26 November 1911: 753). It would turn what Henry
Hetherington had called an "imaginary, impossible, and totally fictitious
offence" (qtd. in Calder-Marshall 132) into a "comic-opera crime" (Foote,
Freethinker, 26 November 1911: 753).

But this, also, despite the apparent triumph of Foote's third defense, was
one result of the *Freethinker* prosecution. "I confess," said Lord Coleridge,
picking his way delicately through the difficulties presented by Foote's
plainspoken and sarcastic literary extracts in his summing-up:

> I confess, as I heard them, I had, and have, a difficulty in distinguishing them
> from the alleged [blasphemous] libels. They do appear to me to be open to the
> same charge, on the same grounds, as Mr. Foote's writings. . . . If it be [so], I
> will make no distinction between Mr. Foote and anyone else; if there are men,
> however eminent, who use such language as Mr. Foote, and if ever I have to try
> them, . . . they shall, so far as my powers go, have neither more nor less than
> the justice I am trying to do Mr. Foote. . . . [T]here is but one rule in this Court
> for all who come to it. (J. Coleridge 29)

The words have a fine liberal sound: all who "use such language" are equally
bound. But though the lord chief justice's painstaking tolerance allowed
Foote the fairest hearing he could have had at the time, it also firmly established the definition centered on "manner," and with it a single standard
of language and public discourse that knowingly discriminated against the
lower classes. With one hand Coleridge waved away the fear of persecution;
with the other he propped open the back door to harassment. "Artisan
atheism" and "vulgar" blasphemy remained proscribed, and would remain
so through the 1922 prosecution of J. W. Gott and beyond. After all, high-
class authors like the ones Foote quoted had only occasional resort to the
weapons of ridicule and plain speech that were the *Freethinker*'s workaday
tools; they chose to use what he had habitually to use.

The key sentence in Coleridge's ruling was disarmingly simple:

> I now lay it down as law, that, if the decencies of controversy are observed, even
> the fundamentals of religion may be attacked without a person being guilty of
> blasphemous libel. (J. Coleridge 28)

The dictum sparked heated argument in legal circles: if the single standard
were fairly applied, and the emphasis on "manner" upheld, an unconscion-
able restraint would be placed upon heterodox literature. Freedom would
be guaranteed only to authors who observed the "decencies," which might
mean anything from refined vocabulary and perfect grammar to tasteful
obliquity. Anyone who used "common," "vulgar," "gross," "shocking," or
"painful" idiom would be liable at law. A blasphemy law so interpreted

was unworkable, as the failure to reach a verdict in the third *Freethinker* trial implicitly suggests. Even commentators who approved the ruling could not find the chain of precedents convincing.

The answer to doubt was to reread legal history and legal documents until the necessary sanction for the new definition could be produced. Such revisionism was of course the governing principle of legal works from Starkie's *Slander and Libel* through the 1841 report; and it now governed the commentaries provoked by Lord Coleridge's ruling, such as the revised edition of W. Blake Odgers's *Libel and Slander* (first published 1881) and G. D. Nokes's 1928 *History of the Crime of Blasphemy*.[42] Revisionism gave rise, in turn, to a vociferous rearguard action by those who either favored the traditional definition for religious reasons or refused to "explain . . . [the law] away in such a manner as to prolong its existence and give it an air of plausibility and humanity" (J. Stephen, "Blasphemy" 315). Abolitionists included the clergymen founders and members of the Committee for the Repeal of the Blasphemy Laws, as well as journalists and members of the legal profession. Lord Coleridge had opted for "expediency" over "authority," declared a leading article in the *Westminster Review* prompted by the "vindictive and happily abortive second prosecution of Messrs. Ramsey and Foote" (July 1883: 2–3, 1); among other eminent judges, Baron Huddleston was "entirely disposed to dissent" from Coleridge's opinion in a minor case of 1886 (Odgers, *Libel and Slander* 472).

The Coleridge ruling could not possibly "provide sufficiently" either for "freedom of religious discussion" or for literary endeavor (J. Stephen, "Blasphemy" 290, 314). It left untouched on the books a statute Coleridge himself found "ferocious" and "shocking" (J. Coleridge 10, 24). And it provided for "the recurrence at irregular intervals of scandalous prosecutions" in common law that very often "afford a channel for the gratification of private malice under the cloak of religion" (J. Stephen, "Blasphemy" 318)—Mary Whitehouse's for the editor, writers, and readers of *Gay News*, for example, nearly a hundred years later. Because no major case of blasphemy was tried for the twenty-five years that followed the *Freethinker* debacle, Coleridge's ruling was not authoritatively challenged in court. It came to be considered " 'the better opinion' in point of law" almost by default (Odgers, *Libel and Slander* 472). "I feel sure," Odgers concluded pragmatically, at the turn of the century, "that it is the only law on the subject which it is possible to enforce in the present day" (472).[43]

Thus, though it seemed that justice was served in April 1883, and though Lord Chief Justice Coleridge appeared so enlightened and class blind in court, he had written an official recipe for discrimination on the grounds of language, "manner," and style. The lower-class role of blasphemous scapegoat had been confirmed at the highest level. And it was no accident of historical timing that this should have happened on the eve of the Third Reform Act of 1884, exactly as two million unrespectable vulgarians acquired a voice in public affairs.[44] It would become hard now to dismiss vox populi as what Francis Galton called it, "the utterance of a mob of nobodies" (69); but progressive loss of faith since the 1840s had put increased pressure on the ideals of civility and gentlemanliness. (Thus, shortly after he became an agnostic in the 1870s, Leslie Stephen wrote, "I believe in nothing, to put it shortly; but . . . I mean to live and die like a gentleman if possible" [Annan 2].) Upper-class, even liberal anxiety about what the mass would say at the ballot box, and fear about how its voice would change or degrade the conversation that is culture, engineered a compensation. The delicate mechanisms of law were ready to hand to check and silence the common man's "own words."

In 1914, spurred by what the *Star* called "recent outbreaks of police interference with the public propaganda of unpopular minorities," a committee for repeal represented the case for abolition to the prime minister (*Prime Minister and the Blasphemy Laws* 16). Its leader, Bradlaugh's daughter, Hypatia Bonner, confirmed that "proceedings in every case" of blasphemy recently tried—Boulter (1908), Gott (1911), etc.—"without exception, have been taken against uncultured men speaking at street corners" or on open land (5). The law had become a "sorry weapon" against "the poor, the defenceless, the ignorant, and the worthless" (6). "It does not seem to be right," seconded the novelist Silas K. Hocking, "that a man should be punished just because he is not a gentleman," since "language, like deportment, is a matter of taste and of gentlemanly feeling" (qtd. 9–10). "In effect," added another member of the deputation, G. Lowes Dickinson, professor of literature, "on the point of language . . . this creates one law for uneducated persons and another for educated persons; one law for one class and another law for another class" (qtd. 8).

In reply, although he was personally sympathetic to abolition, Prime Minister Asquith only reiterated the established position, invoking language that evokes memories of the Carlile prosecutions and the turbulent 1810s: "I think, of course, it is necessary to see that we do not lose any security or safeguard that the law at present provides against . . . *violent or offensive language*" (*Prime Minister and the Blasphemy Laws* 14, my emphasis). The time Parliament would need to debate abolition was strictly rationed in an atmosphere of international tension. No committee for the repeal of the blasphemy laws, however impressive, had ever or was ever to have more effect.

2. TWO CODAS

There are two codas to this first tale of the *Freethinker* case of 1883. One is supplied from an unlikely source. The desire for "security and safeguards" against the vulgar voice of the lower orders cannot be demonstrated any more plainly than by considering a prosecution of the 1880s that never had its day in court.

G. W. Foote was no more immune to snobbery than the society that condemned him. One of his favorite targets was the Salvation Army, whose bands and missionaries had taken to the streets in enormous numbers from the early 1870s. Its enthusiastic excesses featured regularly in the *Freethinker*'s columns. Sometimes the reports were unfair, often (at least to this reader) they were hilarious. At his trial, Foote claimed that a double standard protected the army's language, which was, he declared with some justice, a free mix of "the most brutal language of military camps" and the slang of the streets with the "time-honoured expressions of the creed" (*Three Trials for Blasphemy* 83), the very language "whose sanctity is made the basis of the attack on myself and my co-defendants" (17). Army members called prayer "knee drill"; Salvationist publications were an "Artillery of Words," and so forth.[45] (Before Judge North managed to silence him, he squeezed in a choice quotation to prove his point.) Salvationists even shared the *Freethinker*'s Cockney brand of humor.[46] If society cared so much about the regulation of public discourse, why was the army not prosecuted?

Indeed. Foote was underestimating establishment animus against the lower orders, to whom the Salvation Army addressed itself. Street speaking and meetings in open spaces were techniques Salvationists shared with Secularists, and which in an age of increasing advertisement and commercial display clearly provoked, to a greater degree, the same anxiety over public space and publicity as was expressed in the Paterson and Holyoake trials of the 1840s. When these were banned by the government, the aggravation of the army's noncompliance added to a pile of its offenses against taste and language to make it a very tempting target for blasphemy prosecution.

The army's vulgarity was constitutional, deliberate. William Booth himself, wrote his biographer Harold Begbie, had the appearance of "a middle-aged tub-thumper," or "a clever cheap Jack" drumming up sales with a band in support (*Life* 1: 435). Many establishment and religious organs were judicious in their estimate of the new Christian force: "To men and women of education and refinement," opined the *Tablet* in October 1881, the army's language "must necessarily appear outrageously irreverent. But it appears to be the dialect which goes home more directly to those to whom it is

addressed" (Sandal 143). Other judges made less attempt at accommodation. The army's deemphasis of Bible and sacraments and Booth's excommunication by the Free Churches were not the chief issues. "The charge
most often made was that the methods of the Army were vulgar and irreverent," pandering "to the lowest tastes of the most degraded classes" (Sandal
162, 163). According to a range of newspapers, a Salvationist meeting resembled "a rowdy company in a public-house making game of religion"; "vulgar, senseless noise" was its "staple and essence"; "addresses called prayers
were screamed out . . . irresistibly reminding one of the prophets of Baal"
(qtd. 163).[47]

The loud songs offended most (the very songs Shaw wryly celebrates in
Major Barbara): "Onward! upward! blood-washed soldier!" by Fanny
Crosby; "Ye sons of God, awake to glory," sung to the tune of the "Marseil-
laise" (Sandal 107) and "I've found a Friend in Jesus—He's the lily of the
valley" (207), to the tune of "The old log cabin in the lane," both by the
father of Salvation Army music, Charles W. Fry.[48] The strategy of appropri-
ating well-known tunes developed partly in response to a favorite mob tactic
for disrupting meetings: loudly singing popular songs to drown out Salvationists' voices. It has much in common with the blasphemous parody that
was a staple of *Freethinker* fare, and is one subject of the next chapter. By
early 1882, the year the *Freethinker* was indicted and the peak year for anti-
Salvationist violence and agitation, which was rife from 1878 to 1883, the
bands had moved on from mere popular songs to downright tunes from
the music halls, leading off with a lively new version of the comic hit
"Champagne Charlie" entitled "Bless his name, he sets me free!" (Sandal
110).[49] To outraged middle-class Anglican ears, Booth's simple explanation—Why should the devil get all the best tunes?—hardly seemed ade-
quate justification. One Secularist critic declared that "[a] more flippant,
offensively familiar, irreverent, and blasphemous line" than "We are soldiers
of J.C., / And we sing and pray do we, / Till the day of Jubilee" never
"made its nasal ascent before the astonished Throne of Grace" (*New Ideas
of the Day* 14). An army sympathizer, W. T. Stead of the *Pall Mall Gazette,*
soon to be a bête noire of the establishment, preferred the "concise and
graphic" style of the earliest songs: "The devil and me, we can't agree, / I
hate him, and he hates me" (Sandal 108). There was not much distance
between this and a catchy send-up that begged Jesus to "Stick to my heart /
Like a penny jam tart!" Even Salvationists mistook it for their own (Sandal
111). Bramwell Booth, the general's son and successor, delved deep into the
reasons for the army's offensiveness when he remembered, in 1926, how "It
gave its message through the mouths of quite 'vulgar' people—merchants,

domestic servants, factory girls, farm labourers!" (31); *"It made the dumb speak"* (30, my emphasis).

What was the difference, as Foote might ask, between these vulgarities and the offensive bluntnesses of the *Freethinker?* Not much. It was not long before actual charges of blasphemy began to be made against the Salvation Army. "The religious press," wrote Bramwell Booth, positively "distinguished itself by the eagerness with which it . . . printed any story that came along to prove that we taught false doctrines, promoted irreverence, and encouraged blasphemy, and that the principal result of our work was," in the words of the two hundred blasphemy indictments of the nineteenth century, " 'to bring religion into contempt' " (26). Questions were asked in the House in March 1882 about the danger of rioting posed by the "gross profanity" of Salvation Army meetings (Begbie, *Life* 2: 6); one member of Parliament asked the home secretary to throw the book at a young man prosecuted for street selling of the *War Cry.* April saw an attack on General Booth in the *Times* by a Wesleyan minister. Establishment tactics against the "Sally Army," in fact, exactly replicated actions against "militant" Secularism. Processions were prevented, by Home Secretary Harcourt's express command (Booth 28n); burials were disrupted. "[T]he denunciation reached its height—of absurdity" when Lord Shaftesbury, a staunch advocate of blasphemy prosecution, "solemnly stated that, as the result of much study, he had come to the conclusion that the Salvation Army was clearly Anti-Christ" (Booth, *Echoes* 27). (Lord Coleridge, by contrast, championed the army in the Lords.) On 10 April 1883, while G. W. Foote was preparing for his climactic third trial in the privacy of Holloway Gaol, the bishops of Oxford and Hereford brought further "slanderous charges" in the Upper House of Convocation at Canterbury (Sandal 199). The army was said to have posted "blasphemous handbills"; the exercise called "Creeping for Jesus," in which "the lights were turned down, and men and women, . . . proceeded to crawl upon the floor groping with their hands in the darkness," was denounced as an inducement to sexual immorality (Begbie, *Life* 2: 16). An unfounded statement in the *Globe* of London (June 1885) accused the army of exhibiting a banner at Cambridge bearing "horrible and blasphemous words" (Sandal 199); the story was disproved again and again, but it went the rounds nonetheless. General Booth's organization, the most important flowering of popular Christianity in the late nineteenth century, an army whose charity extended into the slums of darkest London and the human wastes of the empire, was threatened with proceedings on every hand.[50] Upon the blasphemy laws had indeed been concentrated middle-class society's anxieties about "culchaw," class, vulgarity, and the power of words. They were the perfect pretext for prosecution, though in the army's case the trap was never finally sprung.

A second coda is literary, and comes in two parts. Restore to G. W. Foote his place in history, and one can better trace the shape of the paradigmatic novelistic career of the 1880s. George Gissing wrote enthusiastically about Foote's "excellent" "advanced" new monthly, *The Liberal,* to his brother Algernon in January 1879 (*Collected Letters* 1: 142, 153). In February, he heard Foote speak, noting down the heads of his arguments with care (1: 153–54), momentarily stirred by the idea of a career in "public readings" himself (1: 142). He defended Foote's views in an (unpublished) letter to the London *Echo* (1: 154); he entered proudly into a brief correspondence with Foote himself. His note to Algernon about his schoolteacher friend Bertz's response to his *Echo* riposte set the tone of that year. "[O]ne of the daughters of his principal happened to see the passage, & exclaimed: 'Why, here they are discussing whether there is a God or not! I wonder the Queen allows such a paper!' Ha, ha, ha!" (1: 155).

In 1883, Gissing urged Algernon to "read Mr. Justice North's remarks in the Foote case. Very worthy of the middle ages, in sooth" (*Collected Letters* 2: 123). But brash confidence had evaporated. The vulgarity of the *Freethinker* was a shock to the system; the verdict and the national scandal raised specters of the social alienation occasioned by blasphemous atheism. Meanwhile, Bentley was hesitating to publish Gissing's latest novel, impossibly titled *Now or Never, Or Mrs. Grundy's Enemies*. In 1886 Gissing produced the first prize flower in what became a lifelong career in Cockney bashing and fearful reaction against verbal "violence," *Demos;* he returned with a sharp editorial knife to his first novels, *Workers in the Dawn* (1880) and *The Unclassed* (1884), excising all narratorial excess in the handling of his brutal urban material. There is a wide cultural gap between the creative and comic Cockneyisms of Dickens, and the disgusted phonetic transcriptions to which Gissing descended in the *Nether World* (1889): "Ech-ow!" shout his news vendors, "Exteree speciul! Ech-ow! Steendard!" (30). *The Emancipated* (1890) tracks a husband's unstoppable declension from verbal to physical abuse of his wife. *Born in Exile* (1892) climactically turns on a classical pun and a fragment of etymology: to become a *person* lower-class atheist Godwin Peake must train to be a *parson* (1: 53); only through the "clerical career" (2: 91, 105) can he realize all the meanings of Latin *persona;* only thus can he wipe out the shame of his own association with "street-corner rationalism" (1: 195); only thus can he escape the stigma of Cockney-dom, personified by Uncle Andrew, whose opening of "Peak's Refreshment an' Dinin' Rooms" opposite its very gates ignominiously ends Peak's career at college (1: 208), and whose son "massacres" the *Rime of the Ancient Mariner* for family amusement—"The silly buckits *on* the deck / That 'ed so long rem'ined, / I dreamt as they was filled with jew, / End when I awowk, it r'ined" (1: 129).[51] The grammarless hordes are a "squalling mass" and "obscene herd of idiot mockers" (1: 189): "The mere sound of their voices nauseates me; their vilely grotesque accent and pronunciation—bah!" (1: 215). For so endorsing and narrativizing the linguistic class hierarchy of the 1880s, Gissing was finally rewarded with warm reviews: *Born in Exile* was so "obviously not written merely to catch the asses' ears of the duller public" (*Novel Review*, Coustillas and Partridge 211),[52] and in such "pure" and "unexceptionable" English, that it deserved to be judged "one of the cleverest and best written books of the season" (*Daily Chronicle* 201).

Restore to Foote his place in history, and one also understands better what drives the most extraordinary bestseller of the 1880s, *Robert Elsmere*. Mrs. Humphry Ward's eponymous apostate clergyman, bereft of parish living and purpose, has to lean for support against a London lamppost when he sees this advertising placard "flaunting" at a bookshop door (458):[53]

> Read *Faith and Fools*. Enormous success. Our *Comic Life of Christ* now nearly completed. Quite the best thing of its kind going. Woodcut this week—Transfiguration. (*Elsmere* 457)

Mrs. Ward, née Arnold, Matthew's niece, claimed that the "shock" of the Reverend John Wordsworth's Bampton lecture of 1881, which came down hard on religious liberals like "Uncle Matt," "led directly" to her heretical theological romance of 1888 (qtd. in Ashton xii). But Foote's *Freethinker*—especially the 1882 Christmas number—was a more "shocking" goad to prick her into writing, the missing and vulgar link in the famous work's evolution. Ward's husband was a *Times* journalist; she moved in upper-middle-class unorthodox circles; she took in the full outrage of the trials and their context of "militant" Secularism; she shared the panic at seeing Cockney Bradlaugh finally esconced in Parliament in 1886. These are the germs that produce Elsmere's disgusted encounters with ugly agitators of the "common Secularist type" (481), and his classist apotheosis at the end of the novel. Nobly exhausting himself in the "service" of brutalized East Enders, "he pass[es] away" as the founding saint of a new brotherhood of the "human Christ" in "a final flood of light," as Gladstone put it in a lengthy and influential review (*Nineteenth Century*, May 1888: 770). First, however, Elsmere impresses upon "you working men" (*Elsmere* 473) the need for a "new social bond" (548) that can fend off the threats of vulgarity and verbal violence. "I cared about nothing, when you came," gasps a dying gas-fitter, wheeled on for the purpose; "You've been—God—to me—I've seen Him—in you" (498). The strategy, as Gladstone said, "has no relation to the plot," but is a fine "illustration of the great missionary idea of the piece" (*Nineteenth Century*, May 1888: 767). Relentlessly serious and exquisitely reverential, a benchmark of 1880s culture and social belief, Ward's novel is a frontal assault on the "coarse" and "laughing" "brutality" of G. W. Foote's penny paper (457, 458); it fears "the mire of a hideous and befouling laughter" (458); it seethes with class-laden epithets like "mean and miserable mirth" (476). *Robert Elsmere* was an inspired reaction to the blasphemy case that "shocked" the nation, and a fulfillment, as we shall see, of "Uncle Matt's" lifework against that "peculiarly English form of Atheism" that was free-speaking and plainspoken Secularism.

Gissing and Ward suppress the historical point of origin: merely speaking of blasphemy can become blasphemy (see below, 5.3). But Bradlaugh the coal-heaving demagogue with his "offensive purity of Cockney accent" (Gissing, *Born in Exile* 1: 36), whose blunt face and protruding upper lip played into every cartoonist's caricature of the stuttering Lombroso delinquent and speechless ape-man, and Foote the vulgarian, the figure at center of the defining trial of the 1880s, blasphemously possessed of "culchaw," are the shadows that haunt their imaginations and their works. Blasphemy's uses and meanings in the literary world in which they moved are our next concern.

CHAPTER FOUR

LITERATURE AND DOGMA

"The Christian problem" in the Victorian era, wrote Mrs. Ward in 1911, "was first and foremost a literary problem" (introduction to *Elsmere* [1911] xxv). When Foucault hints grandly that the nineteenth century saw a transference of "authority" from the Bible to the "author," one knows better than to hope for a blow-by-blow account of the process. But the history of blasphemy does also provide something of an account. Woven into its telling, cryptic statements like Ward's assume a quality of luminous clearsightedness. This chapter returns to the *Freethinker* case and its contexts from an explicitly literary point of view, consolidating and bringing forward in time the story told in Hone's, Carlile's, Hetherington's, and Holyoake's cases. It presents a last and climactic chapter in blasphemy's transformation into a literary crime, a process deeply imbricated in the shift of "authority" from Scripture to Literature, with a capital L. To read it is, perhaps above all, better to understand the process whereby the Bible entered the nineteenth century as the sacred repository of historical truth and exited it a literary masterpiece, instated at the head of a different "canon," while Literature, in counterbalance, took on the role, as Northrop Frye terms it in a context only a little different, of a "secular Scripture," the subject of serious university study and the cornerstone of mass educational strategy. Reading the *literary* history of nineteenth-century blasphemy allows no escape from the subject of class, but it uncovers an extraordinary interchange between subliterature and the high literature that received wisdom perennially sees recoiling from its touch.

1. "BIBLIOLATRY" AND "BIBLE-SMASHING"

What "militant Secularism" and the whole Freethought tradition most sought to attack was what the laws had for generations most sought to protect: the Holy Bible. The *Freethinker* Christmas number had cast graphic aspersions on Jesus Christ, and Holyoake had questioned the value (and the cost) of religious institutions. But like every one of their predecessors in blasphemous "martyrdom," both men had also challenged the authority of the Book of Books, the BIBLOS, the rock on which the law of England stood. One obscure blasphemer prescribed the burnt ashes of family Bibles as a cure for potato rot (see below, 6.3); Hone parodied sacred text; Carlile promoted Paine's "anti-Bible"; Hetherington stood trial for a work that "renounced" the Bible as "wretched stuff" and an immoral *"insult to God,"* nuggets of deistical offensiveness that were picked out in the indictment (*Trial of Henry Hetherington* 3); Southwell had blown a trumpet-blast to battle with authorities who derived their power from that "monstrous book," the "idol of all sorts of blockheads," "that rubbishing collection of allegories, lies, murders, [and] rapes . . . called 'bible' " (*Oracle*, 27 November 1841: 25); and Holyoake "shunned the Bible as a viper." From the 1810s through the 1840s, it was Freethought's assault on the Bible that most set the martyrs on their collision courses with the courts.

The destructive animus was understandable, at least, in its context of a society founded on the union of state and church—a Protestant Church founded on the Bible. The Victorian drift towards tolerance and secularization, the "progress" of Whig history, was countermanded at every surge by an undertow of religious fundamentalism that found its deepest expression in reverence of the Bible. Swimming against the main stream, a vociferous minority of educated opinion, articulating the gut instincts of a large majority, fought doggedly to preserve the Book's preeminence. There was a wide gap between the liberal ideas the Victorians wrote into law and the mores by which they lived, just as there is today a sharp divide, say, between the freedoms guaranteed by the U.S. Constitution and the codes and taboos of middle America.

It was the insult offered Scripture that had spurred on the heresy case of *Essays and Reviews:* the 1860 volume had tempted the British public with the fruits of Germany's higher criticism of the Bible. The aborted outcome made clerical questionings of Scripture legal, "so long as they do not contradict any doctrine laid down in the Articles or Formularies of the Church of England" (Odgers, *Libel and Slander* 457), but the ground gained was nearly lost in 1865. In that year, following Renan's *Vie de Jesu,* John Seeley published his homegrown English "biography" of Christ, *Ecce Homo:* it was instantly denounced by Lord Shaftesbury as the "most pestilential book ever vomited . . . from the jaws of hell" (qtd. in Chadwick, *Church* 1: 65). In 1865 too, maverick clergyman Charles Voysey published the *Sling and the Stone*, a set of scandalous sermons that pronounced the doctrines of eternal punishment and Atonement "revolting," rejected the divinity of Christ, and insisted that the Bible was not the revealed Word of God. As Broad Churchman Benjamin Jowett remarked, Voysey "looked too far over the hedge" (Conway, *Autobiography* 2: 290).[1] He went on to provide one of the few direct contacts between the worlds of academic and vulgar biblical criticism. Annie Besant was one of many heretics to pass through Voysey's salon, to mingle with respectable doubters like the eclectic minister of South Place Chapel, Moncure D. Conway, and Bishop Colenso of Natal, whose literal-minded calculations about the dimensions of Noah's Ark in *Criticisms on the Pentateuch* bred more scandal.

The reaction that followed the *Essays and Reviews* affair slowed passage of the Test Bill that secured religious freedom in the universities. At the eleventh hour, the House of Lords attempted to insert a clause protecting "the divine authority of the Holy Scriptures" (qtd. in E. Coleridge 2: 54). Not until 1883, the year of the *Freethinker* trials, did the critical study of the Old Testament first appear on the agenda of the annual church congress, much to some members' distress (Chadwick, *Church* 1: 58). As late as 1891, three years after the untroubled publication of *Lux Mundi*, agitation was still intense for what a group of prominent clergymen, in an open letter to the *Times* called "A Declaration," in Parliament, "on the Truth of Holy Scripture" (Royle, *Radicals* 167). There was a solid market for publications like the humorless and lavishly illustrated "militant Christian" *King's Own* (founded 1890), directly aimed at "pretentious" biblical criticism (*King's Own*, 11 January 1890: 3). Innumerable low-brow magazines promised nothing but "plain, simple Gospel teaching," as an advertising flyer for the penny monthly *Friendly Visitor* put it (in JJC).

It was the Book's authority for those over whose heads Providence had set many other powers that was the stickiest sticking point. At the lower levels of society, this was an era of what has been called "rampant" and "crude" Bible worship (Herrick, *Vision* 101), when no poor folk dared turn away from the door the intrusive "missionary" come to read Scripture aloud for their comfort (*Secularist*, January 1856: 1). The "watchword" of the British and Foreign Bible Society was "*The Bible, the whole Bible, and nothing but the Bible!*" (Arnold, *Literature and Dogma* 25). The Bible was the greatest cheap publication of the century: four and a half million copies were sent abroad in the ten years from 1837 to 1847; Africa swam in missionary donations; at home, a Bible sold for sixpence in 1864; and in the year G. W.

Foote left prison (1884) a New Testament could be had for a penny, the
price of his sixteen-page *Freethinker*.[2] Well might Victorians say with God-
dred Gylby in 1561, "men are now a days here in England glutted as it were
with godes word, and therefore almost ready to vomit up againe that which
thei have received" (qtd. in O'Day 25).[3] ("There is something especially
revolting in cheap labor at work on cheap Bibles," said Annie Besant to
horrified clerical colleagues on the London School Board in the late 1880s
[qtd. in A. Taylor].) It was with good reason that G. W. Foote declared
the Bible the preeminent Victorian "fetish" (qtd. in Herrick, *Vision* 39).
He was in good company. The English were an Old Testament people, as
Matthew Arnold knew, their Christianity a "religion of the Bible" (*Literature and Dogma* 7), and their Bible a "talisman to be taken and used literally" (28). One worried clergyman coined a name for the phenomenon in
1850: "Scripture idolatry."[4] Huxley revived a sharper term: "bibliolatry."[5]
    Like fundamentalist Protestantism, as Edward Royle remarks, "militant"
Secularism, its mirror image, "lived by the Bible—*homines unius libri*"
(*Radicals* 167). A platform assault on Scripture always packed the lecture
hall. After all, this was one text audiences would be sure to have read: the
democratizing potential of the great Book persisted even in opposition.
Each leader of the organized Secularist movement cut his teeth on the Bible,
from G. J. Holyoake to Foote's successor, Chapman Cohen. Each of them
drew on the rich Freethought tradition of homespun criticism: Foote's own
Bible Handbook (1888), still available, systematically manhandles chapters
and verses to bring out "Contradictions," "Absurdities," "Atrocities," and
"Obscenities," exactly in the manner of Paine's *Age of Reason*.
    In the 1860s, Bradlaugh fought for Freethought's right to mere legal
existence. The battle joined by G. W. Foote, his lieutenant and successor,
was a last-ditch, all-in campaign of what Bernard Shaw in a letter to the
Freethinker called "Bible-smashing" (1 November 1908: 689). Scripture was
to be swept away in a final explosion of outrage; the Book's authority was
forever to be undermined.
    Foote's campaign was intense, coherent, and sustained. With all the limi-
tations and repetitions it entailed, it became the mission of a lifetime, pursued into the 1890s and the new century. He took every opportunity for
attack—every new church defense of Scripture authority (Dean Farrar's in
1899, for example), every public event and major new book (like Archbishop
Benson's *Christ and his Times* in 1890, received as "high priced wisdom"
[*Freethinker*, 26 January 1890: 37]). Gladstone's debate with American "Infidel" Colonel Ingersoll provoked Foote's dissection of the "Grand Old
Book" that the "Grand Old Man" termed the "Impregnable Rock of Holy
Scripture" (*Grand Old Book* 1). Foote's campaign can be tracked not only

through his career as Sunday lecturer and platform debater, as prolific pamphleteer (two series of the 1870s, *Bible Romances* and *Bible Heroes,* first established his popularity), but also through the magazines he edited and founded: the *Secularist,* the *Liberal, Progress,* and the *Freethinker.* Foote's campaign of "Bible-smashing" was the climax and crown to a long tradition.

It took place in the context of a broader change. This is not the place to describe in detail the shifting relationship between Scripture and literature across the course of the nineteenth century. Under the Evangelical regime by which large numbers of early Victorians lived, there was a near-absolute split between the two: one was truth, the other "fiction." It may be that the opposition was a reaction formation against the years of border crossing that gave birth to the heretical and mythologizing works of Blake and Shelley, prime subjects of Secularist literary lectures like Foote's first efforts. It had legal roots in the Reformation, in the haste with which the government of Edward VI extended the protection of the blasphemy laws to the *Book of Common Prayer,* turning literary production into sacred text. The split produced the most dramatic moment of Charles Southwell's trial for blasphemy in 1842. Taken "as a poetic composition," a description of Minerva and Neptune from Pope's version of the *Iliad* is "innoxious," he declared. But suppose you treated it as a true history? Then "a very different result would be produced." The Bible, by implication, had been read as fact where it should be read as poetry. At this point the prosecuting counsel jumped to his feet to ask "if any limit was to be put to the scope which the defendant took?" (*Trial of Charles Southwell* 54). But Southwell was tenacious. If what Dr. Blair had stated in his famous *Lectures on Rhetoric* (1784) was correct, that the Scriptures are "poetic" productions, "then I have as much right to criticise the Bible as he has" (55). And Blair's declaration that Milton and Shakespeare are equal "in point of poetical and original genius" with the writers of the Old Testament might well "stagger my faith" (*Trial of Charles Southwell* 53).[6]

However, over the course of the nineteenth century, as we have already begun to see, literature—even fiction, most suspect of genres—incrementally graduated from an oppositional to an accessory relationship to Scripture. The development had much to do with Wordsworth's Victorian canonization, consolidated by the posthumous first publication of the much rewritten *Prelude* (1850), and a great deal to do with the high critical standing of George Eliot. Her acceptance of the Wordsworthian role of moral teacher is typographically signaled at the head of every chapter in her novels, in the use of epigraphs (often from Wordsworth, often self-manufactured) that resemble texts for sermons. A close friend of Charles Hennell, she

absorbed the "reverent" tone of his *Inquiry Concerning the Origin of Christianity* (1838); "only the sight of the Christ-image"—a replica sculpture of
the risen Christ that Eliot kept in her study—made "endurable" the sick-
ening task of translating *Das Leben Jesu* (Cross 70). Sympathy and theological training in the commission of acceptable English heresy tempered a
mind that could write successful humanist fiction. The "seriousness" and
"reverence" she epitomized was the antidote for the bane of "ridicule." One
might even say that the leaden gravity of the Victorian "novel-with-a-
purpose" written by her contemporaries was a counterpoise to the long-ago
forbidden pleasures of Hone's parodies and Byron's satires. By the 1870s,
advanced publishers like Kegan Paul would "by no means refuse to publish"
works of "a freethinking or agnostic type"; but they would "sternly reject"
anything that was "merely flippant and written for the sake of destruction"
(*Memoirs,* qtd. in Chadwick, *Church* 2: 465).

Eliot's success spurred the production of pocket volumes with titles like
the *Wit and Wisdom of George Eliot,* which made secular substitution for
Bible words for the day; while already—from the other side of the fence, as
it were—religious tracts telling tales of holy children and infidel shoemakers
blurred the distinction between sacred and profane. Oblique retellings of
Christian story like Kingsley's 1853 *Hypatia* (a luridly different story to the
one Secularists told of the ancient atheist martyr) devolved into premodern-
ist remythologizings like Pater's *Marius the Epicurean* (1885). By the end
of the century the master stories of Scripture freely mingled with fiction
in such extraordinary crossbreedings as *Barabbas* (1893) by Marie Corelli.

A fly-on-the-wall account of the Crucifixion and Resurrection from the
point of view of the robber in whose place Christ ascends the cross, *Barabbas* provides a villainous vamp as the high priest Caiaphas's partner in evil,
and maps on to the sacred story the archetypal plot of maternal melodrama,
climaxing with the doubting hero's generic question to Joseph the Carpenter: "Whose Son was He?" (Corelli 301). Where the biblical text she freely
interweaves is hard to understand, Corelli provides a gloss, so that the novel
explicitly empowers itself as a *reading* of gospel accounts.[7] Repulsively anti-
Semitic, it also imperially reclaims a "dazzling[ly] white" blue-eyed "Egyptian" Christ (50) for the true chosen people: his English Aryan worshippers.[8]
And it begins in and is obsessed with blasphemy. We first meet Barabbas
in prison, "rail[ing] in thick-throated blasphemies" (6); Caiaphas revels in
"terrible language" (279); "ruffianly guards" deride Christ with "mocking
gestures and laughter" that distinctly recall the Christmas's number's strip
cartoon "New Life of Christ" (54); and "Judith Iscariot" damns herself when
she taunts Him in His agony: "Hearest thou me, thou boaster and blasphemer? *If thou be the Son of God, come down from the Cross!*" (112, italics

in original for Bible quotation). The book "aroused in some quarters more violent hostility than any book of recent years," declared a notice in the *Athenaeum* used as a publisher's blurb for the reissue of 1896. But it was the "secular critics" who arraigned Corelli for "bad taste, bad art, and gross blasphemy," and it was an index of Scripture's late-century rapprochement with fiction that "in curious contrast, most religious papers acknowledged the reverence of treatment and the dignity of conception that characterized the work" (inside front cover, 1896). *Barabbas* was the *Greatest Story Ever Told avant la lettre.* From the debate sparked by George Moore's high-literary retelling of the Passion in 1916, *The Brook Kerith,* threatened with a blasphemy prosecution by Wilde's erstwhile lover Lord Alfred Douglas, to the controversy stirred by musicals and movies like *Godspell, Jesus Christ Superstar,* and the *Last Temptation of Christ,* audiences in Britain and America have divided along the battle lines drawn by Corelli's critics in face of the central question: Can Scripture stories survive retelling, translation, modernization, all or any form of reforging in the crucible of literary, dramatic, or filmic creation?

Corelli took seriously what Foote did mockingly. Herein lay the difference between sensational success and prison for blasphemy: the response that the *Freethinker* asked of its reader was utterly dissimilar to the unself-conscious, not to say mindless, suspension of disbelief that *Barabbas* requested. Nevertheless, both enterprises were evidence of a reversal of power relations. In the first half of Victoria's reign, literature was evaluated in terms of how far it reinforced the messages and upheld the authority of Scripture. This was the standard practice of mid-Victorian novel reviewers. In late century, crucially, the Bible came rather to be *supported* by the imaginative strength—even the authority—of Literature.

The method of Foote's "Bible-smashing" showed him fully aware of literature's waxing strength in the contest with Scripture. At first glance it seems surprising, at second glance logical. We find a clue to it in the spasm of outrage that shook bourgeois Tunbridge Wells during the run-up to the *Freethinker* trials in 1883. A young man named Henry Seymour, excited by the news from London, was haled before the courts for a poster advertising the Easter meeting of the town's fledgling Secular Society:

> Great Attractions!
> FUN! FUN! FUN!
> Jumbo and a Trunk!
> Hamlet and the
> Holy Ghost!
> Side-splitting burlesque!
> (qtd. in Calder-Marshall, *Lewd:* 181)

In lieu of the promised platform drama, Tunbridge watched on Easter Sunday as a troupe of policemen trudged from hoarding to hoarding all over town like performers in a latter-day miracle play, carefully pasting over the word "Holy" (Bonner 96). For the marriage effected in Seymour's poster made triviality of a profound taboo. It had exposed the unmentionable affinity between Scripture and Literature. And it had made it *funny*.

What Seymour probably did accidentally, G. W. Foote did systematically. He lived his entire career in the gray area between books and the Book. He had arrived at Freethought by a process of critical thought that is best described as "literary," if we understand by literary criticism the description, analysis, understanding—and the judgment and evaluation—of poetic and prose composition. Doubt first shook him, as it did Bradlaugh and Annie Besant, when he tried to reconcile the discrepancies in the four gospel accounts of Jesus. It sprang up "like a serpent," said Besant, from the chapters over which she toiled in Easter week, 1866 (*Autobiographical Sketches* 32); it grew from Bradlaugh's bitter childhood experience of abandonment by his family for questioning his Sunday school teacher. Foote, who preferred adage to self-revelation, likewise realized that "Searching the Scriptures is the best cure for believing in the Scriptures" (qtd. in Herrick, *Vision* 10). The atheistical conversion narrative was a *literary* experience.

Foote was preeminently a literary man: we encounter here the "other" editor of the *Freethinker*. George Bernard Shaw, who knew him well, felt that the literary career Foote might have had was sacrificed to propaganda. One of only two "uncompromisingly honest" journalists he had ever known, Foote was a "first-rate speaker," and an "able, humane and independent" thinker (*Letters 1874–97* 326); he deserved "a direct relation with the general culture and though[t] of his time" (*Letters 1898–1910* 874).[9] The Bible was only one of his specialties as a lecturer. A "wider-read man than any of the other Secularist leaders," Foote brought to the movement "a poetic and historic sense" (Royle, *Radicals* 99). His first subjects as a Sunday lecturer were Blake and Shelley; he had a literary sense of his project as a magazine editor. He was the bookish blasphemer par excellence. He loved Elizabethan English, "mold[ing]" his style on "Judicious Hooker's" (*Freethinker*, 31 October 1915: 695). He wrote verse "of great power and pathos" (Arthur B. Moss, *Freethinker* 699). (None has survived.) Reciting Tennyson's "Rizpah" from memory, he could bring a laughing and lively assembly to "thrill[ed]" "stillness" (F. J. Gould, *Freethinker* 695). If he "ever had a deity whom he really worshipped, his name was Shakespeare" (J.T., *Freethinker* 691). He knew the works almost by heart; the magnum opus of his life (never finished) was a book on Freethought's Shakespearean "Bible of

Genius." For his conduct of his defense at his trials in 1883, Foote won the support of Herbert Spencer, Frederick Harrison, G. H. Darwin, T. H. Huxley, George Du Maurier, Leslie Stephen, R. H. Hulton of the *Spectator,* P. H. Hill of the *Daily News,* and the many other newspaper editors, literary men, professors, and clergymen who signed the petition to the home secretary for his release from prison. One mourner marked his passing in 1915 in the words of Shelley's lament for the dead Keats, "I weep for Adonais—he is dead!" (*Freethinker,* 31 October 1915: 691).

As much as any cultured doubter or upper-class agnostic of the period, Foote regarded literature as the foundation stone of a revived culture. But dogma was not to be replaced by Literature-as-dogma. His numerous reviews consistently deplore the inartistic machinations of the novel, play, or poem "with a purpose," even a Secularist purpose; Flaubert, "Mrs. Grundy's" bête noir, was the supreme model. Tennyson, for example, stoops to religious tract melodramatics when he bids his atheist commit suicide in "Despair" (*Freethinker,* 13 November 1881: 113); Wilson Barrett's hit play of 1896, *The Sign of the Cross,* is a "dramatic confidence-trick" combining "proselytizing" with "statuesque posings in the scanty costume of ancient Rome" (Foote, *Sign* 12, 9, 8). Foote's colleagues on *Progress* felt the same way: J. H. Shorthouse's best-selling "theological romance" of the seventeenth century has the inartistic shapelessness of a "Tract for the Times" (January 1883: 10); while an article on "Wordsworth as a Teacher" in the same issue wonders whether a poet should be a teacher at all (46–51).

It was inevitable that such a man should give a literary orientation to the movement he came to lead. Foote even staged his own trials for *Freethinker* readers in literary terms:

> Messrs. Dodson and Fogg were set to work in the interest of the outraged Mrs. Bardell of piety, and the honest Mr. Pickwick of Freethought was treated like a designing criminal. (16 July 1882: 226)

It also went without saying that Foote should salute the methods of the German higher criticism: they seemed the belated academic justification of long-held Freethought positions. Literature and literary criticism gave Foote one of his most potent weapons.

The other was laughter. The trials of G. W. Foote—like the 1817 courtroom performances of William Hone—form a case history in how comedy debunks authority, catching it, like the "Comic Bible" cartoon "A Back View," with its trousers down (fig. 12). They are a demonstration of how underdogs who crack jokes can stop feeling like underdogs, at least until the cell door closes. In the *Freethinker's* cathartic pages the unbeliever could imaginatively "say everything," as Foucault says of the condemned man at the executioner's block (*Discipline* 60), and the people might laugh; of Foote, a bird of the same feather as himself, Bernard Shaw would never have said, as he did of Annie Besant, "No truth came to her first as a joke" (qtd. in A. Taylor 184). For a penny a week, Victorians at last came into the "most significant legacy" of the "ultra-radicals" of the 1810s, "a tradition of plebeian . . . irreverence" (McCalmain 237).

All the pieces in the Christmas number and over half the items indicted in earlier issues of the *Freethinker* were jokes or other humorous items. Take this offensive dig at the Salvationists in the "Acid Drops" column for 29 January 1882:

> A lady at church recently said: "Last night I was clasped in the arms of a wicked man. Tonight I am clasped in the arms of my Savior." (36)

It turns up again in the "Profane Jokes" column in 1887, when prosecution was again considered by the Home Office, with the addition of a fully fledged punch line: "A man in the congregation shouted: 'Are you engaged for tomorrow night?' " (20 November: 375). The guffaw solicited is not subtle, but it certainly puts a distance between the reader who laughs and the object of the joke. And it creates that distance in the teeth of the taboo on ridicule, parody, and all suspect laughter that took root in 1817 and reached full flower in the 1880s.

Even burlesque went upmarket in the 1880s, refining itself into musical comedy (M. Booth 198); the high reputation of "kindly cynical" *Punch* cartoonist George Du Maurier through the decade (*Harper's Monthly,* November 1894: 636) represented the logical end point of that institution's paradoxical institutionalization of satire. Lewis Carroll wrote to a young friend whose "anecdote about the Ten Commandments" he declined to hear in 1888:

> I hate to . . . seem uncourteous: but it is a matter of principle . . . to bear . . . one's testimony for the principle of treating all sacred matters seriously. (*Selected Letters* 172)

"[T]here is a terrible amount just now," he added, "of jesting on sacred things" (172). For a time of rigid taboo is often also a time of subversive protest. In the 1880s, parody became the chosen mode of literary decadence (Dowling 144); the cultural wind blowing over from France was salted with ridicule.[10] That climate increased the danger of putting cartoons from *La bible amusante* on the front page of the *Freethinker*.

That offensive strategy was made all the more dangerous by Foote's alterations. His substitution of actual lines of biblical text for Taxil's captions, ignored by commentary, was crucial. The cartoons now became both comic illustrations and implicit visual criticisms of Scripture: "And God spake unto Noah"—Genesis 9.8, in which the Lord (in the clouds) communicates by means of the "Original Telephone," literally pictured (*Freethinker*, 8 January 1882: 9); "And God said, Let there be light: and there was light"— Genesis 1.3, which makes offensive linguistic play of the "divine" smoker's terms "illumination" and "lucifer" (match) (28 May 1882: 171) (fig. 11), while Taxil's text instead embeds its biblical verse in lamely comic narrative: *"Comme il ne tenait pas à faire des bêtises, l'Éternel se dit qu'il lui était nécessaire de commencer par avoir de la lumière. 'Que la lumière soit!' commanda-t-il, et la lumière fut'"* [n.p.]); or (the *Freethinker*'s own image) God's promise to Abraham, "I shall take away my hand, and thou shalt see my back parts"—Exodus 33.23 (*Freethinker*, Christmas no. 1882: 7) (fig. 12). The "Comic Bible" cartoons as the *Freethinker* reconceived them for Protestant England were a frontal assault on divine authorship and verbal inspiration. They mocked fundamentalist Christian faith in the Bible's literal truth. But they also disallowed liberal theology's new acceptance and reliance on the figurative and metaphorical: times had changed since Woolston was imprisoned for an allegorical interpretation in 1728. The cartoons constituted a kind of "lower" criticism. Indeed, Foote's key strategy as Secularism's champion "Bible-smasher" was altogether the literary, and often the parodic, "decomposition" of the Bible.

Thus, for example, the Book of Isaiah becomes "supernatural fiction" (Foote, *Bible Heroes* 178); "Hairy Elijah" "enters the narrative without a note of warning" (145); and the logic of story-telling dictates that we see nothing wonderful in his augury, "Behold, a virgin shall conceive," given that she has just enjoyed "a connubial visit from an able-bodied prophet" (178). A "Short Sermon on Faith" on the text of "Hey diddle diddle" undermines the method of scriptural exegesis (*Freethinker*, holiday no. 1881: 6); "Elisha Ye Prophet" is reduced to prattling (as well as anti-Semitic) simplicity as a "Nursery Tale with a Moral for 'Little Children:' " "Elisha was a prophet / Quite good enough for Jews, / He was the son of Shaphat / And wore Elijah's shoes" (12). A "New Commentary" provides a mock model for interpretation, gathering together glosses on a line of Genesis—"Jacob kissed Rachel, and he lifted up his voice and wept" (29.11)— from twenty-four papers, ranging from the *War Cry* to *Punch, Pink 'Un, Sporting Life,* and *Girl's Own Paper* (30 July 1882: 239). "It is not for us to say," exhorts a pokerfaced "Orthodox Sermon" by "Jehosophat Grimes," "whether Judas first repented, returned the money and hanged himself, and afterwards bought a field with the money and burst asunder in the midst, or whether he first bought a field and falling headlong burst asunder, and then repented, returned the money, and hanged himself. It is for us to receive the oracles of God with unquestioning faith" (9 October 1881: 77).

The Bible was the exclusive target of the *Freethinker*'s 1882 Christmas number, Foote's "budget of blasphemy." In it, holy stories are transformed into comic poem, cartoon strip, mock trial, and fairy tale, that most unprestigious of literary forms: "Elisha the Scalp Hunter" and "Jocular Jehovah"; the cartoon strip "New Life of Christ" (figs. 13 and 14); and a fairy-tale version of the Christian Scheme of Redemption. "The Precious Bible" is a verse inventory of the Good Book's contents: "Three men within a furnace were not fried; / And lots of whopping miracles beside" (14). Mock prayers and parody tracts, Swinburnean Freethought "psalms," alternative parables, and Bunyanesque dream visions provide additional offensive entertainment. "Jehosophat Grimes" enjoys a return engagement: "All difficulties in the Bible, my beloved brethren, may be easily solved by understanding them to be either literal or figurative, or something else" (15). A reminiscence of a "Christmas Panorama" projected by magic lantern is accompanied by a wheezy concertina and a Cockney showman's patter— "all haccordin' to the blessid scripturs" (6).

There is much more at work here than what newspapers and clergymen saw as the apogee of low humor and jeering vulgarity. There is a difference in kind between Foote's literary pranks and the stubborn literal*ism* represented, for example, by Haslam's *Letters to the Clergy*, which leap gleefully on contradiction like that between the prayer book's description of God as "without body, parts or passions" and the Bible's mentions of "finger of the Lord, ears of the Lord, . . . fury of the Lord, vengeance of the Lord," and so on (32–33). In the *Freethinker* was proof, long before Joyce provided it in *Ulysses,* that vulgarity can itself be a literary strategy and parody the most complex literary formation. Moreover, that proof was presented at a time of renewed interest in alternative sacred texts (particularly the Hindu Vedas) and in biblical forgery and apocryphal writings: Andrew Lang exposed the Bible of Alenine, made for Charlemagne in 800 AD, and other scriptural fakes in a *Contemporary Review* essay on "Literary Forgeries" republished in his 1886 *Books and Bookmen;* the forger M. W. Shapira committed suicide in 1884 after failing in his grandest scheme to make one million pounds on a set of leather strips inscribed with the speeches of Moses. Sacred texts treated as mere literary and subliterary constructs are demoted to such. And parody—as William Hone discovered—is the very type of literary "decomposition," a process of reinvention that reveals the problematic inventedness, the *literariness,* of what it parodies. G. W. Foote and his blasphemous *Freethinker* were the "militant" opposite to literature's "reverent" support of Holy Scripture.

2. THE HERETIC TROPE OF THE BOOK

Not all Literature, however. Foote's literary parodic campaign against bibliolatry finds parallels in the works of a wide range of contemporary novelists. Victorian culture had many mechanisms for censoring offensive texts, from trial by review to bans by the circulating libraries to guttings by serial magazines to simple refusals to publish. So it was that a number of Victorian novelists encoded their unorthodoxy in what we might call the heretic trope of the Book-within-the-book, the Book of power. Clergymen had long been considered fair game for satire, and are held up to ridicule by Dickens, Thackeray, Trollope, and the Brontës. But the approach to the national "fetish" required discretion, lest the blasphemous impulse be too easily recognized. Even George Eliot creates the serious joke of Casaubon's "Key to all Mythologies," the book to which Dorothea will be chained by his last will and testament in *Middlemarch* (1871–72), and pointedly bestows on its desiccated clerical author the name of a seventeenth-century scholar of the "false gospels" and Apocrypha.[11] Writers of a later generation took more gleefully to covert "Bible-smashing."

Impudent heretic Wilkie Collins, for example, places in the hands of the *Moonstone*'s narrator Gabriel Betteredge in 1868 a much-thumbed copy of *Robinson Crusoe*. Defoe's classic adventure had caused a scandal on first publication in 1719. He had "impos[ed] on the World" a fake autobiographical document, it was said (*Read's Journal*, qtd. in Haywood 24), and he had done so with the deadpan prefatory "editorial" comment: "the thing [seems] to be a just history of fact; neither is there any appearance of fiction in it" (Defoe 25). Idolized by early Victorians until publication of damaging political material about its author, the paternal ancestor of Victorian realism, *Crusoe* was also the classic example of fictional forgery, and as such stood in a sharply oppositional relationship to the truth of Scripture. This is why Thomas Hardy chooses it as the stylistic model for his heroine's "novel-tellings" in the *Hand of Ethelberta* (1876), a novel that fictionally foregrounds the real-life servant-class perspective, the skepticism, and the cultural claims of its creator (Hardy's mother's maiden name was Hand). *Crusoe* had a courtroom history: the fifth count of Carlile's 1819 indictment marked out as blasphemy Paine's suggestion that Mary and Joseph may "probably" have existed, since "almost all romantic stories have been suggested by some actual circumstance; as the adventures of Robinson Crusoe, not a word of which is true, were suggested by the case of Alexander Selkirk" (indictment in CC; *Age of Reason* 156).

There was considerable point, then, to making *Crusoe* the "amazing" "Book" with a capital *B*, the pseudo-Bible to which narrator Betteredge makes obeisance in Collins's *Moonstone* (110, 236). He discourses on its merits no less than eight times in the course of the novel, and even opens the story proper with a reverent citation: "In the first part of *Robinson Crusoe,* at page one hundred and twenty-nine, you will find it thus written: 'Now I saw, though too late, the Folly of beginning a Work before we count the Cost. . . . ' " (39). *Crusoe* is his "friend in need" (41); those who do not "believe" in it are men of little "faith" (110). Open *Crusoe* at random, Betteredge avers, as many fundamentalist Christians open their Bibles to this day, and you will find the "prophetic" enlightenment you seek (460).[12] At the novel's close, *Crusoe's* parody-prophetic powers even win a "convert" (519). Foote certainly got the iconoclastic point of such parodic idolatry: " 'What does Good Friday mean?' asked one boy of another," reads a joke in his *British Secular Almanack* for 1878; " 'You had better go home and read your *Robinson Crusoe,*' was the withering reply" (38–39). Animus against the exclusive truth claim of the Holy Bible fuels Collins's satire, whose targets also include a "Rampant Spinster" who brandishes tracts with titles like "Satan among the Sofa Cushions" and displays a suspect taste for such highly colored sections of the Bible as gladdened the hearts of more unscrupulous Secularist lecturers, like the account of how "the blinded children of the devil . . . went on with their orgies, unabashed, in the time before the Flood" (249). But that same animus also perhaps compels that different form of narration—that reading from evidence—which makes the *Moonstone* a foundation text of detective fiction. "I am not permitted to improve—I am condemned to narrate," laments the Spinster (241): there is critical bite to the joke.

Yet although Collins's *Moonstone* makes pointed fun of "Scripture idolatry," it keeps within the pale of the permissible. Samuel Butler's heretical autobiographical novel the *Way of All Flesh* is another case altogether.

Pompous clergyman Theobald Pontifex is one target of the novel's anti-Christian, anti-authoritarian satire (the name rings obvious changes on "pontiff" and "pontificate": Butler had recoiled from ordination in 1859). But the Book of Books is all-too-evidently another. Indeed, Theobald's useless clerical lifework is to make a scrapbook "Harmony of the Old and New Testaments" that posthumously "fetche[s] ninepence a barrowload" (425). It may not have been only consideration for those who would recognize its rancorous family portraits that kept the *Way of All Flesh* unpublished from the time revision stalled in 1884 until after Butler's death in 1902.

Self-knowledge of its commission of scriptural literary sins may also have played a part. Butler confided privately to his *Note-Books* that none of the Old Testament books had any "transcendent" literary merit: even Esther and the Song of Solomon (heretically ranked above the rest) "would stand no chance of being accepted by Messrs. Cassell & Co."; and as for David's Psalms, "Mudie['s lending library] would not take thirteen copies of the lot" (*Note-Books* 105). His unpublished novel pushed antibibliolatrous offensiveness and superior literary judgment to further limits.

Butler's composition of the *Way of All Flesh* spanned the course of Foote's "Bible-smashing" campaign from inception to imprisonment, 1871–84. And just as the hapless hero, Ernest Pontifex—Theobald's much-bullied son, another incompetent clergyman—takes his final cue for conversion to atheism from the genial freethinking tinker who rents his landlady's back kitchen, so the text as a whole exploits the range of comic blasphemous possibility produced by such close engagement with the Bible as G. W. Foote criminally perfected.

Ernest moves haphazardly toward literary liberation from the Victorian "fetish" through a first hostile comparison of the Greek tragedies to the Psalms (*Way of All Flesh* 228), an experimental parody of a religious tract, an unintentionally funny sermon on biblical cookery,[13] "furtive" New Testament study meetings (241), and quasi-Puseyite put-downs of scriptural reliability. His mentor in this last stage of development is a "spiritual thief or coiner" who palms "bad threepenny pieces" upon him as the small change of conversation (277) and ends by decamping with all his cash. This is exactly the arc of development once expected of forger-blasphemer Jacob Holyoake (in whose journal the *Reasoner* Butler published a letter on "Mechanical Creation" in 1865 [H. Jones 1: 117]), but neatly and offensively transferred to his Christian opposite.[14] Finally set to comparing the four gospel accounts of the Resurrection by Shaw the tinker, who catches him mixing them up, Ernest hears the words "no, no, no" "ringing up" loudly "from the very pages of the Bible itself" (285). The result is a climactic criminal scene in which he drop-kicks the Holy Book across his room and lunges upstairs to molest a fellow lodger whom he wrongly takes to be a prostitute (425).[15] The comic descent into moral morass proves to be his making, however. Ernest is "retailored" by his prison experience, not as the Kingsley of *Alton Locke* and other "literary garbage" he has been reading would have him be (265), but along the lines of those who really were tailors and shopmen and shoemakers: after his prison apprenticeship he makes his way as a gentlemen's outfitter, burns his sermons, sells his books, and emerges fully fledged as a writer in a parody of *Essays and Reviews* (413).

The Way of All Flesh is above all else an antiscriptural comedy soaked in scriptural idiom. It revels in the most down-to-earth lines, like "THEY DAUBED IT WITH SLIME," which (Butler records), was "one of the few verses of the Bible that I used to like when I was a child" (*Note-Books* 109; *Way of All Flesh* 397). It shares its gift for mockery and its "odious habit of turning proverbs upside down" (*Way of All Flesh* 253) with the *Freethinker:* Ernest's headmaster, Dr. Skinner, has "the harmlessness of the serpent and the wisdom of the dove" (145); while it is eating "sweet" grapes, not "sour," that sets children's teeth on edge, since indigestion makes parents bad tempered (54). The novel takes the same delight in the literal interpretation of Scripture as the "Comic Bible" cartoons:

> He, Adam, went to sleep as it might be himself, Theobald Pontifex, in a garden, as it might be the garden at Crampsford Rectory during the summer months when it was so pretty, only that it was larger, and had some tame wild animals in it. Then God came up to him, as it might be Mr. Allaby [the Rector] or his father, dexterously took out one of his ribs without waking him, and miraculously healed the wound so that no trace of the operation remained. Finally, God had taken the rib perhaps into the greenhouse, and had turned it into just such another young woman as Christina. That was how it was done; there was neither difficulty nor shadow of difficulty about the matter. Could not God do anything He liked, and had He not in His own inspired Book told us that He had done this? (81–82)

Exclusive clerical claims to the right of scriptural interpretation, Butler suggests—with Foote and his predecessors, notably Shakespearean Southwell—rest on such shoddy foundations as these.[16]

But a people who misunderstand literariness and who lay a taboo on parody eventually forget how to read them. Two years into writing the *Way of all Flesh*, Butler pseudonymously published a mock rebuttal of Strauss's *Das Leben Jesu*, *The Fair Haven* (1873): he followed proudly in the footsteps of Defoe, whose ironical *Shortest Way with the Dissenters* had been snapped up by friends and foes alike. But Darwin was right to doubt that "the orthodox will have so good a scent as to detect your heresy" (qtd. in Raby 138). Butler's book was taken seriously. "His exhibition of the certain proofs furnished of the Resurrection of our Lord is certainly masterly and convincing," said the *Rock* in one of two long reviews, a passage Butler quoted in the ironical preface to his second edition in which he revealed his identity (*Fair Haven* xiii). "Again," Butler summarized the reviews, "*The Scotsman* speaks of the writer as being 'throughout in downright almost pathetic earnestness.' While the *National Reformer*"—"Iconoclast" Bradlaugh's organ, a paper not normally mentioned in the same breath—"declares that both orthodox and unorthodox will find matter requiring thought and answer" (*Fair Haven* xv). The critics had swallowed whole passages like the following:

> Let us then follow the sublime example of the incarnation, and make ourselves as unbelievers that we may teach unbelievers to believe. If Paley and Butler had only been *real infidels* for a single year, . . . what a difference should we not have seen in the nature of their work. (62)

They had endorsed a comic refutation of "the hallucination and mythological theories," and pronounced "beautiful" descriptions of "the holy pleasure of a settled faith" (*Rock,* qtd. in *Fair Haven* xiv) that verged on the studied inanity of Theobald's wife's dynastic fantasy of "Heavenly mansions in which they would be exceedingly comfortable" (*Way of All Flesh* 83). But-ler's self-revelation in the second edition of the *Fair Haven* as the satirical author of *Erewhon* (1872), in which "certain ultra-orthodox Christians" had "imagined" an "analogy between the English Church and the Erewhonian Musical Banks," was an exquisite embarrassment (xii).

What is more, there is a curious connection between the man who wrote the *Fair Haven* and the dusty figure at whose trials for blasphemy in 1817 there first had struck root the taboo on parody that obscured the book's reading: William Hone. Hone's name resurfaced in national consciousness a few years after the *Haven's* first publication: Routledge's *Chapters in the History of Popular Progress* (1876) presented him as a press champion; Tegg & Co. reprinted the *Three Trials of William Hone* in 1876 and the *Every-Day Book* in 1878. But, more personally, Ernest's headmaster, "Dr. Skinner," is Dr. Samuel Butler, headmaster of Shrewsbury school, and the archdeacon whom Hone forced to admit his errors in vilifying the *Apocry-phal New Testament* in his 1822 *Charge* to the Clergy of Derby. He was young Samuel Butler's grandfather. The drafts of his letters to William Hone came into the grandson's hands as a family legacy in 1886, and were amongst those he submitted for deposit at the British Museum in 1895 (Jones 2: 345). The younger Butler found them "so cut about" and marked by "trouble" and "abortive beginnings" that it "seemed more proper" to destroy them (Add. Mss. 34,585: 378; 34,586: 1), though not before he made what seem to be full and painstaking copies. The whole incident of the *Charge* and his grandfather's humiliating admission of sloppy scholarship to the "Arch blasphemer" are omitted from the *Life and Letters of Dr. Sam-uel Butler* that Butler published in 1896; all that stands is a polite exchange of Christian courtesies between the "Author of Hone's Everyday Book" and the archdeacon—though he included his notes about the latter's diffi-culties in writing (*Life* 1: 314–16, 329–32). But it is tempting to think that young Samuel Butler had seen the letters before 1886, and followed through

the less decorous trains of thought they provoked in his *Way of All Flesh*—
of the relationship between parody, Apocrypha, and Scripture, and the con-
summate pleasures and dangers of biblical jokes. That temptation is increased when one realizes that Ernest's godfather, the novel's joking narrator (who once turned the *Pilgrim's Progress* into a Christmas pantomime),
shares his name—"John Overton"—with the author of an 1822 *Inquiry
into the Truth and Use of the Book of Enoch*, "Lately found in the Ethiopic
canon" (Overton iii), which anyone who looked up the Hone case in the
British Library would immediately have found, since it was and is bound
up with anti-Hone pamphlets like Rennell's *Proofs of Inspiration*.

The history of blasphemy and "Bible-smashing," however, reveals more
curious connections still. The blasphemers and heretics of the Victorian era,
denizens of the lower-class underworld, turn out to have more unexpected
connections: Annie Besant with Bernard Shaw; Holyoake—more surprisingly—with George Eliot. She called him the "Providence" of the *Leader*
office, where he was employed by G. H. Lewes (MacCabe 1: 165; Holyoake,
Sixty Years 1: 239). He repaid her with personal reverence and a minute
knowledge of her works.[17] "Saturday 5th April," reads his diary for 1884,
"Visited George Eliot's grave" in Highgate Cemetery (in HC). It is not a
coincidence of necropolitan planning that his name was attached to the
plot next door: Holyoake bought it, "that my ashes should repose there,
should I die in England" (*Bygones* 1: 64)).[18] He owed her partner a kind of
writerly redemption: "Lewes included me in the public list of writers and
contributors to the *Leader* . . . when I had only an outcast name, both in
law and literature" (*Bygones* 1: 64). (The inclusion "cost the paper £1,000
to his knowledge" and the loss of contributors like Kingsley [MacCabe 1:
164, 163].) Eliot had shouldered literature's burden of moral teaching with
insight and genius; Holyoake's affiliation with her and her circle profoundly
changed his "Oracular" sense of its uses and mission, and may have informed his suggestion, as Foote put it in the *Freethinker* in 1882, that "the
law of blasphemy should be retained not only for the protection of Christians, but for the aesthetic discipline of Freethinkers" (13 August: 250).[19]

Foote's literary affiliations had no such effect, and he had almost as wide
a range of acquaintance. One longs for details of the long "chat about his
imprisonment" he had with Shaw in 1892, or to know what else they talked
about the evening they were closeted alone in a railway carriage (Shaw,
Diaries 842). Poet James Thomson ("B.V."), whose *City of Dreadful Night*
screws lower-class atheistical alienation to a poetic peak, was a close friend:
Foote propped him up in the last, alcoholic years of his life, publishing

occasional poems and engineering meetings he thought would bring him pleasure.

One of these was with George Meredith. The most surprising relationship between literary figures and blasphemy martyrs across the course of the nineteenth century was perhaps between the subliterary editor of the *Freethinker* and the erudite and sophisticated epitome of the high-literary Victorian novelist. It lasted from 1878 until Meredith's death in 1909, and took in mutual friends like Admiral Maxse.[20] The novelist had had a taste of "militant" Secularism in 1869, when hearing "Iconoclast" speak at the Hall of Science drew from him a sigh of relief. Bradlaugh was "a man of power, and . . . not to be sneered down," he wrote John Morley; "It was really pleasant" for "one suffering from Simon Peter" to "hear those things spoken which the parsonry provoke" (*Letters* 1: 415, 411). Foote had early recognized Meredith as "a great though . . . unknown genius" (*Secularist*, 4 March 1876: 55). As soon as he assumed editorial control, he made space in Secularist magazines for reviews of the novels, extracts, and reprinted poems.[21] His first admiring but critically informed letter, and Meredith's reply, in 1878, was typical of the correspondence that continued through thirty years. "To feel that men like you . . . read and have a taste for what I produce," Meredith wrote, "is full of encouragement to me to write on with good heart" (*Letters* 2: 561). And, "let me add what is of more importance to my mind in communicating with you: that I admire the fight you are making, and class you among the true soldiers" (2: 562). Meredith treated him as one literary man treats another: Foote should "examine rigidly any writing you receive from me" for the *Liberal*, he wrote in 1879, and "not hesitate [to] reject it, should it not be perfectly to your taste" (2: 567). Each man understood the other's public position. Foote was silent about the association until after Meredith's death, lest it damage the novelist's reputation. For Meredith's part, to put his name "at [Foote's] disposal" towards the end of his life (1909 letter, qtd. in *Freethinker*, 31 October 1915: 694), when he had status to lose as the "Sage of Box Hill," was a braver act of generosity than his cash contributions to the *Freethinker* (*Letters* 3: 1695), or the free books he inveigled his publisher into sending its editor. But bravery was to be expected of the man who autographed the copy of his poems he presented to Foote in prison in 1883.

The "brave battle, for the best of causes" (*Letters* 2: 874) that Meredith commended years after Foote's imprisonment was the blasphemous editor's campaign of "Bible-smashing." For this too—discreetly and quietly—was one of Meredith's own fictional objectives. The decision not to publish saved Samuel Butler from potential charges, and Wilkie Collins jokingly concealed his unorthodoxy in the fake book of *Robinson Crusoe.* More

bound than they to a later Victorian literary system that served the reading
needs of the "nuptial curate" and his rector's fifteen year-old daughter (*Letters* 2: 562), Meredith made an art of "inserting edgewise" into his books
(as Hardy later put it [Seymour-Smith 85]) remarks that would pass over
their heads—private jokes "dropped with paradoxical safety into . . . public
text[s]" (Glendinning 18), incapable of detection by the "snuffling moralist
in the British public" (Lindsay 95).[22]

The most important jokes and remarks clustered around the heretic
trope of the Book. Subliterary or not, G. W. Foote had recognized the
affinity: his campaign received an initial impetus from Meredith's taboo
breaking in the *Ordeal of Richard Feverel,* published nearly twenty years
before the first exchange of letters and banned by Mudie's circulating library. Conversely, Meredith's attacks on the Bible in his most high-literary
novels, *The Egoist* (1879) and *Diana of the Crossways* (1885), bear distinct
traces of Foote's influence. To look at the work of the two men side by
side is to witness how powerful class distinctions that informed literary
stance, method, taste, and language could be bridged by the demands of
the struggle against the great "fetish." Three main methods of attack play
through Meredith's career. Like Collins and Butler, but more systematically, he predicates his texts upon the parodic construction of a Book-
within-the-book, a pseudo-Scripture that can be safely and surreptitiously
discredited, with only the predisposed cognoscenti for witnesses; like the
notorious G. W. Foote, he is an expert in the literary "decomposition" of
the Bible's master stories; and (like Foote again) he has a disconcerting turn
for blasphemous ridicule.

Meredith's outspokenly antiprovidential *Ordeal* pivots upon Sir Austin
Feverel's "PILGRIM'S SCRIP." A parody Bible with a scriptural-sounding
name, it is a collection of aphorisms in the style of the Old Testament
Proverbs, with the oracular textbook feel of the parental "words of the wise"
that make up verses 22.17 to 24.22 of that book. The SCRIP is the foundation of Sir Austin's coercive power over his son. After young Richard has
lied to a local farmer, for example, he is "struck . . . in the face" by the
patriarchal saying—"The Dog returneth to his Vomit: the Liar must eat
his Lie. . . . The Devil's mouthful!" (105), a baroque variation on Proverbs
23.8, which warns us not to eat meat with liars, for "The morsel which
thou hast eaten shalt thou vomit up, and lose thy sweet words." The SCRIP
also grants Sir Austin power over a circle of converts like Lady Blandish,
who cites it in copybook legal theological style: "No. 54, C. 7., P. S." (236).
In this Book of power is vested his authority as law, "Prophet" (262), master
of the kingdom-household, "Providence" (71), the "God of the machine"
(388, 522). Indeed, within the text of the *Ordeal,* THE PILGRIM'S SCRIP

assumes a kind of autonomous authority: aphorisms intrude into the text without warning or narrative justification (31, 190, 264, 331, 409, 452, etc.), jolting us into a direct and questioning confrontation with the power of aphorism, verse, chapter, Bible.

The urge to "Bible-smashing" uncovers the connection between the esoteric, ironic *Ordeal* and the "plain story" of a farmer's two daughters that Meredith published eight years later. *Rhoda Fleming* (1865) pits an array of bibliolators against an outspoken few (unobtrusively cast as comic characters, with an eye to Mudie's) who believe "it ain't . . . the best pious ones . . . as is al'ays ready to smack your face with the Bible" (121). "[S]trange, Biblical" (415) Rhoda's belief in the letter of Scripture law leads to her fallen sister's death. She pushes on her sham marriage to a brute who turns out to be a bigamist, with the pious connivance of Farmer Fleming, who "quotes Scriptur' as if he was fixed like a pump to the Book" (266); while the hypocritical local squire searches the Scriptures "to discover a text that might be used against him" if he takes advantage of Fleming's distress to buy up his farm on the cheap (134).

As Meredith's unorthodoxy increased, however, so did the sophistication of its encoding. The attack on bibliolatry in the *Ordeal* and *Rhoda Fleming* is neither subtle nor fully thought through.[23] His most sustained attack comes in the *Egoist,* his light, bright comedy of 1879: one could hardly choose a more "harmless" genre in which to "insert edgewise" one's damning criticism. The Scriptures are erased from the world of the *Egoist,* and an alternate frame of reference substituted: even the Reverend Doctor Middleton, houseguest of Sir Willoughby Patterne, the egoist of the title, spouts not the Bible but the classics. But in their place is another parody Book-within-a-book, Meredith's "Book of Egoism," by which Sir Willoughby justifies and dignifies his actions, "bet[aking] himself to THE BOOK" for comfort in times of need (112). "Now the world is possessed of a certain big book," the novel's second paragraph begins, "the biggest book on earth, that might indeed be called the book of Earth, whose title is the Book of Egoism, and it is a book full of the world's wisdom" (3). The flavor of fairy tale, as in the *Ordeal*'s mocking chapter title, "A Shadowy View of Coelebs Pater going about with a Glass-Slipper" (22), or as in Foote's *Bible Romances* and the 1882 *Freethinker* Christmas number, was part of the intended secret offense.

Diana of the Crossways (1885), written in the immediate wake of Foote's trials, contains no Book-within-the-book. But it does bring to a sophisticated climax Meredith's second "Bible-smashing" technique: it systematically reduces the master stories of the Bible to mere narratives—literary constructs—in a manner reminiscent of G. W. Foote's blasphemous decompositions. The *Ordeal* had made antipatriarchal play with the myth of Atonement, and *Rhoda Fleming* with the story of Eden;[24] while the *Egoist* more comically reworked the Expulsion: Flitch the coachman is last seen "slouch[ing] away" from Patterne Hall "in very close resemblance to the ejected Adam of illustrated books" (282); and the reluctant fiancée that Willoughby imagines has "forfeited" Paradise in his arms (187) ends up with her lover (his secretary) "as happy as blackbirds in a cherry tree, . . . with the owner of the garden asleep" (359). In *Diana,* the master stories of Eden and the Resurrection, along with Jacob's fourteen-year service for Rachel and Judas's betrayal of Christ, decompose under fiction's touch. Eden becomes "the garden of civilized life" (198), while Diana twice experiences a figurative death and rebirth that is explicitly secular and anti-Christian. "To be a girl again," she feels after her husband has cast her off, "[but] with a woman's . . . knowledge of evil, and winging to ethereal happiness, this was a revelation of our human powers" (145); and of her rift with her lover we read, "Her fall had brought her renovatingly to earth, and the saving naturalness of the woman recreated her childlike" (364).

Diana is a novelist concerned with making language new. And as "a woman planted in a burning blush" (321), she imaginatively replaces the Lord who revealed his law to Moses from the heart of a flaming bush. To borrow the terms of Riffaterre, in such a sentence the Bible becomes the ultimate cliché to be "avoided"; the phrase "burning blush" is a power play on words that comically subverts the Word.[25] As such, it is a fine-tuning of Meredith's third strategy in the campaign against bibliolatry, what Foote called the "Profane Joke." The technique is most evident in the *Egoist.* The function of the few biblical references allowed space in this unchristian novel is mere comic relief: they are mere occasional jokes about "Tapestry" (that is, fully dressed) Adams, or Jonah's whale getting indigestion (304), or Solomon giving judgment to a pair of "squabbl[ing]" mothers (308–09). When Sir Willoughby finds that "We cannot quite preserve our dignity when we stoop to the work of calling forth tears," the narrator adds, "Moses had probably to take a nimble jump away from the rock after that venerable Law-giver had knocked the water out of it" (262–63). Meredith might have lifted the style straight out of Foote's early series *Bible Heroes* and *Bible Romances.* Perhaps he did.

There is no question that Meredith—like Butler, like Collins—wrote fictions that play into his own peculiar linguistic strengths, and we would be naive critics not to spot the element of self-aggrandizement in his attack on the Book of Books. After all, the Bible still had a near monopoly over what (like Oscar Wilde) he made best: aphoristic words of wisdom. But in avoidance of the critical cliché that divides high literature from subliterature, we must see in the radical play of Meredith's unindictable novels the same antibibliolatrous impulse, and the same methods, more or less refined, as those that sentenced G. W. Foote to a year in Holloway Gaol.

3. LITERARY LAW AND THE AUTHORITY OF LITERATURE

If the blasphemers of the nineteenth century had some extraordinary literary connections, so too did the lawyers and judges they faced in court, and those connections suggested a very different role for Literature than subversion and biblical decomposition. Even the utilitarian rationalist Fitzjames Stephen, one of the loudest voices in the debate over the *Freethinker* case, was the brother of Leslie Stephen, the uncle of Virginia Woolf, the father of abrasive poet J. K. Stephen, and a powerful critic in his own right. Loss of faith produced different literary effects on his system. He berated Dickens in two famous articles of 1856 and 1857 for political ignorance, pseudo-Christian sentimentality, and vulgar crowd pleasing.[26] Dickens had "fail[ed] to shoulder that burden of responsibility which Literature's burgeoning influence lays especially upon the novelist," abusing his "License" (qtd. in Colaiaco 49). Stephen's terms of judgment recall the terms this study has investigated. So too do his brother's: Dickens could "claim the highest position among English novelists," Leslie Stephen later wrote in the *Dictionary of National Biography,* only "if literary fame could be safely measured by popularity with the half-educated" (*DNB* 15: 30).

John Duke, later Lord Coleridge, was a more fully developed type of the literary lawyer. Like Fitzjames Stephen, he had moved naturally from Oxbridge into the twin worlds of legal and literary London, balancing journalism with his career as a barrister, becoming literary editor of the London Church newspaper, the *Guardian,* in 1849 (he needed the money, too: two hundred pounds a year for his reviews in the 1850s). The legal and the literary weave together at every turn in his correspondence: *The Taming of the Shrew* asserted its right to his attention, for example, even in the middle of the struggle for the University Tests Bill in 1865.[27] Elected to the Literary Society in 1867, Coleridge became its president in 1887. Ironically, he had much in common with the man who stepped into the dock before him in April 1883, G. W. Foote. Both collected books, though the price of the editions varied; both wrote poetry (Foote secretly). With the exceptions of Foote's favorites Meredith, Flaubert, Whitman, and James Thomson, their pantheon of literary greats was the same: Wordsworth, Longfellow, Poe, Hawthorne, George Eliot, Tennyson, Shakespeare, Spenser and the Elizabethans, Homer (about whom Coleridge corresponded with Gladstone), even Shelley, that "audacious blasphemer" (Lord Coleridge, in E. Coleridge, *Life and Correspondence* 1: 242).

Like law, literature was a Coleridge family affair. John Duke's sister, Mary Elizabeth, was a gifted poet. The career of his father, Mr. Justice John Taylor Coleridge, was best summed up by the *Dictionary of National Biography:* "In his judgments, his literary tastes and classical knowledge appear rather than deep learning" (11: 302). Coleridge senior was a long-term contributor to Hone's enemies' organ, the *Quarterly Review,* and its interim editor in 1824. He brought to the family circle of literary intimates not only Pusey, Newman, Thomas Arnold, and the poet John Keble (author of the *Christian Year*), but Southey, Talfourd (a close friend), and William Wordsworth (whose pension he helped secure in 1842).[28]

Then there was the question of the "high poetic name."[29] John Duke Coleridge was indeed the great-nephew of the poet Samuel Taylor Coleridge, whose work he knew intimately, down to the minutiae of composition and revision. Most of all, he took seriously the duties of the family friendship with Wordsworth: publishing scholarly papers; corresponding with readers and "disciples"; fostering the early growth of the transatlantic Wordsworth industry; maneuvering to secure his monument in Poet's Corner in the mid 1850s, an emblematic moment.[30] A letter from W. C. Macready, 14 June 1852, "testif[ies]" to John Duke Coleridge's "faith in the teaching of that 'old man eloquent,' whom we unite in revering" (in E. Coleridge, *Life and Correspondence* 1: 222). As a lawyer in the 1850s, he read Wordsworth in snatches during twelve-hour days at the assizes; and when he entered Parliament in 1865, he took with him an unusual courtroom habit of "illustrat[ing] his arguments" with Wordsworthian quotations (2: 44).[31]

The voyage of Coleridge's life was quintessentially Victorian, and Wordsworth helped largely to smooth its rough passages. In young manhood he complained that Blackstone's *Commentaries* was a "thoroughly low-minded and irreligious" book (in E. Coleridge, *Life and Correspondence* 1: 245); by the 1860s he got "no help from Anglicanism for all my deepest and strongest needs" (1: 264). Doubts gathered while he prepared the case for the prosecution in the 1861 *Essays and Reviews* heresy trial, facing Fitzjames Stephen across the ecclesiastical Court of Arches.[32]

The affair disturbed him because it struck "at the root of 'authority' " (in E. Coleridge, *Life and Correspondence* 2: 112). But while "authority" remained the foundation stone of civilized existence—a constant theme of Coleridge's time as attorney-general (1871–73) and lord chief justice (1880–94)—church and Bible seemed less and less able to supply it. By the 1880s, he wrote in an obituary of Matthew Arnold in the *New Review,* August

1889, Christianity had become a "travesty" (2: 113). But if not in dogma and an established church, where else was authority to be found?

We know the answer already, of course: in Literature. Coleridge's views of its mission and status shifted dramatically between the 1850s and the 1880s. In 1853, he censored Charlotte Brontë's "scornful" *Villette* for its "degrad[ing]" of Christianity (in E. Coleridge, *Life and Correspondence* 1: 207, 206). By the time of the *Freethinker* trials, Coleridge no longer believed in what his father, Keble's biographer, called a "truly Christian literature" (1: 263). Nor did he like the radical idea of literature as a "religion of liberty" (1: 248). In a public address on education, belief in the one Good Book gave way instead to recommending a whole reading list:

> Nothing will . . . tend more to keep you from evil, than the company of good books and the thoughts and counsels of good men. They will fill you with good thoughts, and good thoughts bring forth good deeds, and good deeds are the only true happiness of life. (2: 387)

The essay was a classic example of late-nineteenth-century bibliomania and book collecting in its aspect of replacement or quasi-sacramental activity: "Books That Have Helped Me," "The Blessedness of Books," and so on (qtd. in Altick 139). So too was Lord Coleridge's manuscript list of his "Hundred Best Books" (a journalistic phenomenon of the 1880s) for the *Pall Mall Gazette,* his contribution to a journalistic craze of the 1880s: epitomizing the kind of high-literary censoring mechanisms the new canon would require, it excludes Aristophanes's comedies, since no "splendid genius" can "atone for the baseness and vulgarity of his mind" (22 January 1886, BL Add. Mss. 39,927). Both pieces were typical accompaniments to the decade's push to make standard works on literary history and literary criticism available for nationwide consumption: clergyman Stopford Brooke's primer, *English Literature* (1876, rev. 1880), which sold five hundred thousand copies by 1916; the school textbook *English Poets* (first volume, 1882); H. J. Nicholl's "bold" *Landmarks of English Literature* (1883); Bayard Tuckerman's undiscriminating *History of English Prose Fiction,* which "fills up the vacant niche a good book might have filled" (*Saturday Review,* 17 February 1883: 214).[33] The need for these works was urgently felt: the masses wanted books for "aesthetic culture," "moral culture," "political culture" (J. Collins 148).[34] Literature was now unequivocally asked to provide the authority once found in religion. Wordsworth naturally would figure at the head of the new literary canon, in gratitude for his "purifying influence on the literature of this country," as Talfourd put it in the preface to *Ion* (Tragedies 23), and as the model of the authoritative writer who creates social harmony by "trac[ing] out the links of good by which all human things are bound together" (24).

Such was the cast of mind of the first lord chief justice of all England. Such too was the mind-set of the nation's preeminent literary and cultural critic, the close Balliol friend whose parting Coleridge lamented in 1889: Matthew Arnold.[35] The sea of Christian faith might have ebbed, but faith remained a paramount national necessity. And its survival seemed to Arnold as threatened by secular and Secular*ist* agitation as it was sustained by culture and literature.

Culture and Anarchy, that extraordinary exercise in cultural "discipline," preempted precisely the anomalous identification the 1880s made between blasphemous "militant" Secularism and the Salvation Army. "The *iconoclast,*" Arnold averred, "seems to be almost for *baptizing us all in blood and fire* into his new social dispensation" (*Culture,* in *Portable* 523, my emphasis). His use of the term "iconoclast" was as deliberate as his invocation of the Salvation Army's rallying cry. "Iconoclast" was Bradlaugh's pen name, under which he began editing the *National Reformer* in 1860 and by which he was best known.[36] Behind *Culture and Anarchy* lurks the motivating specter of Secularism's "Chief." Arnold never names him, and his repression has been completed by Arnold criticism. The second chapter, "Doing as One Likes," also reworks with genius the catchphrase smacked on Holyoake's moderate movement around 1863, "Just-what-you-like-ism." It was revived with threatening intent during Bradlaugh's first run for Parliament in 1868, the year before publication of *Culture and Anarchy,* when John Stuart Mill (who had backed Holyoake's pioneer bid for the Tower Hamlets constituency in 1857) notoriously lost his seat because of contributions to the "howling Atheist's" election fund (*Freeman's Journal* 27 May 1880: 5). "I look around me and ask what is the state of England?" Arnold quotes Roebuck's "celebrated definition of happiness": "Is not every man able to say what he likes?" (*Culture* 550). But what Arnold sees in this free-speech "Just-what-you-like-ism" is "a peculiarly British form of Atheism" (550).[37]

Thoroughly unsettled by passage of the Second Reform Act that gave one in three men the vote and threw the 1868 election campaign open, in *Culture and Anarchy* Arnold cast Bradlaugh in the roles a hysterical press had ready-made for him:[38] representative of working-class "excess"; epitome of a "raw" populace demanding its share in the right to do and say what it likes; a compound of "brut[ishness]," "sheer violence," and vehement "ignorance and passion" (536); the inciter of "bawlings" and "blind clamor" in the streets (509, 536). *Culture and Anarchy* is structurally underpinned by repeated and horrified references to the Hyde Park disturbance of 1866, the year the National Secular Society was founded, during which Bradlaugh, the "anarchy-mongering," "notorious tribune" looked the other way when "popular rioter[s]" agitating for universal manhood suffrage tore

PUNCH, OR THE LONDON CHARIVARI.—May 12, 1883.

EXIT CALIBAN

(*After " The Tempest "*).

CALIBAN . . . MR. BR-DL-GH.   ARIEL . . . LORD R-ND-LPH CH-RCH-LL.   [*Act IV. Sc. 1.*

Figure 16. Literature as Establishment weapon. *Punch's* view of the "Bradlaugh Bill's" defeat, 12 May 1883. Compare a 5 May skit on judging submissions to the Royal Academy: "BRADL—— grr! Avaunt! / His coarse brush—confound it! / Hideously doth haunt / All our councils." Or see Home Secretary Harcourt's imaginary "Shakespearean Meditation" on his Government of London Bill, which faced *Punch's* report on the *Freethinker* trial on 17 March 1883.

down park railings (552, 524, 554–55). (This was an unusual event, since Bradlaugh's methods were resolutely nonviolent.) The book's original title, "Anarchy and Authority," accurately represented the importance of class thinking in its conceptualization; and in 1869 the threatening underclass was best epitomized by one man. Restore to Bradlaugh his place in history, and one restores to Arnold's masterpiece the edge of urgency needed to motivate what is in truth an outrageous attempt at character assassination in the cause of Culture. As such it was understood and replicated even by its less high-brow guardians (fig. 16).[39]

The opposite of the iconoclastic "Just-what-you-like-ism" that rushes in to fill the vacuum left by the demise of "Bible-religion," asserts *Culture and Anarchy* in 1869, is "a principle of authority" (511), "center of correct information, taste, and intelligence" (539). In the face of the "inadequacy" of the ruling aristocracy to supply it (515), Arnold turns to an ideal of the state, as the expression of our own "best self" (524); and he regrets, in "the absence of any authoritative center, like an Academy" (539), literature's unsuitability for the role. By the time he published *Literature and Dogma*, only four years later in 1873, the case was altered.

Literature and Dogma is one of the least read of Arnold's works (along with *God and the Bible* [1875], which rebutted the charges it drew down upon his head), yet it is the one to which modern secular culture, certainly modern liberal education, is most deeply indebted. "Iconoclast" broods above a prefatory lament for the burgeoning power of "militant" Secularism (*Literature and Dogma* 7, 9; see also 129, 131, etc.). Yet it is not "Bible-smashing" but the same crude, literal, and pseudo-scientific bibliolatry that G. W. Foote shortly assaulted in the *Freethinker* that most endangers English culture as Arnold sees it, insofar as the "conduct" of the bulk of the people, which is "three fourths of life," is still "inextricably bound up with the Bible and the right interpretation of it" (28).[40] The Bible must thus be saved *for* the masses if society is to be saved *from* the masses. Late Victorians never read the *Way of All Flesh*, and they misread the *Fair Haven*: instead of literary subversion, from the hands of their most acknowledged literary masters they received Literature-as-dogma.

Arnold's "reverent" biblical criticism (*Literature and Dogma* 219) is a sustained act of literary recovery, "as if some simple and saving doctrines, essential for men to know, were enshrined in Shakespeare's *Hamlet* or Newton's *Principia* . . . though the Gospels are really a far more complex and difficult object of criticism than either" (187). It is a masterly exercise in a method "larger, richer, deeper, more imaginative" than the "historic method" of Dr. Strauss (21). Telling the liter*ary* not liter*al* truth about the Bible, reading for "context" (163), "internal evidence" (178), and poetic resonance (180–81), Arnold believed, would lay down for it *"some other source of authority"* (143, my emphasis) beyond miracle and prophecy, beyond exploded claims to consistency and historical accuracy, which the "lapsed masses" would believe (6).

The authority by which *Literature and Dogma* undertakes its task is never explicitly evoked. Rather, the authority of Literature is written into that "most exquisite literary style known among modern writers" (Waite 3); is assumed in the devout joy with which the literary splendors of the Scriptures are proclaimed; it is encoded in the clinching points that finish paragraphs ("Wordsworth says to Duty—" [212], "Shakespeare's explanation is far the soundest—" [176]); it breathes through the superior tone that "literary experience" assumes over scientific and theological abstraction (82, 190,

239, 241, etc.). And superiority is the key to Arnold's argument. Benjamin Jowett had said that the Bible should be read "like any other book" (296); blasphemous Southwell had claimed the right of "poetic" interpretation. Arnold goes further than Jowett, and scouts Southwell's threat. The common man's untrained intellect is not capable of the right criticism of the Bible: it has an "unintelligent . . . fondness for the apocalyptic and phantasmagoric" bits (*Literature and Dogma* 196); and the "impudent" "orthodox theologians" of the day more deserve the label "infidel" for the "bad literary criticism" "which pours every Sunday from [their] pulpits" (188). The Bible belongs exclusively in the hands of first-rate literary critics (186); they shall be the new priests in authority over us.

Literature and Dogma did not succeed in its task of "recast[ing] religion" through the literary rehabilitation and transformation of the Book of Books (10). Rather, in attempting to reauthorize the Bible, Arnold canonized a method, not a text, confirming the Bible in the role in which posterity has inherited it: one of the Great Works of Literature.[41]

4. WHEN "LITERARY DIFFERENCE" BECAME A "CRIMINAL OFFENCE"

The quest for authority brings us back, once more, to the moment in April 1883 when G. W. Foote left his cell in Holloway Gaol for the Court of Queen's Bench, Arnold's friend Lord Chief Justice Coleridge presiding. His third trial was to take an unexpected procedural turn, opening a door into the different future augured but not guaranteed by the law's gradual redefinition of blasphemy and the shift of emphasis from the matter to the manner of the crime.

A defendant with unusual literary sensibility was not likely to let slip from sight the full implications of the legal drama in which he had top billing. Foote knew all along the "great danger" faced in cases like the *Free-thinker*'s, when "there is no statute to be appealed to accurately defining the crime" (*Defence* 21). "This talk about outraging other people's feelings," he declared at his first trial, "is only one way of cloaking . . . hideousness" (*Three Trials for Blasphemy* 29). Against such invocations of sensibility, Foote urged instead that

> It makes no difference in the crime of murder whether you beat out the victim's brains with a crowbar or kill him artistically with subtle poison; and as all murder is murder, so all blasphemy is blasphemy. (*Blasphemy No Crime* 15)

His insistence did not pay dividends with Judge North. Not surprisingly, North bade the jury ignore every reference Foote made to the jury's own "power of defining what is a blasphemous publication" (*Three Trials for*

Blasphemy 37), although this duty was explicitly laid upon them by Fox's Libel Act of 1792.[42]

The vexed issue of definition was not all that North bottled up in court. Sixty-six years earlier, Judge Abbot had tried unsuccessfully to stop William Hone from reciting in court a mock Te Deum that had been distributed to the troops during the Napoleonic wars: "Oh, Emperor of France! We curse thee. / To thee all nations cry aloud, / BONEY, BONEY, BONEY! / Thou art universally execrated, & c. & c." "You have read enough of it," Abbot interrupted. "It is a Ministerial parody," Hone replied. Abbot: "I know nothing of Ministerial or Anti-Ministerial parodies. You have stated enough of that publication for your purpose." Hone protested, in the manner of one spelling out a truism to a backward child: "If this mode of writing has been practiced by dignitaries of the church and by men high in the State, I humbly conceive that that circumstance might be some excuse for my having been the publisher of the trifle now charged as libelous" (*Three Trials* 41). The jury's verdict answered with a resounding "Yes!" the question, "Was it to be endured that a man should thus vindicate his misconduct . . . because he had, as it were, a prescription in crime?" (63). That is how literary—even subliterary—influence works.

For sixty-six years, no such "evidence" was again allowed, no such claim to de facto authority, except in the solitary and exceptional case of Edward Moxon and the complete works of Shelley. Thus, Foote's first and second trials before Judge North were punctuated by interruptions and procedural battles. North's suppressions were so significant, Foote felt, that he reprinted at full length in *Prisoner for Blasphemy* the exchanges they produced (70–74). Quotation in this courtroom was contempt of court:

> Mr. Justice North: What is the name of th[at] book?
> Mr. Foote: The book is *The Autobiography of John Stuart Mill.*
> Mr. Justice North: What are you going to refer to it for?
> Mr. Foote: I am going to refer to one page of it, my lord.
> Mr. Justice North: What for?
> Mr. Foote: To show that identical views to those expressed in the cheap paper before the court are expressed in expensive volumes.
> Mr. Justice North: I shall not hear anything of the sort.
> (*Three Trials for Blasphemy* 19)

These extracts were "not in evidence" (*Prisoner* 78):

> Mr. Justice North: It is a mere waste of time to attempt to justify anything that has been said in the alleged libel by showing that someone else has said the same thing.
> Mr. Foote: In all [slander and libel] trials the same process has been allowed.
> Mr. Justice North: It will not be allowed on this occasion. (20)

Well might Foote have asked his judge, with William Hone, "if you really mean to send me to prison without a fair trial?" (*Three Trials* 86). In 1817, Ellenborough had tried the pure force of legal exclusivity and obfuscation:

> Lord ELLENBOROUGH—You may state what you please; but I tell you, that that shall not be given in evidence which falls within the description of evidence I have mentioned.
>
> Mr. HONE (after a pause)—I really do not understand your lordship; I state it seriously, that I am not aware of the exact meaning of your lordship's intimation.
>
> Lord ELLENBOROUGH—I think what I have stated is intelligible enough to every other person in Court.
>
> Mr. HONE—It certainly is not intelligible to my humble apprehension.
>
> Lord ELLENBOROUGH—I can't help it.
>
> Mr. HONE—I really don't understand what your lordship means by the word *evidence.* . . . If your lordship says, that I am not to read these publications to the jury—if that is your lordship's decision against me, then I have no defense to this information, and I am ready to go with your lordship's tipstaff wherever your lordship may think proper to send me. (*Three Trials* 86–87)

Ellenborough was forced to endure bitterly through two days of hilarious quotation. But sixty-six years had given teeth to law's refusal to entertain literary evidence. A book "in evidence" had to have a direct connection with the case—say, the tome with which a murderer stunned his victim before pitching him out of a window. So that the third trial of G. W. Foote, 1883, before Lord Coleridge, marks an extraordinary cultural moment. As we have seen, at his third trial for blasphemy Foote not only attempted again to make the kind of defense that had been disallowed since Hone walked free, but was allowed by the lord chief justice of all England to do so.

As Foote read aloud, side by side, offensive snippets from the *Freethinker* and extracts from the upper-class "heretics circulated by Mr. Mudie"—Arnold and all the others—he had it in mind not only to expose the classist partiality of the law but to force a public admission of where late Victorian society really got its values. Gesturing to the books strewn on the table before him—books like Hone's, "dusty and tattered volumes that the ushers are quite sure have no law within their moldy covers" (Charles Knight, qtd. in Hackwood 155)—he looked for his evidence and his authority, and Lord Coleridge and the law looked, not to the "higher law" of heaven once invoked by reflex in lawyers' perorations, not to the Book of Books, but to Literature. What was revealed in that moment was that a new cultural consensus had been reached: prisoner and judge ascribed to the same values, bowed to the same authorities. Blasphemous Shelley's revolutionary prediction in the "Defence of Poetry" had come true, and more than true: "Poets" had become the acknowledged "legislators of the world" (*Shelley's Prose* 297). "[W]ho but the Poet first made Gods for men," as Carlyle had asked (with Goethe) in *Sartor Resartus;* "brought them down to us; and raised us up to them?" (219). Between the 1840s and the 1880s, England had indeed discovered the "fragments of a genuine Church-*Homiletic*" (*Sartor* 191) in its Literature, an Arnoldian "center" of authority; literature had provided heroes, "kings," and "articulate voice" (Carlyle, *Heroes* 114). On that literature's authority Mr. Foote of the *Freethinker* also claimed his rights; and Lord Coleridge seemed to offer to grant them.

His landmark ruling in the *Freethinker* case rewards reexamination at this point. "Perhaps the first clear rule upon this subject" (Bonner 105), it made a principle of what long had crept into practice amongst writers, reviewers, publishers; it gave "definite form," as legal historian G. D. Nokes put it in 1928, to the century's "modification" of the offense (66); it penned the death warrant for Hale's famous dictum, "Christianity is parcel of the laws of the land," flatly denied in the Lords in 1917 (Bonner 31).[43] The controversy it provoked was ultimately neither here nor there. Fitzjames Stephen might snap that for Lord Coleridge to talk of an "unseen process of growth" in the law was to ignore the problematics of an institution that was in fact "constructed" ("Blasphemy," 308, 310); but he had sounded the bottom better when he wrote the year before, in his 1883 *History of the Criminal Law,* that "the sentence of the law is to the moral sentiment of the public . . . what a seal is to hot wax" (2: 81).

For if the highest aim of jurist and legislator was to harmonize law and social morality, to make justice fit with real cultural values, Lord Coleridge's was a model among rulings:

> [I]f the decencies of controversy are observed, even the fundamentals of religion may be attacked without a person being guilty of blasphemous libel. (J. Coleridge 28)

Here was the standard of literary value authoritatively and openly planted, and the Bible stripped naked of legal protection. Guilt and innocence were entirely a question of "manner." Finalizing the century's drift towards literary criteria in adjudging blasphemy, Lord Coleridge officially turned religion itself into a matter of manner: "serious" writers, he told the jury at the third trial, were not those who turn our thoughts to religion but those in whom we detect "a grave, an earnest, a reverent, I am almost tempted to say a religious, tone" (qtd. in Odgers, *Libel and Slander* 467). Conversely, the "intent to shock and insult the feelings" of hearers or readers (who might or might not be believers) became "an essential element in the crime" (447). Outraged sensibility at last had full recourse to law.[44]

The gains in this for "serious" literature were clear. The Coleridge ruling signaled the change of climate that made possible a wave of agnostic and atheist confessional fictions and memoirs, from the 1880s through the fin de siècle, by William Hale White ("Mark Rutherford"), Olive Schreiner, Edmund Gosse, and such major figures in the Secularist movement itself as Annie Besant and Jacob Holyoake. It had become legal and safe to say in print "I do not believe" when blasphemy was officially demoted to "no more than the use of immoderate language" (C. Cohen, *Blasphemy* 18). When the authority of the Book had been undermined, other authors could loudly make their claims to influence.

Gosse's high-literary memoir *Father and Son* (1907), for example, played out in full the endgame of Literature's victory over the Bible. The Father is a Plymouth brother and zoologist whose devotion to the letter of scriptural text produces the "literary misfortune" of his ridiculous *Omphalos* (107), which argues God created fossils to test man's faith in the creation myth of Genesis. The Son, however, takes power from the cultured voice of the professional man of letters he was to become, even as he recounts his book-starved early youth. He marshals in a single chapter (ch. 7), against the counterverses of his father (not given), four lengthy quotations from Collins, E. B. Browning, Virgil, and Coleridge, and references to Byron, Dr. Johnson, Kingsley, Horace, Lucretius, Terence, Catullus, and Juvenal. It is quite a battery. A final, nonchalant flurry of phrases in Latin and French completes the ascendancy of the literary son over the biblical "peasant" father (163, 193, 244). Few "lessons for the day" could be more insinuatingly driven home. One is put in mind of Thomas Jefferson's joke about Hale's ruling. That cornerstone of law, he claimed, was actually based on a mistranslation of the 1458 text that gave it precedent: the crucial words *"ancien scripture"* did not mean "Holy Scripture" at all—they meant "old writings," all the inheritance of Literature (50; *Trial of Henry Hetherington* 17).

But G. W. Foote's last day in court was a moment ripe with irony, too. There were subtle but distinct differences between the admissions made in the case of the *Freethinker* and the decisions made in the *Lady Chatterley* case of 1960. In the aftermath of the *Chatterley* case, the slightest pretensions to literary value granted a book virtual immunity to prosecution, even a prostitute's how-to memoir like *Inside Linda Lovelace* (1976). Literariness granted rights. But when Literature in 1883 staked its claim as a positive standard of value, blithely imagined (in Talfourd's words) as "serene[ly]" "elevated" above political conflict (*Speech for the Defendant* 17), it took upon itself rather a kind of duty. It became a yardstick of criminality, the "authority" that controls.

Foote was alert to the danger: to call Shakespeare a "supreme god," or to purchase pocketbooks (as fellow Secularists did) with titles like the *Wit and Wisdom of George Meredith*—or, more disturbingly, the *Pilgrim's Scrip*—was to open oneself precisely to such a construction. Lord Coleridge's ruling stopped short of granting rights to literariness, broadly construed, and certainly did not extend literary status to productions like the *Freethinker* and men like G. W. Foote, who hoped against hope to claim it; it did nothing to break the barrier between literature and the subliterary. Instead it turned to the value system erected by Victorian reviewers and cultural critics (Coleridge, Arnold, et al.) for a set of arbitrary standards by which to judge acceptability and offensiveness; and it ensured that prosecutions would continue to be unpredictable. Convictions would henceforth depend, Foote realized, upon the "tastes" of the jury (*Defence* 23); and, as Bradlaugh had remarked, "what a prosecuting counsel or a bigoted jury may consider ribald or abusive in one case, an enlightened judge and tolerant jury may hold to be fair argument in another" (*Blasphemy and Heresy* 25). Making "decency" of "manner" the basis of law, Foote rightly concluded, "puts a rope round the neck of every writer who soars above commonplace, or has any gift of wit or humor" (*Prisoner* 11). Appointing Literature our policeman "turns a literary difference into a criminal offence" (42).

Foote might believe that he had unmasked classist hypocrisy in the Court of Queen's Bench—as indeed he had. But he also knew that, by making the defense he did make in order to expose it, he had turned for his "authority" to those very upper-class writers against whom he and his class were defined as offensive "other": the oppressed had consecrated the cultural authority of the dominant class; subliterature had confirmed the status, and the difference, of Literature. Claiming his rights by such authority was a gesture embroiled in difficulty. "In a bourgeois culture," writes Roland Barthes, "all that is not bourgeois is obliged to *borrow* from the bourgeoisie" (*Mythologies* 139): Foote's rebellion was contained by the terms of reference it invoked. Like Hardy's Jude the Obscure, graffiti writing on the walls of Christminster, he had made his claim to cultural power in terms borrowed from those who excluded him: "I have understanding as well as you. I am not inferior to you" (Job 11.3; *Jude* 121).[45] It is one of modern literary studies' dirty little secrets that a gain for Literature, such as the *Freethinker* case represented, need not be a gain for democracy. It was the literary redefinition of the crime of blasphemy that allowed for its classist manipulation into the twentieth century.

"The only essential difference," the Reverend Canon Shuttleworth reminded Home Secretary Harcourt in a memorial pleading for Her Majesty's prisoner Foote's release, "between Mr. Matthew Arnold's sarcasms" in
Literature and Dogma "and the caricatures of Mr. Foote is one of refinement."[46] (Lord Coleridge, in a string of letters and articles to Gladstone in
the *New Review* after Arnold's death in 1889, feelingly dissented: for all his
raillery, "there was never . . . the faintest trace of irreverence" in his work
[in E. Coleridge, *Life and Correspondence* 2: 113].) "Within the same week
that I pay a visit to G. W. Foote, the blasphemer, in Holloway Gaol,"
wrote the *Freethinker's* interim editor on 2 September 1883, "we read that
Matthew Arnold, the blasphemer, is to be placed on the Civil List with a
pension of £50 a year" (313). *Literature and Dogma,* like the Christmas number of the *Freethinker* or Meredith dispatching *Coelebs Pater* "with a Glass
Slipper," dismisses the miracle stories of Christianity as "doomed" to "drop
out like fairies or witchcraft, from among matters which serious people
believe" (250); it was in this work (as Foote reminded the court) that Arnold
made his "famous joke" about the Trinity as "three Lord Shaftesburys."
(He "not only left [it] out in his last edition," Lord Coleridge assured Gladstone, "but drew attention to the fact that he had done so, and gave his
reasons for doing it" [in E Coleridge, *Life and Correspondence* 2: 361].) His
dark double and opposite G. W. Foote left the Court of Queen's Bench
in April 1883 to finish his year's hard labor in Holloway Gaol, and to embark
on a lifetime of marginalization and honest toil on low-profile committees
for prison reform, Secular education, and the banning of vivisection. Government was careful, despite severe temptation throughout the 1880s, never
again to lend him a public platform: when he left on Judge North's doorstep
a copy of the first issue published under his resumed editorship, complete
with front-page cartoon and a rousing two-page "Letter to Judge North"
(*Freethinker,* 16 March 1884: 81–82), no one blinked. (The cartoons were
discontinued in 1887.) The new quality journal Foote launched in 1883,
Progress, quickly foundered for want of financing. "He came out of the
furnace as hard as a diamond," as one obituary put it (*Freethinker,* 31 October 1915: 698), to find the bottom about to drop out of the diamond market.
Foote died in harness in 1915, still editor of a penny paper with a dwindling
circulation and president of a shrunken National Secular Society. His moment of history, and Secularism's, had passed. "[Arnold's] blasphemy and
mine," as he remarked in a dry footnote to an 1889 reprint of his triumphant
third speech, "met with very different rewards" (*Defence* 35n).

CHAPTER FIVE

WORDS, WORDS, WORDS

There is another story to tell about G. W. Foote and his blasphemous
Freethinker. It has to do with the raw materials of criminality and the object
of law's rule, the counters of meaning that it is Hamlet's tragedy to see
emptied of significance: "words, words, words." The history of blasphemy
unfolds another "Story of English" than the one celebrated on public televi-
sion and handed down as "triumph" in outdated textbooks. Under its criminal aegis, this chapter brings together five unwritten episodes in linguistic
crisis and resolution.

The consequences of the Victorian philological "upheaval" have remained "much more hidden from Western consciousness" than the effects
of revolution in biology and economics, as Foucault wrote in 1966. Yet
they "have extended much further in our culture" (*Order* 282). The transitional decade of the 1880s was one of the century's three great moments
for "taking stock" of progress in the study and life of language, and of
English in particular, wrote Oxford's first professor of comparative philology, Max Müller (*Science of Thought* xxv).[1] Ferdinand de Saussure started
teaching. Psycholinguistics was born, circa 1883. The audience for writings
on language dramatically widened: popular works like Farrar's *Chapters
on Language* (1861/1865) and Dean Trench's *English Past and Present*
(1855) could be had in six-shilling editions; Müller's *Science of Language*
was reprinted in two fat volumes for sixteen shillings; prescriptions on
literary idiom like Kington-Oliphant's *New English* (1886) competed
with new standard texts like Sayce's *Introduction to the Science of Language*
(1883). The *Junggrammatische* school began to be published in England:
synchronic, speech-focused, grammar-driven, their work laid the founda-

tions for modern linguistics. Crucially, in its leader Carl Abel's *Linguistic Essays* the Romantic idea of language as *Volksstimme*—what Coleridge called "the collective mind of a Country" (qtd. in Dowling 24)—struck scientific root: his reshaping of philology as a "comparative national conceptology" was excitedly welcomed by English reviewers (*Mind*, 30 April 1883: 292).

Above all, in the 1880s historical scholarship began to bear fruit in the *Oxford English Dictionary (OED)*. The most massive philological project ever undertaken, sixty years in the making (1857 to 1928), its first "fascicle" or part volume of 352 pages from *a* to *antyteme* saw the light in January of the year G. W. Foote left Holloway Gaol, 1884.[2] Editor J. M. Murray's emphasis on the "common" core of language, like his admission of newspaper English, troubled early reviewers; they wanted a prescriptive canonical dictionary. But the *OED* did not open a floodgate to revolution as Dowling suggests (181). It swiftly assumed the status of the "ultimate reviewer" desiderated by Riffaterre (D. Taylor 22). Its "repeatedly cited writers and works" testified to "the linguistic centers of authority in the language" (Willinsky 192).[3] Here we might seek for the linguistic standing of Foote (not cited, not mentioned), Bradlaugh (not cited but mentioned), and Holyoake (both mentioned and cited).[4]

Most importantly, any sense of linguistic degradation in the inclusiveness of the dictionary project was outweighed by national pride. The *OED* was no work made for hire like Johnson's dictionary but a communal public project. Seven hundred sixty-two volunteers supplied the quotations that fleshed out entries in that first fascicle; thousands more contributed to the two million finally used. "Ours is a Copious Language," Britons could now pronounce with Podsnappian confidence, "and Trying to Strangers" (*Our Mutual Friend* 179), as they thumbed through the 414,825 headword entries.[5] Moreover, Murray's etymological quest for "Anglicity" produced the rude and hardy Saxons as Englishhood's direct linguistic ancestors, fit progenitors of a master race; Alfred, king of the West Saxons, was crowned a philological King Arthur. Thus dated to circa 800 AD, English assumed apparent historical precedence over its European competitors: German, dated by Grimm to Luther's fifteenth century; French, dated by Littré to the seventeenth. A mania for "Saxon" English swept the country. It held out the promise not only of a return to origins—origins unmuddied by the euphemizations of Norman French (*expectorated* for "spat," *menstruated* for "bled," etc.), a fact with meaning in it for the history of blasphemy—but of racial purity. At its popular worst, the forgotten phenomenon of Saxonism turned into a tracing of superior "Aryan" languages to their "roots," and those roots, in turn, became roots of power.[6] In the

1880s, value and authority, prejudice and patriotism, came to be vested not only in English literature but in the language in which it was constituted. We began to have "faith" in "Englishry," trust in the "English-speaking" "race" and the "English-speaking" "soul."[7] The "science of speech," Sayce assured his readers, was working to change "the Babel of the primeval world into the 'Saturnalia regna' of the future, when there will be a universal language and a universal law" (Sayce 2: 351; Genesis 11.1–9). In the 1880s, remembers the Kenyan writer Ngugi wa Thiong'o, "the weapon of language [was] added to that of the Bible and the sword," and "English was made to look as if it were the language spoken by God" (Willinsky 284, 203), even while level-headed missionaries like Mrs. Booth of the Salvation Army protested: "How do you know that the latest version of English grammar will be the language of heaven?" (Sandal 162). "[W]hoever, through the imposition of hands, whether of his parents or his foreign masters, has received the blessing" of that progress of Indo-European history that culminated in English, Max Müller intoned in 1888, "belongs to that unbroken spiritual succession which began with the first apostles of that noble speech, and continues to the present day in every part of the globe" (*Biographies* 89–90). English, the Imperial English of an empire that became a faith, became a language against which one could sin: this, like its resacralization in the making of the *OED*, restored the potential for word crime. Those facts, too, helped create the cultural climate in which blasphemy must be found out and extirpated.

Thus, the 1880s were a watershed not only in the study but in the life of the English language. The decade's defining linguistic events worked both separately and collectively to recall blasphemy from the national subconscious: they were the other, less obvious cultural conditions for the "crime" of the *Freethinker,* and they are the subjects of this chapter. The ubiquitous Victorian euphemism reached fullest flower in the 1980s, as section 2 discovers: a culture that made it the governing structure of discourse, and a society in which law preserved ancient ideas about the divine origin and "intentionality" of language necessarily also produced its opposite—blasphemy. The endpoint of euphemism was the annihilation of language: section 3 examines the theory and practice of judicial silencing in the blasphemy courtroom from 1819 to 1888. Section 4 details the other life of Jacob Holyoake, "Master of Sentences." Section 5 requires our return to the "fetish" abandoned for literature at the close of chapter 4: publication of the Revised Version of the Bible from 1881 to 1884 dramatically sapped public faith in "Bible English" as the "holdfast" of national language (Coleridge, *Table Talk* 49), and the destabilization this induced fed pervasive anxiety about the significatory power of language, creating the 1880s as a crisis decade for language. The chapter begins, however, with a critical question and an unspeakable subject.

1. MR. FOOTE'S TRIAL FOR OBSCENITY

The dubious Thomas Paterson, bookseller, of Number 8, Holywell Street, London, and the "Blasphemy Depot," Edinburgh, intrudes himself in the role of grotesque prologue. There was a suggestive slippage in his 1843 police court trial for the newfangled crime of "profanity" that disturbed even Paterson himself. In it lies the initial problem this chapter must unravel: What is the relationship between blasphemy and obscenity? What is the meaning of that relationship for our sense of words and the power of language?

Paterson was tried for peddling standard Freethought fare: cheap editions of Gibbon, pamphlets by Holyoake, odd copies of the *Oracle of Reason,* and so on. But Holywell Street was much better known for "indecency, obscenity, and bawdry" (*God v. Paterson* v), and Paterson's crime was instantly apprehended as such: Number 8 was branded a "den of hideous profligacy" (*John Bull,* qtd. 21). Paterson responded, "I have been coupled with the indecent, impure, and immoral, and my writings with obscene publications; I am, therefore, to understand, that is the meaning of the word *profane*" (49). It was an uncomfortable confusion to thrust back in his prosecutors' faces. He did not have to wait long for them to think up new methods of suppression. One of the letters to the *Times* that the case provoked proposed new legislation that would empower police to impound "obscene, indecent, or blasphemous" literature, and magistrates to hand out three- to six-month sentences to offenders. It anticipated very precisely, in short, the provisions of the historic Obscene Publications Act of 1857.

The new act, the first such legislation, was aimed at Paterson's neighbors. Obscene literature, said Lord Campbell introducing his bill, was "a poison more deadly than prussic acid, strychnine or arsenic" (Thomas, *Long Time* 242). The new law was dangerously (or conveniently) short on definitions, the most basic of which was only supplied eleven years later when Chief Justice Cockburn decided the "test of obscenity" was

> Whether the tendency of the matter charged as obscenity is to deprave and corrupt those whose minds are open to such immoral influences, and into whose hands a publication of this sort may fall. (Folkard 475)

The act put an official cap on seventy years' work by the Proclamation and Vice Societies.[8] But it had equally important antecedents in cases like Paterson's "profanity" trial. Suggestively, the 1857 act officially transferred to the crime of obscenity that it had newly constructed the punishment for centuries meted out for blasphemy: burning.[9] The story behind its pas-

sage bears vociferous witness to a blurring of the boundary between the
blasphemous and the obscene.

It was always inexact. Rumors about orgies routinely bolstered medieval
accusations of heresy; the worst blasphemy attributed to the Moriscos of
Spain impugned the virginity of Mary (Lawton 92). Wilkes's *Essay on
Woman* was deemed both an "obscene" and an "impious" libel in 1763
(Starkie 2: 140); sexual possession inexorably gives way to demonic possession in Matthew Lewis's *The Monk*, obscenity to blasphemy, and the author
was charged with both in 1798; an "obscene act," said the Vice Society,
was simply an act "not named among Christians" (Thomas, *Long Time*
197). Obscenity bred blasphemy, and blasphemy could contain obscenity.
The reverse formula, whereby blasphemy could be submerged in obscenity,
waited its time of development. In the mid-nineteenth century mundane
circumstances seemed to conspire to produce it.

Smutty and irreligious books *looked* the same, for a start. Both were
sold under the counter, clandestinely. Both were denied the protection of
copyright. Sentences for obscenity tended to be lighter: Paterson's neighbor
William Strange got only three months in 1857 for *Paul Pry* and *Women
of London;* Dugdale worked hard to rack up a two-year sentence.[10] But the
disparity may only reflect the fact that their offense was more common.
By the mid-nineteenth century, obscenity like blasphemy had undergone
two centuries' parallel progress from religious "sin" to secular "crime."[11]
Both crimes were threats to the status quo. As blasphemy menaced the
established church and public order, so the obscenity of "free" love spelled
anarchy by destabilizing the laws of inheritance. Hence the twin attraction
of Paine and pornography to the rebellious "ultras" of the 1810s and 1820s
(McCalmain, 204–31); and thus the tendency of governments to group
together legislation concerning blasphemy and obscenity, often with enact-
ments pertinent to sedition. Freethinking radical pressmen washed their
hands of smut in the 1830s, but Holywell Street's old hands kept the connection up, issuing a title like the *Amatory Experiences of a Surgeon* as
"Printed for the Nihilists: Moscow" as late as 1881 (Thomas, *Long Time*
226).[12]

Indeed, pornography enjoyed a lascivious renaissance in the early 1880s.
The *Freethinker* competed for notoriety with three underground periodicals
that marked "the heights or depths, according to one's view of the matter"
(Thomas, *Long Time* 275): the *Pearl,* the *Cremorne,* and the *Boudoir,*
launched 1879, 1882, and 1883, respectively.[13] To these expensive publications were added scandal sheets in the same price range as Foote's penny
paper, like the *Ferret* and *Peter Spry*. An angry debate on offensive literature
can be tracked through Home Office papers of the 1880s. "Vulgar," "vile,

and pernicious rubbish," in the words of a constituent's missive to member of Parliament and bookstall magnate W. H. Smith, "like a moral pestilence," was debauching the tastes of "the very lowest class of our fellow men" (HO 45: 9,536/49,022/2). Murder melodramas, obscene publications like *Town Talk,* penny papers like the *Freethinker,* even the *Illustrated Police News* drew the same kind of fire: all were "promiscuous publications" (49,902/73); all appealed to "the debased imagination" (49,022/2). Their advertisements made the streets "unfit for any lady or respectable woman" to walk, especially *Town Talk's* "dreadful contents Bills": *"Fallen Women!" "Prostitutes at the Westminster Aquarium!" "How the women hide their shame!"* (49,902/74).

So closely connected had the two crimes of blasphemy and obscenity become, in fact, that concepts which grew up around the one crime could shift with slippery ease to the other. Hence the arc of connection between the 1840 Moxon-Shelley trial for blasphemy and D. H. Lawrence's posthumous arraignment for obscenity. The stage seemed set in 1883 for the reverse formula to take effect—for blasphemy to be submerged in obscenity, for obscenity to swallow blasphemy.

Extraordinary confusion marked every scandalized letter about Foote's penny paper written to the Home Office, and every note scribbled upon it by Home Secretary Harcourt's staff: it was clearly, commonly, culturally understood that the *Freethinker* should be prosecuted for obscenity. In fact, this was what Harcourt planned. His men pored over the paper from the moment of first publication in hopes of finding grounds for such a prosecution, and only reluctantly admitted, in private, as one assistant undersecretary put it, that "however profane it may be," the *Freethinker* was not obscene (HO 45: 9,536/49,022/79a). Legal nicety never overawed gut instinct, however. Foote's penny paper, Assistant Commissioner of Police James Monro wrote the Home Office in 1887, was a "scurrilous print" (10,406/A46,794/2). The term brings to mind the kind of smutty seaside postcard beloved of Englishmen to this day. Almost every public pronouncement upon the case rankled with like innuendo.

"A pseudonymous correspondent of the *Daily News,*" Foote noted before trial started, "supposed that blasphemy meant the use of indecent language on religious topics" (*Blasphemy No Crime* 11). He might possibly have read the 1841 Royal Commission's Report on the Criminal Law, which first sanctioned the slippage, among its other obfuscations. (It also surprisingly claimed that every case since Woolston's in 1728 had involved the use of sexualized language.) Or the correspondent might have hearkened to the suggestions of Holy Writ. Take Judges 8.3, for example, wherein "the people of Israel . . . played the harlot after Baals." The offense is a religious one—apostasy; the language is sexual. The English, Arnold's Bible-reading people, were apt to make the connection.

Even Holyoake publicly reprimanded the *Freethinker* in the *Daily News* for "violence and obscenity," not for blasphemy (qtd. in *Freethinker,* 13 August 1882: 250). Butcher Henry Varley, the ostensible initiator of the prosecution, regaled members of the House of Commons with a circular that laid on the metaphors with a trowel. "Devise means to stay this hideous prostitution of the liberty of the Press," he urged, "by making these shameless blasphemers amenable to the existing law" (qtd. in Foote, *Prisoner* 22). In court, prosecutor and judge joined the chorus. It seemed to Sir Hardinge Giffard "a prostitution of great names to hear the titles of freedom of the press and liberty of discussion made use of when he had to call attention to such ribaldry" (*Three Trials for Blasphemy* 3). Just as the not-so-dead metaphors of modern English forged a link between words and money, so they invited erasure of the border between blasphemy and obscenity. "Liberty of opinion" became "taking a liberty" or acting the "libertine"; "freedom of speech" became making "free" with words; and what Foote called "literary license" became Judge North's "unbridled license" (45).

This was the classic Grub Street slur, writ large; even "hack" was a slippery, dirty word.[14] It speaks of anxiety over historical shifts in relationship between public and private information: when knowledge becomes "common knowledge" it becomes both vulgar and volatile. "The liberty of the press," pronounced England's chief justice in 1784, "consists in printing without any previous licence, subject to the consequences of law. The *licentiousness* of the press is *Pandora's box,* the source of every evil" (qtd. in Thomas, *Long Time* 111). The early 1880s, twenty years after the introduction of web machines that allowed print runs in the hundreds of thousands, decade of the first mass-market newspapers, inevitably witnessed an upsurge in discomfort.

And in truth, two items in the *Freethinker*'s "hot" Christmas number for 1882 did shave the border between obscenity and blasphemy. One was a mock report of the "Trial for Blasphemy" of Matthew, Mark, Luke, and John (halted for lack of evidence that they wrote the gospels), who, in the inflated language of legal indictment,

> being wicked and evil-disposed persons did publish or cause to be published, certain blasphemous, impious, scurrilous, libelous and scandalous matters, wickedly and profanely devising to asperse and vilify Almighty God, and against his honor and dignity, to the tenor and effect following, to wit, among other matters, that he, Almighty God, did cohabit with or overshadow a certain Jewish virgin named Mary, and hocus her affianced husband Joseph, and that, as a result of such overshadowing an illegetimate [sic] son named Jesus was born. (4)

The second was a tasteless though very obliquely worded piece of "Agony Aunt" advice to "Holy Gh——t" as the father of the same son, in a joke correspondence column: "If it is proved that you are the father of the child you no doubt will have to pay five shillings a week towards its support" (14). Both items flew in the face of the Victorian pact to ignore the sexual dimension of the Scriptures.

In this they signaled their standing in a mutinous tradition. Hone joked but quailed at the thought of holding up the Bible to rebuke; Carlile, with Paine's *Age of Reason* in hand, deliberately planned his assault on "Bible Obscenity."[15] Shop-man Humphrey Boyle worked up a strategic list of lurid examples for his spirited defense of 1822:

> Shall I instance that disgusting scene described as occurring between Lot and his daughters? Shall I take you to the bed-chamber of Onan and Tamar? . . . Can we, for a moment, reflect with serious minds upon the debaucheries of David and his sons, or think without shame of the beastly comparisons made by the book of Ezekiel? (*Report of the Trial of Humphrey Boyle* 15)

These were not rhetorical questions. An undignified scuffle broke out as Boyle announced, "Gentlemen, the first extract I shall read to you is the story of Lot and his daughters" (15). He worked his way solemnly through the whole catalogue: Genesis 19.27–38, 38.9–10; Deuteronomy 23.1; Ezekiel 22.1–21. By the more prudish and pious 1840s, the biblical counterattack was so well known that defendants needed only invoke it to make a stir. Henry Hetherington, for example:

> I have here a list of passages from the Bible, of a highly objectionable character; but as I perceive a number of ladies in the court, I will not pollute their ears, nor shock the feelings of the Jury, by reading them. (*Trial of Henry Hetherington* 18)

Paterson resigned his right to attack with more dramatic effect. "The Bible and other obscene works NOT sold at this shop," read one handbill for the Edinburgh "Blasphemy Depot," which prominently stocked a pamphlet called the *Bible an Improper Book for Youth, and Dangerous to the Easily-excited Brain* (*Trial of Thomas Paterson* 62); he regretted, Paterson said on trial, that a "public court" could not be made an "arena" for the "naked exposure" of "bible beauties" to "the prostitution of the public gaze" (38).

But the Obscenity Act had raised the stakes these men memorably tossed on the table. To break society's vow of silence on the subject of Bible obscenity after 1857 was positively to advertise the fact that the Book protected by the law of blasphemy was potentially indictable under the new law of obscenity.[16] "[I]f a questionable passage can be found in the whole of our pages," Foote claimed with some justice, it can only be by importing into our guarded language the vileness of the "holy Scripture" itself. Yes, there lies the secret of all our "indecency." We have to expose a holy book which reeks with obscenity, . . . and its blind worshippers . . . call us dirty because we point to their own filth. (*Freethinker,* 20 July 1884: 226)

His trials allowed a first opportunity for calling the bluff. The more succinctly offensive item of advice to "Holy Gh——t" was singled out for comment by Judge North. He shared both prosecutor Giffard's opinions and his gift for cliché. "[C]onsider, gentlemen," he urged the jury,

whether the proper term for that [item] would be a controversy or free discussion on a point reasonably considered, or whether the proper description of that would not rather be a piece of ribald obscenity. (*Three Trials for Blasphemy* 40–41)

Giving sentence, with a final metaphorical flourish, he regretted that "a man gifted by God with such great ability" should have chosen "to prostitute his talents to the service of the Devil" (qtd. in Bonner 99).

Foote paid dearly for his two questionable jokes. They facilitated the slippages he protested against before, during, and after his days in court. "I am not prosecuted here on a charge of indecency," he repeatedly reminded his first two juries, "I am prosecuted on a charge of blasphemy." But Giffard nevertheless used the terms "decency and indecency" "at least six times as often" as the word "blasphemy." "I can quite understand," Foote added, "that, by substituting [those words], other associations might be raised and other ideas excited in the minds of the jury" (*Three Trials for Blasphemy* 10).

Indeed. Return to earlier courtrooms, and we uncover the origins of "decency" as the master term of judgment. Jacob Holyoake first felt its full unexpected force: "We would have freedom of inquiry restrained by no laws but those of decency," pronounced Mr. Justice Erskine in 1842 (*Cheltenham Free Press,* 20 August: 270). Such apparent generosity stumped the defendant, who was eager for courtroom struggle. But for his judge, "indecency" was a useful and more neutral substitute for "obscenity." (Victorian law books make no essential distinction between the two terms: they are virtual legal synonyms.) The antonym, "decency," opened a prospect on a world of irreproachable respectability. By the time of the *Freethinker* trials, judicial suggestion had acquired the force of law. Revising Starkie's *Slander and Libel* in 1876, Henry Folkard stated pointblank that "whatever outrages public decency, and is . . . done in contempt of the laws of decency, is indictable" (606).

Such compulsions drove the *Freethinker* case. Lord Coleridge's intermittent efforts at clarification could hardly counterbalance them. He might call the jury to remember, summing up at the end of the third trial, that

Mr. Foote . . . is not a licentious writer in the sense in which Mr. Starkie uses the word licentious. He has not . . . pandered to the sensual passions of mankind. (28)

But such judicious distinctions were featherweights in the scale next to the weighty endorsement of precedent enshrined in his final ruling:

[I]f the decencies of controversy are observed, even the fundamentals of religion may be attacked without a person being guilty of blasphemous libel. (28)

The charge of "indecency" or "obscenity" was one to which Secularism was keenly sensitive.[17] "Young Men," exhorted a Holyoake critic in 1850, "Scorn the coils that would fetter you to the groveling pleasures of infidel sensualism" (Harrison 8). Even in 1883, at eighty years' distance from the French Revolution, an orthodoxy that viewed faith as the foundation of morality need take only a short step to believe that all unbelievers were seducers and pornographers, unworthy of the rights of citizenship. "After our release" from prison, Foote recalled,

[O]ne gentleman actually wrote to ask whether it was true, as his brother-in-law had informed him, that our prosecuted Christmas Number contained a picture of a man openly committing a nuisance. Another person stated that it contained a picture of two Bible characters in the act of adultery. Another . . . [thought] it contained a picture of the Virgin Mary being confined. (*Freethinker*, 20 July 1884: 226)

Just as Huxley had to remind Christian colleagues at University College that "Freethinking does not mean Free love" (Tribe, *One Hundred Years* 227), so Foote found himself defending his heroes and colleagues from sexual slurs into the twentieth century: Tom Paine was an adulterer, claimed the evangelist Reverend Torrey from the stage of the Albert Hall in 1905; Colonel Ingersoll had "assisted in the dissemination of obscene literature" (Foote, *Guilty* 4).

The slur of indecency was personally galling to Foote. His 1876 break with the National Secular Society had been partly dictated by scruples about the "Chief"'s relationship with Annie Besant. The year 1877 saw the "severe test" of Secularist "solidarity" caused by their illegal republication of Knowlton's dry birth control pamphlet, *The Fruits of Philosophy:* sentenced to six months apiece, they went free only on a technicality.[18] The obscene shadow of their prosecution loomed over the *Freethinker* case, and the more its instigators could thicken it, the better.

Yet still Home Secretary Harcourt knew that "we were not prosecuted for obscenity; he knew there was not a suggestion of indecency in our indictment; and he had before him the distinct language of the Lord Chief Justice of England, exonerating us from the slander" (Foote, *Prisoner* 168). "If we were blasphemous it was clean blasphemy" (*Freethinker*, 26 November 1911: 753). Nevertheless, refusing to mitigate sentence against Foote, Ramsey, and Kemp, Harcourt assured the Commons:

> I have seen [the *Freethinker*] and have no hesitation in saying that it is in the most strict sense of the word an obscene libel. It is a scandalous outrage upon public decency. (Foote, *Prisoner* 167)

A liberal minister might have been expected to care for liberty of the press; but the insinuation of obscenity released him:

> [Harcourt] got us locked up in felons' cells as blasphemers, and then piled up against our cell doors a huge heap of filth, . . . in order to scare away all those who might come to our relief. (*Freethinker*, 20 July 1884: 226)

By 1905, the blurring of the boundary between the blasphemous and the obscene was indelibly written into the law books. In order to avoid the charge of blasphemy, W. Blake Odgers wrote in his *Libel and Slander,* the author must "abstain from ribaldry and licentious reproach" (447).

The logic of these slippages—liberty to license, blasphemy to obscenity—is compelling, documented, almost overdetermined. It tempts us to view obscenity as the Victorian crime of crimes, and to consider the *Freethinker* case a locus classicus of the phenomenon whereby all offenses were measured against the great Victorian standard of taboo on sexuality.

A great deal of evidence supports this view. Taboo-driven legislation peaked in the 1880s. The post office "Protection" Act of 1884 allowed recipients of unwanted pornography to lodge official complaints. The Criminal Law Amendment Bill of 1885, which (at last) raised the age of consent from thirteen to sixteen, was altered at the eleventh hour to criminalize homosexual activity.[19] (It was an irony of history that Bradlaugh's fellow member of Parliament for Northampton should have authored the notorious "Labouchere Amendment.") In 1889, serious literature came within scope of the Obscene Publications Act, in direct contravention of its framer's explicit declaration of 1857, made with a copy of *La dame aux camélias* in his hand: respectable seventy-year-old Henry Vizetelly was handed a sentence of three years for publishing Zola in England. And he was prosecuted by an aggressive new antivice organization, the National Vigilance Association (founded in 1886), with the solicitor-general for counsel and future Prime Minister Asquith as his research assistant.[20]

But is the proliferation of legislation, or the political dictate to smear the *Freethinker,* or the ease with which concepts slid across the courtroom floor sufficient reason to accept so grandly totalizing a hypothesis as that all offenses, including blasphemy, were to be measured in the second half of Victoria's reign in terms of the great taboo on sexuality? The problem faced by Mr. Foote is the problem faced by research, interpretation, history.

The very idea that "the customs and values of a society form a totality," a "culture," writes Christopher Herbert, was developed in this period in reaction to a "myth of a state of ungoverned human desire" (29). Was the *Freethinker* unofficially tried for obscenity in press and Parliament because that new crime, like a cultural black hole, irresistibly drew all suspect matter towards it? Or is this a retrospective over-reading by a post-Freudian, post-Foucauldian generation for whom a cigar can never again be just a cigar? The slippage from blasphemy to obscenity is evident. But that is not to say there were no other forces at work in the *Freethinker* scandal. The control of sexuality, the putting-down of obscenity, may turn out to be part of a bigger picture, or may intersect with another dominant cultural matrix, the one Lacan substituted for the sexuality Freud's disciples made the grand key to understanding. That matrix was language.

2. VICTORIAN EUPHEMISM AND THE FEAR OF LANGUAGE

Even a cursory examination of Victorian mores discovers what most made language "decent": euphemism. The Victorians did not invent it, and it was a pan-European problem, as Flaubert's 1881 *Dictionary of Received Ideas* satirically demonstrates.[21] Euphemism is born anew in every generation: "Words that were once chaste," Watts wrote in 1724, "by frequent use grow obscene and uncleanly" (*OED* 10: 656). But there was also a "very rigorous" and deliberate "expurgation" of the "authorized" English vocabulary in the nineteenth century (Foucault, *History of Sexuality* 17); Victoria's reign was the golden age of euphemism. Indeed, so self-evident is the fact that no research has ever been done to ground it, while few theorists except Bourdieu have realized the centrality of euphemism to language as a sociopolitical system. Language loudly disputes with sexuality the role of Victorian master matrix; and Victorian euphemism both avoids and demands the resurgence of its true opposite term: blasphemy.

Under Victoria, "legs" became *limbs;* "w.c." (1810s) became *washroom* (1850s) and *walk* (1870s); "whores" became *fallen women*. Latinisms like *osculate* and *defecate* took hold, along with Frenchified pruderies like *accouchement, lingerie,* and *chemise*. "Trousers" transmogrified into *inexpressibles, inexplicables, indescribables* (as worn by Mr. Trotter in *Pickwick Papers*), and *unmentionables,* the preferred term of the 1880s.[22] As the years of Victoria's reign lengthened, so did the euphemisms, obeying Hugh Rawson's rule, "[t]he longer the euphemism the better" (11): thus "limb" later changed into *lower extremity*. Even sexologists like Isaac Baker Brown, notorious proponent of clitoridectomy, avoided the terms of their trade: his replacement for pseudo-Latin "masturbation" (one which speaks volumes about the suppression of female sexuality) was "peripheral excitement" (case 19, in J. H. Murray 28). Not all euphemism is fraudulent in intent, but in the Victorian period it became hard to tell "the specious moral pickpocket" from "the considerate and soft-spoken idealist" (Adams 55). Aspiration and social anxiety brought as much evasiveness in their train as Victorian "prudery on the prowl."[23] Latinate *emolument, remuneration,* and *honorarium* were words for laundering middle-class money; *emporium,* an inflation of the humble "shop"; *asylum* and *abattoir,* obscuring names for nasty places; *pure-finder,* a pauper's disguise, recorded by Henry Mayhew, for his abject job of dog shit collector (it was used in tanning hides).

Dickens, chary of fiction's blasphemous potentiality, once smiled genially on the national addiction. One stock-in-trade of his humor that has dated badly is the elaborate circumlocution. But in 1855 he sat down to write the most scathing indictment of British euphemism, *Little Dorrit.* The specter of obscenity haunts the novel, to be sure, creating troubling lacunae in reading: we are, for example, withheld for over four hundred pages from the knowledge that diffident hero Arthur Clennam kissed unconscious Little Dorrit on the day her family left the Marshalsea Debtors' Gaol. But despite its dramatic avoidances, *Little Dorrit* chafes more at the tight high-Victorian straitjacket in which it finds language bound; it debars even standard titivations like *trousseau,* sticking to "a vulgar principle . . . of adhering to the language in which it professes to be written" (667). At the novel's symbolic center, the government "Circumlocution Office" smothers national enterprise. Meanwhile, *Dorrit's* men and women fall prey to linguistic ailment. The compulsive and endless chatter of Flora Finching; the cryptic aggressive pronouncements of Mr. F.'s aunt; Mrs. Chivery's "peculiar power of construction" (304); the imperative conjugations of Pancks and Mrs. Merdle ("Keep thou always at it!" [871]): these and more have been much discussed. But what really stops the novel's emotional heart is Victorian euphemism. It governs, more than a verbal tic ever governs in the word-obsessed world of Dickens's fiction, the relationship of Little Dorrit with the father who preys upon her: it is her distinguishing peculiarity to prefer the "plain truth" (551), and William Dorrit's disabling tragedy to be euphemism in person. He hides in it from his shame as the longest-serving inmate of the prison: handouts are "testimonials"; visitors are warned to keep within conversational "bounds" (121); "a man so broken as to be the Father of the Marshalsea," Little Dorrit knows, "could be no father to his own children" (112). The affliction expresses itself physically: writing to Mrs. Merdle about the engagement of their children, Dorrit "surround[s] the subject with flourishes, as writing-masters embellish copy-books and ciphering-books" (658). Mrs. General appeals to him as a chaperone for his girls in his days of prosperity for her ability to "put away" suggestive terms like "husband" (705) and to "stop" unpleasant expressions of capitalist fact, even already-euphemistic "remuneration" (501). (A better phrase, as Mrs. Sparsit decides in *Hard Times,* would be "annual compliment" [141].) The "varnish" Mrs. General is said to dispense is simply euphemism and circumlocution—by another name (503).[24] "Papa is a preferable mode of address," she lessons Little Dorrit:

> "Father is rather vulgar, my dear. The word Papa, besides, gives a pretty form to the lips. Papa, potatoes, poultry, prunes, and prism are all very good words for the lips: especially prunes and prism." (529)

Language is reduced to sound, like elevator music; affect is drained from intercourse. Here is the apogee of what blaspheming Thomas Paterson called "lip purity" (*Trial of Thomas Paterson* 80); here is proof of Hardy's aphorism, "The hall-mark of high civilization" is a "complete divorce between thinking and saying" (*Ethelberta* 149). Mrs. General's advice even embeds another slippage: the word missing from the euphonious list, of course, is not "prism" but "prison." Nevertheless, like his son, Dorrit is irremediably "of the prison prisonous" (105). Resplendent at the banquet that marks his ascent in society, he breaks down into rote repetition of the welcoming speech he once delivered to incoming prisoners: "The space is—ha—limited—limited . . . but you will find it apparently grow larger after a time. . . . This is the Snuggery. Hum. Supported by a small subscription of the—ha—Collegiate body . . ." (708).

As William Dorrit suggests, Victorian euphemism found support in abstraction and inflated language. The one, wrote de Tocqueville, "is like a box with a false bottom; you may put in what ideas you please, and take them out again without being observed" (Rawson 9); the other, as Orwell notes in "Politics and the English Language," "is itself a kind of euphemism" (*Essays* 4: 136). Victorian discourse was suffering a "terrible dilut[ion]," wrote Henry Alford, dean of Canterbury, in a *Plea for The Queen's English* (1863), by "Brummagen sparkle" and "French-paste" (251, 269).[25] "A man going home" is set down by newspaper writers as "an individual *proceeding* to his *residence*" (248); "Good lodgings" are advertised as *"eligible apartments"* (248); and "a man does not now lose his mother: he *"sustains* (this I saw in a country paper) *bereavement of his maternal relative"* (251). Euphemism, abstraction, and inflation muffled all healthy expression. His critics might think it "ludicrous and absurd that a dignitary of the Church of England should meddle with such small matters," Alford responded to the "controversy" his *Plea* excited (xiii); "But the language of a people is no trifle" (5–6). The whole "catalogue" of verbal "swindles and perversions" that Orwell saw choking independent thought, "like tea-leave blocking a sink" (*Essays* 4: 133, 135), was put in place by the Victorians.

The *Plea* went into its seventh edition in the 1880s when writers like "Ouida" took the public fancy. The inflated opening of her *Moths* (1880) would have set the dean's teeth on edge: "Lady Dolly . . . had everything that can constitute the joys of a woman of her epoch," including a marvelous gown "sublimised and apotheosised by niello buttons, old lace, and genius" (Ouida 1). The 1880s were the great age of "Talk and Talkers" (1882 title); and "[n]atural talk, like ploughing, should turn up a large surface of life rather than dig mines into geological strata" (*Talk and Talkers,* qtd. in St. George 63), since (advised another manual) through talk we "maintain class" and "make the time pass agreeably" (qtd. 47, 54). In the 1880s, *Punch* cartoonist George Du Maurier made an art of social slips of the tongue, verbal pitfalls and pratfalls, in popular series with titles like "Things One Would Rather Have Left Unsaid"; Jerome K. Jerome's *Three Men and a Boat* of 1889 achieved nearly instant status as comic classic in part for its clever play on that sort of unmentionable language that "[might] unnerve any man" (137).[26] "Things, Words, and Sayings, to be Avoided in Conversation" were a standard part of conduct books:[27] " 'Shut your mouth,' " summed up "Censor's" best-selling advice of 1884, *Don't, Or, Directions for Avoiding Improprieties of Conduct and Common Errors of Speech* (15). In the 1880s, hardly anyone called a spade a spade; "Generally, people now call [it] an agricultural implement" (W. D. Howells, qtd. in Perrin 11), if not (as Addison joked in 1712) "a well-known oblong instrument of manual industry" (qtd. in Alford 278). Publishers' advertisements that once had read—"*The Pious Country Parishioner* . . . 10d. An allowance will be made to those who give them away," now in truth read—"*The Pious Country Parishioner* . . . A reduction will be made to purchasers for gratuitous distribution" (S. Butler, *Way of All Flesh* 50). The 1880s were the destined noontide of the ubiquitous euphemism.

Euphemism, raised to the status of editorial principle, canonized the "one saint," wrote Chapman Cohen, Foote's assistant and successor, "at whose shrine th[is] Protestant country pays unceasing devotion. . . . Saint Bowdler" (qtd. in Herrick, *Vision* 47). Bowdler's *Family Shakespeare* of 1818 set the century's model for a flood of books expurgated not in response to government or church censorship but in a voluntary access of public-spirited prudery;[28] under Victoria, "bowdlerization" became a euphemism (like earlier "purgation," "pruning," and "chastening") for what the eighteenth century frankly called the "castration," "gelding," and "emascula-

tion" of books. The 1880s were expurgation's golden years. Gilbert and
Sullivan's Psyche advised audiences of *Princess Ida* to "get the[ir classics]
Bowdlerized!" in 1884 (qtd. in Perrin vi); Whitman's denunciation dates
from 1888: "Damn the expurgated books! . . . The dirtiest book in all the
world is an expurgated book" (qtd. vi); Charles Lamb's letters were bowdlerized (for the third time, most thoroughly) in 1888.[29] The period wanted
"retellings" in the euphemistic style of Lamb's own *Tales from Shakespeare;*
one publisher scored a hit in 1886 with a "revised and cleanly edition" of
Gulliver's Travels (Perrin 226, 229). There were seven bowdlerizations of
Shakespeare available before midcentury, but over forty in the 1880s (Perrin
5): Perrin takes the Rolfe and Riverside college editions, 1884 and 1883, as
benchmarks of "lying" discretion, which simply said nothing about their
"unusually savage cuts" (Perrin 112–13).

For the Victorians "mistranslated and expurgated so that Great Books
might live" (Thomas, *Long Time* 247); "No man ever did better service to
Shakespeare" than Dr. Bowdler, averred even Algernon Swinburne (Perrin
85). Nineteenth-century expurgators included Leigh Hunt, Lamb, and
Southey (who cleaned up Chaucer in Middle English in 1831); Lewis Carroll, who "worked intermittently all through the 1880s" on his *Girl's Own
Shakespeare* (Perrin 105n); W. M. Rossetti; Palgrave of the *Golden Treasury;*
Oxford's Professor Quiller-Couch and academician George Saintsbury; Edmund Gosse, who bowdlerized Bowdler's admirer Swinburne's letters;
Wordsworth's nephew; and Fielding's great granddaughter.[30] These literati
too are the ancestors of Orwell's prudish political drones of *1984,* bowdleriz-
ing history for Big Brother, and operating the novel-writing machines.[31]
Victorian canonization of literary saints, and the creation of literature as
standard of value, logically necessitated literature's mutilation. Bowdlerization allowed for mass access, proving true the adage, "the larger the audience, . . . the blander the fare" (Perrin 21).

Accommodating the euphemistic imperative enabled the first great decade of music hall in the 1880s.[32] First words like "cancan" were banned
(since, as a manager said, "in England . . . names excite more horror than
things" [Cheshire 96]), then "NOTICES TO ARTISTES" codified general
principles ("Coarse jests and rough language to be particularly avoided"
[Weightman 93]), until audiences "sigh[ed] in vain," as Max Beerbohm
put it, for the "joyous vulgarity" of yore (*More* 121; "At the Tivoli," qtd.
in Cheshire 89). But vulgarity struck back through euphemistic subversion,
flowering into a private language of "nudge, nudge," "wink, wink": artists
like R. G. Knowles sang "Some Things are Better Left Unsaid" in "a Mysterious Way" (Mander and Mitchenson 90); double entendre (a phrase that
means nothing to Frenchmen) made a star of Little Tich. Repetition and

sing-alongs, as Arnold Bennett observed in his *Journal* (Cheshire 81) fostered a climate of shared knowingness that makes common cause with the construction of rhyming slang. It is the Cockney's knowledge—not disavowal—of four-letter words that supplies meaning and missing rhymes: the "trap" that makes "pony and trap" synonymous with "crap"; the "titties" that make sense of "Bristol [cities]"; the "grunt" that completes "groan and grunt" ("cunt"); the "Pass" that makes "Khyber Pass" not a mere outpost of empire but an eclectic stand-in for "arse."[33] Geographical circumlocution was a favorite trope of the music hall bawdy bashful: "Fiji Fanny, in her little cranny, / Underneath the frangipani tree"; the Girl who might let you "Peek in My Gazebo." "Turns" like these won "UNMISTAKABLE SNIGGERS."[34]

Cockney Marie Lloyd proved most adept at manipulating Respectability's verbal tic. She rose to the top of the bill in the 1880s while still in her teens. "I asked Johnny Jones, so I know now," she sang, got up in a schoolgirl's frock; suggestiveness sauced up songs like "Keep Off The Grass" and "Then You Wink The Other Eye." Her naughtiness is mythic. Did she really once struggle to open her umbrella, then turn to the audience to say, "Oh, what a relief, I haven't had it up for ages?" (Weightman 100). To be the Cockney epitome of the form that (as Raymond Williams has it) gave the people their most authentic voice was to become the Lady of Euphemistic Misrule. Lloyd made "nice" circumlocution "naughty," but "innuendo" on stage proved a slippery concept in law.[35] "It was not what she said, but the way in which she said it" (in reference to "Meet Me by Moonlight Alone"), testimony in a case of 1896, was not grounds for conviction (Pennybacker 131). As G. W. Foote wrote in 1888, "[T]here is a bitter truth in Thackeray's remark that our mouths may be cleaner than our ancestors['], without our lives being purer" (*Freethinker,* 13 May: 154). In the 1880s, euphemism turned out the mother of "blue" invention, babbling volumes about the unmentionable: sex was not its true opposite term.

Music hall's visual equivalent to Lloyd's act offers a further analogy, however. Sheathed in flesh-colored silk, women holding the *poses plastiques* of "classical" artworks looked from a distance entirely nude.[36] The ruse allowed the halls to break, without seeming to break, society's ban on nakedness. And as with bodies, so with language. Verbal fig leaves were de rigueur. Just as Victorians hastened to veil (in fabric, paper, rhetoric) everything from ladies' busts to the "facts of life," so they moved swiftly to swaddle up "naked language": a strange new term entered the vocabulary of disapprobation. One is reminded of Paterson's threat to turn the court into an "arena" for the "naked exposure" of "bible beauties" (*Trial of Thomas Paterson* 70); or one thinks of the president of Yale making protest against writers (like Whitman) who "commit, in writing, an offense like . . . walking naked through the streets" (Perrin 162). The 1857 Obscenity Act spoke not of the "publication" of "Obscene Books, Pictures, Prints," but of their "exposure," as one might speak of the exposure of the unclothed body (precisely what lawyer Henry Folkard does in discussing the act [606]).

The image of "naked language" has a long history. Truth is represented in the emblem tradition as a naked woman looking at the sun; Lacan aptly condenses proverbial sayings into the summary statement, "The truth shows best being naked" (qtd. in Payne, *Reading Theory* 65). The veiling of linguistic nakedness is a motif of the 1880s. G. W. Foote could hardly get a fair answer to his courtroom question of 1883: "If Freethinkers must only strike with kid gloves, why are Christians allowed to use not only the naked fist, but knuckle-dusters, bludgeons, and daggers?" (*Prisoner* 12–13); nor could Fitzjames Stephen expect lawyers to prefer over Lord Coleridge's euphemistic redefinition of blasphemy his own statement of the law in its "natural naked deformity" ("Blasphemy," 300n, 315). The very use of the word "naked" raised opposition in a context that institutionalized euphemism: Victorian law's standard term for "adultery" was "criminal conversation."[37] The vengeful subscribers who got novels banned from Mudie's, wrote a correspondent to the *Pall Mall Gazette* in 1884, were at one with "those . . . imbecile people who . . . blush to mention the 'naked' eye, and . . . adorn the legs of their pianos with drawers" (13 December: 2).[38] Society did not want to know "the whole, or naked body of the facts," pronounced Meredith's unpopular offering of the same year, *Diana of the Crossways* (3). "Bluntness in speech has its votaries, like the nude in art," concluded J. P. Mahaffy, erstwhile tutor to Oscar Wilde, in his 1887 *Principles of the Art of Conversation.* But, "[F]or my part, the less we have of it the better" (30–31); "[t]here is a drapery of speech, as well as a drapery of the body" (28–29).

Yet "[t]he banished of Eden had to put on metaphors, and the common use of them has helped largely to civilize us" (Meredith, *Diana* 231). "The Name" might be "custom-woven, wonder-hiding," Carlyle instructs, but it is also "the earliest Garment you wrap round" you, and "send[s] inwards" its "mystic influences" (*Sartor Resartus* 196, 67). The image of language as the veil that hides nakedness is not merely sexual in valence, and always had a double signification: enabling, avoiding. Having the hope of heaven, preached the apostle Paul, Christians may "use great plainness of speech: And not as Moses, which put a veil over his face," after he came down from Mount Sinai with the Tablets, his features bright with the reflected light of God (2 Corinthians 3.12–13). The veil as Paul sees it keeps understanding at bay; Moses donned it to allow knowledge to approach. Modern linguistics has taken up the image (Allan and Burridge 210). No more than the equivocal evidence of the euphemistic music hall does the concept of "naked language" prove the all-dominance of the sexual matrix. Rather, as Foucault suggests, it was *in words* that sexuality was re-created in the nineteenth century. There was more to the nation's life than the unmentionable, and euphemism governed it all. Even in jail it held sway: Foote's favorite instance was the Holloway chaplain's reference to his cell as his "little room" (*Prisoner* 175).

The 1880s began systematically to study the centrality of human language to mind and society. Building on his cousin Darwin's 1877 "Biographical Sketch of an Infant," Francis Galton began the lines of inquiry that gave birth to psycholinguistics in 1883, the year the disreputable *Freethinker* went to trial;[39] the new journal *Mind* showcased Jesuit father Thomas Harper's elegant demonstration that we need language even to arrive at the idea that "language is the result of a voluntary compact" in the same year (July 1883: 379–80); "No being can be intelligent without language," Max Müller reiterated (*Science of Thought* 2). And language in the 1880s, like Bagehot's English Constitution, was evidently revealed as a system of "checks" and "balances." Then, as now, they worked to preserve what linguists call "face," or community acceptability (Allan and Burridge 5): euphemisms were and are "society's basic lingua *non franca*," writes Hugh Rawson, "embedded so deeply" and so vital to communication "that few of us . . . get through a day without using them" (1). Our capacity for their production is wired into the mind, whose powerful parallel processing enables instant self-censorship.[40] "What I seek in speech is the response of the other," writes Lacan (*Écrits* 86): language always has been and always will be "intersubjective"—or, as speech-act theory puts it, in terms it shares with Holyoake's Rochdale Pioneers, "co-operative."

Given these now-received facts of human language, there might seem no need to seek further reasons for the euphemization of English, particularly in the key decade of the 1880s. But there was another and ancient grand motive at work. The euphemistic Victorians were indeed Arnoldian "Hebrews" in one crucial respect: the religion that in law in 1883 became merely the occasion for blasphemy prosecution gave intelligible shape to a terror so sunken in the subconscious as to be indistinguishable from the primary fears and assumptions of humans as speaking creatures. This terror was the sacred terror of language.

Belief in the divine origin of language survived Locke's rationalist revelations in the *Essay Concerning Human Understanding* (1690) of "Spirit" as "Breath," and "Angel" as "Messenger" (Aarsleff 31); it weathered the etymological reductions ("Heaven," for example, "some place, any place heav-en or heav-ed" [qtd. 63]) of Horne Tooke's radical materialist *Diversions of Purley* (1786/1805).[41] It outlived Herbert Spencer's assumption that language made "progress" (like everything else) in his enormously influential *First Principles* (1862), and Darwin's marshaling of "curiously parallel" "proofs" that "[t]he formation of different languages and of distinct species" were both "gradual process[es]" (*Descent* 90).[42] Moralist Dean Richard Chevenix Trench was the "emblematic figure" of mid-Victorian philology (Dowling 60); and it was for deciding that linguistic change, no less than geological, required many more thousands of years than the Bible decreed had passed since the Earth was created that Rowland Williams, one of the authors of *Essays and Reviews* (1860), stood trial for heresy in the Court of Arches.[43]

Even the "scientific" pronouncements of Max Müller, Oxford's first professor of comparative philology, inadvertently fostered the divine spark in language: "language, articulate and definite language, . . . w[ill] still remain . . . our Rubicon which no brute will dare to cross" (*Science of Language* 1: xxxiv–xxxv). The identification of words and the Word haunts his theory of language's few hundred *"roots"* or *"phonetic types"* or "simply ultimate facts" (1: 527, 528). It was a German Romantic inheritance to believe language neither a reflex response nor a divine revelation passively received but an inner, creative necessity of man's elevated nature.[44] But this new and "radically historical" "metaphysics of the *logos*" (Dowling 11, 14) was first mediated for English readers by S. T. Coleridge's theological sense of words as "moral acts" (qtd. 40), and was stripped of materialist implications by expatriate German Müller. *Roots,* he declared in his famous lectures of 1861–62, "exist, as Plato would say, by nature; though with Plato we should add that, when we say by nature, we mean by the hand of God" (qtd. in Riede 9).[45] "The thread that connect[ed] all my labors," he reaffirmed in his 1901 *Autobiography,* was "the thread that connects the origin of thought and languages with the origin of mythology and religion" (qtd. in Burrow, "Uses" 199); myth was a "disease" of language.[46] The French Societé de Linguistique forbade discussion of the origins of language in 1866; even philologist-clergymen like Frederic Farrar believed "Language a Human Discovery" (chapter title, *Chapters on Language*).[47] But Müller's prominence (Saussure called him "glamorous") sustained general belief in language's divine origin until well into the 1880s in England.

"I am he that doth speak: behold, it is I" (Isaiah 52.5–6): if, in Foucault's words, Freud (and other late Victorians) "brought the knowledge of man closer to its philological and linguistic model" than it had come for near on two thousand years (*Order* 361), a development with profound consequences for twentieth-century thought, still the Gospel writers had first imagined the Son of Man as God's uttered Word, and the Victorians, who lost their faith in God, paradoxically clung to their faith in language; the verse whose authenticity Hone was attacked for questioning in 1821 was dear to the English heart, and missed in the Revised Version of the New Testament published in 1881: "For there are Three that bear record in heaven, the Father, the Word, and the Holy Ghost: and these three are one" (1 John 5.7). "I fear indeed that we shall never rid ourselves of God," Nietzsche confirmed, "since we still believe in grammar" (qtd. in Foucault, *Order* 298): St. Augustine had done his work well when he made a connection in the *Confessions* between the child's acquisition of language and the acceptance of God as Lord; Newman knowingly titled his masterwork the *Grammar of Assent*. The identification of words and the Word speaks even in the titles of popular mid-nineteenth-century works: *A Catechism of English Composition, A Catechism of Elocution*.

Even heretical texts of the 1880s bear the trace of the original fallacy: "How divine is utterance!" exclaims George Meredith's heroine; "As we to the brutes, poets are to us" (*Diana* 154). (Her creator is more careful of his terms: his novel provides grounding and antecedent for every metaphor used. Its idiom is a hermetically sealed system that admits no transcendent Word.) The new journal *Mind* granted Father Harper, S.J., a highly visible platform from which to propound a theory of "the nature and characteristics of the human word" by analogy with the Angelic and the Divine (July 1883: 375), concluding with the inverted proposition that our innate capacity for universal and abstract language demonstrates the existence of God.[48] The essay earned its place, noted the editor, as a sample of "a mode of thought which, having survived all through the modern period, is now asserting itself as an active factor on the philological field" (372n). Derrida and Lacan bear persisting witness to the acuteness of his thought.

The conservative limitations of late Victorian theories worked not only to bolster insistence on the divinity in language but to lay awful stress on the power and "intrinsick meaning" of individual words, as (ironically) the materialist Horne Tooke had put it (qtd. in Aarsleff 250). Scholarly work on the sentence, that is, on the contextual inflection and grammatical creation of meaning, remained a novelty through the 1880s.[49] "[F]or many a young man," wrote Trench, "his first discovery of the fact that words are living powers, has been like the dropping of scales from his eyes" (vi–vii); the purpose of etymology was to recover a living sense of religious experience. As each word was a "fossil" sermon, so it was also a locus of magic, terror, and potential criminality. The sense of "occult learning" attached to Middle English *grammarye*, grammar, lingered on in the word's Scottish form, "glamor" (Ong 93; *OED*). Perhaps Rousseau was right, in his *Essay on the Origin of Languages,* to locate the beginnings of words in "primitive panic."[50]

"Be not frightened of denunciations," Holyoake exhorted working men (*Logic of Facts* 49).[51] But "[t]he majority" were "cheated by phrases," wrote G. W. Foote—by words like "blasphemy" itself, which "carries a host of undefined and evil meanings":

> Words, said Hobbes, are the counters of wise men, and the money of fools. . . . Shibboleths become realities, vague but living, and powerful to attract and repel. An auspicious word lures men like an angel of light; a sinister word scares them like a fiend of darkness. Give a dog a bad name and hang him, says the proverb. The name is enough. It is conclusive. It obviates inquiry, dispenses with evidence, and operates with all the force and authority of an intuition. (*Blasphemy No Crime* 11)

In euphemistic, "Hebrew" England, the name—and the fear it provoked— perhaps was enough. Here was the crux. The Old Testament term "blasphemy" does not only mean reviling God. In the key verses of Leviticus, the sinner who "blasphemed the name of the Lord, and cursed" (24.10) may have done no more than pronounce the sacred personal name of God, "Jehovah," expressed in Hebrew script as the tetragrammaton, *YHVH.* Blasphemy lay in the mere speaking of God's name. So Jehovah becomes "the Lord" and "the Word"; *YHVH* was read aloud in the course of time only by priests during temple services, pronounced *Adonai;* and *Adonai* in time came to be muffled outside the synagogue by the devout euphemism, *Adoshem,* from the Hebrew *Ha Shem,* "The Name" (Allan and Burridge 37). Through euphemism we avoid the New Testament crime of crimes, blasphemy against the Holy Ghost, which, says Mark, shall not "be forgiven unto the sons of men"(3.28–30). "Why asketh thou thus after my name," the angel says to Manoah, Judges 13.18, "seeing it is secret?" In the Holy Communion service of the Anglican Church, the minister recites, "the Lord will not hold him guiltless, that taketh his Name in vain" (*Book of Common Prayer,* n. pag.).

So euphemistic oaths proliferated from the Middle Ages through the close of the nineteenth century, becoming each in their turn "ritualized and conventional behavior" (Allan and Burridge 39) whose origin in terror was long and safely forgotten: *by gad!* (Major Bagstock's stock-in-trade, in *Dombey and Son*); *Crikey! Cripes!* and *Crumbs!* (all avoidances of "Christ!"); *(Good) gracious! Gosh!* and *Golly!*; *by Jove!*; Cockney *Cor!* and *Gorblimey!* (barely recognizable as "God blind me!"); Gilbert and Sullivan's "Big, big D——." All, like the magician's *abracadabra* or the legislator's word rest on the premise, a survival of ancient oral culture and a commonplace of

Romantic poetics, that to *speak* is also to *act*. The Hebrew *dabar* means both "word" and "event" (Ong 32); "God the Father 'speaks' his Son" (75). The logocentrism of the Judaeo-Christian tradition ("distinctive," as Lawton puts it, in its insistence "on blasphemy as an act of language" [*Blasphemy* 5–6]), in its Protestant-Anglican manifestation, helped to make England unique among modern cultures in its susceptibility to the fear of words, and inclined to the worship of language itself.

Thus from the originating wellspring of the Word descends the terror of words that brought three men and a penny paper into the dock, three times, in 1883. Fear to utter the Name, and you will hesitate to name any names. The tendency was reinforced by the classical inheritance that Victorians treasured. "Distrust of language" made part of the etymological development of the late Greek words "blasphemy" and "blaspheme," as used in the Septuagint (Lawton 14). The Hebrew terms for which the verb stood in *(qillel, nakob)* mean on the one hand "pierce, repudiate, insult, abuse" but also to "specify, enunciate, pronounce distinctly" (Levy, *Treason* 22; Lawton 14). Simple Greek "blame" is second cousin to "blasphemy."[52] In his 1881 *Libel and Slander,* W. Blake Odgers twists etymology to reinforce the point (and to align it with literary sensibility): "The word necessarily involves an intent to do harm or to wound the feelings of others," for it is derived from verbs meaning "hurt" and "speak," and "denotes, therefore, 'speaking so as to hurt' " (455). Small matter that the Greek term more precisely means "to speak profanely," or "to speak evil": this is the "hate crime" of the 1990s, the *dysphemism* of modern linguistics, by another— Victorian—name, blasphemy.[53]

Euphemism and blasphemy thus are "obverse sides of the same coin" (Allan and Burridge 7). The "inward anxieties, conflicts, fears, and shames" (Rawson 1) that forbid blasphemy dictate the "outward and visible signs" that are euphemisms. The words are exact etymological opposites. Euphemism is derived from *euphemismos,* the "use of an auspicious word for an inauspicious one," and *euphemos,* "fair of speech" (Burchfield 13);[54] its Latin opposite was also *obscenus,* ancestor of "obscene": "adverse, inauspicious, ill-omened." The classic example of the defensive euphemism prescribed by religious terror is the name *Eumenides,* or "Kindly Ones," for the Furies (Neaman and Silver 1–2). To utter their tabooed name was to invoke their terrible presence. Or, as in the fairy tale of Rumpelstiltskin, retold by philologist Grimm and his brother and explained by Frazer in the *Golden Bough,* "he who possessed the true name, possessed the very being of god or man, and could force even a deity to obey him as a slave obeys his master" (389). The private name was tabooed; designed to "soothe and propitiate" (417), the "public name is a euphemism for it" (Allan and Burridge 33).

The 1880s, the destined noontide of the ubiquitous euphemism, most logically marked the moment when its unmentionable other and true opposite might be summoned from the linguistic underworld to do battle in the High Court of Queen's Bench: *the culture that lives by euphemism must produce blasphemy.* Moreover, a law book technicality suggests the importance of the "obsolete" crime of blasphemy for a people suspicious of, dazzled by, words. It has to do with the relationship between "blasphemous libel," as the crime was also designated in legislation from the eighteenth century, and the laws upon slander and libel—that is, oral defamation of a person, a misdemeanor, and written defamation, a more serious crime.

The relationship is not a straightforward one: no taxonomy or system of information ordering is ever merely neutral. The state need never act as plaintiff in cases of personal slander and libel as it can in cases of blasphemy and must in cases of sedition (Odgers, *Libel and Slander* 7). Nevertheless, English law for a very long time recognized a great deal in common between these differing crimes of language. Most particularly, until nearly the turn of the nineteenth century, all libelous words—the seditious and the blasphemous, as well as those directed against the person—were held, in the terms of a 1703 ruling, to "import a crime of themselves" (qtd. in Nokes 68). Even a lunatic made himself "liable to an action for libel or slander" unless his insanity was "well known to all who hear or read his words" (Odgers, *Libel and Slander* 6). Utterances enjoyed a kind of divine autonomy curiously like that which modern literary theory ascribes to texts.

Fox's Libel Act of 1792 introduced two crucial new concepts, however: "malice" and "intention."[55] They were aimed against the concept *in mitiori sensu* (no metaphysical quirk but an outdated feint to discourage actions for slander), which dictated that words be given "an innocent meaning," the "best" sense possible, if "any amount of legal ingenuity" could find it out (Odgers, *Libel and Slander* 106).[56] In cases of personal slander, "malice" and "intention" needed to be proved; in cases of libel, the "mode and extent" of publication (the wider the more offensive) could be taken as evidence (*Libel and Slander* 4, 323): literacy raised all the cultural stakes. But the case was different with blasphemy. If Hale's dictum held, and Christianity was "parcel" of the laws of the land; "[i]f," as Fitzjames Stephen put it, "the law regards the subversion of Christianity as mischievous," then "an intention to subvert it must"—of necessity—"be mischievous" ("Blasphemy," 313). No need, in such case, to distinguish among the five classes of libelous Words: the "obviously defamatory," the "*prima facie* defamatory," the "neutral" ("i.e., words which are meaningless," like slang or foreign terms, "till some explanation is given"), the "*prima facie* innocent, but capable of a defamatory meaning" (like Holyoake's "thing"), and the

"obviously innocent" (Odgers, *Libel and Slander* 114): only the last category
stood a chance of being judged innocent in a blasphemy court.

In cases of blasphemy, "intention" was irrelevant, and "malice" could
be automatically assumed.[57] In no blasphemy trials was "extrinsic" evidence
of malice—threats, for example—ever offered. No defendant was ever able
to plead as justification for "strong words" (Odgers, *Libel and Slander* 332),
his "honest indignation" (323), or "righteous zeal" (332). Mistakenly to
invoke concepts relevant to slander and libel was to prove oneself amateur. "The law considered," snapped Chief Justice Ellenborough when
Hone ventured in 1817 to say he had "no intention" of "ridicul[ing]" and
"writ[ing] down" the Litany, "that every man intends that which he has
done" (*Three Trials* 133). Besides, "whatever be the *intention* of a publication
attended with a mischievous *tendency,* it is no less a libel" (*Three Trials* 76,
my emphasis), an ominous intrusion of the impersonal term that forty years
later plugged the definitional hole at the heart of the 1857 Obscenity Act.
Trust the text, not the author, wherein intentionality resides, Ellenborough
told Hone's jury: they must decide the issue exclusively "from a review of
the paper before them, and not from the declarations of the Defendant"
(86). (Luckily for Hone the jury ignored the direction.) Hetherington's
refusal to admit he was what the indictment declared him to be, *"a wicked,
impious, and ill-disposed person"* was "idle" in law (*Trial of Henry Hetherington* 3). Carlile shop-man William Turnbridge's dogged attempt to reveal
"malice" as legal euphemism and restore it as meaningful language likewise
fell to the ground.[58] Blasphemy alone remained, of all the language crimes
upon the books, as a survival of older and more fearful philosophies of
language and criminality. Legal technicality assured its role as single conduit
of nineteenth-century England's persisting linguistic anxiety.

Furthermore, in Victorian legal theory, any man had the right to comment on his neighbor—the 1843 Libel Act introduced the sensational idea
that a libel was not a libel if it was true—"provided he does so fairly and
with an honest purpose" (Odgers, *Libel and Slander* 184). These are not
linguistic criteria. The law of slander, most specifically, was and is concerned not with the "manner" of the offense but with "evidence of special
damage" and loss of reputation (2): the "matter" of the crime. To "defame"
is not the same as to "revile." "Merely idle abuse or expressions of contempt
injure no man's credit" (8). Measuredly to call a man a thief or a traitor
is actionable, whereas to hurl at him "a torrent of general vulgar abuse" is
not, though "reducing" it "into writing and publish[ing it] to the world"
may make it so (3). The exact reverse was written into the law of blasphemy
by Lord Coleridge's 1883 ruling on the "decencies" of language, indeed, by
the whole drift of the nineteenth-century history of the crime. "The most

refined and elegant diction" was as liable to be found offensive or innocuous in trials for slander and libel as bad grammar, spelling mistakes, "cant," slang, and general vulgarity (108), all those coarsenesses that were of the essence to the redefined crime of the *Freethinker.*

Blasphemy, then, stood alone on the law books. And a last technicality secured its meaningful isolation. For, unlike actions for obscenity, which had (and have) to begin life in government offices (today, in the director of public prosecution's), blasphemy prosecutions could (and can) be initiated by private citizens. Bulldog Henry Varley, moving force behind the *Freethinker* prosecution, is thus the lineal ancestor of Mrs. Mary Whitehouse, who in 1977 secured the blasphemy conviction of Dennis Lemon, editor of *Gay News,* when government (like Harcourt in 1882) declined to prosecute for obscenity.[59] Legal nicety both made the blurring of boundaries between blasphemy and obscenity inevitable and ensured that the "obsolete" crime of blasphemy, not the new scandal of obscenity, became the legal pressure point or valve through which the decade's anxieties about language could escape.

Only "when we are dealing with religion," wrote Chapman Cohen at the turn of the century, "[does] language, harmless enough in any other connection, become the basis of a criminal prosecution" (*Blasphemy* 19). And what mattered most was the language. The technical shorthand for the offense throughout the nineteenth century was, quite simply, "Words." Its abbreviated and euphemistic effectiveness brings back *Dombey and Son*—"Words have arisen between the housemaid and Mr. Towlinson" (434); or North Country mothers ticking off their offspring for swearing— "language!" ("[V]ulgar," says the *Oxford English Dictionary,* "Short for bad language," dating the term in its first literary usage to 1886.) But it was not a term to raise a smile on the face of a Victorian Freethinker, profane joker or not.

Since the days when Southwell's outrageous *Oracle* went up in smoke, Secularist periodicals from Holyoake's *Movement* (1843–45) and circumspect *Reasoner* (1865–72) to Bradlaugh's *National Reformer* (1860–93) and Besant's upmarket *Our Corner* (1883–88) had played by the rules of linguistic decency. "Plainspeaking," however, was *Freethinker* policy—"not adopted," Foote declared, when bare-faced cheek and naked statement had provoked the expected indictment "in a moment of levity" but "from the first deliberately pursued," in "full conscious[ness] of its dangers" (*Prisoner* 22). "Fearless truth expressed in the plain language of common sense," proclaimed the advertising slogans: "One of the liveliest and most outspoken journals in the world." "Thinking the time had come for a thorough clearing of the ground from the wreck and lumber of the past," wrote Foote's

subeditor J. M. Wheeler, "he started the *Freethinker* with the avowed purpose of . . . destroying hypocrisy by openly speaking out what so many
think secretly" (*Freethinker,* 1 July 1883: 201–02). Contributors used the
coinage "outspeak" as an active verb.[60] The *Freethinker* offended because "it
speaks out plainly what there is a tacit conspiracy to conceal" (*Freethinker,* 6
August 1882: 242).

It was entirely logical that the crimes of blasphemy and obscenity should
be confused in Victorian culture. The slippages that charted the case of the
Freethinker speak to us not of obsession with the body but of the fear of
naming names and the terror of the "unspeakable." Call it blasphemy, call
it obscenity, in a real sense they are a single crime and deserve an Orwellian
name: *word crime.* Historical accident and ancient design converged to
make blasphemy the only means by which widespread fear and linguistic
anxiety could be inscribed in law; here was where the words in which we
create ourselves could be debated, prosecuted, vilified, silenced. The *Freethinker* was not prosecuted for rending the veil of the temple that tore
asunder at the moment that Christ surrendered his human life. It was punished because it ripped to shreds the Victorian veil of language.

The golden thread in that veil was silence. It is as much a signifying
part of language as the zero in mathematics. The word "euphemism" further
evolved in Greek to mean "to keep silent." "If any man among you seem
to be religious," warns James 1.26, "and bridleth not his tongue, . . . this
man's religion is vain." The condensed history in the word offers a kind
of logic to the Victorian institution of silence as the ultimate penitential
euphemism. We must next consider how blasphemous words came to be
"taken as read" in courtrooms, newspapers, and transcripts, across the
course of the nineteenth century, consigned to the oubliette of unspeakability.

3. THE SYSTEMATIZATION OF SILENCE

"[M]y aim," Foucault writes, "is to examine the case of a society which has
been loudly castigating itself for its hypocrisy for more than a century,
which *speaks verbosely of its own silence*" (*History of Sexuality* 8, my emphasis). It is a grand and seductive theory. But it also works best in its French
context. *The History of Sexuality*'s reliance on the Catholic confessional limits its usefulness for English culture. For making charges against that institution, the Protestant Electoral Union was itself charged with obscenity, while
its *Confessional Unmasked, showing . . . the Questions put to Females in Confession* (1867), a compilation from the works of theologians, was recirculated
as pornography.[61] In Wilde's "native land of the hypocrite" (*Picture* 168),

W. T. Stead went to jail in 1885 for breaking the "Conspiracy of Silence" that cloaked a whole slave trade in virgins in the *Pall Mall Gazette*.[62] One wonders if in Victorian eyes the first sin of the Serpent was that he spoke at all.

Law's aim was the same as Dr. Bowdler's: no criminally suggestive "WORD OR EXPRESSION" ought ever to be "SPOKEN, OR WRITTEN, OR PRINTED; AND IF PRINTED, IT OUGHT TO BE ERASED" (17). When the Protestant Electoral Union put out a "chastened" version of the *Confessional Unmasked*, it was promptly again prosecuted, and during proceedings "was not read aloud, but taken as read, and passages in it only, were referred to" (Folkard 611).[63] "I cannot lay down the law as to what is or is not indecent," a judge paradoxically remarked in a case of male-male indecent assault in 1875, "beyond saying that it is what all right-minded men would say was indecent" (Krueger 122).[64] Newspapers similarly established by omission the unspeakability of the Boulton and Park transvestitism and buggery case of 1870–71. The suppression of obscenity offers itself, again, as euphemism's end and opposite term: courtroom procedure and restraints on reporting seem to back its case for priority.

Again, however, appearances are deceptive. The tales of silencing reconstructed by Krueger and others recapitulate a prior story of silencing that was produced first and foremost in the blasphemy courtroom. At first the objective was equally as political as the defendants' decision to speak for themselves. But it devolved into a cultural drive. We would be foolish to take from psychoanalysis and linguistic theory only what it is most obviously tempting to take in the context of blasphemy: a reinforced sense of the crime as a disruptive, orgiastic ejaculation of the "censored" unconscious aggressively asserting itself and the "truth" we habitually repress ("All great truths," as the Shavian aphorism has it, "begin as blasphemies" [*Annajanska*, in *Works* 15: 299]). The dry account of judicial and prison procedures that aimed to stifle word crime, eventually *all* crime, offers rich pickings for the psychology of language.

Any man "may entertain his opinions," Mr. Justice Bayley had declared, passing sentence on Carlile in 1819, "and so long as he confines them to his own breast, he stands harmless and unassailed" (*British Press*, 17 November: 3). "If there were persons so unfortunate as to disbelieve the Scriptures," Attorney-General Denman decided, in 1841, "the law did not interfere with them so long as they kept their opinions to themselves" (*Trial of Henry Hetherington* 21). Unbelief belonged in the closet as much as homosexuality or Catholic "obscenity." The "laws of decency" produced a flat fiat: "don't ask, don't tell."

However, the judges' dicta exposed another problem inherent in the classification of blasphemy with personal slander and libel. There is a point in a man's keeping his "uncharitable thoughts" of his neighbor "to his own breast" (Odgers, *Libel and Slander* 150), though truth would sometimes bid him utter them, and (since 1843) absolve him of crime for so doing. But the man who denies the "truth" of religion in a land where law is founded on that truth has no such recourse, even if God cannot be injured by his words. What use, then, is a "private opinion" on religion that one keeps "to oneself"? Is it even an "opinion" at all?

It was not only the interfering classification of blasphemy with slander and libel that raised the specter of legal paradox. The nineteenth century's drift towards freedom of speech, publication, and religious opinion stirred a deepwater countercurrent; as Mill envisaged, when government checks on the press declined, a censorship imposed by "public opinion" took its place. Prosecutor Alexander found himself caught in the whirlpool where the two currents met during the trial of the bookseller Adams for selling number 25 of the *Oracle:* How to square the imperative of silence with the new standard of "decency"?

> All religious opinions are tolerated but those who hold them must keep them to themselves, or if they do entertain the absurd notion that reason is contrary to revelation, they must at any rate confine themselves to decent language, and not disgust decent people with such language as appears in this book. (*Cheltenham Free Press*, 20 August 1842: 266)

Research treasures such hopeless attempts at legal legerdemain. Alexander's final flurried recourse to the growing threat of obscenity tantalizes with the possibility that canceling blasphemy as true and heartfelt "treason against God" positively coproduced the Victorian obsession with sex; in this scenario, the new Obscenity Act of 1857 follows the achievement of religious tolerance in the 1840s by not many more years than elapsed between the 1689 Toleration Act and passage of the warning statute "for the more effectual suppressing of Blasphemy and Profaneness" in 1698. Just as, in the history of the language, the great vowel shift dictated that every long vowel should change in value, so every shift in the cultural constitution of the country demanded other compensatory movements. "The relevant question at any stage of human history," as Donald Thomas puts it, "is not 'Does censorship exist?' but rather, 'Under what sort of censorship do we now live?' " (*Long Time* 318).

A "catch-22" was written into the plight of the nineteenth-century blasphemer. Magistrate Overbury, sending Holyoake up for trial in Cheltenham in 1842, declared, "Whether you are of no religion *is of very little consequence to us,* but your attempt to propagate the infamous sentiment that there is no God, is calculated to produce disorder and confusion, and is a breach of the peace" (*History of the Last Trial* 10). The italics are Holyoake's. His prosecutor, Mr. Bubb ("a particularly gross, furious, squab-built, vulgar person" [Holyoake, *Sixty Years* 149]), parroted Denman's precedent-setting dictum with a pompous brevity well calculated to bring out its latent quality of chop logic: "The entertaining of opinions is not opposed to law if people keep them to themselves" (18). Statements like this belong in the perverse world of Franz Kafka's *Trial* or on the wall with the other commandments in George Orwell's *Animal Farm,* progressively made madness by the addition of limiting clauses: "ALL ANIMALS ARE EQUAL, BUT SOME ANIMALS ARE MORE EQUAL THAN OTHERS" ("After that," the narrator comments, "it did not seem strange . . . to learn that the pigs had . . . taken out [a] subscription to *John Bull*" [90].) The Bubbian formula has the same flavor of nightmare nonsense verse.

Between 1817 and the *Freethinker* trials of 1883, the imperative to silence the blasphemer progressively inflected and obsessively etched itself into legal procedure and reportage. There were four stages in the process. The first took the standing paradox of the "private opinion" one step further. Not only was the infidel duty bound to keep his opinion to himself, but the construction of law made it impossible for him in any way to defend himself by defending that opinion in court.[65] So Thomas Davison, Carlile's associate, found to his cost in 1821. In the course of his speech in his own defense he remarked, apropos the Old Testament: "Now it so happens that the Deist considers this collection of ancient tracts to contain sentiments, stories, and representations totally derogatory to the honor of a God, destructive to pure principles of morality, and opposed to the best interests of society." For these remarks Mr. Justice Best fined him forty pounds for contempt of court—literally more than his life was worth. Chief Justice Abbott, upholding the fine and the institutionalized loop of logic by which it was demanded, asked to know of the world at large, "Is a judge to sit and hear a man maintain his right to assert or publish blasphemy?" (qtd. in *Westminster Review,* July 1883: 7). No need to guess the answer. It was impossible for the defendant to question the legality of the proceedings against him, and impossible to defend himself without offending anew.[66]

There are times when the blasphemy courtroom of the nineteenth century begs for madder analogies even than the dystopic parables of Kakfa and Orwell. Sometimes it seems a prototype for the theater of the absurd. The defendant speaking in his own defense might think himself possessed of "all the privileges of counsel," an inalienable last right to a "voice," but the silencing dictates of "decency," stricter and stricter as Victoria's century lengthened, often left him practically tongue-tied. There was a political point, of course: the judges' dicta sought to preserve the character of a "Christian country," expelling outlawry from language; the blasphemer of the nineteenth century was the brother in silence of the eighteenth-century Irish Catholic, subject to such humiliations as having his horse summarily taken from underneath him if he dared to admit to his faith, as loud-mouthed Thomas Paterson reminded his judges (*Trial of Thomas Paterson* 21). Prosecutor Chambers "begged to state" at Paterson's "profanity" trial of 1843 that "as a British barrister, I will not consent to have a Court of Justice made the arena of such gross, blasphemous ribaldry" as would result merely from allowing the defendant to speak (*God v. Paterson* 28); and the *Morning Post* took comfort in the fact that the "infamous tenant" of the Holywell Street shop would not dare to institute proceedings against the constable or commissioners who had illegally conspired to smash his windows and damage his business, for if he did, *"what magistrate, what judge, or what jury would listen to him?"* (90, Paterson's emphasis).[67] There was something else in this besides class contempt of the kind that dispatched radical bookseller Thomas Muir (for example) to fourteen years' transportation for sedition in 1793 while his judge dismissed a petition on his behalf with the pregnant words: "no attention would be paid to such a rabble. What right had they to representation?" (Thomas, *Long Time* 139). Magistrate Jardine interrupted Paterson's tirade against the "triple trinity" and the "God-idea": "If you continue to make use of such language, I shall take upon myself to commit you at once; I am not bound to sit here to hear the vilest blasphemy ever uttered" (*God v. Paterson* 22). Officers of the court scuffled to snatch papers from his hands; at one point, having anticipated the seizure, Paterson "coolly" took out a duplicate and continued. The pretender to martyrdom fared no better in Edinburgh in 1844. Robert Owen's *New Moral World* remarked that

> Things are come to a pretty pass indeed, when a judge can with impunity not only frequently interrupt a prisoner while reading his defense, but on its conclusion speak of it [with sarcastic disapprobation], and make its delivery a reason for heavy . . . punishment. (*Trial of Thomas Paterson* 59)

The pattern repeated itself exactly in the trials of Paterson's Edinburgh associates, Thomas Finlay and Matilda Roalfe.[68] Asked if he "kn[e]w the nature" of the books he saw sold, a witness in the last action replied, "I understood they contained something blasphemous." The follow-up question—"What do you consider blasphemy?"—produced the blanket denial: "I never read any blasphemy in my life" (*Trial of Thomas Paterson* 78). "You no doubt intend to put a gag upon my mouth," said Paterson in 1843, deliberately recalling the terminology of repressive legislation; "but you shall not do so without a struggle on my part to prevent it" (*God v.*

Paterson 27). Publication of his half-suppressed speech, in full, was part of the struggle. Holyoake's Anti-Persecution Union notice, printed on the inside back cover of Paterson's trial transcript, asks friends of free speech to help the cause by "Noting or procuring for the use of the committee authentic or official accounts of blasphemy prosecution cases." Their collection and publication had the same kind of importance in the 1840s as the collection of testimony does today for organizations like Amnesty International. Carlile had shown the way: publishing a record of each volunteer's prosecution kept the cause alive, fanning the flames of publicity and public opinion, just as the prison memoir (like Carlile's own *Jail Journal*) redeemed from silence the solitary thoughts of incarceration. But as the years of Victoria's reign lengthened, illegalities and due process calculatedly combined, as Paterson protested, to "bludgeon [blasphemers] into silence" (*God v. Paterson* 15).

As fast as new freedoms opened, the holes they tore in the legal fabric were plugged, lest the blasphemy courtroom leak words to the outside world. The most important of these sprang from the concept of "privilege": here we reach the second stage of the silencing process. On a "privileged" occasion (a trial, a parliamentary debate), a privileged person (counsel for the defense, for example), "may say or write about another person things which no other person in the kingdom can be allowed to say or write" (Odgers, *Libel and Slander* 185). All reports and transcripts were privileged. (So were the "characters" of servants written by their masters: the term is a pocket summary of the politics of representation.) This had allowed Carlile's courtroom masterstroke: reading aloud, in full, the *Age of Reason* in the courtroom, thus enabling his wife's completely legitimate republication of the blasphemous text in her verbatim report of the *Mock Trial.* That loophole was soon stopped. After proceedings in the case of Mary Anne Carlile in 1819 it was ruled illegal to publish "even a correct account of proceedings in a Court of justice, if such an account contain[ed] matter of a seditious, blasphemous, or indecent nature" (*Libel and Slander* 297). A defendant was further prevented, in 1823, from reading the whole of an indicted book out in court "when his declared purpose was not to explain the passages complained of . . . but to repeat the offence" (Nokes 138). To print passages convicted of blasphemy became itself a blasphemous offense.

Then there was the question of reporting court proceedings, or of repeating in the newspapers words indicted but not yet found criminal. "We are happy," declared the *Evening Star* on 15 October 1819, reporting Carlile's trial (in discreet parenthesis), that "no necessity compels us to assist in disseminating" what "it would sully our pages to repeat," that is, the passages that were the basis for the prosecution's charge (n. pag., cutting in

CC). The *Cheltenham Chronicle* likewise refused to report the words it convicted Holyoake of uttering in 1842. But the unwritten rules of journalism were not yet clear. During the press furor over Paterson's "profane" shop placards in 1843, the *Standard* "publish[ed] at length the blasphemies of which [he] has been convicted" (*God v. Paterson* 79). *John Bull*, howling disapproval, contemptuously rejected the *Standard*'s countercharge of excessive concern for mere "lip purity or piety of the ear" (80) with the rhetorical question, ripe with anxiety about the Victorian enlargement of the "public sphere": "[O]nce *print* blasphemy, and who can pretend to circumscribe its course?" (79–80).

The Tory scandal sheet's own report of the prosecution of "a certain newspaper called the *Freethinker*," in 1883, was a not untypical piece of late-century reporting. Dryly approving the prosecution's speech, which takes up three quarters of the article, *John Bull* dismisses Foote at speed ("The defendant then addressed the jury at considerable length"), and inserts unapologetic blanks where quotation of indicted material might stand (3 March: 143). The edition of 10 March fast forwards to the guilty verdict at the second trial, reports in full Judge North's bitter comments to Foote in passing sentence, and pauses for breath only to indulge in the dramatic scene that followed. Less sensational publications, from the *Tablet* to the *Daily News,* muffled that final outcry against injustice in silence too. The Unitarian *Inquirer* was in a small minority in protesting the *News*'s refusal to report a word of Foote's speech in his own defense, as if this too must naturally be blasphemy; few newspapers chose to print letters to the editor on the case; none at any point quoted a single one of the indicted words.

The fourth and final stage concerned simply speaking aloud suspect words within the four walls of the courtroom. At the first trial of William Hone in 1817, the clerk of the court in the normal course of duty read the *Late John Wilkes's Catechism* aloud to the court, with predictably hilarious results: this formed, in fact, "the whole of the case on the part of the prosecution" (W. Hone, *Three Trials* 13). In 1841, during the trial of Henry Hetherington for publishing Haslam's *Letters,* though Attorney-General Sir John Campbell felt it "painful" that the jury should have to hear some "shocking" extracts, they heard them nonetheless. But the pain overwhelmed prosecutor and judge in the Holyoake trial shortly after: they refused at any point to repeat the offending words (*History of the Last Trial* 6, 24, 29–30). It was not to be expected that Judge North and Sir Hardinge Giffard would do anything less in the decent 1880s. But they chose to maintain their silence in a loudly self-conscious manner.

The prosecution would not "outrage public decency," Giffard vowed, by even "referring" to indicted passages (*Three Trials for Blasphemy* 3); he personally would not "be a party publicly to describe the sort of thing he had before him at that moment" (3) but would "spare the ears of the court" (Foote, *Prisoner* 30). The jury's private and silent reading would have to suffice. Only once during the first two *Freethinker* trials did the prosecution bring themselves to read out a single one of the offending sentences. Giffard's assistant was given the nasty job. "As for the Freethinker," he quavered, "he will scorn to degrade himself by going through the farce of reconciling his soul to a God whom he rightly regards as the embodiment of crime and ferocity." Whereupon, Foote recalled, "[a]s Mr. Maloney ended the quotation his voice sank to a supernatural whisper, he dropped the paper on the desk before him, and regarded his lordship with a look of horror, which the worthy magistrate fully reciprocated" (*Prisoner* 30–31). Judge North, with no less fine a sense of courtroom drama, was no more able to bring himself to the sticking point: "The prisoner Foote . . . said, among many other things, a certain thing which seemed to me to be ———. Well, I would rather not touch upon it" (45). The stagy refusal naturally helped jury and audience appreciate how unspeakably awful the indicted extracts were. The gathering silence that brooded over the blasphemy courtroom throughout the nineteenth century thus reached a strategic peak of intensity in the spring of 1883, even while solemnity threatened to succumb to the ridiculous upon which it sat in judgment. It is hard not to smile at how North directed the jury's attention to the tasteless item about "Holy Gh——t" in the magazine before them:

> The learned counsel, who opened this case to you, very wisely refrained from stating in public the particular matters which you have to deal with. I shall do the same. . . . The sixth count relates to a passage at the top of page 14, the second column, the second paragraph from the top. It begins with the word "Holy;" you see what I refer to. (*Three Trials for Blasphemy* 40–41)

But one suspects that no one laughed in 1883.

The *Freethinker* case spurred a final silencing. Within five years, such makeshift repairs to the veil of linguistic decency as North and Giffard supplied in court became things of the past. The 1888 Law of Libel Amendment Act confirmed (again) the 1819 ruling on the illegality of publishing accounts of courtroom proceedings (Odgers, *Libel and Slander* 306). It further provided that in proceedings for obscenity as well as blasphemy, for the purposes of all word crime, forbidden words need never again either be spoken or even silently recorded:

> It is no longer necessary to set out in the indictment the . . . passages in full. It is sufficient to deposit the book, newspaper, or other documents containing the alleged libel with the indictment, or other judicial proceeding, together with par-

ticulars showing precisely, by reference to pages, columns, and lines, in what part
of the book, newspaper, or other document, the alleged libel is to be found, and
such particulars shall be deemed to form part of the record. (section 7, qtd. in
Libel and Slander 473–74)

"Silence in court" indeed. It is one of the ironies of history, and one of
Victorian culture's most logical compensations, that such a provision
should be a by-product of the apparent loosening of restrictions on British
newspapers.[69] Only compare the practice of earlier centuries, and one ap-
preciates how deafening had become the late Victorian silence imperative:
as David Lawton points out, for example, "[p]arliamentary acts against the
Ranters in the Commonwealth period list in full the Ranter blasphemies
they condemn," and the "*Catholic Encyclopedia* entry on blasphemy help-
fully provides . . . examples" of what it defines (4–5).

The "infamous Court of Star Chamber," William Hone reminded the
court, reserved the right to subject any defendant who uttered a word offensive to his judges to having wedges "driven with a mallet into his mouth"
(*Three Trials* 94), an imaginative torture to compare with "bor[ing]" a red-
hot iron "quite thorow" the tongue (Lawton 73).[70] "St. Paul himself,"
Bishop Paley advised, commands us to "stop" the blasphemer's mouth
(Holyoake, "Special Dissertation" 4). Modern procedural "gags" did not
write society's vengeance on the body with the same force and appropriateness, Hone concluded, but they were quite as psychologically "effectual"
(W. Hone, *Three Trials* 94).

It was a prescient remark. From the 1880s, offending words needed never
again at any point in the judicial process be spoken by any actor on the
courtroom stage, nor could any legal document be polluted by their inclusion—an astonishing development. It puts a cap on the subject to add that
the act that exemplifies obsessive English reticence to the outside world,
the Official Secrets Act, was passed the following year, 1889, though it was
rarely invoked until World War I. And if one may judge by the volume
of depositions kept by the Central Criminal Court, the incidence of prosecutions for blackmail, a crime that depends on obsession with unspeakability, surged at exactly this same time.

Languishing in solitary confinement twenty-three hours a day, forbidden
to speak to fellow prisoners, and—until Lord Coleridge intervened—
denied all reading and writing materials except the Bible, Her Majesty's
prisoner Foote got the point (*Prisoner* 135–37). Just as the best way to treat
the unspeakable in court was to stifle it in procedure, so the real punishment for the unspeakable crime of blasphemy was not six months or
a year in jail. It was utter deprivation of voice, words, the power of language. The real punishment for the unspeakable crime was *not speaking;*

the secular word crime of nineteenth-century blasphemy logically bespoke secular excommunication. The outdated law of blasphemy had acquired a new function, enabling what Foucault calls the "normalizing judgment" of a developing "carceral" and "disciplinary" society. The negative function of eradicating "treason against God" gave way to enforcing respect for the silence imperative of respectable bourgeois Victorian England.

The history of blasphemy elucidates the process, in fact, by which silence became the key to the entire prison system. Despite the evidence of architecture (like starfish-shaped Holloway Gaol), the primary method of reformed institutional discipline in the nineteenth century (exemplified also by the workhouse) was not visual or panoptical in the Foucauldian-Benthamite sense but antiverbal and counterdiscursive. Under the "silent system" all inmates became the objects, not the subjects, of language. One of the provisions of the harsh 1865 Prisons Act was the prohibition of speech among prisoners, a provision not rescinded until 1898 and enforced by constant vigilance (Ramsey 6); the only person with whom one might have a conversation was the chaplain, when he visited cells. Oscar Wilde was one of the last victims of the silent system, and it drove him close to a breakdown (Ellmann 506–07). In one model prison warders wore felt slippers, and prisoners donned masks to perform chapel worship in shuttered cubicles (Morris 454).[71] Silence made "a year's hard" in Holloway, 1883–84, a heavier punishment than a longer stretch in " 'terrible Newgate,' as Mrs. Besant calls it": "Solitary confinement and the silent system were not then in vogue, and these have been, not without some justice, described in a parliamentary debate as the worst torture ever devised by human ingenuity" (Foote, *Freethinker,* 28 March 1886: 103). Nothing broke the oppressive stillness "but the voice of some warder calling the numbers of the prisoners who were detailed for some work outside" (Ramsey 12), for—like the name of God—the prisoner's name was tabooed. The system, ironically, depended on literacy: it was from the abstract of regulations pinned up in his room that Ramsey learned "that I must not speak to anybody" (5). In the first month, the prisoner was forbidden all writing and reading materials except the Bible supplied in his cell; in the second, he got a slate and pencil; later, he might have a book a week from the prison library (a provision Harcourt attempted to deny Foote), and use pen and ink to write a letter home.[72] The official form was explicit:

> A prisoner is permitted to write and receive a Letter after three months of his sentence have expired. . . . All letters of an improper or idle tendency, either to or from Prisoners, or containing slang or other objectionable expressions, will be suppressed. (Foote, *Prisoner* 172–73)

Quoting the form wholesale in his prison memoir salved Foote's wounds
and advertised his commitment to linguistic rebellion. This was the culture
and this the frame of mind that cocreated the crime of the *Freethinker.*
Jacob Holyoake, who thought himself the last man "Tri[ed] by Jury for
Atheism in England," was a different case altogether.

4. JACOB HOLYOAKE, "MASTER OF SENTENCES"

Holyoake learned a first linguistic lesson from the guards at Gloucester
Gaol. They refused to spell out the word "blasphemy" on the standard card
pinned to his cell door. Eight years later, in titling his prison memoir, he
eschewed the curtly obvious style of Foote's memoir of 1884, *Prisoner for
Blasphemy,* for the quietly euphemistic *History of the Last Trial by Jury for
Atheism in England.* The aura of "martyrdom" floated about him to the
last, but it became progressively impossible to tell what he had been prosecuted *for:* it was not "atheism," "candor," "explicitness" (his favorite substitute), or "an unusual expression of opinion."[73] The ability to turn blasphemy into its opposite, like Lewis Carroll turning "black" into "white"
in only five moves of a word game, signaled Holyoake's investiture as an
almost-eminent Victorian. And nothing helped Secularism achieve the
modest profile it did under Holyoake in the 1850s and 1860s than the *name:*
preempting Huxley's "Agnosticism" by a full generation, Holyoake's coinage of 1851 was his most successful euphemism. Its credit was canceled by
the "wanton outrage" of the *Freethinker* case (Holyoake, *Present Day,* August 1883: 17): respectable Secularists began calling themselves "Agnostics"
around 1883.[74]

If there was "one thing more repulsive than blasphemy," Holyoake came
to believe, in which the crime was virtually swallowed up, it was "shock[-
ing]" "language," which, "in the interests of society and good-feeling,
should be discouraged" (*Sixty Years* 1: 269–70). It was the deliberate repos-
session of acceptable words that made Holyoake the Secularist movement's
first leader and the father of Cooperativism. His conversion to the idol
Respectability was always and already a specifically *linguistic* process. Martyrdom for blasphemy in 1842 modulated within a decade into a new life
as "this new Master of *Sentences*" (Martin 6, my emphasis). The pun would
prove better chosen than its maker intended.

The linguistic profile of Jacob Holyoake has never fallen into the pur-
view of the biographies; the obscure miscellanea that piece it together are
barely available outside archives in London and Manchester, and if noticed
have been condemned to the dustbin of bibliography. Yet they repay close
attention. Only these allow us truly to read his attempts to rewrite himself

into being: *The History of the Last Trial for Atheism* (1850), rightly subtitled a *Fragment of Autobiography* and obsessively revised in various editions, is correctly described not as a "well-written" but as a "very embellished" account (Lawton 4; Grugel 41n);[75] subsequent memoirs of 1893 and 1905 are as unreliable as they are self-consciously literary. The profile these known and unknown materials construct has an exemplary quality. It might interest linguists and analysts of critical discourse as much as historians of literacy and labor movements; it might seduce Lacanian psychoanalysts who find in language the new "law of the father." Certainly, it speaks directly to this study's central concern with euphemism, silence, and word criminality: the index to the 1878 edition of the *History of the Last Trial* lists the law its author had broken as simply a "Law of Speech and Silence." Within a decade of his imprisonment, blasphemer Jacob Holyoake was more "chastened" by the "law" in language than might have been anticipated even by a nation that summed up political wisdom in Disraeli's dictum, "With words we govern men" (*Safire's* 1).

The process began in silencing. "We refuse to hold an argument," said magistrate Capper, "with a man professing the abominable principle of denying the existence of a Supreme Being" (*History of the Last Trial* 9). This was a small beginning to exclusion from language. Next, there was harassment: "I was treated with the greatest injustice," Holyoake recalled, "as far as language could go, at the police-station" (*Cheltenham Free Press,* 20 August 1842: 267). Awaiting bail, he had to endure a torrent of religious platitudes delivered with an "air of sharp authority" by the police surgeon, Mr. Pinching, who took it upon himself to "reason" with the prisoner (*History of the Last Trial* 11). Lack of response finally turned the man "abusive." Holyoake replied, "Unless you converse with me upon equal terms I shall not answer you" (12). In court, he smartingly recalled how the policemen who illegally "exercis[ed]" against him "the sensual and brutish arm of the law, . . . could not string six sentences together grammatically" (*Trial of George Jacob Holyoake* 30). The same pride in his language power dictated he read aloud, as part of his defense, a turgid little poem he had published in the *Baptist Teachers Tract Magazine* when he was nineteen (*Cheltenham Free Press,* 20 August 1842: 270).[76] In prison, Holyoake's trials of language with the chaplain, eager to exercise on the blasphemer all the force of his twopenny pulpit eloquence, including an inevitable "elaborate peroration on death," were "a ceremony, not a conversation" (*History of the Last Trial* 83). Finally, discreet offers were made of a nice country school when he was released if he could keep his mouth permanently shut (82). This was the one thing he was fated never to do.

The martyr's response to deprivation was revealing. Access to language became a prison obsession. Shut up in the dark of winter for sixteen hours a day, Holyoake "contrived some mitigation" to his punishment "by secreting the cover of a book, sticking pins in the sides at even distances, and running a thread across from side to side," so that "[b]y running a sheet of paper under the threads I could write with a pencil between the lines" (*History of the Last Trial* 173–74). By such means he could keep a prison diary. But the tatty little exercise books in which he scribbled contain not just records of his day-to-day experiences but notes on his progress in literacy. "I studied Justin Brenan on 'punctuation' and 'composition' "; "Read Dr. Johnson's Lives of the poets (4th vol.) with much profit" ("Log Book" no. 1, in HC).

The profit was in the writing. Holyoake's first well-known pamphlet, *Paley Refuted in His Own Words,* a sarcastic riposte to the standard argument for divine design, proudly bears on its title page the reviewer's legend: " 'penned in prison.'—*Cheltenham Free Press.*"[77] There is more in this than prison literature cliché or countercultural hyperbole. The only weapon with which to combat his deprivation was language: the blasphemous voice that could not speak was transformed into the authorial name on the title page. The very title asserted a superior power of linguistic analysis: *refuted in his own words;* it rang satisfying changes on a phrase that rankled: *his own language.*

"The six months are nothing when over," Carlile wrote Holyoake in Gloucester Gaol. "What will you do after is the question" (25 October 1842, in HL). The defining moment of his long afterlife came three years later, when Holyoake entered a competition sponsored by the Manchester Oddfellows (an organization like the Masons but several notches lower on the social scale) for the best lectures upon the themes and degrees of that "Independent Order": Charity, Truth, Knowledge, Science, the Golden Rule. The prize was fifty pounds, ten pounds per lecture. It was a sum worth laboring for. One can almost hear the mind at work in Holyoake's careful phrasing of the principle of plain speech that the blasphemy martyr could not conscientiously eschew but must play down for Oddfellow consumption. "Our Order," according to Holyoake, believes in using only "the simple eloquence of truth" in order to "win you" (*Purple Lecture* 7); it is suspicious of the "dangerous rhetoric of fancy" (8). He had hit the right note and won the competition, beating out seventy-nine competitors, many of them clergymen. The Oddfellows were less than delighted when they learned the identity of their prize author. But they paid up, and used the lectures.[78] The claim to language that had condemned Holyoake's family to penury while he was in prison and his daughter to death now lifted them out of need. Words from his pen were now issued to the world with a stamp of near-holy approval on the title page: "Sanctioned and Approved by the Bristol Annual Moveable Committee, June, 1846" (Holyoake, *Lectures*). The blasphemous "utterer" of counterfeit language was reborn. But to achieve linguistic reempowerment was also to rediscover the law without which there is no power, at least not in language.

Enriched and emboldened, Holyoake struck out on an important second career based on his new mastery of English. Among the cheap self-help books he published from the mid-1840s, manuals of grammar, vocabulary, elocution, and debate dominate the list.[79] Editing infidel journals would not keep food on the table, but he did not merely aim to make extra money by these productions. "The *Spectator* was pleased to say," he recalled of his first, "that I wrote *Practical Grammar* in the spirit of an 'ultra-radical, setting the world to rights'" (*Logic of Facts* viii). The wrongs to be righted were those of classic grammars like Bishop Lowth's (1762) and Lindley Murray's (1795), which "inculcate passive obedience" by means of illustrative examples, "and softly promote the cause of corruption" (Cobbett, qtd. in O. Smith 9).[80] He followed proudly in the footsteps of William Cobbett, for whom writing a common man's *Grammar* was "an act of class warfare" (O. Smith 1); of agrarian insurgent Thomas Spence, who published a phonetic record of *'Import'ant Tri'al ov T'om'is Sp'ens* (1803) eighty years before Pitman and the reformed spelling movement; of the framers of "The Bad Alphabet for the Use of the Children of Female Reformers" ("B" was for Bible, Bishop, and Bigotry [E. Thompson 718]); of William Hone, penning the *Political "A Apple Pie"* (now apparently lost [catalogue, Hone Bath]).[81] Words restored that "power" to the people, Holyoake believed, "they never yet possessed" (*Logic of Facts* vi).

The *Practical Grammar*; the *Handbook* for "Learners"; and his Secular Letter, Word, and Grammar Books for Little Children understand the need for memorable rhymes and illustrative stories: one in the *Child's Word Book* relates a battle between "Mr. Foote and Mr. Headpiece," body and mind. Their well-thought emphases on doing, making, and ordinary life made them modest sellers. "I," for example, is taken as the basis for the "straight" letters of the alphabet: "See, a straight line, like that, standing upright, makes I. When you knock at the door, and Mama says 'Who is there?' you say, 'I.' I begins Ink and Ice" (*Child's Second Letter-Book* 3). The example had the additional practical benefit of encouraging correctness in children who would not say "I" but "me" to their "Mamas," if they had "Mamas." The class consciousness of that little gesture was prophetic.

In 1847, Thackeray's arriviste Becky Sharp threw a prize copy of Dr. Johnson's *Dictionary* out of the carriage window. The year before, Holyoake dared to deny the doctor's all-powerful adage, inherited from Bacon, "Style is the dress of thought," *vestigia mentis.* "Take a man's dress off him, and he is a man still, but take the words away from a sentence, and what becomes of the meaning[?] Style is not the dress of thought, but thought itself embodied in words" (*Practical Grammar* 63).[82] The "dress" could be as plain you liked, even what Johnson called the "degrad[ing]" and "obscure" garb of "rustics or mechanics" (Johnson 380).[83] "Propriety is truth" (65), Holyoake instructed readers, "Language may be considered low, coarse, vulgar, violent, abusive, but it is proper if it is true" (66). "Care nothing about style, nor imitations, nor repetitions," but "be natural, be plain, and make yourself fully understood" (52). The Birmingham autodidact seemed to anticipate the contention of W. D. Whitney, the American philologist, in the 1870s: "The speakers of language . . . constitute a republic, or rather, a democracy, in which authority is conferred only by general suffrage" (qtd. in Dowling 92).

Linguistic radicalism, like all radicalism, however, faded with the 1840s. In the 1850s, Holyoake made extra bread and butter writing promotional leaflets like the *History and Characteristics of Indian and Chinese Teas* for a Glasgow merchant and the *Skin, Baths, Bathing, and Soap* for the Pears company. One might have predicted the move in his bid to "sell" his subject in the *Practical Grammar.* "A person may conceal his ignorance of any other art, but every time he speaks, he publishes his ignorance of [grammar]" (*Practical Grammar* 2). Late twentieth-century salesmen still work the same ploy. "People will judge you," intones the promoter of a product called Verbal Advantage, for your lack of a *"power vocabulary":* late capitalism reduces linguistic wisdom to belief in words as portable property, the bigger the better. ("Call now," radio listeners are admonished: "1-800-547-WORD.") In the 1850s, fellow publisher Henry Vizetelly recalled in 1893, Holyoake was "singularly quiet" (2: 44).

But he also set his sights high. His erstwhile linguistic mentor, Charles Southwell of the *Oracle,* returned from Australasia to a noisy conversion to Christianity, had to admit his "almost unrivaled tact" and "enticing diction" (Southwell, *Impossibility* 8; *Another* 3), phrases annotated with relish in Holyoake's personal copy (HC).[84] Another former colleague pronounced his rebuke to the *Boston Liberator* for "improper" reporting of slavery to be nothing but "cant" (Linton, *Holyoake v. Garrison* 257): "I would have men truthful; he would have them polite, which he thinks is the same as politic" (qtd. in *Young Men's Magazine,* June 1884: 120). The care of words had come to dominate over their utterer and his political objects. The contents list of Holyoake's *Rudiments of Public Speaking* (1853) shows how sharp his sense became for the "good-feeling" and "co-operative" spirit of language: chapter 5—"Discipline"; chapter 6—"Tact," "which may dictat[e]

. . . silence." "[L]et [a man] not forget that fulness [sic] and freedom are both blind; and that without the lights of taste and perspicuity and brevity he may offend, bewilder, and tire" (63).

The files and boxes of the Holyoake Collection speak of a man possessed. Holyoake kept, it seems, every scrap of writing he ever published, or which marked his possession of language power, from Oracular sneers to the editorial encomium passed upon him by the *Liverpool Daily Post:* "[An] eloquent writer and . . . able *litterateur,* [he] us[es] his mother tongue with faultless purity and facile strength" (cutting, 16 August 1879, in HC). He kept the *Biograph and Review*'s inaccurate declaration of 1880, that to "the calm and dignified manner in which Holyoake, eschewing all the arts of the agitator and pseudo-martyr[,] bowed to the decision of the law," England owed the fact that no prosecution for blasphemy had occurred for twenty-five years (cutting, October, in HC). He hoarded his rivals' and enemies' pamphlets. He kept all these things, not only because he believed in himself as "a splendid type" of Victorian "moral chivalry," the Secularist of the century, premier free press campaigner, first labor candidate for Parliament, but because every word mattered to him, in the most literal sense.[85] But while Jacob Holyoake rebuilt himself on their foundation, the words he spoke began to speak him. In becoming "[t]his new Master of Sentences," he proved the truth of a revised adage: language power corrupts.

What happened perhaps went something like this: Schooled in prison and drilled in grammar, as the 1840s passed Holyoake took deeper and deeper to heart the "doctrine of correctness" preached by the eighteenth-century grammarians who were his predecessors, even while he surpassed their prescriptive model and seemed to subvert its class and Christian bias.[86] "Grammar," wrote one sixpenny handbook writer of 1832, "teaches us to speak and write *correctly*" (Oswald 5). To enjoy a *"just"* or "true and appropriate Elocution," the author of a *Catechism of Elocution* put it in 1836, is to acquire a "delivery" that is not merely "EMPHATIC" but "CORRECT, CHASTE, ELEGANT" (3). In these years, English was asked to participate in "that formation of *discipline*" that Latin and Greek once provided (Trench, qtd. in Willinsky 26). The italicized judicial and penal terms (and for "chaste" also read "chastened") echo with suggestiveness; the signifying chain that is language faintly clinks. As we must beware of letting a man's blasphemy stand in for his history, as David Lawton convicts Freud of doing in the case of the "Wolfman" (164), so we must trace Holyoake's linguistic journey to its real end.

For what may well be at the heart of all language study, at the heart of language, and perhaps embedded in the unconscious (if Noam Chomsky and Jacques Lacan are right), is not the impulse to transgression but the will to law.[87] "It is in the power of one individual to change empires," Max Müller declared, "[but] no King or Dictator has ever been able to change the smallest law of language" (*Edinburgh Review,* October 1851: 330). Nineteenth-century philology revealed language to be a trace work of laws, "so regular," as the continental Neogrammarians agreed in the 1870s, "that they admitted of no exceptions" (Dowling 64). The "scientific" study of language, wrote Sayce in 1883, was "the surest means of impressing on the mind the great fact of the universality of law amid all the change and development of nature" (2: 335–36).

Jacob Holyoake rebuilt his life on the power of language that conviction for blasphemy stripped away. But he was no John Clare, clinging to an anarchic denial: "grammar in learning is like tyranny in government. . . . confound the bitch I'll never be her slave" (qtd. in Annan 334). His taming began the moment he picked up the pen to write *Paley Refuted* and his *Practical Grammar.* Each small volume or flimsy pamphlet not only restored his sense of language power but put him *in* the power, subject to the laws of language. There was an auguring appropriateness in the jeu d'esprit he printed for his so-called parliamentary grammar class at the City of London Mechanics' Institute in December 1848: *A Bill for the Better Security of Grammar,* to put down those who do "cut, maim, and murder Her Majesty's English" by denial of its "established rules" and intrusion of their "unauthorized terms" (HC). Holyoake was living Derrida's aphorism 150 years *avant la lettre:* "the access to writing is the constitution of a free subject in the violent moment of . . . its own bondage" (132).

"Access to *writing*": Holyoake's linguistic reinvestment occurred not through "mouthfuls of air" (as Anthony Burgess calls spoken words) but in marks on paper. "I had always been told," Holyoake reflected in prison, "that my voice was too weak to hold out during two hours speaking." As an inspiriting precaution, he breakfasted before trial on "[t]hree eggs beaten in a little rum," with raspberry vinegar to drink ("Log Book" no. 1, in HC). But the "reviews" of his courtroom performance were devastating nonetheless. Holyoake delivered his "prosy incoherent and absurd harangue" in "a shrill discordant voice" (*Times,* undated cutting, in HC); "he had a pronunciation and accent so peculiarly his own, that we were . . . unable to detect the meaning" of his "quotations" (*Illustrated London News,* 20 August 1842, cutting in HL). It was a work of bitterness to copy the verdicts out in longhand (HC, HL).

But the gates of hell he had entered speaking would yield to a written passport. The Gloucester *Calendar of Prisoners* officially recorded that defendant "G.J.H., 25," "r[eads] [and] w[rites] well" (in HC). What Holyoake aimed at in his prison lessons and readings was not the achievement of a

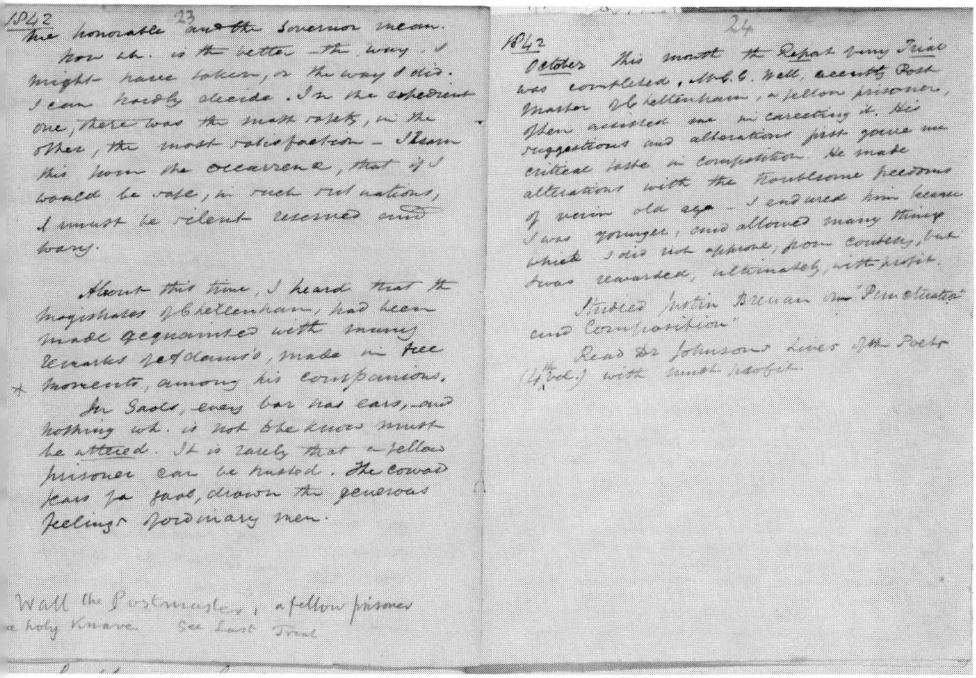
1842 23
The honorable and the Governor mean.
Now wh. is the better — the way I might have taken, or the way I did. I can hardly decide. In the expedient one, there was the most safety, in the other, the most satisfaction — I learn this from the occurrence, that if I would be safe, in such situations, I must be silent reserved and wary.

About this time, I heard that the Magistrates of Cheltenham, had been made acquainted with many remarks of Adams's, made in free moments, among his companions.
In Gaols, every bar has ears, and nothing wh. is not to be known must be uttered. It is rarely that a fellow prisoner can be trusted. The coward fears of a gaol, drown the generous feelings of ordinary men.

Wall the Postmaster, a fellow prisoner
a holy Knave See Last Trial

1842 24
October This month the Report of my Trial was completed, Mr. G. G. Wall, recently Post Master of Cheltenham, a fellow prisoner, then assisted me in correcting it. His suggestions and alterations first gave me critical taste in composition. He made alterations with the troublesome pedantry of vain old age — I endured him because I was younger, and allowed many things which I did not approve, from courtesy, but was rewarded, ultimately, with profit.
Studied Justin Brenan on "Punctuation and Composition"
Read Dr Johnson's Lives of the Poets (4th vol.) with much profit.

Figure 17. Holyoake records his progress in language: two pages from the prison diary. Courtesy of the Bishopsgate Institute Library, National Secular Society Collection.

speaking voice but the acquirement of a writing style. (Keeping notes of his linguistic progress was not a new habit; but the scrappy journal he kept in 1838–39 was elaborately, even desperately, concerned with pronunciation.[88])

> *October.* This month the *Report* of my trial was completed. Mr. G. G. Wall, recently postmaster of Cheltenham, a fellow prisoner [marginal addition: "a holy knave"], then assisted me in correcting it. His suggestions and alterations first gave me critical taste in composition. ("Log Book" no. 1, in HC) (fig. 17)

The man who "maliciously, unlawfully, and wickedly" did "compose, speak, utter, pronounce," and "publish" his blasphemous words "with a loud voice" became a man remade by the printed word. He learned not to "demand . . . unlimited freedom of expression . . . in writing or reading or speaking" (preface, *God v. Paterson* iii), indeed, not to think of speaking and writing as equal and identified activities. Even in a handbook aimed at children Holyoake assumes that the end and ambition of all words is print;[89] his manuscript letters are laid out like printed pages, the next word of the next page always written in the bottom right-hand corner. He continued throughout his life to lecture and debate, though overshadowed from the 1860s by Bradlaugh, and from the mid-1870s by Foote. But it was in print that he existed. If the profit of *Paley Refuted* was in the writing, it was also true that in writing no one could tell how bad his accent was.

Charles Southwell of the *Oracle* had the true "gift of the gab"; it is evident in his ventriloquist's ability to turn establishment rhetoric to blasphemous account.[90] But his own pseudo-Romantic boast of oral power was also quoted against him in court: "I write as I speak, and speak exactly as I think, so that my writings and speeches" are always "hasty, irregular, bold, and enthusiastic" (*Trial of Charles Southwell* 9). Southwell was as obsessed with language and its power as Jacob Holyoake; he boasted to have found that "style" whose lack was "the greatest difficulty to the progress of truth" (Chilton to Holyoake, 21 December 1841, in HL); the one charge he roundly denied at his trial was bad grammar (*Trial of Charles Southwell* 18). But he was inhibited by his own theatricality, and he did not have the same capacity for linguistic self-transformation. The friendship foundered when Holyoake passed austere judgment on some overwritten pamphlets. "[A]s long as [I was] the cock upon the dunghill, I crowed away," Southwell had rightly prophesied from his cell, "but other cocks I find can crow louder and better than I" (19 February 1842, in HL). Holyoake was the better cockerel. Between 1842 and 1850 the man Southwell used privately to tease for unready inarticulateness (Southwell to Holyoake, 19 February 1842, in HL) made a complete transition to print standard literacy and a literary career.

In making that transition, Holyoake also broke the vicious circle in which the cheap press was trapped. His *Reasoner* (1865–72) marked a new era. The working-class radicalism of the first half of the nineteenth century emphasized oratory and the mass meeting; the expectations these generated worked to produce an idiom of the cheap press that necessarily seemed "blasphemous" to middle-class readers whose sense of style (in the problematic but useful terms of Walter Ong) had long been "radically textual" (171). To write as one spoke, as Southwell boasted, was to write criminal English.

Born in 1817, Holyoake rose above the limitations of his generation, which—despite an access to print that was barely imaginable in the 1790s or 1810s—was linguistically insecure in a way that Bradlaugh (born 1833) or Foote (born 1850, a member of the first broadly literate working generation) was not. And he suffered a correspondent need to overcompensate. "One of the first things that literates often study, is language itself and its uses," Ong suggests (9). "Philosophy and all the sciences and 'arts' " to which Holyoake pretended as "Mathematical teacher," writing master, editorial "Reasoner"—even "logic," the catchword that features prominently in several of his titles—may "depend for their existence on writing" (172). Holyoake's investment in print initiated him into another inheritance of its "Art & Mysterie"—the illusion of cold objectivity learnt by the machine-made precision and visual inevitability of the page, as if to say, "That's the way it is" (122). It may have completed his "chastening." It was "print," Ong goes so far as to say (and here some detractors follow him) that directly "fostered the desire to legislate for 'correctness' in language" (130); Dr. Johnson bade us pronounce words as they are written, and the nineteenth century obeyed. This is not to say that in becoming "this new Master of Sentences" Holyoake automatically became conservative and bourgeois. Rather, linguistic reinscription and embourgeoisement turned out to be parallel processes. The Other Life of Jacob Holyoake explodes the logic of Hannah More's promise to her bishop to "allow of no writing for the poor" (qtd. in Webb 16). In obeying the grammarians' injunctions and hearkening to the law in language, the graduate of Gloucester Gaol was more thoroughly chastened than anyone might have anticipated. From indictment for blasphemy he passed to indicting (which also means, merely, *writing*); from hearing sentence to making sentences; from criminal case to grammatical cases; from justifying atheism to justifying lines of type.[91] The hoarded piles of rival pamphlets in the Holyoake collections have been corrected, in pencil, for the satisfaction of the "Master": the archives that remember him are miniature facilities for the penal storage of words.

5. THE VICTORIAN CRISIS OF LANGUAGE

"What will very soon be the language of followers if those who assume to be their leaders talk thus?" So Jacob Holyoake launched a vitriolic attack on G. W. Foote the year after their ill-fated co-editorship of the *Secularist* fell apart in 1877 (*Alien Features* 2). The Master of Sentences had come to hate the blasphemous upstart for deeper reasons than the threat he posed to his own martyr status or Secularism's respectability: for the words in his mouth, the language that shaped his mind. And the crowning irony was that Foote was fighting the *Oracle*'s battles all over again under a standard of belief Holyoake himself had helped to design. Holyoake the ultra-radical had mellowed into a linguistic conservative, and now anathematized the rebel who replaced him in the trenches.

One form taken by Holyoake's conservatism requires our return to the "fetish" abandoned for Literature at the close of chapter 3. The English being a Bible people, with a "slavish" "reverence for [its] letter" (L. Stephen,

Essays on Freethinking 118), the Book was inseparably involved with the midcentury "leap into literacy." In place of the Latinate style dictated by Bishop Lowth's *Short Introduction to English Grammar* of 1762, in the wake of nonconformist religious revival, the nineteenth century substituted a style of English pinned to the biblical rock. Writers like Dickens turned to the King James Bible in hours of stylistic need (little Dombey's death, for example) in the knowledge that "Bible English," as Foote called it (*N.S.S. Almanack*, 1886: 18–19), could speak for him across the full range of his readership. If the Book was the mastering text of Victorian culture, then the language of the Authorized Version was the foundation stone of Victorian idiom—in Müller's phrase, the "palimpsest" of its mind (*Biographies* xxvii). To live "as men worthy your country and your progenitors," as one of Holyoake's critics warned in 1851, Englishmen had to safeguard the Bible's "splendor of thought and diction" (S. Williams 4, 5).

Holyoake had offered real threat to that "splendour" in the 1840s. Cheekily dedicating the first child of his pen to William and Robert Chambers, the dictionary publishers, he lambasted their failure—like the Mechanics' Institutes where he had taught—to stick to their principle of non-partisanship on religion, and concluded by offering them "free and fee-less permission" to pirate his own work as "antidote" (*Paley Refuted* iv). One of the most radical aspects of his word books was their mere secularity: they aimed to break the connection between Scripture and script (*écriture*), writing and Holy Writ, Book and book learning, *Biblos* and *bibliothèque*.

But from the 1850s, Holyoake signaled linguistic rapprochement not merely by succumbing to euphemization, nor only in his wholesale co-option of loaded terms like "decency" and "taste." He also returned to the biblical bedrock. Investigation runs through the land like the "angel" among the "Assyrian hosts" (*Case* 5); Freethinkers must go about, like Nicodemus, under cover of night; and a reverend opponent is exhorted to "go down on thy grateful knees every morning, and thank that Heaven who . . . hast made thy lines to fall in pleasant places, and has, as David says, given thee a goodly heritage" (19). Some usages and allusions are tongue-in-cheek, but all are affectionately respectful.

To the editor of the *Freethinker* this return to "Bible English" was the greatest betrayal of all: it fostered an illusion. Language that seemed divine Foote knew for a relentlessly secular medium. The words in your mouth were not guaranteed by some transcendental "Word"; their meaning and their power were social, cultural, psychological. In the view from Holloway Gaol, Holyoake had reneged on the linguistic struggle of the century, a kind of forty years' war that came to its most public crisis exactly as the *Freethinker* went to trial. There was a corollary to the question, was language proof of mankind's divine origin? It was in itself traumatic: Must we seal ears and lips to the most affecting idiom to which Englishmen could aspire? To G. W. Foote, word rebel and atheist, the verbal beauty of the King James Bible was an immediate and insinuating danger. His campaign of "Bible-smashing" necessarily also involved the desacralization of "Bible English." A Victorian crisis of language plays itself out in the case of the *Freethinker*.

i. The (Un)Making of the Revised Version

In the fantastical preamble to one of many debunking comic "translations" of Scripture into the plain "matter-of-fact" speech of "our scientific, sceptical, matter-of-fact nineteenth century" (Stoker 238), Foote dramatizes the predicament that faced lower-class Secularist writers steeped in the Bible and short on stylistic models.[92] The narrator is given a parchment by "Obadiah," one of the "saints" raised with Christ at the Resurrection, and takes it to a friendly Hebrew scholar for translation:

> A question then arose whether it should be translated into Bible English or into the English of our own period. . . . I preferred to see it rendered into our present vernacular, so that *the deceitful glamour of a consecrated style* might be avoided, and the real facts appear in their naked verity. (*My Resurrection* 7, my emphasis)

An article in the *N.S.S. Almanack* for 1886 lays out plainly the serious argument that informs such impudent returns to the parodic-apocryphal battles of the 1810s and 1820s. The Bible is sanctified by our very susceptibility to language, Foote argues. It has no sacred "essence," but is "embodied" only in its "style." Its appeal rests on the brilliant ability of King James's translators, working in the age of Shakespeare when the language flowered. They had "ears"; their Bible is a "treasury of musical and vigorous" English ("Bible English," *N.S.S. Almanack* 1886: 19). And the emotional hold it establishes over reader and listener has been strengthened by usage and tradition.

To break that hold, Foote employs a battery of strategies. One is more quietly cathartic: familiar phrases are reworked to give echoes that are slightly "off," so that we experience something like an erasure of Authorized language. Thus, say, Foote's refusal to reach for the terms of the parable about the foolish man who built his house upon the shifting sand (Matthew 7.26–27). He writes instead, "Splendour gives no strength to an edifice whose foundations are treacherous" (*Freethinker*, 20 August 1882: 257). Or, in a pamphlet protesting capital punishment, he writes that

> [Like Damocles] Europe . . . sits at its *feast of life*, but the fatal weapon suspended overhead mars its felicity. *Serpents* twine in the dance, arms clash in the song, the *meats* have a strange *savor*, there is a demoniac sparkle in *the wine*, and a poisonous bitterness in *"the dregs"* *of the cup*. (qtd. in Judge 4)

Each one of the potential biblical echoes (italicized) is muffled and distorted: the quotation marks around "the dregs" even point us to the passage's primary mis-echoed intertext from Isaiah 51.17.[93] Meanwhile, the slick parallelisms and swinging rhythms add their effort to obliteration. There is a difference between such desacralization and the inspiriting reformulations of *Sartor Resartus,* say, Carlyle's preacherly call to arms to the nineteenth century: "Work while it is called To-day, for the Night cometh wherein no man can work" (149). The Scottish sage retailored the old clothes of Christianity; Foote shredded them to rags.

The *Freethinker*'s "Profane Jokes" had their part to play in the process of desacralization, exposing the comic possibilities of the Word through wordplay, taking to extremes the gift of verbal tricksiness, shared by all classes of Victorian society, that made popular Carroll's *Alice* and the limericks of Edward Lear. In doing so, they mocked another vulnerable Christian tradition.[94] For instance, a light-minded example of the ever-popular palindrome, a gentlemanly introduction, "Madam, I'm Adam" (*N.S.S. Almanack,* 1885: 63). Or the favorite conundrum of 1882: "Why is the Athanasian Creed like a Bengal tiger? Because of its damnation clause" (*Freethinker,* 30 July: 235). Or "When did David sleep five in a bed?—When he slept with his forefathers" (summer no. 1884: 15). "Why is a muscular Christian no Christian at all?" runs a favorite of 1886: "Because he is a muscle man" (i.e., "Mussulman" [24 January: 32]). "What is the difference between a Secular Hall and a Ritualistic Church? —At the former you get sense, at the latter incense and nonsense" (44). The summer number for 1884 addresses itself to imaginary correspondents like "Auntie Diluvian" and "E. Nock" (7). We may wince, but the jokes stand up well to their models in *Punch.*[95] The desacralizing humor obliterates the constructiveness of once-popular ecclesiastical pseudo-etymologies like *"Pro Te stant, Jesu"* for "Protestant," or, most extraordinary, the favorite Victorian derivation of *"abracadabra"* from the Aramaic *ab,* "Father," *ben,* "Son," and *ruach hakodesh,* "Holy Spirit," with the final syllables based on Hebrew *dabar,* "Word."[96] Language bursts apart in Foote's comic reminiscence of compositorial error: "Adam bruted" for "adumbrated;" "cremation" for "creation." Then there was "the version of the Bible which dropped the *c*," and made 1 Corinthians 15.52 declare that "in the twinkling of an eye" we shall be not *"changed"* but *"hanged"* (3 January: 3). These are only words and letters, arbitrary and feckless, was the recurrent punch line.

Foote's own style aims deliberately at what we might call desacralization by association, or degradation by vernacular proximity. The technique might have been plotted with an ear for the etymological inheritance of the term: *vernacular,* from Latin *vernaculus* (domestic, indigenous), and *verna* (a home-born slave).[97] The crucified Christ, for example, "cr[ied] out with a loud voice and gave up the ghost" (*My Resurrection* 3); the "saints" raised with him vanished, "and the Lord only knows what has become of them" (5); the Harrowing of Hell drags on until "the Lord cut[s] it short" (5); an East End Peter disputes the charge he betrayed Christ—" 'I never denied him, s'w'help me God' " (12). The mix of profane and sacred language jars on the ear, shocks us into laughter. British comedy should recognize its roots: compare the intrusion into a scene of stoning-to-death in Monty Python's comic-blasphemous *Life of Brian,* of a schoolmasterish official (John Cleese at the top of his form) who stops proceedings to harangue the crowd—"No-one is to stone anyone until I blow this whistle . . . even if they say *Jehovah.*" Foote's mix of "Bible English" and Cockney, however, was a far more volatile proposition in the 1880s than Python's fusion of sacred story and middle-class cliché.

The *Freethinker*'s word games are the hostile equivalent of the convoluted redefinitions undertaken by Matthew Arnold. The whole thrust of *Culture and Anarchy* is "to draw towards a knowledge of the universal order which seems to be intended and aimed at in the world, and which it is man's happiness to go along with or his misery to go counter to,—to learn, in short, the will of God," Arnold cuts short circumlocution to say, "[and] make it *prevail*" (*Portable* 475). *Literature and Dogma* effects the metamorphosis of religion into *"morality touched by emotion,"* while God himself becomes the "Eternal" and "the enduring power, *not ourselves,* which makes for righteousness" (48, 80). Such redefinitions aimed to placate orthodox critics and solace conscientious doubters. The strategy was initiated by Feuerbach, and sat oddly with Arnold as the critic who two years before had lamented in print "the sense of want of correspondence between the forms of modern Europe and its spirit" (Arnold, "Heine," *Prose Works* 3: 109); but it spoke to the poet who has come to "epitomize" an "irremediable" Victorian "loss of linguistic plenitude" (Riede 25).[98] Pouring new wine of meaning into the old bottles of "Bible English" conserved the continuity of "culture" (the word, as Raymond Williams remarks, that Arnold most profoundly reworked), and enabled the disciplinary project that was never far from his sight: we should preserve the foundational idiom of the Bible, Arnold contended, because it "come[s] most home to us" (*Culture* 559). Thomas Hardy's view, reading him, was quite different: "When dogma has to be balanced on its feet by such hair-splitting as his," he concluded, "it must be in a very bad way" (*Life and Work* 224). In the old clothes of "Bible English," Foote charged in court, society had discovered how discreetly to veil—or "cloak" or "mask"—its actual lack of religious belief.

The tactic invited cynicism. "Is there a God?" F. H. Bradley imagines a reader asking. "Oh yes," replies Mr. Arnold. "And what is he then?" "Be virtuous, and as a rule you will be happy." "Well, and God?" "That is God," says Bradley's Arnold, "what more do you want?" (*Ethical Studies* 284). Arnoldian redefinition brings to mind the skeptical felicities of Ambrose Bierce's *Cynic's Word Book* (begun 1881): "CHRISTIAN, *n*," for example: "One who believes that the New Testament is a divinely inspired book suited to the spiritual needs of his neighbor" (49–50). It also bred a peculiar kind of panic. "Bible English" had been believed a guarantee against decay and devaluation, inflation and euphemization, at the heart of the *lingua communis*. In this it had fulfilled a function quite different to Milton and Shakespeare. "Our version of the Bible is to be loved and prized for this," Coleridge had said, "that it has preserved a purity of meaning to many terms of natural objects. Without this holdfast, our vitiated imaginations would refine away language to mere abstractions" (*Table Talk* 49). Take that holdfast away, and chaos would threaten, when "what passes for truth in every age" becomes merely a "mobile army of metaphors, metonyms, and anthropomorphisms" (Nietzsche, "On Truth and Falsity," *Early* 180). Thus when Charles Watts debated Secularism with the Reverend Thomas Crow, in the pages of the *National Reformer* in 1876, the debate "turn[ed] in a great measure," wrote Bradlaugh, "upon the signification of words" (*N.S.S. Almanack* [1877] 16). To "dilute high words with weak meanings" (Holyoake, *Logic of Life* 15) was to let them dwindle from Trench's "living powers" into "so many crystallized embodiments of dead and bygone thought" (Sayce 1: 134). (Richard Carlile had had a simpler solution: he banned the words *God, nature, mind, soul,* and *spirit* from the pages of the *Republican*. It was not effective.) From holdfast and rock, "Bible English" had become deadweight and delusive guide in an age when epistemological revolution reenforced our sense of dependence on language.

But what would be the alternative to the grounding of our idiom in the English of the Bible? "The strongest part of our religion to-day is its unconscious poetry," Arnold repeated ("Study of Poetry," in *Portable* 299). It was cause for lamentation that "the voice which most hits our collective thought" should be that of "the newspaper with the largest circulation in England, nay, with the largest circulation in the whole world. . . . the *Daily Telegraph!*" (*Culture,* in *Portable* 488). Better any shift to keep "the sublime and aspiring language of religion," the "grand" idiom of the Authorized Version, from dwindling into the "jargon" of a sect (488, 485, 486). It heartened Arnold to recall Ben Franklin's project to retranslate the *Book of Job,* in which Satan's insinuation, "Does Job fear God for nought?" is rendered as "Does your Majesty imagine that Job's good conduct is the effect of mere personal attachment and affection?" (496–97). Celebrating the national holdfast, Arnold expected the last laugh. But the *Freethinker* camp had it instead.

It was not secular "translation" or desacralizing wordplay but Victorian scholarly tinkering by the twenty-seven men who toiled through 792 days of meetings to produce the Revised Version of the Bible, published 1881–84, that precipitated a sudden subsidence of the verbal ground in the years of the *Freethinker* scandal, shaking the rock of "Bible English" until it cracked in half.

The new Book was a crowning achievement of ecumenical and transatlantic cooperation.[99] The men who made it knew the dangerous delicacy of their task: in 1856, when it was first projected, a revised version was felt to be laden by a linguistic difficulty "such as was 'scarcely capable of being entirely surmounted' " (*Macmillan's Magazine,* June 1881: 156); the "sentiment which strove for long to regard the Authorized Version as something too sacred ever to be touched" had to be "talked and written out" before any action could be taken (*Fraser's,* June 1881: 727).[100] "[W]e do not contemplate . . . any alteration of the language" of the Bible, "except where . . . such change is necessary," read resolution 3, adopted in convocation at Canterbury, when plans were conclusively settled in 1870 (*Revised Version* 5: x). That was to risk the blasphemy of Foote's "Obadiah," rendering his parchment fragment in "our present vernacular." The title "Revised Version" was intended literally (xiv). But recent dramatic discoveries had made available earlier and more authoritative manuscript texts than those available to King James's men. "While the very poorest now have access to advantages and comforts which could not be enjoyed by the wealthiest two centuries ago," asked *Fraser's* in June 1881, "shall we continue to stand, in regard to the purity of the text of God's Word, at the point where our ancestors stood when the Authorised Version was formed?" (731): scholarship, "progress," and consumer pressure united to set the English language a trap.

"[T]he task committed to us," recalled the two "companies" (eight men in Oxford, seven in Westminster) who worked on the New Testament, which was the first volume published, "was to increase its fidelity without destroying its charm" (general preface, *Revised Version* 5: ix). To this end (resolution 4), great efforts were made "to preserve a familiar form of words, or even a familiar cadence," at cost of adding "perplexit[ies]" to the revisers' task (xxv). "Necessary changes" were admitted only in the archaic "style of language employed in the existing Version" (x). Thus Foote and the *Freethinker* readers who had rejoiced at the idea of a "New Version" were at first somewhat disappointed. The revisers of the "New New Testament," decided the *Saturday Review,* "show[ed] excellent taste in rejecting many suggestions of the American Committee," the end of which might have been "the rewriting of the whole in leading-article English" (21 May 1881: 647). Parables, Foote had fantasized, might not have quite the same emotional resonance in the up-to-date lingo of industry favored by the Salvation Army. Matthew 22.1–14, for example: "The kingdom of heaven is like a certain railroad king who made a marriage for his son" (*Freethinker,* 9 October 1881: 76).[101] But there was to be no repetition of the scuffle over Bellamy's new translation of 1818, sanctioned by the Bishops, subscribed to by his "persecutor[s]," and a "tacit admission," claimed Richard Carlile, reading from the work's prospectus in court, "that the old version was wrong"—at which point the chief justice stopped him reading (*Morning Herald,* 16 October 1819: 2).

"The revised version of the New Testament," reported the *British Quarterly Review* in July 1881, "[h]as excited a greater public interest than any book ever published in England. . . . beside which the greatest successes of our popular writers appear insignificant" (128). Reports on progress, dissenting opinions, alternative translations, all had been leaked to the press. The volume was published to fanfare. Over one million copies were sold on the day of publication, 17 May 1881; within a year, the figure had shot to three million, and "[p]eople were soon reading it in the street" (N. Barker 51).[102] In America, printed copies went on sale two days after the text arrived; the 22 May *Chicago Times* "printed the entire text of the Gospels, Acts, and Epistle to the Romans, cabled from New York at a cost of $10,000" (51). The tills rang all day at "Amen Corner," 7 Paternoster Row: since no royal commission and government grant had been forthcoming, Oxford University Press, which along with Cambridge paid expenses, cashed in on its copyright.

Nevertheless, Foote was correct: by the mere fact of revision the "sacredness of the English Bible" was indeed "injured," and there was "a great gain to Freethought" (*Freethinker,* July 1881: 19).[103] On the language now depended the religion, was his radical contention, not the other way round. Publication of the Revised Version provoked a crisis of language that was also a crisis of faith, greater (some claim) than that precipitated by Darwin.[104] The new Book could not but grate on the ear of the faithful; it even afflicted its eye. The sacred text laid out in verses by the "masters of rhythmical prose" in King James's day (*Saturday Review* 21 May 1881: 647) was here reshaped into paragraphs, to "assist the general reader in following the current of narrative or argument" (*Revised Version* 5: xxiii): three generations' worth of novel reading had its consequences.[105] Revision meant the deauthorization of what was authorized, the ultimate desacralization of "Bible English." There was an evident tension between the companies' urge to preserve "an English classic" (1: vi–vii), and "the sincere desire to give to modern readers a faithful representation of the meaning of the original documents" (xv). Attendance on words emptied faith in the Word: Foote could not have hoped for more. "The volume, with all its shortcomings, will do good," thought the *Athenaeum* (28 May 1881: 714). No, disagreed the *British Quarterly:* it was too much to ask of "plain readers" to work through linguistic disturbance to better grounds for belief. Oh, that the revisers had strayed "from the paths of philological integrity" on behalf of "their Mother English" (July 1881: 131). "[O]n the whole," the *Spectator* sighed, "we have what we asked for" (21 May 1881: 665).

Extensive alterations to the Lord's Prayer, most particularly the substitution of "Evil One" in the penultimate phrase, "Deliver us from evil," were "already famous" by the day of publication (*British Quarterly,* July 1881: 137). It might be correct, but it contradicted the widespread and unremarked habit, in Foote's pointedly social phrase, of "dropping the devil."[106] To change the time-honored mysterious phrase "through a glass darkly" to "in a mirror darkly" was "wanton aggression" (*Spectator,* 21 May 1881: 648). "A light for revelation to the Gentiles" was "not a whit more faithful" than "A light to lighten the Gentiles," a "rendering" which came from Tyndale (*British Quarterly,* July 1881: 141), who looms over the disgruntled reviews like the ideal of a modest, single, and literary author, as if the English Bible and "Bible English"—not religion and not the Church—demanded its own authorizing martyr. (Tyndale was strangled and burnt at the stake in 1536, for—amongst other things—compositional errors in his translation of the Bible.)[107] The revisers' insistence on definite articles produced the arhythmical phrase "the weeping and *the* gnashing of teeth" (Matthew 8.12). Even the painstaking voting processes that decided problem passages seemed to open the old text to democratic denigration.[108] Margins to include "very probable" but not "necessary" corrections, variant readings, and the like—generally "too much matter," worried the *Athenaeum* (28 May 1881: 713)—were a suspect novelty. William Hone would have smiled (see above, 1.2). Were these "devils" (text) or "demons" (margin) with which Christ had to deal? Was he "Comforter" or "advocate"? Why should not all "marginal and textual renderings . . . change places" (713)? Margins catapulted the sacred into postmodern relativity.

Above all (since the impetus of the revisers was to revise), there were too many "trifling and apparently gratuitous alterations" groused *Macmillan's* (June 1881: 159)—thirty thousand of them, to which the mind had "a sort of instinctive resentment" (*Spectator,* 21 May 1881: 667), an average in the most heavily affected parts of three per verse. Only one in six alterations was due to improvements in the recovered Greek texts.

To the revisers' credit, few were the result of creeping euphemization, though restraint changed "the sounding of thy bowels" into "the yearning of thy heart" (Isaiah 63.15),[109] and the idols God shall "cast away as a menstruous cloth" (30.22) into "an unclean thing" ("Heb. menstruous," notes the margin, bravely). The American committee's hopeless demand to use "the ineffable Name" in place of "the Lord" was relegated by vote to an appendix. The revisers largely ignored the lead of a slew of unauthorized bowdlerized Victorian Bibles that turned "stones" (that is, testicles) into *secrets* or even *peculiar members* (phrases from Noah Webster's "Improved" Bible of 1833), and "stink" into *ill smell:* "kitsch" and "sanctimonious euphemisms" of which the Reverend Peter Mullen might have said, as he does of twentieth-century revised Bibles, "loss of nerve" tokens "loss of faith" (Mullen 171, 165, 169),[110] and of which Matthew Lewis prophesied (like Boyle and Hetherington, Carlile and Paterson) in his 1796 novel, *The Monk,* in which Donna Elvira puts together a sanitized version for her fifteen-year-old daughter, because "every thing" in the unbowdlerized Bible is "called plainly and roundly by its name" (259).

Instead, the bulk of the new version's revisions were the result of a sweeping and picky insistence on "uniformity" of rendering that showed a "lack of literary perspective" that King James's men would have laughed to scorn (*Saturday Review,* 21 May 1881: 648), and a silly ignorance of the fact that "[t]o Englishmen in general . . . uniformity for its own sake has no charm" (*Macmillan's,* June 1881: 159). The result was repetitive, flattening, "needless spoiling" (*British Quarterly,* July 1881: 141). This was a fault Arnold would not have forgiven. Publishing his own revised version of Isaiah in 1883 he had wanted most "to find that a reader has gone from the beginning of the chapters to the end without noticing anything different from what he was accustomed to, except that he was not perplexed and thrown out as formerly" (introduction, qtd. in ApRoberts 246). Needless to say, Foote seized on the problem with grim delight.

The revisers' decision to render separately as "Hades" (the Greek realm of the dead) and "hell" (or "Gehenna") the two words the Authorized Version translates together as "hell" called out some of Foote's best writing.[111]

> The last chapter of *Mark* is a very straightforward piece of writing in the old version. "He that believeth and is baptised shall be saved: but he that believeth not shall be damned." That's the style! . . . But when we read in the new version that "he that disbelieveth shall be condemned," we miss our fine old full-bodied acquaintance. . . . [T]elling a man to go to Hades sounds like inviting him to dinner. (*Freethinker,* 28 March 1886: 97–98)

The Revised Version represented the culminating phase in the Victorian cult of the Bible, but it also marked the moment of precipitous decline.[112]

After the initial enormous sales, within a few years the bottom fell out of the British Bible market. For the first time, Oxford was left with overstock: they had done well to realize that the publishing future lay instead in the "Authorized Version of the English language" (Willinsky 22) that is the *Oxford English Dictionary.* The threat of "competitive circulation" of old and new versions had been disallowed, since the Revised Version was not immediately licensed for use in church. But it never was "taken home to the hearts of the people" (*Macmillan's,* June 1881: 159). The people were instead "repelled" (160). The revisers had failed in their object (wrote one of their number) "to cause the light of Divine truth to shine with a brighter lustre on the minds of those who are indebted for an acquaintance with it solely to the English language" (Alexander Roberts, *Fraser's,* June 1881: 740), and in so doing they had broken the biblical holdfast of the English language. The linguistic compromise epitomized by the Revised Version barely lasted the century. A *Twentieth Century New Testament,* squarely aimed at "plain readers" and young people, began publication in 1898; numerous other modernizations have met with mixed success.[113] The 1880s were indeed a dangerous decade for the English language.

ii. "Restore to Words Their Primitive Power"

The 1880s were threatened, but they were nostalgic in a manner we never again can be. We are convinced, since Saussure, of the arbitrary nature of language and its role as autonomous symbolic system. We hesitate on the brink of Lacan's leap—"It is the world of words that creates the world of things" (*Écrits* 65). We are dogged, like De Man, by the persistent and troubling sense that language speaks most about language. We are smitten, since Derrida, with shame for our clinging so long to belief in the quasi-magical correspondence between words and the things they represent.[114]

But the metaphysics of presence Derrida excoriates as *logocentrism,* which dates back to Plato's *Cratylus,* had peculiar valance for the "Greek" and "Hellene" Victorians. *Blackwood's* noticed in 1864, for example, the sense of "occult connection between . . . primitive words, and the things signified" latent in Müller's theory of linguistic *roots* (October: 402). Belief in the power of language and literature to elevate or deprave endured: the soul-saving word, the "fatal book."[115] Such contradictory persistence shaped the "moral crisis" of language (Barthes, *Mythologies* 135) that swept England from the mid-nineteenth century. It survived even into the 1880s, when comparativist philology triumphed in Oxford and Cambridge, the *Junggrammatische* school began its challenge for disciplinary domination, and words were reduced to "one object of knowledge among others" (Foucault, *Order* 297).

Here was the threat as well as the comfort inherent in Matthew Arnold's redefinitions of "God" and "religion." Putting the "consecrated style" to euphemistic duty opened wide the gap between words and things, signifiers and what they signified; it was a nasty revelation of the arbitrariness of the sign. For a range of literate doubters and unbelievers, from upper-class Agnostics to disreputable Freethinkers, the revitalization of language was a critical issue: the desacralization of "Bible English" demanded a concomitant return to linguistic basics. And regeneration would have to come from below. "Say what you have to say," advises an 1889 essay on style, "in the simplest, the most direct and exact manner possible, with no surplusage." It reads like an exhortation from the young Holyoake's Word Books. We must "restore to words their primitive power" of delivering to us the world, reestablish "the natural and direct relationship between thought and expression, between the sensation and the term." Both statements are Walter Pater's, the first from his "Essay on Style" (34), the second from his solitary novel of 1885, *Marius the Epicurean,* set in second-century Rome (55). *Marius the Epicurean* registers philology's impact, especially Müller's, even in its vocabulary: Dowling picks out *"clauses* of experience," the *"transitive"* quality of life (132). It offers too a striking literary parallel to the vernacular rebellion with which the editor of the *Freethinker* met late Victorian verbal anxiety.

"[T]he rehabilitation of the mother tongue" is the project of Flavian, a low-born natural leader gifted with "a fine instinctive sentiment of the exact value and power of words" (*Marius* 54). He is the hero of Marius's adolescence, embodiment of Pater's nostalgia for the young aesthete that he was. Reading the story of Cupid and Psyche recounted by Apuleius "in the vernacular" jolts him out of dalliance with the "foppery of words" towards the "secrets of utterance" (30). It makes a rebel of a timeserver, determined to lay open "tarnished and languid" literary language to the "thousand chance-tost gems of racy or picturesque expression" offered by "colloquial idiom" (50, 54).

For "the mother tongue" is "the sole object," Flavian muses, "of the only sort of patriotic feeling proper, or possible, for one born of slaves" (*Marius* 54). From the other end of the social spectrum, Walter Pater, aesthete and classicist, whose euphuistic recastings of language proved a way station on the road to decadence, "the first major writer of Victorian literature in its post-philological moment" (Dowling 5), seconds the lost voice of "vernaculous" Mr. Foote, vulgarian and blasphemer.[116] "The literary programme which Flavian . . . designed for himself would be a work, then, partly conservative or reactionary, . . . partly popular and revolutionary, asserting, so to term them, the rights of the proletariat of speech" (*Marius*

54–55). There is not lacking, even, to make the parallel most suggestive, a sense that pagan Flavian finds, as freethinking Foote perhaps secretly did, a lingering "ritual interest" in "sacred service to the mother-tongue" (56).

A second parallel hails from a source equally as unexpected: the imperial romances of Rider Haggard. To say (as does Wendy Katz) that because he "wrote much of his fiction at a reckless speed" Haggard had "about as much concern for language as a whirlwind for the victims left in its wake" (13) is to let metaphor run amuck. Rather, early contact with "primitive" Zulu unleashed in Haggard a marked nostalgia for that mythical moment when words and things converged.[117] It is its unrecognized, anxious sense of the strangeness of language that keeps *King Solomon's Mines* (1885) fresh to this day. The inaugurating novel of Haggard's best-selling career fantasizes a primal land where words still have absolute power—"the king's word is spoken, the king's doom is done" (143). Here, heroes undergo the apotheosis of word taboo—"your names . . . shall be as the names of dead kings, and he who speaks them shall die," a phenomenon carefully explained in "editorial" footnote (370n).[118] Haggard's surrogate Allan Quartermain penetrates the interior by the aid of a map inscribed by one Da Silvestra, "in the year 1590 with a cleft bone upon a remnant of my raiment, my blood being the ink" (28); home in England he sometimes signs his name with that same "pen" (100).

The most extreme case, however, of the resuturing of symbol and sensation occurs in Haggard's little-known one-gag novel of 1888, *Mr. Meeson's Will*, in which the repentant last testament of a rapacious publisher cast up on a desert island is tattooed on the shoulders of a fellow castaway, Augusta Smithers, a novelist whom he has swindled, with cuttlefish ink and a fishbone: *"I leave all my property to Eustace H. Meeson,"* his once-disinherited nephew (117). The episode speaks to late Victorian fascination with the written body of the New Zealand Maori, recently exhibited in London, recalling the ancient meanings of the verb, *writan:* to score, incise, carve, engrave with a sharp instrument. Rescued to England, Augusta becomes a living "doccymint" (114) who must be "filed in the [court] registry" (182) in the form of a photographic facsimile. (The latter is quickly swiped by newspapermen and erotic perverts [199], so that the case becomes notable for developments in the "law of photographic copyright" as well [201]: thus Haggard, who trained desultorily for the bar from 1880 to 1885, exacts novelistic revenge on that exclusive institution as well as on greedy publishers.) At the book's close, signs are reunited with objects, and Eustace is installed as the patriarchal "owner" of both when he marries Augusta.

Foote could never aspire to Haggard's social and literary acceptance, but he taught himself the same kind of stripped-down plain style that the Zulu romancer employed in now unread and underrated novels like *Nada the Lily* (1892). What colleagues called the "scholarly and studiously polite language" of Foote's early pieces (qtd. in Herrick, *Vision:* 7)—the idiom of the conservative mainstream, "copious" and Latinate, haltingly mastered by an autodidact, even one who worked in a West End library—gave way under pressure of the "Bradlaugh struggle" to economy, clarity, and the deft use of common vocabulary. To survey Foote's writings, from the pamphlets of the 1870s through his work at the *Freethinker* and his dry memoir *Prisoner for Blasphemy,* is to appreciate the development of a conscious polemical stylist. The early version of "The Creation Story," for example (the first in Foote's popular *Bible Romances* series), succumbs to the self-conscious pomposity of the self-taught; the later version supplies full footnotes and scholarly equipment, swelling from eight to sixteen pages, but the heavy-handedness disappears. Some of the changes are minute: "even the clergy mostly disbelieve it" (1882: 1) becomes, more casually and more pointedly, "[they] are beginning to explain it away" (1904: 3).

Nonfiction models for the style he was searching for, if he needed them, were not hard to find. They were a Utilitarian, rationalist inheritance. Jeremy Bentham's hallmark neologisms, purged of ambiguity and historic connection (*codification, international,* among a host of unpronounceable Greek derivatives), and J. S. Mill's plainspoken pleas *On Liberty* and *An Autobiography* were quiet testimony to the power of secular and sparer language. Summing up in his own defense at his climactic third trial, Foote reached out for support to a closer contemporary: Leslie Stephen. "The use of the old phrases and the old forms is still enforced by the great sanction of respectability," declared Stephen's outspoken "Are We Christians?"; those who (like Arnold) "can cheat themselves into using the old charms" are merely "desperate" to "conjure down alarming social symptoms" among the "dangerous classes" (*Essays on Freethinking* 154, 150): such concealment of unspeakable facts in "words . . . which give the least shock" was nothing but euphemistic slipperiness (153). Foote commented, in a phrase richly suggestive of how language becomes belief, "No one who has any knowledge of *the kind of language held by intelligent men* will doubt that such sentiments [as Stephen's] are extremely common" (*Defence* 30, my emphasis).

Face to face, Godless Stephen could be the linguistic "brute" Mrs. Ramsay finds Mr. Ramsay to be in his daughter Virginia Woolf's *To the Lighthouse,* only one step above the "little atheist" he intrudes into the house. Taken to task by Carlyle for not revering the God whose Infinite Love created Hell, Stephen "could only reply," he wrote a friend, "in the words of the good Briton whose parson assured him that whom the Lord loveth he chasteneth, 'I wish he weren't so bloody fond of me' " (qtd. in Annan 236). The quip sounds the true *Freethinker* note, but it was not for general publication. Until he became an associate of the Rationalist Press Association towards the end of the century, Stephen the patrician agnostic had little to do with London's Freethinkers, though he was one of the few to rally to Bradlaugh's defense in the struggle of 1880–86, and, honorably (like his close friend, novelist Meredith), was "at least among those who protested against Foote's harsh sentence after his trial" (Annan 213–14). But he chose his essay titles as carefully as Foote picked his courtroom quotations. They speak, again, an unexpected solidarity with the blasphemous editor's beliefs about language. "Freethinking" and "plainspeaking" were terms Stephen inherited from the eighteenth century whose intellectual history he wrote. To put them together, however, in a title of 1873, *Essays on Freethinking and Plainspeaking*, the book in which he publicly nailed his colors to the mast, was also deliberately to co-opt the offensive labels chosen for themselves by Foote's beleaguered atheistical ancestors of mid-century.[119]

Mill was right to stress that outspokenness would quash ill-founded belief in the ill will of unbelievers, Stephen writes in "An Apology for Plainspeaking" (1873). But: "It is, I venture to remark, still more important to destroy the belief of sceptics themselves that in these matters a system of pious frauds is creditable or safe." "Equivocation," "reticence," and the plain misuse of religious language cannot be other than culturally "effeminating and corrupting" (*Freethinking* 328). Stephen's more famous *Agnostic's Apology* of 1876, published the year after he relinquished holy orders, which made current Huxley's coinage "agnostic" of 1869, exhorted men "to admit openly, what you whisper under your breath or hide in technical jargon, that the ancient secret is a secret still" (41). (By *apology*, Stephen meant not a retraction in the modern sense but the frankest of explanatory apologias.) Stephen himself wrote an English remarkable for its clarity, its literalness, and its refusal to "allow words to carry meanings other than they are given in normal conversation" (Annan 247). Noel Annan accounts for his hostility to the liberal theologian F. D. Maurice entirely in terms of linguistic fervor: by turning denotative into connotative language, literal fact into poetic truth, Maurice was undermining "the logic of language as a means of communication," perverting "the meaning of meaning" (246). He had even invented a new tense, Stephen snorted, "the conjectural preterite" (qtd. 247).[120]

The vehicle by which to revitalize English might be the baldly rational "Enlightened" English of the eighteenth century, as in Stephen's case; it might be the logic of the schools and the legal idiom of the master, Ben-

tham. Or it might be the language of science. It was inevitable that the
new "Revelation" should offer a new linguistic model. Scientific terms, it
was felt, expressed a much clearer relationship to the things for which they
stood, exactly as new scientific knowledge granted a more precise understanding of the material world. At the beginning of his career at the Birmingham Mechanical Institute the young Holyoake made notes towards
teaching his first mathematics class on 31 March 1839, echoing (whether he
knew it or not) the supposition of Locke, as if mathematics were a kind
of unmarked and secular language: "All circumlocution is avoided. No unmeaning word is used. No ambiguous ones. . . . Nothing visionary is admitted" (diary for 1839, in HC). So influential was the scientific model that
its detractors were driven to methods like the *Freethinker*'s. Professor Tait
picked out the most packed sentence in Sir Edmund Beckett's *Origin of
the Laws of Nature* to "translate" into "plain English" in a review of 1879.
Beckett's description of evolution as "a change from an indefinite, incoherent homogeneity to a definite, coherent heterogeneity" became a change
"from a no-howish, untalkaboutable, all-alikeness, to a somehowish and
in-general-talkaboutable not-all-alikeness" (qtd. in Spencer 141). Herbert
Spencer added Tait to his list of linguistic demons (mostly philosophers,
addicted to "verbal fictions" [141]) in an 1880 "Appendix, Dealing with
Certain Criticisms" to his *First Principles.*

Science was fortunate in its two preeminent champions, Darwin and
Huxley, who combined simplicity with eloquence: Darwin, as Desmond
and Moore record, at cost of much vomiting, misery, and crumpled sheets
of paper. The one speaks for himself above, the other (his "bulldog"), Foote
quoted at length in court, savoring lines like, "Extinguished theologians lie
about the cradle of every science as the strangled snakes beside that of Her-
cules" (*Defence* 31). As important in his day was Stephen's friend W. K.
Clifford, whose influence was magnified and sanctified by his early death
in 1879. He employed in the philosophical lectures and writings in which
he strained to lay down a physical basis for social morality the same neutral
and pared-down language he used as scientist and mathematician.[121] "Advanced" writers on all topics aimed at a similar directness.

Yet what a hopeless task it was, this "rehabilitation of the mother-
tongue." The models inevitably were lacking. Her father Leslie Stephen
may have written prose that was "witty and bright without a single dead
sentence in it," Virginia Woolf decided, "Yet he is not a writer for whom
I have a natural taste. Just as a dog takes a bite of grass, I take a bite of
him medicinally" (qtd. in Annan 133). Even scientific language was part of
the problem as Martin Jay construes it, interpreting Foucault: when "scientific language struggles to turn itself . . . into a transparent record of the

observing gaze," all language becomes uncomfortable (188). Language grows, as Lord Coleridge in 1883 claimed that law does, and as philology was dramatically beginning to prove to the whole nation; it is not susceptible to cultivation on petri dishes. Completely invented and unmarked languages, with rules that made plain sense, like Dr. Steiner's brainchild of the 1880s, "Pasalingua," a simplistic mélange of Teutonic and Romantic, were unprofitable enterprises: "When men can buil[d] up a brain in the laboratory," commented Annie Besant in her magazine *Our Corner*, "they may hope to formulate a language in the study."[122]

The quest for models intensified in proportion to the hopelessness of the search. For the new language of freethinking men and secular women did not need only to restore relations with the real world of facts. If that were enough, the parched and emphatic idiom of the Benthamites might have satisfied—Mill without his Wordsworthian revelation, as it were, unmercifully parodied in Dicken's *Hard Times:* "Now, what I want is, Facts" (47). Revitalized English needed also to reflect the full spectrum of human emotion, aspiration, and experience. Thus literature was methodically ransacked not only for its teachings but for the resonance of its language, as if that were a pure function of vocabulary. Here was one source of Shakespeare's power for all Victorians. The same need led to the cult of Swinburne and his richly sensuous poetic language in the Freethought press; it fanned the flames of admiration in England for Emerson's "unhesitating and audacious expressions," as "crisp and precise as proverbs" (*Freethinker,* 7 May 1882: 146); it warmed the Secularist welcome for full-bodied Whitman; it guaranteed a hearty reception, despite its thin-skinned and tenuous quality, for the *Autobiography of Mark Rutherford* and the same sufferer's *Deliverance.* (Hale White's publishers, Trübner's, knew what they were doing when they took advertising space in Holyoake's *Present Day;* they were rewarded with the old man's encomium on White's "singular perfection of style" [September 1885: 25]. Trübner's were Holyoake's own publishers.) The need for a *rich* new language made James Thomson the first "laureate" of Freethought, finding poetry—before *Prufrock* or T. S. Eliot—in the language of the streets, making meaning out of ugliness and vulgarity, in default of beauty, so long as meaning was made.[123] It created ears that might hear what John Davidson was about in rejecting literary language for the reviled idiom of the newspapers and the streets, in his plainspoken urban ballads of the 1890s:

> I ain't blaspheming, Mr. Silver-tongue;
> I'm saying things a bit beyond your art.
> ("Thirty Bob a Week" lines 31–32)

A desperate straining after emotional resonance and spiritual effect makes itself felt in the Secularists' own productions, the "hymn books" and services for Naming of Infants and Secular Funeral like those in "Mr. Gladstone's 'Questionable Book,'" *The Secularists' Manual of Songs and Ceremonies,* over which their best minds toiled. Shelley's idiom informs the new compositions, and Swinburne's *Songs Before Sunrise* were cannibalized for the hymn books, though competition with the Salvation Army may rather have dictated this reworking of "Onward, Christian Soldiers": "Guide us, Truth, thou Star refulgent, / Trav'llers through a darksome land; / We are weak, but thou art mighty / To support our social band" (*Manual* 26). You cannot manufacture aura, as Walter Benjamin told the twentieth century. "Language is the depository of the accumulated body of experience," Farrar quoted Mill in his *Chapters on Language* (297). Cut off from "all former ages," faithless modern man seemed condemned, as the author of the *New Cratylus* put it in 1839, to "the careful but barren elegances of logical prose" (qtd. in Burrow 193). "[The] new order, constructed by the reason," Leslie Stephen wrote in his *History of English Thought in the Eighteenth Century,* "remains colourless and uninteresting, because the old associations have not yet gathered around it" (1: 14). Torn from the holdfast of "Bible English," language seemed to stutter. In the often overloaded and oddly mannered compositions of Secularism, we encounter the same problem of random sacralization in a desacralized world that Baudelaire perceived. "High" and "sub"-literature faced identical problems.

Foote did not escape it, particularly at the beginning of his career, and particularly when he turned aside from the negative work of "Bible-smashing." There is something lumpish in his attempt at pagan reverence in a Christmas address for 1882, for example: "Eat, drink, and be merry; for the sun-god bursts through the womb of winter, and gives promise of another fertilizing spring, ripening summer, and teeming autumn. Your pale-faced Galilean is a thing of yesterday compared with him" (*Freethinker,* 24 December: 401). Meredith put his finger on the problem, although he was not much more adept at avoiding it: *Diana of the Crossways* lives in permanent suspicion of the "plush of speech" that "haunts all efforts to swell and illuminate citizen prose to a princely poetic" (38). The stuttering compositions of subliterary Secularism provide a background for understanding high literature's decadent re-descent into euphemism in the 1890s. *The Picture of Dorian Grey* (1891) makes as much subversive play with respectability's verbal tic as does music hall's Marie Lloyd.

The subject of death produced the greatest strain. "Is not the taboo word *death* above all others," asks the philosopher Jankelevitch, "the unpronounceable, unnameable, unspeakable monosyllable?" (qtd. in Gross 202).

Death seemed to demand euphemism. Eighteenth-century France talked of *journey, voyage,* the *door,* and the *refuge;* Greek and Latin epitaphs imagine death as a *home* or an *inn,* and speak of *nightfall, leave-taking,* and the actor *making his exit* (Gross 208). In England a core group of prettier euphemisms were well established by 1837: *falling asleep, going to meet one's maker, departing this life.* But the euphemistic possibilities proliferated under Victoria, particularly following the Indian Mutiny and the Crimean debacle. Victorians left for *a better life, the beyond,* or *Happier Hunting Grounds;* they were taken to *Abraham's bosom, their last home,* and *eternal rest;* they *joined the invisible choir* and *crossed over Jordan's banks;* they went *to their final rewards, their Fathers,* and *to glory.* The people who buried them were elevated to *undertakers,* burial became *interment,* tombstones became *cemetery monuments.* Death that was the subject of such intensive defensive avoidance was bound to place most strain on the flimsy emotive structures of secular English.

Henry Hetherington's last will and testament offered itself as a model for an ill-fated "genre":

> As I never in thought, word, or deed, wilfully injured any human being, I hope that I shall be forgiven by those whom I may have inadvertently or unconsciously jostled in this world's scramble. . . . I . . . die in the hope and consolation that a time is approaching when the spirit of antagonism will give place to fraternal affection and universal co-operation to promote the happiness of mankind. (Holyoake, *Life and Character of Henry Hetherington* 10)

His death in 1849 left his friends so bereft of appropriate language in which to grieve that they contemplated burying him by the Christian book: "In point of solemnity and decorum," Holyoake fretted, "nothing is gained by dispensing with the Church service," unless "something as carefully considered" is "put in its place" (16). Yet when ladylike Annie Besant sat down to the task of composing an official burial service for the National Secular Society, poetic "plush" crept in to mar the effect: "Sad is death at all times. Sad even when Death comes in the evening of life, to lay on eyes dim with age the poppies of an endless sleep" (*N.S.S. Almanack,* 1884: 33). Even the American Ingersoll could not resist the temptation to strain:

> Again we are face to face with the great mystery that shrouds this world. We question, but there is no reply. Out on the wide waste of seas there drifts no spar. Over the desert of death the sphinx gazes for ever, but never speaks. ("Oration at the Grave of a Positivist," rpt. in *Present Day,* June 1883: 3)

The perils of plainness loomed as large. The much-quoted "almost sacred words" of the inscription on Clifford's tombstone only just hit their mark of stoic restraint: "I was not, and was conceived; I loved and did a little work; I am not, and grieve not" (qtd. in *Freethinker,* 13 October 1881: 97).

"The literature of the Grave, as suitable for those not of the Christian persuasion," Holyoake was left lamenting in the first number of his *Present Day*, June 1883, "is scant and poor, affording small choice as yet" (3).

The problem seemed inescapable: newness meant either overblown strain or disruptive rawness—and maybe prosecution. The old language of biblical echo, cultural resonance, and historical association was inadequate, vague, even contaminated, but it was rich. For Secularists, here was the choice to be made, with much at stake: to risk the traumas of revitalization or to accept the guarantee of cultural continuity that the dominant discourse offered; the linguistic rebellion of Foote or the conservatism of Holyoake.

Evidently, the choice was not for Secularists alone; the blasphemers among them, by whom they defined their tradition, were simply especially attuned to the problematics of words. This was a culturewide crisis, at a turning point in the history of the language: trial for blasphemy was both a product and a symptom. English came under peculiar pressure in the 1880s not only because the language lost its holdfast in "Bible English" or because, as we have seen, the vulgar voice of the common man was battering at the door of suffrage and public discourse. It was in this decade too that English took on the role it pretends to fulfill to this day, that of "universal" language. That turn awaits full academic study. But the crisis of language here traced found immediate and most offensive expression in the final fiction of a lower-class novelist shorn of faith and obsessed by words: Thomas Hardy's *Jude the Obscure*.

CHAPTER SIX

HARDY'S CRIME

Thomas Hardy and *Jude the Obscure,* no other author and no other text, are the fitting final destination of a book called *Word Crimes.* Not a single contemporary notice of Hardy's tragedy of failed love, marital traps, embittered aspiration, child murder, and God-forsaken suicide was pasted into his personal scrapbook of reviews, news, and interviews, still extant in Dorchester Museum. It is not hard to guess why. The horrors of the book's reception in 1895 are the cliché of critical history. Mrs. Oliphant, writing in *Blackwood's* through a haze of maternal grief and failing powers, undid a distinguished career in heaping anathema on anathema;[1] the lunatic fringe of reviewers decided Hardy had "made his home in the slime pits of Siddim" (qtd. in Gittings, *Hardy* 2: 83); the book turned England's "greatest living novelist" into "Hardy the Degenerate" (Lerner and Holmstrom 147). But the hysterical chorus was not without motivation. Blasphemy is both subject and willed effect of Hardy's swan song to fiction.

In the years that followed the *Freethinker* trials, fiction played knowingly with its potential for blasphemy. In *Plain Tales from the Hills* (1885), plain-speaking "hooligan" Kipling refigured blasphemy as both a crime against sacred empire and an escape valve for the manly brutishness that made its builders strong: "the voice we hear is always the voice of the soldier whose God is a cockney 'Gawd,' " charged his most vitriolic critic, "requisitioned for purposes of blasphemy and furious emphasis" (Buchanan 26). Blasphemy as Kipling reimagined it was both waste product and deep structure of the imperial dream.[2] In Wilde's *Picture of Dorian Gray* (1890–91), however, the offense that gives meaning to the plot qua plot ("This is blasphemy, Dorian!" [170]) really exists as an alibi for the seduction of the

reader that the *Picture* as "fatal book" will enact. His "vulgar" outburst kills
painter Basil Hallward, since (as Lord Henry Wotton puts it) "The man
who could call a spade a spade should be compelled to use one" (215), even
to dig his own grave.[3] A few years after *Jude*, the crime's tantalized commission in the *Turn of the Screw* (1898) allowed Henry James's sociopsychologi-
cal reinscription of the "dear old sacred terror" (preface, *Turn* 36). Horror
springs from the words of servants in the mouths of upper-class children,
"appalling" in both senses of the word (*Turn* 246); while it is the governess's
blasphemous bind that only by herself recommitting the crime can she
force little Miles to the "monstrous utterance of names" (213).[4] (The critics'
charge that he had "all too indecently expatiat[ed]" on his unmentionable
subject gave James ironical pleasure [preface, 42; *Turn* 147].) Blasphemy
resurfaced at the close of Conrad's *Heart of Darkness* (1899), as Marlow
assures Kurtz's "Intended" that the "last word he pronounced" was not his
famous reticent whisper—"The horror! the horror!" (68)—but *"your name"*
(76). Marlow thinks the utterance will bring down house and heaven on
his head (76), but the novella's real shock is its conflation of blasphemy
with its opposite, euphemism, a conflation that turns out to have been a
mere "trifle" (76), since words possess no divine trace or ultimate meaning.

None of these texts, however, *focus* on blasphemy like *Jude the Obscure.*
Some critics might call the novel "Jude the Obscene" (Cox 147),[5] just as
the *Freethinker* was pronounced "ribald," but that charge masked the more
heinous accusation. Modern criticism would do well to pay heed: only John
Goode puts a finger, in passing (in the words of his title), on the *Offensive
Truth. Jude* is a Victorian equivalent of the *Pardoner's Tale* anatomized
with incisive clarity by David Lawton. It "condemns blasphemy; produces
blasphemy; and is blasphemy," working a "horror of infinite regression"
(101).

Structured around a sequence of blasphemous scenes, surprisingly innocent of commentary, *Jude* works across the historical registers to invoke
blasphemy both in traditional religious terms and as the class crime of language and offense against literary values that the debacle of 1883 had made
of it. No great Victorian novel was ever more bereft of cultural alibi: *Jude*
eschews every accommodation, every act of self-censorship, of "advanced"
novelists like Mrs. Ward and George Du Maurier; it baffles the graces of
Hardy's own earlier fiction. Most dangerously, in *Jude* blasphemy becomes
a logical response to a universe gone awry: the novel asserts its own and
its hero's right to commit the crime. To make its offensive case, *Jude* plays
variations on the illegal themes of Mr. Foote's penny paper. And it remi-
nisces in painful detail the case of the most "obscure" of all "martyrs" to
the laws of blasphemous libel. In short, *Jude the Obscure* commits blas-

phemy with a vengeance that can have left the perpetrator in no doubt, despite his disclaimers, of the full stop it would put to his fiction career. The *Pall Mall Gazette*'s outraged summary of the action—"dirt, drivel, and damnation" (Lerner and Holmstrom 111)—was not mere glib alliteration but a grimly accurate picture of the blasphemous text that closed the book on Victorian fiction, and opened readers' eyes to the shock of the modernist new.

1. COMMITTING LITERARY BLASPHEMY

The unspeakable charge had been half audible already in Andrew Lang's notice of *Tess*, which led to a public exchange of letters.[6] It was loudly whispered in the reviews of *Jude*. "Throughout the book," said the Christian *Guardian*, in the tone of prosecuting counsel set by the trials of 1883, "a great many insulting things are said about marriage, religion, and all the obligations and relations of life which most people hold sacred" (Lerner and Holmstrom 112). Hardy's own comments marshaled the same terms. Thirty years after the event, he recalled how he was "excommunicated" by the critics, those "Hammers of Heretics," legally licensed to indulge in "contumelious" libels (*Life and Work* 292, 297). The blasphemous echo sounded even in the few journals that came out in his defense. "So active, so malignant have these sanitary inspectors of fiction become," feared H. G. Wells in the *Saturday*, "that a period of terror, analogous to that of the New England Witch Mania, is upon us" (Lerner and Holmstrom 135).[7] Author, attackers, and apologists speak to us in concert, we might even say with complicity, about the crime *Jude* represents.

It was so recognizable partly because the novel's genre was once so familiar. Antithetical *Jude* sets its irreligious irregularities against the familiar background of the Victorian novel of faith and doubt. It did not escape the *Guardian*'s pious reviewer that it is precisely as Jude is thinking "how he might become even a Bishop"—at five thousand pounds a year—"by leading a pure, energetic, wise, Christian life" that the notorious pig's penis, limp annunciator of sex and Arabella Donn, smacks him in the face (Lerner and Holmstrom 112); the novel's miserable denouement plays off the Victorian cliché (best known from Tennyson's "Despair") of the benighted atheist for whom suicide is finally the only option.[8] Religion informs the smallest action: Sue's employer, Miss "Fontover," say, tearing a hole "about as big as a [Communion] wafer" in the brown paper in which Sue has wrapped up her plaster idols of Venus and Apollo (*Jude* 96). Most importantly, *Jude*/Jude's quest for education is entangled in religion's web: *Jude*'s very name for Oxford, "Christminster," points to the city's dual signification, while the college from which Jude receives the practical tip to get back to his stonemason's tools goes by the Huxleyan name of "Biblioll College."

The religious dimension looms largest when we look at *Jude the Obscure* as also the story of Sue. Hardy sent a bowdlerized version for serialization in *Harper's New Monthly Magazine* the year before final volume publication, under the title *The Simpletons* (December 1894 to November 1895). When that title turned out to be the title of another book, he renamed the novel *Hearts Insurgent;* a third change of mind—*The Recalcitrants*—reached the compositors too late to use. All the plural titles were better titles. To stretch the terms of Newman's 1848 title, *Loss and Gain,* as much as this novel is the story of Jude's "loss" of "faith," it is also the ironic counterstory of Sue's "gain."

Gissing had laid some groundwork for such offensive counterpoint in his 1890 *Born in Exile,* in which atheist Godwin Peak seems to change places with Christian Sidwell Warricombe.[9] But another, weightier text had marked out *Jude's* thematic territory: *Robert Elsmere.* Hardy made copious notes on the keynote novel of the *Freethinker* decade when it appeared in 1888 (*Literary Notebook* 211–13); he wrote deferentially of her greater "success" to Mrs. Ward just after *Tess* was published (12 April 1892, *Letters* 1: 263). In making of Sue and Jude a weatherman and a weatherwoman who (like the figures on the old clock) can never be out or in together and at the same time, Hardy parodied Ward's portrait of the "clash of two . . . tendencies of thought" (Ward, *Recollections* 230) in modern Elsmere and his "Bunyan-like" wife Catherine (*Elsmere* 85). Medieval "faithful" Jude moves stage by familiar Victorian stage towards Sue's position of reasoned and ironical Freethought, while Sue descends by degrees through the trauma of her children's death into repentance, penance, conviction of sin, and thence to spiritual prostration, the mortification of the flesh, and a state she herself recognizes, in a last flash of mental clarity, as superstitious "savagery" (*Jude* 361). It is an unflinching study in Christian pathology, couched in grimly "High Churchy" tones, and almost unreadable to pious contemporaries like Mrs. Oliphant.[10]

In *Elsmere,* Mrs. Ward sought to find a new psychological basis for Christianity;[11] in his famous review, Prime Minister Gladstone claimed that the beauty of character of many Christians was proof in itself of the "Christian scheme" (*Nineteenth Century,* May 1888: 784). In *Jude,* the religious spirit is subjected instead to psychological disintegration. Pious feelings are outgrowths of momentary depression (Arabella after Cutlett's death); social climbing (Arabella; Jude the "prospective Bishop, or what not" [42]; and—to a degree—the Phillotson who takes back his estranged wife Sue); ignorant parroting of received ideas (Jude before he meets Sue); sickness and mental breakdown (Jude after the smash-up of his college hopes, when he decides that "obscure" service as a "humble curate" might be "a purgatorial course worthy of being followed by a remorseful man" [133]; Sue, after the children's deaths and her miscarriage); even the sublimation of sexual instincts (Jude's "ecstasy" to think he might find in Sue a "companion in Anglican worship" [93]). "Save-your-own-soulism" is ultimately construed as immoral selfishness, as Jude is left alone to lament, "I'd have sold my soul for her sake, but she wouldn't risk hers a jot for me." (The compound term is surely an offensive memory of Arnold's "Just-what-you-like-ism.")[12] "To save her own soul she lets mine go damn!" (395). Worst, Sue's "conversion" is made retrospectively to justify what the novel shows is pointless: "My children—are dead—and it is right that they should be! . . . their death was the first stage of my purification" (383–84). The orthodox sentiment drops like a stone into a context where it cannot but be questioned. Some have called spiritual autobiography and the novel of faith and doubt the true ancestors of modern psychological fiction:[13] *Jude* sourly proves the lineage.

Inversion came easily to the Victorians who built secular halls and wrote secular hymnbooks. Sue even plays on the unseemly idea that Jude's journey is an anti-pilgrim's progress: "You are in the Tractarian stage just now, are you not?" she asks, "Let me see—when was I there?" (156). Like Dorothea in *Middlemarch,* Jude is a belated saint, "Joseph the dreamer of dreams," martyred St. Stephen, or "a tragic Don Quixote" (215). And while Mrs. Ward's Catherine Elsmere speaks the motto (from John 6.63) that lets her keep faith with her apostate husband—"My Lord is my Lord always; but He is yours too. . . . It is the spirit that quickeneth" (510), a directly oppositional text (2 Corinthians 3.6) provides the epigraph to *Jude:* "The letter killeth." The obvious reminiscence shoved the novel fuller into the reader's face. Jude Fawley is a more subversively powerful model for the common man's experience of loss of faith than is saintly, upper-crust Robert Elsmere.

It was a short step from embittered religious saturation to outright irreligious offensiveness. Much has been said about the long-sustained comparison of "predestinate Jude," for whom there is "no room at the inn" in Christminster, to the suffering human Jesus (indeed, legend gives the name Jude to one of Christ's obscure brothers, as well as to the patron saint of failures). The same analogy lies at the heart of George Eliot's Religion of Christ and of *Robert Elsmere*'s New Brotherhood. But Jude shares his identification with Christ the martyr, prosecuted for blasphemy, with G. W. Foote as well (see *Prisoner* 38, 39, 48, 63, 153, 157). Its climax is Hardy's daring reworking of Mark 15.38, the moment of Christ's death: "And the veil of the temple was rent in twain from the top to the bottom." When Sue declares that she must return to Phillotson, Jude responds:

> "Then let the veil of our temple be rent in two from this hour!"
>   He went to the bed, removed one of the pair of pillows thereon, and flung it on the floor. (373)

It was not for nothing that this scene was cut from the *Harper's* version. There is a point at which *imitatio Christi* slips into blasphemous parody. This scene has certainly reached it.

Jude's affronted reviewers reached instinctively for the punishment the book deserved: burning. Like the *Necessity of Atheism* (1811) by Sue's (and Hardy's) iconoclastic spiritual father, Shelley, and like Froude's *Nemesis of Faith* (1849), publicly burnt at Oriel College, *Jude* fell prey to what Hardy called "the fire-&-faggot system of suppressing heresy" (*Literary Notebook* 62). "Among other appreciations, he received a letter containing a packet of ashes" from an outraged reader in Australia, "which the virtuous writer stated to be those of his wicked novel" (*Life and Work* 288). Then, "at the very height of the [London] season," the Bishop of Wakefield "theatrically" "announced in a letter to the papers that he had thrown Hardy's novel into the fire" (294).[14] The "conflagratory bishop" (Hardy, postscript to *Jude* [1978] 7), as Goode dryly notes, "was surely right to burn Hardy's novel" (141).

Hardy had shown him the way, staging a sequence of sacrificial burnings in the novel itself—first of its heretics' books, then of their clothes, and finally of their bodies: Jude stands over the pyre of his "theological and ethical works" (*Jude* 228) with a fork, an image still more designed to offend than Alec D'Urberville demonically brandishing the required implement at Tess's allotment bonfire; Sue "burn[s] by the flames" the nightgown she bought to please Jude (385); staggering feverish through the Christminster streets after his last earthly sight of Sue's face, Jude comes again on the spot where they first planned to meet: "This—is th' Martyrs—burning place. . . . I remember . . . old Fuller in his Holy State says, that at the burning of [Bishop] Ridley," by "Bloody" Queen Mary, "Doctor Smith—preached sermon, and took as his text 'Though I give my body to be burned, and have not charity, it profiteth me nothing,'—Often think of it as I pass here. Ridley was a ———" (396). Martyr, heretic, blasphemer, pioneer of a new honesty to which the world will not lend ear, there is a weight of meaning behind Jude's final realization: "I'm giving my body to be burned!" (396).

The trope of burning fits strategically into *Jude's* blasphemous framework. Part 1 spotlights two set scenes of worship. In the one, the boy Jude kneels to the holy city enhaloed in the distance; in the second, on the same spot, he humbles himself to the "shiny goddess" (30), the moon: the scenes are equally bred of "impulsive emotion" and "curious superstition" (30). Part 2 deploys similar parallel scenes. In the first, Sue attends a service in Christminster Cathedral. In the second, she conducts her own before her plaster "saints" (105), Venus and Apollo, with Gibbon's chapter on Julian the Apostate for sermon and Swinburne's "Hymn to Proserpine" as song for the day, the very poem that G. W. Foote read in court:

> Thou hast conquered, O pale Galilean: The world has grown grey from thy breath! (97)

(Aptly, Swinburne's lines were an improvisation on the Apostate's dying words, *"Vicisti, Galilaee."*) Meanwhile across the city Jude too is "mumbl[ing]" aloud "strange syllables" with primitive power of "enchantment":

> All hemin heis Theos ho Pater, ex hou ta pant, kai hemeis eis auton. . . .
> Kai heis Kurios Iesous Christos, di hou panta kai hemeis di autou! (97)

The words are from the Greek New Testament (I Corinthians 8.6), a central passage from the creed.[15] But "realism," or literal-minded rationalism, breaks them down into "inexplicable sounds," while the carefully chosen verb "mumbled," placed so near "enchantment" as to infect its meaning, suggests that they are "mumbo-jumbo"—an inane incantation to a primitive idol, the worship of an "object of unintelligent veneration" (*OED*). The term became current in the years between the *Freethinker* case and the publication of *Jude*.

The next count in the novel's indictment concerns the pitiful scene in which Jude, in his cups, recites the Nicene Creed in a Christminster tavern (fig. 18). He is egged on by Tinker Taylor, "who appeared to have been of a religious turn in earlier years, but was somewhat blasphemous now" (122), and introduced like a music hall "turn" by an undergraduate who has come to buy a dog: "The gentleman in the corner is going to rehearse the Articles of his Belief, in the Latin tongue, for the edification of the company" (124). Jude begins:

> "Credo in unum Deum, Patrem omnipotentum, Factorem coeli et terrae, visibilium omnium et invisibilium."

Untranslated, alien, made strange: the words are more mumbo-jumbo. So Jude realizes, turning on his audience: "It might have been the Ratcatcher's Daughter in double dutch for all that your besotted heads can tell!" (125). The reference, which has escaped polite commentary, is to one of the most popular music hall songs of the century: learning and religion are thus at one low blow assaulted.

"JUDE STOOD UP AND BEGAN RHETORICALLY."

Figure 18. Staging blasphemy: Jude recites the creed in a Christminster tavern. One
of Hatherell's illustrations for the serialization in *Harper's*. All except the last
expressed a profound discomfort with picturing Hardy's hero face on.

Next is Jude's solitary death scene, which Goode remarks "surely parodies the climactic funeral of Mr. Gray at Oxford in *Robert Elsmere*" (167).
It goes further, I think, than that. There is an element of blasphemous
imitatio in Jude's intoning of biblical text, while the disconnected "responses" of the holiday crowd outside, watching the boat races, turn the
scene into an anti–church service. Typographical distinction underlines the
liturgical format:

> *"Let the day perish wherein I was born, and the night in which it was said, There
> is a man-child conceived."*
> ("Hurrah!")
> *"Let that day be darkness; let not God regard it from above, neither let the light
> shine upon it. Lo, let that night be solitary, let no joyful voice come therein."*
> ("Hurrah!") (426)

Like Hone and Foote, the Hardy of *Jude* lives by parody. His rewriting of the Ten Commandments may stand with Clough's or Bierce's. Maddened by grief, Sue bursts out, "There is something external to us which says, 'You shan't!' First it said, 'You shan't learn!' Then it said, 'You shan't labor!' Now it says, 'You shan't love!'" (356). Earlier, she and Jude are ousted by local gossips from their job "relettering" the Commandments on the wall of a local church (315). The verb is wonderfully suggestive, and the incident recalls Wilde's flippant mention of the "Twenty" Commandments: as Richard Ellmann puts it, "[t]o miscount was to discount" (63), and to "reletter" was to write down. This is the import of the embedded story a churchwarden tells the gossips: the devil who once finished off the same job for a group of drunken workmen left out all the "Not's" (318). By such errors, as Foote joked, we shall not be "changed" but "hanged": this kind of manhandling of sacred text was a job for "militant" Secularists. There is a careful argumentativeness of structure in such episodes as these (as in *Jude*'s apparently "providential" moments), an awareness of offensiveness—in legal parlance, an *intention*—that makes the offense more.

Jude knows what crime it is he commits as well as his creator. The word *"blasphemy"* had intruded oddly into Hardy's language in the wake of the *Freethinker* case (for example, see the *Woodlanders* [1886–87] 144; 231); in *Jude* it is forced on the reader's attention, in all its new density of meaning(s). "My heart is nearly broken," Jude laments to Sue, "So I have been drinking, and blaspheming, or next door to it, and saying holy things in disreputable quarters—repeating in idle bravado words which ought never to be uttered but reverently! . . ." (126). A fairly accurate traditionalist definition. The head of Sue's teacher training college repeats the same story, in the same terms (147). The fatal word sticks out with rather different effect in Jude's remark to Sue: "Isn't it enough to make one blaspheme" that the composer of a favorite hymn "is one of the most commonplace men I ever met?" (212).

Something is going on here that we cannot ascribe to Satanic inversion or atheistical destructiveness. In *After Strange Gods* (1934), T. S. Eliot lamented that blasphemy in the twentieth century meant precisely what the nineteenth had reshaped it to mean: a breach of good taste, a lapse of language, "bad form" (51). Genuine blasphemy, in its traditional sense, was "a symptom that the soul is still alive" (53), in "reproach" of a secular modern world "in which blasphemy is impossible" (52). Unless the blasphemer "profoundly believes in that which he profanes," he no more blasphemes than a parrot that picks up swear words (52): for this reason, Eliot added, maliciously, it was impossible for Bernard Shaw to blaspheme.

For Hardy it was perhaps possible. He writes in his journal on 29 January 1890 that "I have been looking for God 50 years, and I think that if he had existed I should have discovered him" (*Life and Work* 234). Yet on 9 May he records, "man has done more with his materials than God has done with his" (236). At one moment, God does not exist; at the next he not only exists but is culpably negligent. The entries are typical; they are only two pages apart. As the *Life* confirms, Hardy was determined to let the paradox stand. Half in and half out of the Christian fold, he was a "believing" "agnostic" (Ford 296; Hardy, *Life and Work* 302), an infidel moralist "touched" (as Arnold might put it) by religious "emotion." Patricia Ingham, *Jude's* modern editor, believes its allusions to the Bible "typically contradict the spirit of what he cites" (438). But Hardy is no straightforward "Bible-smasher"; the language and stories of the Bible (a network of Mosaic references recently recovered, for example, or Jude's deathbed scene), remain precariously viable throughout the novel.[16] And so too, therefore, does the crime of blasphemy, even as traditionally conceived.

The danger of Hardy's position was evident. *Jude* painted a "grotesque" and "repellent" view of a "spiteful Providence," thundered the *Athenaeum* (Cox 249). "What has Providence done to Mr. Hardy," said agnostic Gosse in a notice that strained their friendship, "that he should rise up in the arable land of Wessex and shake his fist at his Creator?" (Lerner and Holmstrom 121). For G. K. Chesterton in the *Victorian Age in Literature* (1913), Hardy finds it necessary to "invent" "Him" (i.e. God) in order "to prove how unnecessary"—even "poisonous"—"He is" (144). When Hardy wrote "frankly" to decline nomination as president of the Society of Authors in June 1909, he gave as the single reason for his refusal the fact that

> One of my last poems was called blasphemous by the Guardian, & the Spectator has shaken its head over another. I have had a book burnt by a bishop & the fact announced in the papers. No recent English writer has been so roundly abused by the press as I have been, . . . with the single exception of Swinburne, & he is dead. (*Letters* 4: 28)[17]

And yet, it was not for blasphemy as subject, nor for the novel's blasphemous structure, nor for its utterance of the forbidden word, nor even by dint of the painful trace of lingering faith that infused his self-consciousness of crime that Hardy's novel was incinerated in 1895. There was more to the commission of blasphemy as a specifically literary crime than that. Three weighty reasons secured the verdict of "guilty." First, *Jude* is an ugly, relentless, self-conscious novel that makes no compensatory amends and supplies no alibi for its heretical nastiness. Second, it is a text in which we hear the outlawed voice of the mocking *Freethinker* more distinctly than in any other "serious" literature of the era. Third, *Jude* is excruciatingly plainspoken: a red rag to the bull of class-conscious criticism that alerts us also to the novel's most deeply repressed historical source. The artistic right Hardy claimed in *Jude*—as in his 1891 essay "Candour in English Fiction"—to write the "explicit" novel (*Personal Writings* 132) was nothing other than a recipe for the perfect Victorian word crime.

2. "GET IT DONE AND LET THEM HOWL"

i. No More Alibis

Near the bottom of the outrage over *Jude* was a sense that Hardy had let Literature down. To understand what put a match to smoldering anger, one must look at the novel's lack of the fictional alibis that other transgressive texts tendered their readers.

Jude has no Cockney baiting to make class amends for its sin of unfaith, unlike Gissing's *Born in Exile* (see above, 3.2). It has no ideology of "nice clean English" and inviting provision of French-language scapegoats, unlike the phenomenal hit that preceded it in the pages of *Harper's,* George Du Maurier's *Trilby.* The latter is a sanitized Bohemian romance of a fallen angel who thinks that hell is a fiction, and whose lover spends twelve pages rhapsodizing on Darwin and "snigger[ing]" at the idiocies of church belief (278). It is her "infallible" enunciation (318) of "nice, clean English" (120) through "thirty two British teeth" (72) that redeems the eponymous heroine; while *Trilby's* digressive format and "April day" freshness of style further "swe[pt] away judgment" (*Atlantic,* qtd. in Purcell 68–69).[18] Above all, *Jude* wants the conservative counterweights that made *Robert Elsmere* not only a spiritual succès d'estime but "the most popular novel of the century" (Sutherland, *Ward* 658), a promotional property used to boost sales (amongst other products) of Maine's Balsam Fir Soap (Willey, "*Elsmere*" 57).[19] The very qualities that dated and compromised *Elsmere's* art as a novel secured its accommodating reception. It is perhaps the perfect "control" for Hardy's "experiment."

Elsmere's counterweights included the emotional backdating to the 1840s that made it a theological "cock-crow over yesterday's sunrise" (Conway, qtd. in Peterson 160);[20] a reassuringly "old-fashioned" and "stately" three-decker format (Henry James, *English Illustrated Magazine,* March 1892: 401); the saintly death and class-conscious pronouncements of the apostate hero in whom it bids us have faith (see above, 3.2: *Elsmere* is half novel, half hagiography, a genre in which Ward had trained);[21] its provision of easy targets for reader hostility in the demonic skeptical squire who saps *Elsmere's* faith and his too-pious wife, "the Thirty-nine Articles in the flesh" (*Elsmere* 162); and the workings of its compensatory double-plot mechanism, which supplies punishment for female sin (represented by reckless,

artistic Rose, Catherine's sister) as the narrative price of Elsmere's transgression. *Elsmere's* last strategy, whereby marital reconciliation presents itself
as theological resolution, is a "primitive" novelistic ploy (Sutherland's term,
Ward 125) that looks forward to the simplifications of Hollywood cinema.[22]
Moreover, like its hero the book is " 'earnest' with a vengeance" (*Elsmere*
64), with "[n]ot one least bitter word in it!" (Burne-Jones, qtd. in Ward,
Recollections 245); it observes to the full Lord Chief Justice Coleridge's "decencies of controversy." Even its off-putting density was one of what Gladstone called its "compensations" (*Nineteenth Century*, May 1888: 766): it
was set up in a size of type generally used for religious texts. And critics
like "Mr. G" felt bound to be "very charming personally" to "Dear Mrs.
Ward" (Ward, *Recollections* 237, 238). *Robert Elsmere* launched her career
as "the greatest Englishwoman of our time," as Dean Inge called her at her
funeral in 1920 (qtd. in Peterson 1), Ezra Pound's primly virginal "Great
Mary" (qtd. 3), the actual projector of rescue schemes in the East End first
fantasized in her famous fiction. She had felt herself "born for religion"
(Ward, *Recollections* 230): *Elsmere's* exquisitely reverential manner was that
lost dream's linguistic trace.

Generically distinct from Ward's "propagandist romance" (Gladstone,
Nineteenth Century, May 1888: 766), from Du Maurier's "idealist" fantasy,
even from Gissing's British brand of realism, *Jude* refuses all accommodation, all "alibis." This marked an emphatic change in Hardy's approach.
By the time *Two on a Tower* appeared in 1882, wrote Havelock Ellis, the
"general public" had begun to suspect "that in reading Mr. Hardy's books
it was not treading on the firm rock of convention" (Cox 304). But they
had kept reading, because they were enjoying themselves. *Tess* was his last
great gesture of pleasure giving and public mollification.

The year 1895 was several years into Hardy's newfound status as number
540 of *Vanity Fair's* "Men of the Day." The neglected evidence of "celebrity" interviews in fashionable magazines, pasted into his personal scrapbook, strongly suggests that he may have felt tempted to overplay his hand
in *Jude*. *Black and White's* 1892 "Chat with the Author of *Tess*"—gentleman
magistrate and a "singularly pleasing personality"—is a case in point (27
August: 239) (fig. 19).[23] "Here" at Max Gate, "far from the madding crowd,
uninfluenced by modern conventionalism, unrestrained by Mrs. Grundy,
Mr. Hardy and I," rhapsodizes the writer, "very seriously discussed" the
murder and execution that conclude *Tess:*

> "You cannot imagine how many letters my husband received," said Mrs. Hardy,
> "begging him to end his story brightly." . . . "And why did you not, Mr. Hardy?"
> said I. . . .
> Mr. Hardy shook his head. . . . "One looks for the climax. One is not to be

MR. THOMAS HARDY IN HIS STUDY AT MAX GATE, DORCHESTER

A CHAT WITH THE AUTHOR OF "TESS"

IT will be perhaps the simplest and most interesting procedure on my part that I should tell my readers something about Mr. Thomas Hardy, himself and his surroundings, before going into the weightier matters of the law into which we were compelled in our discussion upon his last production, "Tess of the D'Urbervilles ; a Pure Woman Faithfully Presented." Mr. Hardy is in himself a gentle and a singularly pleasing personality. Of middle height, with a very thoughtful face and rather melancholy eyes, he is nevertheless an

was, I presume, a relative of the novelist—and in whose arms Lord Nelson passed away in the hour of his greatest triumph.

It was by the drawing-room fire that we sat discussing the frail but charming " Tess."

"You cannot imagine how many letters my husband received," said Mrs. Hardy, "begging him to end his story brightly. One dear old gentleman of over eighty wrote, absolutely insisting upon her complete forgiveness and

Figure 19. The "Master" in his study, pictured for fashionable readers of *Black and White* magazine, 27 August 1892. Courtesy of the Bodleian Library, Oxford.

cheated of it by the exigencies of inartistic conventionality. . . . And it is the very favorable reception by the public of this sad ending to my story that has impressed me as a good sign. At one time a publisher would tell you that a tragic ending was always a failure. Now, however, people have studied more fully the fictions of all time, and are infinitely more artistic. (238)

(He may well have underestimated—in his own words—the importance of Tess's "reparation by death for her sin." Sue's disgusting expiations belong in another category.) *Cassell's Saturday Journal* gave Hardy another platform to educate his audience: "some of the greatest poets and others are actuated by the spirit of revolt"; "originality necessarily implies antagonism to convention" (25 June 1892: 945). "One cannot choose one's read-ers," he told both Gosse and Florence Henniker just before publication of the uncensored book version of *Jude,* 10 November 1895 (*Letters* 2: 93,94); but the much-commented stance of blasé indifference is belied by the hope-fulness of the public pronouncements treasured up in the neglected scrap-book. "[D]umb public opinion" was with him, he thought, if not the criti-cal establishment (to Jeanette Gilder, 16 July 1896, *Letters* 2: 126). And he at last had the cash as well as the status to risk rebellion. In 1892 Hardy bought up a block of City of London Electric Company shares; he acquired additional property in Dorchester; he made investments through the bro-kerage firm of Foster and Braithwaite (Seymour-Smith 454). *Tess's* enor-mous sales, and the promise of income held out by the "Wessex" collected edition of his works (of which *Jude's* uncut "first edition" formed part), bankrolled the boldness that a self-made Dorset "peasant" with a middle-class wife to support could not previously afford.[24] But he should have taken warning by the subtext to one of the encomiums collected in his scrapbook:

> The spirit of the time—a spirit of sadness and dissatisfaction—has touched the literature of the time. Now repellent and now attractive, it is nowhere more win-ning than where it blends with Mr. Hardy's brilliancy and humanity. He does not preach his sadness, . . . but its presence lends his works a quiet charm—not distressing you but calling out your fullest and deepest sympathies. (*National Observer,* 7 February 1891; cutting in Hardy Scrapbook)

What makes *Jude* a different novel from *Tess* is also what makes it differ-ent from *Elsmere, Trilby,* and *Born in Exile,* and what makes it entirely unrecuperable by Victorian culture. In the words of his poem "To a Lady, Offended by a Book of the Writer's," probably written after the publication of *Jude* (*Complete Poems* 361), *Jude* cheerfully "yields" its "space" among "cozy cushions" to other and "smugger" things. In *Jude* there is no good Christian, no reconciled Catherine Elsmere, just as there is no Alec D'Urberville to pit against a free-thinking Angel—what G. W. Foote would have called a coarse "scapegoat" for the novel's "respectable agnos-tic." (*Punch,* up to the trick, dubbed Alec a stage villain [Lerner and Holm-strom 84].) The good and evil angels have been uncomfortably combined: at one point Jude even convicts himself of being Sue's "seducer" (362).

Not that she needs one, in the spiritual sense: Sue Bridehead gives fragile body to the profound cultural threat of female unbelief. She herself plays the wicked skeptic to Jude's believer. Even "converted" and bent on self-immolation, she still undermines by negative example the period associa-tion of womanliness with sentimentalized Christianity. "Any offence which the book may contain for timid readers," growled the *Bookman,* arises not from the salacious antics of Arabella, but from the heretical "story of Sue"

(Lerner and Holmstrom 130). Hardy compounds it with unpleasant recognition of the two women's actual likeness: both are "oneyer[s]" who "bolt" from their husbands (283), and get "took in a queer religious way" (376).

That dovetailing is typical of *Jude*. Its plot "almost geometrically constructed," as he wrote Gosse (10 November 1895, qtd. in Page 348n), its tone insistently self-conscious, the book twists the conventions of Victorian realist fiction in a way that disturbs easy reading. The learned stonemason at its center calls for a more complex response than, say, Gissing's morose atheist. At the end of part 1, our hero reminds us that in just seventy pages we have rattled through a utility version of the classic story of youthful dreams and rural "romance." "I am a man," he reflects at age twenty, "I have a wife." More, "I have arrived at the still riper stage of having disagreed with her, disliked her, had a scuffle with her, and parted from her" (73). Or there is the incident of attempted suicide. Jude jumps up and down on the ice at the center of the local pond. When it refuses to crack, he (or the text) wonders what else he can do by way of self-destruction. The answer comes with disconcerting promptness:

He could get drunk. Of course that was it, he had forgotten. Drinking was the regular, stereotyped resource of the despairing worthless. (70–71)

The barely ventriloquized ironic comment would unsuspend the disbelief of the most pleasure-bent naive reader.

Above all, in *Jude* there is no "quiet charm" and "winning" feeling. This was most dangerous of all. For it was the pleasure of losing oneself in "Wessex" and the celebration of "Thomas Hardy," the "supreme poet of the English landscape" (in the words of a modern jacket blurb [qtd. in Widdowson 63, 55]), that had stamped his permit to the title of fictional "Master." The pastoral beauty of *Tess* had neutralized its "worser part" (Mrs. Oliphant, Cox 257). Flatter of tone and set largely in towns and villages that remain bywords for dreariness—Fawley, Reading, Basingstoke, the wrong end of Oxford—*Jude* offers no such compensation. In its place is an unpleasureable emphasis on the "facts of life" (357) and life's "usual squalors" (172). "We want our novelist back among the rich orchards of the Hintocks," Gosse understandably fretted: "In choosing North Wessex as the scene of a novel Mr. Hardy willfully deprives himself of a great element of his strength. . . . physical charm" (Lerner and Holmstrom 118). Moreover, as the *Nation* recalled, "[t]he drama in *Tess* . . . made a direct appeal to passionate emotion well adapted to confuse judgment" (134). *Jude* was "a less immoral book," but "many degrees colder." As a result, "the average intelligence perceives its offensiveness and proclaims dissent" (134). One could look far for a more candid statement of how Victorian fiction normalized its thrills. The case history of *Trilby*, the success of *Robert Els-mere*, had proven the public would bite their tongues not to condemn a book (in the music hall phrase) that was "naughty but nice." *Jude* was uncomfortable and unenjoyable: it was *Jude* that stuck in their throats.

This was not what England had a right to expect. "There may be books more disgusting, more impious as regards human nature, more foul in de-tail," Mrs. Oliphant testified, "in those dark corners where the amateurs of filth find garbage to their taste; but not, we repeat, from any Master's hand" (Cox 257). Hardy had "flouted his readers" (Tyrell, *Fortnightly,* Cox 299). That was a most serious charge in these last years of the novelist's tenure as a public servant, censored and overseen by publishers, circulating libraries, and all-licensed reviewers. "Never in any age or country have writ-ers been asked to write under such restricted conditions" (G. Moore 19). It was the audience that had the rights and the novelists who faced the duties. The "licence" granted genius would take thirty years, the death of the hero, and the birth of a myth of heroic authorship—whereby Hardy comes to rub shoulders with Joyce and Lawrence, Hemingway, and Zola—to establish itself. In the meantime, he had broken his contract to provide pleasure and uplift as pleasure and uplift were understood in 1895. "'Never retract. Never explain,'" Hardy copied into his journal in the late summer; "'Get it done and let them howl.' Words said to Jowett"—one of the seven liberal theologians or *septem contra Christum* of *Essays and Reviews*—"by a very practical friend." The entry immediately following reads: "on the 1st November *Jude the Obscure* was published" (*Life and Work* 286). Blasphemy was a means to frame his critical refusal to peddle pleasure or assume the role of cultural standard-bearer that the trial records of nineteenth-century blasphemy "martyrdom" had so startlingly written into being. But his last novel had a closer connection with offensive actuality. *Jude* has an unmis-takable savor of the unspeakable *Freethinker*.

ii. "Levity at the Lectern"

The deaths of the children, snapped Mrs. Oliphant, are "pure farce . . . only too grotesque to be amusing" (Cox 261). For the *Athenaeum* it was the double remarriage of Sue and Phillotson and Jude and Arabella that was "the crowning absurdity" (251). The *Illustrated London News* put in a nutshell what most disgusted the reviewers: *Jude's* "undercurrent of grim mockery" (Lerner and Holmstrom 124). The critics made Blackstone's legal dictum on blasphemy read like a literary prophesy: "satire and ridicule are what no establishment can endure." It was this final offense that had prompted the conflagratory Bishop's letter to the *Yorkshire Post:* "Sir—Will you allow me to publicly thank you for your outspoken leader in today's issue denouncing the intolerable grossness and hateful sneering at all that one most reveres in such writers as Thomas Hardy" (Lerner and Holmstrom 138). Hardy's mocking description of the "amusing" incident in the *Life*, fits into *Jude*'s own pattern (*Life and Work* 295): "sneering" is one of the keynotes of both heterodox dialogue and skeptical narration.

It was an inheritance of the 1880s. "Comic Bible" cartoons and "Profane Jokes" convicted the *Freethinker* in 1883: what Mrs. Ward labeled "laughing brutality." Its power to offend persisted beyond the century: J. W. Gott earned his first trial for blasphemy in 1911 by selling "Rib-Ticklers, or, Questions for Parsons." Oscar Wilde, who once dreamed of standing trial for heresy in the Court of Arches (Ellman 46), was rebuked as a student at Oxford for his "levity at the lectern" (95); the "sneer" of the decadence he represented in 1895 was culture coded as blasphemous. *Jude*'s reviewers appreciated the connection: the title of the notice in the *National Review* was "Mr. Hardy as a Decadent" (Cox 284).

How far you could go was a moot question in the years between Foote's imprisonment in Holloway Gaol and the publication of *Jude the Obscure*. Gissing tested the limits: "Mockery" is one of the vestigial demonic characteristics of "saturnine" Godwin Peak (see *Born in Exile* 2: 122–23; 3: 178); Du Maurier's Svengali, full of "derisive laughter" (57), stays well within them. In *Jude*, Sue is twice compared to Voltaire, the primal type of the modern skeptic (157, 173), model for Mrs. Ward's squire; his contact with her smashes Candide/Jude's Leibnizian "devotional motto that all was for the best" (224). During the terrible faith-testing scene in Melchester, when Sue describes how she chopped up the Gospels and Epistles into "separate brochures," she allows herself an "ostensible sneer" (154): the incident grimly intuits the spirit in which Hone snipped "the portions which he could believe" out of his Testament (his pious neighbor widely reported), "and pasted them into a book for his own use" (Hone BL 40,121: 89), though it lacks the exuberance with which Bakhtin recounts how the "entire Bible" was "cut up into little scraps" in the parodic *Cena Cypriani* (*Dialogical Imagination* 70). Even as late as the "relettering" scene, while she is pregnant and distressed, Sue can see how "droll" it is "that we two, of all people, . . . should happen to be here painting the Ten Commandments! You a reprobate, and I—in my condition. . . . O dear!" (318). Her response is not found in Hardy's manuscript of *Jude*: like other late additions, as Ingham remarks, it is "a bizarre increase in sophistication" (447n). Jude's own progress in skepticism is an education in sneering. We know his faith is wavering when he makes a joke about Providence (222); and when Sue turns to religion, it is she, as once it was Jude (see 156), who begs, "Don't satirize me: it cuts like a knife!" (371). By the time of his remarriage, mockery's lessons have been thoroughly learnt. One of the "Grundy revisions" Hardy made for serialization in *Harper's* was to cut the howl of "acrid" laughter with which Jude closes the chapter: "It is true religion! Ha—ha—ha!" (405). Rock bottom is reached shortly after (406): in death, "there seemed to be a smile of some sort upon the marble features of Jude" (431). He has become both the satirist and the object of his satire.

The roll call of *Jude's* offenses of "laughing brutality" and skeptical "mockery" reads like a list of similarities to G. W. Foote's *Freethinker;* it adds plentifully to a long list of suspect connections. Arabella's name for Moses, for example, "the Jewish law-giver" (335), is what Foote and South-well would have called him; to Secularists, God was indeed the "savage deity" that the *Athenaeum,* like Chesterton, accused Hardy of mocking in *Jude* (Cox 250). The fate that Sue's statuary meets is given in terms that recall the debate about blasphemy's literary redefinition in 1883: Miss Fontover "stamped on it," says Sue "because it was not according to her taste" (104). Chapter 2 turns on one of the "Contradictions" that formed the richest category of Foote's *Bible Handbook.* The boy Jude is thrashed by farmer Troutham for letting rooks eat the corn in the field he was employed to guard. The pious cliché he offers in explanation—"Mr. Phillotson said I was to be kind to 'em" (10)—only exacerbates the anger of Troutham, who has "largely subscribed" to the "brand-new church tower" (11). For good measure, Hardy adds a parody of the religious tracts on which little boys were brought up that is strongly reminiscent of Foote's essays in the same genre:[25]

> People said that, if you prayed things sometimes came to you, even though they sometimes did not. He had read in a tract that a man who had begun to build a church, and had no money to finish it, knelt down and prayed, and the money came in by the next post. Another man tried the same experiment, and the money did not come; but he found afterwards that the breeches he knelt in were made by a wicked Jew. (16)

Hardy did not need the device of Sue's dead undergraduate friend to hand lessons like this down the class cultural chain. The details surprise, though through the 1880s his fiction had shown a gathering inclination to blasphemous eruption: *Two on a Tower* (1882) was excoriated for its sneering presentation of a cuckolded Bishop, while the *Mayor of Casterbridge* (1886) reveled in Henchard's comic courtroom confrontation with an old woman who has committed a "nuisance" against the wall of the church, the sacrilegious incident that provokes—like the fulfillment of a curse—the shocking revelation of the mayor's past. (Illiterate Whittle, a minor character, incidentally shares his name with the first printer of the *Freethinker.*)

Jude does not shun the most up-to-date jargon in the whole dictionary of commercial English: the offensive idiom of advertising. Graves in the old Marygreen churchyard are "commemorated by eighteenpenny cast-iron crosses warranted to last five years" (6). Vilbert the quack doctor claims that his potent salve can "only be obtained from a particular animal which graze[s] on Mount Sinai" (22). Such transgressive linguistic couplings (the kind associated only with Cockney degenerates in "idealist" works like Stevenson's contemporaneous *Ebb-Tide*) are one of the most striking features Hardy's novel shares with Foote's penny paper.[26] Vilbert's extravagant pitch might take its place among the *Freethinker*'s 1883 summer number's back page of "Sacred Advertisements," packed full of deceptive comic euphemisms:

> PILLS! PILLS!—Use only J.C.'s celebrated Sin-purging Pills. These pills are a combination of the purest Lamb's blood and grace. Warranted to give relief. Patronized by [the murderers] Guiteau, Peace and all the most famous criminals.

Or,

> WANTED, by the Highland Railway Co., a few Christian Excavators with sufficient faith to remove mountains. Good wages.

And,

> SUNDAY TOYS FOR SABBATARIAN CHILDREN.—Noah's Ark, with barking dogs, climbing monkeys and squeaking patriarchs. The Puzzle Cross, 6d. Old Nick-in-the-Box, 5s., very startling; warranted to drive any sensitive child into fits and the arms of Jesus. Superior sort, with real red fire and blazing crackers, 10s. 6d. Infant Jesuses at all prices: wooden 1d., china 2d., wax from 6d. Squeaking Jesuses from 1s. Warranted to roll its eyes and say "Pa-pa" to any Holy Ghost present. (16)

Lest we think these had no models in real life, turn to the back cover of the *Freethinker* for 26 November 1882 for an astonishing coproduction of bibliolatrous naiveté and rampant commercialism, an apparently genuine notice:

> Good News for Believers.
> Arrangements have been made so that every reader of this paper for this month will have an opportunity of possessing a fac simile [sic] of the
> JERUSALEM SHEKEL
> The coin for thirty of which Judas sold Our Savior Jesus Christ. . . .
> It will be sent post free on receipt of the name of this paper and Thirteen stamps. (376)

No wonder Foote's imagination ran riot; the "Thirteen" stamps are a finishing touch. The new mass-produced brand-name products of the 1880s and early 1890s had brought with them a newspaper rash of display advertising aimed directly at customers; the *Daily Mail* (founded 1896) carried sales plugs for women's underwear on the front page. The *Freethinker*'s offenses, again, had run ahead of bitterly resisted change, and Hardy's sneers recapitulated the most offensive aspects of its innovations.

"A sweet, saintly, Christian business!" Jude hardly comprehends his own profane pun. *Jude* the text is not so naive: this is not its sole *Freethinker*-style foray into the world of offensive wordplay. Hardy signals it in his epigraph, "The Letter Killeth," and puts it in action in the "relettering" scene. Alexander Fischler has persuasively argued that *Jude* is founded on a series of interlinked puns on "gin" (meaning both "trap" and "drink") and "spirit" (in the sense both of "otherworldliness" and "strong drink"), which the Victorian reader "could be counted upon" to appreciate (5). To those two words we should add three more that come under pressure in *Jude*: "mean," "vulgar," and "obscure." All are ripe with such associations as landed G. W. Foote in court.

Thus, *Jude*'s landscape is so "meanly utilitarian" (8), its narration so preoccupied with "mean bread-and-cheese question[s]" (84), its spirit so oppressed by "mean" souls (345) that we are tempted to read Little Time's misspelled murder-suicide note—"Done because we are too meny" (355)—as a "grotesque pun" (Goode 159), not on "many" but "mean." For Sue marriage is a "hopelessly vulgarian institution" (*Jude* 285): a usage (frequent in *Jude*) to touch the nerve that pinched status-conscious contemporaries like Du Maurier or the editor of *Harper's*, who protested in August 1894 against the "vulgariz[ing]" of "our literature" by giving "conspicuous place to the sordid and the mean" (476). The frequently used word "obscure" raised the class stakes of wordplay still further. The novel owes it, in part, to the atheistical strain in literature stemming from Gibbon, whose notorious account of the rise of Christianity "makes continual use of the words 'obscure' and 'obscurity'" (Goode 144). But "obscure" means "poor" as well as "unimportant": class enters into *Jude*'s offensive discussion of faith even at the level of title. Hardy will have a use too for the word's third, more abstract sense—"hidden, gloomy, indistinct."

iii. "I Told Him Too Obscurely"

"My first attempt" at fiction, Hardy told the *Pall Mall Gazette* in an 1892 interview, "was a wild sort of manuscript" (2 January, cutting in Hardy Scrapbook). Fundamental problems of plain speaking had dogged him ever since Chapman's reader, Foote's friendly supporter George Meredith, advised him not to "nail [his] colors to the mast" by publishing his outspoken first novel, *The Poor Man and the Lady*, in 1868 (qtd. in Coleman 10). The first novel Hardy published (anonymously), *Desperate Remedies* (1871), similarly turned out "remarkably coarse" in expression (*Athenaeum*, Cox

1). All his working life, as the publisher Tinsley put it in 1875, Hardy "want[ed] a monitor" (qtd. in Seymour-Smith 193]). Leslie Stephen filled the role best, the "book-weighing machine" who conducted the *Cornhill* family magazine against the grain of his own linguistic conscience (qtd. 184). Troy's seduction of Fanny "must be stated," Stephen agreed, in *Far from the Madding Crowd,* but "the words must be careful." When they were instead "embarrassing" or "unhealthy"—classic critical euphemisms for "frank," the sort that made Hardy fume—he stooped to proffering Bowdlerizations; like sheep's "backs" for "buttocks" (Seymour-Smith 186).[27] Hardy's response was instructive: "I may have higher artistic aims some day, and be a great stickler for the proper artistic balance of the completed work" (102).

He never stopped pushing at the limits of the speakable. That popular hit was followed by a novel that even its solitary modern editor has dismissed as "the joker in the pack" (Gittings, introduction xi): *The Hand of Ethelberta* (1876). Peter Widdowson has laid out instead a convincing argument for its centrality to the "other," class-alienated Hardy whose career reached its natural culmination in *Jude the Obscure.* But what most makes this neglected satirical tale of a low-born risqué "Novel-Teller" so central is what has never been remarked: its obsessive interest in plain speaking and sheer bad language. "Never mind the cursing and swearing," the ostler admonishes the milkman, by way of prologue, "or somebody who's never out of hearing may clap yer name down in his black book" (*Ethelberta* 2). The novel does not take his advice.[28] *Ethelberta* is a systematic exploration of the limits of printable language, made more shocking by Hardy's choice as self-surrogate of a woman writer given to "plain English" (102) and "terse candor" (210). The heroine's downfall, for example, follows the discovery that she has written some "ribald verses" (58). " 'Ribald?' " asks Ethelberta, sketching the real-life question Foote put Mr. Justice North in 1883, "I don't think you are aware what 'ribald' means." Her rich patroness replies: "I am not sure that I am. As regards some words as well as some persons, the less you are acquainted with them the more it is to your credit" (58). (Ethelberta is also arraigned for "levity" [39].) The anticipations of Hardy's critics are so close as to make one "pause" a few "semi-colons," like one of the heroine's word-obsessed suitors (38): as Terry Eagleton has cryptically remarked, "it is by 'not writing properly' that [Hardy] lays bare the device" and ideology of bourgeois realism (qtd. in Widdowson 130). *Ethelberta's* linguistic depredations were the logical culmination of the peculiar interest in swear words expressed in the *Crowd* and *A Pair of Blue Eyes* (1873), which both moralize on the health benefits of "cussing" (*Crowd* 51; *Eyes* 77); in 1880, accepting Hardy's *Trumpet Major,* the clergyman editor of *Good*

Words asked in advance that all "swearing shoud be avoided" (Hardy to Sydney Smith, qtd. in Seymour-Smith 253).[29] One is not surprised to learn that in writing *Ethelberta,* Hardy had quarried the manuscript of his outspoken, unpublished first novel, *The Poor Man and the Lady.*

Thinking back to that work, the most original thing "for its date" he ever wrote (qtd. in Seymour-Smith 82), Hardy claimed above all to have been surprised that Macmillan thought it "so aggressive" as to "'mean mischief' almost without knowing it" (*Life and Work* 64). His own obfuscating comments on *Jude* were later so similar as to foster the critical suspicion that in this last novel he was bent on saying what he had wanted to say for thirty years, in "his own words," as martyred Holyoake had put it. That done, he could turn back to poetry, which public neglect left clear of compromise (Wilde, "Soul" 35), to say what "in argumentative prose," Hardy noted in October 1897, "would set all the literary contortionists jumping upon me." "If Galileo had said in verse that the world moved," he added, instantly shifting from the question of language to unbelief, heresy, and the history of religious intolerance, "the Inquisition might have left him alone" (*Life and Work* 302). The "misery" of novel writing, as Gissing wrote Hardy in the mid-1880s, "is that reticences and superficialities have so often to fill places where one is willing to put in honest work" (*Life and Work* 189). Gissing finally dwindled into the urbane and Latinate prose of the *Private Papers of Henry Ryecroft,* his most remunerative work; Hardy ultimately refused to bear the misery.

The critics' and publishers' response to *Tess* had not damaged sales, but it had hardened the will to fight. *Macmillan's* magazine had turned it down, as Hardy put it, "virtually on the score of its improper explicitness" (*Life and Work* 232). One recognizes a familiar phrase—the older Holyoake's favorite euphemism for "blasphemy": Hardy used it himself in the rare critical essay of 1891 in which he claimed the right to write "the explicit novel" ("Candour in English Fiction," *Personal Writings* 132). "I cannot think there should be any theological offence" in the novel, the magazine's editor Mowbray Morris wrote. But there was something the matter, and— as throughout the nineteenth-century history of blasphemy—the matter was "manner" (qtd. in Seymour-Smith 412). Even laboriously "dismembered" and "mutilated" for serial publication, to the degree that (like *Jude*) the text exists in several versions, *Tess* got reviews that gave sustained prophecy of how the unwanted prophet of *Jude* would become outlaw in his own country.[30] The more "daring" the novel, the more the minutiae of language came under scrutiny in the *New Review,* the *National,* and the *Quarterly,* where (reviewing the novel he had declined, under cover of anonymity) Mowbray Morris concluded that Hardy had "gratuitously chosen to tell a coarse and disagreeable story in a coarse and disagreeable manner" (Lerner and Holmstrom 86).

The reviewers knew that Hardy knew what they were talking about. Great exception was taken, said Morris, to Hardy's lambasting in the preface to *Tess* of the "too genteel reader who cannot endure to have it said what everybody thinks and feels" (Lerner and Holmstrom 86). This had too great a flavor of the "outspeaking" *Freethinker.* The reviewers wanted "reticence," the guiding principle of Mrs. Oliphant, later *Jude*'s fiercest opponent. The novel that made her name in 1863, *Salem Chapel,* compounds the secrecy of the melodramatic plot (here involving a speechless sister, apparently fallen, and a silent woman who may have killed) with a legal fear of "incrimination" and a developed psychology of heroic repression; "words the symbols of life," Oliphant preaches, may be "throw[n] . . . like stones" (*Salem* 49, 58). By contrast, "Mr. Hardy le[ft] little unsaid" (Lerner and Holmstrom 66). The conversation about his masterwork *Tess,* like the thwarted movement of Hardy's career through the critically neglected *Ethelberta,* continually refers us to concepts of word criminality as they emerged in the courtroom in 1883. It set in concrete the framework within which *Jude* would be anathematized, while the book's success with the reading public emboldened him to more (not less) "explicitness."[31] Ripping to shreds the veil of language, *Jude* was designed to make smoldering ashes break out into leaping flame.

The 1895 book text of *Jude the Obscure* is more "explicit" than generations of readers have realized. Take the crucial episode of the pig's penis, which Mrs. Oliphant called "more brutal in depravity than anything which the darkest slums could bring forth" (Cox 259). Hardy made changes to the 1903 edition that dramatically detracted from its offensive impact in 1895, as if he were returning to the scene of his word crime, still trying to get the "explicit" balance exactly right. Most strikingly, what in 1903 was changed to read (and still reads) "on the bridge, when he looked at 'ee as if he had never seen a woman before in his born days" (39), in 1895 read, "on the bridge, wi' that piece o' pig hanging between ye—haw-haw! What a proper thing to court over!" (Slack 335).

In 1895, Hardy submitted to the novel's serial "mutilation" with extreme distaste: had there been a route out of his contract, *Jude* would have been withdrawn from *Harper's* (Hardy to Sir George Douglas, 5 January 1896, *Letters* 2: 105).[32] The seventh installment is a classic and painful example of self-bowdlerization. Hardy slashed what might offend the pious as well as the prudes. Thus not only are Jude's kisses in the railway carriage cut but also four pages of dialogue to the end of the chapter beginning "There, dear; don't mind! Crucify me, if you will!" (253). The strategy of "Grundy revision" did him no good with Mrs. Oliphant: "what audience" could want a work that had been serially "introduced . . . into a number of decent houses in England and America, with the most shameful portions suppressed?" (Cox 256). She knew her duty better, and wrote to the Bishop of Wakefield "commending his action" in burning the novel (*Life and Work* 295).

There were limits to the 1895 book text's explicitness. Hardy deleted from the manuscript expressions like "caught in a tom-and-she-cat way" [446n]: the novel does not want to suggest what happens upstairs between Jude and Arabella. It touches Sue's pregnancy with tangential softness: the subject (the word) was near-taboo (one reason why Moore put pregnancy center stage in *Esther Waters* in 1894). Its more "delicate" moments "c[oul]d not be told with more reticence," as Hardy claimed in a letter to Florence Henniker (10 November 1895, *Letters* 2: 95): *Jude* is wary of obscenity. But that is perhaps because its criminal focus is elsewhere.

The formal preface to the 1895 book version restated Hardy's position in terms that make an offensive weapon of blank naiveté. Jeannette L. Gilder's review in the *World*, quoting it (as did the *Pall Mall Gazette*'s reviewer), rose at once to the bait: "Mr. Hardy . . . holds himself exempted from the necessity of 'mincing' his words" (Lerner and Holmstrom 113). "When I finished the story," said Gilder, "I opened the windows and let in the fresh air and I turned to my bookshelves and I said: 'Thank God for Kipling and Stevenson, Barrie and Mrs. Humphry Ward . . . Here are four great writers who have never trailed their talents in the dirt' " (Cox xxxvi). Like Foote, as Judge North might have said, Hardy was "prostituting" his talents. The "eagerness with which every unclean situation is seized upon," said the *Bookman*, "recalls the spectacle of some foul animal that snatches greedily at great lumps of putrid offal" (Lerner and Holmstrom 133). While writers like Mrs. Ward could claim that "the public" had "cooperate[d] in the book" (*Elsmere* [1911] xxix), Hardy had "threatened his readers not merely in their opinions but in their deepest unspoken values" (Howe 397), and at the end of the century, as we have seen, these were most deeply embedded in language. *Jude* acts out the note Hardy made to himself in August 1883, immediately in the wake of Foote's martyrdom: "Write a list of things which everybody thinks and nobody says" (*Life and Work* 168). It exhibited, said the reviewers, an "extraordinary lack of reticence in the telling" (Lerner and Holmstrom 133).

And just as *Jude* comments on its own mockery, so it overtly expresses its concern with "explicit" unreticence. Jude's hardest charge against Sue is not that she is (as the critics have called her) "mysterious" or duplicitous, but that she is "reticent" (272): the term is surely purposefully chosen. The lovers' closeness is measured in terms of how explicit their language becomes: the terms "frank" (215) and "honest" (215, 223) work like signposts; while renascent "prudish[ness]" (222) and a failure in "candor" (251) are apparent in such sophisticated displays of evasiveness as the following:

> "I didn't marry [Phillotson] altogether because of the scandal. But sometimes a woman's love of being loved gets the better of her conscience, and though she is agonized at the thought of treating a man cruelly, she encourages him to love her while she doesn't love him at all. Then, when she sees him suffering, her remorse sets in, and she does what she can to repair the wrong."

To which Jude replies:

> "You simply mean that you flirted outrageously with him, poor old chap, and then repented, and to make reparation, married him, though you tortured yourself to death by doing it."
>
> "Well—*if you will put it brutally*—it was a little like that—. . . ." (253, my emphasis)

Like Dickens's Edith Dombey, eloped with her lover, Sue claims "I didn't mean that!" (250). The resort to euphemism links her (again) to Arabella, who makes intermittent and crude pretense of linguistic propriety. "Mother died of dys——" she cuts herself off—"what do you call it—in the hot weather" in Australia (368). Elegant circumlocution indeed.

The final touch to Hardy's play on the keyword "obscure" is given by "reticent" Sue's self-accusation after the children's deaths. When Little Time asked his fatal question about her pregnancy, she later sobs, she wanted to be "honest and candid" (352): "And yet I wasn't truthful, for with a false delicacy *I told him too obscurely*" (357, my emphasis). Little Time, as a child will, takes Sue and her cruel "facts of life" "literally" (357), so that he acts on the childish plaint to which she accedes: "It would be better to be out o' the world than in it, wouldn't it?" (351). Thus the crowning horror of the novel arises out of linguistic disorder; it is triggered by "obscure" and "reticent" speech. The Victorian compulsion to euphemism, blasphemy's opposite term, laid a heavy constraining hand, we remember, on the publication of birth control information, which the feminist Secularist movement gamely attempted to break. Sue might have gained from their efforts. In the wake of his outspoken novel, Hardy helped his friend Agnes Grove with an article on "What Children Should Be Told" (*Free Review*, July 1896; *Letters* 2: 123n).

The final touch to Hardy's assault on the culture of euphemism turned on how he handled the long-established (though never unproblematic) literary convention of "token speech." It was perennially associated with profanity, as the *Freethinker*'s editor knew when he mockingly penned his offensive Agony Aunt reply to the "Holy Gh——st." But it was also

associated with "violent" and lower-class speech.[33] Thus Mrs. Ward's horrified response to the blasphemies of the *Freethinker* practiced a similar suppression to that which judge and prosecutor imposed in court during the
first and second trials of G. W. Foote (see above, 5.3): the "scroll" seen
"emanating from Mary Magdalene's mouth" in a cartoon of the Crucifixion
"contain[ed] obscenities which cannot be quoted here" (*Elsmere* 458). For
twenty years Hardy had substituted euphemistic versions for truly "profane
imprecations" (Elliott 225): "Odd" for "God," "nation" for "damnation,"
"dang" for "damn," and so on, as in the milkman's outburst in *Ethelberta*.
In the *Mayor of Casterbridge*, he had comically euphemized the old furmity
woman's coarse speech: "I have floored fellows a dee sight finer-looking
than a dee fool like thee, you son of a bee, dee me if I haint" (172). In
Tess, the "merciless polemical syllogism[s]" that Tess heard Angel say and
her ill-fated repetitions to Alec D'Urberville are pointedly omitted. But the
missing arguments are supplied in *Jude*. And so are the long-suppressed
swear words, even on women's lips. "O it is perfectly damnable how things
are!" Sue says when she first learns Jude is married (172). Arabella "bursts
out" of her religious phase to protest to her friend:

> "What right has she to him, I should like to know! I'd take him from her if I
> could!"
>
>   "Fie, Abby! And your husband only six weeks gone! Pray against it!"
>
>   "Be damned if I do! Feelings are feelings! I won't be a creeping hypocrite any
> longer—so there!" (332)

There is a "crude but candid authenticity," as Eagleton says, about Arabella
(69). As for Jude, not until he is moved to agony by Sue's conversion to
"Save-your-own-soulism" does his language stretch to profanity. But then
it becomes the natural idiom of his soul: "I am glad I had nothing to do
with Divinity—damn glad—if it's going to ruin you in this way!" (370).
Drunk and miserable, he consents to follow Arabella home to her father's
house: "Anything—anywhere . . . What the devil does it matter to me?"
(396). One example sets the limits of Hardy's daring: Jude's declaration to
Arabella that "I'd marry the W—— of Babylon rather than do anything
dishonorable!" (402). In *Tess*, Hardy restricted himself to a euphemistic
alteration: Alec calls Tess "you dear damned witch of Babylon" (402),
though Tess protests against "such a whorage as this" during the fatal evening revels that deliver her into her seducer's hands. *Jude*'s "W——,"
which *Harper's* changed to "Woman" (766), was as blunt as Hardy could
get. Elsewhere, forbidden words, typographically "spoken" to almost their
full extent, are a final index of the suffering of his godforsaken characters.
To the reviewers, they were "a shame to the language" and to "English
print" (Mrs. Oliphant, Cox 259). That strident note of patriotism makes

mockery of the modern day marketing of "Thomas Hardy" as a literary
national trust, though one of Hardy's first thoughts for his hero's name,
ironically, was "Jack England." As we shall next see, his sense of nation,
his sense of Englishness, was a far cry from his critics'.

3. HARDY THE DEGENERATE, POOLEY THE OBSCURE

No "mean," "vulgar," or "obscure" aspect of *Jude* went unnoticed in the
reviews. The class-coded jibes of "coarseness," "crudity," and (especially)
"brutality" were all too easy to take personally.[34] "Why should one's club-
acquaintance bring such charges?" Hardy had wondered when the *Saturday*
attacked *Tess* (*Life and Work* 261). The reception of *Jude* called for still
more defensive and arriviste recuperation: Hardy's account in the *Life* is
punctuated by the sound of titled names dropping. But the maneuvers were
unavailing. Even Gissing the jailbird, escaped from the noisy den he shared
with his slatternly wife for a visit to Max Gate, followed a note on Hardy's
"difficulty" with "decent language" in *Jude* with this remark to his diary: "I
perceive that he has a good deal of coarseness in his nature—the coarseness
explained by humble origin. He did an odd thing at breakfast—jumped
up and killed a wasp with the flat of a table-knife!" (*London* 387–88). Admiration was soured by personal contact, and the fall from master to "peasant"
was hard (Gissing to Bertz, 22 September 1895, *Collected Letters* 6: 30).

As the reception, so the inception of *Jude*. Hardy made his deepest denial
of origins in writing that "it was possibly his contact with the stonemason,"
to whom he gave designs for his stonemason father's tombstone in February
1893, "that made him think of that trade for his next hero" (*Life and Work*
267). But the novel itself takes differently the injunction, *"Never betray your
class."* It was as if every moment of public recognition (*Far From the Madding Crowd,* the eventual triumph of *Tess*) produced a recoil of personal
revenge on the literary class system that had bestowed it (*Ethelberta* and
Jude). This is perhaps what drives the compulsive intrusion of pigs and
piggishness into the novel, from Jude's greasy courtship of Arabella, Mrs.
Oliphant's "human pig" (Cox 258), to the brutal scene of the slaughtered
hog, "an act of literary suicide" on which the reviews dwelled angrily.[35] It
is one of the novel's most calculated pieces of class affront. The tabooed
animal was an immemorial byword for filth and appetite, as Stallybrass
and White demonstrate at startling length in their *Politics and Poetics of
Transgression.* The pig is taboo because it is all too much like ourselves:
Cobbett turned the bishop of Landaff's phrase "swinish multitude" in his
1819 letter on blasphemy prosecution into a popular figure for the base
masses; Eaton, who went to prison for the blasphemous *Age of Reason,* was

also prosecuted in 1794 for *Hog's Wash, Or, Politics for the People.* There is a point in the fact that Marygreen's ancient church is broken up to build pigsty walls, or that Jude begs the "converted" Sue not to let him sink back into "wallowing in the mire," like "the pig that was washed," a bluntly offensive echo of 2 Peter 2.22.

However, what goes to the heart of *Jude's* class tragedy of thwarted aspiration is its direct imbrication in the one episode in blasphemy's nineteenth-century history that remains to be told, the one case to come to trial, in 1857, in the forty-odd years between the struggles of the 1840s and the *Freethinker* case of 1883.[36] At its center was a "tall [and] powerful" laborer of about fifty (Holyoake, *Case* 8), who mostly eked out a living by sinking wells around the market town of Liskeard (drought-prone Cornwall has a pagan reverence for its wells). His name was Thomas Pooley. He was a different species of criminal laborer to figure in the folk memory Hardy inherited from his birthplace, from the martyrs to the laws against trades unionism, transported to Australia from the nearby village of Tolpuddle in 1834, to the generically depressed "Dorsetshire Laborer" he memorialized in a biting essay of 1883.

Pooley was a solitary figure, cut off from the community of activism and the tradition of blasphemy martyrdom, and the one rural victim to the law of the century. Hardy left no testimony to the influence of his case; little that criticism could seize on as socially untoward survived his destruction of personal papers before his death. But an accumulated weight of circumstantial evidence offers proof that this national scandal of Hardy's youth returned in memory to increase *Jude the Obscure's* burden of class feeling, refine its psychopathology of bibliolatrous Christianity, and screw to screaming pitch its sense of the grotesque untowardness of things. There is much in Jude of Thomas Hardy. There is something of Horace Moule, the scholarly and alcoholic mentor who committed suicide in 1873.[37] There is more than a touch of Hardy's wild uncle-in-law, "Jack" Antell, the atheistical Puddletown shoemaker who taught himself Latin and Greek before his dreams of learning soured and he took to the bottle, and who finally had himself dragged from his deathbed in 1878 for a remarkable photograph: emaciated by cancer, he poses leaning on a chair "which bears, on a carefully lettered placard, the accusatory words 'SIC PLACET,' addressed presumably to God, Fate, or even the President of the Immortals" (Millgate, *A Biography* 108). But there is much in Jude of Thomas Pooley too.

The *Life and Work* gives a first clue in the trail that leads to his door. One of the titles Hardy drops is not a born aristocrat's but the lord chief justice's: John Duke, Lord Coleridge. On 17 December, 1892, exactly as he was meditating *Jude,* Hardy had "an interesting legal dinner" (*Life and Work* 265) with the eminent judge whose contentious ruling at the third *Freethinker* trial in April 1883 made a class-criminal offense of a "literary difference." Hardy had met him in 1889, and knew him until he died in harness as lord chief justice in 1894. Coleridge was particularly "anecdotic" during that dinner, Hardy recalled (*Life and Work* 265). Perhaps they talked about the *Freethinker* case: it had been the one moment of opportunity in Coleridge's career to make national law; obituaries and later biographies dwelled upon it. But they dwelled on the Pooley case more. That too had the Coleridge imprint.

The upper-class "propagators of heresy" were not prosecuted, Foote charged at the third *Freethinker* trial, because "it would be perilous to touch them" (*Prisoner* 35). Instead, Secularists were made "the *scapegoats* of the cultured agnostics of the day" (34, my emphasis). The term had a particular resonance, and no one was more attuned to it than the judge before whom Foote uttered it. "Scapegoat" was the term that liberal outrage had fastened on Thomas Pooley. And the judge who inflicted on him perhaps the severest sentence for blasphemy in 150 years was Mr. Justice Coleridge, Lord Chief Justice Coleridge's father.[38] His son never forgot the case, or the outcry it occasioned, for more reasons than filial piety. John Duke Coleridge himself had been prosecuting counsel—assigned separately to the case in the normal course of business on the Western Circuit, he said. No defense counsel was appointed.

The press dubbed as uniformly, utterly, *"obscure"* the man the later chief justice helped send to Bodmin Gaol (*Spectator,* 8 August 1857: 834; Holyoake, *Case* 3, 6n). Who would protest his twenty-one months' imprisonment with hard labor for chalking blasphemous "words" on a gate, and "holding blasphemous conversations with a laborer and a policeman," the three successful counts in his indictment (*Case* 31)? For every reader of the *Morning Chronicle,* which called it "A Very Remarkable Sentence" (10 August 1857: 7)—compare a nine-month "stretch" for maliciously stabbing a neighbor handed out at the same Bodmin Summer Assizes (*Cornish Times,* 8 August 1857: 4), or the six months Judge Coleridge gave a Somerset bigamist (*Western Flying Post,* 11 August 1857: 6)—there were ten subscribers to the *Times,* which dispatched the case in eleven lines, or to *John Bull,* which dispatched the prisoner himself as "a dirty-looking excitable man with a grisly beard" (15 August 1857: 526). The *Spectator* turned the tide of indifference. It gave space to denunciation even in the midst of reporting the Indian Mutiny: "Religion is not to be upheld by criminal prosecution, nor is decency to be protected by treating stark simple folly with a tragic retribution" (8 August 1857: 834). No matter what his exact words, Thomas Pooley did not deserve incarceration.

Several versions circulated documenting the "dreadful" things (*Times*, 3 August 1857: 10) he allegedly "did compose, write, and publish" on the stained field gate (fig. 20) that (said Prosecutor Coleridge) "abuts upon the high road" near Duloe, five miles from Liskeard, on the day he trudged over to Sandplace, 22 May, sticking bills for a house sale at Looe, with a tin can in his hand and fustian on his back (*Chronicle*, 10 August: 7). A local carpenter testified only to four simple words, "Jesus Christ" and "T. Pooley" (Holyoake, *Case* 21), so the case would seem at first sight a revival of the Mosaic idea that even to speak the name of the Lord is to commit blasphemy. But the prosecution's star witness recalled a whole sentence: "Duloe stinks of the monster Christ's Bible," with the helpful addendum, "Blasphemy—T. Pooley" (*Chronicle*, 10 August 1857: 7). Both the pathetic *imitatio Christi* and the more shocking testament of rebellion have their relevance for *Jude the Obscure*. No one saw Pooley write, and no one proved his handwriting, a clear failure in law (Holyoake, *Case* 21). And the star witness was none other than the owner of the gate, the rector of Duloe, the Reverend Paul Bush. He tried twice to instigate prosecution, first by filing a charge before another clergyman-magistrate, the curate of Bodmin (Hawtin 18, 18n), the second time in the more usual manner. Pooley was sent forward to the assizes by a vicar called Tatham: "Lord," Jacob Holyoake would pronounce, "deliver the poor man from clerical magistrates" (Holyoake, *Case* 13).

The first, brief newspaper reports stirred up Secularist agitation in London, Birmingham, and the North. Holyoake was dispatched on an official visit of inquiry to Cornwall. The case offered the movement a dramatic platform for public pronouncements and respectable image building, not a fellow martyr to rally around. "Freethinkers, whom we represent," Holyoake declared, "have no sympathy with Pooley's manner of expressing himself." Indeed, "London Secularists" "universally condemned" him (*Case* 6, 3). His "incoherent words" were "bad taste" (7, 6); Bush "might more reasonably indict his parrot for 'cussin' his stableboy" (14). Holyoake's own reports in the *Reasoner* (August 1857 to January 1858), pioneer pieces of investigative reporting, were not only extremely effective, securing Pooley's release from confinement at the end of December 1857, but urbanely well written (see especially his account of his "enchanting" journey from Plymouth to Liskeard [*Case* 3–4]).[39] Before they were reissued as a pamphlet, *The Case of Thomas Pooley, the Cornish Well-Sinker* (1857), Holyoake rewrote "4 lines describing the [Duloe] pigs" at the instance of a friend, since as they

202

THE CASE

OF

THOMAS POOLEY,

THE CORNISH WELL-SINKER,

SENTENCED TO A YEAR AND NINE MONTHS' IMPRISONMENT FOR WRITING ON A
CLERGYMAN'S FIELD GATE.

(A Report made at the instance of the Secularists.)

BY G. J. HOLYOAKE.

THE WRETCHED GATE OF THE REV. PAUL BUSH.

LONDON :

HOLYOAKE & Co., PUBLISHERS, 147, FLEET STREET.

[PRICE THREEPENCE.]

[1857]

Figure 20. Holyoake's sketch of the Reverend Bush's notorious gate, reproduced on
the front cover of the official Secularist report that caused a national scandal.
Courtesy of the Bishopsgate Institute Library, Holyoake Collection.

stood they "disqualif[ied him] from giving any criticism of Mr. Pooley's inelegancies. And *one* sentence of this sort is enough to tarnish the reputation" (letter from S. D. Collet, 24 September 1857, in HL).[40] As Holyoake presents him, Pooley shuffles into history as a "poor, obscure, and oppressed" victim (*Case* 3) from "an obscure village" (6n) who needs the leader of London Secularism to speak for him.

The well-gathered facts of Holyoake's *Case* paint a picture of general illiteracy against which to place its "obscure" victim. One witness, the rector's servant, could not swear to *any* words on the gate; in fact, Mitchell the carpenter and Reverend Bush were the only two who could read (*Case* 21). Cornwall had the lowest literacy rates in the country (Buckle, *Fraser's Magazine,* May 1859: 536): the crime of scrawling on gates in one of its more remote parishes might well seem inconsequential, absurd. But Pooley himself could read and write, though Holyoake calls him "illiterate" (13, 19, 26, 30). His unusual capacity for language is eloquently evidenced in letters home from prison, some of which Holyoake printed; it shows a heart as aspiring towards knowledge as Thomas Hardy's or Jude Fawley's, struggling under the harshest conditions. Pooley had scattered learning enough to compare himself to Galileo, "prisoner for the truth" (letter to Mary Pooley, 16 November 1857, in HL); some years later, he quickly caught the gist of the Colenso controversy (undated letter, in HL). He may not have battened as it was rumored on "the poisonous, infidel publications of the Holyoake school" (*Cornish Telegraph,* 5 August 1957: 3), a charge Holyoake quickly denied (*Case* 8), but he certainly begged for books on his release from confinement (Mary Pooley to Holyoake, December 25 1857, in HL), and sent Holyoake stamps for a subscription to the *Reasoner* (letter, 20 July 1859, in HL) at a time when local employers said they "dare" not offer him work and he seemed to have no recourse but the workhouse (Hawtin 24). The saddest record among the thirty-four items preserved in the Holyoake Collection, Manchester, is Pooley's plea that Holyoake "print this letter" setting out his beliefs and views shortly after he was released (8 January 1858, in HL). He did not. One last paragraph in Pooley's own words appeared in the *Reasoner* on 24 March, in which he thanked London Secularists for his deliverance.[41]

The living of Duloe lay in the gift of Balliol College, and Paul Bush acceded to it in 1850 as a young man of twenty-eight. Cornwall was a backwater where bishops might expect to be billed as "CELEBRITIES," as they are in the indices of the Cornwall Records Office; the fact that Archdeacon Phillpotts had "a field of very fine oats in course of cutting" on 11 July 1857 was front-page news in the *Cornish Times.* Duloe was a fair living, but not a place where a man with a growing family would want to spend his career.[42]

The six acres of Glebe included an arable field with standing buildings by the name of "Old Mowhay." The fatal gate was located either here or next to the rectory, right under Bush's nose. The tithe commissioners' map of 1842 put income from the parish at 632 pounds (CRO). It may not have felt like enough, and may not all have reached Bush's pockets. In 1852 he took on the duties of a newly consolidated chapelry at nearby Heriodsfoot, though it was worth only 65 pounds. (According to Holyoake, Bush also took on the parish of St. Keyne.)

Bush was a fervent man, keen to take up the strong Methodist challenge around Liskeard, where his service book evidences he also preached in 1857 (CRO). A leaflet he prepared in 1889, *The Rectors and Vicars of Duloe,* grandly describes him as "Clerk, M.A., And, at the time of his Institution, a Publick Preacher throughout the Diocese of Exeter" (CRO) while muting its mention of his distinguished predecessors: Charles Atmore Ogilvy, D.D., incumbent 1833–39, who became Regius Professor of Pastoral Theology at Oxford in 1842, and Robert Scott D.D., 1840–50, coauthor of the standard *Greek Lexicon* (1843), who became master of Balliol in 1854. Bush's own ambitions were probably thwarted through his first years. A schoolroom projected in 1851 remained unbuilt in 1857, and lack of public buildings meant a reduction in public influence. But one small success was reported proudly to Scott on 6 May 1857: "we . . . shipped off Edwd. Shelton & John Shelton Junr. to America . . . that we might not have hereafter to transport them elsewhere" (CRO). Bush did not care about the "tribes" of "indelicate" pigs that "prowl[ed] about the cottage doors," Duloe locals told Holyoake. But he was "very strict" about "all our affairs" (*Case* 20). Tall, pale, sandy-whiskered, with "imperious manners" (19), the Rector carried a big "pastoral stick" (20). Pooley's scrawl on his field gate may have seemed a God-given opportunity to lay down some more local law and thrust himself into national prominence. He celebrated his victory in terms appropriate to a crusade in a letter to the newspapers on 1 August 1857: "I cannot help hoping that my successful prosecution of a blasphemer, if made known, may induce others . . . to take the course which I have taken, disagreeable though it be, and enforce the law against blasphemy" (qtd. in *Reasoner,* 18 November 1857: 266).

The flush of success did not last long. Bush made plans to restore his church immediately after the Pooley case. But it took ten years to raise the money, and two years (1859–61) to even draw up the plans. (The new efficient, hierarchical design focused attention towards the pulpit [church plans, in CRO].) The case had no discernible effect on his parishioners' piety. The offertory went up to seventeen shillings and nine pence over Easter, a common pattern, but back to four shillings and sixpence by the end of July, when Pooley went to trial, while the number of communicants slumped from thirty-six to thirteen (service book, CRO). The schoolroom was not built until 1870. The entry for "Bush" in the *Cornish Church Guide* is very small. He was elected honorary canon of Truro Cathedral in 1882, a standard clerical tidbit, and remained rector of Duloe until his death in 1904.

The "avowed infidel" and "scoffer" over whom Bush had triumphed (Bush, *Reasoner,* 18 November 1857: 266) was "a man of strong will" and "eccentric manners," Holyoake wrote, "and the official gentlemen of the neighborhood do not like that sort of thing" (*Case* 4). One freely confessed "that he one day bid a policeman go and flog Pooley with a rope end in the public streets" (11). "[H]ad Mr. Justice Coleridge ordered him to be hung," Holyoake believed, "nobody in Cornwall would have stirred to save him. The awe of clergymen and magistrates is excessive" (4). An instinctive socialist, Pooley frankly equated the one with the other: while the "Clergy Magistrates of Cornwall" lived in "Idleness and splender," he wrote Holyoake and all "Friends of Truth," "the poor man is Robbed of [h]is Honest Labor and He Cant Get no Redress" (letters of 20 July [1859] and 9 January 1858, in HL); "Happy would be Those Days Wen all Men Could Plant Thir own Vines And Eate the fruits Thirof" (26 November 1857, in HL). His daughter summed up: "Sir[,] my father is a poor man . . . and one that likes to enjoy his own opinion" (undated letter to Holyoake [1857]). These were Bush's grounds for thinking him "extremely vain" (letter, 2 January 1858, in HL). "In a remote country district," "individuality" was an "impertinence," and "free opinion a sin" (*Devonport Independent,* 31 October 1857: 8). Pooley's exemplary "moral character" as a teetotalling husband and father who had never been known to use "bad language" (Holyoake, *Case* 7) weighed little by comparison.[43] Even his unusual "long Muntzian beard" was thought an offense (*Case* 10).

The last count in Pooley's indictment was for words uttered as he was dragged off to jail from Liskeard magistrate's court, where he was committed for trial: "If it had not been for the blackguard, Jesus Christ, when he stole the donkey, police would not be wanted. . . . he was the forerunner of all theft and whoredome [sic]" (Holyoake, *Case* 14n). Strong words, but hardly published to the winds, and not admissible in court. Nevertheless, it was for these that Judge Coleridge added nine months to the twelve-month sentence recommended by the jury (six months for each of two other counts) when they "almost immediately returned the prisoner guilty" on 31 July 1857 (*Morning Chronicle,* 10 August: 7). Pooley had been "in the habit of constant writing upon walls and gates blasphemous and disgusting sentences" for fifteen years, argued J. D. Coleridge, prosecuting; and there

Figure 21. Collage of materials in the Pooley case, 1857. *Center* (944) and *behind* (966), letters from Mary Pooley to Holyoake. *Bottom center* and *top right*, densely written letters from Pooley in Bodmin Prison and Asylum. *Left* (924), the indictment. *Right* (1133), copy of the release letter from Under-Secretary Waddington. *Top left* (989), Bush's account of the case. Courtesy of the Co-operative Union, Manchester, Holyoake Collection.

was "the awfully depraved malignity" of his terms to consider (in E. Coleridge, *Life and Correspondence* 1: 249). Those very facts, if true, countered Holyoake, mitigated the offense. They proved delusion, and "[t]here is no crime in disordered words" (6), a moot point in Victorian law.

Public opinion began to be roused (fig. 21). Holyoake addressed over twenty meetings on the Pooley case (Hawtin 20); middle-class Secularist Lionel Holdreth wrote to the *Times,* the *Daily News,* the Law Officers of the Crown, and several members of Parliament; the brother of a Taunton squire upbraided Bush by sending "some of my writings, containing pas-

sages many times stronger than the words employed by that poor, uneducated man" (Hawtin 19). Two thousand copies of Holyoake's report were
printed; by November 1857 every judge in the country and every barrister
on the Western Circuit had one in his hands (*Reasoner*, 4 November: 250).
On 11 December, under pressure of "the Infidel Party within and without
the H[ouse] of Commons" (Bush, letter to W. O'Neill, 2 January 1858, in
HL), Pooley received a full pardon from the Crown. He was released by
the end of the month, when Holyoake brought him up to London to be
"exhibited" (Hawtin 21). Judge Coleridge retired a few months later. But
the story was by no means over.

The Pooley case became a cause célèbre when John Stuart Mill wrote
his condemnation into *On Liberty*. "It will be said that we do not now put
to death the introducers of new opinions," he declared. "But let us not
flatter ourselves that we are yet free from the stain even of legal persecution"
(34). The "tyranny" of public opinion made the "eccentricity" and "mere
refusal to bend the knee" of every man, even a Cornish laborer, a kind of
public duty (74). Reviewing the book for *Fraser's Magazine* in May 1859,
the liberal rationalist Thomas Buckle, one of the founders of modern intellectual history, turned the theme into national scandal: "I could not believe
that in the year 1857, there was a judge on the English bench who would
sentence a poor man of irreproachable character . . . to twenty-one months
imprisonment" (533). It was a clear-cut case of a judge and prosecutor,
father and son, "ferret[ing] out some obsolete law" exclusively for the purpose of "oppressing the poor," and as such explosive, because it fueled the
resentments of the lower classes.

> Why do they not have the learned and eminent indicted and thrown into prison?
> Simply because they dare not. I defy them to it. They are afraid of the odium;
> they tremble at the hostility they would incur, and at the scorn which would be
> heaped upon them, both by their contemporaries and by posterity. (536)

"Let all that heard him," Moses decrees of the blasphemer, "lay their hands
upon his head, and let all the congregation stone him" (Leviticus 24.14).
Pooley was the "victim whose vicarious sufferings may atone for the offences of more powerful unbelievers," the class "scapegoat" (Buckle, *Fraser's*
536) whose ritual expulsion might defuse the tensions endemic to a society
that prided itself both on its tolerance and on its piety, and that was granting ballot box power to the vulgar while it continued to think of itself in
exclusive upper-class terms.[44] Pooley's sentence was "wanton cruelty" (533).
"A great crime has been committed, and the names of the criminals ought
to be known" (535). Buckle's defense of "the poor, crazed, but intrepid well-
sinker," Holyoake declared forty years later, was "the only example . . . in
this century of a gentleman coming forward in that personal way, to vindi-

cate the right of Free Thought in the friendless and obscure" (*Sixty Years* 2: 96).

"[T]he Clergy Magistrates of Cornwall Are Dredfully Harried About Mr. Buckel's writing in Frazer's Magazine," Pooley wrote gratefully to "honest infidles" on 20 July 1859 (HL). The notorious exposé invested the case with "special interest to us, *as lawyers,*" commented the *Solicitor's Journal,* "because it is the first occasion in the long period which has elapsed since society assumed its present settled and refined condition, that the administration of justice, by one of the first class of judicial functionaries, has been openly alleged by persons of education, to have been designedly perverted to the purposes of oppression" (26 November 1859: 45). The profession largely closed ranks against the "reckless ruffianism of free speech" the sentence was passed to put down (*Law Times,* 21 May 1859: 115). In liberal circles, however, Judge Coleridge became the target of outrage.

There was irony in this. Coleridge Senior had once been compared to Jesus Christ in "beauty of character" (Holyoake, *Case* 17); his antagonism to a hate-filled "infidel" like Buckle (journal, 8 May 1859, qtd. in Toohey, "Blasphemy" 329) had not prevented him from delivering the important ruling that there was "nothing unlawful at common law in reverently doubting or denying doctrines parcel of Christianity, however fundamental," as Erskine's fellow judge in the 1842 Unitarian case of *Shore v. Wilson* (Odgers, *Libel and Slander* 448). The judge wanted no public truck with Buckle.

His son was another matter. Privately, John Duke Coleridge told his father that "six months . . . would have done as well as twenty-one" (in E. Coleridge, *Life and Correspondence* 1: 256). Publicly, he was stung not just in his family pride in his father and mentor but in his sense of himself as a "man of character." "I need not tell you," he warned *Fraser's Magazine,* in a sharp open letter to Buckle printed in the June issue, "that [his article] is a libel, nor need I offer you any opinion as to the effect on the character of your Magazine of publishing a tissue of . . . coarse personal malevolence" (635). As for Mr. Buckle:

> [he] will perhaps understand me when I say that . . . he does not comprehend the common feelings of a gentleman . . . . That [he] should have thought [collusion] possible in an English advocate of any standing . . . is a proof that his learning (if he be a learned man) is not education, and has not raised him above the feelings and prejudices of a thoroughly vulgar mind. (638–39)

This was no reply to the "principal charges," Buckle commented in a pamphlet later that month. By leaving them "untouched," Coleridge's letter made "a tacit assumption that they cannot be rebutted" (Buckle, *Letter* 14). But its assumption of class superiority was generally accepted, even where

Coleridge's language was considered too strong. Buckle had "betrayed" himself into "virulent" libel and "indiscriminating abuse," "following the example" of Holyoake's "vulgar" pamphlet (*Law Magazine and Review*, May–August 1859: 282, 270, 276, 279; see also *Solicitor's Journal*, November 1859: 45); his "ungentlemanly tone," said the *Saturday Review*, exuded a "self-sufficiency . . . at once offensive and absurd" (14 May 1859: 585). (By contrast, the *Saturday's* own notice of the elder Coleridge's retirement, which shortly followed the Pooley verdict, discreetly omitted all mention of the contentious case [19 June 1858: 633].) John Duke Coleridge remained obsessed with it: while he "learnt a lesson in Cornwall," as his biographer-nephew remarked (E. Coleridge 1: 251), its exact nature is unclear. Twenty-six years later, one would like to think, the third *Freethinker* trial allowed room to atone for the crime of injustice in which he had conspired; his judgment of 1883 clearly echoed his father's earlier, more tolerant verdict of 1842. A private letter, however, suggests that the trial also granted him an opportunity for more subtly enforcing his class-conscious view of the law: "I am not conscious of having altered my opinion or changed the expression of it since I was counsel in the case of Thomas Pooley," he wrote stiffly to Foote's rival and Pooley's erstwhile defender, Jacob Holyoake, on 29 July 1883. The "controversy in that case" was "discreditable to no one but Mr. Buckle" (HL). His "presumption" and "vulgar swagger" remained unforgiven (Coleridge to Holyoake, 4 May 1886, in HL).

It is wholly possible, then, that dinner with the chief justice in December 1892 brought the Pooley case and the matter of blasphemy to Thomas Hardy's mind. But it was a question, I think, of remembering. Hardy read *On Liberty* in 1867, almost memorizing parts: Sue quotes it freely in *Jude*. But ten years before, he almost certainly saw an earlier analysis of the Pooley case in the *Saturday Review*, to which his mentor Horace Moule introduced him in the year the scandal broke, 1857; he devoured its "brilliantly-written" pages with studious attention (Gittings 1: 39). The case "deserve[d] notice," the *Saturday* felt, "from the legal points which [it] raised," though the "poor half-crazy creature who chalked the walls with offensive remarks" (interestingly, not "the gates") did not merit such "excessive" punishment as he received. "[T]here is a very strong presumption indeed in favor of treating such cases with contempt, and we are sorry that it should have been thought necessary to depart from the established practice" (29 August 1857: 200). The *Saturday's* intervention of 1859 ("Mr. Buckle and Sir John Coleridge") is noticed above; its specific and lawyer-like coverage of the case included the observation, almost nowhere else recorded, that—like Jude reciting the creed—Pooley had "made blasphemous observations, coupling the name of Christ with contumelious reproaches in a public house" (14 May 1859: 586). These were exactly the items to mull over at Fordington Rectory with Moule, or in Hicks the architect's office, where the atmosphere was lively and controversial, and work brought regular contact with West Country clergymen. They were what would be talked up with fervor by Hardy's uncle Antell, the angry Puddletown atheist.

Neither the *Dorset County Chronicle* nor its lively rival the *Dorset County Express* reported the Bodmin Assizes for 1857; and we do not have extant copies of all the newspapers that circulated through Dorchester in that year. But we do know that—in these days before investigative journalism (like Holyoake's pioneering report) and full-blown scandal sheets—trial reports alone satisfied the public taste for dirty linen, and that their lurid stories were regularly recycled through local papers, which may thus be another source for Hardy's knowledge of the Pooley case. (Indeed, the *Express* began extensive trial reports the following year, probably in an attempt to stave off financial collapse.) "Off Wessex," as Hardy called Cornwall, was far from Dorset, but the Pooley case was singular and infamous. Trial reports easily held their own in local papers with the Indian Mutiny, the "Jew measure" (that is, the Oaths Act that would make Rothschild an M.P.), the Married Women's Property Bill, and the Burial Acts Amendment, the hot topics of 1857. They were read with an attention that today seems out of all proportion to their length or detail. And Hardy was one of the closest of close readers, morbidly fascinated from childhood up by the operations of justice. Crime was part of the fabric of his Wessex. "Bloody" Judge Jeffries sentenced eighty men and women to swing on Gallows Hill at one Dorchester Assizes in 1685; Hardy's own duties as a justice of the peace, he told the *World* in 1886, "ke[pt] him in touch with some sterner facts of existence" (cutting, 17 February, in Hardy scrapbook). Moreover, the Pooley case broke midway between the two hangings he witnessed in 1856 and 1858.[45]

And blasphemy was a specific Dorchester memory. It was here that outrageous Richard Carlile served his six years of willful incarceration in the cause of Tom Paine and free publication, 1819–25, founding the nineteenth-century tradition of blasphemy martyrdom. (Sue inherits from the *Age of Reason* her skeptical taste for "Bible Absurdities," masked as an inheritance of cultured agnosticism from Shelley and her dead undergraduate friend.) Carlile's life as the most famous inmate of Dorchester Gaol was the stuff local legend was made of. When "permitted th[e] luxury" of fresh air exercise, "he was led out as a caged animal and exhibited to the gaze of the passing curious" (Foote, *Heroes and Martyrs* 151). He conducted infidel business from his cell, and received delivery of a baby. He was vilified at withering length by the editor of the *Dorsetshire County Chronicle* on 30 December 1824 and 6 January 1825, unusual and arresting items that Hardy might have read as he reviewed the *Chronicle*'s files doing research for the *Trumpet Major* in 1878 and the *Mayor of Casterbridge* in 1884. (The *Republican* for 28 January 1825 is entirely taken up with Carlile's response to being dubbed a "low, illiterate and ignorant person" [qtd. in Foote, *Heroes and Martyrs* 106], a diatribe which the *Chronicle* had refused to print [*Republican,* 4 January 1825: 48].) This history, this legend, would have given weight and meaning to any mention of Pooley's blasphemy to Dorchester citizens in 1857.

We can reconstruct the feel of that year from the pages of the Cornish and national newspapers. They convict one immediately of critical déjà vu. Here, one stumbles over events and details from Hardy's works, together with the cultural contexts that give them poignancy and point: an "unprecedented" rape at Motcombe in Dorset (which reached the London *Observer* on 27 July 1857: 7) such as Tess suffers in *Tess,* while two witnesses and potential saviors (one her cousin) "quietly" passed by; the "SALE OF A WIFE" by a Scotsman for half a pint of gin, such a seed as grew the *Mayor of Casterbridge* (this, like the rest that follow, from the *Cornish Times* around the time of the Pooley trial [22 August 1857: 2]); a horse impaled, like the Durbeyfields' tired old nag, on the "splinter bar" of the oncoming "Fairy" Omnibus while descending a hill in Pound Lane (1 August: 1);[46] new methods for "Killing and Curing Pigs by Steam" (22 August: 4) and a dead baby found in a pigsty, grotesqueries reminiscent of the intrusive piggishness of *Jude* (8 August: 1); the "melancholy" suicide of a clergyman, on the day he first officiated, with a razor (8 August: 4); and an atheist's blighted child miraculously redeemed by the mere fetishistic possession of a Bible ("THE BOOK," 1 August: 4). Finally, there is the accused in another local tragedy timing an egg for breakfast in the minutes before blood is shed, one of the pathetic homely details that precedes the discovery of the children's death by hanging in *Jude the Obscure* (354).

Liskeard, where Pooley lived, lies midway between Plymouth, hometown of Hardy's wife Emma Gifford, and hard-grained Bodmin, where her family removed when its fortunes collapsed in 1860, and where Pooley was tried and jailed in 1857. All the essential drama of his case took place within a small, intensely knowable area: it is fourteen miles from Liskeard to Bodmin; and two days' walk across Bodmin Moor to little St. Juliot on the romantic north coast, where Thomas Hardy came courting and church-restoring for Hicks's successor, Mr. Crickmay, in 1869. The Dorset stranger came to know Cornwall well: this was the first of seven visits. They brought him into a household where the blasphemy of Thomas Pooley, or other local infidels, would have remained a live item of talk: Emma lived with her sister and clergyman brother-in-law in St. Juliot Rectory. Cornwall was a depressed but law-abiding county where offenses were rare and were remembered; they were often the fruits of despair—like that of sixteen-year-old Susan Chinn, charged with murdering her illegitimate baby (the one found in the pigsty).[47]

"On Tuesday last," read the 1 August report on the assizes in the *Cornish Times*, the paper clergymen read, "Mr. Justice Coleridge arrived at Bodmin":

> The calendar for these assizes contained the names of twenty-nine prisoners, some of whom were committed on very serious charges. It included three cases of child murder, one of manslaughter, two for stabbing and wounding, one of assault with intent, two burglaries, one housebreaking, one indictment for blasphemy. (1)

The *Telegraph* was less cagey in its reporting.

> This [last] case has naturally excited very considerable interest, particularly as the learned Judge has referred to it in the following terms, when addressing the Grand Jury: "It was," said his Lordship, "a very unusual charge. He did not know that in his experience of more than 26 years on the judicial bench he had ever found a case of this kind on any calendar." (3)

The enmeshment of church and state is amply given in the paper's preface to its assizes report: Details of attendance by Coleridge's fellow judge at divine service in Bodmin Church, where "an appropriate sermon" was preached on the text from Jeremiah (32.19), "For thine eyes are open upon all the ways of the sons of men, to give everyone according to his ways and according to the fruits of his doings" (4).

The reports of the Pooley case render up details of his "obscure" career deeply suggestive for *Jude the Obscure*. Here recorded are Pooley's unrewarded hard work; his childlike belief (much like the childish Jude's) that the earth "was a living thinking body" (*Spectator*, 8 August 1857: 834); his grief for a small son who died in 1852, whose grave he "decorate[d] with flowers and mineral specimens" (*Cornish Telegraph*, 5 August: 3);[48] the depth of his family affections, despite the clash between his infidelity and his wife's church-going orthodoxy. Penury, sickness, and doggedness, Holyoake's additions, complete the picture (*Case* 8–9). The parallels with Jude's character are plain: there turns out to be a strange truth in G. K. Chesterton's gibe that "heretic[al]" Hardy, the "village atheist," descended to "brooding and blaspheming over the village idiot" (*Victorian Age* 143).

The sense of persecution that drove "wretched" Pooley to "hope that none of the jury were Christians" (*London Times*, 3 August 1857: 10) recalls Jude's howl against the religion that plunges Sue into the symbolic darkness of St. Savior's Church. More secular bystanders believed "Poor Pooley" was "merely insane," though John Duke Coleridge thought him acutely intelligent (in E. Coleridge, *Life and Correspondence* 1: 249) and Bush thought him only unhinged "insofar as every Infidel is insane" (letter to W. O'Neill, 2 January 1858, in HL). (Judge Coleridge Senior more humanely responded to Home Office inquiry that no evidence for "an acquittal on the ground of insanity" had been obvious at the trial, "which on such a charge I should have been very glad to have arrived at" [letter of 2 December 1857; *Fraser's Magazine*, June 1859: 643].) Holyoake thought Pooley's "unusual and abrupt" conduct "denote[d] utter despair or incipient insanity" (6), producing a piece of rock that "fell on [Pooley's] head as he was down a well," two years before, to add to his grief for his son, to explain a recent increase in delusions that "originated" in "want of educating" (*Case* 14). It was better Secularist policy to present Pooley as insane, bereft of the power of language; and the suggestion gave embarrassed authorities a helpful escape clause. We shall never know whether mania dictated the words on the gate. But we do know that trial and imprisonment reduced their utterer to the very brink of sanity.

Fortress-like, Her Majesty's County Prison, Bodmin, still rises on high land above the gray town like a set of carious stone fangs. It is disproportionate to its place, fit for a city six times as large. Plaques on the "execution wall" in the courtyard commemorate the child murderer, the French sailor, the woman who drowned her illegitimate newborn. The cell blocks are five stories high: from the top you can see the moor and the road back to Liskeard. Here Pooley was held before trial. His letter home of 26 July 1857 testifies to the impact of imprisonment upon him. It does not sound deranged.

> Mary, I hope there is nothing the matter. I keep fancying there is something the matter at home. . . . As for me, I am bound in misery. My life is a burden to me. . . . If I was sure I should be bound in this place much longer, I would take poison if I could get it. . . . I am sick of Christian Bible tyranny. What will be the end of this I don't know. (qtd. in Holyoake, *Case* 15)

The treatment deteriorated after sentencing at seven o'clock the next evening. Forbidden to touch his daughter before he was parted from her, Pooley dragged a policeman and the three prisoners to whom he was handcuffed across the courtroom to take her hand. For this he was sentenced to confinement in the dark cells on bread and water for three days (*Case* 16–17); surviving manuscript letters return obsessively to this cruelty. Unable to swallow, Pooley was forcibly fed. Twice he ripped to shreds the prison clothing in which six men forcibly dressed him, and after the second struggle, naked, began to vomit blood. The prison governor feared he might die. On 12 August 1857 Pooley was removed to the pauper wing of Bodmin Asylum as a "criminal lunatic."

This institution was one of the bare handful purpose-built to Bentham's exact panoptic specifications in the nineteenth century. First planned as a leper colony and decommissioned as an asylum in the 1980s, it awaited conversion in 1995 as a condominium complex.[49] In Pooley's time, despite the fields and gardens, it was a closed world of barred upper windows, "fecal disorder" caused by malfunctioning toilets, restricted movement, melancholy "seclusion," and excruciating boredom, marginally relieved by the books and prints provided by a few humane commissioners. Of the seventy-eight patients admitted in 1857, twenty-eight "recovered," twelve did not, and twenty-seven died, all of them pauper patients (reports of 1857 and 1858 in County Asylum Visitors' Book, CRO). Here, Pooley showed more evidence of disturbance. His condition was not improved by the thought of being returned to the jail to complete his sentence if he were declared sane (Buckle, *Fraser's*, May 1859: 534). "I'm afried I should be struck with madness on my Braine," Pooley wrote his wife on 16 November 1857, before degenerating into anguished ramblings about the two shillings and "pice of Cake" he could send her, the gift of the asylum medical officer, Dr. Adams (HL). Yet within a month that same officer, and the governor, certified—as Pooley's official pardon put it—that he could be released with "no danger to himself or others" (letter from Home Office Under-Secretary Waddington, 11 December 1857, in HL). Pooley offers a powerful parallel to Jude's forced descent into the borderland of interchained anguish of body and mind.

But the bare human comfort of sexual loyalty that Pooley can fantasize is denied to Jude (fig. 22). He cannot say, "Mary, I would take poison, poison, if I could but die in your arms" (qtd. in Holyoake, *Case* 15). And again, "Mary, if I could but grasp you in my arms once more, I could die happy. My love for you is not gone, and I hope your love is not gone from me" (26). Hardy's novel turns even this screw of pain: God removes from his heaven, but no human care steps in to salve the wound, as near the close of Arnold's "Dover Beach": "Ah, love, let us be true / To one another!" (lines 29–30, *Portable*). Cruelty and Cornwall were closely associated in Hardy's mind. One of the poems that grew out of a visit to Emma in August 1872, "Near Lanivet, 1872" (the place is three miles from Bodmin), imagines a latter-day crucifixion; in another, a woman laments "The evil wrought at Rou'tor Town" (Bodmin) "On him I loved so true." When he was asked in 1920 what the evil was, Hardy replied, "Slander, or something of that sort" (Seymour-Smith 147). Biographers have struggled to see the

JUDE AT THE MILE-STONE.

Figure 22. Hatherell's final image for the *Harper's* version of *Jude,* November 1895. "The picture is a tragedy in itself," Hardy wrote him, "& I do not remember ever before having an artist who grasped a situation so thoroughly" (*Letters* 2: 94). It hung in Hardy's study until his death.

bearing of this cryptic remark on his own life. But he may not have had himself in mind.

Consider the peculiar nature of Pooley's blasphemy—its quality of public advertisement. It brings back Paterson's sentence for "displaying" a poster in the "public" "thoroughfare" that apparently ran through his shop; it anticipates Seymour's conviction for publicizing a Secularist lecture: "Fun! Fun! Fun! . . . Hamlet and the Holy Ghost!" Pooley's offense was worse, as Holyoake knew: "an offence at law, as defacing property" (6), Reverend Paul Bush's home field gate. (Three burglars tried at Bodmin Assizes were the only prisoners more harshly sentenced [*Cornish Times,* 1 August 1857: 1].) But the fact that Pooley allegedly spelled out his disputed words for all to see, from a public highway, with a handy piece of chalk, was the central fact in the crime: "I may buy and read antichristian books if I please," concluded the *Law Magazine and Review,* "or leave them alone, but I cannot help seeing filthy and contemptuous language publicly inscribed in the streets; and he who forces such on the notice of all his neighbors . . . is guilty of a crime" (May–August 1859: 284); "unnecessary publicity" was later decreed "evidence of malice" in libel law (Odgers, *Libel and Slander* 337).[50] Offense against the Word here takes a peculiarly literal form, revealing, in the signature—"T. Pooley"—an anxiety about authorship and self-representation, something beyond and beside blasphemous *imitatio Christi,* that is suggestive for *Jude.* Pooley groped toward a voice of his own, even scratching a strange meditation on "Death and the Grave" on a slate with a nail the night before he was arraigned before the magistrats: "By the power of this globe, [Bible] tyrants, be careful, for your life is not your own, for in a moment it is gone and called to the grave and receives judgment. Thomas Pooley, July the first" (Holyoake, *Case* 13).

The detail about the chalk sticks in the mind. Jude likewise scrawls his reply to the master of Biblioll College, who has advised him to stick to his trade, graffiti-like "along the wall" that excludes him "with the lump of chalk which as a workman he usually carried" in his pocket:

> "I have understanding as well as you. I am not inferior to you: yea, who knoweth not such things as these?"—*Job* xii 3. (121)

Like the rustic fanatic of *Tess* writing his "killing" letters on fences and stiles ("Thy, Damnation, Slumbereth, Not" [*Tess* 63]); like the Luddites who scrawled their messages of revolution on market walls (E. Thompson 714); like Jude himself as a lad, carving "Thither—J.F." on the milestone that measures his distance from heavenly Christminster (73); but most of all like Thomas Pooley, writing his protest on Reverend Bush's gate, Hardy's hero makes his retort to the world on the world: like the Cornish well sinker's, Jude the stonemason's response to the Divine Word is a direct and tangible counterclaim to authorship. This workingman's notion (in Holyoake's words) of "chalk[ing] his insanities over land and sky" (*Case* 21) sinks in the novel's heart.[51]

Jude's and Pooley's offensive inscriptions recall the terms of the 1889 Indecent Advertisements Act, which gives a definition of "advertisement" that would make a modern lawyer blench: anything from posters and graffiti on walls, gates, trees, buildings, public urinals, to objects "of an indecent or obscene nature" (477) tossed in one's own kitchen area that might with effort be spotted by passersby. The very word "advertisement" welds together the old denotation of "warning" and the modern sense of "publicity" in a manner that warns us of the potential for criminality of all untoward "publication." On this score, the "astounding manner" in which Cornwall's clergy "hunted down this poor lunatic" (Holyoake, *Case* 12) merits brief examination. *Jude's* unholy marriage of Bible English and commercial lingo might also take a cue from the front-page display advertisement placed in the *Cornish Times and General Advertiser* for Saturday, 25 April 1857, cost one shilling and four pence, with perhaps an additional charge for the capitals.

BLASPHEMY.

ANY Person who has seen a man writing Blasphemous sentences on Gates or other places in the neighborhood of Liskeard, is requested to communicate immediately with Messrs PEDLER & GRYLLS, Liskeard, or with the Rev. R. Hobhouse, St. Ive Rectory. (1)

Grylls, an attorney, was clerk to the magistrates who committed Pooley (Hawtin 21). The editor obligingly placed this notice dead center under the masthead, like a bull's eye; it was odd company for the mining and farming notices that surrounded it, and no match for their typographical candor. ("Manure! Manure!! Manure!!!" announces one plug in the rival *Cornish Telegraph,* 29 July 1857; "Arrival!!" of "The Ammoniated Super-Phosphate!" [1].) Sober notices for extraordinary items were a local specialty, however, whether "Self-adjusting trowsers" or "Blasphemy." Both the "criminal" and his pursuers were caught up in the debasement of language (as Horkheimer and Adorno describe it) brought about by the new culture of mass advertisement.

More suggestions of kinship of a more obviously literary kind between the "insane" well sinker and Hardy's stonemason emerge from the archive. Jude Fawley suffers the same intensity of repulsed and anguished engagement with Christianity as Thomas Pooley. Pooley's native Liskeard was a hotbed of activity by the breakaway "Bryanite" or "Bible Christian" sect, extreme Methodists whom Pooley particularly disliked (Holyoake, *Case* 8). Their one way "to flee from the wrath to come" was "Follow Christ according to the Bible," and they placed crucial restrictions upon "taking the Name of God in vain" (*Rules of Society* 1, 3). If *Jude* is in part a meditation on its biblical epigraph, "the letter killeth," the case of Thomas Pooley is an illustration both of what Pooley called "Bible tyranny" (Holyoake, *Case* 13, 15, 29) and what we might call bibliomania. Manuscript letters evidence the fact that Pooley felt he had been directly condemned by "that Book that upholds murder wars vice misery Blasphemy Drunkenness [W]Hordom and upholds All Tyranny and Drenched this Globe with Human Blood" (9 January 1858, in HL). The press evidences his habit of frequent quotation from the Holy Book he later—ritually—placed upon a bonfire. "[I]f folks would burn their Bibles," he told laborer Richard Crapp in a local pub, the *Morning Chronicle* reported, "and take the ashes for dressing

[the fields], it would get rid of the [potato] disease" (10 August 1857: 7).
That comment formed the second count in Pooley's indictment, earning
six months of his sentence, although even John Duke Coleridge thought
it might have been a joke (Holyoake, *Case* 29), and the court recognized
that "the prisoner . . . was never known to write any profane or blasphemous
statement on [his children's] Bibles" [*Cornish Telegraph,* 5 August 1857: 3].)
The weird scene conjured here seemed destined to return in memory to
the man who plotted the blasphemous scene of theological book burning
in *Jude the Obscure* ("theology & burning," as Hardy wrote about the "conflagratory" Bishop, "will continue allies to the end" [*Letters* 2: 125]). Anglo-
Irish courts had ruled in 1852 that "contemptuously to burn a bible" ranked
as a misdemeanor in law (Nokes 117), and three years later the accusation
that he had (inadvertently) burned a Bible in public on a bonfire of licentious works got Father Vladimir Petcherine indicted for blasphemy in Dublin (see Lawton 111–16).

The press felt to the full the grotesque disproportion between Pooley's
status and his crime's, a disjunction that recalls the abrupt shifts of scale
and mood that discountenanced the reviewers of *Jude* (Lerner and Holmstrom 124). "It is evident that [Pooley] cannot be a person whose free transit
about the world can be of any great importance," said the *Spectator,* "but
it is of importance to all of us that no undue severity should be inflicted
upon any man however obscure, and of still greater importance that the
authority of the law should not be damaged by applying its most solemn
machinery to trifles or to getting up a burlesque upon the inquisition" (8
August 1857: 834). Confined to the asylum, Pooley wrote his wife in grandi-
ose terms that have meaning for *Jude:* "There is something wrong with the
human family, and it is time for man to awake, and ask what is divine and
what is not divine. I will walk in solitary [sic], and will ask, what will the
law of man be?" (qtd. in Holyoake, *Case:* 26–27).

There was a pathetic "air of grandeur" in his "proclamation of heroism"
to the court: "If they found it in their breasts to torture him, he would
give up his life's blood, but he would not endure Christian tyranny." " 'My
Lord,' cried the prisoner, with a majesty leant him by the severity of the
sentence, 'I beg of you to put on the black cap at once' " (*Spectator,* 8
August 1857: 834). Holyoake was taken aback by the theatricality of Pooley's
protest. "When he was summoned, on two occasions, before the Liskeard
magistrates, he placed a rope round his neck and walked into the Court
with it, and told the magistrate to pull it and have done with it" (*Case*
6). On another occasion, he undressed and "offered them his garments in
composition of a legal claim upon him" (10–11). What right had a mere
workingman to pose as the hero of his own story? Or to speak—for all his

"address" to the jury might be "rambling" and inconsequential (*Morning Chronicle,* 10 August 1857: 7)—in such a voice as that?

The questions apply equally to Jude. What kind of hero was he to be? The rise of the self-educated proletarian from laboring squalor to citizenship was "one of the most remarkable facts in nineteenth-century English history," but literature was as slow as society to "absorb this remarkable new figure" (Howe 398). *Jude the Obscure* was the first mainstream work of Victorian fiction "from a Master's hand" to present him center stage, to insist "on a recognition of his total humanity" (Eagleton 66). But in what kind of voice should he speak? *Jude* focuses sharply the problem Hardy marked in his copy of Comte's positivist philosophy: "The man who dares to think himself independent of others . . . cannot even put the *blasphemous* conception into words without self-contradiction, since the very language he uses is not his own" (qtd. in D. Taylor 211). The novel posits a progress towards a voice "which is neither Graffito . . . nor mere parody (reciting the creeds)" (Goode 161–62).[52] But at best it achieves a deliberate, awkward hybrid, which took sympathy to hear out. Jude starts the novel mimicking an idiom Sue rightly complains is "too sermony" (273); learns to speak "a kind of University Extension jargon that breaks the heart" (Gosse, Cox 269); breaks out into profanities; and gives his reply to the master of Biblioll in the biblical language that is an instinct of his workingman's blood. The *Bookman* voiced the majority bourgeois verdict: "some of the self-taught man's vanity and his laboriousness of expression are not suppressed" (Lerner and Holmstrom 131). Jude's skeptic's progress has the shape of Foote's career, a paradigm of linguistic rebellion and blasphemous quest for "his own words." Society's urge to "suppress" the coarser voice, which impelled Foote's trials and stiffened the six-year drive to deny Bradlaugh his say in government, haunts Hardy's last and most openly political novel.

The novel does equivocate, however, on this subject of voice. Its final destination is that same uneasy silence in which Foote was shut up in Holloway Gaol. "That is what has been hidden from me," says Catherine Elsmere, "that is what my trouble has taught me; the powerlessness, the worthlessness, of words" (Ward, *Elsmere* 510). *Jude*'s movement towards silence traces itself first in a persistent and destabilizing confusion of letters with actors: the much-discussed Christminster "ghosts"—the disembodied voices and airborne quotations Jude hears in the streets on his first and last days in the city—are part of a network that includes thirty-two notes, the "letters" Sue writes for Miss Fontover ("Alleluja" as artifact, emptied of divine power), and the "relettered" Ten Commandments. Second, just as Jude's painfully acquired gobbets of Latin and Greek are dropped untranslated into the text and unassimilated into its flow—like the boldly capital-ized title of the Greek Testament, set off alone as a paragraph entire in itself "Η ΚΑΙΝΗ ΔΙΑΘΗΚΗ" (40, 41, 46)—so the classical languages never become a means of truly human communication: Jude is excluded from Christminster's theater on Remembrance Day, and thereby from the Latin ceremony and the discourse of class power (347). Thirdly, the novel's strenuous effort to represent the full range of human experience stutters through difficult scenes (see 251, 366, 383) to end in frustration: Hardy declines to print the "terribly profane language about social conventions" Jude resorts to "in his mental agony" (423), or the "striking epithets" he "vent[s]" in the face of Vilbert the quack doctor. The movement towards silence and the subtext of blasphemy converge as history might have pre-dicted they would. Mrs. Edlin makes the "reticent" final comment: "Poor chap, he got excited, and do blaspeam [sic] terribly" (423). The last notes sounded are the negative notes of blasphemy and literary blasphemy (as that final misspelling announces), intermixed.

Last: Jude's Pooley-like scrawl on the wall of Biblioll College is not made (unlike Pooley's) in "his own language." Jude makes his counterclaim against the bibliolatrous master who denies him the power of knowledge in a language of power to which he is denied a right: *"I have understanding as well as you. I am not inferior to you"* (Job 12.3). The lines are disconcertingly italicized, estranged from the body of the text. Almost all working-class radicals, with mixed success, attempted to appropriate Bible English in the nineteenth century, excepting only Foote and (for a time) Richard Carlile; its appropriation is not achieved in Hardy's novel. Jude's claim is as much hopeless as it is subversive.

The same may be said of his dying words. It is perhaps important that they were added after the novel was complete: originally, Jude had ended in utter silence, like his own pig, whose windpipe Arabella cuts through to stifle his dying scream. Now, Jude dies speaking in a voice that is clearly, typographically, not his own. In fact, like the scriptural claim Jude turns into graffiti (*"I have understanding . . ."*), the words are Job's, from what Leslie Stephen called the agnostic's book of the Bible. Hardy cited Job frequently (most recently in *Tess*), and "feared the Job-cum-Ezekiel moralist loomed too largely" behind *Jude*'s "would-be artist" (*Letters* 2: 96). His title may even be read as a scripted pun: *Jude the OBscure, Job's cure*, the *Obscure JoB*.[53] Job, the book that gave biblical bowdlerizers one of their greatest challenges, had a direct linguistic attraction. In the chapter from which Jude's dying words are taken, Bildad tries to quiet Job, and his comforters try to "break me in pieces with words" (Job 19.2), while God stands ar-raigned for his silence. Job and *Jude* continue:

Let the day perish wherein I was born, and the night in which it was said, There
is a man child conceived.

Let that day be darkness. . . . let no joyful voice come therein.

Why died I not from the womb? Why did I not give up the ghost when I
came out of the belly? . . . For now should I have lain still and been quiet. . . .
There the prisoners rest together; they hear not the voice of the oppressor. (Job
3.3–18; *Jude* 426–27)

On the one hand, the words lead us back to wordlessness—the desire for
annihilation figured as silence. On the other, they are an extraordinary
outpouring, a rush of accusatory utterance, language used in rebuke of the
Word, an ancient talking cure, compulsive "sin with [the] lips" and
"scourge of the tongue" (Job 2.10, 5.21). "Dying is no gammon," as Pooley
said (Holyoake, *Case* 27). "Therefore," says Job, "I will not refrain my
mouth" (7.11), for "if I hold my tongue, I shall give up the ghost" (13.19).
The Book of Job ends when the Lord cuts short all conversation with the
simple assertion of his power and the uselessness of "darkening" (or "obscuring") counsel "by words without knowledge" (38.2). Job assents: "Behold, I will lay mine hand upon my mouth" (40.4). *Jude* ends on the Book
of Job's midnote of protest against that silencing, and as such may well be
read as a blasphemous parody of Job's legend of the enduring man whose
life is made the sport of inexplicable powers.

"Oh that my words were now written," wishes Job, "oh that they were
printed in a book! Oh that they were graven with an iron pen and laid in
the rock for ever!" (Job 19.23–24)—like the words of Thomas Pooley, scribbled on slates and gates, as if to ape the Lord who wrote his Commandments on tablets of stone. That cry reverberates through *Jude the Obscure.*
Jude as the blasphemous lower-class scapegoat reconfigured as fictional hero
proves ultimately unbookable; and—like the Secularists who lived by the
Book, in a mirror-image world of their own anti-Christian making—
Thomas Hardy the novelist writes himself into silence. *Jude the Obscure* is
the swan song of Victorian fiction in more ways than one.

It is not recorded when or where Thomas Pooley died. There is nothing
of him left in Liskeard and Duloe; his marriage cannot be traced in the
parish records; the assizes' records have been lost; time has obliterated his
son's grave. The outspoken protest of *Jude the Obscure,* its "blaspeaming"
offensiveness, and the silence into which it dwindles, turns out to echo
other men's struggles besides Hardy's own, and a class's and a culture's
crisis. "We were all of us obscure persons," as Francis Place wrote of the
committee of radicals that changed voting patterns in Westminster, 1807
(E. Thompson 465); Jude the martyr, patron saint of failures, lived on in

the dogged tradition of the Secularist—and the desperate—martyrs to the law. Sometimes the world listened, briefly, when they spoke out.

4. MODERN WORDS, MODERN CRIMES

It is obvious already that Hardy the novelist-poet, who revised his *Jude* across manuscript, serial, 1895, 1903, and 1912 ("Wessex") editions, and died leaving notes on his copy, had an intense interest in language and a deep-rooted feeling for its nuances. The friend he met in 1857 and remembers in the figure of the dead undergraduate shared that feeling: long-dead Horace Moule was collector of entries for the letter "H" for the *Oxford English Dictionary*. In the year 1865, from which he dated his loss of religious faith, Hardy himself began a notebook in which he kept lists of various usages of the same word: the Word lost its hold, but words kept their power, and the unprescriptive description of what they said was a subversive business. The "deep" "mental influence" (*Life and Work* 42) of Leslie Stephen was a joint effect of their linguistic struggles over his *Cornhill* serials and his public pronouncements on "Freethinking and Plain-speaking."[54]

A third connection cemented the link between unbelief and linguistic devotion. Hardy's close friend from at least 1890 (*Letters* i: 237), the wealthy banker Edward Clodd, was both the popular author of works like the *Story of the Alphabet* (1900) and *Magic in Names* (1898/1920) and one of the "militant" rationalists who "with Huxley, Bradlaugh, Foote the atheist, Ingersoll and others, destroyed revealed religion" in the 1880s (Ford 296). Clodd respectfully cites "Foote the atheist" in his *Memories* of 1916 (154), he signed the petition to Home Secretary Harcourt for Foote's release from prison, and he probably knew Foote personally. The *Freethinker*'s editor was a well-known public figure and national type (Clodd collected them), and they had Meredith's friendship in common. Clodd quotes Foote's obituary notice of Meredith in the *English Review* for March 1913: Meredith "aided with money," Clodd recalled in 1916, the year after Foote died, "the aggressive methods of the late Mr. Foote, to whom was addressed the last letter that he wrote, promising support to the *Freethinker*" (*Memories* 154). Foote would have wholeheartedly endorsed Clodd's conviction that linguistic superstition "has played, and still plays," an "important part" in "savage and civilized belief and ritual" (*Magic in Names* ii). Through Clodd, perhaps, with whom he shared the acquaintance of Huxley, Clifford, Gissing, and other less reputable unbelievers, Hardy too knew G. W. Foote.

It is fitting that a tie, if it existed, should be traced through the medium of language. Language was the dominant theme in the three provocative essays on the writing and reading of fiction that Hardy published in the years 1888–91, immediately before he wrote his last novels. Fiction might break the Ten Commandments if it does so "in a genteel manner" (Hardy, "Candour in English Fiction," *Personal Writings* 129); writing for the "young Person" forces novelists to wear "a common livery in style and subject" (132): the servile imagery brings back *Ethelberta* and its linguistic offenses. (Hardy copied into his *Literary Notebook* about this time Müller's description of written language: "free speech 'in a state of domestication' " [Wickens 19]). Hardy the writer, at the height of his powers, combined Foote's linguistic rebelliousness with a different conservatism from Holyoake's. English, he said, was not a "dead language—a thing crystallized at an arbitrarily selected stage of its existence" (qtd. in Elliott 20); and "purity" in language "almost always means ignorance" (20). Gathering in the richness of the past, he also wanted to make the language new. In *Jude* Hardy opened the "Great Tradition" of the novel (from which Leavis would later exclude him) to the whole hierarchy of the nation's language, from polished top to "brutal" bottom, without residual regard for what the reviewers called the "homogeneity of his utterance" (Lerner and Holmstrom 76): "Bible English," the resonant language of Shakespeare and of the past, the idioms of science and philosophy, newspaper and magazine English, coinages of his own making, Dorset dialect, commercial jargon, colloquialism, and slang. This was linguistic desacralization by association on the grand scale. Refusing to "speak like a book" (Gissing, *Born in Exile* 1: 38) was to align himself with the blasphemers. But it was also to step into the future.

In a novel that shifts location from lush pastures and windswept heaths to the "meanly utilitarian" sub-urban landscape of North Dorset, Hardy's "racy Saxon of the West-country" (qtd. in D. Taylor: 161) could no longer function predominantly as local color, comic relief, and vessel of folk wisdom. There is far less dialect in *Jude* than in *Tess,* but what there is spreads itself across a larger cross-section of characters (even schoolmaster Phillotson speaks it) and a broader range of human experience. Its use contradicts the standard assumption of Hardy's favorite *Saturday Review,* as revealed in its notice of the *Imperial Dictionary* on 27 January 1883, that "the ordinary rustic gets along with the use of from three to five hundred words" (118). (Hardy was omitted from the dictionary's "exhaustive list" of literary sources [119].) Dialect carries some of the deeper and most rebellious meanings of *Jude the Obscure.* "Goddy-mighty" (7) lives at the level of local superstition. Arabella's imperfectly euphemized curse, "Od damn it all!" (64), turns the Lord of Hosts into a fragment of demotic speech. The "grotesque element" in phonetic representation Hardy abjured in an 1878 note to the *Athenaeum* was what he wanted in *Jude* ("Dialect in Novels," *Personal*

Writings 91); the novel resists the class-coded literary convention by which virtuous characters (like Dickens's Oliver Twist) speak standard English.

Hardy's defense of dialect as "intrinsically as genuine, grammatical, and worthy of the royal title" as "the Queen's English," the "uniform tongue" ("Dialect in Novels," *Personal Writings* 93), is well known. It seems to have escaped critical notice, however, that in his last novel it was not so much the Dorset dialect he advanced to space and status as the "impure" language of the unwashed urban underclass. Hardy "had not the slightest intention of writing for ever about sheepfarm[ers]" (*Life and Work* 105), nor perhaps in their idiom alone. As the interviewer for *Cassell's* magazine remarked in 1892, Hardy was "much more of a town bird than many of his readers may think," who spent half of his working life to 1893 in London, and took a "West End flat every season" (25 June: 944). The Arabella who gets the privilege of closing the narrative, in dialect, has picked up more than her fair share of bastard Cockney and "hateful modern slang" in her peregrinations through the bars of Empire (Patmore, *Woodlanders* review, Cox 149). Hardy asks us to focus on her language, not her body: "Well—I should not have called Arabella coarse exactly," says Jude, "except in speech" (275). The demotic idiom of the "human pig," still more than the half-formed utterance of the self-schooled Jude, strikes *Jude's* loudest note of linguistic rebellion. The urban drawl of Hardy's language has more consequence even than the "urban invasion" (Widdowson 65) signaled by *Tess's* threshing machine or the city sprawl of "Aldbrickham's "'s dreary streets.

"[F]inished" by London life, Arabella's voice rings with the true note of the fin de siècle trollop who dreamed of being a Gaiety Girl and queued for the cheap seats at the Empire. (Hardy records visits to music halls during the writing of *Jude*, winter 1892–93 [*Life and Work* 265, 269]; advertisements in the Dorsetshire papers remind us how easy the railway made it to soak in their atmosphere.) "O, Mr. Cockman, now!" she says, "How can you tell such a tale to me in my innocence! . . . Mr. Cockman, what do you use to make your mustache curl so beautiful?" (187); Mr. Cockman, in reply, merely "whiff[s]" on his cigar (187). She even drops a Cockney aitch in her final judgments on Jude: "He's a 'andsome corpse" (430). This was not the kind of prose the public wanted of "Thomas Hardy" of "Wessex." To make things worse, Arabella's vulgarisms often hit the nail on the head. Consider her all-too appropriate epithet, as Arabella shows off the wedding ring after her remarriage to Jude: "There's the padlock, see . . ." (404). She reaches the heights of "expressive" coarseness when she ticks Phillotson off for "dirting" his "nest" (334), and in tipping Sue to get properly "spliced," so that if her man "cracks her noddle with a poker" she will have some recourse at law (283). Cliché and shopworn proverbial wisdom mix with colloquialism in a style that brings literary dialogue closer to speech—the grounds for Hardy's approval of the young Kipling's contemporaneous "experiments" in his "penny-farthing yarns" (*Life and Work* 246), partly driven by urban life and the impact of music hall. ("People haven't yet realized," Kipling wrote in 1934, "how much [music hall songs] had to do with the national life" [Cheshire 89].)

Jude's own urban, London, music hall, public house notes linger in memory. Unless Jude is kept "cheerful" (400)—a euphemism for "drunk"—Arabella fears, "I shall be left in the lurch" (400). The "snob-screens" that divide the bar where she works "prevent topers in one compartment being put to the blush by the recognitions of those in the next" (186); the cash register emits a "ting-ting" every time a coin is dropped in (186). Even Sue's description of marriage recalls the notice that law requires over pub doors: "licensed to be loved on the premises" (271).

"The imperfect digestion" of scientific and philosophic vocabularies, said one of *Tess's* reviewers, "could not more potently destroy our illusions if they were steam whistles" (Cox 178–79). *Jude* signals its more uncomfortable modernity by loud blasts on that very instrument. The novel is literally shaped by the conditions of lower-class modern life: for the first time in history, working people are granted mobility by the agency of the train. *Jude's* "modern vice of unrest" is spoken in a modern voice of unrest: people do not merely "arrive," they "arrive by train" (178)—"up-train," "down-train," and "excursion-train" (304); and their comings are "timed" (219) by the railway timetable. The courses of lives intersect like railway tracks: Sue and Jude arrange to meet "by the up-train which crossed his down-train at [Alfredston] station" (184), and Jude arrives to see the composer of "The Foot of the Cross" by "a series of crooked railways" (202). History is divided into the time "before railway days" (303) and the time after. Conversations take place in railway time. Sue, for example, must break off intimacies with, "But I have to go back by the six o'clock train" (221). Prosaic modernity and the compulsion of circumstances in a machine age mingle at such moments. The railway penetrates even to the level of metaphor (and Hardy makes sure we notice it does): so Sue talks of her marriage with Phillotson as being "accelerated, as the railway companies say of their trains" (176). Judge North or Mr. Justice Coleridge would have viewed the usage as painful "levity."

But it anticipates precisely the urban tones of *The Wasteland,* T. S. Eliot's modernist manifesto. Hardy in *Jude* exemplifies Herbert Spencer's stylist of the future, who will take into account "the increasing heterogeneity in our modes of expression" (qtd. in Wickens 114). "Here," said W. H. Auden, "was a 'modern' rhetoric which was more fertile and adaptable to different themes than any of Eliot's gas-works and rats' feet" (Elliott 352–53).

T. S. Eliot disliked Thomas Hardy. His "Primer of Modern Heresy," *After Strange Gods* (1934), helped sustain the critical charge of blasphemy well into the twentieth century. The author of *Jude* is a primary target in a text that also points the reader at the "history of blasphemy, and the anomalous position of that term in the modern world" (51). Significantly, Eliot coupled his remarks about Hardy's lack of "any institutional attachment" or "submission to any objective beliefs" with a devastating and snobbish attack upon his peculiar voice and language: "He seems to me to have written as nearly for the sake of 'self-expression' as a man well can; and the self which he had to express does not strike me as a particularly wholesome or edifying matter of communication"; Hardy was "indifferent even to the prescripts of good writing" (54). The charge of blasphemy was not just a matter of Catholic faith, but the index of Eliot's refusal to see that the modern literature he himself helped (or hoped) to epitomize was founded on the shock of word crime and the concomitant admittance of the vulgar, the frank, the democratic-demotic, even of the four-lettered word: admit Hardy into the canon, and you had to admit this also. Eliot could "testify" for Kipling's oeuvre (in Gilbert, *Kipling and the Critics* 118), even the *Plain Tales* and *Barrack-Room Ballads*. He edited Kipling's verse for Faber, under fire, in 1941. But he must ignore his unlooked-for resemblance with Hardy. Kipling's and Hardy's careers had traced opposite arcs from the moment when both launched their books of the late 1880s and early 1890s: Kipling from "hooligan" blasphemer to the laureate who taught empire to "think in English," to "reassure [it]self" (*Kim* 154, 180); Hardy from "Master" novelist read by the family hearth to "degenerate" soiling the national language. Eliot could even write an obituary panegyric on Marie Lloyd (see *Selected Prose* 173, 172), recognizing her "living Music Hall" as Kipling's "inspiration and refreshment" (*Choice of Verse* 10). Kipling the ritualist, Kipling the conservative, even Lloyd the vulgarian patriot, were recuperable; Hardy the "pro-Boer," Hardy the humanitarian, Hardy the blasphemer who kept alive his class loyalty to brutish "Hodge" was not.

The persisting power of the penalties upon blasphemy were "a challenge," as the 1914 deputation for repeal put it, "to every new-born thought" (*Prime Minister* 11), a bar to linguistic and literary innovation. Yet, just as blasphemy brooded over the birth of the Victorian novel, so "militant" Secularism's blasphemous urge towards linguistic revolution stiffened the adversarial stance of modernist writers who aimed to shake up their audience with "the shock of the new." ("Shocking" was of course one of the epithets flung against *Jude* [Howells, Cox 255].) The "vulgar" *Ulysses* that Eliot's friend Virginia Woolf declined to publish at the Hogarth Press takes a loud cue from Jude's drunken recital of the Nicene Creed in the low-life Christminster tavern. We cannot miss the heretical implications of "coarse" and "mocking" Buck Mulligan's shaving ritual (*Ulysses* 14, 3), the novel's annunciatory Ur-modernist moment. Compare Jude, nearing the end of his recitation, with the help of three pence worth of Dutch courage, raising his whisky glass "with the manner of a priest leading a congregation." Mulligan, Stephen Dedalus, Jude, all are alike "horrible example[s] of free thought" (*Ulysses* 17). Joyce's *Ulysses* and Hardy's *Jude* share the impulse to gross parody as they share risk-taking shifts of scale and idiom; both mingle the urge to outrage with a broad appeal for sympathy on behalf of unheroic mankind.[55]

What is more, Mulligan's "Ballad of Joking Jesus" is lifted straight from the pages of the indicted *Freethinker,* whose penny paper crudities, so history and criticism would have had us think, have nothing at all to do with canonized Literature:

> I'm the queerest young fellow that ever you heard.
> My mother's a jew, my father's a bird.
>
> (*Ulysses* 16)

"We oughtn't to laugh," says Haines the Englishman, "He's rather blasphemous" (16). But "laughing brutality" is the keynote of the novel's first movement. *"Qui vous a mis dans cette fichue position?" "C'est le pigeon, Joseph"* (34). Though Stephen credits Leo Taxil with the joke, the *Freethinker* is a much closer source; and it was a homegrown Dublin paper in the *Freethinker* style that published the comic new *Vie de Jésus* he cites, while Foote went to prison for putting Taxil's *Bible amusante* into circulation. "Sea-death, mildest of all deaths known to man. . . . Prix de Paris: beware of imitations" (42): blithely Joyce cements the unholy linguistic marriage of high style and advertising lingo (medium of Bloom's profession) that added to *Jude*'s and the *Freethinker*'s offenses. Blasphemous "rogueword"-play launches *Ulysses* on its quest for a revived and encompassing language, which shall not serve the worshipful imperial British state whose "big words . . . make us so unhappy" (39, 26). "Come forth Lazarus! And he came fifth and lost the job" (87); "Madam, I'm Adam" (113): these are the *Freethinker*'s own "Profane Jokes." "Naughty boy: punish," Bloom thinks as he fingers a flirtatious invitation: "afraid of words, of course. Brutal, why not? Try it anyhow. A bit at a time" (64). Shem the penman, "bawd of parodies," might have learned a few tricks from the *Freethinker*'s exuberant

"Skeleton Sermon" on the text of Luke 6.39—"Can the blind lead the blind? Shall they not both fall into the ditch?":

> IV. *The ditch.*—Ditch handy. Bountiful Providence. Why ditch? Why not pond? Might be drowned in pond. Mercy of god. Wet or dry ditch? According to weather and degree of sinfulness of the fallen. Picture discomfort of two blind men mixed up in a wet ditch. Also priest seeing four feet projecting from ditch and then passing by on the other side (Luke x., 31). Point out that he might think they were fore-feet. Couldn't help a quadruped out. Send for the nearest pound. Animal clearly forfeit. . . .
>
> VI. *Moral.*—The ditch is human depravity. Pitch into it. (22 April 1883: 126)

The Hardy who filled in *Jude*'s token speech blanks is older brother too, to the modern writer who spelled out the "ugly" and "dirty" four-letter words in *Lady Chatterley's Lover*, D. H. Lawrence (Allan and Burridge 23). When Penguin Books went on trial for its free publication in 1960, T. S. Eliot, O.M., "twenty five years a Churchwarden" and "a Vice-President of the Church Union" (besides Nobel prize-winning author of poetry, plays, and "Essays on Religious, Social and Literary subjects") was asked for a deposition. Perusing the manuscript of his attempt in the Lawrence Archive of Nottingham University Library (La R 415/2) is a lesson in how to saw a critic in half. Never used, the document was only deposited after Eliot first scored through, neatly ripped away, or simply underlined as not his exact wording every overstrong statement about the "value" of Literature and Lawrence's meaning for it that a solicitor named Rubinstein wrote up in legal form for the defense after their interview. "[O]ur concern was speech," Eliot had written in *Little Gidding*, "and speech impelled us / To purify the dialect of the tribe" (lines 124–25). It was not to be expected he could come unhesitant to Lawrentian literature's call. "Lawrence was a man of intense seriousness and sincerity and had an important message," the deposition reads (last words underlined), "good for all those who can see and understand his view point." In the margin Eliot added the proviso: "For those who cannot, LADY CHATTERLEY'S LOVER is a novel which may be in part very boring and in other parts shocking, but not, I think, in any way harmful" (3). The Lawrence-Hardy connection may well have been present to his mind as he set about his difficult task. The deposition partly renounces the "violent and sweeping" views on literary "tradition" and "orthodoxy" of sensibility that Eliot had expressed in *After Strange Gods* in 1934 (2). In that work, Lawrence figured as "an almost perfect example of the heretic" (38), and Hardy—though Eliot strove to deny the relevance of his crime for the modern world—was featured as the "Arch-blasphemer," while Eliot shuttled disconsolately between the two, finally awarding Lawrence the palm for greater genius and lesser "morbidity."

The "obscenity" of *Lady Chatterley,* as has been seen, was close kin to
the "blasphemy" of the *Freethinker;* its initial reception resembled the bonfire laid on for *Jude.* Lawrence's novel was "the most evil outpouring that
has ever besmirched" English language and literature (*John Bull,* collected
in Draper 278). The magistrate's case of Lawrence's "ribald" nude paintings,
seized from the Warren Street gallery in June 1929, offered a visual analogy
for the word crime of which he was accused: "the hair" was "clearly shown
on the private parts," the test of obscenity that Chief Inspector Drew had
explained to the Select Committee on Indecent Advertisements in 1908
(qtd. in Thomas, *Long Time* 289). Similarly, in *Lady Chatterley* Lawrence
had spelled out all the words—whether to the detriment of his art remains
a question: Yeats said they burned holes in the pages (Epstein 67). The
parallels with the offenses of Foote and Hardy are clear. It is not a coincidence that Lawrence next put down on paper, to finish his life as man and
writer, the blasphemous tale the *Escaped Cock* (also known as the *Man Who
Died*), another "New Life of Christ," nor that the pivot on which his career
turned was his 1914 *Study of Thomas Hardy.* Its finest critical moments
concern *Jude the Obscure.* "Blasphemy" as *Jude* presents it, Lawrence argues,
lies in the perversion of natural sexual relations (117, 120–21). The "tragedy
of Hardy, always the same," was "the tragedy of those, who, more or less
pioneers, have died in the wilderness whither they had escaped for free
action, after having left the walled security, and the comparative imprisonment, of the established convention" (*Study* 21).

For the "Great Tradition" from which Leavis excluded Hardy we should
substitute something like Richard Carlile and the shopmen's "Little Honorable House of Blasphemers": as Widdowson writes, Leavis "had to write
Hardy out," deny the claim made for him in the early 1920s as the preeminent representative of the "modern consciousness," because "he seemed to
counter everything Eliot stood for" (27); he has always had, Terry Eagleton
adds, "a profoundly unnerving effect upon the dominant critical ideologies"
(qtd. in Widdowson 5). That alternative tradition includes a late-Victorian
reader of novels and re-maker of narratives who turned most dramatically
on his cultural fathers, "re-invent[ing] and partly rewrit[ing]" blasphemy,
Sigmund Freud (Lawton 84); it includes a work that trespasses across the
borders of nations, thus adding to the demotic modern mix, to stake its
author's considerable claim to the status of "greatest living writer" in English, Salman Rushdie's *Satanic Verses. Jude* is that blasphemous tradition's
literary point of origin: the novel's current standing and its central place
in the Hardy oeuvre would have flabbergasted the critic who voiced the
consensus view, from the retrospect of 1910, that *Jude* was simply "the worst

novel he has ever written," if not the most degenerate work "from the hand of a Master" England had ever been offered (W. L. Phelps, in Cox 398).

In the same year, 1910, on the front page of the *Freethinker* for 12 June, G. W. Foote placed "terrible" *Jude,* with the tragedy of *Tess,* at the pinnacle of Hardy's achievement. He sent his sharp analysis to the novelist, "with the writer's comp[limen]ts": it labels "the first of living English writers" an out-and-out Freethinker (869). Writing at once cordially to thank him, Hardy called it a "generous appreciation" (*Letters* 4: 96).[56] Foote's piece is the only commentary on his last novel Hardy preserved in his personal scrapbook. He wrote a note to himself of the author's address, in pencil, at the foot of the page. As we have tacitly endorsed a modernist requirement of "shock" in great literature—the new norm that connects splenetic Martin Amis, say, to Bret Ellis Easton—so we may also have—I may here have—elevated *Jude* among Victorian novels by very dint of its uncomfortable againstness, precisely because it is, in all senses, blasphemous. The study of blasphemy helps us understand *Jude the Obscure* in its conflicted historical moment. But it also helps us understand ourselves, and the desires of our time. The forgotten story of Mr. Foote's subliterary rag turns out to have a lot to offer, after all.

Notes

INTRODUCTION

1. The N.S.S. copy of the *Freethinker* has been microfilmed at the instigation of historian Edward Royle.

2. "There lives more faith in honest doubt, / Believe me, than in half the creeds" (Tennyson, *In Memoriam* stanza 96, lines 11–12). The prestige of utilitarianism and Comtean positivism allowed more emphatic Victorian "doubters" like John Stuart Mill and John Morley to rise to prominence as legislators and men of letters. On the imagery of "theft," see the vicar's response to a Darwinist in George Du Maurier's *Trilby:* "Sir, you're—you're a—you're a *thief,* sir, a *thief! You're trying to rob me of my Savior!"* (286).

3. For some pre-Reformation thinkers, blasphemy was the vilest form of heresy; for others, including Thomas Aquinas, "[h]eretics blaspheme[d] against God by following a false faith" (qtd. in Levy, *Treason* 331). Returning to the Biblical concept of blasphemy became a means for Protestant "heretics" to "defin[e] themselves religiously" (Levy xiv).

4. The 1698 Blasphemy Act did explicitly include within scope of the crime any "writing, printing, teaching, or advised speaking" that should "deny any one of the persons in the Holy Trinity to be God" or "deny . . . the holy scriptures of the old and new testament to be of divine authority" (*Statutes at Large* 10: 177).

5. The requirement that "nonconformist" ministers (Methodists, Wesleyans, Baptists, etc.) subscribe to most of the Church of England's Thirty-nine Articles was abolished in 1779. Emancipation of Roman Catholics, begun in 1778, was completed in 1829; the Catholic hierarchy was reestablished in 1850. Quakers were relieved. The "Trinity Act" of 1813 relieved Unitarians (see Levy, *Blasphemy* 341–45 on its precarious passage); their position in common law was settled by a decisive ruling in the *Shore v. Wilson* case of 1842. Compulsory church attendance was abolished in 1847, well after the law mandating it became unworkable, though "no fewer than ten persons were sent to prison for this offence" in 1839 (Hunter, *Heresy Laws* 15). Scandal surrounding the blasphemy prosecution of a Cornish well sinker named Thomas Pooley seemed to render the law obsolete in 1857.

6. *Vision and Realism: A Hundred Years of The Freethinker,* edited by Jim Herrick, is a collection of articles from the *Freethinker.*

7. Unless otherwise noted, citation is from the 1850 edition of *History of the Last Trial,* reprinted 1972.

8. *Thomas Hardy and His Readers: A Selection of Contemporary Reviews,* edited by Lerner and Holmstrom.

9. Each of the three volumes could be rented out separately, thus tripling profits. Mudie's annual subscription fee of one guinea was comparatively low but nevertheless "excluded lower-class people who could read fluently" (Coustillas 11). Free public libraries were few until the end of the century. Matthew Arnold called Mudie's "a machinery for the multiplication and protection of bad literature" (1880 *Fortnightly Review* article, qtd. 14), since mediocre talent could readily survive on print runs of a few hundred copies if the libraries bought them.

10. See Pierre Coustillas's introduction to *Literature at Nurse,* and Guinevere Griest's *Mudie's Circulating Library and the Victorian Novel.*

11. Moore vows to "issue my next book at a purchasable price" to "appeal direct to the public" (qtd. in Coustillas 4); Foote appeals to "the great court of public opinion." Foote the low-life blasphemer demands a "voice" in public life, while Moore incites a revolution in the literary system that "would be as far-reaching in its effects, as the biggest franchise-bill ever planned" (qtd. in Coustillas 22); and so on.

12. Descriptions of Bradlaugh (*Freeman's Journal,* 22 May 1880: 5) and Kipling (Buchanan 20–32), respectively.

13. Thanks for this economic metaphor to Tim Wandling.

14. Unlike the Church of England, the Church of Scotland had forced through its Protestant reformation *against* the will of the Crown, and had different feelings about its relationship to the state. In 1834 the General Assembly ruled that no pastor should be intruded upon a congregation against its will, a "veto act" that made "[a] smashing of the union between Church and State" inescapable (Chadwick, *Victorian Church* 2: 225). Scotland was subsequently divided between a weak established church and a free church "strong in the great cities and formidable in the Highlands and Hebrides," which took away 474 of 1,203 ministers (2: 225).

15. Three American prosecutions for blasphemy were brought between 1968 and 1971: for swearing profanely; for calling Jesus a "bastard" in an underground high school newspaper; and for displaying a poster in a shop window that read, "Jesus Christ—Wanted for sedition, criminal anarchy, vagrancy, and conspiracy to overthrow the established government" (Levy, *Treason* 336–37). Fifteen U.S. states had a blasphemy law on the books in 1970; six in 1982.

16. Bradlaugh's 1889 bill for repeal was rejected on a second reading in the Commons by a resounding 143 to 48; the bills of 1913 and 1914 failed even to reach that stage. Repeal attempts of the 1920s were sponsored by a society for abolition formed in response to the third verdict against J. W. Gott in 1922. A Blasphemy Laws Amendment Bill was granted a second reading in 1930 but died partly for lack of support from a minority government and partly because of an overreaching amendment by the Catholic solicitor-general.

17. J. M. Browne was convicted of sending blasphemous and obscene material through the post in 1897; three Freethinkers were unsuccessfully prosecuted in 1903.

18. A Bradford merchant who edited the *Truthseeker* in his spare time (1894–1905), Gott was prosecuted a total of four times, and was first imprisoned in 1911. Amongst other productions that caught the authorities' eye was his *Rib-Ticklers, Or, Questions for Parsons.* Lemon's 1977 sentence was overturned on appeal. For trenchant discussions, see Sutherland, *Offensive Literature,* and Walter, *Blasphemy: Ancient and Modern* (1990) and *Blasphemy in Britain* (1977).

19. The Church of England reported 1995 Christmas Day communicant figures per 1,000 population (aged 15 and older) of 96 in Hereford, the country's "holiest" diocese, and 20 in both Birmingham and Sheffield, the lowest figures reported. Figures for usual church attendance in Britain now stand at just under 1.1 million.

20. A final twist is supplied by the realization that the offense never existed under the Imperial Raj.

CHAPTER ONE

1. A few persisting anomalies were removed by an 1855 act that eliminated concurrent jurisdiction. Hereafter, "no blasphemous publication, which is punishable in the secular Courts" could "be taken cognizance of in the ecclesiastical" (Odgers, *Libel and Slander* 457).

2. The Nonconformists were the first to attempt to cope with the trauma of industrialization, "a task for which the Church of England . . . had neither the organization nor the zeal" (G. Trevelyan 507). The dedicated "slum parson" and "Anglican Christian Socialist" like F. D. Maurice and Charles Kingsley did not come into being until the 1840s.

3. Until the mid-nineteenth century, when figures rose slightly, an annual income of 90 pounds brought one into the ranks of the lower-middle classes; the middle-class range was 150 to 400 pounds.

4. The Tithe Commutation Act stopped payment in kind in 1836. In 1891 tithes were made payable by the landowner. The Anglican Church of Ireland was disestablished in 1871.

5. Arnold's "wild" proposals for an ecumenical Protestant national church, *The Principles of Church Reform* (1833), cost him promotion and friendships. The disestablishment he feared was averted by Robert Peel, whose new Ecclesiastical Duties and Revenues Commission embarked upon a fifty-year program of incremental reforms in 1835.

6. Phrases, respectively, of Bradlaugh's opponent, Lord Randolph Churchill (Arnstein 198), and his successor in Parliament, Freethought historian J. M. Robertson (*Charles Bradlaugh* 9).

7. The shoemakers' unusually strong union was "virtually a Jacobin organization" (E. Thompson 702). Their descendants enthusiastically supported Republican Bradlaugh in the 1860s and 1870s. According to a review of William Winks's *Lives of Industrious Shoemakers* (1883), "Sir Robert Peel is said to have declared that shoemakers were at the head of every conspiracy or political movement" (*Saturday Review,* 3 March: 288).

8. The 1851 census estimated that 5.25 million people who could have attended church or chapel on the Sunday before census day did not attend (Chadwick, *Church* 1: 366). Of those who did attend, 4,536,264 were Dissenters; 5,292,551 were Anglicans.

9. The word *imprimatur* on the title page previously signified a "licensed" and permitted publication: "let it be printed."

10. The three parodies were first published in December 1816. Olivia Smith claims only the *Creed* was Hone's, but the bulk of evidence points to his sole authorship, which he never repudiated.

11. Unless otherwise noted, citation is from William Tegg's 1876 reprint of Hone's *Three Trials* (1818). Cross-checking with newspaper reports and legal records reveals that partisan reporters generally took reliable notes of blasphemy trials: the craving for "truth" induced scrupulousness. A shorthand writer was probably supplied for Hone's trials by Francis Place (see Hone BL 37,949: 46).

12. Alas, the three thousand pounds collected seeped away on projects like publication of Hazlitt's *Political Essays,* on which Hone took a risk at a time when Hazlitt desperately needed assistance (Rickword 22).

13. Hone's *Register* ceased publication on the eve of his trials. The advertising address Place drafted for it was "a clear attempt to rescue the reform movement from the influence of the [universal] manhood suffrage policy" (E. Thompson 613). Place was a shadowy figure behind the cases of Carlile and Hetherington as well as Hone's.

14. "Triangle, s.," reads Hone's footnote on Castlereagh's soubriquet, "a *thing* having three *sides;* the meanest and most tinkling of all musical *instruments;* machinery used in military *torture.* DICTIONARY" (*Sinecurist's Creed* 3n).

15. *A Political Catechism, dedicated, without Permission, to . . . the Earl of Liverpool, Lord CASTLEREAGH, and Co.,* "By an Englishman," also published by Hone in 1817, eschews laughter altogether for an extremely factual analysis of the "Unnatural" state of the country—election bribery; bartering for seats; a family tax burden of 40 pounds (*vs.* 3 pounds in America); state pensions of 38,754 pounds to Lord Arden, 23,093 pounds to Earl Camden, and so on—concluding, "READER—HAST *THOU* SIGNED THY NAME TO A PETITION FOR REFORM?" (8).

16. Hone's one foray into the political use of Scripture after 1817 was the *Form of Prayer, with Thanksgiving to Almighty God, To be used daily by all devout People throughout the Realm, for the Happy Deliverance of Her Majesty QUEEN CAROLINE from the late most Traitorous Conspiracy* (1820). "READER," he closed the pamphlet, "It seemeth meet to acquaint thee that the foregoing Form of Prayer . . . hath been wholly compiled from *Scripture,* and from . . . the *Book of Common Prayer*" (*Facetiae* n. pag.).

17. Unless otherwise noted, citation is from the edition of *Bullet Te Deum* published by Hone in 1817.

18. Judgment of the editors of Dickens's *Letters:* Madeline House, Graham Storey, and Kathleen Tillotson (3: 337).

19. The forty indictments by "information" in the three years from 1808 have been called "the most daring invasion of public liberty attempted since the time of the Stuarts" (Hackwood 111).

20. The suppression was thorough, and may have been aided by official expunging. The British Library holds only a proof copy of *John Wilkes's Catechism,* marked up in

Hone's hand, in its manuscript collections; outside the Berg collection, I have been unable to trace either the *Sinecurist's Creed* or the *Political Litany* in the United States. It is for this reason that they are here cited both in original editions and as reprinted (verbatim) in Hone's *Three Trials*.

21. He may have been pricked by the example of T. J. Wooler, who cleared his *Black Dwarf* of seditious libel in June 1817.

22. See Olivia Smith, 190–201. Her account of Hone (as Patten suggests [1: 438n]) is flawed by misunderstanding of blasphemy's political meanings but is nonetheless interesting. Hone was already "an experienced writer of trial literature" (O. Smith 177), including the *Trial of Lord Citroen of Guildford* (a radical member of Parliament), and *Hone's Interesting History of the Memorable Blood Conspiracy,* concerning government payments to informers who incited crimes.

23. Only the Reverend Samuel Parr was privy to his beliefs. Hone described in a letter of 4 April 1825 how Parr bearded him in his study: "You must answer me a question, & answer it *honestly* and *truly*—what is your *creed*?" (Hone BL 34,586: 4).

24. Before the Great Reform Act of 1832, there were four open districts in the country: "safety valves," E. P. Thompson dubs them (471). All freeholders could vote in Middlesex. Wilkes attributed the notes to his *Essay on Woman* (a romping parody of Pope's *Essay on Man*) to Bishop Warburton; it earned him a year in prison and a five-hundred–pound fine in 1763. He was again sentenced in 1769 for a piece entitled *Veni Creator paraphras'd, Or, the Maid's Prayer.*

25. One seller of Hone's parodies, Robert Swindells, was dragged from his home and the place torn apart while his naked pregnant wife cowered in terror. Eventually released without charge, he returned to find she had suffered a miscarriage and died (W. Hone, *Three Trials* 95n–96n).

26. Hone BL 40,108: 208 is a poster entitled "JURORS: 'Men who have dared to be Honest in the Worst of Times.'" By an act of George II the master of the Crown Office presented prosecution and defense with forty-eight names from a list of potential special jurors. Each side could strike out twelve, a right the Crown Office attempted to deny Hone (*Trial by Jury* 19). On Hone's and other radicals' protests against the system, see J. Ann Hone, *For the Cause of Truth* (333–35).

27. "The passion of laughter is nothing else but *sudden glory* arising from some sudden *conception* of some eminency in ourselves, by comparison with the *infirmity* of others" (Hobbes 4: 46).

28. See, for example, Canning's "Soldier's Friend," an imitation of the radical young Southey: "Come, little Drummer Boy, lay your knapsack here: / I am the soldier's friend—here are some books for you; / Nice clever books by Tom Paine the philanthropist" (Jerrold and Leonard 93). Hone dedicated the *Man in the Moon* "to the Right Hon. George Canning, Author of Parodies on Scripture, to Ridicule his Political Opponents" (*Facetiae* n.p.).

29. Phrases from an 1831 letter to Thomas Hood, regarding his projected *Comic Annual,* by Hartley Coleridge (BL Add. Mss. 40,856: 104).

30. Noah gets drunk, Pilate brings water for guests to wash themselves, and so on (M. A. Rose 147–48). Bakhtin calls the work pure "pileata Biblia," by which "a correspondence of all details to Sacred Writ is strictly and precisely observed," while "at the

same time the entire Sacred Writ is transformed into carnival" (*Dialogical Imagination* 70).

31. Also never finished was a projected study of Horn-Books, the forerunners of children's primers. Hone's notes eventually became the basis for Andrew Tuer's 1896 *History* (Shepard n. pag.).

32. The Corpus Christi play, for example, is based on the apocryphal Gospel of Nicodemus and the Discourse of St. John the Divine (Kolve 308n, 298n).

33. The "Apocrypha"—that is, "secret" or "hidden"—books were so called by Jerome in the fourth century, being those works in the Greek Old Testament (the "Septuagint") that were not found in the Hebrew. The Council of Laodicea (AD 343–89) outlawed all of the apocryphal books except Baruch; the Council of Hippo reversed the decision. The Old Testament Apocrypha was finally condemned to provisionality by the Council of Trent (1645–65). The 1947 discovery of the Dead Sea and Qumram Scrolls, which contain parts of the texts, has not yet re-promoted the Apocrypha to "inspired status" (Haywood 15).

34. The key works on the apocryphal Gospels and Epistles available at the time were John Albert Fabricius, *Codex Apocryphus Novi Testamenti* (1719); Nathaniel Lardner, *Credibility of the Gospel History* (1727), which laid out the argument for authentication; and Paley, *Evidences of Christianity* (1794), which included an abridgment of Lardner. The "oppugners" included Hobbes and John Toland, in his *Defence of Milton's Life* (1699).

35. Modern commentators believe that the four synoptic Gospels and Paul's correspondence were available to churches by the middle of the second century. The New Testament canon "became a reality" around AD 190 and "closed" in AD 405 (Du Toit 103). Some eighteenth- and early-nineteenth-century scholars pushed canon formation back as early as AD 94, by which date (writes Archdeacon Butler) only Revelations and the five "Catholic" or "general" Epistles remained to be "received" (Dr. Butler 18–19). Hone was not far wrong, however, in ascribing the drive to "close" the canon to the need to combat heresy, a central concern of the Council of Nice (*Apocryphal* iv). Hebrews was disputed until the fourth century; the Ethiopian canon includes several works deemed apocryphal in AD 405.

36. E. Hancock republished Hone's text as the *Suppressed Gospels and Epistles* in 1863, having issued the same in serial parts a few years before as the *Forbidden Books*.

37. The word "compilers" was added to the subtitle late in the day; it is missing from an undated draft title page in Hone's hand (Hone WA).

38. The verse of "three heavenly witnesses" was omitted by Luther, and gained ground only between 1566 and 1580. The *Quarterly* reviewed various "Vindications" between January 1822 and December 1825. The verse was dropped in the Revised Version of the Bible, 1881.

39. Joseph Hone, a lawyer and Tory, hoped to emigrate to America by raising eight hundred pounds from anti-Hone well-wishers like the chief justice and the attorney-general, who both subscribed (*Aspersions* 8). In the event, he went out as a judge to the criminal colony of Tasmania.

40. Hone publicly preserved his reviewer's anonymity. He was the Reverend Hugh James Rose (Lawley, "Cruikshank and Hone," in Hone Berg, n. pag.).

41. Hone sent an early copy of *Aspersions Answered* direct to Archdeacon Butler "deeming it uncourteous that you should be first acquainted with the mention of your name, in a pamphlet by me, through the ordinary course of publication" (12 February 1824, Hone BL 34,585: 318).

42. Butler had charged, for example, that Hone "induced" his reader to think there was something wrong with the Creed by "willfully" and "fraudulently" omitting a note in his source, Mr. Justice Bayley's edition of the *Prayer Book* (Dr. Butler 28–29). The charge actually rested on his own sloppy reading (Hone BL 34,585: 378). As to his objection to the language of the translations, the Archdeacon should have opened the copy of Jeremiah Jones that stood on his own library shelves (379).

43. "Never mind the *Quarterly*," wrote another friend: "you are in good company" (Hone BL: 40,856: 11). The periodical had advertised its delight in "[its] favorite amusement, the sacrifice of asses—Hone, Hunt, Hazlitt," Shelley, Keats, and the rest (*Quarterly*, October 1821: 103). Hone's irritation at persistent disbelief in his authorship dictated the dramatic scene that introduces his collected *Facetiae and Miscellanies* (1827): a lady customer exits his shop *"in a rage"* when she discovers that Hone not only sells but is himself the author of his publications (vii).

44. Holyoake's phrase, quoted in *God versus Paterson* vi; see also his 1874 pamphlet, *The Limits of Atheism, Or, Why Should Skeptics Be Outlaws.* "If an informer can carry the words to persons interested in their suppression," he wrote of his own case, "if policemen can be sent to apprehend, without warrants, the man who publicly expresses his opinions—if he can be handcuffed like a felon, and thrust into gaol . . . then, I say, this [liberty-law] is a mockery" (*History of the Last Trial* 31–32). Similarly, the post office colluded with police to spy on Foote's mail in 1883 (*Three Trials for Blasphemy* 60–61), and an illegal order was obtained to pry into Bradlaugh's bank account in an attempt to link him to the *Freethinker* (Foote, *Prisoner* 34).

45. Acts of 1855, 1869, and 1870 stated as a principle that a person with no religious belief was competent to give evidence, but in practice magistrates could simply refuse to administer secular affirmations. Affirmation bills failed in 1861 and 1863. Thus, before 1888 the right to affirm was restricted to conscientious objectors like Quakers, Separatists, and Moldavians who believed oath taking violated Biblical injunction.

46. Hone's literary educative instinct was evident even in his political squibs. *The Queen's Matrimonial Ladder*, for example, features apposite epigraphs from the Old Testament; Cowper; Shakespeare (*All's Well That Ends Well, Cymbeline, Coriolanus, Henry VIII*); Southey, *Minor Poems;* Sheridan; and Byron (most of the words discreetly asterisked out), though a picture of the king rolled away in a wheelbarrow is set off with the small-type subliterary epigraph " '*Cat's Meat!*'—*English Cry*" (*Facetiae* n. pag.).

47. The *Grub Street Journal* said of serial publication on 26 October 1732: "This method of weekly Publication allows Multitudes to peruse Books in which they would otherwise never have looked" (qtd. in Dickson 9). Approximately 150 works were issued in numbers before 1750, including *Robinson Crusoe* and the plays of Shakespeare. Before Hone's venture, the most striking serially issued works published were probably Pierce Egan's twelve-part *Life in London* (1820–21), and the twenty-six-part *Microcosm of London*, on which Thomas Rowlandson and Charles Pugin collaborated (1808–10). Never-

theless, the success and impact of the *Every-Day Book* was as "unprecedented and stunning" (Dickson 9) as posterity has described *Pickwick*'s.

48. Dickens attempted to stick out for 120 pounds; he agreed to terms on 11 August. On 22 August, Bentley offered him a two novel deal, and Dickens pushed up the price from 400 to 500 pounds (*Letters* 1: 165n); *Barnaby Rudge* was its first fruit. Tegg's children's book was eventually published in 1839 as *Sergeant Bell and his Raree-Show* under the pseudonym "Peter Parley" (1: 163n).

49. "Timothy Twigg" features in Thomas Hood's 1834 novel *Tylney Hall*, which Dickens read in 1846. "The man drawn to the life from the *pirate bookseller*" (Forster's substitution) "is wonderfully good" (Dickens to Forster, 5 July 1846, *Letters* 4: 579).

50. *Charles Dickens: Critical Assessments,* edited by Michael Hollington, is a collection of reviews and articles, many of which are cited in *Word Crimes*.

51. In *Edwin Drood* the text is "When the wicked man turneth away from his wickedness . . . he shall save his soul alive" (P. Collins 297). For extended discussion of Dickens's biblical inheritance, see Larson, *Dickens and the Broken Scripture*.

52. The power of this maneuver was testified to in Lionel Bart's musical *Oliver!*: Sikes's one song is a long threat to utter what "strong men tremble" to hear— *"My Name."* The number was dropped from the 1968 film version both for reasons of length and because director Carol Reed realized the effectiveness of removing Sikes altogether from the musical's linguistic economy.

53. *Twist* may also be indebted to one of Hone's earliest publications, the gruesome *Confession of Thomas Bedworth* (1815), a vivid prefiguration of Bill's sexualized murder of Nancy and his haunted flight from her bloody specter through London streets and into the country. Surrendering to be hanged and "put out of his misery," Bedworth told the justice: "She has followed me everywhere night and day." *"There!"* he screamed, "She's by me now" (qtd. in Rolleston 26–27).

54. Hone's daughter repeated the claim (Hackwood 190). Patten accepts Hone's primary role even in creation of some of the more visual squibs, like their fake "Bank Restriction Note."

55. See Patten 2: 213. Hone paid sixty pounds for the illustrations to various facetiae, and thirty-six pounds for the twelve pictures Cruikshank supplied for the *Every-Day Book*. The sums do not compare with twelve pounds a plate for *Oliver Twist,* but they were not mean at the time.

56. See, for example, Hone's whimsical 4 January 1823 letter to Mr. Rhodes of Lyons Inn, requesting a peek at a rare volume. If he cannot lend it, Hone writes, "I desire no reason—such a collection as yours ought not to be assailable by every Tarquin, and if I thought myself one because you had permitted me a flirtation I ought to set about the abduction in another way" (Hone Bath).

57. One of Dickens's illustrators on the *Old Curiosity Shop,* Samuel Williams, also worked on Hone's *Every-Day Book* from 1825 to 1827. Another Hone publication, *Poor Humphrey's Calendar* (1828), inspired Mayhew and Cruikshank's *Comic Almanacks,* and has a flavor of Dickens's *Master Humphrey's Clock*.

58. A veteran Deist publisher with seven prosecutions under his belt, Eaton was prosecuted in 1812 for selling a supplementary tract of Paine's under the title of the "Third Part" of the *Age of Reason*. He served eighteen months, but "escaped another

sentence, by death," immediately afterwards for publishing D'Holbach's atheistical account of Jesus, *Ecce Homo* (*J. S. Mill on Blasphemy* 15). Eaton's humiliation by pillory backfired when an "immense crowd of people cheered him during the whole hour" (Cobbett, *Political Register*, 27 January 1820: 770), the spectacle making "a sort of an *appeal to the People*" (772). The pillory was abolished immediately after.

59. The Vice Society initiated more than fourteen prosecutions for blasphemy in the years 1817–25. One of Carlile's supporters called them, "officious eave droppers" (J. Jones 10–12). (I am grateful to Kevin Gilmartin for alerting me to this pamphlet, as also to T. J. Wooler's *Dialogue.*)

60. "Men kept those writings hidden away," W. J. Linton said of the *Age of Reason* in 1880, for example, "as their fathers had kept the first English Bible" (*Watson* 10). Brendan Clifford, introducing *Blasphemous Reason: the 1797 Trial of Tom Paine's AGE OF REASON,* makes the extraordinary claim that Paine's "assault on the Bible carried all before it" (3).

61. The "Wealth / That lay / In the House that Jack built" consisted precisely in those rights and civil liberties whose erosion accelerated in 1817. The skit reputedly sold over one hundred thousand copies.

62. See, for example, the *Times,* 14 October 1819: "I cannot listen to any discussions" of the Old Testament, the chief justice told Carlile. "I do not believe the truth of that history," he returned. "Here," the *Times* noticed, "a gentleman behind Carlile uttered an exclamation of horror, which drew down the animadversion of Orator Hunt" (2).

63. Carlile's zeal may have been directly responsible for the arrest of Wooler's publisher; certainly, when Carlile offered to take his place, Wooler declined. Some of the bolder editorials Sherwin signed were actually written by Carlile.

64. As such, the *Republican* (circulation fifteen thousand at its peak) shared honors with Cobbett's *Political Register* (circulation forty to sixty thousand in 1816–17) and Wooler's *Black Dwarf* (which sold twelve thousand copies a week in 1819). The mayor of Exeter ordered it publicly burned in 1819. Carlile's other journals were *Deist* (1819–20), *Lion* (1828–29), *Prompter* (1830–31), *Gauntlet* (1833–34), and *Scourge* (1834–35).

65. Hone wrote to Attorney-General Shepherd on 23 November 1817 disavowing Carlile's re-publications (J. Hone, *For the Cause* 333). Authorship of the parodies has persistently been misattributed to Carlile because of his piracies and imitations.

66. Carlile immediately saw the subversive potential of Hone's *Apocryphal New Testament.* He prefaced his own "faithful & authentic translation" of the book *Toldoth Jesu* in the *Republican* with a vow to "unfold the whole history of Christianity" without "Hocus Pocus tricks" (23 July 1824: 3). Shelley's letter to the *Examiner* of 3 November 1819 pointed out that, "the Unitarian . . . considers whole passages of the Bible as interpolations & forgeries. He admires the book of Job & Solomon's song as he admires Aeschylus or Anacreon" (*Letters* 2: 140).

67. There was both pragmatism and fanaticism in Carlile's emphasis on martyrdom. "This little imprisonment of yours," he gloated to a faint-hearted colleague some years later, "has done more work in our way, than we could have done in a year without it" (letter to Robert Taylor, 1831, in HC). But he also came to "suspect . . . the qualifications of every man who had not taken out a diploma from the Attorney-General" (Holyoake, *Life and Character of Richard Carlile* 39).

68. The agitators who gathered at Carlile's Fleet Street shop in the summer of 1819 included Thistlewood, Ings, and Davidson, executed in 1820 for their parts in the Cato Street Conspiracy to assassinate members of the cabinet. Carlile was an "injudicious participant in some of their conversations" (Wiener 39). The two to three hundred "dedicated" ultras were political descendants of the revolutionary Jacobins and belated disciples of Thomas Spence (d. 1814), who had advocated an early form of agrarian socialism. For details of Wedderburn's blasphemous Hopkins Street "chapel" and his relationship to Carlile, see McCalmain, *Radical Underworld* (132–47, 185–88).

69. Besides running his publishing business, Carlile also read his way through James Mill, Bentham, Hume, Locke, and Gibbon in Dorchester Gaol. The bulk of the volunteers who kept his London shop open were Zetetics; their *Newgate Monthly Magazine* (1824–26) is an impressive miscellany on materialist atheism, birth control, and political economy.

70. For unfathomable reasons, the *Principles of Nature* is recorded in some history books as a birth control manual.

71. The *Times,* which opposed the government over Peterloo, was unusual in reporting it. The *New Times* was founded and edited by John Stoddard, dismissed from the *Times* in 1816. Hone and Cruikshank's *Slap at Slop* appeared in the broadsheet format of the *New Times,* complete with a mock newspaper tax stamp depicting a cat's paw and with the motto, "On Every Thing he Claps His Claw." Direct payments to journalists by government reached a peak under the Tories in the 1820s.

72. These are the bits that mislead scholars into applauding Carlile's courtroom performance. Hone denied providing them, but the evidence is extant at the Huntington Library (RC 544, in CC). The heartfelt laments for his lack of eloquence, all of which Carlile used, must have given Hone pleasure in the composition.

73. Carlile would have been glad to find himself listed in the British Library catalogue as *dissenter*. Foote's title of 1874, *Heroes and Martyrs of Freethought,* in which Carlile figures largely, is perhaps modeled on the Religious Tract Society's 1869 production *Heroes and Martyrs of the British Reformation.*

74. The *Monitor* took Paine seriously, however, printing weekly replies to his assault on the Bible from 24 October to 12 December 1819 (4).

75. One of the witnesses Carlile was not allowed to call was a "dotty old clergyman" ready to testify that Chief Justice Abbott had been a Deist at college (Levy, *Blasphemy* 366). Gifford was widely believed to be a Unitarian, perhaps even a Deist. "If he had really blasphemed," Carlile claimed, "he had done so with the Attorney-General" (*Statesman,* 15 October: 1). The subpoenaed dignitaries were not compelled to attend unless their expenses were paid beforehand. Robert Owen refused Carlile's subpoena.

76. This remark is attributed by Wiener to John Jones, *Republican,* 2 February 1822, but I have been unable to verify it.

77. In January 1821 Jane Carlile was sentenced to two years for selling the *Republican,* the transcript, and other works. Mary Anne was fined five hundred pounds and sentenced to twelve months' imprisonment in July for publishing Carlile's *New Year's Address to the Reformers of Great Britain.* Carlile played the family card energetically in the reports on blasphemous proceedings that formed the main substance of the *Republican* in early years.

78. Prosecutions against street vendors were undertaken in all of these cities. The list, of course, is not exhaustive. The number of 150 prosecuted and imprisoned was the total accepted by Holyoake and written into Secularist histories. Working from contradictory and incomplete government records, Levy records 96 to 99 accusations against seditious and blasphemous libelers for the year 1819; 30 to 50 in 1820; and a total of 245 between 1817 and 1822. Of these, approximately half were prosecutions for blasphemy. Thompson puts the national total lower at 160 prosecutions in the period 1819 to 1821. Whatever the true figures, as Levy remarks, "they were unprecedentedly huge" (*Blasphemy* 355), and the vast majority were for the *Age of Reason.*

79. The Constitutional Association was founded in May 1821 with the express purpose of curbing press "licentiousness." It broke up in 1822, after a year of "frenzied activity" (Wiener 94). The Vice Society alone pushed on the later Carlile prosecutions.

80. The subscription list included on any sample day, say 25 January 1822, eleven shillings and four pence from "The Ropemakers of Shadwell" (regular contributors); "A Coal-heaver's Weekly Subscription" of sixpence; half a crown each from anonymous contributors with messages like "I'll Call for a Book Some Day"; and a half crown from "A Conscientious Attorney."

81. "You must allow . . . how much I have at stake," Carpenter told the jury; "[but] it is only by enduring additional imprisonment that I can hope to atone for the unpardonable crime of poverty" (*Republican,* 18 July 1824: 777) For this dignified impertinence, he was sentenced to three years in prison (799).

82. Holyoake refused prison dress and offered his jailers the choice either of exempting him from religious observance or of carrying him bodily into chapel, which "will not edify the remainder of your congregation" (*History of the Last Trial* 60).

83. "Precedent should not be put for law; nor is custom law," the volunteers declared, "[for] in all cases in which power is concerned, custom and precedent will always be made use of, in favor of power, and for the subjection of the people" (*Report of the Proceedings against William Turnbridge* 12). The argument was made cruel classist mock of by the prosecution: "Under what law do you charge me?" they imagined the prisoners saying. "The Common Law." "Oh! That is nothing. What you call common law is an unjust restriction of natural rights. All property was originally common. I have a right to pick your pocket" (*Times* report of Carlile's trial for *Elihu Palmer's "Principles of Nature,"* 16 October 1819: 2).

84. Nine shopmen remained in prison after Carlile himself was released, the men of May 1824.

85. The Carlile case was also important in setting the precedent that "a publication induced by the prosecutor is sufficient in a criminal case," that is, that vendors can legitimately be tricked into selling (Odgers, *Libel and Slander* 172).

86. Brougham personally "rejoiced" at the putting down of a "mass of the grossest and most criminal matter" (qtd. in E. Thompson 744), but principle was principle. Hume lambasted the Constitutional and Vice Societies as "little better than conspiracies against the subject" (*Debate on Mr. Hume's Presenting a Petition* 27).

87. "Deism, unnoticed, is harmless," wrote Wooler. "It has no charms for the populace. It offers them none of those motives for enthusiasm which are to be found in other Creeds" (7). Mill's estimate of one hundred thousand was based on sales of twenty

thousand, with each copy ("as . . . it is notorious") having multiple readers (*Mill on Blasphemy* 16). His *Westminster Review* article was reprinted by G. W. Foote in the run-up to his trials of 1883, from which pamphlet it is quoted here.

88. The charge of sedition laid against Carlile himself for his report on the Peterloo Massacre was allowed to lapse. Large numbers of detainees had to be released for lack of evidence at the end of 1819, when the act suspending habeas corpus expired.

89. Two hundred thousand was the estimate of the *Gentleman's Magazine*. "I[t] would take me a whole day and a quire of paper to give you anything like detail," Keats wrote to his brother George: "The whole distance from the Angel Islington to the Crown and anchor was lined with Multitudes" (*Letters* 2: 194).

90. A very short act of four articles, the statute gave courts authority to order the immediate seizure of any condemned work, even if an appeal had been lodged (Halevy, *Triumph* 71). Besides further restricting the press, the other acts confirmed the outlawry of assemblies for the purposes of drilling or other military exercises; the bearing of arms, a traditional English liberty; and any gathering of over fifty people that might discuss "any grievance of a public character, any economic or professional matter, or any question which concerned Church or State" (70).

91. Hone caught the new tone. He wrote Manchester antiquarian W. D. Clipsham about items of local custom for the *Year Book:* "what has come shall go in except the 'last shift' [i.e., undergarment]—I studiously avoid vulgarities, or what *refined* people might so deem of [sic]. If the Year Book were for Antiquarians only I should give many curious things which from the general nature of the work I am constrained to omit" (27 September 1831, Hone Bath).

92. Catnip to ladies, Taylor later married a moneyed widow and settled down to a new life in France. For details of his career, including the "sermons" that got him convicted in 1828, one of which described Christ as the "Jewish Vampire," see Calder-Marshall, *Lewd, Blasphemous, and Obscene;* for details of his idiosyncratic anticipations of later allegorical, mythological, and comparative interpretations of Christianity, the *Syntagma* and the *Diegesis* (written in prison in 1828–29), see Cutner's *Robert Taylor.* Charles Bray, author of the important *Inquiry Concerning the Origin of Christianity* (1838), called the *Diegesis* "witty, abusive" and impressively learned (Cutner 52). Taylor initially bounced back from his first imprisonment by undertaking a "lecture tour" with Carlile; he commenced it by nailing a Latin thesis to the door of the Cambridge Divinity School. This widely publicized scandal, Desmond and Moore argue, powerfully fed Darwin's anxieties about his evolutionary research, leading to extreme slowness of publication and debilitating nervous illnesses (see especially 70–73 and 84–85). Carlile's journal *Lion* gives an account of the "Infidel Mission"; he published the Rotunda lectures of the "Devil's Chaplain" as the *Devil's Pulpit* in 1831–32. On the "Swing" Riots, see Hobsbawn and Rude, *Captain Swing.*

CHAPTER TWO

1. Hone gave the slogan great currency in an illuminated colored transparency displayed in his shop window and seen by thousands following press agitation that helped restore Caroline to her rights as queen in 1820 (*Facetiae*, n.pag.).

2. The *Guardian* carried over a dozen articles denouncing the Reform Act of 1832.

Sales reached sixteen thousand during the crisis of its passage, and fell to five thousand in later years.

3. Many of the unstamped campaigners had similar flair. One, Henry Berthold, claimed in court that his *Political Handkerchief* could not be prosecuted as an illegal newspaper because it contained no paper: it *was* a handkerchief (Hollis, introduction to *Poor Man's Guardian* 1: xxvii). Hetherington delegated day-to-day editing of the *Guardian* to the Irish lawyer and journalist James Bronterre O'Brien. But O'Brien was kept out of the limelight and out of prison: there was no question who the "Guardian" was.

4. The stamp tax was finally abolished on 20 June 1855. The price of paper had risen from twenty-one shillings a quire in 1794 to fifty-five shillings in 1845, before falling to forty shillings after abolition of duty in 1850. Paper became truly cheap only after the introduction of wood pulp and esparto grass in the 1860s.

5. See, for example, the *Guardian's* opening address, which anticipates that the reward for defiance may be "the cross of agony itself, on which Christ *expiated his* 'SEDITION'" (9 July 1831: 1).

6. The preamble to the act directed it against "Pamphlets and printed Papers" that have "lately been published in great Numbers, and at very small Prices, and [which] it is expedient should be restrained" (qtd. in Hollis, introduction to *Poor Man's Guardian* 1: xiii*n*).

7. The Society for the Promoting of a Cheap and Honest Press turned into the London Working Men's Association, which in turn became one of the sponsors of the People's Charter. The intertwining of political and religious protest is also evident in the support tendered the unstamped press by the Radical Reform Association, which grew directly out of the Civil and Religious Liberty Association after the achievement of Catholic Emancipation in 1829. After his expulsion from the Freethinking Christians sect in 1827 and a falling out with Carlile, who disliked his newfangled politics, Hetherington joined the Civil and Religious Liberty Association in 1828 and became secretary of the Radical Reform Association in 1829. Carpenter, a former nonconformist preacher, was typical in not only moving from the *Age of Reason* struggle to the War of the Unstamped (as well as into the cooperative movement), and from thence to Chartism (editing *Charter* from 1838 to 1840), but also in returning to blasphemy as a method of political protest in the 1840s (see below, 2.2).

8. The novel was one of Holyoake's sacred texts. He copied out the hero's "Last Words" on the reverse of a flyer about himself, reprinted from the *Men of the Times* series in 1872 (in HC). Cooper's atheism was well known in the 1840s, when he wrote the *Purgatory of Suicides.* He was reconciled with Christianity in later life.

9. Another unstamped publication targeting the Church of England was the *Christian Corrector.* Carpenter's *Slap at the Church* summed up their position, which was anticlerical rather than antireligious: "The Savior lived and died *for* man / To live upon him is the Bishops' plan" (qtd. in Hollis, introduction to *Poor Man's Guardian* 1: xxiv).

10. Cleave evaded the 1789 law that forbade the hiring out of newspapers by selling the *Times,* the *Chronicle,* and the *True Sun* for half price the day after publication. He worked with Carpenter on the *Slap at the Church* and the *Church Examiner.*

11. The Court of Exchequer had demanded six hundred thousand pounds for Holyoake's publication of *War Chronicles* during the Crimean fiasco.

12. The Great Reform Act of 1832 restricted the vote to 10-pound urban householders, and to 50-pound leaseholders in the counties. This effectively enfranchised only those with incomes of over 150 pounds a year. "It appeared that of the working classes not more than one in fifty would be enfranchised by the Bill," canvassers reported to Lord John Russell. But "even this estimate would appear to have been excessive" (E. Thompson 818). In Leeds, for example, with a population of 124,000, government returns of May 1832 showed that only 355 better-off workmen would be admitted to the franchise.

13. Heywood had served his time for the unstamped *Poor Man's Guardian,* however, and Queen Victoria refused to visit Manchester while he was mayor later in the century (Holyoake, *Sixty Years* I: 102–03).

14. Title words of undated poster advertising "A Select Course of 4 Public Lectures . . . by the Rev. Dr. West" (in HC).

15. "Religion, the keystone of education," Sir James Graham declared to Brougham in 1841, "is in this country the bar to its progress" (qtd. in G. Trevelyan 531). The population doubled from seven million to fourteen million between 1751 and 1821, and reached twenty-six million by 1871. The principal rivals in elementary education before 1870 were the British and Foreign School Society and the National Society for Educating the Poor according to the Principles of the Established Church; their efforts were anticipated by a widespread Sunday school movement. Supplementary measures of 1876 and 1880 were needed to realize the "ideal" envisaged by Forster's Act of 1870. There was no state provision for education whatsoever before 1833, when the government voted twenty thousand pounds towards school buildings for the voluntary societies.

16. Popularization of the words spoken in Parliament by Robert Lowe, Viscount Sherbrook, on 15 July 1867: "I believe it will be absolutely necessary that you should prevail on our future masters to learn their letters" (*Oxford Dictionary of Quotations* 429). One in every three men was granted the vote by the Second Reform Act of 1867.

17. "Everyone must be able to read," adds Lévi-Strauss, "so that government can say: Ignorance of the law is no excuse" (300). Such a conspiratorial view insufficiently accounts for the lag of a century in Britain between the Industrial Revolution and Forster's Education Act. One contributing factor may have been Britain's tardiness, in marked contrast to France, in establishing bureaucratic systems of state control; another was certainly the short-term greed of individual employers, who undercut the prices of philanthropic rivals who tried to educate their child and sometimes their adult workers. Godzich's large contention, based on analysis of contemporary developments in the United States, remains persuasive, however, and finds obvious parallels in Britain: that a concern with mass literacy can be a convenience to antipopulist and antidemocratic thinking, even when masked as an alternative to academic "theory" or high culture.

18. The Taunton Act of 1868 anticipated that ten children out of every thousand would go on to secondary eduation, eight of them to schools of the "third grade," suited to the "needs" of the lower middle classes (R. Williams, *Revolution* 159). Of a child population of 4 million, 64,000 would thus enjoy either a classic upper-middle-class

liberal education or a "second grade" education to age sixteen, suitable for the creation of civil servants and army officers, while 256,000 would receive practical technical schooling. "It is obvious," the commission commented, "that these distinctions correspond roughly . . . to the gradations of society" (qtd. 159).

19. One mid-Victorian estimated that there were 3,454,327 literate adults against 1,759,148 illiterates at midcentury. The number of children in school rose from 900,000 of 2.6 million in 1833 to nearly double that figure by 1851; by 1861 approximately 2.5 million of a possible 2.75 million children "may have been in some form of school attendance" (R. Williams, *Revolution* 157).

20. "The future historian of the Religious Tract Society," founded 1799, "in a prize essay of 1850, cited figures to show how much greater was the circulation of the unstamped press on the side of 'moral corruption' than that of the entire religious output," writes R. K. Webb (27). "Infidel publications showed a real knowledge of the people for whom they were intended; that could be said of no religious publication" (28). Working people often did not read the tracts pressed upon them, but either preserved them "for the inspection of the clergyman or the visitor," or devoted them to "base but vital domestic purposes which religious writers would understandably not care to mention" (Webb 27). By midcentury, five hundred million tracts had been distributed, it was estimated by a short-lived publication called *Freethinker* (1 June 1850: 9).

21. "English atheism became conceptually possible under the auspices of the Protestant Reformation," writes David Riggs. "The same institutional apparatus simultaneously produced believers and nay-sayers. The historic transformation commenced in the 1530s, when the Protestant reformers' faith in Bible-reading, the widespread availability of cheap printed texts, and King Henry VIII's desire to impose a standard creed on all his subjects, created the impetus for the first program of universal education in English" (5).

22. The monitor system allowed a single master to control a thousand pupils, all learning by rote. Dickens in *Hard Times* compared it to the manufacturing of piano legs (53).

23. The cylinder steam press was invented in Germany in 1806; the *Times* became the first newspaper to employ it in 1814. Technology enabled the S.D.U.K.'s *Penny Magazine* to "stand upon the commercial principle alone." Without the new machines, "it would have taken a single press, producing a thousand perfect copies each day, one hundred and sixty days" to produce the 160,000 copies of the first number (Charles Knight, preface, 18 December 1832: iv).

24. Watts and Co., Secularist publishers, were still using the series title "Pamphlets for the Million" in 1912.

25. Imitations were of all sorts: the *Penny Gazette,* the *Penny Punch,* the *Penny Times,* and so forth. Knight's original survived until 1845, then floundered forward for one last year as *Knight's Penny Magazine* before folding in 1846. The title was revived later in the century as the *New Penny Magazine.*

26. Hetherington bought a Napier double cylinder machine that could print two thousand sides an hour when he was left money under the will of Julian Hibbert, Carlile's supporter in earlier days. O'Brien estimated in 1837 that Hetherington had five thousand

pounds in stock, a press worth fifteen hundred pounds, and business of a thousand pounds a year. Yet "he died so poor in 1849 that his executors could not meet the claims on his estate" (Hollis, introduction to *Poor Man's Guardian* xxv).

27. The "Cabinet" may have been modeled on the penny reprint "Library of Reason" put together by William Chilton, one of the notorious *Oracle of Reason* circle (A. Barker 47).

28. The cheap reprint was not new: earlier Freethinkers had published Gibbon in sixpenny numbers. But while Chandos, for example, claimed to have sold 3.5 million volumes of reprinted classics between 1868 and 1884, Rationalist Press Association reprints substantially consisted of new books still within copyright.

29. Much of canto 6 and all of canto 7 was omitted in Moxon's 1839 edition, together with many of Shelley's notes, which were pieced together from the pamphlet that got him expelled from Oxford in 1811, *The Necessity of Atheism*. "I don't like Atheism," Mary Shelley wrote Leigh Hunt on 12 December 1838, when Moxon got cold feet, "nor does he *now*. Yet I hate mutilation—what do you say?" (M. Shelley, *Letters* 2: 304). Eventually she decided she could in conscience "leav[e] out the expressions which Shelley would never have printed in after [life]" (2: 305). When Hunt, Trelawny, and others protested, on publication, she confided to her journal: "I . . . wish I had resisted to the last—but when I was told that certain portions would injure the copyright of all the volumes to the publisher," for which he was paying five hundred pounds, "I yielded" (2: 310n). She prevailed on Moxon to reinstate the omitted passages in 1840 partly by pointing out that this "would improve the sale" (2: 311). He complied grudgingly (2: 324). Keen for Shelley's work to reach a wide audience, including "the religious," who "particularly like [him]," she herself omitted his "too shocking" essay "On the Devil and Devils" from her edition of Shelley's prose, also published by Moxon (2: 326). She became actively interested in Moxon's proposals for an edition of the poetry as a means of "exert[ing] pressure to stop the publication of Shelley's works in [cheap serial] numbers" in 1834 (2: 198n).

30. There is evidence that he may have been released after only six weeks.

31. See Bonner 66, and *Trial of Thomas Paterson* 58 for judicial comments on protecting the young.

32. In Norman England, lawyers were called "counters" or "narratores." The "inquisitorial" style of French criminal procedure was less fertile ground for literature.

33. One author began libel proceedings in retaliation for the *Athenaeum*'s description of his "attempt at a novel" as "the very worst . . . that has ever been perpetrated," for "vulgarity," "profanity," and "indelicacy" (Odgers, *Libel and Slander* 203).

34. Unspotted orphan Ion nerves himself to the duty of slaying Adrastus, tyrannical king of Argos, only to discover he is himself his long-lost son. After Adrastus conveniently dies (repentant) by another hand, a hereditary curse descends to Ion, and he kills himself in the temple to relieve the plague it brings upon his people, bidding them "Swear . . . / That ye will seek hereafter in yourselves / The means of sovereign rule" (Talfourd, *Tragedies* 119; 5.3.86–88). Circulated in manuscript in 1835, *Ion* was published on the day Macready staged it at Covent Garden in May 1836. Talfourd's lack of a university education may have been one motivating and compensatory factor in his choice of preferred literary genre.

35. Notice of 20 May 1837 affixed to the title page of *Speech of Serjeant Talfourd on Literary Property*.

36. The *Oracle of Reason* gang promptly set about reprinting them in the Library of Reason.

37. The phrase *"Is there a God?"* was footnoted by Shelley: "This negation must be understood solely to affect a creative Deity. The hypothesis of a pervading Spirit, coeternal with the universe, remains unshaken" (*Poetical Works* 25).

38. Moxon did not quite match up to Dickens and Talfourd's ideals of gentility. He gave away the "secret" of Talfourd's authorship of *Glencoe* immediately before the first performance in 1840, a bit of promotional showmanship Dickens (with a fine sense of period class insult) called "coarse and vulgar blabbing" (letter to Talfourd, 22 May, *Letters* 2: 71).

39. The act of 1710 established fourteen-year copyright, and the 1814 measure a twenty-eight year period or life. On the latter act's muddled progress through Parliament, largely caused by publishing trade opposition to the legal deposit of eleven copies to Britain's main university libraries, a side issue that dominated discussion from 1808, see Feather, *Publishing, Piracy and Politics* 100–12. On eighteenth-century copyright theory's dependence on the Lockean concept of literary property, see M. Rose, *Authors and Owners* 113–29.

40. A year's deliberations by a divided select committee produced a muddled report, and reform of copyright was shelved until 1836, when publishing trade advocates pushed through a measure that reduced the number of deposit copies from eleven to five. Thus the ground was cleared for Talfourd to introduce his first bill.

41. Despite this, "Robert Southey, Esq.! LL.D.!! POET LAUREATE!!! & c.!!!!" (W. Hone, *A Slap at Slop*, in *Facetiae* 46) later warmed up to Hone. "I am sorry to learn that you are still, in the worldly sense of the word, an unfortunate man," he wrote on 26 April 1830. "When I am next in London, I shall seek for you, that I may have the satisfaction of shaking you by the hand" (Hone BL: 40,120: 345).

42. At four pence, less than a sixteenth of the original cost, Hone's prose *Corsair* "brought Byron, or at least [Hone's] version of Byron, to [a] working-class but literate populace" (Manning 223) whilst cleaning up much of the morals. Hone claimed to be a "thorough" "hater" of "this species of robbery" to a friend at the *Edinburgh Review* (letter, 15 November 1823, in Hone BL 41,071: 10), and Hackwood (245) believed his *Lord Byron's Poems* and *Wat Tyler* were his only forays into literary piracy. (Hone claimed the latter was "Reprinted, Verbatim, page for page, word for word, and letter for letter, and carefully collated with the Original" [advertisement, in *Official Account* 15].) But the Berg collection holds copies of Hone's 1816 Popular Cabinet Edition of *Guy Mannering* and his generically refigured version of *Bertram, or the Castle of St. Aldobrand, being the romance of the Tragedy By the Rev. R. C. Maturin*, and Hone was also forgetting the "mutilated volumes of Jones" and other theological works that he had "pillaged in the most shameless manner" for his *Apocryphal New Testament* (*Quarterly Review*, July 1821: 355).

43. "Thou shalt believe in Milton, Dryden, Pope; / Thou shalt not set up Wordsworth, Coleridge, Southy; / Because the first is crazed beyond all hope, / The second drunk, the third so quaint and mouthey," and so on. Hone's pamphlet ended with three

pointed sentences: "Lord Byron's [ironical] Dedication of *Don Juan* to Lord Castlereagh, was suppressed by Mr. Murray, from delicacy to Ministers. *Q.* Why did not Mr. Murray suppress Lord Byron's *Parody* on the Ten Commandments? *A.* Because it contains nothing in ridicule of Ministers, and therefore nothing that *they* could suppose, would be to the displeasure of Almighty God" ("*Don John*" 40).

44. Southey had pictured Byron at the head of a "Satanic" school of writers in his 1821 *Vision of Judgment.* See Marchand 2: 933.

45. Byron was neither so bold nor so apparently ignorant of law on other occasions. He wrote Murray after Hone published his spurious third canto: "Eldon will decide against you—were it only that my name is in the record.—You will also recollect that if the publication is pronounced against on the grounds you mention as *indecent and blasphemous* that *I* lose all right in my daughter's *guardianship* and *education*—in short, all paternal authority" (4 December 1819, *Letters* 6: 252).

46. Byron briefly considered privately printing the work in hopes that it would be pirated (Wickwar 272).

47. As late as 1874, however, an "orthodox missionary" sought to justify his piracy of the Unitarian minister Page Hopps's *Life of Jesus,* "a book written in a reverent spirit," by the plea "that it was a blasphemous publication and therefore incapable of copyright" (Odgers, *Libel and Slander* 470).

48. Carlile copied *Mab* out by hand twice while he was in prison for selling Hone's parodies in 1817, and "in the summer of 1819, . . . made an effort to obtain the consent of its author to its publication, but did not succeed" (*Republican,* 1 February 1822: 147). Bookseller William Clark put out an edition in 1821. Shelley "tried to get an injunction to suppress it, but privately approved" (Walter, *Blasphemy in Britain* 3), while the Vice Society's secretary warned Clark "that he needed not to plead ignorance of the quality of the publication after having so long served as shopman in Carlile's shop" (*Republican,* 1 February 1822: 146). *Mab* was suppressed when Clark gave recognizances to his good behavior and withdrew the publication, a "scandalous compromise" in Carlile's eyes (146). (After Shelley's death, he was imprisoned for four months.)

49. Lamb had recently introduced him to Wordsworth as "my one admirer" (*DNB* 55: 343). Talfourd was "converted" to Wordsworth by a fellow lawyer, Mr. Baron Field.

50. I am grateful on this point for an early reading of Woodmansee's unpublished manuscript, "The Cultural Work of Copyright: Legislating Authorship in Britain 1837–42."

51. Talfourd was inexperienced (he was first returned for Reading in 1835), but not, I think, incompetent. Reception of his speech in Moxon's defense puts in question Feather's judgment that he was a "poor and unconvincing speaker" (143).

52. Talfourd reflected bitterly in January 1842 both on how his bill was "thrown out in one night by Macaulay" and on how his income had dropped by a thousand pounds since 1840 (journal, qtd. in *Letters of Charles Dickens* 2: 18n). "Literature's own familiar friend, in whom she trusted, and who had eaten of her bread, had lifted up his heel against her" (G. Trevelyan 159). Macaulay's hostility to copyright reform may have had some relation to his mission to bring the light of English reason and literature to India, on a budget, though he did not respond to the imperial strain in Talfourd's arguments (*Speech of Serjeant Talfourd* 15).

53. Wordsworth took the post in 1813, and held it until his entry into "that great book of life" called "the *Pension List*" (W. Hone, *Slap at Slop, Facetiae* 46) at three hundred pounds per annum in 1842. John Hunt's *Yellow Dwarf* commented on Wordsworth's "elevation": "Snug's the word. St. Peter is well at Rome; and Mr. Wordsworth is attached to the Excise" (3 January 1818: 4). In fact, the position was no sinecure, and never brought in the four hundred pounds a year Wordsworth initially hoped it would. He was also generously concerned that his works be made more cheaply available to wider circles of readers (see Merriam 136–40).

54. The publication of Johnson's *Lives of the English Poets* (1779–81) and Wharton's *History of English Poetry* (1774–81) first "brought to the British marketplace the attractive notion of a national literary heritage" (Willinsky 25) that assured Englishmen of their superiority.

55. Wordsworth left his *Prelude* unpublished at his death partly to have something of value to bequeath to his family (Feather 126). For details of early Victorian "pilgrimages" to Wordsworth's Lakeland home at Rydal Mount, and his appeal to a broad range of believers, see Gill, *William Wordsworth* 385–99.

56. Talfourd was Lamb's executor under his will, and assumed total editorial control. On his "mutilation" of materials, see the 1905 Bibliophile Society edition, *Letters of Charles Lamb, in which many mutilated words and passages have been restored to their original form.* The "unsigned essays" Lamb had contributed to Hone's *Every-Day* and *Table Books* did not appear amongst his works until 1876.

57. See Moxon letters of 1827 (Hone BL 40,120: 294; 41,071: 20). Moxon knew Hone well enough to play a practical joke on him in 1825 (Merriam 62). Moxon married Lamb's adopted daughter in 1833. For details of his heavy dependence on the Lamb circle and the postmortem Lamb estate in the early years of his business, see Merriam 25–74.

58. Dickens wrote Moxon on 27 October 1840, "Will you have the goodness to send me at your earliest convenience, a copy of each of your famous reprints? . . ." (*Letters* 2: 139). The series began with Samuel Rogers's *Pleasures of Memory,* Campbell's *Poetical Works,* and Lamb's *Essays of Elia.* It was praised in the *Examiner* on 15 March as showing that the copyright bill need be no bar to cheap publications.

59. History had its revenge in 1852 when Moxon had to withdraw Shelley's *Letters* on discovering that most of the texts were forgeries.

60. Phrases, respectively, from Carlyle's petition to the House, and Wordsworth's open letter to the *Kendal Mercury,* 1838 (*Letters of Charles Dickens* 1: 161n; Feather 133). Tegg wrote two pamphlets against Talfourd's bill, in 1837 and 1840.

61. "Heaven helps those who help themselves," Smiles prefaces his first paragraph; help "from without" is "enfeebling in its effects" (*Self-Help* 1). Reformist legislation can therefore work moral evil (2).

62. An 1854 circular in HC records that only one hundred of the twelve hundred–pound set-up costs had been subscribed by that date.

63. The *Tablet* called Holyoake's *Movement* a "small vehicle for condensed blasphemy" (note, in HC). The *Reasoner* was published without interruption from 1846 to 1861, when Bradlaugh launched the *National Reformer.* It was then issued intermittently until 1872.

64. Holyoake lists himself among the "Defiant Syndicate of Four," but it is unclear

whether his connection with the *Oracle* dates from inception. The other members were Southwell, Malthus Questell Ryall, W. J. Linton, and printer-subeditor William Chilton, "the only absolute atheist I have ever known" (Holyoake, *Sixty Years* 1: 142), who shirked martyrdom in favor of Holyoake in 1842 (letter, 24 December 1841, in HL). Circulation dropped quickly from an initial high of four thousand to approximately seven hundred. The *"O"* expired in 1843, after fruitless efforts to "get [it] to London" (Ryall to Holyoake, 4 January 1842, in HL). One reader at least found it profoundly exciting, writing in the margin of the copy now held by the Bodleian Library next to a statistical item on the burning of heretics (10,220 by Torquemada alone), for 27 November 1841 (32–33): "Open your eyes, o ye people, calling yourselves Christians, read the book ye call holy with your understandings. . . . See how ye have been blinded and what Asses ye are!"

65. See Holyoake's 1845 pamphlet, *The Value of Biography*.

66. "Dare to be wise yourselves, and SWING shall be, / If you approve, THE PEOPLE'S TRAGEDY" (prologue, *Swing* 8). Despite Taylor's relentless self-advertisement, he had some skill, and made a hit with his character the archbishop of Cant, whose expostulations on "weekly trash" and blasphemous pamphlets (9–10; 1.1) strongly recall Hone's *Political House That Jack Built* and *Man in the Moon*. The play was Taylor's response to "Richard the God's" arrest for seditious libel (11). It is undoubtedly a coincidence that Meyerbeer achieved his greatest success in 1831 with his opera *Robert le diable;* Taylor may have known the opéra comique on which the sinister production was based. The copy of *Swing* in the British Museum is inscribed, "The Rev. Mr. Taylor respectfully gratifies his own vanity with the hope of affording some entertainment to Mr. Kemble on this specimen of *what the Drama should be*" (Cutner, *Robert Taylor* 64).

67. See Haywood, *Faking It* (77). Trumping his rivals' editions, Collier's *Notes and Emendations* sold four thousand copies in 1852. Collier makes strange company with the notorious William Henry Ireland, whose fake Shakespeare play *Vortigern and Rowena* was laughed off the stage at Drury Lane in 1795, and who may have been a "youthful literary revolutionar[y] bent on undermining the authority of the cultural establishment" (71). His father (his first dupe) was a noted bardolator, and entrapped him in perpetuating his crime by exhibiting his "finds" to fellow worshippers. Boswell knelt down and cried, "I now kiss the invaluable relics of our bard: and thanks to God that I have lived to see them!" (Ireland 96). G. T. Lawley drew special attention to Hone's correspondence with Ireland (Hone BL 40,108: 40).

68. Other passages found criminal were taken from an article on "Symbol Worship," which concluded a disquisition on the birth of the Hindu deity Ganesh with the verdict that "th[is] history" was "to the full as reasonable as that of Tom Thumb, Baron Munchausen, or Jesus Christ" (*Trial of Charles Southwell* 3).

69. For Southwell's histrionic career and failed attempt at theater management, see his *Confessions* 91–93.

70. Luther is Southwell's favorite: "The Pope was born out of the devil's posteriors," he quotes, "he is Antichrist, the greatest of pimps, the governor of Sodom" (*Oracle of Reason*, 27 November 1841: 27).

71. It is one of the ironies of history that Holyoake later received two government grants of a hundred pounds each towards the trip to America that resulted in his 1884 *Settler's Guide Book*.

72. His former colleagues begged him to "consider if there be not a better way of removing the wall of obstruction to what you deem the spread of truth, than the *breaking your head against it*" (Rodgers to Holyoake, 19 June 1842, in HL). His *Oracle* editorship commenced with number 8 and lasted fourteen weeks.

73. Holyoake consulted several lawyers. He wrote his wife on 22 July 1842 that "[they] all think my cause a very good one and that I shall not be imprisoned for long if at all" (in HL). Attempts to move the trial to London were unsuccessful.

74. Judge Erskine regretted that evidence of Holyoake's authorship was not laid before the court, and Prosecutor Alexander risked repeated rebukes to ensure that the jury guessed it. See *Cheltenham Free Press,* 20 August 1842: 266. Number 36 of the *Oracle* carried Holyoake's sequel to the "Jew Book" article.

75. The Anti-Persecution Union was formed in response to Holyoake's and Adams's cases.

76. "I was near the door; he was the length of the room from me," emphasized the prosecution's witness, James Bartram; "I heard [the words] distinctly; they were spoken in a distinct voice" (*Cheltenham Free Press,* 20 August: 266).

77. The full text is as follows: "You have been convicted of uttering language, and although you have been adducing long arguments to show the impolicy of these prosecutions, you are convicted of having uttered these words with improper levity" (Holyoake, *History of the Last Trial* 64).

78. Holyoake had ended every letter to his wife, "Kiss Mad[eleine] for me." One damaged letter, from the day before the trial, is noted by him in pencil as "Eaten by Madeleine, or torn with her teeth" (9 August 1842, in HL). He made preparations for suicide in prison, mathematically calculating where he would have to lie on the floor to "be able to tilt up [his metal] bed," and "pull it down so as to drive the leg through his brain" (*Sixty Years* 1: 84).

79. The forty or fifty counterfeit mints in operation at the end of the eighteenth century (Foucault, *Discipline* 86) remained active until cash payment (suspended 1797) was resumed in 1821; 17,885 forged pieces of paper money were presented at the Bank of England in 1816. At first glance, Hone and Cruikshank's "restriction note" looked like a forgery. Then one took in the full force of the parody: the main image of men and women hanging in a row, like counters; the "stamp" showing Britannia eating her children; the rope-looped "signature" of the public hangman.

80. Technically, lawyer Alexander explained to the jury, "uttering" language meant originating and authoring the words, as opposed merely to "publishing" them (*Free Press,* 20 August 1842: 266).

81. Shell's main concern is "the tropic interaction between economic and linguistic symbolization and production" (*Money, Language, and Thought* 4). On the introduction of coinage in Greece in the sixth and fifth centuries BC, for example, some thinkers came quickly to "recognize interactions between economic and intellectual exchange, or money and language" (2). Greek *sēme* means "word" as well as "coin" (2), just as German *übertragung* means both "economic transference of property" and "linguistic transfer of meaning" (85); the "Economics of Translation in Goethe's *Faust*" are particularly worth examination (84–130). Paper money more resembles language than coinage in that it is a symbol "entirely disassociated from the commodity that it symbolizes" (105).

82. According to the *Oxford English Dictionary*, the verb "to coin," in its sense of "to make money by stamping metal" dates from circa 1330; the figurative use of the term, as in "to coin a phrase," dates from circa 1580. The more common sense of "to utter," relating to speech and language (as in "He uttered the words with feeling"), dating from circa 1400, precedes the financial sense of "to give currency to; to put into circulation as legal tender" by almost a century. "To utter" also in the mid-sixteenth century could mean "to issue by way of publication; to publish;" and in the early nineteenth century developed the meaning "to announce for sale."

83. Compare the double roles of Mr. Pancks in Dickens's *Little Dorrit*: "teller" of fortunes and money.

84. Marlowe was accused of apostasy and counterfeiting by Richard Baines in 1592; he was taken with a fake shilling in 1593, when Baines also delivered to the authorities a detailed Note on his atheism. Marlowe's sister was charged with blasphemy as well. (I am grateful for clarification on this point to my colleague David Riggs.) Marlowe's forgeries were not limited to coins: he also conjured on stage (and so into the "real" presence of theatrical space) a counterfeit Helen of Troy whose lips will "suck forth" the soul of Dr. Faustus (5.1.100). Victorian scholars, intent on moral rehabilitation, dismissed the Note as the "Baines libel."

85. Southwell complained loudly to Holyoake that he was "treated very like a thief" (letter, 20 August 1842, in HL).

86. The response to this from the bench was: "You are very insolent, therefore [!!!] you are committed to three months' imprisonment" (Barker 12–13, exclamation original). The personal price Swann paid for free and cheap publication was a total of four and a half years in prison.

87. "The petitioners have a full and immovable conviction," submitted a group from Yorkshire, "that the House doth not, in any constitutional or rational sense, represent the nation; that, when the people have ceased to be represented, the constitution is subverted; that taxation without representation is slavery." "[I]f such language were tolerated," Canning replied, "there was an end to the House of Commons" (qtd. in O. Smith 32).

88. The law invoked was the 1839 Metropolitan Police Act, later reinforced by the Town Police Causes Act of 1847.

89. The combination acts of 1800 were repealed in 1824–25, but six laborers of Tolpuddle, Dorset, who formed a trade's union in 1833, became that movement's first martyrs only months later. They were convicted of "conspiracy" for having taken an oath and asked for "a voice in the British nation" ("Martyr" George Loveless, qtd. in *Tolpuddle* 7). The Tolpuddle Union was noticeably anticlerical.

90. Unless otherwise noted, citation is from the 1889 edition of Foote's *Defence of Free Speech*.

91. Slipped between "BLANK VERSE" and "BLAST FURNACE" one finds the S.D.U.K.'s verdict that "the true crime of blasphemy" consists in "hurtful, injurious, and insulting speech," rather than the denial of religious doctrine (*Penny Cyclopedia* 3: 507). "All things are not really sacred which many agree to call so," the entry continues, "Satire and ridicule may reach where plain argument would not go" (3: 508). Given the

availability of the 1833 *Cyclopaedia* to lower-class families, it is highly likely that these remarks had an impact.

92. Holyoake did much to produce the show of unity. In pretrial letters to Holyoake, Carlile urged delaying his trial, so as to avoid a winter in prison (11 July 1842, in HL); he was so moved by Holyoake's speech that "I could scarcely restrain myself from jumping into the dock to embrace you" (11 August 1842, in HL).

93. "[W]ithin the last week," Southwell wrote Holyoake from prison on 14 March 1842, "I have been . . . flooded with notes of letters, some condoling and some most heartily abusing me" (in HL). He was kept well supplied with stamps, and also enjoyed a regular supply of luxury items, courtesy of subscriptions, including cigars, two new night caps, bear's grease for his hair, a refurbished suit, and a silk handkerchief (list of "Necessaries" supplied by T. Whiting, jailer, in HL).

94. See Paterson's *Devil's Looking-Glass, or Mirror of Infidelity!* (1848) and *Letters to Infidels* (1846).

95. Organized Secularism has been well served by the historians. See especially Royle's *Victorian Infidels* (1974) and *Radicals, Secularists, and Republicans* (1980), which provide a careful explication of the movement's internal dynamics; see also Walter Arnstein's *Bradlaugh Case* (rev. ed., 1983). Jim Herrick (*Against the Faith*) and David Tribe (*One Hundred Years of Freethought*) chronicle Freethought from within; Warren Sylvester Smith's 1967 *London Heretics, 1870–1914* locates the Secularists on the crowded urban map of unbelief; Owen Chadwick's *Secularization of the European Mind in the Nineteenth Century* lays the philosophical and political groundwork; Susan Budd's 1977 *Varieties of Unbelief* traces the social fate of atheism and agnosticism from 1850 to 1960. At the local level, David Nash's 1992 *Secularism, Art and Freedom* has devoted the attention it deserves to the Leicester Secular Society.

96. Of fifty-five Secularists in the period from 1865 to 1915 for whom Edward Royle collected details of past allegiances, "two-thirds had been Owenites and one-third Chartists" (*Radicals* 129).

CHAPTER THREE

1. These are the labels given six large cocoa-nuts in a *Punch* cartoon for 26 May 1883, "A Shy at the Sticks." "The Government Bill might give us Mohammedans, Hindoos, Buddhists, Chinese, and Fetish worshippers in addition," the Tory *John Bull* reported of the Affirmation Bill, "but the immediate object is to admit Atheists, and specially the notorious BRADLAUGH" (3 March 1883: 137). "The name of God was to be shut out of the House of Commons, in order to get Bradlaugh into it" (*Spectator,* 28 April 1883: 533). The nation was becoming too "tolerant of anomalies," declared the Anglican *Rock,* which ran advertisements for "Forms of Petition" against the bill (9 March 1883: 156). The bill was the key to "Incipient Profanity" (editorial, 16 March: 173): "The Apostle JAMES knew something of the matter when he wrote 'the tongue is a fire, a world of iniquity' " (173).

2. An "Holympian" fantasy by "Jeames" the Cockney servant, fresh from reading "*Hovid*—in translashun I must own," closes out the obsessive theme of several years (*Punch Almanack,* 1884: 22).

3. Rapid technological advances quickly outmoded many of the docks built before the 1840s, so that in the second half of the century more were built: the Royal Albert, West India South, and Tilbury Docks; docks deep and wide enough to handle the new steamships; docks with hydraulic lifts. The result was that by the 1880s London was massively overdocked. The Great Strike of the London Dockers occurred in 1889.

4. The aims and methods of the N.S.S. are best summed up in the fourth clause of the program put together in 1866: "That human improvement and happiness cannot be effectually promoted without civil and religious liberty; and that, therefore, it is the duty of every individual . . . to actively attack all barriers to equal freedom of thought and utterance for all" (qtd. in Royle, *Radicals* 6). The poet James Thompson put membership figures much higher, at 1,192 in 1876 (qtd. 19).

5. Some local groups emphasized activism; others stressed the provision of a community to members who were self-excluded misfits in society at large. In Leicester, for example, as surviving ephemera demonstrate, a well-organized society with an unusual degree of family involvement duplicated all the benefits of dissenting chapel life: coffee-shop, reading room, and sewing circle; Sunday excursions and children's classes; Secularist choir and hymnbook; "naming" and burial ceremonies. See David Nash, *Secularism, Art and Freedom,* and materials extant in the John Johnson Collection of the Bodleian Library, Oxford. Thankfully, the members did not pursue the suggestion of a Stalybridge Secularist to write a Freethought libretto for the *Messiah* (Royle, *Radicals* 137).

6. The Christian Evidence Society was founded in 1870 by prominent Evangelicals, including Lord Shaftesbury, to combat "the present prevalence of scepticism or of unbelief in various classes of society" (*National Reformer,* qtd. in Royle, *Radicals* 301). The Christian Evidence League, headed by Bradlaugh's estranged brother, was a much less respectable body.

7. See Budd (103–13) for some accounts of the moral and social, as well as intellectual, motives for conversion, from reading Paine or rereading the Bible to experiencing sudden light during one of Bradlaugh's orations.

8. See also the controversy about the deathbed of Emma Martin, memorialized in Holyoake's *Last Days of Mrs. Emma Martin* (1851).

9. The most famous case of legalized breach of contract was the *Cowan v. Milbourn* case of 1867. The contract between the secretary of a local atheistical organization and the proprietor of a hall was deemed unenforceable because it was drawn up for an illegal purpose, that is, the dissemination of atheistical opinions in public lectures.

10. Not until the Bowman case (commenced 1915) went up to the House of Lords on appeal in 1917 was the right to will property for Secularist purposes securely established in law. The total budget of the N.S.S. was under five hundred pounds even in the mid-1880s: the *National Reformer* and other journals frequently ran editorial begging letters and special appeals. "To leave money to an atheist," as Royle wryly remarks, "could be taken to signify an unsound mind, thus nullifying the will" (*Radicals* 186).

11. Bradlaugh was lucky in his employer, Thomas Rogers, a Fenchurch Street solicitor. Desperate to hang on to his clerk's talents, he asked him only not to let propaganda injure the business. Hence Bradlaugh's adoption of his notorious pseudonym, "Icono-

clast." The *National Reformer* began life in 1860; Bradlaugh edited it alone from 1866 to 1881, then with Annie Besant from 1881 to 1887. It combined quality with low price—sixteen foolscap pages for only two pence; circulation doubled to six thousand by 1872. "That so many people . . . read it is a remarkable testimony to the intellectual abilities and appetites of some Secularists" (Royle, *Radicals* 159). Besant's *Our Corner* later veered towards socialism; G. B. Shaw's *Irrational Knot* (written in 1880) and *Love among the Artists* (1881) were serialized in 1885–87 and 1887–88.

12. Aveling decamped from the N.S.S. to the Social Democratic Federation and the embraces of Marx's daughter Eleanor in the early 1880s. His treatment of her was a contributory factor in her later suicide.

13. Bradlaugh edged Holyoake off the staff of his *National Reformer* in 1863 at the cost of paying thirty-nine weeks' salary of two pounds and two shillings a week, whether Holyoake delivered his two columns or not. See *Mr. Holyoake's Disconnection with the "National Reformer."*

14. Foote was a founding member (1875) of the Sunday Society for Opening Museums, Art Galleries, Libraries, and Gardens, in the distinguished company of Dean Stanley, the second president, Huxley et al. He was one of the selected speakers at the society's first public annual meeting, 27 May 1876.

15. Besant began editing the *Reformer* on 7 May 1881. Given the amount of lead time needed to set up Foote's new venture, I do not think jealousy at her appointment can have been a large factor in the launch of the *Freethinker* or the shape the publication took.

16. Different *Reformer* columns carried clear notices of "legal responsibility" for contents. Writers of "Reports of Meetings," for example, were "to be considered Responsible for the Facts and Opinions stated therein" (sample issue, 27 March 1881: 220).

17. Thwaite's Liver Pills were one exception to the general ban. They were also advertised in the *Secular Chronicle*. Victorian Freethinkers may have suffered largely from dyspepsia.

18. The *Freethinker* was launched in May 1881, the *Evening News* in July. *Tit-Bits* began publication on 22 October, and was an instant success. Imitations included Northcliffe's *Answers,* the profits from which funded launch of the halfpenny *Daily Mail* in 1896; they had poor news quality but a "marked" emphasis on popular education (R. Williams, *Revolution* 225). The leading weekly of the period was *Lloyd's Weekly News,* which reached a circulation of nine hundred thousand in the 1890s, partly by dint of blanket coverage of the Jack the Ripper murders; the *Daily Mail* sold 989,000 by 1900. A sign of the times, *Public Opinion: A Comprehensive Summary of the Press throughout the World* began publication (in Washington) in 1886.

19. The *Star* sold 142,600 copies on the first day of issue. Items included "Another 'People's Palace' Wanted" and "The Pugilistic Revival. What an Old Hand Thinks." The paper carried enormous display advertisements.

20. A boycott by W. H. Smith lasted until 1906. Compare suppression of *Private Eye*'s Princess Diana obituary issue in 1997.

21. The *Librairie* also published cheap editions of *La Pucelle* (*"ouvrage célèbre de Voltaire"*) and *La Religieuse* (*"célèbre roman de Diderot"*), together with other clearly

indecent volumes: *Le Convent de Gomorrhe; Les amours secretes de Pie X;* and so forth. Nevertheless, these productions were claimed to be openly sold "chez tous les marchands de journaux" (advertisement, back cover of *La Bible amusante*).

22. Taxil's text to this image reads, for example: "Comme il ne tenait pas a faire des bêtises, l'Éternel se dit qu'il lui etait nécessaire de commencer par avoir de la lumière. 'Que la lumière soit!' *commanda-t-il, et la lumière fut*" (n.pag.).

23. The *Tomahwak, A Saturday Journal of Satire,* was edited by Arthur à Beckett under the motto "Culpam Invitat Qui Peccatum." Full-page cartoons in January 1870 included "Christian Charity!" and "The Cure for Murder. Or, Justice Clings to the Gallows." J. W. Gott continued the *Freethinker* tradition in his Bradford *Truthseeker,* which declined into purely cartoon offensiveness after Gott's prosecution for blasphemy in 1903.

24. "According to Mrs. Besant . . . it was owing to the commencement of these caricatures that in November, 1881, the [Freethought Publishing] company gave up the publication of the paper. She did not . . . care to be responsible for what she could not defend" (*John Bull,* 21 April 1883: 254).

25. See, for example, the rector of Bethnal Green's letter to the *Rock,* 22 March 1883: "In my parish, the 'Comic History of the Bible,' and the 'Comic History of the Life of Christ,' the *cramba repetita* of French infidelity, are exposed for sale in the shop windows," where "boys and girls especially delight" in them (182).

26. Foote and Ramsey were put on hospital diet two months into their sentences but lost a great deal of weight nonetheless (Ramsey 15). Both reacted with distaste to the earthy potatoes and wooden spoons, a security precaution.

27. Such were the signatories of a letter of complaint from members of the National Club, 1 Whitehall Gardens, S.W. The secretary notes on the reverse: "A worse number than usual" (HO 144, piece 114/A25,454/495).

28. When Lady Bracknell inquires about Miss Prism in the *Importance of Being Earnest,* "is [she] a female of repellent aspect, remotely connected with education?" and Canon Chasuble replies, "She is the most cultivated of ladies, and the very picture of respectability," Wilde's grande dame can only conclude, "It is obviously the same person" (*Writings* 533). A play that so flaunted its lack of respectability naturally once included a scene in which the hero is arrested; Wilde cut it just before opening night, only to live the scene through a few days later.

29. Harcourt was explicitly asked "what steps the Government would take to put down" the *Freethinker* in the Commons in 1882 (*Freethinker,* 23 March 1884: 89).

30. See Attorney-General Sir Henry James's letter and Harcourt's private note (HO 45, pieces 9,536/49,902/79 and 79a).

31. A man was sentenced to fourteen days at Glasgow in 1885 for selling the *Freethinker* (HO 45, piece 10,406/A46,794/8).

32. A new hundred-pound property requirement of each special juryman ironically guaranteed greater "independence" of judgment.

33. Charges against Whittle were dropped.

34. There was considerable money at stake. The conscientious new member of Parliament had voted over two hundred times.

35. "Small towns in Cornwall recorded in many cases thirty per cent of their adult population in signatures for release," reported Reverend Sharman of the Association for Repeal (*Freethinker*, 23 March 1883: 92). A two-page letter to the Unitarian *Inquirer*, however, protested the general lack of "sympathy" for the "blasphemers," together with "creeping pharasaic respectability" (14 April 1883: 247), though the British and Foreign Unitarian Association's Council withdrew a resolution to censure the *Freethinker* sentence.

36. Following the *Secularist* debacle, Holyoake seconded a motion to expel Foote from the N.S.S. at the National Conference of 1876, after Foote had launched a demand for greater democracy within the power structure. The animosity lasted a lifetime.

37. Holyoake followed the letter with a note to Bradlaugh's enemy, Henry Varley, reassuring him that, "My letter to Sir William V. Harcourt was a plea for *abatement* of sentence[,] not questioning the grounds of it" (30 August 1883, in HL). He also wrote to Lord Coleridge to acknowledge his own errors and "the great service rendered by your Lordship to conscientious discussion" (in E. Coleridge, *Life and Correspondence* 1: 250).

38. "In a word, *R[ex] v. Hetherington* reaffirmed in 1841 the doctrines laid down in *R[ex] v. Woolston* more than a century before." And that case itself, was "remarkable on account of the emphatic way in which it makes the matter and not the manner of the publication the gist of the offence" (J. Stephen, *History* 2: 471).

39. The traditional definition centered firmly on "matter" was still considered workable by the prosecution in Holyoake's case the following year. It was invoked in the case of *Cowan v. Milbourn* in 1867, although Barons Martin and Bramwell disagreed with their senior's ruling, preferring the view of another "learned judge" that "blasphemy is more in the manner and spirit of treating the subject than in the actual matter itself" (J. Stephen, *History* 2: 464).

40. "The whole tone of th[is] passage," Stephen remarked, "is that the unbeliever is a poor, vulgar, ignorant wretch, whom it may be well to treat with contemptuous lenity as a rule, but whom you can always punish if he makes himself offensive by imputing to him bad motives, a malicious intention, or indifference to the public interests" ("Blasphemy" 313–14).

41. At Paterson's Edinburgh trial in 1844, the lord justice clerk found authority for the definition centered on "manner" by rereading the second clause of the indictment. Thus the publication of words intended to "asperse, vilify, ridicule," or bring into "contempt" became not an amplification but an alternative charge to "denial of the truth and authority of the Holy Scriptures or the Christian religion" (*Trial of Thomas Paterson* 55).

42. "It must, of course, be admitted," conceded Odgers in the 1905 edition of his *Libel and Slander*, "that the law laid down by Lord Coleridge in *Rex v. Ramsey and Foote* cannot be reconciled with every one of the earlier decisions." However, "It is in no way the duty of a judge to accept all the *dicta* of his predecessors and to apply them literally" (471).

43. After this period of inactivity, between 1908 and 1914 the law was "accepted, and extended, by five judges in succession" (*Prime Minister and the Blasphemy Laws* 4).

44. The bill eventually passed without great agitation while the nation was preoccu-

pied with General Gordon's fate in Khartoum and events in Ireland. It was followed by an act of 1885, which broke up two-member boroughs into single-member constituencies, making it "less easy to drill or corrupt the constituents" (Young 139).

45. When "Lijah" Cadman, former chimney-climbing boy, started signing his reports "Yours in the King's Army, Lijah" (Bishop 66), Booth recognized the publicity value of the military imagery; it also summed up his feelings about the nature of his mission, founded 1865. He adopted the name "Salvation Army" in 1878; annual general meetings became known as war congresses; the *Salvationist*'s name was changed to the *War Cry!*; bands, flags, and uniforms were introduced. One of Bramwell Booth's later pamphlets was entitled *Bible Battle-Axes;* one of Catherine Booth's *Aggressive Christianity;* and pamphlets of 1920 and 1944 *Christ, the Aggressor* and *Religion with a Punch!*, respectively.

46. The *Tablet* for 17 March 1883 noted, "We do not know whether 'General' Booth considers the *War Cry* in the light of a comic paper. . . . One warrior invokes 'apt alliteration's artful aid,' and rejoices in the name of Sergeant Sally Slee, while one incident in what is termed a 'Cockney Conflict' at Notting-hill is thus described: 'One head was broken by the enthusiastic drummer, but fortunately it belonged to his drum' " (407).

47. The army was a favorite *Punch* target too. The 24 March issue that imagines Foote contributing an article on "The Limits of Belief" also includes a hostile item suggesting the army was absconding with supporters' money (142). A property-owning society is liable to label all outsiders "thieves."

48. The first collections of army songs were entitled the *Hallelujah Book* (1880), "containing 107 of the 'merriest songs' of the Army" (Sandal 123), and *Hosanna Songs* (1880). Both were priced at a penny.

49. Mob violence against the army was often incited by the brewers whose trade they threatened. Figures for 1882, Bramwell Booth recalled in *Echoes and Memories,* were 642 assaults (some very serious) and 60 damaged buildings. But, "There was no redress. We could obtain neither protection nor reparation" (25). Extreme hostility dated more or less from the bishop of Carlisle's attack on Salvation Army tactics in an October 1880 sermon on the text of 1 Corinthians 14.33, "For God is not the author of confusion, but of peace."

50. General Booth's personal testament, *In Darkest England and The Way Out,* was published in November 1890. (It was partly edited and ghostwritten by W. T. Stead of the *Pall Mall Gazette.*) Ten thousand copies sold on publication day and two hundred thousand within a year. As the bishop of Durham realized, "William Booth has rediscovered the lost ideal of the Church—the universal compulsion of the souls of men" (Bishop 93), bringing "the submerged tenth" of society to light (94). Booth also championed legal aid for the poor.

51. Gissing's *In the Year of Jubilee* (1894) similarly makes a centerpiece of vulgarian Bradlaughite Barmby's reading of *Paradise Lost*—" 'Ail, orrors, ail! and thou profoundest Ell / receive thy new possessor!' " (213–14)—while outside "sound[s] the wailing shout of a dustman," like "the voice of a soul condemned to purge itself in filth" (263).

52. *Gissing: The Critical Heritage,* edited by Pierre Coustillas and Colin Partridge, is a collection of reviews.

53. Unless otherwise noted, citation is from *Robert Elsmere,* edited by Rosemary Ashton, 1987.

1. The Broad Church party was dismayed when Voysey rejected pleas for silence and appealed against deprivation of his living. His defense before the chancellor of York enjoyed a lively sale. It was drafted by Fitzjames Stephen.

2. Needless to say, the British and Foreign Bible Society sold below commercial rates. The penny Testament sold eight million copies by 1903.

3. I am grateful for this reference to my colleague David Riggs.

4. Title of a pamphlet by T. Wentworth Higginson, minister of the Worcester Free Church in the United States, the second in the series *Secular Miscellany* (1854).

5. In the late Victorian period the term came to mean "Bible worship" rather than simple self-prostration (to paraphrase the *OED*) before the letter of Biblical law, in which sense the word was used by De Quincey in 1847.

6. Southwell's analysis devolved naturally into an assualt on scriptural canonicity, drawing both on Hone's *Apocryphal New Testament* and (it seems) on Jeremiah Jones. Two long pages of transcript simply list books like "The Song of the three children in the fiery furnace"—"allowed as Canonical, of late," like the rest of the Apocrypha, "by the Church of Rome." There must once have been literary decisions about the canon, Southwell implied; and there would be again. "Recently," he quoted one authority, "the *Canticles* have . . . been rejected by Whiston, and *Jonah* and *Daniel* by Eickhorn, Aikin, & c., as 'legends and romances' " (*Trial of Charles Southwell* 45).

7. See for example, Corelli's gloss on Christ's address to the sorrowing women before the Crucifixion, Luke 23.31 (*Barabbas* 78).

8. Other anti-Semitic ploys include the provision of an Aryan reader-in-the-text, mysterious prophetic Melchior the Egyptian, and the recasting of remorseful Pilate as an imperial administrator horrified by the natives' savagery.

9. Shaw's view was shared by many (Judge 2). Shaw chaired the Foote-Besant public debate "Is Socialism Sound?" in February 1887; he stood against Foote (half in jest) for the presidency of the National Secular Society in 1890; and he engaged in a lively two-day public debate with him on the "Legal Eight Hours Question" in 1891. The two men often sat on the same committees, for free speech and prison reform, for example. Shaw published a defense of his belief in the "life force" on the front page of the *Freethinker* in 1908 (1 November: 689–90), and wrote to Chesterton, apropos "Shavianism: a Religion": "Foote is still bewildered about me imagining that I am a pervert" (*Letters 1898–1910* 762). The other "uncompromisingly honest" journalist was another prominent literary Freethinker, John Mackinnon Robertson (Shaw, *An Autobiography* 119; *Letters 1898–1910* 874).

10. "Some of the most important [new] periodicals" of the 1880s and 1890s "depended upon the comic in their effort to offer an alternative to established values, institutions, writers, critics, and literary works" (Hannoosh 61). They included *Le chat noir* (1882–92), *Lutece* (1883–86), *L'Hydropathe* (1879–80), and *Le Scapin* (1885–86).

11. Compare Paine's reply to the New Jerusalemites who claimed to have found the

true "key" to Scripture, "lost above four thousand years": "it must have been very rusty" (Carlile, *Life of Paine* xxxi).

12. The practice dates back to the *Sortes Virgilianae* or "Virgilian lots," a method of divination by opening Virgil's *Aeneid* at random and construing what is found on the open page.

13. His bishop is not amused when the spirit moves Ernest to unfold from the pulpit "what kind of little cake it was that the widow of Zarehath had intended making when Elijah found her gathering a few sticks" (Butler, *Way of All Flesh* 291). (Seed cake, he decides.)

14. "If you begin with the Bible," says Pryer, "you are three parts gone on the road to infidelity," since "[a] more unreliable book was never put on paper (Butler, *Way of All Flesh* 261). Ernest surpasses him in dismissing Zechariah as "poor stuff, full of Yankee bounce" (262). The novel is explicit in its reference to the Freethought and Secularist tradition. When Ernest moves into Mrs. Jupp's boardinghouse to live sanctimoniously among the poor, he finds that "by far the greater number" of his neighbors "were practically infidels, . . . while many were avowed Atheists—admirers of Tom Paine, of whom he now heard for the first time" (272).

15. Ernest first visits pretty Miss Snow, who *is* a prostitute, going upstairs "with his Bible under his arm, and a consuming fire in his heart." He "knew well enough what he wanted" after that aborted encounter, "and as for the Bible, he pushed it from him to the other end of his table. It fell over on the floor, and he kicked it into a corner" (*Way of All Flesh* 289).

16. Number 87 of the *Tracts for the Times* endorsed the revival of the exclusive historical right of the Catholic church "as the interpreter of Scripture," Southwell reminded the court (*Trial of Charles Southwell* 83). Deny his "equal right" to examine the Scriptures, he warned, and "the danger which you yourselves run" as Christians, Protestants, and nonconformists of being denied direct interpretive access to the Bible was plainly clear (44, 83).

17. See, for example, Holyoake's comments on the social "usefulness" of *Romola* in *Bygones Worth Remembering* (2: 94). He remained disappointed at Eliot's positivist reluctance to see the people act for themselves, quoting the line from *Felix Holt:* "Ignorant power comes in the end to the same thing as wicked power" (*Bygones* 1: 277).

18. Holyoake was eventually interred in Kensal Green; perhaps his lease on the Highgate plot ran out.

19. Extant in HL is extensive correspondence with Bray, Eliot's friends the Hennells, Charles Dilke, John Morley, Thomas Hughes, and J. H. Shorthouse, author of what Foote's reviewer called "John Inglesant's Tour in Search of a Religion" (*Progress,* January 1883: 10), besides Gladstone, Herbert Spencer, and (extensively) John Stuart Mill. Holyoake used his books as calling cards, sending Ruskin (for example) his *Limits of Atheism* in 1884. He was proud to count the Tennysons among his friends.

20. Maxse wrote to the *Daily News* on 1 May: "Sir,—Mr. Foote's brilliant defense last week will probably have awakened some fastidious critics to their error in having depicted him as a low and coarse controversialist. . . . I know something of Mr. Foote, and I am quite certain he would not say anything to shock a refined interpretation of religion" (*Freethinker,* 6 May 1883: 138). (The letter was not printed by the editor.)

21. Foote printed extracts from *Vittoria,* for example, in the *Secularist* (4 March 1876: 55); he reprinted a Meredith sonnet in the *Liberal* (November 1879: 495) and an extract from *In the Woods* in the *Secularist* (13 January 1876: 20). His personal taste was for the poetry.

22. Glendinning gives the example of the character "Onesiphorus Dunn" in the *Last Chronicle of Barset:* Trollope invented him, she claims, "simply so that he could write that Mr. Dunn was 'usually called Siph by his intimate friends'" (17). The name was shorthand for "syphilis."

23. Some of the *Ordeal's* aphorisms, for example, have some positive function, and its kept woman, Belladonna, is traditionally imagined as devil and serpent, an excess of biblical resonance that Meredith later wipes from his work. Likewise, in *Rhoda Fleming* Meredith pushes towards subversive reversal by presenting the fallen Dahlia as a "nun-like" and martyred Magdalen (326), but also simply upholds inclusive Christian charity above the letter of scriptural law.

24. Sir Austin's conceit of playing God inevitably casts his son in the scapegoat role, so that when his educational "experiment" appears to have failed, "all humanity's failings fell on [his] shoulders" (*Ordeal* 389). In *Rhoda Fleming,* fallen Dahlia (as her flower name prophesies) returns to her father's garden in spite of his fiat: she names two trees she can see from its confines "Adam" and "Eve," because—in ambiguous phrase (is this a reference to a spurned display of beauty, or to the repelling "flaming sword" of Genesis 3.24?)—they seem to be "turning away from the blaze of Paradise" (8; see also 431, 492).

25. Exodus 3.2 is the intertext here: the line is a Derridean antipun on the Biblical "bush [that] burned with fire" and yet "was not consumed," while the "deviant" verb "plant" ensures that we half hear the word with which it truly belongs, "bush," as well as the verb which more naturally belongs with "b*l*ush"—"pant" (Meredith, *Diana* 321).

26. *Little Dorrit* is labeled an "ignorant and mischievous libel" of government in the *Saturday Review* (qtd. in Colaico 54, 57), and Dickens is said to "gloat . . . over [Little Nell's] death" in the *Old Curiosity Shop* "as if . . . it was some savory dainty" in the *Edinburgh* (qtd. 57). Fitzjames Stephen's review of a *Tale of Two Cities* was once called "the most infamous, perhaps, in the whole record of English criticism" (qtd. 55).

27. A note to John Bright, 3 June 1877, best conveys Coleridge's fine, almost precious literary sensibility: "I have left for you at the Athenaeum a little parcel with *Love is Enough* in it which I think a *very* beautiful and pathetic thing—in a very difficult metre for any one without a very delicate ear to manage but which Morris has managed very successfully" (BL Add. Mss. 43,389: 226).

28. For records of his easy friendships with Southey and Wordsworth, see BL Add. Mss. 47,553 (especially fol. 115) and 47,553: 148.

29. See J. C. Sharp's commemorative poem, "Balliol Scholars" (in E. Coleridge, *Life and Correspondence* 1: 53). Coleridge read too much poetry, it was said, to get a first-class degree at Oxford. Nevertheless, in 1843 he was offered a fellowship at Exeter College, which brought him the acquaintance of J. A. Froude. Arnold, Jowett, Stanley, and the agnostic poet Arthur Hugh Clough were Balliol friends.

30. See Carpenter, *House of Kings* 288. Poets' Corner acquired its character during the seventeenth and eighteenth centuries. Shakespeare's monument was raised in the nineteenth century. The Victorians also raised monuments to Dr. Johnson, Burns,

Thomas Campbell, S. T. Coleridge, Southey, and James Thomson. Eighteen monuments were raised from 1827 to 1836; the space began rapidly to fill up. Wordsworth was thus lucky: only two monuments were erected between 1856 and 1865; Stanley (dean from 1864) actively discouraged them. Blake had to wait for national memorialization until 1957.

31. We may trace the legal habit of literary quotation to Talfourd and Coleridge. Shakespeare remains the favorite source. During one hearing in the O. J. Simpson trial of 1995, defense lawyers shrugged off criticism with, "Much ado about nothing," and "You just take the slings and arrows" (*Time,* 6 February 1995: 59).

32. Coleridge was retained by the bishop of Salisbury against the Reverend Rowland Williams, vice-principal and Hebrew lecturer of St. David's College, Lampeter, who held a living within the bishop's jurisdiction. In court, Coleridge dodged the broader issues to focus narrowly on the legal point, that a clergyman who had signed the Thirty-nine Articles had no right to private judgment.

33. Brooke's other titles included *Theology in the English Poets* (1872; 6th ed. 1880), *Religion in Literature and Religion in Life* (1901), *English Literature from the Beginning to the Norman Conquest* (1898), and studies of Tennyson and Browning. He sat on the Committee for the Repeal of the Blasphemy Laws 1912–14. H. J. Nicholl's verdict that "much of the literature of the past is rubbish" was too strong for the *Saturday Review* (20 January 1883: 88), but his *Landmarks* was nevertheless immediately usable.

34. On the "hopeful equation of literature and civilization that lay at the heart of the Victorian ideal," see Dowling, *Language and Decadence* 3–103 (quotation 51).

35. Earlier, Coleridge's 1854 review of Arnold's *Poems,* in which he regretted the "high, distinct" separation of Arnoldian poetry from the "everlasting conflict of our Lord and Satan" (in E. Coleridge, *Life and Correspondence* 1: 209), proved almost too strong for friendship.

36. Compare *Punch's* patriotic poem of 14 April 1883, in which "King Mob" unfurls his "blood-stained banner" and "Proclaim[s] . . . his gospel of dynamite"—"He spread the terror of force and fist, / And flattered the impudent Atheist" (170). On 30 June, Bradlaugh is featured at the center of a cartoon called "The Westminster Wax-Works," "In the same clothes as worn by him 3 August 1881," the day he entered Parliament (301), that is, virtually in rags.

37. "Just-What-You-Like-ism" was also the title of an 1863 propaganda leaflet, number 4 in the series *Helps to Belief* (1863).

38. Leslie Stephen calculated that only two members of Parliament could be said to represent working-class interests in 1867, while roughly 500 of the 658 members of the Commons belonged to the landed interest (Annan 58).

39. Thus the halfpenny *Evening News* in its first issue (26 July 1881) drew a sharp contrast, in commenting on Dean Stanley's funeral, between Arnold as representative of literature "in its very broadest aspect of 'sweetness and light' " (26 July: 2) and the Bradlaugh threat of "plentiful" and "cheap" "street democrats" (2).

40. The Holloway chaplain's sermon "which came nearest to causing a breach of the regulation, which enjoins 'reverent behavior in chapel,' " was his disquisition on the "tongues of fire which sat upon the disciples," said W. J. Ramsey. "It never occurred to him that any figure of speech was intended. He said, 'This is what happened, the

tongues were shaped like this' (here he held up his right hand closed except for two fingers, which he extended and spread open like a letter V)" (10).

41. Later works, even clerical standards like R. L. Ottley, *Aspects of the Old Testament* (1897), assume what many of the martyrs to blasphemy law went to prison for: that Genesis is "poetical," not historical; that the legend of the Fall dealt with the *character* of human sin, and so on (see Chadwick, *Church* 1: 60). The early Christians, wrote the Secularist scholar J. M. Robertson, simply did not have a "literary conscience" (*The Jesus Problem*, 1917, qtd. in Paull 21).

42. Fox's Libel Act provided only that a judge might give his opinion to the jury upon the question of libel or not libel. When Ellenborough gave his, at his second trial, William Hone declared: "let me say . . . that, after all, it is but the opinion of *one* man, it is but his lordship's opinion. Of course I speak this in no offensive sense. (loud huzzaing)" (*Three Trials* 90).

43. The denial occurred in the context of the Bowman bequest case of 1917. It was one of Foote's major achievements as president to have restructured the National Secular Society in 1898 as the Secular Society Limited, paving the way for this legal victory.

44. For G. D. Nokes writing in 1928 the three *Freethinker* trials "were really remarkable as embodying an unqualified judicial recognition of the new intention to shock" (94). In the only passage in his summing up in which he used his own words exclusively, Coleridge insisted on the intention to "insult the feelings" (Nokes 94). Though it might be "preposterous . . . to say it shall be an offence to hurt people's feelings," G. Lowes Dickinson, professor of literature, told Prime Minister Asquith in 1914, "such was now the settled state of the law" (*Prime Minister and the Blasphemy Laws* 8–9).

45. Unless otherwise noted, citation is from *Jude the Obscure*, edited by Patricia Ingham, 1985.

46. These phrases are given in undated cuttings from *Knowledge* and the *Times* (HO 144). Shuttleworth wrote on behalf of the pro-abolition Church of England Guild of St. Matthew.

CHAPTER FIVE

1. There is little literature on the subject; Linda Dowling (*Language and Decadence*, 1986), John Willinsky (*Empire of Words*, 1994), and Dennis Taylor (*Thomas Hardy's Literary Language*, 1993) have made valuable partial explorations; Aarsleff mapped the period from 1780 to 1860 in *The Study of Language in England* (1967).

2. The first full volume was published in 1888. Trench had first proposed to collect "unregistered" words into a new dictionary worthy of the language in an 1857 paper to the Philological Society, *On Some Deficiencies in our English Dictionaries* (49). The title *Oxford English Dictionary (OED)* was first used in 1895; it is used here for convenience. In terms of genesis, compare the one hundred and more years spent on Grimm's *Deutsches Woerterbuch* (commenced in 1838 and published 1854–1961) and the fifty years the Academie Francaise spent on the letter A.

3. The "over-representation of the patriarch," Shakespeare, who accounts for two percent of all citations in the first edition of the *OED*, is a large part of Willinsky's investigation (63).

4. Works of Holyoake, including the *Reasoner*, are cited for the words *co-operation*,

co-operative, secular, delivery (of a speech), *dynamitist, errorless, forfend, workful, stamp* (verb), and *preachy. Oxford English Dictionary* entries record Bradlaugh's imprisonment in the Houses of Parliament's *Clock Tower;* he is mentioned also for the legal terms *maintenance* and *tortiously,* and in newspaper extracts illustrating the words *lark, trickster,* and *disallow.*

5. Dickens's Podsnap exactly parodies Herbert Coleridge, first editor (1858–61) of the *OED* (Willinsky 30).

6. Müller himself had made the "reckless" identification of "blood" and "language" he laments in his 1888 *Biographies of Words and the Home of the Aryas* (122, 108). The nineteenth-century jargon of philology, penetrating deeply into consciousness, had long insinuated the idea that when we talk about language we are also talking of race: *root, stock, stem, purity, kinship, family.*

7. "Englishhood" was the 1883 coinage of Mrs. Lynn Linton, author of the *True History of Joshua Davidson, Christian and Communist* (1872). Other compounds of the 1880s included "English-born," "English-managed," and "English-minded." The *OED* records a first usage of the term "English-speaking" in 1873 (though see the title of George Wainwright's 1860s *Appeal to the English-speaking Public on Behalf of a New English Dictionary*); it gained general acceptance around 1887.

8. The Proclamation Society was so called for the "Proclamation for the . . . Preventing and Punishing of Vice, Profaneness, and Immorality" which it persuaded George III to issue from the throne on 1 June 1787. The Vice Society, founded in 1802, brought 159 cases against pornographers in its fifty-five years (by Lord Campbell's estimate), resulting in 154 convictions.

9. The supplementary act of 1820 "for the more effectual Prevention of Blasphemous and Seditious Libels" first enabled the judge or court, after verdict, to order the seizure of "all copies of such libels in the possession of the defendant" (Folkard 603) but did not order them burnt.

10. When Dugdale's Holywell Street emporium was raided in 1851, police took away 882 books; 870 prints; 110 catalogues; 9 pounds of letterpress, lithographic stones, and copperplates, as well as lewd snuff boxes and toothpicks (Thomas, *Long Time* 281).

11. Ecclesiastical prosecutions for adultery and fornication were still technically possible in the Victorian period, and incest remained an ecclesiastical offense, "the only reason which I can assign," Fitzjames Stephen notes, "why . . . in its very worst forms [it] is not a crime by the laws of England" (*History* 2: 430). The Court of King's Bench decisively ruled in the 1727 case of the publisher Curll for *Venus in the Cloister* that obscenity, like blasphemy, was "punishable at common law" as "an offence against the peace, intending to weaken the bonds of civil society, virtue, or morality" (Odgers, *Libel and Slander* 463).

12. J. W. Gott kept the connections alive into the twentieth century: prosecuted three times for blasphemy, he was also tried for offenses under the wartime Defence of the Realm Act, as well as for sending obscene books through the post.

13. Production of pornography declined during the 1840s from a peak in the 1830s, and there were few prosecutions in the 1850s and 1860s, despite much more activity. Nevertheless, between 1834 and 1868, "the Vice Society was responsible for the seizure . . . of no less than 129,681 obscene prints; 16,220 books and pamphlets; five tons of

letterpress in sheets; 16,005 sheets of obscene songs, catalogues, and handbills" (Thomas, *Long Time* 284–85).

14. "Hack" or "hackney," as in "hackney cab," an old word for *horse,* could also mean "prostitute" in later Victorian parlance. So could "mot," but the word derived not from French *mot,* but from Dutch *mott-kast* or harlotry, according to Hotten's *Slang Dictionary* of 1874.

15. The first count of Carlile's indictment quotes Paine's notorious assertion (60): "Whenever we read the obscene stories, the voluptuous debaucheries, . . . with which . . . the [Old Testament] is filled[,] it would be more consistent that we called it the word of a Demon than the Word of God" (indictment, CC). "If [this] can be justified," Carlile noted, "then that which the jury will avoid placing in the hands of their children, is the work which contains those voluptuous stories" (*Report of the Mock Trials of Carlile* 33–34). Foote gleefully repeats as finale to his piece "Are We Obscene?" the story that the *Age of Reason* "was once stopped at an American custom-house, because the official eye had detected some 'obscenities' in it; but on investigation it turned out that every one of these passages was a quotation from the Bible" (*Freethinker,* 20 July 1884: 226).

16. This is the whole thrust of Annie Besant's revengeful pamphlet of 1880, *Is the Bible Indictable?*

17. Hetherington typified the Freethought publisher of midcentury in "claim[ing] no exemption from punishment if I sell any obscene publication" (*Trial of Henry Hetherington* 7).

18. Veteran publisher Edward Truelove was sentenced to four months in 1883 for another well-worn effort, Robert Dale Owen's *Moral Physiology.* Carlile had made birth control a plank of freethinking radical policy when he published *Every Woman's Book* in the 1830s. On the Bradlaugh-Besant case, see Chandrasekhar, *"A Dirty, Filthy Book."* A late Victorian medical handbook in the author's possession discreetly dispenses advice on ailments like virginal "green sickness" under the title *Works of Aristotle.*

19. Standard sentence was set at twelve months: "Compared to [this]," remarked Bernard Shaw during an 1897 prosecution, "the punishment of a man who batters his wife to death is a trifle" (Calder-Marshall 217). Foote and Holyoake campaigned with him for George Bedborough, charged for selling a copy of Havelock Ellis's *Sexual Inversion.* Separate laws on buggery and sodomy were unaffected by the new act. Sodomy was a capital offense until 1861; the last execution, however, was in 1836. Rape was decapitalized in the 1840s. Homosexual acts between consenting adults were illegal in mainland Britain until 1967.

20. Asquith later recalled how he spent "the best part of a fortnight . . . with scissors and a pot of paste at hand, in a diligent quest for the most objectionable passages in M. Zola's voluminous works" (Thomas, *Long Time* 268). Vizetelly himself initiated the game by sending to the treasury solicitor a set of *Extracts Principally from the English Classics.* He had perhaps made himself vulnerable also by publishing the unexpurgated Mermaid series of Renaissance drama. A previous conviction for publishing translations of *La Terre, Pot Bouille,* and *Nana* was dropped when he withdrew the books from circulation and paid a hundred-pound fine. Vizetelly was egged on by George Moore, "Zola's ricochet in England."

21. "Confinement" becomes "happy event"; "belly" is "replace[d] by . . . 'abdomen' " (Flaubert 299, 295); and so on.

22. Or trousers might literally not be mentioned. "I got softly out of bed," says Giles the butler in *Oliver Twist*, "drew on a pair of ————"

"Ladies present, Mr. Giles," murmured the tinker. "———— of *shoes*, sir," said Giles, turning upon him and laying great emphasis on the word. (176)

23. A catchphrase of 1890s newspaper reporting, caricaturing Mrs. Ormiston Chant's crusade against Music Hall *poses plastiques* (Weightman 78).

24. "The Varnisher" was Hone's nickname for Southey, for example in the *Political Showman* (*Facetiae*, n. pag.).

25. Alford was the author of a standard set of notes on the Greek New Testament used by clergyman in explaining "difficulties."

26. See, for example, Jerome's description of being given the cold shoulder by a courting couple—"they give you a look that says all that can be said in a civilized community" (110), and the results of his dog chasing a cat through the streets—"enough bad language wasted in ten seconds to last an ordinary respectable man all his life, with care" (122).

27. Section title in Emily Thornwell's *Lady's Guide to Perfect Gentility*. The *Illustrated Family Gymnasium*'s further recommends "reciting . . . with a gag placed vertically between the teeth" as a corrective to poor enunciation (qtd. in Macdonald 21).

28. Bowdler's *Family Shakespeare* was actually based on a privately printed volume of 1807 by his bluestocking sister Harriet, who snipped out of Shakespeare (her preface declares) the ten percent of his lines that might "raise a blush on the cheek of modesty" (qtd. in Perrin 62): her name had to be suppressed, lest the world should know that she knew what to cut. Longman's kept the *Family Shakespeare* in print until 1925. The volume of expurgated books increased "right up until the war," Perrin records (246), though by 1914 the cultural consensus was gone.

29. The first edition, of course, was Talfourd's: he changed Lamb's habitual "damn him!" to "hang him!" and excised profane flights of fancy like "[the] Right Reverend tears of Earl Nelson" (Fitzgerald xiv).

30. Miss Fielding succeeded in scissoring *Tom Jones,* a novel so indecent, announced Frederic Harrison in 1886, "that a Bowdlerized version of it would scarcely be intelligible" (qtd. in Perrin 6n).

31. Harriet Bowdler's friend, the Reverend Plumtre, recommended replacing "the entire repertoire" of Elizabethan, Restoration, and eighteenth-century drama by expurgated "Plumtre versions" (Perrin 141), and then destroying the originals.

32. The building of the London Pavilion, completed 1885, "inaugurated a fresh era in music-hall history" (1895 remark, qtd. in Mander and Mitchenson 48). Fourteen million annual visits were made to thirty-five of London's halls by the end of the decade (Pennybacker 118).

33. Interestingly, London slang also specializes in anti-euphemisms like "kick the bucket" (i.e., die), motivated by a "real or pretended disdain for a taboo" on dangerous words (Allan and Burridge 15).

34. *Daily Mail* headline of 1912 (Cheshire 95). See the collection, *Elsa Lanchester Sings Bawdy Cockney Songs.*

35. Compare the title of George Robey's 1908 memoir, *My Life Up Till Now: A Nautibiography*. Even the *Freethinker*'s "Profane Jokes" (despite Foote's prudish protestations) picked up the technique of euphemistic subversion: "At a recent church entertainment in Surrey the following item was seen on the programme: 'Miss Fisher—*Put me in my little bed*, accompanied by the curate' " (10 January 1886: 136).

36. *Poses plastiques* were introduced at the Palace Theatre in Cambridge Circus in 1893. See Weightman 81–95.

37. The 1824 Vagrancy Act similarly made it an offense for a man to be caught "willfully, openly, lewdly and obscenely exposing his person . . . with intent to insult any female" (Pannick 145). Legal euphemism backfired in 1892 when Lord Coleridge quashed as inexplicable a sentence for "walking" (i.e., publicly fornicating).

38. The writer, Robert Langstaff De Havilland, author of the banned novel *Enslaved*, was responding to George Moore's campaign against Mudie's "irresponsible censorship," launched in the *Pall Mall Gazette* on 10 December 1884. In *Literature at Nurse* Moore pointedly set out to "examine the clothing of some of the dolls passed by our virtuous librarian as being decently attired" (4).

39. Darwin's pioneer essay was based on diary notes of his baby son Doddy's progress from "instinctive cries" to the "expressive use of intonation," "words of a general nature invented by himself," and—finally—intelligible language. Doddy's compound word *"black-shu-mum"* (licorice), for example, is a mélange of learned adjective, a childish abbreviation for "sugar," and Doddy's own word for food, "mum" (*Mind*, July 1877: 293). Galton's view was not sanguine: "We inherit our language from barbarous ancestors, and it shows traces of its origin in the imperfect ways in which grades of difference can be expressed" (*Inquiries* 33). His intriguing comments about the triggering of abstract ideas by spoken words include the testimony of an "authoress" that "the interrogation 'what?' " always "excites" the disciplinary idea of a fat man cracking a long whip (183, 157–58). On evolution and the dependence on language of conscience, memory, and imagination, see John Macrone, *The Ape that Spoke*, passim.

40. See Jean Aitchison, "Psycholinguistics," *Oxford Companion to the English Language* (820). It may be, Allan and Burridge summarize, that taboo vocabulary "is stored or accessed differently in the brain," a theory for which Tourette's syndrome and coprolalia provide some evidence (24).

41. *"Truth"* becomes that which a man *"troweth."* "These are the sleights of hand by which [Tooke] robs those who give heed to him of that for which all the silver and gold in the universe would be no compensation," wrote the liberal clergyman F. D. Maurice ("On Words," in *Friendship* 50); he was "the very best and cleverest specimen of a modern leveler" (37). A leader of the London Constitutional Society, Tooke was tried for treason in 1794: see O. Smith, *Politics of Language* 110–53.

42. Darwin endorsed Herder's notorious *"Bow-wow"* theory of onomatopoeic origin in the *Origin of Species* [1859], also revived by (amongst others) the Reverend Farrah, in *Chapters of Language* (1865), although it had repeatedly been pronounced dead since its first publication in 1772. The theory was demolished by Max Müller in an 1873 series of Royal Institution lectures, in which he also pooh-poohed the *"pooh-pooh"* theory of Abbe de Condillac (1746), whereby words like *"foul"* and *"filth"* were derived from interjections like "faugh! foh! fie!" (*Science of Language* 1: 510).

43. Williams's source, Baron Bunsen, asked for twenty to twenty-five thousand years: see "Bunsen's Biblical Researches," *Essays and Reviews* 45–83, and Burrow's "Uses of Philology in Victorian England" 193–95.

44. Burrow refers on this point (187n) to Sir Isaiah Berlin's article on Herder in *Encounter* 25: 1 (July 1965). On Romantic philology generally, see Dowling, *Decadence* 3–45.

45. Rival Dr. Murray went much further, reducing the roots of language to *ag, bag, dwag, cwag, lag, mag, nag, rag, swag* (Müller, *Science of Language* 1: 530n); while Dr. Schmidt derived "all Greek words from the root *e*, and all Latin words from the arch-radical *hi*" (1: 530n). Darwin denied that the "power of forming general concepts" was exclusive to man (*Descent* 88): "as Mr. Leslie Stephen observes, 'A dog frames general concepts of cats or sheep' " (89).

46. Müller's ex-student Oscar Wilde commented: "Better *Endymion* than any theory . . . of an epidemic among adjectives!" (*Artist as Critic* 418–19).

47. *"On the human origin of language, the voice of the Bible coincides perfectly with the voice of reason and of science"* (F. Farrar 8). Müller's "roots" were merely "ultimate etymologies" in modern disguise, the *"caput mortuum"* of philology (96–97); other critics lampooned the idea as the *"ding dong"* theory. Dean Richard Trench decided that the primal linguistic scene of Genesis, in which God brought the animals before Adam to be named, was "the clearest intimation of the origin, at once divine and human, of speech" (15); man was gifted by God not *"with names,* but *with the power of naming"* (14). Thus language and the gift of reason neatly collapse on one another, as suggested (Müller later argued) in the co-origin of the words "name," "know," and *"natus"* or "son" (*Science* 1: 520), a sophisticated variant on the well-worn Greek pun on logos (1: 527).

48. A child, Harper explains, grasps words in their broadest senses, so that, for example, it will recognize *all* roses as "rose" (*Mind,* July 1883: 393). This was a clever extrapolation from the "old controversy among philosophers, whether language originated in general appellatives, or in proper names," the controversy of the *primum cogitum* and *primum appellatum* (Müller, *Science of Language* 1: 512).

49. The "import of the sentence" was first significantly theorized only around 1810 (Aarsleff 104). It was a primary concern of the *Junggrammatische Schule.*

50. See Gerald L. Bruns, "Language, Pain, and Fear," 131–32.

51. Holyoake was repeating the warning of W. J. Fox in his Unitarian Lectures to the Working Classes.

52. "Blaspheme" came to mean "revile" or "reproach" in late Latin.

53. Dysphemism: "an expression with connotations that are offensive either about the denotatum or to the audience, or both" (Allan and Burridge 26).

54. Euphemism is not to be confused with "euphuism," or the substitution of pleasing alternatives (dating from Lyly's *Euphues,* 1578), though by late century the word was a functional euphemism for "euphemism" (Fowler and Fowler 22).

55. By "malice" in law is strictly meant "the absence of lawful excuse" or "privilege," or "any improper motive" for the publication (Odgers, *Libel and Slander* 320–21).

56. Words were henceforth to be taken "in the plain and popular sense in which

the rest of the world naturally understands them" (Odgers, *Libel and Slander* 108). But in practice this was difficult to achieve: law had not a moment's trouble with "*pettifogging shyster'* when applied to a lawyer," Odgers reports (112, 116) but stumbled over the popular epithet *"welcher"* (115). And the "witty conception of lawyers," as one exasperated judge put it, took a long time dying (*Libel and Slander* 106–07).

57. Intention could be assumed in cases of libel and slander only if words were "obviously defamatory."

58. "A law may be made to build a church, to pay the priest a salary, to give him the tithes of the produce of the land and the agricultural laborer," Turnbridge declared, "but a law cannot be made to say that a man shall believe, *that certain words have certain meanings which they have not*" (*Report of the Proceedings against William Turnbridge* 24).

59. Lemon had published an imagined meditation on the body of Christ by a homosexual Roman centurion. He was an easier target than the author, James Kirkup, a professing Christian and a member of the Royal Society of Literature listed in *Who's Who:* "he turns out to be rather more substantial than we had supposed," read an internal memorandum of Whitehouse's Viewers and Listeners Association (Sutherland, *Offensive Literature* 153). The poem's title (what else?) was a play upon the euphemistic keynote of the poem by Lord Alfred Douglas that Wilde meditated upon with eloquence under cross-examination in 1895: "The Love That Dares To Speak Its Name." Lemon was sentenced to nine months. Mrs. Whitehouse considered an action against the BBC comedy series, *Till Death Do Us Part,* in 1972: her target was its "strong" language and vulgar Cockneyisms ("Wot ababht yer virgin birf, then?" [Sutherland 149]). The BBC's code for broadcasters still warns against "strong" language.

60. See, for example, Aveling's description of the "mass meeting for the Release of G. W. Foote": "Mr. Symes delighted everyone by his outspeaking" (*Freethinker,* 22 July 1883: 225).

61. The prurient confessional was a well-established trope of gothic and pornographic fiction, like the *Awful Disclosures of Maria Monk* (1836). That title perhaps gave rise to another obscene bit of Cockney slang, *Maria Monk* (presumably "spunk," that is, semen).

62. This phrase was repeatedly used during publication of Stead's serial revelations (6–10 July 1885), "The Maiden Tribute of Modern Babylon." His three months' sentence was ostensibly the price of having proven that a man could buy a girl for immoral purposes, by doing it: he was prosecuted by the very attorney-general he had pressured to pass the Criminal Law Amendment Act. It was General Booth who led Stead to the former procuress, Rebecca Jarrett, who introduced him to thirteen-year-old Eliza Armstrong.

63. The reprinting of adultery and assault trial transcripts was another Holywell Street enterprise. See the reports (some very distressing) included in the *Pearl,* July 1879 to December 1880.

64. By comparison with the female, only an "impoverished" narrative can be pieced together from male-male indecent assault depositions, Krueger observes. It always culminates in the strategic formula "he laid hold of my privates," which, while it invokes the laws of property, maintains the plaintiff's freedom from implication in his own story

(126). The issue in rape cases was rather to establish the victim's credibility. One is tempted to represent the situation in a simple formula: narrativization = criminalization.

65. Before the act of 1843, the problem was partly referable to the libeler's general inability to plead the truth of his libel.

66. This was the opinion given when counsel attempted to move in arrest of judgment in the 1728 Woolston case; similar questionings met with similar responses in the cases of Carlile in 1819, Hetherington in 1841, and Southwell in 1842.

67. A "Young Man" smashed Paterson's shop window, knocked down his shop boy, threatened him with violence, and seized some of his books. He was the son of a former vice-chancellor of England, Knight Bruce. Law's official response was to ask him to pay for the glass (*God v. Paterson* 22). The *Globe* opined, "We do not think that the respectable part of the public should have no other protection against annoyance from blasphemous publications, than to go about breaking windows in order to attract the attention of the persons whose duty it is to put an end to the nuisance" (undated quotation, 84). "Why not crush the reptile?" concluded the *Morning Herald* (undated quotation, vi).

68. Finlay's legal adviser opened the case for the defense by claiming "it could be no crime in the defendant to vilify and deny" a religion that its "professors" would not "vindicate" against charges of obscenity and cruelty (appendix, *Trial of Thomas Paterson* 63). At this point "the sheriff interfered and refused to allow Mr. Macora to say another word" (63). Finlay remarked, "I think it very unreasonable that I should be expected to submit . . . without wishing for, and insisting on the right to open my mouth, or my books in my own defense" (65).

69. Section 3 of the 1888 act privileged any "fair and accurate report in any newspaper of proceedings publicly heard before any court, . . . if published contemporaneously with such proceedings. . . . Provided that nothing in this section shall authorize the publication of any blasphemous or indecent matter." "Fair and accurate reports of judicial proceedings . . . were already privileged at common law," Odgers worried, "and I cannot believe that this section creates any *absolute* privilege" (*Libel and Slander* 306–07). The very word "privilege" was struck from the original bill, while the troublesome concepts of "public concern" and "public benefit" were introduced, the former a new legislative expression (307, 315). There was real scope here for quiet social control.

70. The latter was a classic example of the "transparent" or "telling" penalty (Foucault, *Discipline* 104, 114) linked to its criminal origin by a kind of infallible "poetics" of mutilation. One of the founders of the Society of Friends, Naylor was whipped, pilloried, branded, and dispatched to prison for an indefinite term for riding into Bristol in imitation of Christ entering Jerusalem.

71. Perfected in Pentonville, London, the silent system was notably tested in eighteenth-century Philadelphia, writes Eric Cummings, where "solitude . . . was envisioned as the paramount cure for criminals. . . . [O]ne of the more spectacular instruments of 'correction' was the iron gag, a device fixed to the head and shoulders of an inmate with an attachment that gripped the tongue. Long a valued implement in the repertoire of torturers, [it] was one of the few sanguinary punishments the Philadelphia inventors of the prison preserved from the past" (4).

72. This provision created the format of Wilde's *De Profundis,* couched (with the help of some creative rule bending by the governor of Reading Gaol) in the form of an

epistle to Alfred Douglas (Ellmann 510), in whose silence it had its origin. Harcourt took a month to reply to Foote's request for books, and then merely replied (by form letter): "that the Secretary of State saw no reason to accede to my request" (*Freethinker*, 2 March 1884: 67). Foote went two and a half months without reading before the prison commissioners intervened.

73. Interviewed in the *Millgate Monthly* for its series "Modern Influences" near the end of his life, Holyoake claimed that imprisonment for "explicitness" provided "six months' schooling in candour" (October 1905: 6).

74. "The term 'Agnostic' has changed the character of controversial theology among all educated thinkers," Holyoake wrote in the *Agnostic Annual and Ethical Review* for 1901 (88). The *Annual* began publication in 1884, and was largely responsible for popularizing Huxley's 1869 coinage; the *Secular Review* changed its name to the *Agnostic Journal* in 1887; a journal called the *Agnostic* was briefly published in 1885. Despite widespread acceptance, by 1893 Holyoake's colleagues on the Propagandist Press Fund felt the need of a still more positive label, and in that year adopted Gould's coinage of 1888, becoming the "Rationalist Press Committee" (prospectus, qtd. in Gould 16). The term "wanton outrage" was a period avoidance for rape, assault, or (terrorist) attack: Holyoake was undoubtedly aware of all the innuendoes.

75. The revisions are not explicable simply in terms of the shift in standards of printed propriety from mid- to late century. In the fifth edition of the *History of the Last Trial* in 1878, for example, a second subtitle is dropped ("Submitted for the Perusal of Her Majesty's Attorney-General and the British Clergy"); the line "I revolt at the touch of a Christian" is followed (in parenthesis) by the feeble gloss: "Their touch at that time meaning imprisonment" (14); the phrase "I do not believe there is such a thing as a God" earns a lengthy disclamatory footnote (13n); a quotation from the *Cheltenham Chronicle* containing the capitalized title "HOLYOAKE THE BLASPHEMOUS SOCIALIST LECTURER" (1850: 7) is cut; the line, "I must say that I was an atheist" (15), is qualified as "I had begun to think I must be an atheist" (1878: 25n); and Holyoake's original apology for his potentially offensive style—no longer needed—is cut.

76. This first publication, "The Reign of Time" (*Baptist Teachers Tract Magazine*, October 1836; 342), survives in HC.

77. Holyoake singles out as dangerous Paley's "homely eloquence" and "charming lucidity" (*Paley Refuted* 9). Besides defending Christianity in his enormously influential *View of the Evidences of Christianity* and *Natural Theology*, Paley contributed *Reasons for Contentment* to the conservative cause in 1793, and "was rewarded for it with a prebend at St. Paul's by the Bishop of London" (O. Smith 70).

78. The Oddfellows were nearly excluded from the Friendly Societies Act of 1852 because of Holyoake's authorship.

79. This was an important trend among the publishers of the 1830s and 1840s. See, for example, the string of cheap books and pamphlets on language put out by the Edinburgh company of Oliver and Boyd, such as Alexander Reid's *Rudiments of English Grammar;* "For the Use of Schools"; or the Reverend John Oswald's *Etymological Manual of the English Language*, one shilling and sixpence from Longman, and the same author's *Helps to the Orthography of the English Language*.

80. Murray's grammar, the *ur*-text of English grammar books, sold two million cop-

ies in over three hundred editions. Cobbett objected to insinuating examples like, "Patriotism, morality, every public and private consideration, demand our submission to lawful government" (qtd. in O. Smith 9).

81. Wesley also wrote a ten-page chapbook *Short English Grammar,* in 1748; Adam Smith, author of the *Wealth of Nations,* lectured on rhetoric. Charles Knight's SDUK *Penny Magazine* produced a series "On the Meanings of Words" in 1832. It turned out to be traditionally prescriptive, though it began with a warning against "wordy sophistry, whether found in books, or proceeding from the mouth of one invested with authority" (21 July 1832: 155), words Southwell echoed in his opening address as first "Priest" of the *Oracle.*

82. See also Holyoake's 1853 *Logic of Facts* for a commonsense demonstration of "reason's" dependence on language.

83. "As the compiler of the *Dictionary,* founder of literary criticism, and author of a prose style that was avidly read and imitated," writes Olivia Smith, "Johnson was a uniquely important popularizer of [eighteenth-century] ideas which emphasized the distinction between refined and vulgar English" (13, 20).

84. "Notwithstanding," Holyoake pencils neatly in the margin, "few Christians would touch it with a pair of tongs" (Southwell, *Another* 8, Holyoake's copy, in HC).

85. Joseph McCabe's phrases, in his graveside address (qtd. in *South Place Magazine,* March 1906: 86).

86. Holyoake's work gives prescient notice to the new descriptive linguistics: "Dr. Priestley lays down the doctrine that the grammarian's province is not to invent rules, but to discover them. He is not to dogmatise as to how men shall talk, but to find out how they do talk" (*Practical Grammar* 66).

87. Chomsky's revolutionary *Syntactic Structures* (1957) first made the contention that children in learning language make successive hypotheses about the rules that underlie speech, and may indeed be "wired" with an innate hypothesis-making device. Childish efforts to speak "properly" represent the replacing of hypothesized laws by general laws; thus it is, for example, that children will regularize irregular verbs ("breaked," "thinked," etc.). What is innate is the will to law. See Jean Aitchison's useful summary chapter (105–24).

88. "When the vowels are preserved long and open by the final *e,* four of them always have sounds which exactly correspond with their names; thus *e* in theme, *i* in time, *o* in tone, and *u* in tune, and *a* should be pronounced as heard in face" (note of March 14, 1839, "Log Book," in HC).

89. See the section on "Writing for the Press" in the *Handbook of Grammar.* Similar pronouncements more than counterbalance what might seem disclaimers, like Holyoake's dictum in *Practical Grammar,* "The secret of good writing is talking with the pen" (60).

90. "[D]o not . . . suppose," for example, "that . . . I am not as tremblingly alive to the necessity of laws for the protection of society, in our present state, as the learned counsel himself is," and so on (*Trial of Charles Southwell* 32).

91. Trained on Latin, earlier grammarians knew what connections to make between grammatical "case" and criminal cases. The term is derived from Latin *casus,* or "fall." Vocative, accusative, genitive, dative, and ablative were thus imagined as successive "fall-

ings away" from an upright nominative. (I am grateful to my colleague Patricia Parker for bringing this connection to my attention.)

92. Foote tapped into a well-established tradition of mock "translation." At his first trial, Hone cited a sophisticated parody of a chapter of Ezekiel in the October 1816 issue of *Blackwood's Edinburgh Magazine,* claiming to be "a translation of a Chaldee manuscript preserved in a great library at Paris" (*Three Trials* 24); Carlile presented his sub-Hone parody of 1817, *The Order for the Administration of the Loaves and Fishes,* as "Translated from an Original Greek MS, lately discovered in the Neighborhood of a certain DEN OF THIEVES, in Westminster" (title).

93. "Awake, awake, stand up, O Jerusalem, which hast drunk at the hand of the Lord the cup of his fury; thou hast drunken the dregs of the cup of trembling, and wrung them out" (Isaiah 51.17). Compare also the climactic reworking of the image during Christ's trial in the Garden of Gethsemane: "Abba, Father, take away this cup from me" (Mark 14.36).

94. Word games were important to early Christianity. Christians recognized each other by means of the symbol of the fish, whose Greek name—*ichthys*—spells out the first letters of the words "Jesus Christ, the Son of God, the Saviour" (Augarde 32). Several of the Psalms are acrostics (33).

95. Compare, say, the motto produced by anarchist scares in 1883: "Right is Might, and Wrong is Dyna-mite" (*Punch,* 17 March: 133).

96. Compare Max Müller's "scientific" etymology of the word "human": "The Latin word *homo,* the French *l'homme,* which has been reduced to *on* in *on dit,* is derived from the same root that we have in *humus,* the soil, *humilis,* humble. *Homo,* therefore, would express the idea of a being made of the dust of the earth" (*Science of Language* 1: 524). The "petrified philosophy in language" (1: 520) thus "naturally" endorsed Christian Revelation.

97. Petronius in his *Satyricon* likewise needles Roman anxieties about the language in which the elite constructed themselves as elite, although it was taught them by domestic slave tutors. The Romance languages descend from their vernacular, not from the idiom of Cicero frozen through the Renaissance by the ideologues of *Latinitas.* The nineteenth century saw an explosion of variants (*OED*): "vernacularly" (1808); "vernacularism" (1846); "vernacularity" (1842, 1867); "vernacularization" (1873). (I am grateful to classicist Martin Bloomer for the insights that started this train of association.)

98. Arnold's key phrases, writes J. Hillis Miller, are not "pregnant" but "empty" linguistic "shells": "Their repetition empties them further of meaning, and testifies to the fact that though there is something to which the words refer, that something is not named by the words" (265).

99. All denominations, even the Unitarians, were involved; only the Catholics declined to take part. The entire text twice crossed the Atlantic to incorporate suggestions by the American committee.

100. The revisers eventually claimed an "honored" precedent, contending that the "form in which [the Bible] has now been read for 270 years" was "the result of various revisions made between 1525 and 1611" (*Revised Version* 5: v).

101. Salvationist leaders offered to guide sinners to the "Salvation Factory" (Sandal 166). A tombstone in Ely Cathedral likewise plays on the idea of a Holiness Express:

"[I]f you'll repent and turn from sin, / The Train will stop and take you in" (qtd. in Morris 204).

102. Compare 1,000,000 Bibles and prayer books printed by Oxford in 1860 to 127,000 in 1780 (Amigoni 77).

103. The *Freethinker* was issued monthly from May to August and weekly from 4 September 1881.

104. See, for example, Lance St. John Butler, *Victorian Doubt:* 6.

105. For this novelty too the revisers claimed "the precedent of the earliest English Versions" (*Revised Version* 5: xxiii).

106. See also the notices in the *Athenaeum* (28 May 1881: 713–14) and *Fraser's* (June 1881: 733). *Macmillan's Magazine* complained also that the Revised Version dropped, as spurious interpolations of later date, the phrases "which art in Heaven," "Thy will be done as in Heaven so on earth," and "but deliver us from evil" (June 1881: 154).

107. See, for example, *Macmillan's,* June 1881: 152–53; 157–58.

108. A simple majority on first revision and a two-thirds majority on a second. There were eventually seven full revisions.

109. Arnold was braver in his translation of 1872/1883. He retained the phrase but added a misleading note: "The metaphor is from strings tightly stretched, and giving, therefore, a louder and deeper sound" (qtd. in ApRoberts 255).

110. In the Revised Standard Version in common use in the 1950s the dead Lazarus who "stinketh" in the Authorized Version and Revised Version merely emits "an odour" [John 11.39]. "Stink" was uniformly erased from Bible vocabulary: Nelson's Complete Concordance to the Revised Standard Version [1957] contains only one entry for the word, and it relates to a fisherman's catch.

111. This hotly disputed decision provoked a dissenting article by a breakaway member of the revising company, Dr. Vance Smith, in the *Nineteenth Century* (June 1881).

112. Optimists like Dean Howson in *Good Words* (September 1881: 594–99) believed the Revised Version would usher in a new era of intensive Bible study. He was in the minority.

113. The Revised Version was never adopted in English churches. The American Standard Edition based upon it became the basis for the widely adopted Revised Standard Version published in America 1946–57. Britain finally opted for outright modernity with the *New English Bible* of 1970. (It should be added that it took the Authorized Version fifty years to win acceptance, and Tyndale was killed the year before the idea of Bible translation was finally accepted.)

114. The common assumption that language is a "list of terms corresponding to a list of things," observed Saussure, rests on the presupposition that ideas exist independently of words, and masks the nature of the sign, which consists of a concept (signification) and a sound pattern (signal); "the link between signal and signification is arbitrary" (65, 67). See also Derrida, *Of Grammatology.*

115. On Victorian beliefs about the direct physiological effects of reading pornography, see Thomas, *Long Time* 241–45.

116. "Vernaculous": Ben Jonson's coinage, in *Volpone,* for "low-born, scurrilous" (*OED*). Compare Irishman George Moore's ecstatic response to *Marius:* it was "far more

... than a mere emotional experience," carrying him "into the genius of my own tongue" (qtd. in Gray 131).

117. For a satirical variation on the theme, see Sir Richard Burton's suppressed 1865 *Stone Talk: Being Some of the Marvellous Sayings of a Petral Portion of Fleet Street.*

118. Haggard returns to the phenomenon numerous times. Interestingly, "Khiva" and "Ventvogel," loyal servants who die in the course of the novel's action, were in real life Haggard's own servants, murdered in 1877, and "he deliberately preserved their names in *King Solomon's Mines*" (Butts's editorial note, 323).

119. See, for example, the author's sneer at Holyoake et al. in the *Creed of Error* (1851): "a spurious mental independency has taken hold of a class of men, who call themselves 'Free-Thinkers' and 'Plain-Speakers' " (S. Williams 3).

120. The vagueness Stephen charges Maurice with perpetuating is directly connected to Maurice's unshaken belief in God as the source of language, and his rejection of any idea "that words are arbitrary signs of ideas" ("On Words," 1838, in *Friendship* 34).

121. See the second volume of Clifford's *Lectures and Essays,* especially, "On the Nature of Things-in-themselves" and "On the Scientific Basis of Morals" (2: 1–51, 52–73). Frederick Pollock's biographical introduction strikes the keynote both stylistically and scientifically: "It is an open secret to the few who know it, but a mystery and a stumbling block to the many, that Science and Poetry are sisters" (1: 1).

122. A classic artifical language, "Pasalingua" anticipated Esperanto: "from ta hausa, the house, can be derived:—ta haus-osa, the large house; ta haus-illa, the small house; ta haus-al, the wretched house" (*Our Corner,* January 1887: 56).

123. Raymond Williams seems to be one of the few to have made the connection between "B.V." [James Thomson]'s *City* and the urban idiom of the *Wasteland:* see *The Country and the City* 236–41.

CHAPTER SIX

1. The last of Mrs. Oliphant's six children died in 1894. In 1882, as Elisabeth Jay records, Hardy had welcomed "direct communication with a writer I have known in spirit so long" (*Autobiography of Margaret Oliphant* xvi); in his 1912 postscript to *Jude* he laughed off her critique as "the screaming of a poor lady in *Blackwood*" (xvi).

2. See, for example, the extraordinary story "The Conversion of Aurelian McGoggin," in which the title character is "struck dumb" by an aphasic judgment that actualizes his blasphemous nickname (*Plain Tales* 101), the "Blastoderm," in retribution for "thrusting" his religious belief "down other men's throats" (97): Kipling's imperial code reconfigures blasphemy as manly swearing and unreticence as blasphemous failure to keep a stiff upper lip.

3. Kipling's 1891 novel *The Light That Failed,* published seven months after Wilde's *Picture* in the pages of the same journal, *Lippincott's Monthly,* answers it with a developed allegory of reconfigured imperial blasphemy. In both works, the *ekphrastic* figure of a soul-changing painting allows access not only to the "closet" of homoerotic or (in Kipling's case) misogynist desire but to the censored realm of the blasphemous and the unspeakable.

4. Quint and Jessel are the Victorian unspeakable spoken: the man's name is a com-

bination of "squint" and "quim" (a Cockney synonym for "cunt"), the woman's is a distant play on "hussy" and "Jezebel." The point holds, I think, despite Edel's and Tintner's revelation that the *Turn* reworks a potboiler called *Temptation*, which James read at the age of eleven, with a villain called "Peter Quin."

5. *Thomas Hardy: The Critical Heritage*, edited by R. G. Cox, is a collection of articles, many of which are cited in *Word Crimes*.

6. Lang declared the closing reference to the "President of the Immortals" as having "finished his sport with Tess," to be either blasphemous or "meaningless": "I cannot say how much this phrase jars on one" (Cox 196).

7. Wells is identified as the *Saturday's* reviewer by Seymour-Smith (564).

8. See Foote's 1881 pamphlet *Atheism and Suicide: A Reply to Alfred Tennyson.*

9. Gissing also began a novel under the title the *Insurgents* in February 1888 (*London* 209n).

10. "High Churchy": Hardy used the term over and over again in 1895 letters to friends and acquaintances (*Letters* 2: 97, 98, 99).

11. Ward's day-to-day details are most touching, like Elsmere's mechanically stooping to put away their baby's bricks after his wife, crushed by his confession of apostasy, has literally recoiled from his touch (*Elsmere* 355).

12. Hardy was fond of such compounds. In a *Pair of Blue Eyes* we read of the St. Launce's "Every-Man-His-Own-Maker Club," in *Tess* Marian talks overfamiliarly about the " 'That-it-may-please-Thees' " in the church service, and in *Far from the Madding Crowd* drinkers pass a tall two-handled mug called a "God-forgive-me."

13. Mrs. Ward herself argued in 1884 that the rise of the "Literature of Introspection" was a direct result of the decline of Christian orthodoxy. This was the title of her two-part review of journals by Xavier Thiriat and Henri-Frederic Amiel from January to February 1884 in *Macmillan's Magazine;* her first book was a translation of the latter's *Journal Intime* (1885).

14. The "scandalized prelate," Hardy relates (quoting the Bishop's official *Life*), also "took an envelope out of his paper-stand and addressed it to W. F. D. Smith, Esq. M.P.," librarian Mudie's rival, of railway bookstall fame. "The result" was the book's "quiet withdrawal" (*Life and Work* 294).

15. "But to us there is but one God, the Father, of whom are all things, and we in him; and one Lord Jesus Christ, by whom are all things, and we by him."

16. I am grateful for this reference to Sam Prestridge (unpublished ms., "Hardy's Use of the Moses Saga in *Jude the Obscure*").

17. Hardy eventually accepted the position, which was largely honorary. He called the society a "trades union" (*Letters* 5: 190).

18. Half-English, half-French Du Maurier solved the problem of linguistic "indecency" by coding it as un-English, so that circumspect readers believed that "all the bad part is in French" (*Trilbyana* 24). *Trilby* was deeply indebted to Henri Murger's *Scènes de la vie bohème* (1845), he told Henry James, "only the British public does not know that" (Ormond 445): "French book" was a period code word for pornography. The "New Testament lovingness of *Trilby*" (*Atlantic*, qtd. in Purcell 68) became a favorite subject for sermons; Du Maurier's association with *Punch*, "puffed" within the text, helped cancel out his aggressive agnosticism. *Trilby* gained *Harper's* a hundred thousand new

subscribers, Du Maurier thought, although "she has cost 30,000 old [ones]" (Ormond 477). *The Heresy of Trilby* (1897), a propagandist flyer distributed free by the Freethought Federation, fell on stony ground.

19. Published in England on 24 February 1888, *Elsmere* sold about forty thousand copies in Britain and two hundred thousand (most of them pirated) in America that year alone. By 1911, it had reputedly sold nearly a million copies (Ward, *Recollections* 252).

20. Ward dates the action 1882–86, but family history drew her to the 1840s, which saw her father's traumatic conversion to Catholicism and ignored her grandfather Thomas Arnold's plea for an all-embracing national church.

21. Her early researches on Spanish saints in the Bodleian Library left Ward convinced that "[t]here is no approaching the idea for the masses except through the human life" (*Elsmere* 553).

22. Ward reuses the ploy in her inferior 1911 "sequel," *The Case of Richard Meynell*, in which the hero, on trial for heresy in the Court of Arches, successfully courts Elsmere's daughter Mary.

23. Hardy became a justice of the peace for Dorchester in 1884, and was appointed a county justice of the peace in 1894. "We can only hope that he will never be tempted to try any Desperate remedies for the reformation of local poachers," commented the *Dorset Chronicle,* "or be led away from the strict administration of justice by a Pair of Blue Eyes" (12 April 1894, cutting in Hardy Scrapbook).

24. See Hardy's gloat to Clodd after Lang's punitive review of *Tess,* 4 February 1892: "You will be glad to know that there is no check to the sale of the book. Mudie keeps ordering more and more" (*Letters* 1: 257).

25. See especially "A Wonderful Infidel Shoemaker," *Freethinker,* 11 September 1881: 46.

26. "Beer it is!" cries a drunk in Stevenson's *Ebb-Tide.* "Any number of persons can use it (like Lyon's tooth tablet) with perfect propriety and neatness" (29).

27. The *Quarterly* reviewer of Tess, Hardy noted, "says *inartistic* when he means *unorthodox,* & *uncleanly* when he means *unfavorable to the vested interests by which he thrives*" (*Letters* 1: 265).

28. Mischievously, Hardy even picks up (as Gittings remarks) on Leslie Stephen's well-known habit of swearing half audibly under his breath (introduction xviii; see *Ethelberta* 227, 109, 279).

29. *Good Words* was the only magazine approved by the Society for Purity in Literature; it refused Trollope's *Rachel Ray* in 1861 because it contained a dancing scene. It was printed by Virtue & Co.

30. Hardy's terms in titles to chapters of the *Life* describing the trials of *Tess* and *Jude.* Hardy concludes his narration of *Tess's* "dismemberment": "It may be mentioned that no complaint of impropriety in its cut-down form was made by readers, except by one gentleman with a family of daughters, who thought the blood-stain on the ceiling indecent—Hardy could never understand why" (*Life and Work* 232–33). One wonders whether the comment is a sly (and indecent) joke, or a moment of real naiveté.

31. Hardy also "used his reputation over *Tess* to make some of the sexual expressions in [his] other novels more frank. For the first time," in the corrected edition of 1895,

"the heroine of *The Woodlanders* was allowed to say to her rival, 'O, my great God! He's had you'" (Gittings, *Hardy* 2: 79).

32. Compare the "N.B." Hardy wrote on his manuscript of a *Group of Noble Dames* (1891): "The above lines were deleted against the author's wish, by compulsion of Mrs. Grundy" (qtd. in Seymour-Smith 393).

33. When fierce Clem Peckover shouts "It's a ——— lie!" in Gissing's *Nether World* (1889), the narrator can only comment, "Clem's epithet was too vigorous for reproduction" (35).

34. Hardy was well aware of the class implications of the critics' catchword, "brutality": see "The Science of Fiction" (*Personal Writings* 136). Mowbray Morris in the *Quarterly* had called the idiom of *Tess* "a style for which he was assuredly not born" (Lerner and Holmstrom 87).

35. See Jeannette Gilder in the *World* (qtd. in Lerner and Holmstrom 113). Besides the pig's penis scene, Jude and Arabella's courtship includes a cross-country chase after piglets and the couple's reacquaintance above her father's sausage shop. Jude further tells the Christminster crowds: "a man without advantages . . . should be . . . as selfish as a pig to have a really good chance of being one of his country's worthies" (*Jude* 344).

36. A man named John Thompson was committed for trial on the prosecution of a local clergyman in November 1868 for publishing some ramblings about the second coming, but the case was abandoned (Odgers, *Libel and Slander* 452).

37. Moule's illegitimate son by a local girl who "was shipped off to Australia" was later hanged there (Seymour-Smith 49), a fact that may have contributed to the creation of Father Time.

38. The Pooley sentence is repeatedly referred to as the severest single sentence served in 150 years. But one of the Carlile volunteers, Joseph Rhodes, was given 2 years in 1822, though it is not known if he served the full term, and Campion was sentenced to 3 in 1824.

39. Pooley "received a free pardon from the Crown" (Mill, *On Liberty* 34n). Materials in the Holyoake Collection, Manchester, reveal that it was grudgingly given (HL; see also Hawtin 23).

40. Holyoake had originally written, "Pooley is quite wrong in saying Duloe stinks of the Bible—it stinks of pigs" (*Reasoner*, 23 September 1857: 205). This sentence was struck from the pamphlet version, and the inflated substitution made that "I found the physical aspects of the village far from bearing marks of the same pastoral supervision which is exercised over its theological condition" (*Case* 20).

41. Pooley's daughter's letter of thanks, dated 14 March 1859, was given at greater length (*Reasoner*, 24 March: 91). He was sent five pounds that week.

42. A photograph of the Bush family outside the rectory in the 1880s shows nineteen people (CRO). The first baby was born in 1851.

43. "One of his masters told me that he kept his family supplied with better food than any other laborer of his station in Liskeard. In the winter he would rise first, make the fire, and prepare his wife's breakfast" (Holyoake, *Case* 7). Pooley wrote bitterly of the "Drunken Parson In Bodmin Gaol" (letter to Holyoake, 26 November 1857, HL).

44. A gentleman who had recently written up jokes about the Edenic angel's commands to an Irish Adam could be convicted of "revolting blasphemy" by the *Saturday*

Review (qtd. in Holyoake, *Case* 28) but still remain a contributor to the *Edinburgh Review* and an educator of gentlemen's sons.

45. The first, of a woman, embedded an imaginative and erotic seed that germinated in *Tess* (Seymour-Smith 32–33).

46. Just such a sale and just such an accident were also reported in the *Dorsetshire County Chronicle* at different times, as was the "indecent" incident of the blood-stained ceiling (Gittings 68; Millgate, *Hardy: His Career* 265).

47. Chinn was tried by Judge Coleridge immediately after Pooley. Despite evidence that she had abused the child, she was found not guilty. The proportion of committals per head of Cornish population was 1 in 626 in 1857, compared with 1 in 255 in lusher Devon (*Cornish Telegraph*, 5 August: 4).

48. "Christians" kept stealing the better stones, Mrs. Pooley told Holyoake (*Case* 7). Pooley called the grave "the one spot he could call his own," and lay on it to weep while the magistrates debated sending him up for trial (*Case* 7). It had been a struggle to get permission for cemetery burial (8).

49. I am grateful to the asylum caretakers for allowing me access to the premises and providing this information.

50. Words written on a postcard, copied by a clerk, set up in type by a compositor, or sent by telegraph—even words addressed to the person defamed—likewise became libelous because they could potentially be read by third parties (Odgers, *Libel and Slander* 153–55; 235–37).

51. Compare the imagery as Jude first realizes Arabella's sensuality: "as by the light of a falling lamp one might momentarily see an inscription on a wall before being enshrouded in darkness" (*Jude* 39).

52. Revealingly, with the money he made from *Jude*, Hardy designed an extension to Max Gate: a new attic suite for Emma, to remind her of her girlhood, and a large study for himself positioned directly over the new kitchen, so that day by day he would hear the voices of cook and housemaid below.

53. I am grateful for development of this point to my colleague Robert Polhemus.

54. It was Hardy whom Stephen asked on 23 March 1875 to witness his signature to "a deed renunciatory of holy-orders under the act of 1870" (*Life and Work* 108).

55. Swinburne's "pale Galilean," who haunts both *Jude* and the third Freethinker trial, turns up in *Ulysses* as Stephen's "pale vampire" (40, 109).

56. "I am much obliged to you for sending the copy of the *Freethinker,* in which I have read with much interest the article entitled 'Views and Opinions' & the generous appreciation it shows of my own defective writings" (Hardy, *Letters* 4: 96). The remainder of the letter discusses the two men's common interests in humanitarian causes and the ethical consequences of Darwinism.

ABBREVIATIONS AND ARCHIVAL COLLECTIONS

Undated items, difficult of reference, are separately listed by number (if given); all other items are listed by date.

BL Add. Mss.: British Library. Manuscript materials held in the Additional Manuscripts Collection.

CC: Carlile Collection, Huntington Library, San Marino, California. Primarily letters, manuscript notes, scrapbooks, newspaper cuttings, and miscellanea; selected items given by collection number, preceded by the letters RC (for "Richard Carlile").

CRO: Cornwall County Records Office, Truro, England. Tithe map and service books for Duloe parish; records of country clergymen; Bush family papers; Bodmin Asylum Visitors' Book; handbills.

Hardy Scrapbook: Thomas Hardy's personal scrapbook of reviews, interviews, etc. Hardy Collection, Dorset County Museum, Dorchester.

HC: Holyoake Collection, Bishopsgate Institute, London. Primarily annotated pamphlets, undated cuttings, manuscript notebooks, and diaries.

HL: Holyoake Collection, Co-operative Union archive, Holyoake House, Manchester, England. Manuscript letters and personal memorabilia relating to the trials of George Jacob Holyoake, Charles Southwell, and Thomas Pooley.

HO: Home Office papers, Public Records Office, Kew, London.

Hone Bath: Bath Public Library, England. Manuscript letters and annotated *Catalogue of Books, Prints & c. collected for a History of Parody by Mr. William Hone.*

Hone Berg: Berg Collection, New York Public Library. *Album of original sketches, proofs,*

and plates (most of them for works published by William Hone) and of letters from
[George] *Cruikshank to Hone* (2 vols.). Also G. T. Lawley's manuscript of an unpublished monograph on Cruikshank and Hone, rare copies of Hone squibs, and a manuscript letter pasted into Jerome Kern's copy of the *Every-Day Book.*

Hone BL: British Library. Additional manuscripts relating to Willliam Hone, listed by
volume and folio number. Manuscript memoirs, letters, "History of Parody," corrected proofs, etc.

Hone WA: William Hone Papers, Washington State University Libraries, Pullman.
Miscellaneous manuscript letters and contributions to the *Every-Day Book,* etc., together with bound manuscript by G. T. Lawley entitled the *Purely Literary Productions and Correspondence of William Hone and His Friends.*

Howell Collection: Freethought and Secularist printed material, housed at Bishopsgate
Institute, London.

JJC: John Johnson Collection of printed ephemera, Bodleian Library, Oxford.

National Secular Society Archives, North London.

National Secular Society Library, Bishopsgate Institute, London.

Nottingham University Library, D. H. Lawrence Archive. T. S. Eliot's (unused) deposition in the case of *Lady Chatterley's Lover;* newspaper cuttings.

Aarsleff, Hans. *The Study of Language in England 1780–1860.* Princeton: Princeton UP,
1967.

Ackroyd, Peter. *Dickens.* New York: Harper, 1990.

Adams, Robert M. "Soft Soap and the Nitty-Gritty." Enright 44–55.

Addis, William E., and Thomas Arnold. *A Catholic Dictionary.* Rev. T. B. Scannell and
P. E. Hallett. 15th ed. London: Routledge, 1951.

Aitchison, Jean. *The Articulate Mammal: An Introduction to Psycholinguistics.* 3rd ed. London: Unwin, 1989.

———. "Psycholinguistics." *Oxford Companion to the English Language* 820–21.

Alford, Henry. *A Plea for The Queen's English.* London: Routledge, 1881.

All About The Salvation Army. London: S. A. Book Stores, 1882.

Allan, Keith, and Kate Burridge. *Euphemism and Dysphemism: Language Used as a Shield
and Weapon.* New York: Oxford UP, 1991.

Altick, Richard. *The English Common Reader.* Chicago: Chicago UP, 1957.

Amigoni, David. "Matthew Arnold and the Colenso Controversy: The Bible in 'The
Republic of Letters.'" *Matthew Arnold: Between Two Worlds.* Ed. Robert Giddings.
London: Vision, 1986. 75–99.

Annan, Noel. *Leslie Stephen, The Godless Victorian.* London: Weidenfeld, 1984.

ApRoberts, Ruth. *Arnold and God.* Berkeley: U of California P, 1983.

The Arents Collection of Books in Parts and Associated Literature: A Complete Checklist.
New York: New York Public Library, 1957.

Arnold, Matthew. *Literature and Dogma: An Essay Towards a Better Apprehension of the
Bible.* New York: Burt, n.d.

————. *The Portable Matthew Arnold.* (Including *Culture and Anarchy.*) Ed. Lionel Trilling. Harmondsworth, Eng.: Viking-Penguin, 1980.

————. *The Prose Works of Matthew Arnold.* Ed. R. H. Super. 11 vols. Ann Arbor: U of Michigan P, 1962.

Arnstein, Walter L. *The Bradlaugh Case.* Rev. ed. Columbia: U of Missouri P, 1983.

Ashton, Rosemary. Introduction. H. Ward, *Robert Elsmere* (Oxford) vii–xvii.

Aspland, Lindsey Middleton. *The Law of Blasphemy, being a Candid Examination of the Views of Mr. Justice Stephen.* London: Stevens, 1884.

Aspland, Robert. *An Inquiry into the Nature of the Sin of Blasphemy.* London: Hunter, 1817.

Augarde, Tony. *The Oxford Guide to Word Games.* Oxford: Oxford UP, 1984.

Ayto, John. *Dictionary of Word Origins.* New York: Arcade, 1990.

Bakhtin, Mikhail. *Problems of Dostoevsky's Poetics.* Ed. and trans. Caryl Emerson. Minnesota: U of Minneapolis P, 1984.

————. *The Dialogical Imagination: Four Essays.* Ed. Michael Holquist. Trans. Caryl Emerson and Michael Holquist. Austin: U of Texas P, 1981.

————. *Rabelais and His World.* Trans. Helene Iswolsky. Bloomington: Indiana UP, 1984.

Barker, Ambrose G. *Henry Hetherington 1792–1849.* London: Pioneer, 193[?].

Barker, Nicholas. *The Oxford University Press and the Spread of Learning 1478–1978.* Oxford: Clarendon, 1978.

Barthes, Roland. *S/Z: An Essay.* Trans. Richard Miller. New York: Hill, 1974.

————. *Mytholgies.* Sel. and trans. Annette Laves. St. Alban's, Eng.: Paladin, 1976.

Beerbohm, Max. "Ouida." *More.* London: Lane, 1899. 101–15.

Begbie, Harold. *Broken Earthenware.* London: Hodder, 1909.

————. *The Life of General William Booth, The Founder of the Salvation Army.* 2 vols. New York: Macmillan, 1920.

Bentham, Jeremy. *Introduction to the Principles of Morals and Legislation.* Ed. J. H. Burns and H. L. A. Hardt. 1782. London: Athlone, 1970.

Besant, Annie. *An Autobiography.* 2nd ed. London: T. Fisher Unwin, 1893.

————. *Autobiographical Sketches.* Rpt. of *Our Corner.* London: Freethought, 1885.

————. *Is the Bible Indictable? An enquiry whether the Bible comes within the ruling of the Lord Chief Justice as to Obscene Literature.* London: [Freethought?], 1880.

Bierce, Ambrose. *The Cynic's Word Book.* London: Bird, 1906.

Bishop, Edward. *Blood and Fire! The Story of General William Booth and the Salvation Army.* Chicago: Moody, 1964.

Bivens, Leslie. "Nineteenth Century Reactions to the *O.E.D.:* An Annotated Bibliography." *Dictionaries* 3 (1980–81): 146–52.

Blackstone, William. *Commentaries on the Laws of England.* 2nd ed. 4 vols. 1765–1769. London: Strahn, 1783. Rpt. New York: Garland, 1978.

Blake, William. *Selected Poetry.* Ed. Michael Mason. Oxford: Oxford UP, 1996.

"Blasphemy." *Westminster Review* 108 (July 1883): 1–11.

Bloom, Harold. *The Visionary Company: A Reading of English Romantic Poetry.* Ithaca: Cornell UP, 1961.

Bolinger, Dwight. *Language—the Loaded Weapon*. London: Longman, 1980.

Bonner, Hypatia Bradlaugh. *Penalties Upon Opinion; Or Some Record of the Laws of Heresy and Blasphemy*. Rev. and enl. F. W. Read. 3rd ed. London: Watts, 1934.

The Book of Common Prayer. Oxford: Oxford UP, 1833.

Booth, Michael R. *Theatre in the Victorian Age*. Cambridge: Cambridge UP, 1991.

Booth, William. *How to Reach the Masses with the Gospel*. London: Morgan, [1870].

———. "What is the Salvation Army." *Contemporary Review* 42 (August 1882): 175–82. *Eclectic Review* NS 36 (July–December 1882): 482–87.

Booth, William Bramwell. *Echoes and Memories*. London: Hodder, 1977. London: Salvationist, 1926.

Bourdieu, Pierre. *Language and Symbolic Power*. Ed. John B. Thompson. Trans. Gino Raymond and Matthew Adamson. Cambridge: Harvard UP, 1991.

Bowdler, Thomas. *A Letter to the Editor of the British Critic*. London: Longman, 1823.

Bradlaugh, Charles. *The Laws Relating to Blasphemy and Heresy*. London: Freethought, 1878.

———. *Speeches by Charles Bradlaugh*. Ed. John M. Robertson. 2nd ed. London: Watts, n.d.

———. *When Were Our Gospels Written?* London: Austin, [1864].

Bradley, F. H. *Ethical Studies*. London: King, 1876.

Brantlinger, Patrick. *Rule of Darkness: British Literature and Imperialism, 1830–1914*. Ithaca: Cornell UP, 1988.

British Parliamentary Papers, Report from the Royal Commission on the Criminal Law 1834–1841. Eds. P. Ford and G. Ford. 6 vols. Facsimile reprint. Shannon, Ire.: Irish UP, 1971.

Brontë, Charlotte. *Jane Eyre*. Ed. Richard J. Dunn. 2nd ed. New York: Norton, 1987.

Brook, G. L. *The Language of Dickens*. London: Deutsch, 1970.

Bruns, Gerald L. "Language, Pain, and Fear." *Iowa Review* 2.2–3 (1980): 131–32.

Bryant, Arthur. *Macaulay*. [London]: Davies, 1932.

Buchanan, Robert. "The Voice of the Hooligan." Gilbert 20–32.

Buckle, Thomas Henry. *A Letter to a Gentleman respecting Pooley's case*. London: J. W. Parker, 1859.

———. "Mill on Liberty." *Fraser's Magazine* May 1859: 509–42.

Budd, Susan. *Varieties of Unbelief: Atheists and Agnostics in English Society 1850–1960*. London: Heinemann, 1977.

Bunce, Oliver Bell. *Don't, Or, Directions for Avoiding Improprieties in Conduct and Common Errors of Speech*. N.p.: Boudoir, 1891. Chapel Hill: Algonquin Books, 1984.

Burchfield, Robert W. "An Outline History of Euphemisms in English." Enright 12–31.

Burgess, Anthony. *A Mouthful of Air: Language, Languages . . . Especially English*. New York: Morrow, 1992.

Burke, Edmund. *Reflections on the Revolution in France*. Ed. J. G. A. Peacock. Indianapolis: Hackett, 1987.

Burrow, J. W. "The Uses of Philology in Victorian England." *Ideas and Institutions of Victorian Britain*. Ed. Robert Robson. New York: Barnes, 1967. 180–204.

Burton, Sir Richard. *Stone Talk: Being Some of the Marvellous Sayings of a Petral Por-*

tion of Fleet Street, London, to One Doctor Polyglott, Ph.D. London: Hardwicke, 1865.

Butler, Lance St. John. *Victorian Doubt: Literary and Cultural Discourses.* London: Wheatsheaf, 1990.

Butler, Dr. Samuel. *The Genuine and Apocryphal Gospels Compared: A Charge, delivered to the Clergy of the Archdeaconry of Derby.* London: Longman, 1822.

Butler, Samuel. *The Fair Haven: A work in defence of the miraculous element in our Lord's ministry upon earth.* 1873. Introd. Gerland Bullett. London: Watt's, 1938. Rationalist Press Association Thinker's Library ed.

———. *The Life and Letters of Dr. Samuel Butler.* 2 vols. 1896. New York: AMS, 1968. Facsmile rpt. of the 1924 ed. *Works of Samuel Butler.* vols. 10 and 11.

———. *Samuel Butler's Note-Books:* Sel. and ed. Geoffrey Keynes and Brian Hill. London: Cape, 1951.

———. *The Way of All Flesh.* Ed. James Cochrane. Harmondsworth, Eng.: Penguin, 1966.

Byron, George Gordon. *Byron's Don Juan.* Eds. Truman Guy Steffan and Willis W. Pratt. 4 vols. Austin: U of Texas P, 1957.

———. *Byron's Letters and Journals.* Ed. Leslie Marchand. 12 vols. London: Murray, 1973–82.

———. *The Complete Poetical Works.* Ed. Jerome McGann, with Barry Weller (vol. 6). 7 vols. Oxford: Clarendon, 1980–93.

———. *Lord Byron's Cain.* Ed. Truman Guy Steffan. Austin: U of Texas P, 1968.

Calder-Marshall, Arthur. *Lewd, Blasphemous, and Obscene: Being the Trials and Tribulations of Sundry Founding Fathers of Today's Alternative Societies.* London: Hutchinson, 1972.

Campbell, [John], Lord. *The Lives of the Chief Justices.* 7th ed. 4 vols. New York: Cockcroft, 1878.

Carlile, Richard. *Jail Journal: Prison Thoughts and Other Writings.* Ed. Guy Aldred. Glasgow: Strickland, 1942.

———. "The Life of Thomas Paine." *The Political and Miscellaneous Works of Thomas Paine.* London: Carlile, 1820.

———. *The Order for the Administration of the Loaves and Fishes; Or, The Communion of Corruption's Host.* London: Carlile, 1817.

Carlyle, Thomas. *On Heroes, Hero-Worship and the Heroic in History.* Ed. Carl Niemeyer. Lincoln: U of Nebraska P, 1966.

———. *Sartor Resartus.* Ed. Kerry McSweeney and Peter Sabor. Oxford: World's-Oxford UP, 1987.

Carpenter, Edward, ed. *A House of Kings: The Official History of Westminster Abbey.* New York: Day, 1966.

Carroll, Lewis. (Charles Lutwidge Dodgson.) *Selected Letters of Lewis Carroll.* Ed. Morton N. Cohen, with Roger Lancelyn Green. London: Papermac, 1982.

Catalogue of Books, Prints, & c. collected for a History of Parody by Mr. William Hone, containing an Extensive and Remarkable Assemblage of Extraordinary Parodies. Printed for Southgate's Auctioneering Rooms, 22 Fleet Street. N.p.: [1828].

Chadwick, Owen. *The Secularization of the European Mind in the Nineteenth Century.* Cambridge: Cambridge UP, 1990. Canto ed. First published 1975.

———. *The Victorian Church.* 2nd ed. 2 vols. New York: Oxford UP, 1970.

Chandrasekhar, S. *"A Dirty, Filthy Book": The Writings of Charles Knowlton and Annie Besant on Reproductive Physiology and Birth Control and an Account of the Bradlaugh-Besant Trial.* Berkeley: U of California P, 1981.

Chapman, Raymond. "'A True Representation': Speech in the Novels of Thomas Hardy." *Essays and Studies* 36 (1983): 40–55.

Cheshire, David F. *Music Hall in Britain.* Newton Abbott, Eng.: David, [1974].

Chesterton, G. K. *Charles Dickens.* London: Methuen, 1906.

———. *The Victorian Age in Literature.* New York: Holt, 1913.

Civil Equality. Speech of Sir John Trelawny, Bart., M.P. On the Second Reading of the Affirmations Bill. House of Commons, 11 March 1863. London: "Friends of Affirmations," 1863.

Clifford, Brendan, ed. *Blasphemous Reason: The 1797 Trial of Tom Paine's AGE OF REASON.* N.p.: Bevin, 1993.

Clifford, William Kingdon. *Lectures and Essays.* 1879. Eds. Leslie Stephen and Sir Frederick Pollock. 3rd ed. 2 vols. London: Macmillan, 1901.

Clodd, Edward. *Magic In Names and In Other Things.* London: Chapman and Hall, 1920.

———. *Memories.* New York: Putnam's, 1916.

———. *The Story of the Alphabet.* 1900. New York: Appleton, 1907.

Cockshut, A. O. J., ed. *Religious Controversies of the Nineteenth Century: Selected Documents.* Lincoln: U of Nebraska P, 1966.

———. *The Unbelievers: English Agnostic Thought.* London: Collins, 1964.

Cohen, Chapman. *Almost an Autobiography: The Confessions of a Freethinker.* London: Pioneer, 1940.

———. *Blasphemy: A Plea for Religious Equality.* London: Pioneer, 1922.

Cohen, Ed. "Writing Gone Wilde: Homoerotic Desire in the Closet of Representation." *PMLA* 102 (October 1987): 801–13.

Colaiaco, James A. *James Fitzjames Stephen and the Crisis of Victorian Thought.* London: Macmillan, 1983.

Cole, G. D. H. *Richard Carlile, 1790–1843.* London: Gollancz, 1943.

Coleman, Peter. *Obscenity, Blasphemy, Sedition: Censorship in Australia.* Brisbane, Austral.: Jacaranda, [1964].

Colenso, John Williams. *The Pentateuch and the Book of Joshua Critically Examined.* 7 vols. London: Longman, 1862–79.

Coleridge, Ernest Hartley. *Life and Correspondence of John Duke, Lord Coleridge.* 2 vols. London: Heinemann, 1904.

Coleridge, John Duke, Lord. *The Law of Blasphemous Libel: The Summing-Up in the Case of Regina v. Foote and Others.* London: Stevens, 1883.

Coleridge, Samuel Taylor. *Table Talk and Omniana.* Ed. T. Ashe. London: Bell, 1884.

Collet, Collet Dobson. *History of the Taxes on Knowledge: Their Origin and Repeal.* 1899.

London: Watts, 1933. Rationalist Press Association Thinker's Library. First published 1899.

Collet, Sophia Dobson. *George Jacob Holyoake and Modern Atheism: A Biographical and Critical Essay*. London: Trübner, 1855.

Collier, Richard. *The General Next to God: the Story of William Booth and the Salvation Army*. New York: Dutton, 1965.

Collins, John Churton. *The Study of English Literature: A plea for its recognition and organization at the universities*. London: Macmillan, 1891.

Collins, Philip. *Dickens and Crime*. Bloomington: Indiana UP, 1968.

Collins, Wilkie. *The Moonstone*. Ed. J. I. M. Stewart. Harmondsworth, Eng.: Penguin, 1966.

Collison, Robert. *Dictionaries of English and Foreign Language*. 2nd ed. New York: Hafner, 1971.

Colonel Ingersoll on Mr. G. J. Holyoake. N.p.: Philip Dawson, 1883. Rpt. from the *Boston Investigator*.

Connell, Robert. *Catechism of English Composition*. Edinburgh: Oliver, 1839.

Conrad, Joseph. *Heart of Darkness*. Ed. Robert Kimbrough. 3rd ed. New York: Norton, 1988.

———. *The Mirror of the Sea and A Personal Record*. Ed. Zdzislaw Najder. Oxford: Classics-Oxford UP, 1988.

Conway, Moncure D. *Autobiography, Memories and Experiences*. 2 vols. Boston: Houghton, 1904.

———. *Blasphemous Libels*. Lessons for the Day No. 24. London: Allen, 1883.

Corelli, Marie. *Barabbas: A Dream of the World's Tragedy*. 1893. Philadelphia: Lippincott, 1896.

Court, Franklin E. *Institutionalizing English Literature: The Culture and Politics of Literary Study, 1750–1900*. Stanford: Stanford UP, 1992.

Coustillas, Pierre. Introduction. Moore 9–24.

Coustillas, Pierre, and Colin Partridge, eds. *Gissing: The Critical Heritage*. London: Routledge, 1972.

Cox, R. G., ed. *Thomas Hardy: The Critical Heritage*. London: Routledge, 1970.

Craik, Henry. "The Study of English Literature." *Quarterly Review* 156 (July 1883): 187–215.

Cross, J. W., ed. *George Eliot's Life as Related in Her Letters and Journals*. New York: Crowell, n.d.

Cruikshank, George. *George Cruikshank's Omnibus*. Ed. Laman Blanchard. London: Tilt, 1842.

Cummings, Eric. *The Rise and Fall of California's Radical Prison Movement*. Stanford: Stanford UP, 1994.

Cutner, H. Introduction. Foote, *Defence of Free Speech* (1932) 3–7.

———. *Robert Taylor*. London: Pioneer, n.d.

Darwin, Charles. *The Descent of Man*. 1871. 2nd ed. 1874. New York: Appleton, 1879.

———. *The Origin of Species*. 1857. 6th ed. 1872. London: Oxford UP, 1963.

Davidson, John. *John Davidson: A Selection of His Poems.* Ed. Maurice Lindsay. London: Hutchinson, 1961.

Davidson, Randall T. "The Methods of the Salvation Army." *Contemporary Review* 42 (1882): 189–99.

The Debate in the House of Commons on Wednesday, March 26, 1823; on Mr. Hume's Presenting a Petition for Mary-Anne Carlile. London: Moses, 1823.

Defoe, Daniel. *Robinson Crusoe.* Ed. Angus Ross. Harmondsworth, Eng.: Penguin, 1965.

Derrida, Jacques. *Of Grammatology.* Trans. Gayatri Chakravorty Spivak. Baltimore: Johns Hopkins UP, 1976.

Desmond, Adrian, and James Moore. *Darwin: The Life of a Tormented Evolutionist.* New York: Norton, 1991.

Dickens, Charles. *Bleak House.* Eds. George Ford and Sylvere Monod. New York: Norton, 1977.

———. *David Copperfield.* Ed. Trevor Blount. Harmondsworth, Eng.: Penguin, 1966.

———. *Dombey and Son.* Ed. Alan Horsman. Oxford: Clarendon, 1974.

———. *Hard Times.* 1969. Ed. David Craig. London: Penguin, 1985.

———. *The Letters of Charles Dickens, 1820–1829.* Vol. 1. Eds. Madeline House and Graham Storey. Oxford: Clarendon, 1965.

———. *The Letters of Charles Dickens, 1840–1841.* Vol. 2. Eds. Madeline House and Graham Storey. Oxford: Clarendon, 1969.

———. *The Letters of Charles Dickens, 1842–1843.* Vol. 3. Eds. Madeline House, Graham Storey, and Kathleen Tillotson. Oxford: Clarendon, 1974.

———. *The Letters of Charles Dickens, 1844–1846.* Vol. 4. Ed. Kathleen Tillotson. Oxford: Clarendon, 1977.

———. *The Letters of Charles Dickens, 1847–1849.* Vol. 5. Eds. Graham Storey and K. J. Fielding. Oxford: Clarendon, 1981.

———. *The Life and Adventures of Nicholas Nickleby.* Ed. Michael Slater. Harmondsworth, Eng.: Penguin, 1978.

———. *Little Dorrit.* Ed. John Holloway. London: Penguin, 1985.

———. *Oliver Twist.* Ed. Kathleen Tillotson. Oxford: Oxford UP, 1982.

———. *Our Mutual Friend.* Ed. Stephen Gill. London: Penguin, 1971.

———. *The Pickwick Papers.* Ed. Robert L. Patten. Harmondsworth, Eng.: Penguin, 1995.

———. *Sketches by "Boz."* Ed. Dennis Walder. Harmondsworth, Eng.: Penguin, 1972.

Dickson, Sarah Augusta. Introduction. *The Arents Collection of Books in Parts 7–20.*

Dictionary of National Biography. Eds. Leslie Stephen and Sidney Lee. 63 vols. London: Smith, 1885–1900.

Disher, W. Willson. *Winkles and Champagne.* London: Batsford, 1938.

D'Israeli, Isaac. *Curiosities of Literature.* 1823. New ed. Ed. Benjamin Disraeli. 3 vols. London: Routledge, 1859.

The Dorchester Guide; Or, A House That Jack Built. London: Dene and Munday, [1819].

Dowling, Linda. *Language and Decadence in the Victorian Fin de Siècle.* Princeton: Princeton UP, 1986.

Draper, R. P. *D. H. Lawrence: The Critical Heritage.* New York: Barnes, 1970.

Du Maurier, George. *Trilby*. New York: Harper, 1894.

Du Toit, Andrie B. "New Testament." *Oxford Companion to the Bible*. 102–04.

Eagleton, Terry. "The Limits of Art." *Thomas Hardy's Jude the Obscure*. Ed. Harold Bloom. New York: Chelsea, 1987. 61–71.

Edel, Leon, and Adeline Tintner. "The Private Life of Peter Quin[t]: Origins of *The Turn of the Screw*." *Henry James Review* 7.1 (1985): 2–4.

Eliot, George (Mary Ann Evans). *Middlemarch*. Ed. W. J. Harvey. Harmondsworth, Eng.: Penguin, 1965.

Eliot, T. S. *After Strange Gods: A Primer of Modern Heresy*. London: Faber, [1934].

———. *Complete Poetry and Plays of T. S. Eliot*. London: Faber, 1969.

———. *Selected Prose*. London: Faber, 1975.

Elliott, Ralph W. V. *Thomas Hardy's English*. Oxford: Blackwell, 1984.

Ellmann, Richard. *Oscar Wilde*. New York: Vintage, 1988.

Emerson, Edwin, and Marion Mills Miller. *The Nineteenth Century and After*. 3 vols. New York: Collier, 1906.

Enright, D. J., ed. *Fair of Speech: The Uses of Euphemism*. Oxford: Oxford UP, 1985.

Epstein, Joseph. "Sex and Euphemism." Enright 56–71.

Essays and Reviews. Leipzig: Tauchnitz, 1862.

Farrar, Frederic. *Chapters on Language*. London: Longman, 1865.

Farrer, J. A. *Literary Forgeries*. Introd. Andrew Lang. London: Longman, 1907.

Feather, John. *Publishing, Piracy and Politics: An Historical Study of Copyright in Britain*. London: Mansell, 1994.

Felstiner, John. *The Lies of Art: Max Beerbohm's Parody and Caricature*. New York: Knopf, 1972.

Fischler, Alexander. "Gins and Spirits: The Letter's Edge in Hardy's *Jude the Obscure*." *Studies in the Novel* 17 (Spring 1984): 1–19.

Fish, Stanley. *Doing What Comes Naturally: Change, Rhetoric, and the Practice of Theory in Literary and Legal Studies*. Oxford: Clarendon, 1989.

Fitzgerald, Percy. Editor's Preface. Lamb, *The Life, Letters, and Writings of Charles Lamb* xi–xvi.

Flaubert, Gustave. *Bouvard and Pecuchet, with the Dictionary of Received Ideas*. Trans. A. J. Krailsheimer. Harmondsworth, Eng.: Penguin, 1976.

Folkard, Henry Coleman. *The Law of Slander and Libel: Founded upon the Treatise of the Late Mr. Starkie*. 4th ed. London: Butterworth, 1876.

Foner, Philip S. Introduction. Paine 7–42.

Foote, George William. *Arrows of Freethought*. London: Kemp, 1882.

———. *Atheism and Suicide: A Reply to Alfred Tennyson, Poet Laureate*. London: Freethought, 1881.

———. *The Atheist Shoemaker and the Rev. Hugh Price Hughes*. London: Forder, [1894].

———. *Bible Heroes*. (Serial parts.) London: [Forder?], [1887?].

———. *Bible Romances*. London: Freethought, 1882.

———. *Bible Romances*. London: Secular Society, 1904.

———. *Blasphemy No Crime*. London: Kemp, 1882.

———. *Blasphemy No Crime: The Subject Treated Legally, Historically, and Morally*. London: Progressive, n.d.

————. *The Book of God in the Light of the Higher Criticism, with Special Reference to Dean Farrar's New Apology.* London: Forder, 1899.

————. *Christianity and Progress, a reply to W. E. Gladstone.* London: [Forder?], 1888.

————. *Christianity or Secularism, Which is True? The Verbatim Report of a Four Nights' Debate between the Rev. Dr. James McGann and Mr. G. W. Foote.* London: Progressive, 1886.

————. *Comic Sermons and Other Fantasias.* London: Forder, 1893.

————. *Death's Test, Or, Christian Lies and Dying Infidels.* London: Besant, 1883.

————. *Defence of Free Speech.* Introd. H. Cutner. London: Pioneer, 1932.

————. *Defence of Free Speech, Being a Three Hours' Address to the Jury in the Court of Queen's Bench before Lord Coleridge on April 24, 1883.* London: Foote, 1889.

————. *Flowers of Freethought.* London: Forder, 1894.

————. "George Meredith: Freethinker." *English Review* 13 (March 1913): 602–16.

————. *The Grand Old Book. A Reply to the Right Honorable W. E. Gladstone's The Impregnable Rock of Holy Scripture.* London: Progressive, 1891.

————. *Guilty or Not Guilty? An Open Letter to the Rev. R. A. Torrey.* London: Pioneer, 1905.

————. *Infidel Death-Beds.* Rev. and enl. A. D. McLaren. London: Pioneer, n.d.

————. *Letters to the Clergy.* London: Progressive, 1890.

————. *Letters to Jesus Christ.* London: Progressive, 1886.

————. *My Resurrection: A Missing Chapter from the Gospel of Matthew.* London: Forder, 1892.

————. *The Philosophy of Secularism.* London: Progressive, 1889.

————. *Prisoner for Blasphemy.* London: Progressive, 1886.

————. *Secularism Restated.* London: Ramsey, 1874.

————. *Shakespeare and Other Literary Essays.* London: Pioneer, 1929.

————. *The Sign of the Cross, a Candid Criticism of Mr. Wilson Barrett's Play.* London: Forder, 1896.

————. *What is Agnosticism?* London: Freethought, 1902.

Foote, George William, and W. P. Ball, eds. *The Bible Handbook for Freethinkers and Inquiring Christians.* 1888. 11th ed. New York: Arno, 1972.

Foote, George William, and Charles Watts. *Heroes and Martyrs of Freethought.* London: Watts, 1874.

Ford, Ford Madox. *Return to Yesterday.* New York: Liveright, 1932.

Foucault, Michel. *Discipline and Punish: The Birth of the Prison.* Trans. Alan Sheridan. New York: Random, 1979.

————. *An Introduction.* Trans. Robert Hurley. Vol. 1 of *The History of Sexuality.* New York: Vintage, 1980.

————. *The Order of Things: An Archaeology of the Human Sciences.* New York: Vintage, 1990.

————. "A Preface to Transgression." *Language, Counter-Memory, Practice: Selected Essays and Interviews by Michel Foucault.* Ed. Donald F. Bouchard. Ithaca: Cornell UP, 1977. 29–52.

Fowler, Eric. *Modern English Usage.* Oxford: Clarendon, 1926.

Fowler, H. W., and F. G. Fowler. *The King's English.* 3rd ed. Oxford: Clarendon, 1930.

Frazer, Sir James. *Taboo and the Perils of the Soul. The Golden Bough* 2. 3rd ed. London: Macmillan, 1911.

Froude, James Anthony. "The Oxford Counter-Reformation." *Short Studies on Great Subjects.* 1882. 4th ser. New York: Scribner's, 1910. 151–236.

———. *The Nemesis of Faith.* London: Chapman, 1849.

———. *Shadows of the Clouds.* London: Ollivier, 1847.

Frye, Northrop. *The Secular Scripture: A Study of the Structure of Romance.* Cambridge: Harvard UP, 1976.

A Full Report of the Trial of Henry Hetherington. London: Hetherington, 1840.

Fuller, Thomas. *The Church History of Britain from the Birth of Jesus Christ, Untill the Year MDCXLVIII.* 11 vols. London: Williams, 1655.

Galton, Francis. *Inquiries into Human Faculty and Its Development.* London: Macmillan, 1883.

Gibson, James. "Hardy and his Readers." *Thomas Hardy: The Writer and His Background.* Ed. Norman Page. New York: St. Martin's, 1980. 192–218.

Gilbert, Eliot, ed. *Kipling and the Critics.* New York: New York UP, 1965.

Gill, Stephen. *William Wordsworth: A Life.* Oxford: Clarendon, 1989.

Gilman, Sander L. *Nietzschean Parody: An Introduction to Reading Nietzsche.* Bonn: Bouvier, 1976.

Gilmour, J. P., ed. *Champion of Liberty: Charles Bradlaugh Centenary Volume.* London: Watts, 1933.

Gissing, George. *Born in Exile.* 3 vols. London: Black, 1892. New York: AMS, 1968.

———. *Collected Letters of George Gissing.* Eds. Paul F. Mattheisen, Arthur C. Young, and Pierre Coustillas. 8 vols. Athens: Ohio UP, 1990–96.

———. *Demos: A Story of English Socialism.* Ed. Pierre Coustillas. Brighton, Eng.: Harvester, 1987.

———. *The Emancipated.* Introd. John Halperin. London: Hogarth, 1985.

———. *George Gissing's Commonplace Book.* Ed. Jacob Korg. New York: New York Public Library, 1962.

———. *In the Year of Jubilee.* Introd. John Halperin. London: Hogarth, 1987.

———. *London and the Life of Literature in Late Victorian England: The Diary of George Gissing.* Ed. Pierre Coustillas. Hassocks: Harvester, 1978.

———. *The Nether World.* Ed. Stephen Gill. Oxford: Classics-Oxford UP, 1992.

———. *New Grub Street.* Ed. Irving Howe. Boston: Riverside-Houghton, 1962.

———. *The Private Papers of Henry Ryecroft.* Introd. John Stewart Collis. Notes Pierre Coustillas. Brighton, Eng.: Harvester, 1982.

———. *The Unclassed.* Ed. Jacob Korg. Brighton, Eng.: Harvester, 1976.

———. *Workers in the Dawn.* Ed. Pierre Coustillas. Brighton, Eng.: Harvester, 1985.

Gittings, Robert. Introduction. Hardy, *The Hand of Ethelberta* xi–xxii.

———. *Young Thomas Hardy and Thomas Hardy's Later Years.* 1975. 1978. 2 vols. in one. New York: Little, 1990.

Glendinning, Victoria. "Naming Names." *Trollopiana: The Journal of the Trollope Society* no. 13 (May 1991) 16–21.

God v. Paterson: The Extraordinary Bow-Street Police Report. London: Clarke (for the Anti-Persecution Union), [1843].

Godzich, Wlad. *The Culture of Literacy.* Cambridge: Harvard UP, 1994.

Goldberg, Jonathan. *Writing Matter: From the Hands of the English Renaissance.* Stanford: Stanford UP, 1990.

Goode, John. *Thomas Hardy: The Offensive Truth.* Oxford: Blackwell, 1988.

Gordon, J. H. *Just-What-You-Like-ism.* "Helps to Belief" No. 4. Leeds: Harner, 1863.

Gosse, Edmund. *Father and Son: A Study of Two Temperaments.* Ed. Peter Abbs. Harmondsworth, Eng.: Penguin, 1983.

Gott, J. W. *Rib-Ticklers, or Questions for Parsons.* Bradford: [1900?].

Gould, Frederick J. *The Pioneers of Johnson's Court: A History of the Rationalist Press Association.* London: Watts, 1929.

Graff, Gerald. *Professing Literature: An Institutional History.* Chicago: U of Chicago P, 1987.

Gray, Tony. *A Peculiar Man: A Life of George Moore.* London: Sinclair-Stevenson, 1996.

Gregor, Ian. "Contrary Imaginings: Thomas Hardy and Religion." *The Interpretation of Belief.* Basingstoke, Eng.: Macmillan, 1986. 202–24.

Griest, Guinevere L. *Mudie's Circulating Library and the Victorian Novel.* Bloomington: Indiana UP, 1970.

Gross, John. "Intimations of Mortality." Enright 203–20.

Grugel, Lee E. *George Jacob Holyoake: A Study in the Evolution of a Victorian Radical.* Philadelphia: Porcupine, 1976.

Guerard, Albert J. *Thomas Hardy: the Novels and Stories.* Cambridge: Harvard UP, 1949.

Guillory, John. *Cultural Capital: The Problem of Literary Canon Formation.* Chicago: U of Chicago P, 1993.

Habermas, Jürgen. *The Theory of Communicative Action.* 2 vols. Boston: Beacon, 1984–87.

Hackwood, Frederick William. *William Hone: His Life and Times.* London: Unwin, 1912.

Haggard, H. Rider. *Allan Quartermain.* London: Longman, 1887.

———. *King Solomon's Mines.* Ed. Dennis Butts. Oxford: Classics-Oxford UP, 1989.

———. *Mr. Meeson's Will: A Novel.* New York: Harper, 1888.

———. *Nada the Lily.* New York: Longmans, 1918.

———. *She.* Ed. Daniel Karlin. Oxford: Classics-Oxford UP, 1991.

Halevy, Elie. *A History of the English People 1815–1830.* Trans. E. I. Watkin. New York: Harcourt 1924.

———. *The Triumph of Reform, 1830–1841.* 1923. Trans. E. I. Watkin. Rev. ed. London: Benn, 1950.

———. *Victorian Years, 1841–1895.* Trans. E. I. Watkin. London: Benn, 1951.

Hall, S. C. *A Book of Memories of Great Men and Women of the Age, from Personal Acquaintance.* 2nd ed. London: Virtue, 1877.

Halliday M. A. K. "Anti-languages." *American Anthropologist* 78 (1976): 570–84.

Hannoosh, Michele. *Parody and Decadence: Laforgue's Moralites legendaires.* Columbus: Ohio State UP, 1989.

Hardy, Thomas. *The Collected Letters of Thomas Hardy.* Eds. Richard Little Purdy and Michael Millgate. 7 vols. Oxford: Clarendon, 1978–88.

————. *The Complete Poems of Thomas Hardy.* 1976. Ed. James Gibson. New York: Macmillan, 1978.

————. *Far from the Madding Crowd.* Ed. James Gibson. London: Everyman, 1993.

————. *The Hand of Ethelberta: A Comedy in Chapters.* Introd. Robert Gittings. 1975. London: Macmillan, 1986.

————. *Jude the Obscure.* Ed. Norman Page. New York: Norton, 1978.

————. *Jude the Obscure.* Ed. Patricia Ingham. Oxford: Classics-Oxford UP, 1985.

————. *The Life and Work of Thomas Hardy:* "An edition upon new principles of the materials previously drawn upon for *The Early Life of Thomas Hardy 1840–1891* and *The Later Years of Thomas Hardy 1892–1928* published over the name of Florence Emily Hardy." Ed. Michael Millgate. Athens: U of Georgia P, 1985.

————. *Literary Notebook.* Ed. Lennart A. Björk. 2 vols. New York: New York UP, 1985.

————. *The Mayor of Casterbridge.* Ed. James K. Robinson. New York: Norton, 1977.

————. *A Pair of Blue Eyes.* Ed. Roger Ebbatson. Harmondsworth, Eng.: Penguin, 1986.

————. *The Personal Notebooks of Thomas Hardy.* Ed. Richard H. Taylor. London: Macmillan, 1978.

————. *Tess of the D'Urbervilles: A Pure Woman Faithfully Presented.* Ed. David Skilton. Harmondsworth, Eng.: Penguin, 1978.

————. *Thomas Hardy's Personal Writings.* Ed. Harold Orel. London: Macmillan, 1966.

————. *The Woodlanders.* Ed. Dale Kramer. Oxford: Classics-Oxford UP, 1985.

Harper, Thomas. "The Word." *Mind* 8 (July 1883): 372–401.

Harrison, J. *The Logic of Life, In reply to G. J. Holyoake's Logic of Death.* Newcastle: Barkas, [1850].

Haslam, C. J. *Letters to the Clergy of All Denominations.* Manchester: Heywood, [1840].

Hawtin, Gillian. "The Case of Thomas Pooley, Cornish Well-Sinker, 1857." *Notes and Queries* NS 21 (January 1974): 18–24.

Haywood, Ian. *Faking It: Art and the Politics of Forgery.* New York: St. Martin's, 1987.

Hennell, Charles Christian. *Inquiry Concerning the Origin of Christianity.* London: Smallfield, 1838.

Herbert, Christopher. *Culture and Anomie: Ethnographic Imagination in the Nineteenth Century.* Chicago: U of Chicago P, 1991.

Herrick, Jim. *Against the Faith.* New York: Prometheus, 1985.

Herrick, Jim, ed. *Vision and Realism: A Hundred Years of The Freethinker.* London: Foote, 1982.

Hobbes, Thomas. *English Works of Thomas Hobbes.* Ed. William Molesworth. 11 vols. London: Bohn, 1839.

Hobsbawn, Eric. *The Age of Empire: 1875–1914.* New York: Pantheon, 1987.

Hobsbawn, Eric, and George Rude. *Captain Swing.* New York: Pantheon, 1968.

Hodge, Robert, and Gunther Kress. *Language as Ideology.* 1979. 2nd ed. London: Routledge, 1993.

Hoggart, Simon. "Politics." Enright 174–84.

Hollington, Michael, ed. *Charles Dickens: Critical Assessments.* 4 vols. Mountfield, Eng.: Helm, 1995.

Hollis, Patricia. *The Pauper Press: A Study in the Working-Class Radicalism of the 1830s.* Oxford: Oxford UP, 1970.

————, ed. *The Poor Man's Guardian 1831–1835.* Rpt. with introd. 4 vols. London: Merlin, 1969.

The Holy Bible, Containing the Old and New testaments translated out of the Original Tongues: Being the Version set forth A.D. 1611 compared with the most ancient authorities and revised. 6 vols. Oxford: Oxford UP, 1881–85.

Holyoake, Austin, and Charles Watts, eds. *The Secularist's Manual of Songs and Ceremonies.* London: Austin, 1871.

Holyoake, George Jacob. *Alien Features of Secularism.* N.p.: privately printed, [1877].

————. *Bygones Worth Remembering.* 2 vols. London: Unwin, 1905.

————. *The Case of Thomas Pooley, the Cornish Well-Sinker.* London: Holyoake, [1857].

————. *The Child's Second Letter-Book, for Teaching Reading and Writing at Once.* London: Watson, 1853.

————. *The Government and the Working Man's Press.* N.p.: Free Press, [1853].

————. *Handbook of Grammar: For the Use of Teachers and Learners.* London: Watson, 1846.

————. *History of Co-operation in England.* 1858. 2 vols. London: Trübner, 1875–79.

————. *The History of the Last Trial by Jury for Atheism in England: A Fragment of Autobiography.* 5th ed. London: Trübner, 1878.

————. *The History of the Last Trial by Jury for Atheism in England: A Fragment of Autobiography, Submitted for the Perusal of Her Majesty's Attorney-General and the British Clergy.* London: Watson, 1850. New York: Arno, 1972.

————. *The Last Days of Mrs. Emma Martin, Advocate of Free Thought.* London: Watson, 1851.

————. *The Lectures Used by the Manchester Unity, of the Independent Order of Odd Fellows.* London: Hornblower (printer), 1846.

————. *Life and Character of Henry Hetherington.* London: Watson, 1849.

————. *The Life and Character of Richard Carlile.* 1849. London: Austin, [1870].

————. *Life and Last Days of Robert Owen.* Centenary ed. London: *Trübner,* 1871.

————. *The Limits of Atheism, Or, Why Should Sceptics Be Outlaws?* London: Brook, 1874.

————. *The Child's Ladder of Knowledge.* London: Frederick Farrah, 1864. Rpt. of *The Little Child's Word Book, for Teaching Spelling, Meaning, and Grammar at Once.*

————. *A Logic of Facts: Or, Plain Hints on Reasoning.* London: Watson, 1853.

————. *The Logic of Life, Deduced from the Principle of Freethought.* London: Newsagent's, [1861].

————. *The Origin and Nature of Secularism.* London: Watts, 1896.

————. *The Outlaws of Freethought: The Policy Which May Secure an Affirmation Bill.* London: [Holyoake, 1861].

————. *Paley Refuted in His Own Words.* London: Watson, 1850.

————. *Plain words about Secularism.* [London]: Privately printed, 1882.

————. *Practical Grammar.* 1846. London: Watson, 1852.

————. *The Principles of Secularism Briefly Explained.* London: Holyoake, 1859.

——. *The Principles of Secularism Illustrated.* 4th ed. Rev. London: Watts, 1881.

——. *The Purple Lecture Used by the Manchester Unity of the Independent Order of Oddfellows.* London: Hornblower (printer), 1846.

——. "Richard Carlile." *Dictionary of National Biography.* Ed. Leslie Stephen and Sidney Lee. 3rd ed. London: Smith, 1908. 3: 1009–12.

——. *Rudiments of Public Speaking and Debate: Or, Hints on the Application of Logic.* 1st American ed. New York: McElrath, 1853. Rpt. of 2nd London ed.

——. *Secularism the Practical Philosophy of the People.* London: Holyoake, 1854.

——. *Self-help a Hundred Years Ago.* London: Sonnenschein, 1888.

——. *A Short and Easy Method with the Saints.* London: Hetherington, [1843].

——. *Sixty Years of an Agitator's Life.* 1893. 3rd ed. 2 vols. London: Unwin, 1900.

——. "A Special Dissertation on Blasphemy Prosecutions in General." *The Trial of Thomas Paterson.* 3–8.

——. *The Spirit of Bonner in the Disciples of Jesus; Or the Cruelty and Intolerance of Christianity Displayed, in the Prosecution, for Blasphemy, of Charles Southwell.* Sheffield: Hardcastle, [1842].

——. *The Value of Biography in the Formation of Individual Character, Illustrated by the Life and Writings of Charles Reece Pemberton.* London: Watson, 1845.

——. *Working-class Representation.* London: Secular, 1868.

——. *The Workman and the Suffrage.* London: [Holyoake?], 1859.

Hone, J. Ann. *For the Cause of Truth: Radicalism in London 1796–1821.* Oxford: Clarendon, 1982.

——. "William Hone (1780–1842), Publisher and Bookseller: An Approach to Early 19th Century London Radicalism." *Historical Studies* (Melbourne) 16 (1974): 55–70.

Hone, William. *Ancient Mysteries Described, especially the English Miracle Plays, founded on Apocryphal New Testament Story.* London: Reeves, 1823.

——. *Another Article for the Quarterly Reviewer.* London: Hone, 1824.

——, ed. *The Apocryphal New Testament, being all the Gospels, Epistles, and Other Pieces now Extant, attributed in the First Four Centuries to JESUS CHRIST, His Apostles, and their Companions, and Not Included in the New Testament by its Compilers.* London: Hone, 1820.

——. *Aspersions Answered: An Explanatory Statement, addressed to the Public at Large, and to Every Reader of the Quarterly Review in Particular.* London: Hone, 1824.

——. *The Bullet Te Deum, with the Canticle of the Stone.* London: Carlile, 1817.

——. *The Bullet Te Deum, with the Canticle of the Stone.* London: Hone, 1817.

——. *"Don John," Or Don Juan Unmasked; being a Key to the Mystery, attending that Remarkable Poem.* London: Hone, 1819.

——. *The Early Life and Conversion of William Hone [the elder].* London: Ward, 1841.

——. *The Every-Day Book; Or, Everlasting Calendar of Popular Amusements, Sports, Pastimes, Ceremonies, Manners, Customs, and Events, incident to each of the Three Hundred and Sixty-Five Days, in Past and Present Times . . . For Daily Use or Diversion.* 2 vols. London: Hone, 1826.

——. *Facetiae and Miscellanies.* With 120 engraving by George Cruikshank. London: Hone, 1827.

————. *The Late John Wilkes's Catechism of a Ministerial Member; taken from an Original Manuscript in Mr. Wilkes's Handwriting, never before printed, and adapted to the present Occasion.* London: Hone, 1817.

————. *Official Account of the Noble Lord's Bite.* London: Hone, 1817.

————. *The Political Litany, diligently revised; to be Said or Sung, until the Appointed Change Come, throughout the Dominion of England and Wales, and the Town of Berwick upon Tweed. By Special Command.* London: Hone, 1817.

————. *The Sinecurist's Creed, or Belief; as the same can or may be Sung or Said throughout the Kingdom. Quicunque vult.* London: Hone, 1817.

————. *The Table Book.* London: Hunt, 1827.

————. *The Three Trials of William Hone, for publishing Three Parodies.* London: Hone, 1818.

————. *The Three Trials of William Hone, for publishing Three Parodies.* Introd. William Tegg. London: Tegg, 1876.

————. *The Year Book.* Introd. and Bibliog. Leslie Shepard. Facsimile rpt. Detroit: Gale, 1967.

————. *The Year Book of Daily Recreation and Information, concerning Remarkable Men and Manners, Times and Seasons, Solemnities and Merry-Makings, Antiquities and Novelties.* London: Tegg, 1832.

Hotten, John Camden. *Slang Dictionary, Etymological, Historical, and Anecdotal.* London: Chatto, 1874.

Howe, Irving. "A Distinctively Modern Novel." *Jude the Obscure.* Ed. Norman Page. New York: Norton, 1978. 395–406.

Hunter, W. A. *The Blasphemy Laws: Should They Be Abolished?* Plymouth: Assoc. Repeal of Blasphemy Laws, 1884.

————. *The Past and Present of the Heresy Laws.* London: Sunday Lecture Society, 1878.

Hutcheon, Linda. *A Theory of Parody.* New York: Methuen, 1985.

Hutchinson, Horace C. *Portraits of the Eighties.* London: Unwin, 1920.

Ingersoll, Colonel Robert E. *Heretics and Heresies.* London: [Freethought], 1877.

————. *Real Blasphemy.* London: Progressive, 1885.

Ingham, Patricia. Introduction. Notes. Hardy, *Jude the Obscure* xi–xxvi, 433–51.

Inglis, K. S. *Churches and the Working Classes in Victorian England.* London: Routledge, 1963.

Ireland, William Henry. *The Confessions of William Henry Ireland.* Introd. Richard Grant White. New York: Bouton, 1874.

James, Henry. *The Aspern Papers and The Turn of the Screw.* Ed. Anthony Curtis. London: Penguin, 1984.

————. "George Du Maurier." *Partial Portraits.* 1888. Introd. Leon Edel. Ann Arbor: U of Michigan P, 1970. 327–74.

————. *The Question of Our Speech; The Lesson of Balzac: Two Lectures.* Boston: Houghton, 1905.

————. *The Turn of the Screw.* Ed. Robert Kimbrough. New York: Norton, 1966.

James, Louis, ed. *Print and the People 1819–1851.* London: Lane, 1976.

James, Montague Rhodes. *The Apocryphal New Testament, Being the Apocryphal Gospels, Acts, Epistles, and Apocalypses.* Oxford: Clarendon, 1924.

Jay, Martin. "In the Empire of the Gaze: Foucault and the Denigration of Vision in Twentieth-century French Thought." *Foucault: A Critical Reader.* Ed. David Couzens Hoy. Oxford: Blackwell, 1986. 175–204.

Jefferson, Thomas. *The Writings of Thomas Jefferson.* Ed. Andrew A. Lipscomb with Albert Ellery Bergh. vol. 16. Washington: Thomas Jefferson Memorial Assoc., 1903.

Jerome, Jerome K. *Three Men in a Boat.* Harmondsworth, Eng.: Penguin, 1957.

Jerrold, Walter, and R. M. Leonard, eds. *A Century of Parody and Imitation.* London: Oxford UP, 1913.

Johnson, Samuel. *Samuel Johnson: Selected Poetry and Prose.* Eds. Frank Brady and W. K. Wimsatt. Berkeley: U of California P, 1977.

Jones, Henry Festing. *Samuel Butler: A Memoir.* 2 vols. Macmillan, 1919. New York: Octagon, 1968.

Jones, Jeremiah. *A New and Full Method of Settling the Canonical Authority of the New Testament.* 3 vols. Oxford: Clarendon P, 1798.

Jones, John Gale. *Substance of the Speeches of John Gale Jones, delivered at the British Forum, March 11, 18, & 22, 1819, On the Following Question, "Ought the prosecutions instituted against Mr. Carlile and others, for the publication of Paine's AGE OF REASON, to be approved. . . . ?"* London: Carlile, 1819.

Jowett, Benjamin. "On the Interpretation of Scripture." *Essays and Reviews* 289–372.

Joyce, James. *Ulysses.* The Corrected Text. Ed. Hans Walter Gabler, with Wolfhard Steppe and Claus Melchior. New York: Vintage, 1986.

Judge, Mark H. *A Lover of Freedom: George William Foote, 1850–1915.* London: Pioneer Press, [1915].

Katz, Wendy. *Rider Haggard and the Fictions of Empire.* Cambridge: Cambridge UP, 1987.

Keats, John. *The Letters of John Keats, 1814–1821.* Ed. Hyder Edward Rollins. 2 vols. Cambridge: Harvard UP, 1958.

Kennedy, Arthur G. "Odium Philologicum, or, A Century of Progress in English Philology." *Stanford Studies in Language and Literature.* Ed. Hardin Craig. Stanford: Stanford UP, 1941. 11–27.

Kenny, Courtney. "The Evolution of the Law of Blasphemy." *Cambridge Law Journal* 1 (1922): 127–42.

Kingsley, Charles. *Alton Locke, Tailor and Poet.* Ed. Elizabeth A. Cripps. Oxford: Oxford UP, 1983.

Kington-Oliphant, T. L. *The New English.* 2 vols. London: Macmillan, 1886.

Kipling, Rudyard. *A Choice of Kipling's Prose.* Ed. Craig Raine. London: Faber, 1987.

———. *A Choice of Kipling's Verse.* Ed. T. S. Eliot. 1941. London: Faber, 1983.

———. *Kim.* Ed. Alan Sandison. Oxford: Classics-Oxford UP, 1987.

———. *The Light that Failed.* Ed. John M. Lyon. London: Penguin, 1988.

———. *Plain Tales from the Hills.* Ware, Eng.: Wordsworth, 1993.

———. *Something of Myself.* Harmondsworth, Eng.: Penguin, 1977.

Kolve, V. A. *The Play Called Corpus Christi.* Stanford: Stanford UP, 1966.

Kristeva, Julia. *Revolution in Poetic Language.* New York: Columbia UP, 1984.

Krueger, Christine. "Naming Privates in Public: Indecent Assault Depositions, 1830–60." *Mosaic* 27 (December 1994): 121–40.

Lacan, Jacques. *Écrits: A Selection*. Trans. Alan Sheridan. New York: Norton, 1977.

———. *The Four Fundamental Concepts of Psycho-analysis*. Trans. Alan Sheridan. Harmondsworth, Eng.: Penguin, 1979.

Lamb, Charles. *Charles Lamb: Prose and Poetry, with Essays by Hazlitt and De Quincey*. Ed. George Gordon. Oxford: Clarendon, 1921.

———. *Letters of Charles Lamb, in which many mutilated words and passages have been restored to their original form*. Ed. Henry Harper. 5 vols. Boston: Bibliophile, 1905.

———. *The Letters of Charles Lamb, with a Sketch of His Life*. Ed. Thomas Noon Talfourd. London: Moxon, 1837.

———. *The Life, Letters, and Writings of Charles Lamb*. Ed. Percy Fitzgerald. London: Gibbings, 1903.

Lang, Andrew. *Books and Bookmen*. 1886. London: Longman, 1892.

Larson, Janet. *Dickens and the Broken Scripture*. Athens: U of Georgia P, 1985.

Lawrence, D. H. *Lady Chatterly's Lover*. New York: Black Cat-Grove, 1982.

———. *Study of Thomas Hardy and Other Essays*. Ed. Bruce Steele. Cambridge: Cambridge UP, 1985.

The Laws Against Religious Liberty: A Statement and an Appeal. London: National Secular Society, 1892.

Lawton, David. *Blasphemy*. Philadelphia: U of Pennsylvania P, 1993.

Leavis, F. R. *The Great Tradition*. Harmondsworth, Eng.: Penguin, 1948.

Lerner, Laurence, and John Holmstrom. *Thomas Hardy and His Readers: A Selection of Contemporary Reviews*. New York: Barnes, 1968.

Lévi-Strauss, Claude. *Tristes Tropiques*. Trans. John and Doreen Weightmann. New York: Athenaeum, 1974.

Levy, Leonard W. *Blasphemy: Verbal Offense against the Sacred*. New York: Knopf, 1993.

———. *Treason Against God: A History of the Offense of Blasphemy*. New York: Schocken, 1981.

Lewis, Matthew. *The Monk*. Ed. Howard Anderson. Oxford: Classics-Oxford UP, 1980.

Lindsay, Jack. *George Meredith: His Life and Work*. London: Head, 1956.

Linton, W. J. *Holyoake versus Garrison: A Defence of Earnestness*. London: J. Watson, [1853]. Bound offprint from *The English Republic*.

———. *James Watson: A Memoir of the Days of the Fight for a Free Press in England*. Manchester: Heywood, 1880.

Lipking, Lawrence. *The Ordering of the Arts in Eighteenth-Century England*. Princeton: Princeton UP, 1970.

Locke, John. *Essay Concerning Human Understanding*. Ed. Maurice Cranston. New York: Collier, 1965.

———. *A Letter Concerning Toleration*. Ed. Mario Mantuori. The Hague: Nijhoff, 1963.

Lowndes, John James. *An Historical Sketch of the Law of Copyright*. London: Saunders, 1840.

Macaulay, Thomas Babington. *Speeches by Lord Macaulay*. Sel. and introd. G. M. Young. London: Classics-Oxford UP.

MacCabe, Joseph. *Life and Letters of George Jacob Holyoake*. 2 vols. London: Watts, 1908.

Macdonald, Gerard, ed. *Dear Prudence: Being the Correspondence between Prudence and many Troubled Inquirers*. London: Century, 1985.

MacDonnell, J[ohn]. "Blasphemy and the Common Law." *Fortnightly Review* 33 (January–June 1883): 776–89.

Macrone, John. *The Ape that Spoke: Language and the Evolution of the Human Mind.* New York: Morrow, 1991.

Mahaffy, J. P. *Principles of the Art of Conversation.* London: Macmillan, 1887.

Maison, M. M. *Search Your Soul, Eustace: a survey of the religious novel in the Victorian age.* London: Sheed, 1961.

Mander, Raymond, and Joe Mitchenson. *British Music Hall.* Rev. ed. London: Gentry, 1974.

Manning, Peter J. *Reading Romantics: Texts and Contexts.* New York: Oxford UP, 1990.

Manvell, Roger. *The Trial of Annie Besant and Charles Bradlaugh.* London: Elek/Pemberton, 1976.

Marchand, Leslie. *Byron: A Biography.* 3 vols. New York: Knopf, 1957.

Marlowe, Christopher. *The Complete Plays of Christoper Marlowe.* Ed. J. B. Stean. Harmondsworth, Eng.: Penguin, 1967.

Martin, William. *The Logic of Holyoake's "Logic of Death;" Or, Why the Atheist Should Fear to Die.* Glasgow: Blackie, 1854.

Maurice, F. D. *The Friendship of Books and Other Lectures.* Ed. Thomas Hughes. 2nd ed. London: Macmillan, 1874.

McCalmain, Iain. *Radical Underworld: Prophets, Revolutionaries, and Pornographers in London, 1795–1840.* Oxford: Clarendon, 1993.

McGann, Jerome, ed. *The New Oxford Book of Romantic Period Verse.* Oxford: Oxford UP, 1993.

Mearns, Andrew. *The Bitter Cry of Outcast London.* London: Macmillan, 1883.

Meredith, George. *Diana of the Crossways.* New York: Norton Library-Norton, 1973.

———. *The Egoist.* Ed. Robert M. Adams. New York: Norton Critical-Norton, 1979.

———. *The Letters of George Meredith.* Ed. C. L. Cline. 3 vols. Oxford: Clarendon, 1970.

———. *The Ordeal of Richard Feverel.* Ed. John Halperin. Oxford: Classics-Oxford UP, 1984.

———. *The Ordeal of Richard Feverel.* 1859. Introd. Lionel Stevenson. New York: Modern Library, 1950.

———. *The Pilgrim's Scrip: Or, Wit and Wisdom of George Meredith.* 1888. Folcroft: Folcroft, 1978.

———. *Rhoda Fleming: A Story.* London: Constable, 1914.

Merriam, Harold Guy. *Edward Moxon, Publisher of Poets.* New York: Columbia UP, 1939.

Mill, John Stuart. *Autobiography.* Ed. Jack Stillinger. Boston: Riverside-Houghton, 1969.

———. *J. S. Mill on Blasphemy.* London: Progressive, 1883. Rpt. of "Religious Persecutions." *Westminster Review* 2 (July 1824): 1–27.

———. *On Liberty and Other Essays.* Oxford: Classics-Oxford UP, 1991.

Miller, D. A. *The Novel and the Police.* Berkeley: U of California P, 1988.

Miller, J. Hillis. *The Disappearance of God: Five Nineteenth-Century Writers.* Cambridge: Harvard UP, 1963.

Millgate, Michael. *Thomas Hardy: A Biography.* New York: Random, 1982.

———. *Thomas Hardy: His Career as a Novelist.* New York: Random, 1971.

Mitch, David. *The Rise of Popular Literacy in Victorian England: The Influence of Private Choice and Public Policy.* Philadelphia: U of Pennsylvania P, 1992.

Modern State Trials. Ed. William Townsend. 2 vols. London: Longman, 1850.

Monty Python's Life of Brian. Dir. Terry Jones. Warner, 1980.

Moore, George. *Literature at Nurse, Or, Circulating Morals: A Polemic on Victorian Censorship.* Ed. Pierre Coustillas. Hassocks, Eng.: Harvester, 1976.

Morgan, William W. "The Novel as Risk and Compromise, Poetry as Safe Haven: Hardy and the Victorian Reading Public, 1863–1901." *Victorian Newsletter* 69 (Spring 1986): 1–3.

Morris, James. *Heaven's Command: An Imperial Progress.* 1973. Vol. 1 of the *Pax Britannica* trilogy. Harmondsworth, Eng.: Penguin, 1979.

Mosheim, John Lawrence. *An Ecclesiastical History, Ancient and Modern.* Trans. Archibald MacLaine. 6 vols. London: Vernor, 1803.

Moxon, Edward. *The Prospect, and Other Poems.* London: Longman, 1826.

———. *Sonnets.* London: Bradbury, 1843.

Moyles, R. G. *A Bibliography of Salvation Army Literature in English, 1865–1987.* Lewiston/Queenston, ON, Can.: Mellen, 1988.

Mr. Holyoake's Disconnection with the "National Reformer." London: Holyoake, [1863].

Mullen, Peter. "The Religious Speak-Easy." Enright 159–73.

Müller, Friedrich Max. *Biographies of Words and the Home of the Aryas.* London: Longmans, 1888.

———. *Chips from a German Workshop.* 4 vols. London: Longman's, 1867–75.

———. *The Science of Language. Founded on Lectures Delivered at the Royal Institution in 1861 and 1863.* 2 vols. New York: Scribner's, 1891.

———. *The Science of Thought.* New York: Scribner's, 1887.

Murray, Charles. *A Letter to Mr. George Jacob Holyoake; Containing a Brief Review of that Gentleman's Conduct.* London: Pavey, 1854.

Murray, J[ames] A[ugustus]. *The Evolution of English Lexicography.* Oxford: Clarendon, 1900.

Murray, Janet Horowitz, ed. *Strong-Minded Women and Other Lost Voices from Nineteenth Century England.* New York: Pantheon, 1982.

Murray, K. M. Elisabeth. *Caught in the Web of Words: James A. H. Murray and the Oxford English Dictionary.* New Haven: Yale UP, 1977.

Nash, David. "Blasphemy in Victorian Britain? Foote and the *Freethinker.*" *History Today* 15.10 (1995): 13–19.

———. *Secularism, Art and Freedom.* Leicester: Leicester UP, 1992.

Neale, Eskine. *Sunsets and Sunshine; or, Varied Aspects of Life.* London: Longman, 1862.

Neaman, Judith S., and Carole G. Silver. *Kind Words: A Thesaurus of Euphemisms.* 1983. Rev. ed. New York: Facts on File, 1990.

A New Catechism for the Use of the Swinish Multitude. Necessary to be had in all Sties. "By the late Professor Porson, from the *Examiner.*" London: Carlile, n.d.

New Ideas of the Day. London: Freethought, 1887.

Nietzsche, Friedrich. *Early Greek Philosophy and Other Essays.* Trans. Maximilian A. Muegge. New York: Russell, 1964.

Nisbet, Robert. "The State." Enright 185–202.

Nokes, G. D. *A History of the Crime of Blasphemy.* London: Sweet, 1928.

Northey, James. *Caught Red-Handed (Everyday Sayings: Their Origins and Spiritual Applications).* London: [Salvationist] IHQ, 1987.

———. *My Best Togs (Everyday Sayings: Their Origins and Spiritual Applications).* London: [Salvationist] IHQ, 1985.

O'Day, Rosemary. *The English Clergy.* Leicester: Leicester UP, 1979.

Odgers, W. Blake, with J. Bromley Eames. 1881. *A Digest of the Law of Libel and Slander.* 4th ed. London: Stevens, 1905.

———. "The Law Relating to Heresy and Blasphemy." *Modern Review* 4 (July 1883): 586–608.

Ogden, C. K. *Debabelization.* London: Kegan Paul, 1931.

Oliphant, Margaret. *The Autobiography of Margaret Oliphant.* Ed. Elisabeth Jay. Oxford: Oxford UP, 1990.

———. *Salem Chapel.* Introd. Penelope Fitzgerald. New York: Virago-Viking, 1986.

Olmstead, John Charles. *A Victorian Art of Fiction: Essays on the Novel in British Periodicals, 1851–1869.* 4 vols. New York: Garland, 1979.

Ong, Walter. *Orality and Literacy: The Technologizing of the Word.* London: Methuen, 1982.

Orel, Harold. Preface. Hardy, *Thomas Hardy's Personal Writings* vii–xii.

Ormond, Leonee. *George Du Maurier.* Pittsburgh: U of Pittsburgh P, 1969.

Orwell, George. *Collected Essays, Journalism, and Letters.* 4 vols. Eds. Sonia Orwell and Ian Angus. New York: Harcourt, 1968.

———. *Animal Farm: A Fairy Story.* 1945. Vol. 8 of *The Complete Works.* Ed. Peter Davidson. London: Secker, 1987.

Oswald, John. *Outlines of English Grammar.* Edinburgh: Oliver, 1832.

Overton, John. *Inquiry into the Truth and Use of the Book of Enoch.* London: Printed for the author by Simpkin, 1822.

Oxford Companion to the Bible. Eds. Bruce M. Metzger and Michael D. Coogan. Oxford: Oxford UP, 1993.

Oxford Companion to the English Language. Ed. Thomas McArthur. Oxford: Oxford UP, 1992.

Oxford Dictionary of Quotations. Ed. Angela Partington. 4th ed. Oxford: Oxford UP, 1996.

Oxford English Dictionary. Prepared by J. A. Simpson and E. S. C. Weiner. 2nd ed. 20 vols. Oxford: Clarendon P, 1989.

"Oxoniensis" [Rev. Henry John Todd]. *A Remonstrance Addressed to Mr. John Murray, Respecting a Recent Publication.* London: Rivington, 1822.

Pack, Ernest. *A "Blasphemer" on "Blasphemy." The latest Leeds police fiasco.* Bradford: N.p., [1903].

———. *The Trial and Imprisonment of J. W. Gott for Blasphemy.* Bradford: Freethought, [1910?]

Page, Norman. *Speech in the English Novel.* London: Longman, 1973.

Paine, Thomas. *The Age of Reason.* Ed. Philip S. Foner. Secaucus: Citadel, 1974.

Palmer, D. J. *The Rise of English Studies.* London: Oxford UP, 1965.

Palmer, Elihu. *Elihu Palmer's "Principles of Nature."* Text and commentary Kerry S. Walters. Wolfeboro: Longwood, 1990.

Pannick, David. "The Law." Enright 135–50.

Parrinder, Patrick. *Authors and Authority: English and American Criticism, 1750–1990.* 1977. Rev. ed. New York: Columbia UP, 1991.

Pater, Walter. *Appreciations, with an Essay on Style.* London: Macmillan, 1889.

———. *Marius the Epicurean.* Ed. Ian Small. Oxford: Classics-Oxford UP, 1986.

———. *The Renaissance.* London: Macmillan, 1910.

Paterson, Thomas. *The Devil's Looking-Glass, or Mirror of Infidelity!* London: Paterson, [1848].

———. *Letters to Infidels.* London: Paterson, 1846.

Patten, Robert L. *George Cruikshank's Life, Times, and Art.* 2 vols. New Brunswick: Rutgers UP, 1992, 1996.

Paull, H. M. *Literary Ethics: A Study in the Growth of the Literary Conscience.* New York: Dutton, 1929.

Payne, Michael. *Reading Theory: An Introduction to Lacan, Derrida, and Kristeva.* Oxford: Blackwell, 1993.

Paz, D. G. *The Politics of Working-Class Education in Britain, 1830–1950.* Manchester: Manchester UP, 1980.

Pearce, Harry Hastings. "Charles Southwell in Australia and New Zealand." *New Zealand Rationalist* 18.10 (1957): 8–11.

Pearson, Hesketh. Introduction. Wilde, *De Profundis and Other Writings* 9–16.

Pennybacker, Susan. " 'It was not what she said, but the way in which she said it': The London County Council and the Music Halls." *Music Hall: The Business of Pleasure.* Ed. Peter Bailey. Milton Keynes: Open UP, 1986. 120–40.

The Penny Cyclopaedia of the Society for the Diffusion of Useful Knowledge. 16 vols. London: Knight, 1833.

The Penny Revival Hymn Book. Comp. William Booth. N.p.: N.p., n.d.

Perrin, Noel. *Dr. Bowdler's Legacy: A History of Expurgated Books in England and America.* London: Macmillan, 1969.

Peterson, William S. *Victorian Heretic: Mrs. Humphry Ward's Robert Elsmere.* Leicester: Leicester UP, 1976.

Platt, Isaac Hull. *The Ethics of Trilby: with a Supplemental Note on Spiritual Affinity.* Philadelphia: Conservator, 1895.

A Political Catechism, dedicated, without Permission, to His Most Serene Highness OMAR, Bashaw, Dey, and Governor, of the Warlike City and Kingdom of ALGIERS; the Earl of Liverpool, Lord CASTLEREAGH, and Co. By an Englishman. London: Hone, 1817.

Posner, Richard. *Law and Literature: A Misunderstood Relation.* Cambridge: Harvard UP, 1988.

Post, Robert. "Cultural Heterogeneity and the Law: Pornography, Blasphemy, and the First Amendment." *California Law Review* 76 (March 1988): 297–335.

The Prime Minister and the Blasphemy Laws: Verbatim Report of the Speeches at the Recent Deputation. Issued by the Committee for the Repeal of the Blasphemy Laws, May 1914.

The Prosecution of Messrs. Foote and Ramsey for Blasphemy. [Transcript of third trial.] London: Aveling, 1883.

Purcell, Edward. "*Trilby* and *Trilby*-mania: the Beginning of the Bestseller System." *Journal of Popular Culture* 11 (Summer 1977): 62–76.

Pure English. San Francisco: Carson, 1884.

The Queen v. Charles Bradlaugh & Annie Besant. London: Freethought, 1877.

Raby, Peter. *Samuel Butler. A Biography.* London: Hogarth, 1991.

Railton, George Scott. *The Authoritative Life of General William Booth.* New York: Hodder, 1912.

Ramsey, W. J. *In Prison for Blasphemy, Or, Nine Months of Christian Charity.* London: Forder, n.d.

Rawson, Hugh. *A Dictionary of Euphemisms and Other Doubletalk.* New York: Crown, 1981.

Reade, Winwood. *The Martyrdom of Man.* 1872. London: Kegan Paul, 1892. First published 1872.

Renan, Ernest. "Qu'est-ce q'une nation?" *Nation and Narration.* Ed. Homi K. Bhabha. London: Routledge, 1990. 8–22.

Rennell, Thomas. *Proofs of Inspiration, or the Grounds of Distinction between the New Testament and the Apocryphal Volumes.* London: Rivington, 1822.

A Report of the Proceedings, in the Mock Trial of an Information, . . . against William Turnbridge. London: Carlile, 1823.

The Report of the Proceedings of the Court of King's Bench, in the Guildhall, London, on the 12th, 13th, 14th, and 15th Days of October; being the MOCK TRIALS of Richard Carlile. London: Carlile, 1819.

Report of the Trial of Humphrey Boyle, Indicted at the Instance of the Constitutional Association, as "A Man with Name Unknown." London: Carlile, 1822.

Rickword, Edgell, ed. *Radical Squibs and Loyal Ripostes: Satirical Pamphlets of the Regency Period, 1819–1821.* New York: Barnes, 1971.

Riede, David. *Matthew Arnold and the Betrayal of Language.* Charlottesville: U of Virginia P, 1988.

Riffaterre, Michael. *Semiotics of Poetry.* Bloomington: Indiana UP, 1978.

Riggs, David. "Marlowe's Quarrel with God." Unpublished essay, 1995.

"The Rival Armies." *All The Year Round* 29 (July 1882): 485–88.

Roberts, William. *A Catechism of Elocution.* Edinburgh: Oliver, 1836.

Robertson, J. M. *Charles Bradlaugh.* London: Watts, 1920.

———. *A History of Freethought, ancient and modern.* 1899. 4th ed. London: Watts, 1936.

———. *A History of Freethought in the Nineteenth Century.* London: Watts, 1929.

Rolleston, Frances. *Some Account of the Conversion from Atheism to Christianity of the Late William Hone.* 2nd ed. London: Rivington, 1853.

Rolph, C. H., ed. *The Trial of Lady Chatterly: Regina v. Penguin Books Limited.* Baltimore: Penguin, 1961.

Room, Adrian. *Dictionary of True Etymologies.* London: Routledge, 1986.

Rose, Margaret A. *Parody: ancient, modern, and post-modern.* Cambridge: Cambridge UP, 1993.

Rose, Mark. *Authors and Owners: The Invention of Copyright.* Cambridge: Harvard UP, 1993.

Rossiter, W. "Artisan Atheism." *Nineteenth Century* 21 (February 1887): 262–72; 22 (July 1887): 111–26.

Routledge, James. *Chapters in the History of Popular Progress, Chiefly in Relation to the Freedom of the Press and Trial by Jury, 1660–1820.* London: Macmillan, 1876.

Royle, Edward, ed. *The Bradlaugh Papers: A Descriptive Index.* Wakefield: EP Microform, 1975.

———, ed. *The Infidel Tradition from Paine to Bradlaugh.* London: Macmillan, 1976.

———. *Radicals, Secularists, and Republicans: Popular Freethought in Britain, 1866–1915.* Manchester: Manchester UP, 1980.

———. *Victorian Infidels: the Origins of the British Secularist Movement 1791–1866.* Manchester: Manchester UP, 1974.

The Rules of Society, Or, a Guide to Conduct, for those who desire to be Armenian Bible Christians. Launceston: Eyre, 1818.

Safire's New Political Dictionary. New York: Random, 1994.

The Salvation Soldier's Song Book. Comp. William Booth. London: Partridge, [1880].

The Salvation War, under the Generalship of William Booth. Yearly publication. London: S.A., 1882–86.

Sandal, Robert. *The History of the Salvation Army.* Vol. 2 (1878–86). London: Nelson, 1950.

Saussure, Ferdinand de. *Course in General Linguistics.* 1916. Ed. Charles Bally and Albert Sechehaye. Trans. Roy Harris. La Salle: Open Court, 1986.

Sayce, A[rchibald] J. *Introduction to the Science of Language.* 1883. 3rd ed. 2 vols. London: Kegan Paul, 1890.

Scott, Harold. *The Early Doors.* London: Nicholson, 1946.

Selincourt, Ernest, ed. *The Letters of William and Dorothy Wordsworth. The Middle Years, Part II, 1812–1820.* 2nd ed. Rev. Mary Moorman and Alan G. Hill. Oxford: Clarendon, 1970.

Seymour-Smith, Martin. *Hardy.* New York: St. Martin's, 1994.

Shaw, George Bernard. *Collected Letters 1874–97.* Ed. Dan H. Laurence. New York: Dodd, 1965.

———. *Collected Letters 1898–1910.* Ed. Dan H. Laurence. New York: Dodd, 1972.

———. *Collected Works of Bernard Shaw.* 30 vols. New York: Wise, 1930–32.

———. *The Diaries.* Ed. Stanley Weintraub. University Park: Penn State UP, 1986.

———. *Shaw: An Autobiography 1856–1898.* Sel. Stanley Weintraub. New York: Weybright, 1969.

Shell, Mark. *The Economy of Literature.* Baltimore: Johns Hopkins UP, 1974.

———. *Money, Language, and Thought: Literary and Philosophical Economies from the Medieval to the Modern Era.* Berkeley: U of California P, 1982.

Shelley, Mary Wollstonecraft. *The Letters of Mary Wollstonecraft Shelley.* Ed. Betty T. Bennett. 3 vols. Baltimore: Johns Hopkins UP, 1980–88.

Shelley, Percy Bysshe. *The Letters of Percy Bysshe Shelley.* Ed. Frederick L. Jones. 2 vols. Oxford: Clarendon, 1964.

———. *The Poetical Works of Percy Bysshe Shelley.* Ed. Mary Shelley. London: Moxon, 1840.

———. *Shelley's Prose, Or, The Trumpet of a Prophecy.* Ed. David Lee Clark. Albuquerque: U of New Mexico P, 1954.

Shepard, Leslie. Introduction. W. Hone, *The Year Book* (Gale) [i–iv].

Shorthouse, J. H. *John Inglesant: A Romance.* London: Macmillan, 1905.

Slack, Robert C. "Hardy's Revisions." *Jude the Obscure.* Ed. Norman Page. New York: Norton, 1978. 331–39.

Slop's Shave at a Broken Hone. London: Wright, 1820.

Smiles, Samuel. *Self-Help.* 1859. London: Murray, 1905.

Smith, F. B. "The Atheist Mission, 1840–1900." *Ideas and Institutions of Victorian Britain.* Ed. Robert Robson. London: Bell, 1967. 205–35.

Smith, Olivia. *The Politics of Language 1791–1819.* Oxford: Clarendon, 1984.

Smith, Warren Sylvester. *The London Heretics 1870–1914.* London: Constable, 1967.

Songs of the Salvation Army. Comp. William Booth. 3rd ed. London: S. A. Book Depot, 1884.

Southwell, Charles. *Another "Fourpenny Wilderness," in which may be found more Nails for the Coffin of Nonsense called Atheism.* London: Watson, [1852].

———. *The Confessions of a Freethinker.* London: Printed for the author, n.d.

———. *The Impossibility of Atheism Demonstrated.* London: Watson, [1852].

Speech of John Gale Jones, delivered at the British Forum, held at the Crown and Anchor Tavern in the Strand. London: Carlile, 1819.

Speech of Mrs. Susannah Wright, before the Court of King's Bench, on the 14th of November, 1822. London: Carlile, 1822.

Spencer, Herbert. *First Principles.* 1862. 4th ed. Chicago: Rand, [1880].

Stallybrass, Peter, and Allon White. *The Politics and Poetics of Transgression.* Ithaca: Cornell UP, 1986.

Stang, Richard. *The Theory of the Novel in England, 1850–1870.* New York: Columbia UP, 1959.

Stanley, Arthur Penrhyn. *Life and Correspondence of Thomas Arnold, D.D.* Seventh edn. 2 vols. London: B. Fellowes, 1852.

Starkie, Thomas. *A Treatise on the Law of Slander and Libel, and Incidentally of Malicious Prosecutions.* Rpt. from 2nd English ed., 1830, with notes and ref. American cases and English decisions since 1830 by John L. Wendell. 2 vols. Hartford: Wendell, 1858.

The Statutes at Large, from the Eighth Year of King William III to the Second Year of Queen Anne. Vol. 10 of 109. Cambridge: Bathurst, 1764.

The Statutes of the United Kingdom of Great Britain and Ireland, 60 Geo. III. & 1 Geo. IV. 1819–1820. London: Butterworth, 1820.

Stein, Gordon. "The Blasphemy Laws." *Free Inquiry* 1 (1981): 18–19, 35.

———. ed. *The Encyclopaedia of Unbelief.* Buffalo: Prometheus, 1985.

———. *Freethought in the U.K. and the Commonwealth: A Descriptive Bibliography.* Westport: Greenwood, 1981.

Stephen, Sir James Fitzjames. "Blasphemy and Blasphemous Libel" *Fortnightly Review* NS 35 (March 1884): 289–318.

————. *A Digest of the Criminal Law: Crimes and Punishments.* London: Macmillan, 1877.

————. *A History of the Criminal Law of England.* 3 vols. London: Macmillan, 1883.

Stephen, Leslie. *An Agnostic's Apology, and Other Essays.* 2nd ed. London: Smith, 1903.

————. *The English Utilitarians.* 3 vols. New York: Putnam's, 1900.

————. *Essays on Freethinking and Plainspeaking.* London: Longmans, 1873. Farnborough: Gregg, 1969.

————. *The History of English Thought in the Eighteenth Century.* 2 vols. London: Smith, 1881.

Sterling, Leonard. *The Doctrine of Correctness in English Usage: 1700-1800.* 1929. New York: Russell, 1962.

Stevenson, Robert Louis. *Dr Jekyll and Mr Hyde.* Ed. Jenni Calder. Harmondsworth, Eng.: Penguin, 1979.

Stevenson, Robert Louis, in collaboration with Lloyd Osborne. *The Ebb-Tide: A Trio and Quartette.* Ed. David Daiches. London: Everyman, 1994.

St. George, Andrew. *The Descent of Manners: Etiquette, Rules and the Victorians.* London: Chatto & Windus, 1993.

Stoker, Bram. *Dracula.* Ed. A. N. Wilson. Oxford: Classics-Oxford UP, 1983.

Stonehouse, J. H., ed. *Catalogue of the Library of Charles Dickens from Gadshill.* London: Piccadilly, 1935.

Stuart, Charles Douglas. *The Variety Stage.* London: Unwin, 1895.

The Suppressed Gospels and Epistles of the Original New Testament. London: Hancock, 1863.

Sutherland, John. "Macmillans and *Robert Elsmere.*" *Notes and Queries* 34 (March 1987): 47–48.

————. *Mrs. Humphry Ward: Eminent Victorian, Pre-Eminent Edwardian.* Oxford: Clarendon, 1990.

————. *Offensive Literature: Decensorship in Britain, 1960–1982.* London: Junction, 1982.

Talfourd, Thomas Noon. *Critical and Miscellaneous Writings.* New York: Appleton, 1864.

————. *Speech for the Defendant, in the prosecution of the Queen v. Moxon, for the publication of Shelley's Works.* London: Moxon, 1841.

————. *Speech of Serjeant Talfourd on Literary Property, Delivered in the House of Commons, on the 18th May, 1837.* London: Sherwood, 1837.

————. *Tragedies.* London: Routledge, 1889.

Taxil, Leo [Gabriel Jogand-Pages]. *La Bible amusante, pour les grands et les petits enfants.* "401 dessins par Frid'rick." Paris: Librairie anti-clericale, [1881–82].

Taylor, Anne. *Annie Besant: A Biography.* Oxford: Oxford UP, 1992.

Taylor, Dennis. *Hardy's Literary Language and Victorian Philology.* Oxford: Clarendon, 1993.

Taylor, G. H. *A Chronology of British Secularism.* London: National Secular Society, 1957.

Taylor, "Reverend" Robert. *Swing, Or, Who are the Incendiaries? A Tragedy, Founded on Late Circumstances, and as Performed at the Rotunda.* London: Carlile, 1831.

Tegg, William. Introduction. W. Hone, *Three Trials of William Hone* i–v.

Tennyson, Alfred Lord. *The Complete Poetical Works.* Ed. T. Herbert Watson. Rev. and enl. Frederick Page. London: Oxford UP, 1971.

Thomas, Donald. *A Long Time Burning: The History of Literary Censorship in England.* New York: Praeger, 1969.

———. *Swinburne: the Poet in His World.* London: Weidenfeld, 1979.

Thompson, E. P. *The Making of the English Working Class.* New York: Vintage, 1966.

Thompson, F. M. L. *The Rise of Respectable Society: A Social History of Victorian Britain 1830–1900.* Cambridge: Harvard UP, 1988.

Thornwell, Emily. *The Lady's Guide to Perfect Gentility.* New York: 1856. Reprod. Huntington Library, CA, 1984.

The Three Trials for Blasphemy of Messrs. G. W. Foote, W. J. Ramsey, and H. A. Kemp. London: Progressive, [1883].

Tillotson, Kathleen. Introduction. Dickens, *Oliver Twist* vii–xiv.

Tolpuddle. An historical account through the eyes of George Loveless. London: Trades Union Congress, 1984.

Toohey, Timothy J. "Blasphemy in Nineteenth-Century England: The Pooley Case and Its Background." *Victorian Studies* 30 (Spring 1987): 315–33.

———. *Piety and the Professions: Sir John Taylor Coleridge and his Sons.* New York: Garland, 1987.

Trall, R. T. *The Illustrated Family Gymnasium.* New York: Wells, 1879.

Trench, Richard Chevenix. *On Some Deficiencies in our English Dictionaries, being the Substance of Two Papers read before the Philological Spciety, Nov. 5, and Nov. 19, 1857.* 2nd ed. London: Parker, 1860.

Trench, Richard Trevenix. *On the Study of Words and English Past and Present.* New York: Dutton, 1927.

Trevelyan, G. M. *English Social History: A Survey of Six Centuries, Chaucer to Queen Victoria.* 1942. Harmondsworth, Eng.: Penguin, 1967.

Trevelyan, George Otto. *The Life and Letters of Lord Macaulay.* 4 vols. Leipzig: Tauchnitz, 1876.

Trevelyan, Janet P. *The Life of Mrs. Humphry Ward.* London: Constable, 1923.

Trial by Jury and Liberty of the Press. The Proceedings at the Public Meeting, December 29, 1817, at the City of London Tavern, for the purpose of enabling WILLIAM HONE to surmount the difficulties in which he has been placed by being selected by the Ministers of the Crown as the Object of their Persecution. London: Hone, 1818.

The Trial of Charles Southwell, (Editor of "The Oracle of Reason") for Blasphemy. Rept. William Carpenter. London: Hetherington, 1842.

The Trial of Henry Hetherington. London: Hetherington, 1840.

The Trial of George Jacob Holyoake. London: Anti-Persecution Union, 1842.

The Trial of the Reverend Robert Taylor, A.B.M.R.C.S. upon a Charge of Blasphemy. London: Carlile, 1827.

The Trial of Thomas Paterson, for Blasphemy, before the High Court of Justiciary, Edinburgh, with the Whole of his Bold and Effective Defence. Also, The Trials of Thomas Finlay and Miss Mailda Roalfe (for Blasphemy) In the Sheriff's Court. With notes and "A Special Dissertation on Blasphemy Prosecutions in General" by the Secretary of the Anti-Persecution Union [G. J. Holyoake]. London: Hetherington, 1844.

Tribe, David. *One Hundred Years of Freethought.* London: Elek, 1967.

———. *President Charles Bradlaugh, M.P.* London: Archon, 1971.

Trilbyana: the rise and progress of a popular novel. The York: Critic, 1895.

Trollope, Antony. *An Autobiography.* Eds. Michael Sadleir and Frederick Page. Introd. and notes P. D. Edwards. Oxford: Classics-Oxford UP, 1980.

Vanden Bossche, Chris R. "The Value of Literature: Representations of Print Culture in the Copyright Debate of 1837–1842." *Victorian Studies* 38 (Autumn 1994): 41–68.

Vincent, David. *Literacy and Popular Culture, England 1750–1914.* Cambridge: Cambridge UP, 1989.

Vizetelly, Henry. *Glances Back Through Seventy Years: Autobiographical and Other Reminiscences.* 2 vols. London: Kegan Paul, 1893.

Waite, Robert. Introduction. Arnold, *Literature and Dogma* 3–4.

Waldron, John P., ed. *The Salvation Army and the Churches.* New York: S.A. Literature Dept., 1986.

Wall, Stephen, ed. *Charles Dickens: A Critical Anthology.* Harmondsworth, Eng.: Penguin, 1970.

Walter, Nicholas. *Blasphemy: Ancient and Modern.* London: Rationalist Press Association, 1990.

———. *Blasphemy in Britain: the practice and punishment of blasphemy, and the trial of Gay News.* London: Rationalist Press Association, 1977.

Ward, Aileen. "Keats's Sonnet, 'Nebuchadnezzar's Dream.'" *Philological Quarterly* 34 (1955) 177–88.

Ward, Mrs. Humphry. *The Case of Richard Meynell.* Garden City: Doubleday, 1911.

———. *Robert Elsmere.* Ed. Rosemary Ashton. Oxford: Classics-Oxford UP, 1987.

———. *Robert Elsmere.* Westmoreland ed. Vol. 1 of 16. Boston: Houghton, 1911.

———. *A Writer's Recollections.* London: Collins, 1918.

Wayside Points for New Roads: Or, Defenses of Freethinking. No. 1. London: Watson, 1852.

Webb, R. K. *The British Working-Class Reader, 1790–1948: Literary and Social Tension.* London: Allen, 1955.

Webster, Richard. *A Brief History of Blasphemy: Liberalism, Censorship and The Satanic Verses.* Southwold, Eng.: Orwell, 1990.

Weightman, Gavin. *Bright Lights, Big City: London Entertained 1830–1950.* London: Collins, 1992.

Welsh, Alexander. "Burke and Bentham on the Narrative Potential of Circumstantial Evidence." *New Literary History* 21 (1990): 607–27.

———. *Strong Representations: Narrative and Circumstantial Evidence in England.* Baltimore: Johns Hopkins UP, 1992.

White, R. J. *Waterloo to Peterloo.* London: Heinemann, 1957.

Whitehead, John. *This Solemn Mockery: The Art of Literary Forgery.* London: Arlington, 1973.

Whitney, W. D. *Max Müller and the Science of Language: A Criticism.* New York: Appleton, 1892.

Whom to Believe and What to Believe about the Salvation Army. London: S.A., [1882].

Wickens, G. Glen. "Victorian Theories of Language and *Tess of the D'Urbervilles.*" *Mosaic* 19 (Winter 1986): 99–115.

Wickwar, William H. *The Struggle for the Freedom of the Press, 1819–1832.* London: Allen, 1928.

Widdowson, Peter. *Hardy in History: A Study in Literary Sociology.* London: Routledge, 1989.

Wiener, Joel H. *Radicalism and Freethought in Nineteenth-Century Britain: The Life of Richard Carlile.* Westport: Greenwood, 1983.

Wilde, Oscar. *The Artist as Critic: Critical Writings of Oscar Wilde.* Ed. Richard Ellman. New York: Random, 1968.

———. *De Profundis and Other Writings.* Introd. Hesketh Pearson. Harmondsworth, Eng.: Penguin, 1976.

———. *The Picture of Dorian Gray.* Harmondsworth, Eng.: Penguin, 1975.

———. "The Soul of Man under Socialism." *De Profundis and Other Writings.* 17–54.

———. *The Writings of Oscar Wilde.* Ed. Isobel Murray. Oxford: Oxford UP, 1989.

Willey, Basil. "How *Robert Elsmere* struck Some Contemporaries." *Essays and Studies* 10 (1957): 53–68.

———. *More Nineteenth Century Studies: A Group of Honest Doubters.* London: Chatto, 1956.

Williams, Raymond. *The Country and the City.* New York: Oxford UP, 1973.

———. *Culture and Society: 1780–1950.* 1958, New York: Columbia UP, 1983.

———. *Keywords: A Vocabulary of Culture and Society.* London: Fontana, 1975.

———. *The Long Revolution.* Harmondsworth, Eng.: Penguin, 1965.

Williams, S. *The Creed of Error; A Reply to Holyoake's "Logic of Death."* London: Partridge, [1851].

Willinsky, John. *Empire of Words.* Princeton: Princeton UP, 1994.

Wolff, Robert Lee. *Gains and Losses: Novels of Faith and Doubt in Victorian England.* New York: Garland, 1977.

Wood, T. Martin. *George Du Maurier, the Satirist of the Victorians.* New York: McBride, 1913.

Woodmansee, Martha. *The Author, Art, and the Market: Rereading the History of Aesthetics.* New York: Columbia UP, 1994.

———. "The Cultural Work of Copyright: Legislative Authorship in Britain 1837–42." Unpublished essay, 1995.

———. "On the Author Effect: Recovering Collectivity." *The Construction of Authorship: Textual Appropriation in Law and Literature.* 15–28.

Woodmansee, Martha, and Peter Jaszi, eds. *The Construction of Authorship: Textual Appropriation in Law and Literature.* Durham: Duke UP, 1994.

Wooler, T. J. *A Dialogue on the Approaching Trial of Mr. Carlile, for publishing the Age of Reason.* London: Wooler, 1819.

Woolf, Virgina. *To the Lighthouse.* New York: Harcourt, 1955.

———. *A Writer's Diary. Being Extracts from the Diary of Virginia Woolf.* Ed. Leonard Woolf. 1953. London: Grafton, 1978.

Wootton, David. "The Fear of God in Early Modern Political Theory." *Historical Papers* (Canada) 17 (1983): 56–80.

Wordsworth, William, and S. T. Coleridge. *Lyrical Ballads*. Eds. R. L. Brett and A. R. Jones. 2nd ed. London: Routledge, 1991.

The Works of Aristotle, The Famous Philosopher. Containing his Complete Masterpiece and Family Physician; his Experienced Midwife, his Book of Problems and his Remarks on Physiognomy. London: Moritz, n.d.

Young, G. M. *Portrait of an Age: Victorian England*. 2nd ed. London: Oxford UP, 1953.

Index

Abbott, Charles (judge): at first Hone trial, 32; attempts to block speech, quotations, 198; as Chief Justice, charged with unorthodoxy at Carlile trial, 68, 338n.75; sweeping ruling of 1819, 36–37; and institutionalized loops of logic, 233 affirmation. *See* oath

Age of Reason, The: overview, 60–77; as rationalist anti-Bible, 6, 10, 30, 60–62, 170, 172, 181–82, 211; as handbook for agitators, 61, 337n.60; as symbol of "blasphemous" free publication, 19; and French Revolution, 61; 1797 prosecution, 19, 61; inheritance of "vituperation," 61; republished by Carlile, 61, 65–69; huge sales, 67, 69, 71. *See also* Carlile, Richard; Eaton, Isaac Daniel; Paine, Thomas; plain speech; privilege; volunteers

agnosticism: as "honest doubt," 5; as upperclass privilege, 156; agnostic writers immune to prosecution, 156; dangers of attempts at same, 156. *See also* Huxley, Thomas Henry

Alford, Henry (Dean): on threat of euphemism to "The Queen's English," 217–18; defends concern with language, 218; clerical credentials, 364n.25

anti-Semitism: widespread in Victorian culture, 81, 113, 307; as Freethought tactic,

113, 179; in "Comic Bible" cartoons, 113; in *Freethinker's* "New Life of Christ," 145 figs. 13 and 14; and Foote's Jewish successor as editor, 113. *See also* Corelli, Marie; Southwell, Charles

Aphorism: 188–90. *See also* Bible, Holy; Meredith, George

Apocryphal New Testament, The: accidental discovery by Hone, 41–42; text of "three Heavenly Witnesses" (Father, Son, and Word), 224; in English translation, 43–44; in Jones's *New and Full Method for Settling the Canonical Authority of the New Testament,* 43–44; relation to mystery plays, 41–42; history and character, 42–43; Hone's scholarship in presenting, in *Ancient Mysteries Described,* 43–45; as assault on canonical Scripture, 44–48; as revenge on, 30; as "forgery," 46, 48; clerical critics' outcry, 44–49, 186, 335n.43; errors in, 45, 47–48, 185; assumption of Hone's impostordom, 49; populist tendencies of his publication, 44; margins and relativity, 45–46; crime of scriptural style, 46; Hone's *Aspersions Answered,* 47–49, 54, 335n.41. *See also* Bible, Holy; Butler, Dr. Samuel; Butler, Samuel; Byron, George Gordon, Lord; forgery

Arnold, Matthew: religious liberalism of, 167; on circulating libraries and literary mediocrity, 330n.10; *Culture and Anarchy,* on need for authority, 194–96; as response to Second Reform Act, 194; as assault on Salvation Army, 194; on "Just-what-you-like-ism" (i.e. Secularism), 194–96, 273; and on "Iconoclast" Bradlaugh, 194–96, 360n.39; *Literature and Dogma* as same, 196; literary reclamation of Bible in, 172, 196–97; supercedes historical method of Strauss, Feuerbach, 196; joke quoted by Foote in court, 154–55; rebuked, defended, 203; cut from later editions, 155; Arnold awarded state pension, 203; redefinitions of "God," "religion," 253–54, 260, 371n.98; satirized, 253–55; Arnold's translation of Isaiah, 258; euphemism in, 372n.109; *God and the Bible,* twentieth-century influence of, 196; rejection of parody, 38; on anti-Semitism, 113. *See also* Arnold, Thomas; *Jude the Obscure;* Ward, Mrs. Humphry

Arnold, Thomas: on Church corruption, 20; penalized for advocating ecumenical reform, 331n.5; rejection of parody, 38

Aspland, Robert (Unitarian minister): as Hone supporter, 35; *Inquiry into the Nature of the Sin of Blasphemy,* and biblical ridicule, 35; charges Byron with parody, 101

atheism: persisting penalties on, through 1880s, 132–33; as threat to society, justice, 21, 132; the word as weapon, 21; bogey "artisan atheist," 21; stock tales of infidel deathbeds, 132–33; atheism and moral breakdown, pornography, 213; contrast of toleration for theism, 7, 329–30n.6. *See also* Southwell, Charles

authority: as Victorian desideratum, 192–93; of Literature, 193; consecrated in court, 199–200, 201–2. *See also* Arnold, Matthew; Carlyle, Thomas; Coleridge, John Duke; Lawrence, D. H.; literature; Shelley, Percy Bysshe

Bentham, Jeremy: on "public interest," in *Introduction to the Principles of Morals and Legislation,* 19; and Carlile, 19; support of Hone's *Reformist's Register,* 26; Bentham's

idiom as linguistic model, 262, 263; panoptical prison plans, 146, 311. *See also* Society for the Diffusion of Useful Knowledge

Besant, Annie: as type of female "heretic," 14–15; gifted speaker, 134; rise through N.S.S. ranks, 135, 137, 353n.15; "questionable" relations with Bradlaugh, 213; careful editorship of *Our Corner,* 133, 229; writes "official" N.S.S. funeral service, 267; and confessional memoirs, in safety, 201; on language, 265; on Bible and bibliolatry, 172, 176, 363n.16; and London heretics, 171; as birth control advocate, 14, 137; sentenced for *The Fruits of Philosophy,* 213. *See also* birth control; Shaw, George Bernard

Bible, Holy: and English culture, literature, 169–91, 195–97; stripped of legal protection, 200–201; as Victorian "fetish," 8, 170–72; and instrument of class, imperial power, 171–72; nineteenth-century oaths, proclamations, of belief in, 110, 171; mass production of, 171–72; as blasphemers,' law's, focus, 170; and Secularist "Bible-smashing," 170–72; and alternate Victorian words, books, of wisdom, 173–74, 190–91, 202; allegorical interpretation of, 18–19, 179; Bible and literacy, 84, 85, 249–50, 343n.21; ridicule in the Bible, 35; shifting relations with literature, fiction, 169, 173–75; transformation into "masterpiece," 169, 173–75; obscenity as treated in the Bible, 209–10; as charged against the Bible, 106, 210–12, 363n.15; Bible's euphemistic imperative, 225–26; limitations to, in translation practice, 258; Bible and language, 249–59, 366n.43; "Bible English" as linguistic "holdfast," 249–51, 255, 266, 268; Tyndale burned for compositional errors in, 257. See also *Age of Reason, The; Apocryphal New Testament, The;* Arnold, Matthew; Butler, Samuel; Carlile, Richard; Carlyle, Thomas; Collins, Wilkie; Corelli, Marie; Eliot, George; *Essays and Reviews;* Foote, G. W.; *Freethinker, The;* Gladstone, William Ewart; Gosse, Edmund; Hardy, Thomas; Hetherington, Henry; "Higher Criticism"; Holyoake, George Jacob; Hone, William; Meredith,

George; Moore, George; Owenism; parody; Paterson, Thomas; Pooley, Thomas; Revised Version; Shakespeare, William; Southwell, Charles; Taxil, Leo

bible amusante, La. See Taxil, Leo

birth control: tradition of Freethought writing on, agitation for, 6, 293, 338nn.69–70, 363n.18; and female heretics, 14; birth control as "obscenity," 137; The Fruits of Philosophy case as "test" of Secularist solidarity, 137, 213. See also Besant, Annie; Bradlaugh, Charles

Blackstone, William: on ridicule, 36, 284; authority of legal Commentaries, 21, 158; as "irreligious" book, 192

blasphemy: traditional meanings of, 8; in the Bible, Judaeo-Christian tradition, 18, 225–26, 304; and name taboo, fear of Words, 225–26, 230; as an "act" of language, 226; Greek and Hebrew terms for, 226; as "dysphemism" and "hate crime," 226, 366n.53; as "truth," 7, 231; blasphemy as indefinable, 6; historical failure to define, 6–7, 197–98; distinction from heresy, 6, 18; blasphemy as repressed history, 8; in formation of working-class identity, 72, 74; secularization of, co-produces Victorian sex obsession, 232; politicization of, 9, 18–21; as disruption and claim to community, 121, 123; 234; blasphemy and 1810s "ultra-radicals," 66, 121; as infidel "trade," 48, 69; Anglican exclusiveness of law of blasphemy, 16–17; attempts at abolition, 16; in 1914, 162; blasphemy as literary crime, 8, 169, 175–81; as literary act, 95; law as "aesthetic discipline," 186; literary redefinition of, 91–94; allows class discrimination, 158; confirmed by Freethinker case, 93, 160; "matter" v. "manner," 92, 158; new criteria of "seriousness," "feeling," "taste," 92–93, 202; style as "reverence," 200–201; compare reviewers' standards, 93–94; applied to "coarse and brutal" Jane Eyre, 93; "scornful" Villette, 193; intent to "shock," 93, 97–98; blasphemy as class crime of language, 8, 127; as "words" (in technical shorthand), 229; and the unspeakable, 7, 230; as original word crime, 9, 230; "explicitness" as euphemism for, 290; as requirement of modern, postmodern, fiction, 326–27; blasphemy law as sole conduit for linguistic anxiety, 228–29; allows private prosecution, 229. See also copyright; euphemism; Foote, G. W.; forgery; Freethinker, The; Gay News; Hale, Matthew; Hardy, Thomas; language; Lawton, David; Levy, Leonard; libel; literature; obscenity; piracy; Royal Commission on the Criminal Law; Salvation Army; Starkie, Thomas; statutes; Stephen, Sir James Fitzjames

Booth, "General" William. See Salvation Army

Boulter, Harry: prosecuted 1908 and 1909, 16

Bowdler, Thomas: as English "Saint," 218–19; on "erasure" of language, 231; suppression of sister's work on Family Shakespeare, 364n.28. See also Carroll, Lewis; Gosse, Edmund; Hunt, Leigh; Lamb, Charles; Lewis, Matthew ("Monk"); Shakespeare, William; Swinburne, Algernon Charles

Bradlaugh, Charles: childhood loss of faith, 176; legal genius, battles, 6, 149, 172; founder-editor of National Reformer, 132, 133, 184, 352–53n.11, 353n.13; linguistic, legal caution in, 229, 353n.16; pseudonym "Iconoclast," 194; promotes "militant" Secularism, 129; founds, leads National Secular Society, 6, 126, 129, 134; as charismatic working-class "hero," orator, 5, 134–35, 136; as "howling" atheist, "devil," 134, 330n.13, 360n.36; with Cockney accent, 168; caricatured as Caliban, 195 fig. 16; identified with Affirmation Bill, 128, 135, 195 fig. 16; breaks securities system, 83; struggles to take seat in parliament, 128, 135, 148–52; implicated in Freethinker case, 143; escapes trial, 6, 149; moves first Freethinker trial to Queen's Bench Court, 149; "put[s] his FOOTE in it," 151; sentenced for The Fruits of Philosophy, 213; on blasphemy as indefinable, 7. See also Arnold, Matthew; Besant, Annie; Foote, G. W.; Freethinker, The; Giffard, Sir Hardinge; Gissing, George; Holyoake, George Jacob; Meredith, George; Morley, John; National Secular Society; Oxford English Dictionary; Tyler, Sir Henry; Varley, Henry

Brougham, Henry: petitions for Carlile volunteers' release, 72, 339n.86; founds Society for the Diffusion of Useful Knowledge, 87; on scapegoating of vulgar unbelief, 157. See also Society for the Diffusion of Useful Knowledge

Burdett, Sir Francis (M.P.): protests suspension of habeas corpus, 27; "political persecution" of Hone, 31; imprisonment of Carlile and volunteers, 72

Butler, Dr. Samuel: arch-deaconal Charge against Hone's Apocryphal New Testament, 44–47; recantation and errors, 48–49, 335n.42; read by biographer-grandson, 185–86

Butler, Samuel: The Way of All Flesh and biblical parody, 182–86, 358nn.13–15; in Freethinker style, 183–84; Erewhon as satire on Church of England, 185; Fair Haven mistaken for serious Bible criticism, 184–85, 196; Butler family connections to Hone, 185–86

Byron, George Gordon, Lord: and Richard Carlile, 66; piracies of, 102; and William Hone, 25; piracies of, 100–101; create Byron's role as revolutionary, 101, 346n.46; caricatured as blasphemer, 103; claims responsibility for publication, 103; but knows better, 346n.45; parody in Don Juan, 101, 107, 345–46n.43; irony as weapon, 157; blasphemy of Cain, 10, 100–102; prefatory nods at Hone's Apocryphal New Testament, 101; disapprobation of king, critics, 102–4; Cain devoid of copyright, 101; "Byron effect" on copyright law, 104; stopped by death, 104. See also Aspland, Robert; Carlile, Richard; Gifford, William; Hone, William; Hunt, John; Murray, John; pornography

Canning, George (President of the Board of Control): caricatured by Hone and Cruikshank, 23 fig. 2; as "right honorable" parodist, 33–34, 37

Carlile, Jane: as female blasphemy martyr, 14, 338n.77; and inspiration to volunteers, 14; gives birth in Dorchester Gaol, 69

Carlile, Mary Anne: as female blasphemy martyr, 14, 338n.77; and inspiration to volunteers, 14, 69

Carlile, Richard: overview, career, 10, 60–77; hawks Black Dwarf, 65; publishes Sherwin's Register, 65, 337n.63; sells Wat Tyler, 100; pirates Queen Mab, 104, 346n.48; and Byron's Cain, 102; republishes Hone's parodies, 65–66, 337n.65; reports "Peterloo Massacre," 63, 64 fig. 4, 340n.88; indicted for blasphemy, 62; finds vocation of jailhouse "martyrdom," 14, 63, 65–66, 68–70, 146, 235, 337n.67; edits Republican, 65, 71, 79, 337n.64; bans words God, soul, etc., 254, 317; other journals, 82, 337n.64; as "Anti-Christ" of "Printing Press," 66; putting out trial transcripts, Jail Journal, 72, 235; as exemplary autodidact, 66, 338n.69; as champion of Paine, 72, 73 fig.5, 75; Age of Reason, 67–69; read aloud in own defense, 69, 235; and therefore republishable, 69; but lack-lustre courtroom performance, 68, 338n.75; though misreporting of trials, 67, 235; Carlile as volunteers' "General," 70; on "crime" as political protest, 72; and "unstamped" cheap press, literacy, 79–82, 87; on "Bible Obscenity," 211, 363n.15; and biblical translation, 256, 337n.66, 371n.92; as Dorchester Gaol celebrity, 307–8; epitome of plain speech, linguistic "violence," 74–75, 157; but not physical force, 66, 76, 338n.68; public slur on Carlile's literacy, 308; trial assistance to Jacob Holyoake, 123, 242, 351n.92; Holyoake's Life and Character of Richard Carlile, 71. See also Age of Reason, The; Byron, George Gordon, Lord; Church of England; freedom of press; freedom of publication; Hone, William; Hunt, Henry ("Orator"); Levy, Leonard; martyrdom; "Peterloo Massacre"; volunteers; Wooler, T. J.

Carlyle, Thomas: on Literature as "Church-Homiletic," 106, 200; and authority, 200; and language as veil, 221; and reformulations of "Bible English," 252; supports copyright bill, 107

Carpenter, William: as Age of Reason volunteer, 71, 339n.81; as Poor Man's Guardian volunteer, 82; edits unstamped *Slap at the Church,* 82, 341n.9; reports Southwell trial, 123; joins cooperative movement, 124; as example of political blasphemer, 341n.7

Carroll, Lewis (Charles Lutwidge Dodgson): and transgressive nonsense, language, 37, 240; and refined taboo on laughter, 1880s, 178; and "Girl's Own" (expurgated) Shakespeare, 219

censorship. *See* freedom of press; freedom of speech

Chartism: as premier working-class political movement, 6, 76, 78; but interwoven with free press struggle, 70, 82, 341n.7; Chartist Shakespeare worship, 112; "monster" petitions to parliament, 121; Secularist inheritance, 124, 351n.96. *See also* Shakespeare, William; Shelley, Percy Bysshe

cheap press: in 1840s and after, 78–90; in 1880s and after, 139–40, 148; as "unstamped," illegal "pauper press," 78–80; flair and ingenuity of, 341n.3; the cheap press as "blasphemy," 79, 81–82; government animus against, 83–84; idiom of, 248; the slogan "Knowledge is Power," 10, 80, 84, 122; cheap publication as blasphemy against Literature, 106; and high price of books, 84; coincidence of low cost and "gross purpose," 84–85; Secular Book Depot, 89; Watts's *Literary Annual,* 89–90; origins of Rationalist Press Association, 90; book clubs and paperbacks, 90. *See also* Bible, Holy; Carlile, Richard; copyright; Dickens, Charles; Foote, G. W.; freedom of press; *Freethinker, The;* Hetherington, Henry; "Higher Critcism"; Holyoake, George Jacob; Hone, William; literacy; Moxon, Edward; piracy; Society for the Diffusion of Useful Knowledge; "taxes on knowledge"; Tegg, Thomas

Church of England: corrupt condition before 1834, 19–20; but social prestige of, 20; neglect of poor, 21; bishops burnt in effigy, 20; political parsons, 20; clerical magistrates, 20; and "Peterloo Massacre," 63, 64 fig. 4; in Pooley case, 298, 302, 305; church rates, refused by Carlile, 73 fig. 5; ecclesiastical courts, and heresy, 170–71,

285; and sex crimes, 362n.11; Church of England state privileges, "Articles and Formularies," 170; Anglican exclusiveness of law of blasphemy, 16–17; clerical "celebrity," 300–302. *See also* Arnold, Thomas; Butler, Samuel

circulating libraries: covert censorship of "tradesman" Mudie, 9, 12, 183, 188, 221, 330n.10, 365n.38; and literary mediocrity, 330n.10; Mudie targeted in court, 1883, 154, 199; likewise W. H. Smith, 12, 154, 374n.14. *See also* Moore, George

class: and nineteenth-century history, 21; assumptions of Carlile prosecution, 62; and language, terms of judgment, 117–18; and classification, at base of language, 120–21. *See also* Coleridge, John Duke; 1880s; euphemism; Foote, G. W.; *Freethinker, The;* Holyoake, George Jacob; Lawrence, D. H.; property

Cleave, John: as *Poor Man's Guardian* volunteer, 83; evader of press restrictions, 341n.10; piratical publisher, 108; cooperator, 124

Clifford, W. K.: as linguistic model for Secularists, 264; early death, 264; tombstone's "almost sacred" words, 267

Cobbett, William, 19; invents "twopenny trash," 22, 79; *Political Register,* 26; on "vulgarity," literacy, in "Letter to the Bishop of Landaff," 74–75, 79; on language, 243; on the phrase "swinish multitude," 295

Cockney: vilification by R. L. Stevenson, 287, 292, 375n.26; shared knowingness of rhyming slang, 220; Cockney anti-euphemism, 364n.33. *See also* Bradlaugh, Charles; Coleridge, John Duke; Dickens, Charles; Gissing, George; Hardy, Thomas; Kipling, Rudyard; music hall; Salvation Army

Coleridge, John Duke, Lord (Lord Chief Justice): parliamentary and legal career, 152; as critic and bibliophile, 191–92, 193, 359n.27, 359n.29; and literary family, 192; and Wordsworth industry, 192; on Tichbourne case and Cockney vulgarity, 120; loss of faith, 192–93; and conduct of Voysey heresy trial, 192, 360n.32; need for

Coleridge, John Duke (*continued*)
  authority, 192–94; in Literature, 199–200;
    friendship with, influence of, Arnold, 192,
    194, 360n.35; defense of "reverence" in,
    203; interest in *Freethinker* case, 152; lib-
    eral conduct of, 144, 152; criticized, 152–
    53; praise of Foote, 154; momentous rul-
    ing, 7–8, 16, 93; and literature, "manner,"
    class, "feeling," 93, 159–62, 197, 361n.44;
    master-term of "decency" in, 93, 212–13,
    228, 280; ruling criticized, 160–61, 200;
    but supported by legal revisionism, 161; re-
    examined in literary terms, 199–202; the
    ruling as euphemism, 221; Coleridge pre-
    vents fourth trial, 153; softens prison condi-
    tions, 147, 238; as friend of Hardy, 296–
    97, 306; as prosecutor in Pooley case,
    296–97, 298, 302–3, 310; class, emotional,
    impact of scandal, criticisms, 305–6
Coleridge, John Taylor (judge): best known
    for literary tastes, 192; as *Quarterly* editor,
    192; conduct, scandal, of Pooley case, 297,
    298, 302–3, 304, 309–10; undermines aura
    of "Christlike" gentleness, 305; retirement,
    306
Coleridge, Samuel Taylor: caricatured by
    Hone, 27; and Coleridge family circle,
    192; on language, 205; theological sense
    of, 223; on Bible as linguistic "holdfast,"
    254
Collins, Wilkie: and Bible parody in *The
    Moonstone*, 181–82, 187, 188
"Comic Bible" cartoons. See *Freethinker, The;*
    Taxil, Leo
common law. See law
Conrad, Joseph: conflation of euphemism and
    blasphemy, in *Heart of Darkness*, 270
cooperation: and community, among blas-
    phemy martyrs, 123; their prominence in
    Cooperative movement, 123–24. See also
    Carpenter, William; Cleave, John; Hether-
    ington, Henry; Holyoake, George Jacob
copyright: from 1810s to 1840s, in relation to
    blasphemy, 98–109, 346n.47; in eigh-
    teenth century, 99, 345n.39; perpetual,
    107; as patrimonial right, 99; as security
    against circulation of literature, 98; and
    undeserving mass, 108; cancelled by blas-
    phemy, or charge of, 99–100; idea of the

"non-book," 100; acts, debates, 1808–1836,
    345n.39, 345n.40; failed bills of 1837–1841,
    99; 1842 Act, proposed by Mahon, 99;
    modified, 105–6, 107; copyright and
    Moxon case, 91, 104–9. See also Byron,
    George Gordon, Lord; forgery; Macaulay,
    Thomas Babington; Shelley, Percy Bysshe;
    Talfourd, Thomas Noon; Tegg, Thomas;
    Wordsworth, William
Corelli, Marie: *Barrabas* as Bible melodrama,
    174–75; and anti-Semitism, 113, 173,
    357n.8; and obsession with blasphemy,
    174–75
Cruikshank, George: relationship to Dickens,
    56–57; mentored by Hone, 57–60; repudi-
    ation of parodies, 60; illustrations for, 57,
    63, 64 fig.4, 143; and for *Every-Day Book*,
    57, 336n.55; "Bank Restriction Note," 118,
    349n.79; presence at trials, 57; life marked
    by friendship with Hone, 60; pictured
    with, 58 fig. 3
culture: reform and education as threats to,
    128–29; *Punch* cartoons, 128, 131 fig. 10; as
    determinant of acceptable language, 157;
    as fake "culchaw," 14; in blasphemy prose-
    cution and threats of, 165–66. See also
    Arnold, Matthew; Salvation Army

Darwin, Charles: on origin, evolution, of lan-
    guage, 223, 365n.42; on its acquisition in
    childhood, 222, 223, 365n.39; language not
    exclusively human, 366n.45; psychoso-
    matic price of own stylistic clarity, 264
decency. See obscenity
Defoe, Daniel: *Robinson Crusoe* as forgery,
    181–82; as parody Bible, in Wilkie Col-
    lins's *Moonstone*, 181–82, 187; *Crusoe* and
    Carlile trial, 181–82; in Secularist jokes,
    182; *Shortest Way with the Dissenters*, un-
    read irony of, 184
Deism: and blasphemers before 1840, 21. See
    also Paine, Thomas
Denman, Thomas (Chief Justice): conduct of
    Hetherington trial, 84–85, 92, 159; on ridi-
    cule in, 37; conduct of Moxon trial, 97–
    98; dedicatee of Talfourd tragedy, 97; on
    paradox of the "private opinion," 231, 233
Dickens, Charles: relationship to George
    Cruikshank, 56–60; connection with and

career parallels to William Hone, 10, 51–
60, 336n.48; attends Hone's deathbed, 58–
59; caricatures funeral, 59; overlap of
Hone, Dickens, literary circles, 56; urban
inspiration, 51–52; *Every-Day Book* as gold-
mine for method, materials, 52–53, 335–
36n.47; Dickens's copy, 53; Dickens and
"innocent" pleasure, laughter, 37, 54; as
cautious parodist, 54–55; warned against irreligion, 54; anti-clericalism, 181; Bible reverence, 250, 336n.51; charged with vulgarity, 54; and abuse of fiction's socio-critical
"license," 191, 359n.26; popularity *v.* critical contempt, 55; dedicates *Pickwick* to
Talfourd, 98–99; blasphemy and euphemistic avoidance in *Oliver Twist*, 55–56,
336n.52, 364n.22; standard English in, 321;
Hone as bookseller in, 56; other Hone influences on, 336n.53, 336n.57; Hone as
Copperfield's Micawber, 57–58; Dickensian
comic Cockney, 166; Bakhtinian "double-
voicedness" in *Little Dorrit*, 38, 54–55; euphemism in, 216–17; linguistic commentary, parody, in *Hard Times*, 217, 265;
Podsnappery in *Our Mutual Friend*, 93;
and the *OED*, 362n.5; the Shakespearean
trace in *Great Expectations*, 112. *See also*
Cruikshank, George; *Every-Day Book*;
Talfourd, Thomas Noon; Tegg, Thomas

Dugdale, William. *See* pornographers

Du Maurier, George: as "kindly cynical" cartoonist, 178; art of verbal pit- and pratfalls, 218; "nice, clean English," 279,
374n.18; "idealist" romance of *Trilby*, 280;
Svengali, "derisive laughter of," 285; class
concerns, 288

Eaton, Isaac Daniel: prosecuted for "Third
Part" of the *Age of Reason*, 61, 158, 336–
37n.58; publisher of populist *Hog's Wash*,
295–96

education. *See* literacy

1880s: neglected transitional decade, 9; class
and cultural unrest in, 128–29, 130 fig. 9,
131 fig. 10; and "heroic" Secularism, 129;
refined taboo on laughter in, 178; biblical
forgeries in, 180; bibliomania of, 193; as
watershed for language, philology, 204,
222; as golden era of euphemism, 206,

215–16, 218, 221, 231; pornographic renaissance in, 208–9; taboo on sexuality in,
214; bowdlerization in, 219; 1880s crisis of
language, signification, 255–68. *See also*
statutes

Eliot, George: as moral teacher, 173–74; as
translator of Strauss, 83–84, 174; anti-
biblical animus of *Middlemarch*, 181; Eliot
on Jacob Holyoake, 186; her anti-populist
impulse, 358n.17; "Religion of Christ,"
273. *See also* "Higher Criticism"

Eliot, T. S.: on genuine *v.* modern (secular)
blasphemy, in *After Strange Gods*, 2, 277;
urban tones of *The Wasteland*, 322–23; dislike of "blasphemer" Hardy, 323, 326; support for Kipling, 323; Marie Lloyd, 323;
on the *Lady Chatterley* case, 325

Ellenborough, Edward Law (Chief Justice): as
butt of Hone's satire, 27, 34; seeks courtroom revenge, 28, 32; conduct of case, issue of parody, 32–36, 41; attempts to
block defense, quotations, jury deliberation on Hone's "intentions," 199, 228,
361n.42; outwitted, 34, 198

Erskine, Thomas (judge): and Holyoake case,
117–18; on "reverence," 92; "law" of "decency," 212; impact of 1797 *Age of Reason*
trial, 92–93

Essays and Reviews: ecclesiastical trials for heresy, 156–57; as offense against Bible, 170–
71; against language, divine theories of,
223; Jowett on Bible in, 197; advised to
"Get it done and let them howl," 284

euphemism: and fear of language, 215–30; destined noonday of 1880s, 206, 215–16, 218;
and prudery, 215–16; as "lip purity," 217,
236; and class anxiety, inflation, abstraction, 216, 217–18; and Latinisms, Norman
French, 205; and expurgation (of books),
218–19; in 1880s, 219; necessary to sacred
status of Literature, 219; euphemism and
"naked language," 220–21; in 1880s, 221;
and motif of linguistic "veiling," 221–22,
230; and community "face," in linguistic
theory, 222; and divine theories of language, 222–24; sacred fear of, 224–25; and
ritualized oaths in, 225–26; euphemism's
demand for blasphemy, 206, 215, 229; as
blasphemy's opposite, 9; etymologically

euphemism (*continued*)
and structurally, 226; the terms "Secularism," "agnosticism" as euphemisms, 240, 369n.74; redefinition, "dilution," of "high words," 254; weak alternatives to "Bible English," 254–55; decadent redescent into euphemism in 1890s, 266; euphemism and death, 266–67; legal euphemism, 221, 365n.37; "euphuism" as euphemism, 366n.54. *See also* Alford, Henry; Bible, Holy; blasphemy; Bowdler, Thomas; Cockney; Dickens, Charles; Hardy, Thomas; Holyoake, George Jacob; Hone's parodies; Meredith, George; music hall; plain speech; Respectabilty; silence; Stead, W. T.; Stephen, Leslie; Wilde, Oscar

Every-Day Book, The: overview, 25, 30–31; "originality" and "vernacular character," 51–52; serial publication, 1825, 52–53, 55, 84, 335–36n.47, 336n.57; mixed audience, close relationship with, 52–53, 54; succeeded by *Table* and *Year* Books, 52–53; as "antidote" to parodies' "bane," 53; taken over by Thomas Tegg, 53; reprinted 1878, 185; inspiration for S.D.U.K., *Penny Magazine*, 88. *See also* Cruikshank, George; Dickens, Charles

Farrar, Frederic (Dean): popular *Chapters on Language*, 204, 266; secular vision of, 223
Feuerbach, Ludwig. *See* "Higher Criticism"
Finlay, Thomas: "Scotch" trial for blasphemy, 15, 123; "gagging," 234, 368n.68
Foote, G. W.: overview, 3, 7–9, 135–36, 319; character and early career, 135–37, 353n.14; and "polite," "scholarly" style, 137; Foote as Secularist lecturer, 136–37; "playful imagination," 137; doomed co-editorship of *The Secularist*, with Jacob Holyoake, 133, 153, 249, 355n.36; edits *Liberal*, 166,187; literary gifts, 176–77; Shakespeare worship, 176–77, 202; literary friendships, 186–88; Foote as N.S.S. Vice-President, 137; President, 136, 203; rift with Bradlaugh, 137, 213; but joins the "Bradlaugh struggle," launching the *Freethinker*, 137, 143; its task of "purging satire," 139; Foote the martyr, 4 fig. 1; ambition overemphasized, 144; real conditions and price of imprisonment, 144, 146–47, 150, 152–53, 203, 238–40, 354n.26; Foote as populist vulgarian, 127, 137; as literary critic, 127; who rejects literature-as-dogma, 177; Foote's "Bible-smashing," 172–73, 175–81, 182, 187–88, 277, 286–87, 363n.15; literary methods of, 175–81; as parodic "decomposition," 179–81; the *Freethinker* trials: overview, 7, 143–66; prosecution as anti-Bradlaugh plot, 17, 143–44, 148, 149; as assault on bourgeois mores, Respectability, 126, 147–48; private action, 146 fig. 15, 148–49, 229; first indictment, 149; "hot" Christmas number, 149; and parody, 180; separately prosecuted, 149, 150; and first tried, 150; twice, 150; charges of "obscenity" by press, public, government, 208–10; vulnerability of two "hot" items, 210–15; courtroom slurs, 212, 236–37; "excessive" sentences, 150; curtailment of reporting, 236; Foote's response to sentence, 150; punishment by silencing, 238–40; hostile and muffled press coverage, 150–52, 236; class sneers in, 151; Foote's attempts to delay third trial, 152; climactic speech at, 7–8, 154–56, 159–60; applauded, 8–9, 127, 154; reads literary quotations in court, 154–55, 160, 198–99; charges discrimination against "penny" blasphemy, 127, 155–56; against plain speech, 127, 156, 159–60; argues against literary redefinition of blasphemy, 197, 202–3; trial's hung verdict, 152; but remission refused, 153; despite support of literary men, 177; Foote confirmed as subliterary scapegoat, 202–3, 297; post-acquittal inuendoes, 213–14; lifelong marginalization, 203; later threats of repeat prosecution, 16; Foote on the fear of words, 225; desacralization, translation, of "Bible English," 250–53, 256, 258, 317; attempts to revitalize language, 261–62; failure of, 266; edits *Progress*, 151–52, 203; Foote as snob, 13; and outlaw archetype, 13; claims Hardy as Freethinker, 327; admiration of *Jude*, 327; *Bible Handbook*, 172, 286; *Bible Heroes*, 190; *Bible Romances*, 189–90, 262; *Heroes and Martyrs of Freethought*, 71, 338n.73; memoir *Prisoner for Blasphemy*, 3, 8, 9, 144, 152, 198, 240, 262.

See also blasphemy; Coleridge, John Duke, Lord; *Freethinker, The;* Hardy, Thomas; *Jude the Obscure;* Kemp, Henry; martyrdom; Meredith, George; *Oxford English Dictionary;* plain speech; Ramsey, W. J.; Salvation Army; Sharman, Reverend; Shaw, George Bernard; Tyler, Henry; Varley, Henry

forgery: and economic anxiety, 118–20, 349n.81; and "coining," 120, 350n.82; and parody, 46, 180; and Christopher Marlowe, atheist, 120, 350n.84; and Hone and Cruikshanks's "Bank Restriction Note," 118, 349n.79; of Shakespeare manuscripts, folio, 112, 348n.67; and terms of language, blasphemy judgment, 118–20; and Bible, in 1880s, 180; the blasphemer as human forgery, impostor, 49–50; provisions for civil disablement, 49–50. See also *Apocryphal New Testament;* copyright; Defoe, Daniel; illegality; parody; piracy

Foucault, Michel: on transgression, 7; "disciplinary" and "normalizing" law, 8, 49, 239; authority, 169; free speech of the executee, 178; language and philology, 204, 222–23, 259, 264–65; sexuality and silence, 206, 230

freedom of press: threatened 1817, 22; in case of Hone, 22–39; in case of Carlile, 63, 65; and relation to Chartism, 82; as "license" and "prostitution," 210; censorship and concepts of "publishing," 65, 232; and Carlile's volunteers, 69–70. *See also* Bradlaugh, Charles; cheap press; Foote, G. W.; freedom of speech; Holyoake, George Jacob; Lawrence, D. H.; Secularism; silence; Woolf, Virginia

freedom of speech: as "reckless ruffianism," in Pooley case, 305. *See also* Foote, G. W.; Holyoake, George Jacob; martyrdom; self-representation; silence; Taylor, Robert

Freethinker, The: as response to "Bradlaugh struggle," 17, 137, 353n.15; as "blasphemous" forerunner to tabloid newspapers, 139–40; title, 122; "outspeaking" in, 137, 229–30; plain speech in, 138, 154–56, 160; signed articles in, 139; the forbidden weapon of ridicule, 137–39; "Profane Jokes," linguistic methods of, 253; Cockney offensiveness, 252–53; and Secularist community, 138; "Sacred Advertisements," 287–88; lasting success, 140; notorious "Comic Bible" cartoons," 140–43, 141 fig. 11, 142 fig. 12, 149, 177; changes from *La bible amusante,* 140, 142, 178–79; offensive visualization in, 143; assault on Bible text, inspiration, 140–42, 141 fig. 11, 142 fig. 12, 178–79; as subversive laughter, 177–81. *See also* anti-Semitism; Butler, Samuel; Foote, G. W.; Joyce, James; *Punch;* Taxil, Leo; Ward, Mrs. Humphry

French Revolution: as motive for upper-class piety, 20–21; for lower-class unbelief, 21. See also *Age of Reason, The*

Freud, Sigmund: and Wolfman case, blasphemy, 142, 245, 326; and obscenity, cigars, 215; and language, philology, 223; *Fruits of Philosophy, The. See* birth control

Gay News: 1977 trial of editor Dennis Lemon, 16, 98; prejudice as motive in, 161, 367n.59; private prosecution by Mary Whitehouse, 229

Giffard, Sir Hardinge: as Bradlaugh foe, 150; as prosecutor in *Freethinker* trials, 150; suggestive courtroom slurs, 210, 212, 236–37

Gifford, Robert (Attorney-General): in case of Richard Carlile, 62, 67, 68

Gifford, William. See *Quarterly Review*

Gissing, George: admiration of Foote, 166; until trial for blasphemy, 166; Foote influence suppressed, 168; Cockney-bashing and fear of language, 166–67, 279; rewarded with warm reviews, 167; Bradlaugh-bashing, 168, 356n.51; "mockery" in *Born in Exile,* 285; offensive counterpoint in, 272; compare *Jude the Obscure,* 272; remunerative Latinisms, in *The Private Papers of Henry Ryecroft,* 290; Gissing on Hardy's "peasant" "coarseness," 295

Gladstone, William Ewart: 1880s administration, troubled, 129; on affirmation and toleration, 135; on state religion, 20; as defender of Scripture, 172; on *Robert Elsmere* and Christian psychology, 167–68, 272; on *Elsmere's* "compensations," 280; on Secularists' "questionable" *Manual of Songs and Ceremonies,* 266

Gosse, Edmund: high-literary *Father and Son*, 201; enacts Literature's ascendancy over Bible, 201; as bowdlerizer of Swinburne, 219; friendship-straining review of *Jude the Obscure*, 278; as Hardy confidant, 282–83

Gott, J. W.: three "stretches" for blasphemy, 16, 331n.19; jokes in *God v. Gott* and *Rib-Ticklers, or, Questions for Parsons*, 16, 285; cartoons, 354n.23; vulgarity, 160; imprisonment and death, 16, 146; and obscenity, official secrets, 362n.12

Haggard, Rider: on resuturing of words and things, Zulu, Saxon, 261–62, 373n.118

Hale, Matthew: 1676 ruling, "Hale's law," 18, 227; denied 1917, 200, 361n.43; based on mistranslation, 201

Harcourt, Sir William (Home Secretary): thwarted desire to prosecute Foote, 148, 149; for obscenity, 209; accusations of same against *Freethinker*, 213–14; refuses to mitigate sentences, 161, 203, 214; exacerbates conditions of imprisonment, 239, 368–69n.72; acts against Salvation Army, 165

Hardy, Thomas: overview, 11, 12, 13; labeled "heretic" by Chesterton, 278, 309; on reviewers' "privilege," 271; personal scrapbook, celebrity interviews, 269; as evidence of overconfidence, 280–82, 281 fig. 19; refuses role of cultural standard-bearer, 284; snobbery and denial of origins, 295; suspicion of Arnoldian "hair-splitting," language, 253; lifelong urge to plain speech, bad language, 288–91, 295; explicitness in *The Poor Man and the Lady*, 288, 290; "coarseness" in *Desperate Remedies*, 288; "cussing" in *A Pair of Blue Eyes*, 289; and *The Trumpet Major*, 289–90; "unhealthy" language in *Far from the Madding Crowd*, 289; *The Hand of Ethelberta*, 289–90; and problem model of Defoe's *Crusoe*, 181; and swearing in, 289–90, 294, 320; *Two on a Tower*, reviewers' suspicions of, 280, 286; *The Woodlanders*, and the word "blasphemy" in, 277; *The Mayor of Casterbridge*, trace of blasphemy in, 286; comic euphemism in, 294; Hardy on euphemism as principle of civilization,

dogma, 217, 253; hostile reception of *Tess of the D'Urbervilles*, 271, 290–91, 295; its "improper explicitness," 290–91; demonic and anti-biblical imagery, scenes, 274, 313; dialect and "modern" language in, 320, 322; "mutilation" of serial text, 375n.30; differences from *Jude*, 280, 281, 282, 283, 294; success of *Tess* allows risk-taking, 282; the essay "Candour in English Fiction," "explicit" agenda of, 279, 290; and other essays on fiction, language, 319–20; Hardy's motives for abandoning the novel, 290; knowledge of Pooley case, 296–97; from John Duke Coleridge, 296–97, 306; from *Saturday Review*, local press, local memory, 306–10; in Cornwall, 308–9, 311–12; personal links to G. W. Foote, 319, 327; linguistic and philological associations of, 319; "The Dorsetshire Labourer," 296; *Life and Work*, 278, 285, 295–96. *See also* Carlile, Richard; Coleridge, John Duke; Eliot, T. S.; Foote, G. W.; Gosse, Edmund; Joyce, James; *Jude the Obscure*; Lawrence, D. H.; literature; Meredith, George; novel; Stephen, Leslie

Haslam, C. J.: indicted *Letters to the Clergy*, 37, 83; offensive cheapness of, 84–85; power of perversion overemphasized, 85; "sincerity" in, 92; "shocking" language in, 93, 236; Bible-smashing literalism of, 170, 180. *See also* Hetherington, Henry

Hennell, Charles Christian. *See* "Higher Criticism"

Hetherington, Henry: championship of the cheap and "unstamped" press, 10, 79–84, 88–89, 155; and working-class literacy, 84–90, 108–9; *The Poor Man's Guardian*, 78–84, 86, 89, 120, 124; theatrical conduct of, 78, 80–81; *Guardian's* assault on "Abuses of Religion," 81–82; Hetherington indicted, tried, for blasphemy of Haslam's *Letters*, 37, 83–85, 92–93, 228; argues cheap publication the real crime, 84, 155; scale of his printing operations, 89, 343–44n.26; tests law by indicting Moxon, 90–92, 104, 106; Hetherington as "insect" "abuser of the press," 95, 97; pirates *Queen Mab*, 104; blasphemes against Literature, 106, 108–9; assists Southwell at

trial, 123; as cooperator, 124; on "Bible Obscenity," 211, 363n.17; Secularist model of
his will and funeral, 267; co-opted by Holyoake, 125–26. *See also* cheap press; Haslam, C. J.; Moxon, Edward; Society for
the Diffusion of Useful Knowledge; Talfourd, Thomas Noon; Taylor, Robert
"Higher Criticism": greater impact than Darwinism, 256; "reverence" of English strain,
especially Hennell's *Inquiry Concerning
the Origin of Christianity,* 92, 173–74;
Strauss's *Life of Jesus* in Chapman edition,
83; immune to prosecution, 83, 156;
though refused *Times* advertising space,
84; but at threat when put out in cheap
numbers, 83; mock rebuttal by Butler,
184; Renan's *Vie de Jésus,* 170; outcry
against Seeley's *Ecce Homo,* 170–71;
against Voysey's *The Sling and the Stone,*
171. *See also* Arnold, Matthew; Bible,
Holy; Butler, Samuel; Eliot, George; *Essays and Reviews*
Holyoake, George Jacob: overview, 6, 11; Holyoake and the oath, 50; services to education and cheap publication, 109–10, 243–
44; to free press, 83; first R.P.A. president,
109; early life, 110; joins, repudiates Chartists, 110, 126; on mathematics as "language," 264; as "Social Missionary," 110,
114; resigns, 114; defends, edits *Oracle of
Reason,* 110, 114, 349n.72, 349n.74; Cheltenham lecture and arrest, 114–16; trial,
114–21, 124–25, 232–33, 235–36, 349n.73;
indicted words, 115, 117, 349n.76; claim to
"his own" language, 114–15; to "unlimited
freedom of expression," 115; hostile press,
115, 117; class vilification by, 121; "convicted of uttering language," 118–19,
349n.77; imprisonment, 118, 339n.82,
349n. 78; death of daughter, cost of martyrdom, 118, 119 fig. 7, 349n.78; edits
Movement and *Reasoner,* 110, 248, 347n.63;
careful language of, 137, 229, 298; Holyoake as "Father" of Cooperativism, 123–
24, 235–36; of Secularism, 124–26; as
"pet" of "all respectables of society," 124–
26, 125 fig. 8; and "intelligence franchise,"
126; reverence for George Eliot, G. H.
Lewes, 186, 358n.17, 358n.19; earnestness,

37, 92; coins euphemisms for "blasphemy," 240; coins term "Secularism,"
240; linguistic conversion to Respectability, 240–49; begins in silencing, 241; creates prison obsession with words, "composition," 241–42, 247 fig. 17; pride in,
claim to language power, 241–43, 245; restored by writing Oddfellow lectures,
242–43; "ultra-radical" *Practical Grammar,*
243, 244, 370n.86; and other word books,
success of, 243; new concern for "tact,"
"politeness," in, 244–45; chastening by the
"law" in language, 245–46, 249; move
from criminal speech to "correct" writing,
print, 246–48; repudiation of Foote, linguistic, 152, 153–54, 249, 355n.36, 355n.37;
charges *Freethinker* with "violence and obscenity," 210; rival journal *Present Day,*
133, 265, 268; defers to "Bible English,"
249–50; laments inadequate secular "literature of the grave," 267; campaigns for release, pardon, of Thomas Pooley, 298–
300, 299 fig. 20, 303–4, 310; and advances
own claim to language, respectability,
298–300, 376n.40; rift with Bradlaugh,
National Reformer, 134, 353n.13; "Cabinet
of Reason," 109, 344n.27; *The Case of
Thomas Pooley,* 298; urbane style in, 298–
300, 376n.40; *Child's Word Book,* 243; *History of Cooperation,* 112; *History of the Last
Trial for Atheism,* 11, 115, 240–41; euphemistic rewritings of, 241; *The Logic of
Facts,* 109, 118–19; *Paley Refuted in His
Own Words,* 242, 248; *Rudiments of Public
Speaking,* 244; *Self-Help by the People,* 124;
Skin, Baths, Bathing, and Soap, 244. *See
also* Chartism; cooperation; Eliot, George;
Foote, G. W.; Kingsley, Charles; *Oxford
English Dictionary;* Owenism; Secularism;
Smiles, Samuel; Southwell, Charles; Vizetelly, Henry
Hone, William: overview, 10; and religion, Bi-
ble, 30–31; in Hone family punishment,
30; revenged in parodies, 30; Bible's role
in later "conversion," 31; Hone's political
times, 21–22; Hone as government target,
22; to be "crushed," 28–29; for *Reformist's
Register,* 26; for biblical parodies, 26–27,
332n.16; inventiveness of, 26–27; "cru-

Hone, William (*continued*)
  dity," 26; political pedigree of, 31–32;
  Hone as threat to literary "purity," 24–26,
  41; mixes literature and politics, 25; MS
  collector Lawly on Hone's "dual" life, 25,
  41; three trials of, 24–39; as public event,
  32; as comic carnival, 7, 32–34; literary
  event, 29–30, 333n.22; Hone speaks in
  own defense, 28–29; quotes parodies in
  court, 198–99; despite judges' protests,
  199; protests "gags" and silencing, 238; assists Richard Carlile, 67, 338n.72; as conscious "martyr," 24, 29–30; courage of,
  28; acquittal of, 32, 34; subscription for,
  24–25; friendship of Rev. Parr, 25, 40,
  333n.23; branded "arch blasphemer," 25,
  31; by brother Joseph, 334n.39; publishes
  Three Trials, 34, 39, 112; Hone repressed,
  misrepresented, by critics, 25–26; by biographer Hackwood, 25; Hone's "History of
  Parody," genesis, 39–40; as model for
  study of popular literature, 40–41; radical
  view of language, 243; but later anxiety
  about "vulgarity," 340n.91; Hone's hand
  in S.D.U.K. *Penny Magazine,* 88; and educative instincts, 335n.46; bankruptcy, 40–
  41, 53; Hone's place in publishing history
  22–26; pirate editions of Southey, Byron,
  100–101, 345n.42; "unmasks" latter's publisher, blasphemy, 101; antiquarian instincts, 41; restored to memory in 1870s,
  25, 185. See also *Apocryphal New Testament, The;* Bentham, Jeremy; Bible, Holy;
  Butler, Dr. Samuel; Butler, Samuel; Byron, George Gordon, Lord; Carlile, Richard; Cruikshank, George; Dickens,
  Charles; Ellenborough, Edward Law;
  Every-Day Book, The; forgery; Hardy,
  Thomas; Hone's parodies; Hunt, John;
  Lamb, Charles; martyrs; parody; Place,
  Francis; Routledge, James; Society for the
  Diffusion of Useful Knowledge; Tegg,
  Thomas; transcripts
Hone's parodies: frontispiece to 1827 collec-
  tion, 58 fig. 3; *Buonaparte-phobia* (1815),
  26; *The Late John Wilkes's Catechism*
  (1817), 24, 26, 31, 38; read in court, 32–33,
  236; as critique of euphemism, 35; *The Po-
  litical Litany* (1817), 24, 26; charged as "se-

ditious libel," 31; bookseller persecuted
  for, 36–37; as vulgar subliterature, 38, 107;
  The Sinecurist's Creed (1817), 24; as Trinitarian satire, 26–27; *The Bullet Te Deum*
  (1817), 27, 38; *The Political House That
  Jack Built* (1819), 37, 63, 64 fig. 4, 103;
  The Man in the Moon (1820), 23 fig. 2, 39;
  The Political Showman (1821), 39
Hunt, Henry ("Orator"): close relationship to
  Carlile, 63, 74; *imitatio Christi,* 74; and
  traditional radicalism, 81
Hunt, John: as Hone's friend and supporter,
  28; as editor of *Yellow Dwarf,* 28; as publisher of Byron's *Don Juan,* 101; libel conviction for *Vision of Judgement,* 104
Hunt, Leigh: and protests against prosecutions of 1810s, 22, 74; and Dickens circle,
  56; as literary expurgator, 219
Huxley, Thomas Henry: quoted by Foote in
  court, 155, 264; as secular linguistic model,
  264; but immune to prosecution, 156;
  coins term "agnosticism," 240, 263; revives
  term "bibliolatry," 172; defends Freethought *v.* obscenity charge, 213; published in *Agnostic Annual,* 89; in R.P.A.
  "Thinker's Library," 90. See also agnosticism; Rationalist Press Association

"Iconoclast." *See* Bradlaugh, Charles
illegality: in nineteenth-century blasphemy
  cases, 50; Carlile raids, thefts, 68. *See also*
  forgery
impostordom. *See* forgery
information, *ex officio:* anachronistic proceeding, 27; use for repression, 27–28; against
  Hone, 27–28; punitive cost of, 28
Ingersoll, Colonel Robert: on blasphemy, 7;
  debates Bible with Gladstone, 172;
  charged with obscenity, 213; stylistic temp-
  tations of, 267

James, Henry: blasphemy in *The Turn of the
  Screw,* 270, 373–74n.4
Jowett, Benjamin. See *Essays and Reviews*
Joyce, James: and vulgarity, parody, 180;
  "rogueword"-play, 324–25; in *Freethinker*
  style, 324–25; likelier source than Taxil's
  Vie de Jésus, 324. See also Swinburne, Al-
  gernon Charles; Woolf, Virginia

Jude the Obscure: as fictional blasphemy, 269–327; summary of offenses, 270–71; as novel of faith and doubt, 271–72; offensive context of, 11; critical outrage at, 269, 271, 272, 278, 279, 283–85, 292, 326–27; burned by bishop, 274, 284–85; charge of obscenity, 270; class terms of criticism, 295; graffiti writing on walls, 202; the name "Biblioll College," 272; the phrase "Save-your-own-soulism," 273, 373n.12; *Jude*'s pathology of religion, 272–73; offensive *imitatio Christi,* 272–73; staged scenes of burning, 274; blasphemous scenes of worship, 274–76; Shelleyan reference in, 274, 307; the *Age of Reason* in, 307; offensive music hall echoes, 275; parody of Ten Commandments, 276–77, 320; ambiguous Bible citation, 278; intrusion of the word "blasphemy," 277; conscious commission of crime, traditionally conceived, 277–78; confrontational failure of fictional alibis, 278–84; offensive claim to plain speech, 278–79, 291–95; decried by critics, 292; "mutilation" of serial text, 282, 291–92, 375n.30; did not palliate critics, 292; threat to readers' values, 292; offense of female heresy, 282–83; self-conscious uneasiness, 283; lack of pastoral charm, 283; rebuked by critics, 283–84; *Freethinker* parallels, influences, 284–88; including phrases, names, 286; and offensive commercial jokes, wordplay, 286–88; "levity" disgusts critics, bishop, 284–85; "mocking" Sue cuts up Testament, 285; the hero's progress in sneering, 285–86; "obscurity" v. "explicitness" in fiction, language, 288–95; Sue's crime of "reticence," euphemism, 292–93; *Jude*'s refusal of token speech, 293–95; *Jude* as offense against English, 294–95; as revenge on literary class system, 295–96; real-life models for anti-hero: atheist uncle, Horace Moule, 296, 306–7, 319, 376n.37; but close reminiscence of Pooley case, 309–16; in emphasis on graffiti, 312–14; and tragic theatricality, 315–16; bibliomania in *Jude the Obscure,* 313–15, 317–18; *Jude* and Job, 317–18; and the lower-class voice, 316–17, 377n.52; limitations on, silencing, 317–18;

martyrdom, 318–19; modern language in *Jude,* 319–27; mixed utterance, in, 320; dialect in, 320–21; urban slang, Cockney, in, 279, 321–22; language of modernity, railway, in, 322–23. *See also* Gissing, George; Hardy, Thomas; Kipling, Rudyard; novel; Pooley, Thomas; Stephen, Leslie; Swinburne, Algernon Charles; Ward, Mrs. Humphry

juries: "packed" (corrupt) "special" juries 32; at Carlile trials, 67; at Hone trials, 32, 333n.26. *See also* libel; self-representation

Keats, John: applauds William Hone, 24; sonnet "Nebuchadnezzar's Dream," 24; on Carlile trials, 67, 69, 340n.89

Kemp, Henry: as *Freethinker* printer, replacing Whittle, 149; three-month sentence, 150; no mitigation of, 214

Kingsley, Charles: *Alton Locke* as "literary garbage," 183; hero modeled on Chartist-atheist Thomas Cooper, 82; *Hypatia,* 174; objects to Holyoake, 186

Kipling, Rudyard: and "cockney 'Gawd,'" in *Plain Tales from the Hills,* 269, 373n.2; manly/imperial blasphemy, in *The Light That Failed,* 373n.3; linguistic "experiments" of, 322; as "hooligan" blasphemer, 323, 330n.13. *See also* Eliot, T. S.

Knight, Charles. *See* Society for the Diffusion of Useful Knowledge

Lacan, Jacques: on matrix of language, 215, 221, 222; priority of, 259; language and the "law of the father," 241, 245–46

Lamb, Charles: dedicatee of *The Every-Day Book,* 25; connection suppressed, 107; blackballed for "levity," 37; as literary saint, 107–8; letters bowdlerized by executor Talfourd, 219, 347n.56, 364n.29

language: philological, linguistic, watershed of 1880s, 204–7; birth of psycholinguistics, 222, 365n.39, 365n.40; divine, Romantic theories of language, 222–24, 366n.44; survival to late century, 223; theorized in *Mind,* 222, 224, 366n.48; Protestant logocentrism, 226; Derrida on, 259; language and power, 121; and class, "dress," 243–44; and/as democracy, 244, 367n.58; radical

language (*continued*)
  grammars and "Bad Alphabets," 243, 246;
  Sayce's *Science of Language,* 204, 206, 246;
  and language as law, 241, 245–46; as *Volksstimme,* 205; and nation, English, 205; English as "universal" language, 9, 206; as
  "language of heaven," 206; "English-
  speaking" race, soul, 206, 362n.6, 362n.7;
  arbitrary nature of language, "sign" (Saussure on), 259, 372n.114; 1880s crisis of language, signification, 255–68; attempts at
  linguistic revitalization and revolution, Secularist, 254, 260–68, 323; in fiction, 26–
  62; nonfiction models, 262–64; utilitarian,
  rationalist, 262–64; scientific, 264–65; failure of artificial languages, 265; limitations
  of models, 265; straining for literary, spiritual, resonance in language, 265–67; in
  Secularist writing, 251, 266; particularly on
  death, 268–69; Secularist urge to revolution, 323–24. *See also* Alford, Henry; Bentham, Jeremy; Besant, Annie; Bible, Holy;
  blasphemy; Carlile, Richard; class; Clifford, W. K.; Cockney; Coleridge, Samuel
  Taylor; Darwin, Charles; Dickens,
  Charles; Du Maurier, George; *Essays and
  Reviews;* euphemism; Farrar, Frederic;
  Foote, G. W.; forgery; Foucault, Michel;
  Freethinker, The; Haggard, Rider; Hardy,
  Thomas; Holyoake, George Jacob; Hone,
  William; Huxley, Thomas Henry; Lacan,
  Jacques; libel; Maurice, F. D.; Mill, John
  Stuart; Müller, Max; Oliphant, Mrs.; Orwell, George; *Oxford English Dictionary;*
  Paine, Thomas; Pater, Walter; plain
  speech; property; Revised Version; Salvation Army; Southwell, Charles; Spencer,
  Herbert; Stephen, Leslie; Swinburne, Algernon Charles; Thomson, James; Tooke,
  Horne; Trench, Richard Chevenix; violence; Ward, Mrs. Humphry; White, William Hale
laughter: overview, 177–81: Bakhtin on popular laughter, 51; and subversive 1810s, inheritance of, 178; refined taboo on, in
  1880s, 178, 284–85. *See also* Carroll, Lewis;
  Du Maurier, George; Foote, G. W.; *Freethinker, The;* parody; Shaw, Bernard
law: characteristics of English common law,

  15–16; and cultural consensus, 200–201;
  literariness of Victorian law, 94; and literary lawyers, 94–95; literary connections of
  nineteenth-century (blasphemy) lawyers,
  191–94. *See also* Abbott, Charles; atheism;
  blasphemy; Blackstone, William; Coleridge, John Duke; Coleridge, John Taylor;
  copyright; Denman, Thomas; Ellenborough, Edward Law; Erskine, Thomas; Giffard, Sir Hardinge; Gifford, Robert; Hale,
  Sir Matthew; Harcourt, Sir William; illegality; information; juries; Levy, Leonard;
  libel; Mill, John Stuart; North, Mr. Justice; oath; obscenity; privilege; Reform
  Acts; Royal Commission on the Criminal
  Law; self-representation; Shepherd, Sir
  Samuel; Sidmouth, Henry Addington; Society for the Suppression of Vice; Starkie,
  Thomas; statutes; Stephen, Sir James Fitzjames; Talfourd, Thomas Noon; "taxes on
  knowledge"
Lawrence, D. H.: *Lady Chatterley's Lover,* self-
  publication of, 65; obscenity trial of Penguin Books for, 11, 70; parallels to Moxon
  case, 98, 209; literary immunity and authority, 201; and language, class, obscenity, blasphemy, Hardy, 325–26. *See also*
  Eliot, T. S.
Lawton, David: on blasphemy as linguistic
  act, 12; as threat to community, 15; on
  Ranters' blasphemies, 238; on "blasphemy"
  of Freud's "Wolfman," 245, 326; of the
  Pardoner's Tale, 270
Levy, Leonard: on blasphemy, 8; on Carlile as
  inadequate "theorist," 65; Foote as sleaze-
  monger, 5
Lewis, Matthew ("Monk"): and blurring of
  blasphemy and obscenity, 208; and biblical bowdlerization in *The Monk,* 258
libel: blasphemy as "blasphemous libel," 227–
  29; libel and ancient theories of autonomous language, 227; inapplicable to "blasphemous libel," 227–28; Fox's Act (1792),
  22; gives definitional power to juries, 32,
  198, 361n.42; introduces concepts of "malice" and "intention," 227, 366n.55; quashing concept of *mitiori sensu,* 227, 367n.56;
  1792 Act unconcerned with "manner,"
  228–29; 1843 Act and truth of utterance,

228, 368n.65; libel law and the "private opinion," 232, 377n.50; as paradox in the case of religion, blasphemy, 232–33; 1888 Law of Libel Amendment Act confirms curtailment of privilege, 237, 368n.69

limits of study: overview, 13–16; and religious fervor, 13–14; and gender, 14–15; and nation, 15–16

literacy: and eighteenth-century cases, 19; and Paine's *Age of Reason*, 75; and Wordsworth's *Lyrical Ballads*, 75; and democracy, 78; educational reform, religious bars to, 86, 133, 342n.15, 342–43n.18; courtroom denial to "unthinking working classes," 85; literacy and industrial conditions, 85; and extension of franchise, 85–86, 342n.16; and social control, 86, 342n.17; and vulgarization of learning, 130 fig. 9; working-class "leap into literacy," 86–87; indebtedness to blasphemers, 86–90, 343n.20; statistics at midcentury, 343n.19; generational differences, 248; concept of the "fatal book," 259; literacy in Cornwall, Pooley case, 300. *See also* Bible, Holy; Carlile, Richard; Holyoke, George Jacob; language; *Penny Magazine;* Society for the Diffusion of Useful Knowledge; Southwell, Charles

literature: as blasphemy, 1810s, 106; but shortly no longer "truly Christian," 193; as new standard of cultural value, 8–9, 98, 106–8; as authority, 193; in *Freethinker* case, 197–203; bibliomania of 1880s, 193; need for standard works on literature, 1880s, 193; and for critics as priests, 197; literature as courtroom "evidence," 33, 198–200; and Hone's quotations, 33, 198–99; and subliterary other, in case of Hone, 36; of Moxon/Hetherington, 107; of Foote, 202–3; literature with a capital "L," 95; confers immunity to prosecution, 95, 107; "growth of Poet's mind," 96; literary context and criminality, 96–97; sacred person of author, preferably dead, 96, 106–7; Literature *v.* literacy, 108; loss of faith as literary experience, 176; literary connections of nineteenth-century blasphemers, 186–87. *See also* agnosticism; blasphemy; Byron, George Gordon, Lord; Carlyle,

Thomas; Foote, G. W.; Gosse, Edmund; Lamb, Charles; law; novel; Shakespeare, William; Shelley, Percy Bysshe; Wordsworth, William

Lloyd, Marie. *See* music hall

Macaulay, Thomas Babington: "conversion" to copyright, 105–7, 346n.52

"manner." *See* blasphemy; Coleridge, John Duke; Foote, G. W.; libel; literature; Starkie, Thomas

Marlowe, Christopher. *See* forgery

martyrdom: free speech tradition of, 6, 9, 154; and dissenting tradition, 67, 67, 338n.73; and rhetoric of *Poor Man's Guardian*, 81; intellectual demands of, 123; government stop to, 123; trial as political "representation," 29; as publicity stunt, 148; length of sentences, 376n.38; subversive transformation of prison, punishment, 70–71, 144; passive resistance, 70–71, 339n.82. *See also* Carlile, Richard; Foote, G. W.; Gott, J. W.; Hetherington, Henry; Holyoake, George Jacob; Hone, William; *Jude the Obscure;* Pooley, Thomas; self-representation; volunteers

Maurice, F. D.: charged with "perverting" meaning, language, 263; on God as basis of language, 373n.120

Meredith, George: praise of Bradlaugh, 187; of Foote, 187–88; who reprints poems, extracts, 359n.21; mutual friends, influences, parallels, 187–90, 358n.20; as parodist, "Bible-smasher," 187–91; in *The Ordeal of Richard Feverel*, 188–89, 190, 203, 359n.23; *Rhoda Fleming*, 189; *The Egoist*, 189–90; *Diana of the Crossways*, 189–90; Meredith and "master stories" of Bible, 189–90, 359n.24; and power-plays on the "Word," 190–91, 359n.25; and aphorism, 190, 202, 359n.23; and euphemism, "veiling," 221; and power of metaphor, 224; and "plush of speech," 266; Meredith as Hardy's reader, 288; as *Freethinker* backer, 263, 319

Mill, John Stuart: 1823 *Westminster Review* article on blasphemy law, Carlile prosecutions, 72, 157, 159, 339–40n.87; influence of *On Liberty* 13, 132, 304, 306; Buckle's

Mill, John Stuart (*continued*)
  review of, 304–6; Mill on censorship by
  "public opinion," 232; on working-class literacy and legal vulnerability, 85, 157, 159;
  on "persecution" in Pooley case, 304; the
  oath, 50; Mill backs Holyoake bid for parliament, 194; loses own seat, 194; *Autobiography* quoted by Foote in court, 154–55,
  198–99; plain idiom as linguistic model,
  262–63, 266
Milton, John: and *Paradise Lost* as holy text,
  96, 101; as blasphemous model, 103–4
money. *See* property
Moore, George: on censored "trade" of fiction, in *Literature at Nurse*, 12, 284,
  330n.12, 365n.38; *The Brook Kerith* threatened with blasphemy prosecution, 175
Morley, John: unorthodoxy and prominence,
  329n.2; quoted by Foote in court, 155; immune to prosecution, 156; because "speaks
  differently" to Bradlaugh, 157
movies: and popularity, blasphemy, of *Godspell*, 175; *Jesus Christ, Superstar*, 175; *Last
  Temptation of Christ*, 175; comic blasphemy in *Monty Python's Life of Brian*,
  253; profane wordplay in *Singin' in the
  Rain*, 36
Moxon, Edward: as high-class publisher,
  unique blasphemer, 10–11, 90, 345n.38;
  publishes *Complete Works of Shelley*, 90–
  91, 344n.29, 347n.59; trial for blasphemy,
  90–98, 104; verdict, 91, 98; copyright, 91,
  104–9; model series of cheap reprints,
  108, 347n.58; and Dickens, Lamb, Hone,
  circles, 56, 345n.38, 347n.57. *See also*
  Hetherington, Henry; Lamb, Charles;
  Shelley, Percy Bysshe; Talfourd, Thomas
  Noon
Mudie's Library. *See* circulating libraries
Müller, Max: on philology and 1880s, 204; on
  linguistic "laws," 246; language as mental
  "palimpsest," 222, 250; linguistic "roots,"
  223, 259, 362n.6, 365–66n.45, 366n.46;
  divine trace in theory, 223, 366n.47;
  "spiritual succession" of Anglo-Saxon heritage, 206; demolishes "bow-wow" and
  "pooh-pooh" theories of language, 365–
  66n.42; Müller's "glamor," influence, 223,
  260

Murray, John: attempts to water down *Don
  Juan, Cain*, 101–3; removes names as publisher, 101; threatened with prosecution,
  102–3. *See also* Byron, George Gordon,
  Lord
music hall: accommodation of euphemism,
  219; subversion, 219–20, 365n.34, 365n.35;
  Marie Lloyd as mistress of, 220, 266. *See
  also* Eliot, T. S.; *Jude the Obscure*

National Secular Society (N.S.S.). *See* Secularism
Newman, John Henry (Cardinal): and novel
  Loss and Gain, 5, 272; and Coleridge circle, 192; and title *Grammar of Assent*, 224
North, Mr. Justice (judge): biased handling of
  Freethinker trials, 144, 150, 151, 154, 158,
  163, 166, 197–98, 203; refuses quotation in
  court, 198–99; accuses Foote of obscenity,
  210, 212; suggestive courtroom slurs, 236–
  37
novel: as measure of Victorian culture, 11–12;
  disciplined and censored, 12–13; alibis and
  compensations in, 12–13, 187–88, 189,
  279–80; serial publication of, 12; blasphemy in and as fiction, 1880s–90s, 269–
  70; modern myth of heroic authorship,
  284; Victorian conditions of production,
  284; constraints on novel compared to poetry, 290. *See also* Butler, Samuel; circulating libraries; Collins, Wilkie; Conrad,
  Joseph; Dickens, Charles; Du Maurier,
  George; Gissing, George; Haggard, Rider;
  Hardy, Thomas; James, Henry; *Jude the
  Obscure;* Kipling, Rudyard; Lawrence,
  D. H.; Meredith, George; Moore, George;
  Oliphant, Mrs.; Pater, Walter; Stephen,
  Leslie; Ward, Mrs. Humphry; Wilde,
  Oscar

oath: as bedrock of social process, 50; and hypocrisy, 50; Affirmation Act of 1888, 50,
  133; failed Bill of 1883, 128, 351n.1; earlier
  acts unenforceable, 135. *See also* Bradlaugh,
  Charles; Holyoake, George Jacob; Mill,
  John Stuart
obscenity: overview, 207–15; as Victorian
  crime of crimes, 214; in 1880s, legislation,
  214; and National Vigilance Association

(f. 1886), 214, 363n.20; relationship to blasphemy, 98, 207–15; historical-conceptual confusion with, 208; progress from "sin" to "crime," 208, 362n.11; Holywell Street as focus of nineteenth-century pornography, 207, 208; penalties of seizure, burning, 207, 362n.9; Obscene Publications Act (1857), 207–8; definitional problems in, 207; solved by concept of "tendency," 207, 228; "exposure" in Act of 1857, 221; obscenity and achievement of religious toleration, 232; and indictability of the Bible, 211, 363n.16; of medical textbooks, 97; surreptitious pornography titles, 122; porn activity, 1830s–60s, 362–63n.13; porn renaissance of 1880s, 208–9; Home Office correspondence on, 208–9; obscenity and English metaphor, 210; "decency" as master-term of judgment, from 1840s, 212; in *Freethinker* case, 212–13; obscenity as charge against Secularism, 213; confusion with blasphemy written into lawbooks, 214; linguistic logic of confusion, and taboo on confessional, 230–31, 367n.61; but obscenity cannot include blasphemy, 214–15. *See also* atheism; Bible, Holy; birth control; Coleridge, John Duke; Foote, G. W.; freedom of press; *Freethinker, The;* Giffard, Sir Hardinge; Harcourt, Sir William; Hardy, Thomas; Holyoake, George Jacob; Lawrence, D. H.; Lewis, Matthew ("Monk"); North, Mr. Justice; Paterson, Thomas; pornographers; Royal Commission on the Criminal Law; Society for the Suppression of Vice; Stead, W. T.; Vizetelly, Henry

Oliphant, Mrs.: anathematization of *Jude the Obscure,* 93, 269, 272, 284, 291–92, 373n.1; "reticence" in *Salem Chapel,* 291; linguistic patriotism of, 294–95; on Arabella as "human pig," 295

Oracle of Reason. See Southwell, Charles

Orwell, George: "Politics and the English Language," 217–18; *1984* and censorship, word crime, nonsense, 5, 219, 230, 233

Owenism: Robert Owen's 1817 declaration, 110; accommodation and (ir)religious tensions in movement, 110, 111, 113; oath of belief in Bible, 110; Owenism as "dev-

ilism," 11, 118; as Secularist inheritance, 6, 124, 351n.96; *New Moral World's* report of Paterson trial, 234. *See also* Holyoake, George Jacob

Oxford English Dictionary (OED): publication details, 361n.2; desire for authority, prescription in, 205; and citation, mention of Foote, Bradlaugh, Holyoake, 205, 361–62n.4; and Anglo-Saxonism, national pride, 205–6; as replacement Bible, "Authorized Version of English Language," 9, 259. *See also* Dickens, Charles; Hardy, Thomas; Shakespeare, William; Trench, Richard Trevenix

Paine, Thomas: as archetypal infidel artisan, 60; urged to flee England by Blake, 60; as linguistic revolutionary, 19, 62–63, 74–75, 77; *Rights of Man,* 60; Paine and literacy, 86; death-bed propaganda, 132–33; class sneers, 151; accusation of adultery, 213

Paley, William (Bishop): influential *Natural Theology, Evidences of Christianity,* 369n.77; conservatism and "homely eloquence," 369n.77; "refuted" by Holyoake, 242; on need to gag blasphemy, 238

parody: tradition of biblical, 24; fear of, 25, 34–35, 371n.92; as "sedition" and "treason," 35, 36, 39; as people's voice, 36, 38; as blasphemy, 35–36; taboo on, 34–38; as "literary misdemeanor," 38; parody and forgery, 46, 180; and "serious" Victorianism, 37–38; decadence, 178; divorced from politics, 37–38, 54; nineteenth-century theories, 34–35; origins, 38; parody as literary "decomposition," 38–39, 45; Bakhtin on, double vision of, 38–39, 51; high-literary parodies of Bible, 181–91; Victorians forget how to read, 184–85. *See also* Butler, Samuel; Byron, George Gordon, Lord; Canning, George; Collins, Wilkie; Cruikshank, George; Dickens, Charles; Foote, G. W.; forgery; *Freethinker, The;* Hone, William; Joyce, James; *Jude the Obscure;* laughter; Meredith, George; piracy; Salvation Army

Pater, Walter: on revitalization of language, 260; in *Marius the Epicurean,* 260–61; remythologization of Christianity, 174

Paterson, Thomas: dubious "gift of the gab,"
15, 121–22; vulgar language, 93; London
"profanity" trial, 121–22; and issue of public *v.* private, 122, 163, 236, 312; Edinburgh
trial for blasphemy, 234–36; imprisonment, instability, 121, 123; and obscenity,
profanity, 207; and the Bible, 211, 220;
combats courtroom silencing, 234–36
penalties on opinion. *See* atheism
Penny Magazine. See Society for the Diffusion
of Useful Knowledge
"Peterloo Massacre": as context to Carlile
trial, 63, 340n.88; memorialized by Hone
and Cruikshank, 64 fig. 4. *See also* Hunt,
Henry ("Orator")
piracy: in 1810s, 99–104; makes literature
cheap "common property," 100; and plagiarism, 98. *See also* Byron, George Gordon, Lord; Carlile, Richard; copyright;
Hetherington, Henry; Hone, William;
pornographers; Shelley, Percy Bysshe;
Southey, Robert; Tegg, Thomas
Place, Francis: as Hone supporter, 26, 332n.11,
332n.13; petitions for Carlile volunteers,
72; advises Hetherington, 90; on radical
expedients, "obscurity," 80, 318
plain speech: as "intellectual vernacular," 10,
62; in Woolston case, 18–19, 157; of
Paine's *Age of Reason,* 62–63; political import of, 62–63; criminalized by Carlile
prosecutions, 74–76; drive to suppress in
eighteenth and nineteenth centuries, 157–
58; confirmed 1914, 162; unfairness of "single standard" for language for working
classes, 157–60; "verncularity," 252–53; literary and spiritual perils of plain speech,
267–68. *See also* Bentham, Jeremy; Clifford, W. K.; Darwin, Charles; euphemism; Foote, G. W.; *Freethinker, The;*
Hardy, Thomas; Holyoake, George Jacob;
Hone, William; Huxley, Thomas Henry;
Jude the Obscure; language; Mill, John Stuart; Paine, Thomas; Southwell, Charles;
Stephen, Leslie; Thomson, James; violence; Woolston, Thomas
Pooley, Thomas: as "obscure" "scapegoat," 11;
so dubbed by press, 297, 315, 318–19; dismissed by all, except *Spectator,* 297–98,
309, 315–16; facts and confusion in evi-

dence, 298–300, 299 fig. 20, 302; Secularist agitation and denigration, 298–300,
303–4, 310, 376n.41, 376n.43; but Pooley's
unusual capacity for language, 300; animosity of Bush, local clergyman, 298,
300–302; but his ambitions thwarted,
301–2, 304; Pooley's "eccentricity" and "independence," a local problem, 302; case
becomes national scandal, 303–5, 303 fig.
21; taken up by Mill and Buckle, 304–6;
reported in *Saturday Review,* 306–7; local
press, 307–8, 309; Pooley believed "insane," 309–11, 377n.48; prison breakdown,
310–11; pardon, 376n.39 *imitatio Christi,*
blasphemous, 313; claim to authorship,
313; as offensive publicity, 313; class and
"Bible tyranny," 298, 310, 313, 314–15;
Pooley as anti-hero, 315–16. *See also* Coleridge, John Duke; Coleridge, John Taylor;
Hardy, Thomas; Holyoake, George Jacob;
Jude the Obscure; Mill, John Stuart
Poor Man's Guardian, The. See Hetherington,
Henry
pornographers: Dugdale pirates Byron's *Don
Juan,* 101; as famous pornographer, 208,
362n.10; Benbow pirates Byron's *Cain,*
100; insurgent pornographers of 1810s,
208
pornography. *See* obscenity
printing press: as symbol of popular power,
66, 86–87; steam printing, 87, 89,
343n.23, 343–44n.26. *See also* Carlile, Richard; Hetherington, Henry
prison. *See* martyrdom
privilege: allows legal republication of *Age of
Reason,* 69, 235; curtailed by silence imperative, 235–36. *See also* Hardy, Thomas;
self-representation; silence
property: "honest doubt" and infidel "theft,"
5, 329n.3; property, money, and language,
rights to, 118–20; capitalist accumulation
of words, 244; property and "voice," in
political discourse, 120–21. *See also* class;
forgery; language; piracy; public space
public space: violated by Holyoake, 121; by
Paterson, 121–22; by *Freethinker,* 122; and
working people, 122; and cult of bourgeois
privacy, 122; *débacle* of Tunbridge Wells
poster, 175–76, 312. *See also* Hardy,

Thomas; Pooley, Thomas; Swinburne, Algernon Charles

Punch: as *Freethinker* model, 137–38; as bourgeois organ, 128–29, 130 fig. 9, 131 fig. 10; institutionalization of satire, 178; commentary on Bradlaugh, Foote, 151

Quarterly Review: anonymous review of Hone's *Apocryphal New Testament,* 44–49; Gifford comes out against Byron's *Cain,* 103

Ramsey, W. J.: as codefendant in *Freethinker* trials, 149, 150; names names of high-class publishers, 155; prison experiences, 146, 150, 152–53, 239, 354n.26

Rationalist Press Association (R.P.A.): present-day pronouncements on blasphemy, 74; blasphemous/Secularist inheritance, 90; role of Charles Watts, 89–90. *See also* cheap press; Holyoake, George Jacob; Huxley, Thomas Henry; Stephen, Leslie

Reform Acts: First (1832), 20, 28, 81, 83, 120–21, 340n.2, 342n.12; Second (1867), 85, 194; Third (1884), 128; as mob threat to culture, 121, 128; as motive for *Freethinker* prosecution, 8, 162, 268; women's suffrage and Secularism, 14. *See also* Arnold, Matthew

Renan, Ernest. *See* "Higher Criticism"

Respectability: as idol, 8, 124–26; as motive force in *Freethinker* trials, 8, 147; and for Secularist opponents of "outspeaking," 153; including the Marquess of Queensberry, 153; respectability and euphemism, 220, 262. *See also* Holyoake, George Jacob; Wilde, Oscar

Revised Version (of Bible): overview, 9, 206; the (un)making of the Revised Version, 255–59; resolutions to protect "Bible English," 255–56; earlier translations, 256; fanfare of publication, 256; but provokes a crisis in language, faith, 256–59; though refusal of euphemization, 258; critical outcry against alterations, renderings, margins, 257–59. *See also* Bible, Holy; language; *Oxford English Dictionary*

Roalfe, Matilda: Edinburgh prosecution, 15, 123, 234; and femininity, 14

Royal Commission on the Criminal Law: sixth report (1841), on blasphemy, obfuscations of, 91–92, 159; confusion of blasphemy and obscenity, 209

Rushdie, Salman: publication of *Satanic Verses,* 5; fatwah against, 8; international controversy, 16–17; Viking paperback, 70; Rushdie as quintessential modern "blasphemous" writer, 326

Salvation Army: success of, 165, 356n.50; similarities to, competition with Secularist movement, 163, 165, 266; "militancy" and martial language, 356n.45; appropriation of popular songs, 164, 356n.48; "irreverent" Cockney vulgarity, 163–64, 165, 356n.46, 371–72n.101; parody, 164; attacks on, 356n.49; in *Punch,* 356n.47; plain speech of, 13, 163, 164–65; satirized by Foote and *Freethinker,* 13, 149, 163, 178, 256; William Booth as "tub-thumper," 163, 164, 165; *In Darkest England,* 356n.50; charges of blasphemy in Convocation, parliament, 165; by Lord Shaftesbury, advocate of blasphemy prosecution, 165; Bramwell Booth on language, blasphemy, 164–65; Mrs. Booth on privileged English, 206. *See also* Arnold, Matthew

Saussure, Ferdinand de. *See* language

Secularism: overview, 3, 6; philosophical sources, 124; respectability under Holyoake, 126; liability to slurs, 213; "militant" Secularism, 13, 129–32; and the diehard Secularist "type," 132; as "scapegoat" for "cultured agnostic[s]," 16, 156; inverted world of Secularism, 172, 202, 273, 318; emphasis on press freedom, publication, 76, 81, 89, 133–34, 139–40; long struggle for a public voice, 154; "heroic" decade of 1880s, 129–32; membership and audience of National Secular Society (N.S.S.), 1880s, 129–32; objectives, 352n.4; N.S.S. *Almanacks,* 251, 267; legal obstacles to N.S.S. solvency, 133, 352n.10, 361n.43; support for women's suffrage, 14–15; Secularist periodicals of 1880s, 133; stylistic caution of, 229; lectures and oratory, 133–34; news value, impact, of Secularist issues, 134; and "Bible-smashing," 172; moment

428   INDEX

Secularism (*continued*)
of history past, 203; the term as euphemism, 240. *See also* Arnold, Matthew;
Bible, Holy; birth control; Bradlaugh,
Charles; Foote, G. W.; Holyoake, George
Jacob; language; obscenity; Pooley,
Thomas; public space; Respectability;
Salvation Army
self-representation, 13; by Hone, 28–30, 198–
99, 238; by Carlile, 67–69; by Southwell,
122–23; by Holyoake, 114–19; by Foote,
149–56; limits on, 233–34
Shakespeare, William: as nineteenth-century
radical prophet, 111–12; works as "Bible of
Humanity," 112, 196; as linguistic source,
251, 265, 320; as model for blasphemy, 112;
Hamlet, 111–12; and the "Holy Ghost,"
175–76; the exclusive Shakespeare Society,
112; Shakespeare as establishment possession, weapon, 97, 195 fig. 16; on "profanation," 156; Victorian expurgation of, 219;
OED overrepresentation of, 361n.3; courtroom quotation of, 360n.31. *See also* Bowdler, Thomas; Bradlaugh, Charles; Carroll,
Lewis; Chartism; Dickens, Charles; Foote,
G. W.; forgery; Southwell, Charles
Sharman, Reverend: as secretary of National
Association for the Repeal of the Blasphemy Laws, 153; petitions for Foote, 153,
161
Shaw, George Bernard: and Secularism,
Foote, close relations with, 5, 6, 172, 186,
357n.9; on his literary talents, 176; blasphemy of *Blanco Posnet*, 6; Shaw as theater reviewer, 133; novels serialized in *Our
Corner*, 133, 353n.11; and Annie Besant,
133, 178, 186; on Bradlaugh, oratory, 134,
135; on truth and jokes, 178; as aphorist,
on blasphemy, 231; as impossible blasphemer, 277
Shelley, Percy Bysshe: contributes to Hone
subscription, 24; protests Carlile "persecution" in *Letter to Lord Ellenborough*, 61;
protests "despotism," "Peterloo" Massacre, 22, 63; on "vulgar" language, 74;
drowned, 104; Moxon *Complete Works*, 10,
90; includes *Queen Mab*, 10; quintessential underground, pirate text, 90, 104–6,
346n.48; "Chartists' Bible," 112; deletions

in Moxon's edition, atheistical, 91,
344n.29, 345n.37; restored, indicted, 91;
involvement of Mary Shelley in, 91,
344n.29; Moxon/Shelley trial, 94–98, 198,
209; Shelley's posthumous elevation to
"angel," 96, 105–7; safe republication of
Mab, 109; prophecies of literary authority
in the *Defense of Poetry* fulfilled, 112, 199–
200; Secularist admiration, 173, 266. *See
also* Carlile, Richard; copyright; Hetherington, Henry; *Jude the Obscure;* Moxon,
Edward; Talfourd, Thomas Noon
Shepherd, Sir Samuel (Attorney-General): mis-
guided conduct of Hone trials, 32–33;
wins right to regulate literary expression,
35–36, 38
Sidmouth, Henry Addington (Home Secretary): suspends *habeas corpus*, 22, 27; circular to magistrates, 22; spurs Carlile, 65;
Sidmouth as target of Hone's satire, 23
fig. 2, 26–27
silence: as end objective of euphemism, 230–
40; and "obscene" confessional, 230–31; as
courtroom imperative, 231–40; dictates in-
defensibility of irreligious opinion, 233–35;
and publication of transcripts, speeches,
235; and press reports of proceedings, 235–
36; as bar to reading indictment, quotation, 236–37; confirmed in law, 1888,
237–38; silence and new standard of "decency," 232; imposes limits on self-representation, legal "privilege," 233–34; silence
as ancient torture, 238; as punishment for
blasphemy, 238–389; and Victorian penal
system, 239–40; and Official Secrets Act,
blackmail, 238. *See also* Foote, G. W.;
Holyoake, George Jacob; Hone, William;
Paterson, Thomas; Wilde, Oscar
slander. *See* libel
Smiles, Samuel: *Self-Help*, 347n.61; rejects,
loses, Holyoake manuscript, 109
Smith, W. H. *See* circulating libraries
Society for the Diffusion of Useful Knowledge (S.D.U.K.): utilitarian objects of, 87,
88; Charles Knight, 87–88; steam printing, editorial innovations, and format of
Penny Magazine, 87–88, 343n.23; *Magazine* and fear of working-class literacy, 88;
and unchecked violation of Stamp Act,

88; imitations of, 343n.25; but initial indebtedness to Hone, 88; to Henry Hetherington, 88–89; actual middle-class audience of, 89; *Magazine* series "On the Meanings of Words," 370n.81; *Penny Cyclopaedia*, definition of blasphemy in, 123, 350–51n.91; blasphemers' parody promotion of "Really Useful Knowledge," 88. *See also* Bentham, Jeremy

Society for the Suppression of Vice: as motive force in blasphemy prosecution, 61; of Richard Carlile, 67, 68; Vice Society's relationship to Constitutional Association, 69–70, 339n.79; Proclamation Society, 207, 362n.8; and anti-obscenity actions, 207–8, 337n.59, 362n.8; against literature, 97, 102, 104

Southey, Robert: as Laureate, target of Hone's satire, 27, 364n.24; forgiven, 345n.41; *Wat Tyler* indictable, 97, 99–100; on "Satanic" school of poetry, 346n.44; expurgation of Chaucer, 219

Southwell, Charles: as aspirant actor, 111, 348n.69; edits *Oracle of Reason*, 110–11, 347–48n.64; signed articles in, an innovation, 111, 139; Shakespearean private language, 111–12; no. 4 and the "Jew Book" article, 112–13, 170; anti-Semitism in, 112–13; but see Southwell as Shylock, 113; other criminal items, 348n.68; his "abominable" plain language, blasphemy, 113–14, 229; sentence, imprisonment, 114, 146, 351n.93; Southwell as Holyoake's mentor, 110; his "gift of the gab," 121; learned speech in own defense, 122–23, 357n.6; on Bible "poetry," 173, 197, 358n.16; conversion and rift with Holyoake, 244; fatal boast of oral power, 248; incapacity for linguistic self-transformation, 248. *See also* Shakespeare, William

Spencer, Herbert: quoted in court by Foote, 155; immune to prosecution, 156; on linguistic "progress," 223; "verbal fictions," 264

Starkie, Thomas: influential definition of blasphemy, in *Law of Slander and Libel* (1812), 18, 19, 84; shifts emphasis to "manner" of crime, 159; legal revisionism, 161; of Starkie's work, 212; Starkie and Royal Commission, 159; on the oath, 50

statutes: blasphemy act (1698), 15, 329n.5; as "ferocious and shocking," 161; confirmed "Hale's law," 18; abolished 1969, 16; Trinity Act (1813), 68; act "for the more effectual Prevention . . . of blasphemous and seditious libels" (1819), 74–75, 79, 108, 362n.9; statutes and sexuality, 214; Obscene Publications Act (1857), 207–8, 221, 232; Criminal Law Amendment Act (1885), 214, 363n.19; Fox's Libel Act (1792), 22, 32, 198, 227, 228–29, 361n.42; Libel Act (1843), 228, 368n.65; Law of Libel Amendment Act (1888), 237, 368n.69; Official Secrets Act (1889), 238. *See also* copyright; law; Reform Acts; "taxes on knowledge"

Stead, W. T.: as Salvation Army supporter, 164, 356n.50; breaks 1880s "Conspiracy of Silence" on sexual slavery, 230–31

Stephen, Leslie: quoted by Foote in court, 154; immune to prosecution, 156; Stephen and moral ideal of gentlemanliness, 162; and linguistic loss of cultural resonance, 266; and non-ideal of literary "popularity," 191; on Job as the agnostic's book of the Bible, 317; idiom as linguistic model, "brutal" and anti-euphemistic, 262–63, 264; Stephen as R.P.A. associate, 263; as patrician agnostic, 263; but protests *Freethinker* sentences, 177, 263; *Essays on Freethinking and Plainspeaking*, 263; Stephen as Hardy's "monitor," 289, 319; calls him to witness self-defrocking, 377n.54. *See also* Woolf, Virginia

Stephen, Sir James Fitzjames: leading legal theorist, historian, 7; literary critic, 191; anti-Dickens, 191, 359n.26; judicial pronouncements on blasphemy ("obsolete"), disingenuous, 158–59, 200, 227; work on Voysey heresy case, 357n.1

Strauss, David Friedrich. *See* "Higher Criticism"

suffrage. *See* Reform Acts

Swinburne, Algernon Charles: blasphemes at Arts Club, 122; no action taken, 122; quoted by Foote in court, 154–55; by Hardy in *Jude*, Joyce in *Ulysses*, 275, 377n.55; but immune to prosecution, 156; supports expurgation of Shakespeare, 219; stylistic importance to Secularism, 265–66

Talfourd, Thomas Noon: and copyright, 11, 104–7, 346n.52; as type of the Victorian literary lawyer, 94–98, 112; verse tragedy *Ion,* 94, 344n.34; relationship to Wordsworth, 11, 105–7, 346n.49; on apolitical "purity" of (Wordsworthian) literature, 193, 201; review of *Cain,* 103–4; "celebrated" defense of Moxon and Shelley, 94–98, 346n.51; debt to Byron, *Cain,* 104; courtroom speech as literary act, 95; "gorgeousness" of diction, 96; debt to Wordsworth's *Prelude,* 96, 105; parallels to copyright speeches, 105. *See also* copyright; Denman, Thomas; Dickens, Charles; Lamb, Charles; Moxon, Edward; Shelley, Percy Bysshe

"taxes on knowledge": stamp duties, acts of 1815/1819, 79–81; securities system, 79, 83; copyright law as tax on knowledge, 109. *See also* Bradlaugh, Charles; Cobbett, William; Hetherington, Henry; Society for the Diffusion of Useful Knowledge

Taxil, Leo: *La bible amusante,* 140; English attempts at suppression, 140, 143; smut and toilet jokes in, 140; Foote's alterations to, 140, 142, 178–79. See also *Freethinker, The;* Joyce, James

Taylor, Robert: as Carlile's comrade in blasphemy, 76–77, 340n.92; lectures at Rotunda Theater, 76–77; trial reported by *Poor Man's Guardian,* 77, 82; two years' solitary, 77; as dramatic author of *Swing,* 111, 348.66

Tegg, Thomas: son William republishes Hone's *Three Trials,* 25, 185; Hone as Tegg house author, 53; Thomas Tegg approaches Dickens, 53; repudiated by Dickens, Carlyle, 53, 108–9, 336n.49, 347n.60; and piratical *Parley's Penny Library,* 108; resists copyright passage, 108, 347n.60

Thomson, James: quoted by Foote in court, 154; relations with Foote, 186–87; *The City of Dreadful Night,* 186, 191; as linguistic model, for T. S. Eliot's *Wasteland,* 265, 373n.123

Tooke, Horne: as radical politician, 32; as materialist philologist, 223, 224, 365n.41

transcripts: self-published by Hone, 34; and Carlile publicity mill, 72; selling power, 72; and press freedom, 123, 234–35. *See also* freedom of press; self-representation; silence

Trench, Richard Chevenix (Dean): impact of *English Past and Present,* 204; as "emblematic" figure of Victorian philology, 223; on words as "living powers," 224, 254; but language as both human and divine, 366n.47; as originator of *OED,* 361n.2

trial. *See* martyrdom; self-representation

Tyler, Sir Henry (M.P.): Bradlaugh foe and backstage manager of *Freethinker* prosecution, 143, 147, 148–49

Varley, Henry (butcher): Bradlaugh foe and front man for *Freethinker* prosecution, 148–49; privately brought, 229

violence: fear of linguistic, 60; Carlile and, 75–76; volunteers' choice of "word" over "sword," 76; misread metaphors, 76; technical meaning, 76; Hetherington and "violence," 83, 158. *See also* Holyoake, George Jacob

Vizetelly, Henry: prosecuted for "obscene" Zola translations, 214, 363n.20; on "singularly quiet" Holyoake, 244

volunteers: for the *Age of Reason,* 10, 69–72, 339n.78; ingenious tactics of, 72; beliefs and language of, 71, 76; sentences, 70; William Campion, 71; Humphrey Boyle ("Man with Name Unknown"), 71; Boyle on "Bible Obscenity," 211; parliamentary petitions for volunteers' release, 72, 339n.86; volunteers win end to prosecution, 71–72; volunteers for *Poor Man's Guardian,* 80–83; as veteran blasphemers, 82–83; Abel Heywood, later snubbed by Victoria, 83, 342n.13; Joseph Swann, on his "voice" in taxation, 120–21, 350n.86. *See also* Carpenter, William; Cleave, John; Watson, James

Voysey, Charles. *See* "Higher Criticism"

vulgarity: term's new pejorative meaning, 74–75. *See also* Cobbett, William; Cockney; Coleridge, John Duke, Lord; Dickens, Charles; Gott, J. W.; Joyce, James; plain speech; Salvation Army; Shelley, Percy Bysshe

Ward, Mrs. Humphry: and problem of female heresy, 14; direct response to *Freethinker* case, in *Robert Elsmere*, 167–68; unacknowledged, 168; Ward targets "coarse" and "laughing" "brutality," 168, 285; "obscenity," 294; Ward on Christianity's "literary problem," 169; influence of "Uncle Matt," family history, 168, 375n.20; *Robert Elsmere* as anti-model for *Jude the Obscure*, 272, 273, 276, 374n.13; alibis and counterweights to transgression in, 279–80, 375n.22; Mrs. Ward and "Religion of [human] Christ," psychology of, 167–68, 272, 273, 375n.21; and "cooperation" of readership, success, 292, 375n.19; and limitations of language, 316. *See also* Arnold, Matthew; Gladstone, William Ewart

Watson, James: as *Poor Man's Guardian* volunteer, 82, 83; as Freethought publisher, 89; and cooperative movement, 124

White, William Hale ("Mark Rutherford"): confessional agnostic fiction of, 201; and "perfection of style," 265

Wilde, Oscar: as epitome of Victorian scandal, 17; and Respectability, 124, 147, 266, 354n.28; and prison conditions, 146–47; enforced silence, breakdown, 239; and writing of *De Produndis*, 368–69n.72;

Lord Alfred Douglas on blasphemy, 175; *The Picture of Dorian Grey,* play on euphemism in, 230, 266, 270; blasphemy, seduction in, 269–70; Wilde on the "Twenty" Commandments, 277; "levity at the lectern," 285

Wooler, T. J.: trial for "seditious" *Black Dwarf,* 22, 333n.21; declines Carlile's assistance, 337n.63; satire on Carlile trial, 68

Woolf, Virginia: on publishing "freedom" and Hogarth Press, 65; on "brutality of father's idiom, 262, 264; refuses to publish *Ulysses,* 324; relationship to Fitzjames Stephen, 191. *See also* Stephen, Sir James Fitzjames; Stephen, Leslie

Woolston, Thomas: 1728 prosecution, 18–19; plain speech and precedents of, 63, 157, 159, 209

Wordsworth, William: and legal-literary Coleridge circle, 192–93; caricatured by Hone, 27; sister Dorothy disapproves Hone acquittal, 34; potential offense of *Lyrical Ballads,* 75; posthumous publication of *Prelude,* 347n.55; Wordsworth's influence on copyright law, 99, 105–8; campaigns in person, 107; Victorian canonization, 105–7, 173, 177, 196, 359–60n.30; "purifying influence" on literature, 193; post as Distributor of Stamps, 106, 347n.53. *See also* Coleridge, John Duke; Talfourd, Thomas Noon